# GODS, GUNS AND MISSIONARIES

# GODS, GUNS AND MISSIONARIES

## The Making *of* the Modern Hindu Identity

# Manu S. Pillai
### Winner *of* the Sahitya Akademi Yuva Puraskar

An imprint of Penguin Random House

ALLEN LANE

Allen Lane is an imprint of the Penguin Random House group of companies whose addresses can be found at global.penguinrandomhouse.com

Published by Penguin Random House India Pvt. Ltd
4th Floor, Capital Tower 1, MG Road,
Gurugram 122 002, Haryana, India

First published in Allen Lane by Penguin Random House India 2024

Copyright © Manu S. Pillai 2024

All rights reserved

10 9 8 7 6 5 4 3 2 1

The views and opinions expressed in this book are the author's own and the facts are as reported by him which have been verified to the extent possible, and the publishers are not in any way liable for the same.

Please note that no part of this book may be used or reproduced in any manner for the purpose of training artificial intelligence technologies or systems.

ISBN 9780670093656

Typeset in Adobe Caslon Pro by Manipal Technologies Limited, Manipal
Printed at Thomson Press India Ltd, New Delhi

This book is sold subject to the condition that it shall not, by way of trade or otherwise, be lent, resold, hired out, or otherwise circulated without the publisher's prior consent in any form of binding or cover other than that in which it is published and without a similar condition including this condition being imposed on the subsequent purchaser.

www.penguin.co.in

*To the one in the grove*
*The one with the roof*
*The one who lay forgotten*
*And to the thousand-year-old*
*in Neduvaramcode.*

*And above all,*
*to my mother*
*Pushpa*

# CONTENTS

*Introduction: A Brief History of Hinduism*   xiii
1. Monsters and Missionaries   1
2. 'Heathens' and Hidden Truths   45
3. Governing the Gentoos   87
4. 'An Indian Renaissance'   126
5. For God and Country   168
6. 'Native Luthers'   213
7. Drawing Blood   259

*Epilogue: What Is Hinduism?*   313
*Acknowledgements*   327
*Notes*   331
*Index*   551

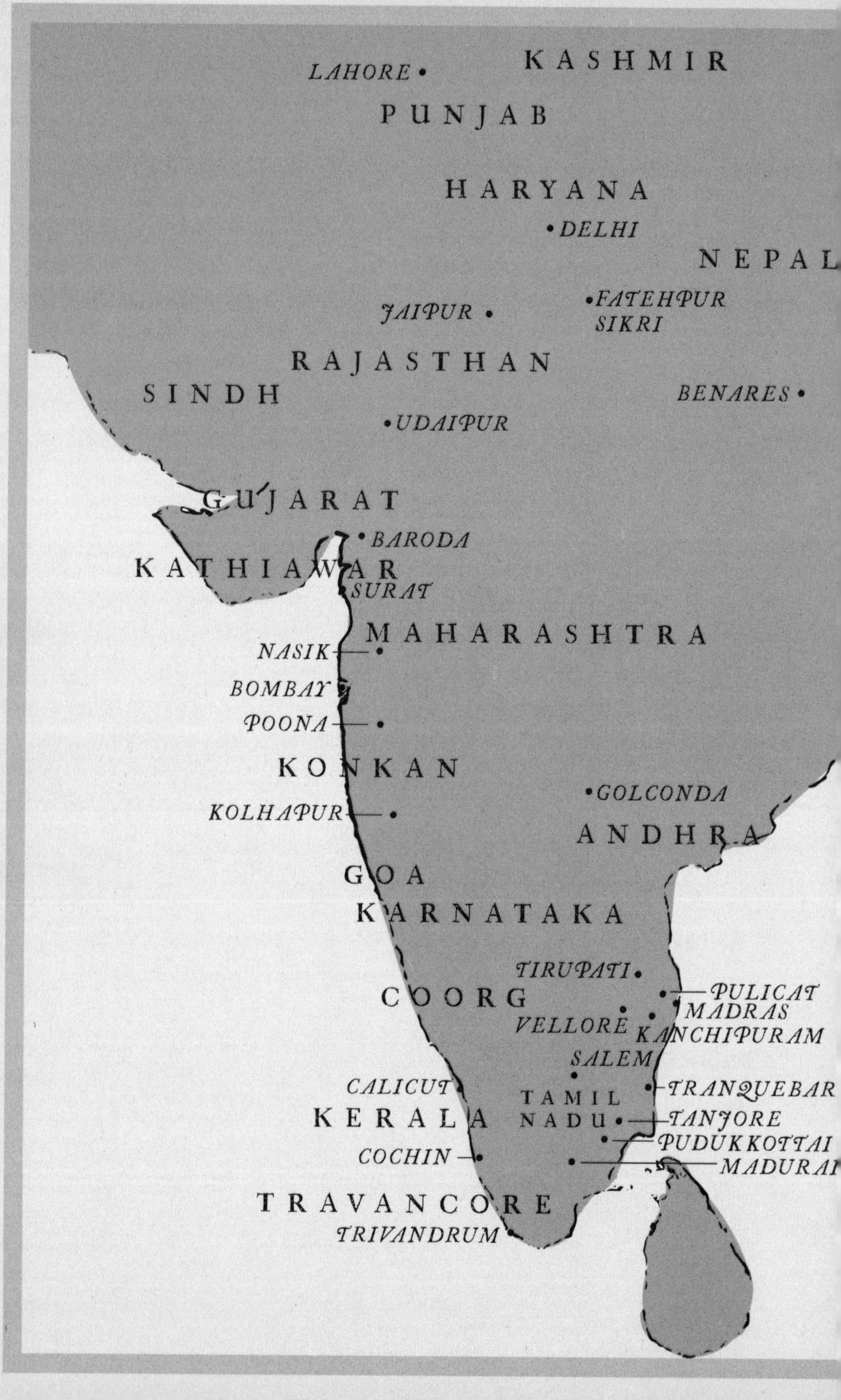

## Map of India

- KASHMIR
- LAHORE
- PUNJAB
- HARYANA
- DELHI
- NEPAL
- JAIPUR
- FATEHPUR SIKRI
- RAJASTHAN
- SINDH
- BENARES
- UDAIPUR
- GUJARAT
- BARODA
- KATHIAWAR
- SURAT
- MAHARASHTRA
- NASIK
- BOMBAY
- POONA
- KONKAN
- GOLCONDA
- KOLHAPUR
- ANDHRA
- GOA
- KARNATAKA
- TIRUPATI
- COORG
- PULICAT
- VELLORE
- MADRAS
- KANCHIPURAM
- SALEM
- CALICUT
- TRANQUEBAR
- KERALA
- TAMIL NADU
- TANJORE
- COCHIN
- PUDUKKOTTAI
- MADURAI
- TRAVANCORE
- TRIVANDRUM

BIHAR

ASSAM

BENGAL
· CALCUTTA

ORISSA
· PURI

This map is a perception of the author specifically created for explaining his views in this book. The boundaries, topographical and geographical features depicted therein, whether historical and contemporary, are neither purported to be correct nor authentic. The map is drawn to scale.

# INTRODUCTION

## A BRIEF HISTORY OF HINDUISM

In the summer of 1902, when the maharajah of Jaipur set sail to attend the coronation of King Edward VII in London, parked in his steamer was a team of Indian cows. The cow, venerated by orthodox Hindus, had for generations now enjoyed a place of eminence in the overseas retinues of high-born 'natives'. In 1831, Raja Ram Mohun Roy, the celebrated Bengali thinker and spokesperson of the Mughal emperor, landed in England with a cow.[1] Just under two decades later, Rana Jung Bahadur of Nepal also travelled West with cattle, allowing Indian attendants alone to milk them, lest they lose their sacred quality.[2] The Gaekwad of Baroda got on a ship to Europe in 1887 with two cows, though in this case, the adventure sadly proved taxing for the animals—they died before the vessel docked in Aden.[3] Such tragedy notwithstanding, the cow did preserve its status in the international rosters of itinerant Hindu princes. It served, after all, not only as a source of ritually pure milk on foreign shores but also as a breathing totem of custom and faith for men wedged between traditional religiosity and colonial modernity.

It was a conundrum Madho Singh II of Jaipur (1862–1922) felt keenly when he accepted his invitation to the coronation. He was an old-fashioned man, who only recently had censured a courtier for crossing the 'black waters' of the ocean and going abroad—an undertaking prohibited to good Hindus.[4] And now he was himself called upon to travel to London and pay homage in person to his English suzerain. Naturally, the maharajah turned to his priests for advice—the issue was not *if* he could go as much as *how* he might do so without causing violence to the sensibilities of his people and the religious sanctity of his position. The Brahmins did not take long to give the ruler their counsel: It was decided that if the maharajah went with his family deity, Sri Gopalji, he could bypass the injunction against international travel.[5] For that way, technically, it would be the sanctified image that went to England, and as a good devotee, Madho Singh would only be 'following' Sri Gopalji from his Jaipur shrine to the headquarters of the empire. Where mortals could not directly flout custom, god would show the way.

What followed was elaborate preparations for Sri Gopalji and his princely escort, joined by 125 less exalted others, to sail. The SS *Olympia*, a sparkling new (and thus, undefiled) steamer, was acquired and customized for Jaipur's purposes. Two dozen Brahmins travelled to Bombay in advance to 'purify' the ship, and six months' worth of water from the Ganga, India's most sacred river, was transported in silver urns—that way, the maharajah was spared the abhorrent prospect of swallowing English water.[6] Baggage weighed at 2000 *maund*s (about 70 tons) was heaped into eight wagons of a train; this being done, Madho Singh himself set out from Jaipur. In Bombay, a second round of rituals followed to venerate the sea-god, copying, reportedly, the precise protocol established by Rama, the hero of the epic Ramayana, in some imprecise mythical time. This involved dropping gold and silver onto the waves, not to speak of 'raw rice, cocoanuts, flowers and milk'.⁷ Having thus traced 'the footsteps of his ancestor', the ruler, who claimed descent from both Rama and the sun, finally went forth to the land of his white masters, in the all-validating shadow of god.⁸

Arriving in London after a series of memorable incidents—such as in Marseilles where Madho Singh distributed mangoes to a French crowd—this marriage between expediencies of the age and stage-managed custom resumed. When the maharajah started from Victoria station, it was Sri Gopalji's image that occupied the first carriage, Madho Singh following behind—a sight that caused, according to a chronicler, public amazement.⁹ Newspapers, the account stresses, praised the maharajah's devotion to his deity, and the reader is constantly reminded of how he upheld every Indian habit and tradition in his daily routine.¹⁰ Madho Singh did, of course, go to the opera, the races, to the Crystal Palace, Madam Tussaud's and other still-popular tourist spots in the capital of *Inglistan*, but all with Sri Gopalji's blessings. Indeed, when the coronation was postponed after Edward VII became unexpectedly ill, the maharajah 'appealed day and night' to his Hindu deity, who magnanimously intervened, we read, and restored the Christian king to strength.¹¹ If the crowning took place at all, that is, it was because an Indian god, with his royal camp follower, happened to be in London to save the day.

By September, the maharajah was home, presumably with his cows in reasonable good health. Madho Singh had proved his loyalty to the Raj not only by attending the coronation in person but also, it was said, by calling at Buckingham Palace every day during Edward VII's illness.¹² The story goes that while other visitors used the time to holiday in Scotland and Paris, the ruler of Jaipur refused to leave London till the British *padshah* (emperor) recovered. He also ensured there was little criticism at home for breaching custom—Brahmin pandits, a Muslim aide and men of the commercial classes had accompanied him, creating a stake (or culpability at any rate) in the escapade for multiple interests.[13] Or as an English daily explained, this 'true Oriental' who identified with 'all the ancient religious traditions' that were 'so unspeakably dear to the souls of the Hindus', had nevertheless proved 'absolutely faithful to his duty as a vassal of the King-Emperor'.[14] For Madho Singh occupied two very different worlds, and with the services of sympathetic priests and a mobile deity, maintained a fine balance between both.

One of the brightest gifts of the Indian priest is the ability to bypass awkward corners between theory and reality through the manipulation of tradition. For centuries, kings were consumers of this marvellous Brahmin talent. Nearly each time a peasant chief or warrior achieved a degree of power, for instance, it was the Brahmin he turned to, seeking legitimization through an upgrade in caste and ritual status. Cows were, as always, critical: One ceremony required the aspirant to wait inside an artificial gold bovine while his priests chanted mantras. And at the appropriate moment, the man would spring from the womb of his new 'mother', reborn into the superior rank he sought. In a 1659 episode, a freshly minted monarch of Tanjore reportedly even sat in the lap of the priest's wife, bawling like a baby, lest there be confusion about the proceedings.[15] Either way, for the Brahmin ritualist, this reaffirmed his unique right to bestow status; for the would-be king, meanwhile, it was elevation from an ordinary provenance into a league of semi-divine proportions.[16] And once both sides had got what they wanted, the cow was dismantled, the priests taking home (most of) its pieces.[17]

But droll as this sounds, it marks also a more serious dynamic. India is a civilization raised up on astute compromises. It could be no other way, given the linguistic, ethnic, geographical and cultural diversity of the land. Keepers of the song and lore which shaped its national narrative confronted such dizzying contingencies that a degree of plasticity was integral to holding it all together.[18] After all, in the 3000 years preceding Madho Singh's journey to Europe, the country had witnessed wave after wave of change. Vedic culture, with its fire altars and sacrifices, promoted by Indo–Aryans, met competition from cults that venerated gods in images; this encounter caused Hindu practice to emerge by the end of the first millennium CE as a grand system of temple worship.[19] Buddhism and Jainism sponged away patronage, and though they faded, these too marked the landscape with hybridity. Then came Islam from overseas: It could neither be defied, given its proximity to power, nor absorbed into one of India's capacious traditions—here a more uncertain adaptation appeared. Finally came the trauma of colonialism, backed by withering evangelical Christian attacks—the theme of this book—birthing yet another face for Hinduism. All throughout, Brahmin texts lamented this *kali yuga*—a black age of corruption and doom—when the undeserving sat on thrones and 'order' (as they defined it) took a leave of absence.[20] But formal cries aside, they adjusted each time, maintaining a façade of continuity while actively innovating, blending old with new.

This, in fact, is patent from the beginning. In ancient times, as Indo–Aryan culture fanned out from the Indus Valley in the subcontinent's north-west, to the eastward Gangetic heartland of India, it stumbled onto groups with varied social beliefs.[21] For Brahmin promoters of the Vedic religion, these were originally *mleccha*s, or barbarians, regardless of whether they were advanced urban people or tribes deep in the forest. Why, even eaters of garlic—taboo for many Brahmins even now—were mlecchas.[22] Most of present-day India, tellingly, was branded mleccha-*desa*, or barbarian country, including Gujarat and Sindh in the west, Bengal and Bihar in the east, and the southern peninsula; to visit these places was to commit 'sin through the feet'.[23] But, in practice, with the rise of new kingdoms, opening up of commercial links, migrations sparked by intra-Aryan conflicts, and that plain old human attraction to fresh avenues, Brahmins *did* set foot in such territories. The idea of the mleccha-desa remained, but mutated quietly from a geographical definition to the more versatile concept of a place where the Brahminical order was not in vogue.[24] And naturally, it fell upon Brahmins to propagate their system wherever they went, transforming assorted mleccha-desas into lands receptive to them and their four holy texts, the Vedas.[25] Or as the father of Hindu nationalism would later put it, there began a 'process of assimilation, elimination, and consolidation', outlining what we today call Hinduism.[26]

Necessarily, however, this was only possible through a give and take of principles and positions. The orthodox tradition of Brahmin elites envisioned a world of four caste groups, functioning in carefully policed harmony. At the top sat, of course, Brahmins themselves, guarding the gates of divine access. Then came Kshatriyas, or a ruling class, whose duty was to protect Brahmins and the world they had designed. The Vaishyas were the productive classes, followed by a fourth set in the Sudras, or a general mass, to serve everybody else. In actual fact, though, this division never existed in such perfection in most of India.[27] It was an aspiration—the portrayal of an ideal Brahmin world—rather than reality as it existed. Tradition wrote off troublesome details of this type as a defect of the kali yuga. Better epochs did, it was claimed, exist, but these had (conveniently) passed in the time of mythical heroes and legendary kings. Now, there were only Brahmins and problems, and a fight to 'restore' the correct way of things—a stance that not only justified the selling of Brahminical ideas in virgin territories with all the gloss of a sacred mission but also, simultaneously, relieved Brahmins from the pressures of rigidity, allowing sensible bargains. For their vision of the world was mostly theoretical, its practical enactment proving messier than official narratives allow. Hinduism, as it would emerge, was not so much what Brahmins wanted; instead, it is the story of their *negotiations* with a bewildering variety of counter-thoughts and alternate visions. Change is coded into its DNA.

Of course, Brahminical ideas held leverage too, and as monarchies emerged in India, dynasts found this creed attractive.[28] Its theories on social stratification, the portal various rites opened to the gods and its means to supply legitimacy established a reciprocal (if also tense) bond between power and religion.[29] Or as a key text offers: 'The Kshatriya does not flourish without the Brahmin, and the Brahmin does not prosper without the Kshatriya'—hence such rituals as of the golden cow to invent Kshatriyas where there were none.[30] Unsurprisingly, Brahmins frowned upon areas following non-monarchical systems and were, therefore, disinterested in their ideology.[31] Moreover, contenders appeared in the form of Buddhism and Jainism, growing popular with those segments excluded from the accord between Brahmins and royalty. Focused not on pleasing gods as much as ethical living, these Sramanic ('striving') schools elevated non-violence, good conduct and the purity of the soul— simpler narratives capable of appealing to broader interests.[32] Once institutionalized, Sramanic traditions competed fiercely with Brahmins—one Buddhist text ranks dogs above Brahmins[33]—and Megasthenes counted both among the class of 'philosophers' he encountered in India. Indeed, the third century BCE edicts of the emperor Ashoka, personally a Buddhist, admit these tensions and, wisely, advocate tolerance.[34]

The rise of the Mauryan empire in India in this period, and the access it provided to unexplored pastures meant, additionally, that the field was open for missionaries.[35] Buddhism, for example, spread out not only westwards and south, but also overseas, its growth causing lasting anxieties to Brahmins. The empire itself emerged from an erstwhile mleccha-desa, absorbing 'purer' Aryan territories as it grew; thus, before reconciliation was reached, an early emperor, branded a lowly Sudra, was recorded as a slayer of (legitimate) Kshatriyas.[36] The advent of Greeks, Indo-Scythians and other foreign tribes in the north-west meant that unforeseen political and cultural ideas were also entering the fray from a different direction, adding to the competitiveness of the religious market. In the circumstances, Brahmins had again to adapt—they could either fade into irrelevance, blaming mlecchas for their decline, or co-opt those aliens, arriving at nimble compromises.[37] Already, as their Indo–Aryan ancestors abandoned nomadic ways for settled agrarian life in the Gangetic belt, their religion had changed: Its emphasis slid from the ritual act to philosophical reflections collected in the later Vedic corpus, the Upanishads—which, in turn, may have been catalysed by exchanges with other indigenous groups.[38] Anchors were still maintained in the Vedas but much perched outside was also accepted. One method enabling this was hierarchy: All ideas were welcome, but those closest to the Brahmins' own were deemed higher or superior, and those more grating, lower.[39] This was tolerance but within certain parameters.

Either way, as Christianity dawned in the Middle East, in India too religion was transformed. Old gods of the Vedic age, such as Indra and Agni, made way for two powerful deities, Vishnu and Siva, with their own mythologies and strategies to counter Sramanic ambitions.[40] Siva, for one, is believed to represent the combination of a pre-Vedic Indic divinity with a Vedic god,[41] while Vishnu went from a 'one-act' figure in the Vedas to a 'god of colossal proportions'.[42] In many ways, it was a case of mix and match: Non-Vedic gods could be merged with Vedic counterparts, and Brahmins accepted popular elements from the other side, while cladding it in their theological principles. Ideas were transmitted through hugely appealing epic poetry, which held clues as to such adaptation. The Mahabharata, for instance, sells the (Brahmin-approved) concept of monarchy over other systems,[43] but the polyandrous marriage of its five heroes to a single wife suggests un-Aryan influences too.[44] Into the first millennium CE, then, what we frame within the blanket term 'Hinduism' had shed most of its Vedic appearance,

Vishnu by Pierre Sonnerat in his *Voyage aux Indes Orientales et à la Chine* (1782), courtesy of the Library of Congress, Rare Book and Special Collections Division.

Siva by Pierre Sonnerat in his *Voyage aux Indes Orientales et à la Chine* (1782), courtesy of the Library of Congress, Rare Book and Special Collections Division.

becoming a more mixed commodity known as the Puranic religion.[45] Originally shaped by bards through oral traditions, this was codified by Brahmins into a Sanskrit corpus—the Puranas—varnished with their own philosophical preoccupations.[46] And their dissemination far and wide, where they assimilated diverse traditions and wove these into a shared religious frame, coincided with the next great imperial phase in India.

Under the Gupta dynasty—possibly of Brahmin descent[47]—by the fifth century, Brahminical culture entrenched itself in faraway corners of the land, carrying pet precepts while seeking to reconcile these with a landscape of mindboggling diversity.[48] On the one hand, the Puranas reveal a rivalry between adherents of the two big gods—where the *Sivapurana* exalts Siva and presents Vishnu as awestruck, the *Vishnupurana* pays back in kind, showing its own protagonist as the superior.[49] But that aside, they were knitting all kinds of regional cults and beliefs into a comprehensible whole. Siva's family and retinue offered a means, evidently, to incorporate local divinities, including totemic animal gods such as the part-elephant Ganapati.[50] Vishnu's partisans, meanwhile, built on the theory of avatars to locate in *his* camp other regional gods. Ten incarnations are popular, while the total of twenty-four is supposedly inspired by Jainism's tradition of that many spiritual teachers.[51] Individual avatars' prehistories signal much: The boar incarnation, thus, syncretized a pre-Aryan cult, while the man-lion merged an animal deity into the tradition.[52] Why, as Buddhism—despised with a vehemence by Brahmins once—declined, the Buddha too was recast as an animal-friendly form of Vishnu, albeit a 'deceptive' one, sent to bamboozle the wicked by vending falsehoods.[53]

By design, therefore, the Puranas were quite flexible. Or as a Brahmin wrote in 1804, through 'their equivocal style, our devine [sic] Legislators gave us an opening to reform any part . . . as change of circumstances and vicissitudes of time may suggest'.[54] As ever larger tribes and societies were drawn in, more and more redactions appeared, including sub-Puranas for distinct regions and castes.[55] The longest in the scheme, the *Skandapurana*, has even been described as a 'scrap-bag'. In the indologist Wendy Doniger's words, every time someone 'came upon a story that seemed to be . . . old but did not . . . have any known provenance, he could remark, without fear of contradiction, "It's in the Skanda Purana"'.[56] To modern minds, trained to look for chronological exactness, this could be frustrating. One *sthala* Purana—linking a sacred site to the grand narrative—was found repeating a late corruption of a city's name, instead of its historical identifier, causing a nineteenth-century man to demand that, if nothing else, the 'holy' text 'surrender its insolent pretensions to antiquity'.[57] All sthala Puranas, he warned, 'profess to be integral portions of the old [main] 18 Puranas, but it is an open secret that their manipulation can scarcely be said to have yet ended'. Indeed, there were even in the colonial-era 'bards' who supplied Puranas 'on order' in convincing verse.[58] The *Bhavishyapurana*, an 'ancient' text about the future, notes not only India's Muslim sultans, thus, but also a certain Victavati—Queen Victoria.[59]

But quibbling about historiographical wantonness is to miss the point, for the Puranas are works of genius. They acquired their fluid form not to meet present-day scholarly standards but to tie the local with the pan-Indian, and the evolving with the stable; to universalize what was provincial, while seeding the parochial with the universal.[60] Rising above geographical and cultural plurality, everything was accommodated in an (admittedly cluttered) Sanskrit master narrative. Even if tenuously, they established links, unified disparate elements, all while giving the Brahmin vision of society immortality by *owning* traditions that otherwise might rise in opposition.[61] As Vedic ritualism faded, thus, and new gods and cultural spaces appeared on an ever-widening horizon, Brahmins linked this present to freshly forged pasts of myth and tradition.[62] Indeed, Brahmin culture too was transformed; 'like a python swallowing its prey whole, Brahmanism's feats of incorporation changed and distended its [own] shape'.⁶³ That is, as Puranic Hinduism ingested diverse peoples and gods through its 'gargantuan powers of assimilation', its effects travelled along a two-way street, leaving its Sanskrit synthesizers also altered.⁶⁴ Or as was stated with a more negative spin, 'Brahmanism having failed to conquer', was itself 'conquered by the multitudes'.⁶⁵ It was entirely natural, then, that the resultant product—Hinduism—became a 'macro-reality of organically united micro-realities':⁶⁶ a detail that would cause controversy, even shame, in the colonial period, when under European influences religion was imagined as more neat and coherent.⁶⁷

The examples are fascinating. The Chenchu tribe in Andhra territory became part of the great narrative after a myth invented a union between an avatar of Vishnu and a Chenchu woman.⁶⁸ In Assam, the Ahom kings of Southeast Asian Tai descent were Hinduized from the fourteenth century, the process requiring hundreds of years.⁶⁹ Meanwhile, in merging the local goddess cult with the Sanskritic, its 'left-handed' mode of worship (featuring liquor and meat) was not only endorsed but adopted even for Brahmin deities (who ordinarily receive flowers and milk).⁷⁰ In Tamil country, a leading god, Aiyanar, was transformed into Siva's son born of a beguiling female form of Vishnu (horrifying a touchy European who felt Vishnu could hardly be respectable if he committed 'uncleanness' with a man).⁷¹ In Maharashtra of the twelfth century, a pastoral deity, Vitthal, who to this day commands love, became a Vishnu avatar, despite contestations by Jains who claimed him as theirs.⁷² Indeed, the process is still in play—the Musahar community in Brahminism's Gangetic home have two brother deities; these have lately been recast as the sibling heroes from the epic Ramayana, drawing this marginalized caste more firmly into the Brahminical order.⁷³ Unsurprisingly, all this had its politics too: In Kerala—a region where Brahmin ascendancy occurred relatively late—a goddess who liked human sacrifice was persuaded to pull on with substitutes. But in the process, her non-Brahmin custodians were also ejected to make way for Brahmin priests.[74]

Equally for Brahmins, however, while they attempted to construct narrative unity, their own identity was sliced. Far from being a uniform, well-oiled machine working in coordination, they imbued local colours and peculiarities; different groups cultivated distinct traits and markers in a concession to regional sensibilities. Thus, there were Brahmins entitled to study the Vedas but also Brahmins denied it; there were vegetarian Brahmins as there were those who ate more than grain and greens;[75] and there were Brahmins who buried their dead, while most chose cremation.[76] For the societies Brahmins penetrated also made demands of them. Namboodiris in Kerala, for instance, adopted not only superficial aspects linked to dress but also, initially, the local system of matrilineal succession.[77] Even native candidates for Brahminhood had to be accepted, the process masked by Puranic tales. One tells, thus, of how Brahmins on the Konkan coast were 'created' by a Vishnu avatar from the 'funeral pyre of sixty men', so he could have assistance during a ritual.[78] Others in Maharashtra—supposed, at some point, to have presided over human sacrifice—were formed from camel bones, fertilized by the semen of an ass, this origin myth obviously manufactured by rivals to denigrate.[79] Tribal priests, absorbed into the Hindu scheme, were upgraded as Brahmins,[80] and Iranian 'sun-priests' too were welcomed and rebranded as Maga Brahmins in Rajasthan and Bihar.[81] It is not surprising, therefore, that even on the cusp of modernity there were feuds about whether some Brahmins were Brahmin at all.[82] Brahminhood *itself* became a contested, jumbled category—this was not one caste, but many: a factor that would cause inordinate confusion to India's British rulers in times ahead.[83]

Understandably, negotiation, including through economic and social relations, underpinned all this. Country powers often invited Brahmins to settle, not just to cement kingship but also for extending an organized agrarian political economy, which held material incentives.[84] Thus, in north Kerala, different groups-turned-castes slowly grew dependent on one another, this reflecting in their gods occupying slots in shared groves. As the scholar Dilip Menon observes, 'Deceased ancestors, local heroes and heroines, gods of the Vedic pantheon, and nature gods all rubbed shoulders in a seamless fabric of worship.'[85] Families moving from the plains to tribal uplands accepted carnivorous forest gods, the tribes reciprocating with room for incoming vegetarian deities.[86] A Tamil story in which a Brahmin figure's severed head is attached to an outcaste's body, transforming her into a goddess, also hints at such 'fusion'.[87] In the same region, not only was an androgynous goddess turned into Siva's wife,[88] but at the festival marking this 'marriage', another god appears as a 'guest'. Deity to the Kallar tribe, he was reimagined as Vishnu, his inclusion in the tale having something to do with bringing a refractory people under control.[89] Things did not always work out, though: At Devarapura in Karnataka, the Kurubas celebrate the Kunde Habba (Ass Festival). Drunk and dressed in drag, men hurl expletives at the deity for abandoning them and eloping with a goddess, perhaps echoing a reluctant compromise.[90] Tellingly, even in the eighteenth century, Brahmins were unwelcome here, risking torture in politically fractious times.[91]

The bigger point, then, is that while Puranic culture grew into 'a vast ocean', it is important to remember that 'the Brahmanical stream, no matter how big and forceful, still [represented] only one amongst numerous others flowing into' it.[92] What made the difference, however, was that Brahmins went out of their way to identify each river and claim for it a common source with others; in creating an overarching explanatory frame, they sought unity while maintaining a formal supremacy for themselves and their ideas. Indeed, though the Vedas became less and less relevant to the everyday practice of Hinduism even for Brahmins, Puranic texts that did actually matter were legitimized by constructing links, even if largely nominal, with the Vedas.[93] And so long as the Vedas were not denied and the caste superiority of Brahmins were accepted, practically anybody—holding a variety of ideas—could be brought into the frame.[94] That way Vedic texts remained *formally* supreme even if it was a later, more mixed corpus that better represented religious reality—a situation we might describe as a 'win-win'.

It is this many-faced, multi-layered system that we today call Hinduism. This was not a religion with one book or one fount. But what did press it together was belief in similar myths and legends, told and retold in multiple forms and languages. There was always a hill nearby where Rama rested, or where characters from the Mahabharata dwelt; there was always a Puranic story in which local people were part of a great cosmic event.[95] Indeed, such was the popularity of the Puranas that the far-removed Vedic system—theoretically Hinduism's foundation—had little bearing on the lives of most people considered Hindu. While an understanding of the Vedas endowed scholars with respect, the fact that it had little immediate relevance even led to jokes. A twelfth-century intellectual likened Brahmins to load-bearing donkeys, with their archaic books,[96] and the term *chandasa*, for Vedic experts, also acquired a pejorative connotation, as 'a stupid ritualist who does not understand the ways of the world'.[97]

But the Brahmin *did*, quite patently, understand the ways of the world. He had to make room for gods he did not first recognize and for ideas that rose up from other traditions. He did have to concede space to beliefs from beyond his Sanskrit universe, shrewdly deploying the lament of the awful kali yuga to excuse such pragmatism. So much so that most of what constitutes Hindu culture today is 'not . . . the offspring of Brahmanism as its [child] by adoption'.[98] It was not the ideal scenario, of course, but it did give Brahmin ideologies a foothold in many localities. Equally, the provincial was not beholden to Brahmins, for it too shaped this narrative.[99] But Brahmin elites—linked across regions by a shared language in Sanskrit and a veneration for the Vedas—attempted to integrate the ideas of even rivals into an amorphous whole, claiming every innovation as unblemished tradition.[100] While Hindus had many ways and practices, then, it was arguably Brahmins who helped sculpt Hindu*ism*. And most importantly, this endowed this class with control over the pan-Indian narrative—a source of immense power, which would in time catalyse Hindu nationalism.[101] Simply put, every time new forces emerged, the Brahmin was equipped, in return for preservation, to provide from his all-encompassing bag of myths, material tailored to fit the moment. Indian civilization, after all, is built on stories—and if it met anything unfamiliar, it simply absorbed it and told yet more stories.

By 1000 CE, India's cultural landscape was on the verge of fresh transformations. Until then, just as Brahmins wooed all varieties of groups, Buddhists and Jains too had employed similar strategies, often working from an overlapping toolkit. For instance, if Buddhism evolved its own gods and rites, to the extent of sometimes appearing like a mirror of its rival,[102] the idea of a Buddha-yet-to-come found a Brahmin parallel in Vishnu's prophesized final avatar.[103] Many similarities extended even to metaphysics and philosophy—the noted eighth-century theologian Sankara is in friendly accounts cast as Siva-incarnate, born to decimate Buddhists, while others (including critics from rival Hindu schools) accused him of having simply dressed the Buddhist wolf in Brahmin clothing.[104] Suspicion of Sankara's philosophy—that the godhead is formless, eternal and infinite; that the tangible world, including deities and rituals, is illusory—is not surprising. Leaving aside theological hair-splitting, traditions built around Siva, Vishnu and increasingly the supreme female energy, Shakti, prevailed on the ground; to suggest these were illusory was controversial. All agreed, of course, that there was only one paramount being, and that others were subordinate manifestations. But depending on one's leanings, for most, that being was either Siva or Vishnu or Shakti—and these gods were perfectly capable of acquiring different forms and personalities, touching the (equally non-illusory) human world.¹⁰⁵

Part of this commitment to a personified god, as opposed to the abstract entity, was the result of *bhakti*, or devotionalism. While local cults appear to have always showed an affection for sacred spots with images, into the early centuries CE pan-Indian faiths, including Sramanic traditions, embraced the temple.¹⁰⁶

Shakti, the great goddess, by Pierre Sonnerat, in his *Voyage aux Indes Orientales et à la Chine* (1782), courtesy of the Library of Congress, Rare Book and Special Collections Division.

A complex system of worship would develop over the next millennium, as gods, after due ceremony, took up residence in images of wood, stone or metal. Worship was no longer about fire sacrifices to invisible deities, or a philosophical acceptance of the almighty; the emphasis moved to the individual *beholding* divinity. Gods were humanized: They could be cajoled, flattered, reprimanded, loved, spurned, threatened but always embraced by emotion.¹⁰⁷ There were child gods, and adult gods; gods who were angry in one shrine, benign in the next. Temple rites saw deities being roused in the morning, taken around in processions and for baths (including post-menstrual dips),¹⁰⁸ celebrate marriages, and do all that humans did—but on a scale befitting their status. Soon, royalty became sponsors of temples: Valuable real estate was bestowed, and rulers, advertising their power, assumed protectors' duties.[109] In the peninsula, thus, under the Pallava kings, great edifices began to emerge.[110] In time, the temple evolved roles as banker, cultural timekeeper, economic engine and a supplier of stability when political sands shifted. And as Brahmins adapted to endorse and co-opt these novel forms of worship—which many first scorned—bhakti received theological certification as a legitimate route to liberation.[111]

Moreover, by the medieval period, early shoots of sectarian identities—as defined now, where people perceive themselves as followers of a specific faith—started making their appearance. As the historian Manu Devadevan argues in the case of Karnataka, '(w)orshipping a deity was [hitherto] simply a part of everyday life, not a marker of identity'; just as 'wearing cotton clothes, residing in a thatched hut or making love never produced identities like cotton-wearer, thatched-hut-dweller, or love-maker, so also the worshipping of Siva or Visnu . . . did not confer identities'.[112] This was a spiritual bazaar where multiple groups peddled religious wares, to an audience buying from all. Kings too, even when they had favourites,[113] tended to balance groups: Inscriptions in Andhra style a Vishnukundina ruler as a devotee of Siva in one record, while praising him as pro-Buddha in another. Bengal's Palas built Hindu temples even as they supported Sramanic monks.[114] In Kerala, an Ay king preferred Vishnu but gave to Siva too, while his heir aided Jains and Buddhists.[115] The Western Gangas claimed Brahmin descent but served as patrons of Jainism without hesitation.[116] While seemingly paradoxical, this mix and match had a logic: Even Buddhist royalty had an incentive in upholding Brahmin theories on caste, for example, viewed more as a sociopolitical instrument than as a religious principle.[117] Temples entrenched this: The control of land meant that shrines developed patronage networks, supporting musicians, priests, dancers, farmers, artisans and, over time, whole communities, all while injecting into these specific social ideologies.[118]

Aiding this process of religious identity formation, especially at elite levels, was the energy with which Puranic stories welded together diverse physical temple sites. The result was the creation of what the scholar Diana L. Eck has called a 'sacred geography', with pilgrimage becoming a popular means to experience divinity; a path that did not involve asceticism or monkhood.[119] Thus, in present-day Kurukshetra, a banyan tree marks the 'exact spot' where Krishna in the Mahabharata imparted wisdom to Arjuna, in his great preamble before battle.[120] Chadayamangalam on the west coast is where the vulture Jatayu fell as he tried to prevent the evil Ravana from abducting Rama's wife in the Ramayana; and once Rama had killed his enemy, it was at Rameswaram on the *east* coast that he cleansed himself, consecrating a temple. Dantewada in Chhattisgarh, known for a goddess of tribal origins, was linked to Shakti and cast as the spot where a *danta* (tooth) from the corpse of Siva's wife fell as he danced with it in furious agony; her genitals fell in Assam in the north-east, her navel in Tamil country, her hair in Karnataka, a breast in Bihar and a hand all the way north in Kashmir. A single story, thus, entwined temples across vast reaches, reinforcing the claim of an essential unity.[121] By encouraging devotees to travel to such sites, not only were they told that they could gain spiritual release, but it also generated a culture of commonality despite different vocabularies, tongues and histories. Viewed this way, latter-day India's slogan of 'Unity in Diversity' acquires a different origin.[122]

That said, if there were currents binding temples and their surrounding communities into a grand narrative, its politicization, elite domination and growing ritualism (with attendant paranoias around caste purity) meant dissent was not far away either. It was among Tamils, in the Tamil language—which rivals Sanskrit in claims to literary antiquity—that bhakti emerged. Indeed, poetic expression of this constitutes the oldest Hindu literature *not* in Sanskrit.[123] Over several centuries, the songs of Tamil poet-saints celebrated sacred spots. But when this devotionalism spread to

Karnataka, it featured criticism. Here, Virasaiva thinkers eschewed temple worship, adoring Siva through stone *ishtalingams* carried by each believer instead. Virasaiva ranks featured washermen, barbers, toddy-tappers, cobblers, sex workers and burglars—sections less invested and likely to be included in temple culture.[124] Basava, its leading voice, dismissing religious complexes,[125] wryly remarked, 'The rich will make temples for Siva. What shall I, a poor man do? My legs are pillars, the body the shrine, the head a cupola of gold. Listen, O lord . . . things standing shall fall, but the moving shall ever stay.'[126] On extravagant Brahminical rites and mantras, he quipped: 'Parrots recite. So what? Can they read the Lord?'[127] Such bhakti, which would engulf the subcontinent in diverse shapes, is often romanticized as 'Indian analogues to European protestant movements'; as a religious culture 'of and for the underdog'.[128] In other words, even in devotional spaces, there was no one way, and diversity of approach remained—a different dynamic from that stereotype of India as unchanging and timeless.[129]

Was there, however, no conflict at all as these varied paths crossed each other? Today, religious tension in India is imagined along a Hindu–Muslim axis: There was an all-encompassing Hindu identity to which cruelty was done by an invading faith. In actual fact, however, feuds were not uncommon between partisans of Siva and Vishnu (Saivas and Vaishnavas), and of both against Jains and Buddhists. Saiva poetry, thus, presents Vishnu as subject to Siva; as one who cannot presume to even comprehend that god.[130] Vaishnavas returned the favour by showing Siva as Vishnu's appointment, his followers 'ignorant innocents'.[131] One Saiva saint is eulogized for defeating Buddhists in a debate only to lose face when jousting with a Vaishnava.[132] In a temple chronicle, the twelfth-century Vaishnava saint Ramanuja flees Saiva persecution in one area, only to convert the Jain king whose land he enters.[133] Even in the twentieth century, Vaishnavas could 'boast' of having never patronized Saiva shrines.[134] That said, agents of Vishnu and Siva still worked within a common 'religious ethos' with 'ubiquitous Puranic myths'; Sramanic rivals, on the other hand, were more alien.¹³⁵ Even in the oldest Tamil poetry, thus, the bigger enemy is the Jain or Buddhist.¹³⁶ Rivalries between Siva and Vishnu sought to *subordinate* one to the other; feuds with Sramanic religions aimed to vanquish them. Trenchant disputations were routine. A seventeenth-century account claims, for example, that when once a Jain gave a dressing down to his Brahmin rivals, they were so hopelessly emasculated that it was a surprise 'the townspeople did not lust after them as if they were women'.¹³⁷

By the eleventh and twelfth centuries, after sacred sites became significant factors, such rivalries assumed violent proportions. Saiva hagiographies are a case in point: In them, Vaishnavas are murdered for telling 'lies' about Siva and an image of Vishnu is melted by a Saiva's power.¹³⁸ A bloody twelfth-century royal succession in Andhra saw two factions backed by rival sectarian groups,¹³⁹ while in 1598, Saiva priests jumped off a tower to protest the amplification of Vishnu in a prominent Tamil temple town.¹⁴⁰ In 1789, Vaishnava and Saiva ascetics in Maharashtra clashed over precedence during a ritual dip.¹⁴¹ In fact, as late as the 1860s, the predecessor of Madho Singh of Jaipur—who we met at the start of this chapter—launched a campaign of oppression against Vaishnavas after pledging his loyalty to Saivism.¹⁴² Even so famous a temple as Tirupati—among India's most popular—witnessed disputes about the identity of its deity. The image evidently features matted hair and serpents—aspects typical of Siva—while a smear of sandalwood paste on the forehead is said to conceal that god's third eye. Though the deity holds objects associated with Vishnu, that these are supposedly detachable sparked suspicions. By the twelfth century, at any rate, Vaishnavas were in control, arguing that Vishnu too in some contexts sports matted hair, and that the articles were picked up by the deity personally. As for the sandalwood mark, it does not conceal a third eye but a wound Vishnu received when he took a blow to save a cow!¹⁴³ Yet again stories came to the rescue.

What can be inferred, then, is that from major shrines to obscure ones, it was possible to reclaim and reinvent them according to shifting patterns—something that direly affected the Sramanic religions once they lost out to Puranic rivals.[144] Thus, what is now a Hindu temple in Nagercoil used to be Jain in the sixteenth century.[145] Long before, kings in the Deccan converted Buddhist shrines in Ellora chiselling out Buddhas to ensconce Vishnu—those figures that were spared were, by the nineteenth century, visualized as Hindu anyway.[146] Lord Curzon, viceroy of India, was startled in 1903 when visiting Gaya—location of the Buddha's enlightenment—he found its temple in Saiva hands.[147] At Kandiyur in Kerala, home to a ninth-century Siva, a Buddha was discovered buried nearby.[148] To the north, at Paruvasseri, a Jain image, meanwhile, became Vishnu.[149] Violence and natural calamities often tilted the balance: In Karnataka, it is estimated that as many as 2000 Jain sites were destroyed or repurposed in the late medieval period.[150] Saiva stories buttress such speculations: They show their heroes coming across towns with 'new Jain monasteries and temples', while Siva suffers 'like a small fish in a pond surrounded by hungry herons'. Rousing others to challenge the Jain 'dogs', they 'uproot and shatter' their 'dolls'.[151] Though the numbers are inflated, a single Saiva saint is credited with killing 32,000 Jains, while another slaughters 8000.[152] Tamil poetry has a Vaishnava steal a gold Buddha to fund a temple for Vishnu,[153] while another declares: 'Snatch the rice from the mouths of those who burden the earth! Stuff them with grass instead!'[154] In fact, as recently as a century ago, Tamil temple processions featured images 'representing a Jain impaled on a stake'.[155]

India's religious universe—both within the Puranic system as well as in its dealings with faiths of the Sramanic kind—was clearly, thus, of extraordinary complexity. Saivas and Vaishnavas baited one another, while Buddhists and Jains were reduced to submission.[156] Caste became a stringent part of existence, with some segments cast as so ritually impure as to be untouchable. Even proponents of bhakti, while democratizing devotionalism and access to god, hesitated to challenge caste in secular settings.¹⁵⁷ What is remarkable is that Brahmins nearly everywhere won towering social positions, though again, this too was not without criticism. The thirteenth-century *Basavapurana* from the Andhra region is full of hostility for them, for example. Here, Brahmins are cast as the 'real' untouchables: In one story, a lady, when brushed by one, takes a cleansing bath; in another, an untouchable covers his (meaty) lunch to save it from a Brahmin's polluting (vegetarian) eyes, reversing the hierarchy. In the first tale, the saint even has a dog recite the Vedas, to curdle Brahmin pride.¹⁵⁸ As usual, however, enmity was tamed into compromise; near contemporaneous with the *Basavapurana* is another work, by a Brahmin, to soften militant Saivism.¹⁵⁹ More effort would be invested in this direction so that by the fifteenth and sixteenth centuries, retellings of Saiva saints' lives not only expunged dislike but proactively brought them in line with Brahminical ideals.¹⁶⁰

For Brahmins, though, there was no happy ending. For by then, India's religious and cultural landscape had been disrupted by another new force: the creed of Muhammad.

Among the legendary rulers of Kerala on the western seaboard, with its maritime history, were some who disappointed Brahmin chroniclers. One king bought into Buddhist doctrines, we are told, until challenged by Brahmins to a great debate. When his team lost, the man was banished from the country.¹⁶¹ Then there was another. Having committed an injustice, he was denied atonement by the religions at hand; so, he took reprieve in an option fresh off foreign merchants' boats, called Islam.¹⁶² Later retellings are more colourful. Admiring the evening sky, this king one day witnesses the splitting of the moon. Learning of Muhammad's miracle from some Arab traders, he divides his lands among vassals, boards a ship to the Middle East and becomes a Muslim.[163] Whether or not the legend bears truth, the tale of the convert king caught on. On the one hand, it legitimized a dozen Hindu dynasties along the coast as beneficiaries of the king's partition of territories.[164] But, on the other, it also carved out space for the presence of a Muslim community in Kerala. Indeed, just as Brahmins claimed they were settled in these parts by a Vishnu avatar, the story of the convert rajah opened narrative windows for Islam also to smoothly slide into local imagination.[165] As Muslims familiarized themselves with the land, in other words, they too deployed stories comparable to those in the Puranas.[166]

Islam's advent in the *north*, however, was not via networks of maritime commerce but through battlefields—a bloodier setting where incentives to blend in through creative writing were not urgent. Tales were, of course, woven, but for foreign audiences— the eleventh-century raids of Mahmud of Ghazni were magnified disproportionately in Arabic texts so as to valorize him in the Islamic world as the bane of infidels. Though Gujarat's Somnath temple, which he plundered, was not special, it was positioned before Muslim powers as the Mecca of idolatry. Indeed, in one account, the Prophet having failed to destroy what becomes the idol in Somnath (!) is asked by an angel not to fret; this specific deity is reserved for our king.[167] Mahmud set a gold standard for Muslim raiders, among whom parading and breaking idols proved a commitment to monotheism.[168] India, viewed as the nerve centre of polytheistic image worship was fertile territory, thus,[169] for his successors to both enrich themselves and to construct legitimacy. So, while Somnath survived Mahmud's iconoclasm, it kept attracting copycats. Memories of these desecrations would acquire a life of their own. Not only would the British attempt to 'avenge' Hindus in the Victorian age but postcolonial India's first president also laid the foundation stone personally for the present temple, as if correcting a historical wrong.[170] Unlike in Kerala, then, where mythmaking eased

Islam's entry, in the north, it would come to be perceived by some as a devourer of Hindus, and a civilizational adversary.

Understandably, responses to Islam see-sawed between these extremes, depending on who was speaking. It was, as one mind frames it, a 'strange combination of acceptance and rejection'.[171] An eleventh-century Buddhist text, for instance, irreverently suggests that advocates of the Vedas might gel gloriously with Islam, given their shared fondness for violence.[172] But jibes aside, Brahmin intellectuals struggled, not least because it was tough to draw the Muslim neatly into the Puranic universe. For already evolved and packaged in the Perso–Arabic world, his religion was unlikely to succumb to the typical overtures. Some of it was about principles—if Brahmins ordered the world into castes, Islam, in theory, proposed egalitarianism.[173] And while there was no single pan-Indian Hinduism, Brahmins had, as we saw, formed a 'consciousness' of unity, to which Muslim power posed a threat.[174] As a faith, Islam had, of course, been part of India's spiritual platter for some time, and by the eighth century, the term *musalmana* (Muslim) found its way into Sanskrit.[175] But joined to and reinforced by autonomous *power*, with alternate ideals of kingship, god and self-expression, it loomed as a rival to Brahminism and its umbilical ties to political authority. 'For the first time in her history' (or in a long time at any rate), 'India was to reconcile to the existence [and possibility] of a *separate* culture-community'—something that, given the abruptness with which it happened, triggered mixed feelings, its worst coming to a head with the subcontinent's partition in the 1940s.[176]

But this sense of separateness appears early on. For instance, in twelfth- and thirteenth-century literary coverage of clashes between a Hindu king and an invading Muslim counterpart. In his own courtly production, the former is presented as Vishnu-incarnate, here to quell all the chaos unleashed by foreign savages.[177] Their misdeeds include crashing temple rites, eating meat, treating Brahmins with contempt and following a lifestyle repellent to Hindu eyes.[178] On the Muslim side, meanwhile, a Persian text employed comparable strategies: The Hindu is Satan's instrument; the sultan was fighting 'enemies of the faith'; and he sought not material profit but to advance the 'Islamic way of life'.[179] Both professed divine validation, posing as defenders of order. Such tall claims, in fact, would become formulaic. Thus we have a fifteenth-century sultan described in Persian accounts as such a zealous infidel-killer that each time he liquidated 20,000, he would throw a party.[180] So too a fourteenth-century Hindu inscription is predictable when it reports how the 'darkness of the Turks' having 'enveloped the world', the country, 'tortured' by the halting of temple rites, was akin to 'a forest engulfed by a rampaging fire'.[181] While this reveals tension, how much reflected real violence and how much polemics—as in feuds between Jains and Buddhists, Saivas and Vaishnavas—is debatable.[182] And yet the existence of such tension is itself telling.

In any case, once Islamic power settled in India, as opposed to making periodic visitations, its appetite for temple-smashing was much reduced. By the thirteenth century, a Muslim dynasty was entrenched in Delhi, and its armies would overwhelm most of the subcontinent. In the process, kingdoms were conquered, Hindu royalty toppled and temples reduced to rubble.[183] But thereafter, as a foreign elite ruling over a populous country, compromises were inevitable. Or in the words of a vizier, Muslim power was like salt in a dish—desirable but best sprinkled in moderation.[184] Sultans issued coins with Sanskrit inscriptions and, over time, formed a policy of tolerance, even if only out of practical considerations.[185] Parallel acts of desecration did occur but as the scholar Richard Eaton phrases it, Hindu sites suffered 'on the cutting edge of [the sultanate's] moving military frontier' as it expanded into new territories.[186] Yet, the threat was ever-present: 400 years later, thus, the formidable Tipu Sultan in his home provinces was a patron of shrines, honouring Hindu spiritual heads and having temple rites performed in his name. But when he invaded Kerala next door, without irony the same man deployed violent rhetoric, shattered idols and proved a terror.[187] The reverse too occurred—Chhatrapati Shivaji, founder of the Maratha state, in his seventeenth-century kingly narrative is Vishnu manifested to destroy 'unruly Muslims'.[188] This while his father was apparently named after a local Muslim divine.[189] Accommodation and suspicion, then, coexisted—a situation sustained into the present.

Better impulses did, of course, assert themselves, then as today. Indeed, while contradictions were stressed during conflict, in everyday terms, constructive exchange was inevitable. In the Deccan, thus, a Muslim notable, impressed by Hindu thought in the sixteenth century, found himself a guru. His desire to become a Brahmin was foiled, but Murtaza did reincarnate himself in Sanskrit as Mrityunjaya.[190] In Bengal, the cult of Satya Pir has its central figure combine Brahmin religious markers with the garb of a Muslim fakir.[191] Seventeenth-century Karnataka was home to a miracle-working Hindu, raised by Muslims,[192] while in Andhra, a Hindu king and his Muslim vanquisher were reimagined as forms of Siva and Vishnu.[193] In Maharashtra, similarly, the deity Khandoba received Muslim veneration,[194] while in Sindh, some portrayed Ali as Vishnu's newest avatar.[195] In Benares—Hinduism's most sacred city—a traveller saw Muslims abandon Islam for the Brahmin's faith.[196] Equally, the Muslim saint Kabir grew so popular with Hindus that some posthumously gave him a Brahmin pedigree.[197] Meanwhile, at the court in Delhi, the Mughal emperor Akbar celebrated Hindu festivals and had a Veda and the Mahabharata translated into Persian.[198] Pleased Brahmins issued panegyrics likening him to a deity.[199] As for Somnath, once tormented by Islamic powers, it soon became custom for local Muslims en route to Mecca to 'pay their *respects*' here.[200] Why, attempts were made to concoct Puranic origins for Islam itself: In one account, the Prophet springs from Vishnu, while another suggests it was Siva who gave Muhammad leave to propagate a new religion.[201]

Islam, then, was different but not 'inexpressibly alien', not least because Muslims in India were themselves diverse and the opposite of a monolith.[202] Matrilineal Muslims in Kerala had more in common with their matrilineal Hindu neighbours, for example, than with Deccan Muslims, whose food, culture and general being was of a different order. For the most part, people managed to live together, transcending disagreements. One enabler was simply the country's diversity. While Islam was distinct, this, in a society full of plural identities, was not unusual. If Muslims were in Sanskrit narratives described as *asura*s (demons) and mlecchas, the terms were also used at times by Hindus against other Hindus.[203] Where Muslim rulers destroyed temples, Hindu kings too—even if they did not demolish or break idols—occasionally plundered them.[204] So also while the sixteenth-century philosopher Eknath produced a dialogue in which a Hindu and Muslim trade barbs, in another he challenges (intra-Hindu) caste prejudices.[205] That is, Hindus did not think of themselves as *only* Hindus, viewed in contrast to Muslims—that claim appeared in the modern period. Until then, identities were shaped by multiple parameters such as caste and region and language, religion being one of many factors. Thus, two persons might share a linguistic identity as Telugu speakers, and yet have little intercourse if one were Brahmin, the other 'untouchable'. In fact, the Brahmin might deal more regularly with Muslim authorities, serving as a bureaucrat or cultural middleman, transacting in courtly Persian.[206]

Yet, the religious divide was not artificial or a colonial invention, as is sometimes argued by the well-intentioned, who seek to bridge current religious cleavages in India. For at an intellectual level, notions of 'Us and Them' always persisted between Muslims and Hindu elites. After all, even in efforts to reconcile Islam with Hinduism, recognition of each as dissimilar is implicit.[207] Even under the kindest sultans, temple worship was tolerated, not endorsed; Brahmins were respected, but no Muslim power was likely to admit their pretensions to superiority.[208] A steady undercurrent of suspicion remained, then.²⁰⁹ And there was no shortage of violence. In 1244, 'Muslims were killed following an assault . . . by the Hindus during *Id* prayer' in Haryana.²¹⁰ Despite Kerala's culture of tolerance, a mosque was attacked in the fourteenth century for tiling (as opposed to thatching) its roof, and by this claiming parity with a temple.²¹¹ Fifteenth-century Kashmir saw Hindu and Muslim shrines set ablaze, in addition to provocative cow slaughter.²¹² A Hindu rajah in Rajasthan, was, for opposing Mughal inroads, saluted in religious language: he denies 'the kalamam (*kalima*)' and elevates the 'veda-purana'.²¹³ In seventeenth-century Karnataka, conflict occurred when Hindus took an idol of Ganapati by a Muslim shrine; they were decried as 'infidels' with an 'accursed' deity.²¹⁴ Some decades earlier, in a Telugu text, a southern emperor is shown viewing both the Hindu king of Orissa and a neighbouring sultan as enemies; but the former is a notch better for keeping faith in the right gods.²¹⁵ One especially graphic statement comes from a Bihar-born poet in the early 1400s:

> The Hindus and the Turks live close together.
> Each makes fun of the other's religion.
> One calls the faithful to prayer. The other recites the Vedas.
> . . . The Turks coerce passers by into doing forced labor.
> Grabbing hold of a Brahmin boy, they put a cow's vagina on his head.
> They rub out his *tilak* [forehead mark] and break his sacred thread . . .
> They destroy temples and construct mosques.²¹⁶

To sum up, then, ingredients always existed in India to support a binary between Muslims and non-Muslims. And in some contexts and spaces, this alerted Hindus—despite their various differences—to the *possibility* of political oneness. That is, if Brahminism held a 'consciousness' of unity, faced with an opponent, that feeling would slowly harden. In the modern age—which pushed political integration, introduced technology such as the press and the need

Emperor Akbar [Jahangir's father] and Gosain Jadrup [Chitrup], Folio from the 'St Petersburg Muraqqa', Harvard Art Museums/Arthur M. Sackler Museum, Gift of Grenville L. Winthrop, Class of 1886, Photo © President and Fellows of Harvard College, 1937.20.

to stand up to colonialism—new meaning was invested in broad-based labels. Two ideas appeared of the Indian nation: a pluralistic one with room for all, celebrating syncretic aspects of the Hindu–Muslim encounter. And another, equating India with a Hindu nation, galvanized by memories of persecution by Muslim kings and, as we shall see, Christian colonialists. Logic could be found for both. Emperor Jahangir, for example, was transfixed by a Brahmin ascetic called Chitrup in 1617.[217] 'Without exaggeration,' he diarized, 'it was hard for me to part from him.'[218] They bonded over spiritual issues, finding plenty of common ground—evidence that Hindu and Muslim could get along.[219] And yet, the same monarch also once, almost on a whim, destroyed a temple and its 'hideous' idol—confirmation for the cynical that Islam could never be truly trusted.[220] Chitrup too affirmed his separate identity. When asked what he thought about the Prophet, he replied: 'You yourself say he was sent by God. He is the guide of the people to whom the True King has sent him. He need not trouble himself about us, courtiers of the Almighty.'[221] Islam had value for those who believed in it, he seemed to argue. But for those who met god through other paths, the divine message was already clear.

As always, in India, even if the destination were the same, the road could never be one. And as much as this could be read as pluralism, ever present was also the prospect of disunion.

It is possible that by now the reader of this rambling essay will relate to an eighteenth-century padre's frustration. 'These heathens,' he grumbled, 'are very shifting in their discourses. One tells me one thing and another something different.'[222] Or perhaps we declare too many things at once, all of which happen to be true. He deserves sympathy, either way, for Indians also are likely to find the country's religious evolution bewildering.

Masked under that disarmingly plain term 'Hinduism' is a many-layered phenomenon—from a leaner Vedic personality, it became something richer in the Puranic age; exchanges with tribal cults, Buddhism, Jainism and Islam activated fascinating transformations. Things were perplexing enough by the early modern era, until the arrival of European powers—and, in their wake, politically backed Christianity—slapped on a fresh coat of complexity. Alongside came other upheavals. The Mughals stretched their power to its limits, and when Akbar's great-grandson died in 1707, their empire went into decline. Emboldened vassals shook themselves free, and in the resultant flux, a petty overseas venture—the English East India Company—inched out from its coastal enclaves to become a great hegemon. It is the story of Hinduism in this period that makes up the rest of this book; or specifically, the context in which Hindu nationalism—Hindutva, so dominant now in India—found its raison d'être. This is not, then, a study of the religion across the ages but a survey of 400 years at most—a span that supplies the historical setting and much of the emotional stimulus empowering present-day Hinduism.

It is often argued, however, that Hinduism is a Western 'invention'; that before the modern era, there were just castes, sects and a heap of contradictory traditions, possessing none of the streamlined clarity associated with Christianity and Islam. Certainly, 'Hinduism' as a term is of recent vintage. It appeared first as a label for foreigners to lump together unfamiliar people. And yet, once created, Hindus seized that expression, recognizing something familiar there. To suggest this was passive acquiescence in a foreign-made identity is simplistic.[223] As we saw, the encounter with Islam had initiated a feeling of oneness among Hindu thinkers, building on an older unifying Brahminical impulse. Confronted by colonialism, such instincts grew firmer, and Hindus themselves invested substance in the outsider's name tag. Hinduism was not 'invented'; it represents the latest milestone in a long-running religious process. Like a river that might originate in small streams, this one too had many beginnings. But it has been flowing for long, only picking up a new name at a bend along the way. So, while the name is modern, the river is old. Besides, to compare Hinduism in a blanket sense to Christianity and Islam is to presume that religions must all fit one template to qualify; that anything which does not meet certain parameters—prophets, a core set of codes—is somehow a pretender. The fact, however, is that religions can emerge in different forms in different places, just as they might borrow from one another.[224] Historically, Hinduism did not fit the mould of book-based religions, though in its modern form, it does appropriate many of the latter's features. In the past, it was like an ever-expanding tapestry of uncertain shape; modern dynamics, however, hastened the stitching-up of its outer borders.

This closing of the door is the principal focus of this book. And, as we shall see, it was born of a sustained and often painful interaction with the colonial West. We will begin with Europe's early encounters with Hindus—a phase in which white men met a new culture but treated it not with open minds but jaundiced eyes. Indeed, European ideas of Hinduism were in good measure shaped by their own cultural and political preoccupations; they saw what they *wished* to see and interpreted Hindu culture to suit predetermined priorities, as highlighted in the first two chapters. By itself, this would not have mattered—on the contrary, Christianity looked like it was growing worryingly Hinduized in India. But having gained power, white men's slanted perceptions acquired force. Hindus would now begin to look at themselves in a mirror crafted by foreign hands, seeing a somewhat distorted reflection: The making of this mirror is the theme in chapters three and four, as brown men under white rule came to terms with what was being projected. And yet, 'native' minds were not blank slates. Or as an annoyed missionary put it, 'It is possible for a Hindu to have his whole soul apparently absorbed in a subject, and yet for his real thought to be as far from it as the east is from the west.'[225] With growing assaults on Hindu culture—the subject of the fifth chapter—'native' agency asserted itself. And as the final two sections of the book demonstrate, this took the form of both an internal soul-searching, as well as external resistance, leaving Hindu society transformed yet again. That is, if the British had certain ideas, Hindus too had distinct motivations; in remaking themselves, they ingested part of the colonial fare—strategically finding parallels within their traditions—refusing to swallow the rest. The result was a hybrid: old in many respects but also renewed to survive the modern world and its pressures.

There is a saying, though, that to look for the ancestry of saints, and the origins of rivers is an enterprise fraught with peril, bringing, as it does, mainly disappointment. The same could apply to investigating modern Hinduism. The religion today has a grand, linear narrative which, to its most rigid believers, is the only truth. They see an eternal faith, above history and even the possibility of scholarly scrutiny. To try and study how all this acquired its current appearance under the domination of strangers,[226] is possibly hopeless at best, controversial at worst. But I take the risk, for it is a remarkable story, featuring mahatmas and polemicists, missionaries and 'natives', little gods and great gods, text and tradition, and, of course, foreigners of different persuasions. There is battle, of men and ideas both. There is the ascent of prejudice, which did more damage than wars of conquest. There is colonization not only of land and resources but also of the mind and its frameworks. But it is a story of defiance too, aspects of which are bloody, others cerebral. Crucially, colonialism seeded a feeling among many Hindus that their identity needed muscle; and in forging this defensive frame, they would position themselves against the West and Muslims both. That colonialism gave Hinduism a new look is just another turn in a history full of reinvention. Yet, its *political* consequence is also an exclusionary creed. This, to some Hindus, is an aberration:

the repulsive offspring of a saintly mother. Advocates of militant Hinduism, however, view things differently. Faced, they would argue, with dangerous rivals in Islam and Christianity, Hindus cannot but fortify their new, unified identity. Pluralism sounds charming, but regimentation is essential to survival. That wrathful child was born for a reason, they insist, and in the following chapters we examine its advent.

What this book is *not* is a history of Hindu philosophy or of the lofty ideas of ancient sages. It is not a study of the Vedas and holy texts, or a quest to unearth deep meanings obscured in theological traditions. It is only an investigation into human action and reaction, in a context of political conquest, cultural domination and resistance. For those who prefer happier, more syncretic aspects of Hinduism's history—which are, without question, inalienable parts of it—or a romantic celebration of the faith, proceed no further. The pages ahead offer something rather less reassuring.

But while this is not a comforting account, it will, hopefully, prove interesting. And in its own way, illuminate why things are the way they are in the land of the Hindus.

ONE

# MONSTERS AND MISSIONARIES

In November 1579, three devout Christians set out from the Konkan coast for the capital of Akbar the Great in upper India. They were servants of the Society of Jesus, an order of Catholic priests founded a few decades before, and locally headquartered in the Portuguese enclave of Goa. The leader of the party was Rodolfo Acquaviva, scion of one of Italy's wealthiest noble houses, who had jettisoned all aristocratic pretensions for the Jesuit's cassock. With him were Francis Henriquez and Antonio Monserrate—the former a Persian convert and the latter a Catalonian.[1] Their combined quest was to win over the Mughal emperor himself, whom they knew as Zelaldinus Equebar (Jalaluddin Akbar). He had, after all, personally summoned them, asking that they bring Christian texts 'in order that we may learn the Law and its full meaning and perfect truths in every respect'.[2] Upon arrival in February 1580, they were welcomed formally first and then at a private reception, where the emperor, to general amusement, appeared in European cloak and hat. Habitually,

Akbar offered his guests a mass of gold, but riches did not excite the missionaries; instead, it was his warmth that made an impression. As Monserrate reported ecstatically, 'these signs foretold the speedy conversion of the king to the true religion and the worship of Christ'—a case of wishful thinking if ever there was one.[3]

The season in which the Jesuits arrived was bubbling with controversy, the emperor having irritated the Muslim *ulema* (clergy) at court. Only recently he had obtained a document from the most prominent of them, ceding him authority in adjudicating religious disputes—a decree signed unwillingly by many who thought it a scandalous encroachment. But it was hardly the first time Akbar deviated from orthodox ideals: A few years earlier, he had also established a 'house of worship' where rival disputants debated theological ideas. Alongside Muslims, this *ibadat khana* also hosted Brahmins, Jains, Zoroastrians and others, who could loudly express scepticism and challenge one another's beliefs. When our three Jesuits arrived, therefore, they were invited to also join, though their passion—and unfamiliarity with court etiquette—meant it was a disaster: The emperor had to take them aside and ask them to mind their language after an outrageous inaugural performance.[4] Nonetheless, Acquaviva and his friends remained hopeful. On receiving the Bible, not only did Akbar kiss and raise each volume over his head, he also asked which one contained the gospel and 'showed yet more marked reverence to it'.[5] Soon, they were requested to translate the text into Persian, while the emperor, to the horror of some, placed one of the imperial princes under the visiting fathers' tutelage.[6]

This intellectual climate in the Mughal court flowed chiefly from Akbar's uncommon keenness to interrogate received wisdom and ancestral convictions of all stripes. Ruling over a diverse, multicultural society, imperial policy had evolved into one of *sulh-i-kul* where, as his heir wrote, 'there was room for practitioners of various sects and beliefs', on the understanding that 'all religions have a place within the spacious circle of God's mercy'.[7] Even the grand gateway to the chief mosque in the capital, Fatehpur Sikri, carried an inscription celebrating the teachings of Jesus,[8] with the quote: 'The world is a bridge; pass over it but build no house upon it.' When Zoroastrians brought a holy fire, Akbar publicly prostrated before it to show respect.[9] And, of course, there was Hindu influence that upset conservative Muslim courtiers, their resentment an ill-concealed secret; one merry Hindu writer even claimed that Akbar's was really a Hindu government.[10] To the Jesuits this was all quite confusing. As they recorded—in a way revealing as much about themselves as their subject—given the emperor's attitude, it was surprising that 'Zelaldinus has not yet been assassinated'.[11] For they too viewed Akbar's heterodoxy as a character defect. 'He cared little,' Monserrate reported grimly, 'that in allowing every one to follow his own religion he was in reality violating all religions.'[12]

At a personal level, of course, Akbar remained very encouraging of the Jesuits, which kept them motivated in their endeavour to bring him to Christ—he was once seen walking with an arm around Acquaviva's shoulders, a mark both of ease and favour.[13] They accompanied him on a major military campaign also: a rebellion by his brother in Afghanistan orchestrated by some of the ulema as a concrete measure against Akbar's alleged heresies. Why, the emperor entertained their unsolicited advice even on topics not their concern: Once the pious fathers encountered a group of transgender people and were apoplectic that 'such a class' were allowed in the capital. They recommended that 'these libertines' be banished 'as though they were a deadly plague' or 'burnt up by devouring flames'. Amused, Akbar laughed.[14] But his tolerance of ideological diversity was certainly a perplexing substance, and the Jesuits had no desire to evaluate their own dogmas against the emperor's yardstick of reason. Debates in and out of the ibadat khana could grow heated, and Akbar, while venerating Mary and Jesus, steadfastly refused to believe god had produced a son through a virgin.[15] Frustrated, Acquaviva soon complained: 'Nothing, Father, and I say it with tears, nothing strikes the air but that diabolical name [of Muhammad]. Scarcely ever do we hear the most sweet name of Jesus. For the Moors only call him Jesus the Prophet, and say that he is not the Son of God.'[16]

It was late in the day before the fathers realized that Akbar had no intention of converting at all—his interest lay in grasping the principles of each competing faith to craft a new philosophy for himself as a monarch, and in scrutinizing all religions fairly. Even as he discussed Christian thought, he was bowing to the sun, drinking holy Ganga water, banning animal slaughter[17] and otherwise flirting with multiple traditions—a 'fickleness' unbearable to the Jesuits.[18] It also did not help that Mughal officers in the south were soon at war with the Portuguese; when the emperor explained that it was triggered by local provocations, Monserrate dismissed this on the grounds that 'no reliance must be put on the oath of a Musalman, since Muhammad himself teaches that it is lawful to swear falsely to an enemy'.[19] In the end, the Jesuits withdrew, for they did not wish to give the emperor 'the pearls of the Gospel' simply so he could 'tread and crush [them] under his feet' to satisfy some ungodly curiosity.[20] Henriquez took off in 1581 and the next year Monserrate followed; by the time Acquaviva departed in 1583, their chief consolation was the 'discovery' of Tibet further north, where 'a great harvest' of 'white' heathens, untarnished by Muslim influence, could, it was hoped, be reaped.[21]

That, however, was a task for others. For soon after his return to Goa, Acquaviva was hacked to death when some companions and he planted a cross at the site of a smashed Hindu temple. At a time when the Inquisition promoted militant orthodoxy (more on that later) in Portuguese dominions, the fathers had been free to speak as they wished in the Mughal court: The Prophet was 'a wicked and impious villain';[22] Islam was merely 'the superstition of Muhammad';[23] the Quran was 'stuffed with countless fables' and 'extreme frivolity';[24] and, since polygamy was sin, even Akbar's wives, save one, were 'courtesans and adulteresses'.[25] In fact, the Jesuits themselves were surprised they got away with such potentially life-threatening declarations. 'Will these Musalmans never martyr us?' cried Acquaviva, yearning for a glorious Christian end.[26] No, sighed his colleagues gloomily, for Akbar was too fond of them, so 'no one dare[s] touch us'.[27] It was far away from Zelaldinus and angry 'Moors', then, that the heroic death Acquaviva sought came to him, from a mob of Hindus in that broken Goan temple. When news of his violent end reached Fatehpur Sikri, the emperor was upset. 'Alas, Father!' he is reported to have exclaimed, 'Did I not tell you not to go away? But you would not listen to me.'[28] Perhaps it was because a lot of what Akbar had to say seemed ahead of its time; and for his single-minded Jesuit friends this was too much to bear.

While the chief antagonists of the Jesuits in the Mughal court were its Muslim scholars, on the way there, the three fathers had observed some Hindu practice too. To begin with, they were annoyed that their escort spent a long time resting in the port of Surat, waiting for the stars to realign auspiciously before resuming the journey—a delay made less infuriating only by the sight of people arriving to look at their images of Mary and Jesus and according these the same honour Akbar would.[29] In Mandu, they were puzzled to see 'a fragment of a huge iron gun' being worshipped,[30] while the festival of Holi, witnessed in Narwar, scandalized them: Where men and women celebrated the advent of spring, splashing each other with water and colours—a tradition still alive—the fathers saw 'savage and degraded' public conduct.[31] Thereafter in Gwalior, 'thirteen rude statues' provoked their ire, though this may be because they suspected these monumental Jain sculptures as representing Christ and his apostles.[32] Muslim sites too were decried, of course: Islamic 'religious zeal' from earlier times meant the horizon featured numerous ruined temples, substituted with 'shrines of wicked and worthless Musalmans' who were 'worshipped with vain superstition as though they were saints'.[33] All in all, in their view, there was nothing to report on the way to Akbar but idolatry and fraud. India was a pagan land governed by only marginally better Islamic power.

Of course, everything the Jesuits conveyed passed through specific lenses of cultural difference and missionary exaggeration—a pattern built over several years. This was partly to loosen the purse strings of wealthy patrons at home, reminding them of the 'barbaric' conditions in which the fathers toiled but partly also to entertain

Broken image of Surya, the sun god, in Konch, by Thomas Fraser Peppé (1870), from the James Fergusson Collection of Photographs of Indian Architecture, Boston Public Library via Digital Commonwealth.

with tales of the unusual and exotic. After all, as the founder of the Society of Jesus wrote, there was a massive appetite in Europe for news of foreign lands. And such information—'sauce for the taste of a certain curiosity'—was to be generously supplied.[34] In a 1593 Jesuit encyclopaedia by one of Acquaviva's contemporaries, a section was, thus, dedicated to the art of letter writing, and the need to know one's audience. As the author explained, citing Cicero, the Roman statesman, there was 'one method of writing letters for republics, another for princes or monarchs, and yet another for those who guide the Church'.[35] The result was that the Jesuits knew what, featuring sufficient quantities of bravado and 'sauce', would appeal to general readers, and what made for sober internal circulation. Criticism of such tilted narratives emerged within the order itself, with complaints that these generalizations led to 'features of one particular case' being applied across the board, birthing all varieties of stereotypes,[36] while translation, editing and selective excerpting also served to sensationalize, not enlighten. But, grumbling notwithstanding, the Jesuits' letters remained a powerful source of knowledge about India, in the process cementing clichés that still endure.

Many of these stereotypes, to be sure, were not inventions of the Society and its fathers. For centuries prior, information about India, much of it spurious and even laughable, had been trickling West. Marco Polo's diary from the thirteenth century was an influential model, for instance. As the art historian Partha Mitter notes, Polo was among the first to describe *devadasi*s, or female temple servants, when he wrote of 'abbeys in which are gods and goddesses to whom many young girls are consecrated', who on holy days, 'sing and dance before the idol with great festivity'.[37] By the fifteenth century, this found visual representation through a Parisian illustrator, except that, having never witnessed what he drew, the picture was a peculiar mash: The devadasis took the form of European nuns, complete with robes and veils, dancing before an image, also dressed like a Catholic sister. This 'putting [of] European clothing on an Indian subject' became a 'constant feature of the early Western image of Indian gods' as well.[38] For few Europeans had direct experience of the topics they described, with the result that unChristian subjects were pressed into ready-made, more familiar Christian templates. As multi-armed, many-headed Hindu deities were heard of, these too were retrofitted into available medieval categories. Or as Mitter tells, 'classical monsters and [pagan] gods, Biblical demons and Indian gods were all lumped together' in one universal master class: that of 'monsters'.[39]

This perception of pagan gods as devils lay in Europe itself, and in Christianity's early phase of expansion. In seventh-century Rome, for example, when the Pantheon was seized and turned into a church—which it still remains—the gods who resided there were branded a 'multitude of devils'. So also, early missionaries to Britain found locals conducting animal sacrifices; the deities receiving these were lumped under the same term.[40] Idols were bad, and memoirs of pious Christian figures often speak of their breaking these, physically as well as via miraculous powers. One sixth-century bishop in France could not understand why pagans were so 'angry' when men with the 'thought of God' burned their shrines and asked them to stop praying to trees and springs. In resisting, they were 'deserting the light and running to darkness'.[41] The prevailing Christian belief, after all, was that pagan gods were attendants of Satan who had been cast out from heaven; it was demonic powers that 'persuaded men to build them temples, to place there images or statues of wicked men and to set up altars to them, on which they might pour out the blood not only of animals but even of men'.[42] In St Augustine's words, 'pagans were under the power of demons . . . [who] wanted to pass themselves off as gods.'[43] Stories abounded, especially as idols in pre-Christian Europe were destroyed, of the foul forces concealed within. In one case, 'flies of unusual size' flew out of a broken image; elsewhere a 'demon in the shape of a dark animal' sprang from a shrine that was dismantled.[44]

Received (un)wisdom of this variety was to go a long way in framing India and its culture in the West now.[45] Thus, for example, by the time the Dutchman Jan Huyghen van Linschoten joined Portuguese service in Goa in the year of Acquaviva's death, it was normal to describe gods in temples as demons. Or as the man wrote, Hindu shrines housed 'Idoles' that were 'cut most ugly, and like monstrous Devils'. Indeed, the devil *spoke* through these images, which was why Hindus venerated him and made offerings: 'to keepe friendshippe' and ensure 'hee should not hurt them'. Their religion, in other words, was not about finding the light as much as cowing to darkness—the opposite of Christianity.[46] Once van Linschoten passed by some villages and 'at everie hil, stonie Rocke or hole' there was a 'Carved Pagode, or rather Devils, and monsters in hellish shapes'. An image he saw on this journey was 'so mishaped and deformed' that that it surpassed all the ugliness so far suffered— the deity (probably Narasimha, the man-lion form of Vishnu) had 'hornes, and long teeth that hung out of his mouth, down to the knees, and beneath his Navel and belly it had an other such like face, with . . . tuskes'. There was on its head something 'not unlike the Popes triple crown' so that 'in effect it seemed to be a monster [of the] Apocalips'.[47] No matter which way he looked, van Linschoten saw in Hindu gods the very creatures Christian mythology warned the faithful to beware. To Indians, of course, these images were 'visual theologies' and 'visual scriptures',[48] but, made of black stone and housed in dark sanctums, outsiders conjured up unpleasant associations.

Interestingly, these descriptions were recycled formulaically by European travellers, resulting in a standardized (and negative) image of Hindu culture.[49] Indeed, there is a strong chance that our Dutchman plagiarized his reports from a man who preceded him by decades. Ludovico di Varthema, an Italian, in an account published in 1510 spoke of gods on the Kerala coast. 'The King of Calicut is a Pagan,' begins the relevant section, and he worshipped a 'devil' called Deumo—a distortion of the Malayalam *deivam*, or god.[50] On the doors of Deumo's shrine were wooden devils, but the chief idol was

Engraving of Vishnu in his incarnation as Narasimha, the man-lion (1672), from the Wellcome Collection.

metal. Revealingly, di Varthema added how this particular deity had 'a crown made like that of the papal kingdom, with three crowns; and it also has four horns and four teeth, with a very large mouth, nose and most terrible eyes'. Its hands were like 'a flesh hook, and the feet like... a cock'.[51] While van Linschoten's description of what he saw is suspiciously similar (as is Johan de Mandelslo's from the seventeenth century, which may, in turn, have been 'borrowed')[52], di Varthema himself was hardly being original. He claimed to have also seen a Sathanas (Satan) seated in a flame of fire, 'wherein

Deumo, the Devil of Calicut, as depicted in Jacques Collin de Plancy's *Dictionnaire Infernal* (1818), courtesy of the Library of Congress.

are a great number of souls', one drawn into its mouth, and another ensnared by hand. As Mitter notes, this was just a lazy description of Satan as painted in pictures of hell in *Europe*.[53] In other words, even as travellers related sights they had seen in Hindu lands, they also consciously manufactured material, inspired by medieval tropes, in the interests of titillating their audience.[54]

In fact, though things had improved from the age when India was thought to be home to talking serpents and one-eyed beings, there was yet much nonsense published overseas. Leaving aside Marco Polo's bundle of overstatements, there was one like Odoric Mattiussi who in the early fourteenth century described in coastal India an idol 'which is half man and half ox' and 'giveth responses out of its mouth'. This god, the Italian friar insisted, consumed 'the blood of [exactly] forty virgins' regularly, so that if in the pure Christian world parents vowed to give children to church service, in India fathers and mothers pledged their offspring's heads.[55] He also reported in Kerala a tradition of widow burning; that is, if a dead man left a wife, 'they burn her alive with him, saying that she ought to go and keep her husband company'.[56] It is an odd remark, for while sati was indeed practised in many places in India, Kerala is one region where it was explicitly prohibited.[57] As late as the nineteenth century, when a migrant wished to burn herself thus, local authorities denied permission, offering to escort her to a neighbouring territory instead where the act was acceptable.[58] Could it be that Mattiussi was mechanically recycling Marco Polo,[59] in an attempt to seem 'authentic', only to accidentally apply his claim to the wrong geography? In any case, sati quickly became an essential ingredient in travelogues, down to the British era, with the consequence that a real but hardly national custom, limited to certain classes and places,[60] was identified as a defining feature of Hinduism—a rhetorical handle that in time justified the British Raj's own quest to 'civilize' India.

Additionally, given that such travelogues were sparse in number, each possessed the capital to launch stereotypes. Mattiussi, thus, claimed to have seen on the east coast a 'wonderful idol' of gold, seated on a gold throne, in a temple—throwing originality to the wind—also constructed of 'pure gold'. Every year, this deity, 'as big as St Christopher is commonly represented', drove out in a 'fine chariot' for a procession. Alongside music and gaiety, there was, however, a bloody custom of ritual suicide that saw hundreds 'cast themselves under the chariot so that its wheels may go over them ... and cut them in sunder'.[61] This, then—which in all likelihood was mostly a misreading of accidents or occasional overzealousness—became the latest staple in travel diaries, its horror inspiring a heap of supposed eyewitness accounts. Nicolo de Conti, in the fifteenth century, thus, claimed that in Vijayanagara—where the emperor maintained a humanly impossible 12,000 wives—there was a festival in which devotees were run over,[62] and van Linschoten in the next century similarly told of people being madly 'crushed to peeces'.[63] Then came Adolph Bassingh in the 1600s noting not only 'curious and horrific' idols in India but also the by now familiar mode of voluntary death by chariot wheel.[64] At this time, these processions were associated with unnamed southern shrines, but by the British era, the ritual came specifically to revolve around the temple at Puri in Orissa, inspiring a hundred missionary pamphlets lambasting the savagery of Hindu idolatry.[65]

Such repeated confirmation in travel accounts of India's barbarity was essential to promoting in Europe its own sense of civilization.[66] Often, it also had more to do with events and anxieties in Western societies than a curiosity about the East. Sati, for example, was repeatedly presented as a custom invented to prevent wives from poisoning their husbands and running off with lovers—a theory first offered by ancient Greeks. Van Linschoten asserted so, noting matter-of-factly that since Indian women were 'leacherous and inconstant', they disposed of their men 'to have the better means to fulfil their lusts'.[67] Less than twenty years after him, another man adapted the story to Rajputs in the north, claiming they burned widows because of an epidemic of murderous wives.[68] In 1689 an English chaplain could not resist writing on that 'libidinous disposition' which tempted brown women to liquidate their spouses.[69] However, as more than one scholar has shown, this interpretation of sati as a preventive to homicidal female tendencies may well have been Western eyes giving a European logic to an Indian custom, absent as it is in Hindu and Islamic accounts. For in late medieval *England*, women who conspired against their husbands were burned alive,[70] and in continental Europe too, there were cases of female poisoners. White men observing sati in India, that is, seem to have imported for it an origin myth from their own shores.[71] Many were also keen to play hero, with travellers competing to claim they tried to dissuade sati-elects.[72] Indeed, in one tale, a gallant (but conveniently anonymous) 'Christian soldier', unable to save a lady, falls into a fevered state and himself dies.[73]

At any rate, if Hindu women were not paying for their murderous propensities by being set alight, they were allowing desire to run amok, letting European observers indulge in all kinds of fantasies. John Ovington wrote in the seventeenth century that in Surat, women possessed clandestine networks to pick men off the streets to pleasure them—in one case a lady discovered unhappily that a person so brought to her bed was her lawfully wedded husband.[74] There was a festival, a later account adds, in which women fornicated with strangers, risking incest, and left behind handkerchiefs as trophies.[75] When in 1621, a grandson of Akbar's was killed, another traveller explained how a shrine built to the dead prince attracted many. Except that this became a means for 'secluded ladies', otherwise trapped and sexually starved in harems, to give their passion 'the food for which it hungered', choosing from a buffet of male pilgrims.[76] In Calicut, meanwhile, the king allowed his Brahmin priests to sleep with his wife before he touched her;[77] and among the region's polyandrous Nairs, not only did women simultaneously maintain ten husbands, these men were 'Slaves' to the sinister 'Charms' of their oversexed wives.[78] Hindu girls even congressed with idols: Before virgins were wed, they offered their 'mayden-head' to stone, ivory or metal genitals of gods. Their bridegrooms clapped like buffoons, and blood gleamed off the 'Divellish idol'.[79] While it is possible that several women in India were sexually adventurous, and that there were spaces where norms were transgressed, it is equally likely that these graphic stereotypes reflect more their writers' fetishes than a comprehension of everyday local happenings.[80]

Then, of course, there was the unsavoury presence of ascetics and fakirs. This class of 'Ashmen', so named after the 'abundance of Ashes with which they powder their Heads' and bodies were a 'very disagreeable and sordid Aspect'. Both Muslims and Hindus had variants of these, but what was appalling was sadhus who walked naked; Ovington was horrified that women spoke freely to these men, unaffected by their nudity.[81] An eighteenth-century account

An Indian widow being led to suttee [sati] (1811), by François Balthazar Solvyns, from the Wellcome Collection.

censures such 'sanctified Rascals' who made 'a great Shew of Sanctity' when in reality they revelled in 'Nastiness and an holy Obscenity': One sadhu left a European voyeur transfixed with revulsion as he flaunted a golden penis-piercing. Many 'young married Women' came to see this holy man, it was added, and 'taking him [i.e. his member] devoutly in their Hands, kiss'd him, whilst his bawdy Owner stroak'd their silly Heads, muttering some filthy Prayers'.[82] Sadhus and yogis performed austerities that sometimes inspired awe but generally seemed an embarrassment: In the south, one man saw them worship 'an Altar with a Dildo in the middle'—the phallic *lingam*, a representation of Siva—offering 'Rice and Cocoe-Nuts to the Devil.'[83] In due course, the British would discover that many of these men were warriors too, who fought with a ferocity capable of stupefying their enemies, already likely startled by their abbreviated sense of dress.[84] But on the whole, as with women and their allegedly unpoliced passions, these ascetics too were branded pure evil, and India as home to yet more exotic—and revolting—people.[85]

Finally, local gods and goddesses were no better. One seventeenth-century missionary related half-baked notions he claimed had local authority. Siva, he said, as the historian Ines G. Zupanov translates, owned an enormously long penis, a mark of his limitless desire. But it served a practical purpose also in that it was used to 'plough the earth' and shape seas, hills and other geological details. His desire, in the meantime, mutated into a female, attached to his back, and when he said *Om* (a sacred syllable; here, misrepresented as the query, 'Do you desire?'), the woman replied with *Am* ('I desire').[86] A fellow Jesuit continued the account in which the lady-on-the-back manages to separate herself so they can copulate, only to find that Siva's divine penis is impossibly sized. It was cut, therefore, into eighteen pieces. Then came the problem that the goddess had no genitals herself, so Siva had to create it with a finger: From the blood of this vagina were born planets, the sun, moon and other stars, not to speak of flowers used in Hindu rituals.[87] Such tales of 'divine debauchery', Zupanov

A Sadhu (1799), by François Balthazar Solvyns, from the Wellcome Collection.

points out, may have been derived from local retellings of mythology (for Puranic accounts do present gods as possessing carnal instincts) but as usual also had much to do with the roused fancies of the men relating them. They were 'part and parcel of the missionary strategies of deriding and ridiculing',[88] and succeeded, either way, in sustaining the idea of the irrational, sexually unfettered heathen, in urgent need of spiritual rescue and Christian salvation. The West had to save the East not only from its own men and women, that is, but also sham gods and demonic forces.

From the end of the medieval times, down to the colonial age, then, there was an information network that duplicated certain clichés about India and Hindus, helping Europeans construct a self-image of themselves as better.[89] Certainly there were shrines where human sacrifice was offered, and by all means, it is likely that women had lovers and killed husbands (in one eighteenth-century attempt, by crushing glass into dough).[90] But the elevation of the specific as a timeless standard perpetuated the idea of India as a savage Other to Christendom; something akin to suggesting that because Henry VIII had a habit of shedding wives, all Christian kings were predisposed to depriving their spouses of heads. Even stepping into the country was fraught with personal, moral and religious peril, which with the Jesuits was heightened. As we learn, their letters had 'an unavoidable tripartite narrative structure'. First, en route to India, they would encounter turbulent seas, suffer near-death experiences and recall their mortality; when they reached the subcontinent, its tropical climate came as a shock; this, then, led to a 'divine ordeal' of bodily agony to prepare them for sacred service in a strange country.[91] Jesuits, after all, trod treacherous roads into bewildering lands, 'now through muddy paths, now over innumerable streams . . . ever haunted by the fear of pagan governors' threatening execution.[92] It did not matter that this image sat in contrast with the warm welcome at Akbar's court, and, as we shall see, in 'heathen' kingdoms too. For, even if reality were one thing, rhetoric served its own purpose.

As for the Hindus, at first India's residents could not have cared for what itinerant Europeans were writing about them, their gods and culture. But as the white man's political power grew in the country, his skewed narratives—and the prejudice these came to represent—acquired the ability to afflict their world. And so, these would slowly become a threat, till in time Hindus themselves were forced to answer the question: Who were they, really? If not devil-worshippers, what was their religion truly about? In a world where other (unfriendly) cultures could scrutinize their identity, how might they articulate their self-image? It was in the construction of these answers that Hinduism took its contemporary, modern form, drawing pride and confidence from certain aspects of its past and shame from others.

The story of Hindus' life under Western authority begins in 1498. In May that year, after many months at sea, a group of half-starved, exhausted Portuguese sailors landed in Kerala on the Indian coast. It was a momentous turn in history, these men heralding the dawn of colonialism in the country. In fact, Europeans stamped the land before even the Mughals—when Vasco da Gama and his crew arrived, Akbar's grandfather was still a teenager in Uzbekistan, decades away from conquering Delhi. Interestingly, after coming ashore, da Gama and his men found themselves in a temple. Oblivious that they were doing homage to a goddess—the place was assumed to be a chapel to Mary—they participated in its rites, accepted holy ash and dismissed frescoes depicting multi-armed beings with big teeth as just Christian saints imagined locally.[93] Clearly then, as the anthropologist Joan-Pau Rubiés observes, not *all* Europeans instinctively branded Hindu gods as monsters; where di Varthema would see devils, his predecessors were willing to visualize the mother of Christ.[94] This has an explanation. For one, with rumours that Kerala was home to a lost Christian tribe, da Gama had reason to keep an open mind. But equally, there was economics: The Portuguese hoped to win special terms of trade from the local rajah. It was when this did not happen, that things turned bitter. So, by the time di Varthema was writing a few years later, not only was the king confirmed as hostile, the Portuguese had narrative incentives in branding him a devil-worshipper. Politics tinted their gaze, and in the process, the aforementioned stereotypes came in handy.

Importantly, the Portuguese fixed early on against being just another set of merchants; 'from the start [their] effort was based on compulsion and force, not peaceful competition.'[95] After all, Portugal's elite and royalty were propelling the venture: Unlike traders, incentivized to keep their heads down, minimize risks and turn profits, these aristocratic backers hoped to acquire that extra commodity called glory.[96] They had 'the gun in [their] hand and', they were certain, 'god on [their] side', all this stemming from a religious fervour inflecting politics in their own part of the world.[97] It helped that inland powers in India took little interest in maritime affairs, allowing the Portuguese to militarize international waters. Armed aggression in disrupting pre-existing networks also turned them into predatory extortionists.[98] Soon, toeholds were obtained in Kerala and Goa, the second a prized possession till the twentieth century. While some coastal rulers resisted, mainland powers were willing to parley.[99] The Portuguese's foreignness was no handicap. In 1505, their envoy to Vijayanagara, south India's greatest state, reported that its king had even offered to transmit a bride for Manuel I, in turn expecting the Christian monarch to reciprocate by shipping into *his* harem a sister; this way, 'the blood of the two royal houses would mingle', producing a union.[100] While this did not come to be—Manuel I probably had reservations about getting in bed with pagans—the overtly political nature of Portuguese trade meant that it was not long before religion entered the fray in India too. They had come not to just buy and sell but to make history—

something which would happen in time with the British also, albeit at a slower pace and greater scale.

With the establishment of a white ruling class in their tracts, the Portuguese came into everyday contact with Hindus, armed with scarce knowledge but copious pre-judgement. The encounter took barely a generation to turn violent.[101] One factor was that the colonizer's rigid religiosity had grown stiffer still in reaction to the anti-Catholic Reformation occurring in Europe.[102] That is, with the emerging Protestant movement accusing the Catholic church of perverting the faith, Catholic powers had a special necessity to demonstrate unequivocal Christian credentials. And here, their newly acquired Indian enclaves offered a parade ground, packed as they were with devil-worshipping pagans. As early as 1522, a bishop had declared it a 'mistake to continue to show favour to [i.e., tolerate] idolatry', urging the flattening of temples.[103] Though a shrine was destroyed in a stray incident,[104] this was not yet policy—the Portuguese had Indian collaborators and were in no hurry to alienate them. Indeed, local Hindu elites had aided the Europeans in taking Goa from its previous (Muslim) masters.[105] They would regret this, though, for no sooner were their new rulers secure than they proved worse than the last regime. In 1540–41, hundreds of temples were razed, their assets appropriated for Christian institutions.[106] By the decade's end, John III ('John the Pious') outlawed Hinduism, commanding that since 'idolatry is such a big offense against God . . . I will not tolerate it to exist'; Goa's idols, 'in public and in hiding', must, he demanded, be crushed.[107] Ecclesiastical authorities backed this diktat to 'extinguish the sect of Maphamede and Gentilica [Hinduism]',[108] and the Inquisition too—targeting Jews originally—was imported to India.[109] Rapidly, not only were many Hindus dragooned into the Catholic faith,[110] there was also an exodus of gods from the area.[111]

As a pattern, this flight of deities was not unprecedented. In previous times, as Muslim power first washed across the subcontinent,

Hindu gods often went into exile to avoid detection. Many were lost—idols from a Tamil temple concealed in the fourteenth century were only retrieved in the twentieth, for example.[112] Between the sixteenth and eighteenth centuries, as Bengali, Mughal and Andhra sultans clashed over power in Orissa, its most celebrated deity, Jagannath, had to hide repeatedly, for a total of thirty years.[113] In future too, there would be occasions for deities to disappear: Under Emperor Aurangzeb (1618–1707), whose iconoclasm still generates controversy, one particular god was hosted by a chain of Hindu princes in Rajasthan, birthing the expression, 'In whose turban does the lord reside?'[114] To be clear, Hindu dynasts seized gods too, and as far back as the seventh century we see proof of this.[115] Near-contemporaneous with the Portuguese, a Vijayanagara ruler appropriated gods from neighbouring lands, thus.[116] And if in 1072 CE, a Tamil shrine was plundered during an intra-Hindu caste conflict,[117] a Kerala king would act similarly in the eighteenth century.[118] But Hindu princes tended to *wrest* deities; non-Hindu powers threatened their destruction.[119] So, new strategies were invented: Some gods were hidden behind walls, others in ponds; occasionally decoy gods were planted to mislead. Why, certain Hindu deities were secreted away disguised as corpses.[120] One medieval text even offers a protocol for burying gods, where the priest apologetically states: 'As long as there is danger, O [lord], please lie down in a bed with the goddess Earth.'[121]

Something similar transpired in Goa now, as gods looked for sanctuaries from white tyranny. Temples, after all, were being 'demolished stone by stone', the deities within 'burnt', 'beaten into pulp' or, if they were metal, melted for reuse as church objects and chandeliers.[122] So, a goddess from Chimbel was extracted to Bicholim and deities from Sirula went to Mulgaon.[123] The Portuguese were not pleased: By the 1580s, they were attempting to block temple-building in neighbouring lands and to prevent locals from spending money earned in Goa on banished divinities.[124] Pointed offence was given: When breaking the temple where Acquaviva would be murdered, they added to the provocation by slaughtering a cow in the precincts.[125] As late as 1619, it was recorded—by an anti-Portuguese observer, admittedly—how priests in Goa had 'a lot on their hands' turning people 'Christian by force'.[126] Resistance was ruinous. In 1565, thus, when a padre went to a village, its residents appeared 'with weapons and loud shouts', beating up his aide. In retaliation, seven temples were burned, with orders issued that 'none should dare to rebuild them'.[127] In this reign of a nervous bigotry, local habits too were suspect, ranging from squatting to urinate to entering homes barefoot.[128] Hindus offered even to pay to celebrate festivals but to no avail.[129] Like their gods, many fled in the end, travelling hundreds of miles away, and a number died in the process: mauled by animals, drowning or because they ran into arms-bearing 'Jesuit students' lying in wait.[130] The irony, of course, as the scholar Alexander Henn reminds us, is that Catholics were striking at Goa's idols—and idolaters—in the same period that Protestants attacked their icons in Europe under the charge of idolatry.[131] But precisely for this reason, there was no sympathy; the Portuguese had to demonstrate with fire and blood that they were authentic Christians.[132] And Hindus suffered in the process.[133]

Banner of the Inquisition in Goa, engraving by Bernard Picart (1722), from the Wellcome Collection.

This Catholic dogmatism, revealingly, however, extended to some brown Christians too, who were 'Hindu in culture, Christian in religion, and Oriental in worship'.[134] Kerala was home to the Nasranis, who claimed descent from converts left by the apostle St Thomas in 52 CE.[135] They were, that is, a community which believed itself to have been Christian for as long as Europe.[136] Our traveller Mattiussi encountered them in the fourteenth century, foreshadowing in tone the Portuguese when he lamented how St Thomas's grave elsewhere in the peninsula was 'filled with idols' because of 'vile and pestilent heretics'.[137] Reference was to the influence of the Church of the East, deemed dissident by Catholics, on the Nasranis; Kerala's Christians received bishops not from Rome but Persia, while archdeacons were confirmed in their posts by Hindu rajahs.[138] Though these spiritual heads were held in 'Reverence both by Christians and Infidels', the Portuguese deemed all this adulteration.[139] At first, they sought to shepherd Nasranis into the Catholic fold through persuasion, but most of the sheep—who, like Hindus, made cock sacrifices to their saints[140]—had neither heard of the pope, nor were they anxious to discard long-standing customs.[141] So by the mid-sixteenth century, things grew heated. As with Goa's temples, tombs of two Nasrani spiritual heads were allegedly destroyed.[142] In 1599, after their Persian bishop died, the community was coerced into accepting Catholic suzerainty. As their new leader promised, they 'abjured all the Errors' of their forebears hereon, saw past guides as 'cursed Hereticks, that are burning in Hell for their Errors' and swore instead 'Obedience to the Pope as St Peter's Successor and Christ's Vicar on Earth'.[143]

Supervised by Goa, a synod was called. In the Portuguese view, because Nasranis lived 'among so many Heathens' and were 'subject to Idolatrous Kings', it fell to white men to 'purge out the Heresies and false Doctrines' debasing their faith.[144] After all, they performed similar rituals as Hindus, had notions of caste purity, and maintained links with temples—a syncretism which to Europeans was scandal.[145] Other decrees aimed at 'literary extirpation', banning books.[146] For instance, in *The Infancy of Our Saviour*, Nasranis held that Jesus was a naughty child, went to a Jewish school and that his father had had a first marriage. These and 'a thousand other Fables and Blasphemies' were cancelled.[147] A list of books was supplied so they could be 'corrected, or destroyed'.[148] Catholic positions and customs—such as requiring celibacy of priests—were imposed; soon, the Kerala church was subordinated to Goa. But in the end, compulsion had its limits. In 1653, after the Portuguese ambushed a Persian on his way to reclaim the Nasranis, many rebelled.[149] One faction declared autonomy, forged ties with the Patriarch of Antioch in Ottoman Turkey (as opposed to Rome), threw off the Portuguese yoke and began installing brown archbishops.[150] It divided Kerala's Christians but enough in the community clung to the old ways: The cock sacrifices continued, as did traditions in which figures like St George are cast as siblings to fiery goddesses like Kali.[151] Indeed, as late as 1806, when a local rajah was informed that the British and Nasranis were of the same faith, he remarked that this 'could not be the case, else he must have heard it before'—so different was the 'native' Christian from the European.[152]

In all this, the nascent beginnings of something powerful is visible. Among Hindus, persecution by an alien race wielding a foreign faith would, at one level, spark a soul-searching of sorts. It was clear to most in Goa that what the Portuguese were doing was not merely politics; religion was enmeshed in it. If the white man's government was unkind, it stemmed from a 'blueprint of imperial thinking' supplied by a parallel cast of associates: missionaries.[153] Goa hosted four orders: First came the Franciscans after its conquest, then the Jesuits, Dominicans, and finally, the Augustinians by the middle of the sixteenth century.[154] That these fathers encouraged a hard-line position was clear. In a 1560 conference of Hindu village heads, thus, we find debate on how the community might respond to pressures to convert. One speaker suggested exile: 'It is better to lose our property than our souls.' Another urged cautious patience. 'I do not think,' he felt, 'that the fervour of Christianity will last beyond the reign of this Viceroy', who was a zealot; Hindus should cling on as best as they could until someone nicer came to the helm. But the 'seniormost' man saw things clearly. Political agents of the Portuguese crown would trot in and out, but it was 'fathers of the Company of Jesus' who mattered; and these 'will never leave or stop making Christians'. This was the reality Goa faced—survival inside a long-term pressure-cooker, where as a royal letter stated, missionaries must be valued 'more than many of the warriors'.[155] In the old man's view, the best option, then, was to become Christian—a proposal accepted by 200 souls from fourteen families. Not wishing to abandon their homes or surrender social and material privileges, these 'heathens' chose to bend.[156]

And yet, the fact that twenty years later, Acquaviva was brutally murdered suggests that not *all* Hindus were prepared to submit to this 'catechism through fear'.[157] Herein lies the impulse that would mark political Hinduism. Life in Goa was tough, with employment, political status and much else made contingent on Christianization.[158] 'The Portuguese,' we read, pressed a transfer of religious loyalties even to recognize 'groups within their political body', and many Hindus acquiesced if only to gain a plank to reclaim influence or negotiate for better terms.[159] But those who resisted were resolute too. Besides violence—one of Acquaviva's friends in that 1583 massacre was ordered to bow to an idol, and upon refusal, killed, with his blood smeared on the deity—there were creative strategies also to bypass the imbalance in power.[160] Parking gods just miles outside Goa's limits, for instance, Hindus wooed converts, encouraging apostasy.[161] Brahmins manufactured rites to *re*-convert lapsed Hindus: You could bathe in the sea or wash yourself with Ganga water.[162] Shrines outside Goa where exiled deities now resided were often grander than their original seats, in visual defiance of the Portuguese.[163] Within the region too, Hindus who remained were a problem. They 'persevere', a 1580 record tells, 'in their idolatry and abominable errors'; this despite decades of state hostility,[164] where the authorities could even invade private homes at will.[165] Demolished temples were rebuilt and, though fully aware of the risks, villagers refused to remit taxes in some parts, even conspiring with enemies of the Portuguese.[166]

In the end, the government relaxed its grip, not least because its policies had proved bad for business.[167] Besides, the Portuguese never did acquire the power to translate their edicts into unchallenged reality, especially in peripheral districts.[168] And, as this shift occurred, old habits of coexistence reappeared. Many deities returned to Goa, and Catholics and Hindus began sharing festivals, Christian saints receiving veneration from the latter,[169] and Hindu goddesses winning Catholic devotees.[170] Local culture, it would seem, ultimately triumphed over decrees of the foreigner. But for future Hindu nationalists this was exactly it—Hindus, they would argue, were naively large-hearted. Alien faiths, on the other hand, with the slightest power in so small a quarter as Goa, tended towards aggression. Hindus, it would be lamented, were habitually prepared to forgive the worst horrors; tolerance on their rivals' part, however, was based only on practical calculations. Old patterns, therefore, would no longer do. After all, even if harmony returned to Goa, the place itself was transformed. In Salcete alone, in the late sixteenth century, there were 8000 Christian converts against a population estimated at 80,000. By the eighteenth, however, the numbers had switched: There were now 1,00,000 Christians and barely 3000 of other faiths.[171] So, as would be urged in time, the idolaters had to be on their guard. To prevent old horrors from recurring, they could neither forgive nor forget. And memories of persecution—and resistance—would one day supply the raw material for articulating a unified, combative Hinduism; one aspiring not only to defend itself but of actively going on the offensive.

Within decades of the establishment of Portuguese rule in India, missionaries who shadowed them realized—despite immense support and firepower from Goa—that this country was going to prove a challenge. Typically, when white men in robes set out for the East, it was with a degree of professional optimism. As Francis Xavier (1506–52) of the founding class of the Society of Jesus, wrote in 1540, two years *before* reaching India, the prevailing sense was that 'native tribes are very well disposed to accept the religion of our Lord Jesus Christ'. All that was lacking was competent preaching, so that an ambition to 'convert two or three kingdoms of idolaters' in a few years was not unreasonable.[172] When he actually arrived, however, he found the situation dire. To start with, most missionary activity was limited to the coast (where Portuguese ships offered protection) and its non-elite classes. In Tamil country, thus, there were thirty villages of Paravar converted a decade before via another man's labours. But this was not because Jesus appealed to this low-ranking group of fishermen, and boat- and salt-makers. Facing competition from rivals in the pearl-fishing sector, the Paravar had sought Portuguese security and were claimed wholesale in a quid pro quo—a commercial rather than spiritual transaction. When Xavier asked: 'what more they believed now than when they were Infidels,' beyond the appellation of being Christian, they had not a clue.[173] Journeying with a translator from village to village, the father launched a valiant effort to impart knowledge to his less than sterling flock, but apprehensions lingered. And far from converting whole kingdoms, even communicating to the interested minority was trying, given linguistic and other limitations.

It is not surprising, then, that shortcuts were employed. On the one hand, there was fear that converts might relapse into idolatry (bans on drinking and polygamy were disincentives against sustained faith),[174] but equally, there was also need to shore up numbers. In a 1545 letter, Xavier announced how in 'the space of one month I made Christians of more than ten thousand'. His method was necessarily dubious. 'As soon as I arrived in any heathen village where they had sent for me to give baptism, I gave orders for all, men, women, and

Francis Xavier preaching to Indians, seventeenth-century engraving by G. Edelinck after J. Sourley, from the Wellcome Collection.

children, to be collected in one place. Then, beginning with the first elements of the Christian faith, I taught them there is one God.' This elementary lesson having been imparted, he would communicate the sign of the cross and recite a prayer in the local language (which he would have 'learned . . . by heart'). Thereafter, he gave them 'articles of the Creed and the ten Commandments'. When it seemed like the mass of people were 'sufficiently instructed to receive baptism', he proceeded with the ceremony and wrote 'each [convert's new] name on a ticket'. After a round of destroying idols and bringing in the converts' families, he bid them goodbye and set off for his next station.[175] 'In this way,' concluded Xavier, 'I go all round the country'.[176] Indeed, at times he was unable to use his hands or voice 'from the fatigue of baptizing', for 'in a single day I have baptized whole villages'.[177] But shallow successes notwithstanding, the father encountered an obstacle: the hold of a 'perverse and wicked set' of 'liars and cheats' known as Brahmins.[178] Or as Xavier admitted, were it not for these people, India's pagan masses would easily be 'embracing the religion of Jesus Christ'.[179]

As it happened, Brahmins were a tantalizing, incomprehensible entity for Europeans. One early Portuguese writer, despite all the cultural and racial difference between Hindus and them, had observed that this *specific* group among the former shared ideas in common with Christians.[180] For, as the Portuguese writer Duarte Barbosa added in 1516, at their core, Hindus offered prayers not to diverse gods (or devils) in idols but one 'God, whom they confess and adore as the true God, Creator and maker of all things'. This was not simple polytheism—if there was a variety of gods in shrines, these were all 'under' a formless great being.[181] Even van Linschoten, after talking of the usual 'divilish superstitions', added how Brahmins believed 'their [sic] is a supreame God above, which ruleth all things'.[182] This now created a quandary: The assumption that Hindus were a photocopy of Europe's polytheists could not hold.[183] Like former idol-worshippers in the West, brown people had a list of deities, yes; and yet they *also* acknowledged a single power. Without irony, their paganism was tethered to a monotheism.[184] Idolatry itself, in fact, was represented differently by Brahmins. There were no feared forces inside, the images only representing god (singular) in various manifestations (as gods, plural). Or as a text explains: 'Even if the cow's entire body were filled with milk, it could secrete it only through the teat'; images were that divine teat.[185] Nobody important believed idols were gods; they only *symbolized* divine power.[186] For missionaries, this more sophisticated glimpse of Hindu ideas generated a problem, for they could no longer simply traffic in stereotypes.[187] They would, instead, have to apply themselves to gathering real knowledge before they could debunk the Hindu system.[188] Land was easier to conquer; a conquest of souls warranted more meticulous efforts. And in the process, Brahmins would become key to missionary imagination—and the principal defendants for Hinduism, as we shall see in the next chapter.[189]

While this class was met with even in areas under Portuguese control—so much so that the Goa government too relied on Brahmins for administrative support[190]—it was in Hindu-ruled territories that Jesuits clashed with them on more equal terms. The fathers were welcome in coastal courts, which entertained them partly from curiosity but also out of fear of Portuguese terror.[191] Thus, about 1600, a Jesuit called Giacomo Fenicio not only debated Brahmins in Calicut but also prepared a guidebook on Hindu mythology and its gods.[192] His language, to be clear, was violent, given how the text was intended for European priests,[193] but it is patent that the author spent much time cataloguing and digesting the Puranic tradition—something Xavier neglected, using vitriol to compensate for ignorance, until giving up on India three years into his stay. Fenicio and his peers, on the other hand, recognized that the age of blanket dismissal was over; attacking local gods as devils confirmed European biases but did not unsettle Hindus or bolster conversion. Knowledge, therefore, was imperative to spiritual dominance. So, as Akbar's ulema were baffled when Jesuits cited the Quran and used it to challenge them on their own turf, the father in Calicut combined missionary zeal with a command (even if at times garbled) of Hindu mythology. His objective was transparent. 'I have,' Fenicio explained, 'occupied myself with studying [the Hindus'] religion', and not mere superficialities like deities with 'six faces and twelve hands'. He had ventured deeper to identify material of more *intellectual* value, to help 'in refuting these Hindus'.[194] In other words, while the goal of winning converts and smashing idols remained, experience dictated that mapping the local position, on its own terms, was a critical first step.[195]

Interestingly, as with Acquaviva and his friends at Akbar's court, Fenicio also had the freedom to argue his case in Calicut. But as with the Mughals, its Hindu ruler too was not convinced. For instance, told about Christianity's superiority, the rajah asked how Jesus could be divine, when he was 'gibbeted on a cross and killed by the Jews?'[196] And if idolatry were bad, how come Christians adored images of the Virgin? Was *that* not idolatry? This being precisely one of the charges Protestants tossed at Catholics, the father 'flung into a passion' and a 'vehement peroration'. Lacking a direct answer, he attacked the deity Krishna instead, a god to whom even Akbar's Jesuit friends took exception.[197] According to Puranic mythology, Krishna was full of mischief. Jesus suffered in his mortal aspect to atone for mankind's sins, but what, asked Fenicio, did Krishna do? Flaunting his research, he dished out a caustic account of the deity's exploits: He broke pots and pans, was thrashed by his mother 'with a churn-staff', hid the clothes of bathing women and acted in ways unbecoming of any god.[198] The Hindus' personalized deity—who could be loved and chided—was an undignified rogue in Jesuit eyes. Others like Ganapati defied logic: He had an elephant's head, a prodigious belly, but somehow managed to commute on a rat. Even allowing for annoyance, one imagines the king and his court would have been impressed with Fenicio's homework.[199]

For the father in turn, while missionary success was slight, he was able to aid Portuguese strategic interests. He converted the rajah's nephew, for instance, concealing the fact so the prince could spy on his uncle.[200] And as an appalled authority wrote, Goa's religious leadership, 'instead of condemning' the Jesuits for 'this scandalous dissimulation, actually confirmed it'.[201]

This overlap between Portuguese political concerns and the missionaries was a continuation of a culture where there was no 'distinction between religion, economics, and politics'.[202] Thus, when the Dutch sailed into Calicut, it was Fenicio who represented Goa with the rajah, aiming to thwart Portugal's rivals.[203] With the Mughals, it was bluntly stated that Jesuit presence at court was a source of intelligence.[204] This could even embarrass missionaries: In the 1540s, Goa contemplated an ambitious voyage to loot the Tirupati temple, which was under protection of the Vijayanagara emperor. Though ships sailed out, inclement weather aborted the operation; so instead, they attacked a temple south of the Calicut rajah's territories.[205] This, ironically, was done even as Xavier received support from the province's Hindu ruler.[206] It did not end double-dealing: in 1615, there was another Jesuit encouraging the Portuguese in their programme of intimidation. In his blandly titled *Historia do Malavar*, Diogo Goncalves lists the locations of temples in southern Kerala, estimates of their treasure, resources of the surrounding countryside and offers ideas on how the Portuguese might attack these places—shrines (and the occasional mosque) by the beach were close enough to be blown up from ships, for example, while others would require disembarking. Happily, the father surveyed the terrain in advance and supplied ideal landing spots.[207] It really did look, then, as far as the Portuguese were concerned, as if god and the gun went hand in hand. And Hindu powers noticed this; while Nasrani churches were acceptable, European ones sometimes found themselves under attack in Kerala. For they represented not merely faith but also white men's imperial presumptions.[208]

As Jesuits moved into the interior, however, further away from Portuguese arms, these overt connections with politics backfired. In 1598, a mission went to the new capital of Vijayanagara at Chandragiri. It was welcomed with an elephant parade and Venkata II, the reigning *raya* (emperor), gave permission to 'build a Church, erect Crosses, and convert men'.[209] Of course, he had his motives: A predecessor had tried and failed to hammer out a deal for the exclusive supply of warhorses with the Portuguese.[210] Nor were the fathers innocent of worldly causes—scuttling overtures from the Dutch would soon become one of their mandates.[211] So the court flattered the Jesuits, while the latter reciprocated: A European artist they introduced not only painted Hindu gods but also, apparently, an erotic picture of Venkata in a pool with women (for which he promptly got into trouble).[212] As with Akbar and the Calicut rajah, this potentate also listened to the Jesuits with an open mind: They could assert the falseness of idol worship without fear, angry Brahmins being silenced.[213] That is, till Portuguese *political* excesses tested royal tolerance: Venkata's warmth dissipated in 1606 when news arrived of a skirmish between the state's authorities and white soldiers on the east coast. Though peace was restored, the Jesuits were dropped, and in 1610, the emperor transferred his favour to the Dutch, challenging Portuguese monopoly of the seas.[214] Shortly after, the fathers departed.[215] By too openly mixing religion with politics, they had failed their mission. Fresh lessons would need to be learnt—though old mistakes would in time recur under the British, with painful consequences again.

In 1577, an Italian couple called Pier and Clarice had a boy they named Roberto. He was their firstborn, and as such expected to follow in the military tradition of his paternal ancestors. After all the de Nobilis were—no pun intended—nobility: They claimed descent from a Holy Roman Emperor, and Pier personally was decorated for fighting Protestant armies under the banner of the Vatican.[216] Roberto, however, wished to serve Rome in a different format: By his teens, he had fixed on becoming a missionary. His family thought him silly, till the boy simply left one day, found a patron at a sufficient distance from his relations, finished his theological education and became a Jesuit. In 1603, he was certified as ready to serve in the East, and set out for India soon after. It was an unusually long journey: His vessel was wrecked, and the young man found himself stranded in Mozambique for months, awaiting further conveyance. But in the end, he landed in Goa, intact. After preliminary training in Kerala and on the Tamil coast, he was soon posted to the inland Vijayanagara town of Madurai. And it was in this great Hindu centre, at the heart of which towered a grand temple, that de Nobili would expend his life, achieving a certain celebrity (and to critics, notoriety). Or as a contemporary proclaimed, 'Touched by the deplorable blindness of these people . . . filled with the great notion that Jesus Christ came for the salvation of all men', de Nobili threw himself into service. This language was typical, of course, but Roberto was not, steering clear of the path Xavier and others had paved, with their aversion towards Hindus. Instead, in what would prove controversial, he announced: 'I shall become an Indian to save the Indians.'[217]

The Italian was on to something. After decades in India, Catholic missionaries were grappling with uneasy questions. Without Portuguese heft would their message appeal to 'heathens'? Could Hindus be wooed by methods less stick, more carrot? Experience recommended to some that a purely evangelical policy, actively distanced from Goa's politics, was preferable. Several Jesuits arrived at the conclusion that Hindu culture need not be condemned; their pitch was spiritual transformation, not cultural or bodily imitation. It did not matter if people sat on their haunches to urinate, so long as they accepted Christ. Instead of savaging all they encountered, the fathers needed to be circumspect; they would have to understand

Hindu culture, and then make their case in forms intelligible to intended converts. Thus, de Nobili's older contemporary Thomas Stephens, composed the *Kristapurana* ('Christ Purana') in a blend of the Marathi and Konkani languages. Instead of inflicting Latin alone and patronizing lectures, the man crafted a vehicle for Christian ideas, imitating Hindu devotional poetry.[218] Indeed, until the Bible was translated a century later, this Purana remained 'the closest text available to the complete Bible story in [any] Indian language'.[219] So too around 1599, one Alesandro Leni, during preaching excursions, assumed the appearance of a Hindu yogi, divorcing himself visibly from Jesuit hostility.[220] Or as one of the fathers in Venkata II's durbar declared, it was preferable 'to dress oneself, to eat, and to keep other social customs', as Hindus did; to have an impact, missionaries must match the local image of holy men.[221] So, where Europeans so far clumsily pushed Eastern concepts into Western moulds—and damned them for not fitting—they now attempted the reverse, veiling imported spiritual cargo in 'native' fabric.

De Nobili would become the most committed advocate of this inculturative strategy. Madurai had been home to a Jesuit outpost for a decade, but with little to show; it had not made a single convert, let alone any of exemplary merit. The problem was clear: Catholics were linked too closely with the Portuguese, who, to Hindu elites, lacked dignity. The *Parangi* (a corruption of 'Frank', for Europeans) was pegged with drinking, rowdiness (thanks to sailors), inferior castes (like the fishermen

Roberto de Nobili, Wikimedia Commons.

Xavier converted), and, rumour had it, eating children fried in butter (for Indians possessed their own stereotypes about white people).[222] Besides, as another Jesuit wrote, thanks to Portuguese tyranny, missionaries were viewed not with 'opposition' alone but as a 'pestilence'.[223] As far back as the 1520s, it was lamented that even as pious fathers went about sermonizing, their secular compatriots' 'scandalous lifestyle' punctured the effect.[224] And it was true that, outside Goa, most converts were of lower caste; a reason why even the Nasranis hesitated to adopt Catholicism.[225] It was hardly shocking, then, that when asked if they would entertain the *Parangi Margam* ('Parangi faith') by black-robed fathers, Hindus of status recoiled; the Jesuits were offering tainted goods.[226] Some, like de Nobili's colleague in Madurai plodded on, but the Italian decided on a reinvention. Hindus, he believed, might welcome the Bible if it looked browner—by which he meant a specific 'respectable' shade of brown. What a future Jesuit called 'the Dregs of the Populace'[227] did not interest him, given how they dragged Catholicism down into a tarnished Parangi-ism.[228] Instead, de Nobili turned his gaze to the cream of Hindu society. For if *they* were wooed, prestige would encase Christianity.[229] It was critical, that is, to aim high and pluck from the top.

One of de Nobili's first innovations, therefore, was to discard the cassock. Instead of expecting Indians to become European in all but complexion, he embraced *their* sartorial tastes, dressing hereon like a *sanyasi* in saffron robes—the 'native' godman's uniform even today. *Sanyasam*, or renunciation, is a normative goal for orthodox Hindus—assuming the look of an ascetic Brahmin, the Catholic father exalted here an ideal straight out of Sanskrit textbooks.[230] Where Jesuits stigmatized everything pagan, de Nobili argued that battling 'external' details was a waste when there was a war of souls to win. All he challenged was religious aspects of Hinduism, not its social and civil usages.[231] He even restyled the Christian message—he spoke not of the Parangi Margam but *Satya Vedam* ('true religion'), with himself as *tattvabodhakar* ('teacher of truth'). By 1610, his Jesuit bosses in Goa learnt that he had acquired a sacred thread, worn by Brahmins across the torso, and that he no longer ate meat.[232] So much so that many believed he was preaching a new religion; to locals, he was no Parangi for they 'had not heard him pronounce the name of Jesus'.[233] And men were drawn to this indigenized Christianity and its spokesman. De Nobili even invented new rites: When a Brahmin came on, he cut his old sacred thread, and gave him a 'Christian' one with a cross. Like Hindus, Madurai's new Catholics continued to apply sandalwood paste to the foreheads, and before mass, the father performed puja, or worship as in temples.[234] Most significantly, he was addressed as *aiya* ('sir', an honorific typically applied to Brahmins), and everyone thought *he* was the head of the church; if the pope showed up in Madurai, his scandalized, more conventional colleague warned, they would view His Holiness as only a stray Parangi, not the great governor of the Catholics.[235]

This complainant had good reason to resent the Italian. De Nobili's fellow missionary was an older, working-class Portuguese ex-soldier. Soon after the former's arrival, he was cast aside. That is, to bolster his claims to high status, de Nobili invented a veritable caste system between them. After all, he wrote, 'I professed to be an Italian Brahmin'; a figure of his august standing could not mingle on equal terms with a Parangi.[236] He would not dine with the man, and the latter, if he wished to confer with the Italian, was compelled to do so in secret.[237] In effect, de Nobili was endorsing the Hindus' poor opinion of Jesuits to design a better one for himself; by discrediting his colleague, he ennobled himself. Naturally, the other father was glum. De Nobili, in a flash of his own aristocratic origins, also sneered at his colleague's lack of education, and played up nationality, hinting that it was an insecure Portuguese faction raking up trouble.[238] For them, de Nobili suggested, missionary fervour was subordinate to patriotic loyalty, whereas Jesuits from lands other than Portugal could separate faith from political interest.[239] As for being a Brahmin, his colleague's panic was silly. It merely meant de Nobili was of 'an order of learned men', not that he had become an idol priest.[240] The sacred thread was a badge of status, not paganism. 'Did anyone,' the Italian demanded, 'ever pronounce superstitious the wearing of the golden bulla, the toga bordered with purple, or the tunic with the broad stripe, which were the distinguishing marks of [Rome's] patricians'?[241] No, and the same logic applied here in Madurai.[242] Besides, it was necessary to live sanyasi style 'for if these people did not see me do such penance, they would not receive me as one who can teach them the way to heaven'.[243]

Annoyingly for de Nobili, Goa sided with his disgruntled colleague: It was not wise to encourage the belief that the Portuguese were a beastly people. Some flexibility was tolerable—after all, Nasranis who did accept Catholicism retained Hindu customs despite every pressure from above[244]—but modification beyond basics was a threat. As Zupanov notes, at a time when the church had closed ranks to battle the Reformation in Europe, de Nobili was skating alarmingly close to inventing a brand-new headache.[245] In 1612, they asked him not to separate his high-caste Christians from those 'reeking with the stench of fish'[246] serviced by his partner; that all Christians must pray together was not negotiable. The Italian obeyed the letter of the command but violated its spirit by seating converts in separate rows by caste.[247] Goa was affronted again when on a visit the father took along a Brahmin cook, declining to sit at their (Parangi) table; he was not just playing fancy dress but had internalized his argument.[248] And with good reason: Early on, de Nobili was blackmailed by a Brahmin, who threatened to expose him as a Parangi in disguise.[249] Naturally, criticism within the Jesuit order continued about his 'false and absurd method',[250] till in 1619, the Italian was forced to deploy family influence and lobby the Pope.[251] Now, to the irritation of his adversaries, the Vatican *endorsed* his style. It helped that by way of results, the father was vindicated. 'I long most keenly to travel about these vast spaces . . . to win their innumerable peoples for Christ Our Lord,' he wrote,[252] and by the time of his death in 1656, the Madurai mission commanded the loyalty of thousands. There were, unfortunately, not many Brahmins,[253] but other high-born groups were attracted.[254] To his naysayers, then, the Italian Brahmin's success was its own answer.

In the broader scheme of things, these happenings in Madurai mark an astonishing shift from earlier attitudes. In Goa, Jesuits insisted on not just Christianization but also a Europeanization. Or as one of de Nobili's associates explained, 'The Portuguese try to turn all their converts not only into true Christians but also into genuine Portuguese.'[255] Ex-Hindus were told to discard 'native' clothes, customs, habits and even names. No, vegetarianism was *not* acceptable; no, local musical instruments may *not* be played at weddings.[256] In contrast, here in the Tamil south, as Catholics operated outside the protection of a Christian state, the reverse occurred: Converts could retain everything from their past lives, including caste prejudices, so long as they replaced Hindu gods with Jesus and Mary. In one Indian writer's words, it was a case of *murti Christachi, mandira Hinduche:* placing an idol of Christ in a Hindu temple.[257] So where as late as 1736 Goa was still attempting to outlaw 'native' influences in converts' lives,[258] Jesuits in the Madurai mission wore loincloths like Hindu ascetics and ate vegetarian meals off plantain leaves. They absorbed not just broad norms but specifically Brahmin ones. Indeed, an observer confirmed, the people did not view them as Parangis at all; and were 'the Natives to have the least Notion of this, the Fathers would be obliged to quit the Country'.[259] This inculturation grew so strong that when in 1744 Rome withdrew support, it was simply too late—Tamil Catholics were not amenable to European micromanagement. Their faith, while theologically distinct from that of Hindus, shared a 'common religious idiom'—it had ensconced itself into a Hindu terrain.[260] Or as a Protestant critic would sigh, all the 'silly observances of Paganism' with its 'ghastly superstitions' had invaded the papal religion in this corner of India.[261]

Essentially, then, Christianity was altered. The Portuguese attacked Nasranis for appearing too Hindu; ironically now, their Catholic faith was succumbing to the same influences. Its greatest proof was the centrality of caste to 'native' Christians. In the 1840s, thus, when a Jesuit went to a village of Parayars (described once as 'the refuse of the whole nation')[262] for their ritually 'polluting' caste status), he kept them standing outside the church.[263] As late as 2008, low-caste Catholics would complain that they were still 'refused the honor of reading scripture, serving at the altar, or joining the choir', and endured 'separate seating', 'separate funeral biers' and demarcated cemeteries.[264] Tamil Christians, like Hindus, had chariot processions, 'except that the image of the Virgin' replaced goddesses. There was the 'the same noise of trumpets', 'the same blaze of rockets', and 'the same dancers, with ... marks of sandal-wood and vermilion on their naked bodies' as in temples. At the shrine of one of de Nobili's successors, it was perfectly Christian to sacrifice goats too,[265] and when another built a new church, it was with 'an image of the Blessed Virgin Mary in the native dress'.[266] Tellingly, this brand of Christianity was less menacing to Hindu powers—unlike the Portuguese alternative—and they willingly extended patronage.[267] In Sarukani near Sivaganga, for example, village revenue was allocated to a church, described as a *sarvesvara kovil* ('temple of the almighty'). The document was quintessentially Hindu: The grant was to endure 'until the extinction of the sun [and] moon',[268] and it was equal to sponsoring Brahmins and lighting 'lamps in one hundred thousand temples'. To upset it, however, was tantamount to the 'crime of killing the sacred black cow'.[269] The sanctity of the cow, that is, was summoned here to shelter Christian interests.

One wonders whether de Nobili intended to go this far. What he had in mind was a 'balancing of much acceptance with some rejection'; he could never fully endorse Hinduism, for then his own merchandise, Christianity, would not find buyers. So, his intent was to naturalize himself and his faith with the people while positioning

Jesus as a more refined alternative to Hinduism.[270] Ultimately, the goal was still to convert. To an extent this succeeded, but equally, Christian saints simply joined a general cast of gods and goddesses in these parts. Just as Hindus prayed at the tombs of Muslim sufis for children, they now also went to shrines to the Virgin.[271] And for Christians too, a transfer of allegiance to the Bible did not mean a negation of the past; Tamil Catholics continued to make offerings to village goddesses.[272] Hinduism did not absorb Christianity as it once had tribal cults. Meanwhile, the latter, for its part, while staying separate, maintained a 'native' appearance, not posing as pointed a threat as the church in Goa. In fact, by the nineteenth century, Catholics were sometimes called Hindu-Christians, or as a leading judge preferred, Christian-Hindus.[273]

For future Hindu *nationalists*, though, there was cause for worry, nevertheless. On the one hand, it was clear that political power made all the difference. Goa's Christianization and demographic transformation, after all, was a result of Portuguese control of the state. The lesson, then, was that Hindus must always retain a grip over authority. But the Madurai formula was no better. Xavier and more aggressive Jesuits were at least honest about their goals. The Italian, on the other hand, was a 'conman'. He Hinduized Christianity, yes, but fundamentally what he ran, they would argue, was a scam.[274] The irony, of course, is that this strategy—of much acceptance with some rejection—was how Brahmins too planted their ideas across the subcontinent over the centuries, synthesizing countless groups and tribes into the Hindu order. Viewed this way, de Nobili was following an Indian tradition; the white Brahmin was, inadvertently, enacting the brown one's playbook, albeit for a religious system of faraway origins. And in this, perhaps, lay the recipe of his success—he was doing something quite well known to Hindus.[275]

In the end, the challenge to Jesuits in India came not so much from Hindus as Christians of a different denomination. Starting in the eighteenth century, a fresh crop of missionaries began to trickle into the country—except these were Protestants. The schism between Catholics and forces of the Reformation in Europe was institutionalized by now, and charges levelled by Jesuits against 'natives' were seized on by the new entrants to brand *Catholics* illegitimate—Protestants accused Catholics of idolatry, superstition, and of burying the faith under 'an innumerable multitude of rites, ceremonies, traditions, and errors'.[276] On the face of it, this has parallels with Hindu critiques of Jesuits, as we saw with the questions raised to Fenicio. Indeed, one of the quarrels even between Nasranis and the Portuguese came from brown Christians' denial of Catholic images, which Jesuits argued was heresy.[277] Then there were miracles. Even as they censured Hindu superstition, Catholic faith in divine interventions was unquestionable. Xavier claimed a miracle when a lady with prolonged labour pains delivered after he converted her,[278] and hagiographies show him bring people back from the dead, now by baptising a drowned child, and next by applying spittle to a snake bite.[279] The result was that the fathers themselves gave their Protestant rivals 'a very good Opportunity of representing the Jesuits as egregious Liars'.[280] To Jesuits, Hinduism was a lie; in Protestant eyes, Jesuits were also frauds. In fact, from their perspective, Catholic complaints against idolatry were a case of pot versus kettle, a point seemingly confirmed by the ease with the papal faith could be Hinduized.[281]

Naturally, the Jesuits smelled danger. When the first Protestant fathers landed nearby, Madurai denounced them as 'heretics'; when they published books, subverting Catholic teachings, these were declared as 'full of errors'. Amusingly, just as high-caste Hindus claimed that only the worst of their lot had reason to convert, Jesuits argued that men 'of the lower strata of society, some pariahs, enticed by the love of rupees' alone fell for Protestant propaganda.[282] And if extremist Hindus even today slander Christians as 'rice-bag' converts, eighteenth-century Jesuits insisted that 'a large number of neophytes' had 'sold their souls' to Protestants to escape 'pangs of hunger'.[283] All along, Indian Christians—demonstrating that 'natives' had their own calculations—exploited the feud: If unhappy with Catholics, they could transfer allegiances in 'a truly diabolical treason'.[284] In one case, after a man shifted to the Protestant camp, there were murderous reprisals even.[285] So that as a Jesuit warned in 1731, the 'danger of heresy' was constant, and Protestants, 'intent on the ruin of souls, roam about the fold, seeking whom they may devour'.[286] It was a dying cry, though, for by the end of that century, Jesuits would be marginalized in the very evangelical space they helped create.[287] And by the Victorian age, a British (Protestant) official would write them off decisively as 'a perfect scandal to the religion which they profess'.[288]

It was Protestants who now began to build a following in India, reinforced not long after by the might of the English East India Company. And under British rule, Hindus across a much larger geographical expanse were to find their lives—and religion—under scrutiny and attack.

TWO

# 'HEATHENS' AND HIDDEN TRUTHS

On 31 January 1708, the son of a German corn merchant stopped at an unnamed rest house in the Indian peninsula. Armed with lessons from the Bible, not to speak of good old-fashioned missionary zeal, he found a captive audience among the children in a school attached to the building. Who, demanded the European father, was their god? Siva, the startled Hindu boys replied, only to be notified that this was a horrible lie—no deity with a wife and issue could be entertained seriously; the *actual* lord of the universe was unmarried. Of course, the missionary clarified, this true god had had a son named Jesus, but there was no spouse, and he advised the students to 'be guided and instructed by his holy Laws' or contemplate eternal damnation. 'Our Business,' replied the children with forgivable cheek, 'is to learn to read and write', and their schoolmaster, at any rate, never troubled them with such 'abstruse' riddles as whose god was real and whose an imposter. So next, the corn merchant's son turned on the poor teacher. It must all have caused a commotion, for in the end, a temple dancer resting nearby asked the man to take his quarrel to Brahmins, who might answer his 'puzzling Questions'—and more to the point, to cease harassing tired travellers and bewildered little children.¹

Bartholomäus Ziegenbalg must have made a strange sight in eighteenth-century Tamil country. For all his magisterial speeches about god, delivered with force and conviction, he was less tall and imposing, and more round and ample,² saddled also with a stomach ailment that would kill him. Unlike the Madurai Jesuits who adopted local dress, and despite the heat and humidity of the south Indian coast, he moved around in a long black coat, chasing debate and, now and then, manufacturing discord. He once attended, for instance, the court of a celebrated Muslim mystic, insulting everybody there by refusing to take off his shoes in the holy presence. When the old sufi told him that even the local rajah came before him barefoot, Ziegenbalg declared the mystic too proud and coolly lectured him on the merits of humility. Predictably, he was not permitted entry the next time.³ But such reverses did not dull our man's avidity. He had, after all, come all the way from Europe to spread the gospel, braving the worst of official bureaucracy and mission politics, not to speak of Catholic resentment. And while he had no desire to become a martyr, he was determined to see his task through, even if it upset a few crabby 'natives' and gave him a reputation as an irritating Protestant.

Ziegenbalg was born in 1682⁴ in Saxony into a middle-class family. Both his parents died when he was a child, but not before his mother first pointed him towards the Bible. By his teens, young Bartholomäus had formed a sincere interest in religion. His studies in Berlin were interrupted by dismal health, but in 1703, he managed to transfer to Halle to learn from a highly regarded clergyman. Despite his less than robust constitution, when intelligence arrived that the king of Denmark was keen to ship Protestant missionaries to assorted (Catholic-dominated) corners of the world, Ziegenbalg was nominated with another student. Neither was thrilled at the prospect

Bartholomäus Ziegenbalg, courtesy of the Hamburger Kulturgut Digital.

of life in Africa as proposed, though, and even failed examination by a bishop in Copenhagen. But royal will prevailed: In a second appraisal, the tester quietly modified his prior assessment, endorsing Ziegenbalg and his colleague, Heinrich Plütschau, as fit for service. An audience with the king followed, but in an unexpected twist, it was decided that the Germans should pack their bags for India, not Africa, as missionaries of His Majesty of Denmark.[5]

Unlike the Portuguese in Goa, however, with whom Catholic missionaries possessed clout, the Danish East India Company was less than delighted by the priests who knocked on their doors in 1706. Ziegenbalg had already got into trouble with his ship's captain after berating him for pestering a woman on board. In response, Plütschau and he were restrained on the vessel for days after arrival, with 'stale bread and foul water' for nourishment.[6] When they finally found a boat to bring them ashore to Tranquebar on India's east coast, these first-ever Protestant missionaries in the land[7] discovered that Company men were unfriendly—their Danish chaplains disliked Germans,[8] while officials thought all missionaries flies in the mercantile ointment. After being made to wait an age to see the chief, they were swiftly abandoned in a street—it was a junior merchant's sympathy that helped them find shelter. Official hostility, in fact, would continue for almost all their time in India: On New Year's Day in 1707, for example, when Ziegenbalg sermonized about 'the sins . . . and the omissions of Christian Governments', it was (accurately perhaps) interpreted as a broadside against the Company. Immediately, he was accused of 'inciting to rebellion'. On another occasion, the father spent four months in confinement after a second slight, imagined or real.[9] No wonder many missionaries believed they were fighting eternally against the odds, what with fellow Christians turning spiteful.

Patience, however, was key to winning the souls of strange brown 'heathens', misled twice over thanks to papal agents. And lack of support, while rendering an initial jolt, did not prevent the missionaries from launching their enterprise. Plütschau was evidently less proactive, with the result that much of the work was inspired by Ziegenbalg. Given Portuguese dominance at sea during previous centuries, theirs had become the language of commerce, 'spoke here by many Heathens'—this, naturally, had to be learnt.[10] Alongside also commenced Tamil lessons from a local called Alagappa ('Aleppa'), with whom they got along fabulously. Their other teacher, though, was more of a challenge, for he tended to 'argueth daily with us' about religion. 'We hope,' wrote Ziegenbalg, 'to bring him over to Christian Knowledge', while the Indian was bent on taking the white men to Siva.[11] Either way, by August 1707, Ziegenbalg was confident enough to preach in the local tongue,[12] though this was a colloquial Tamil, and not its courtly cousin mastered by de Nobili in the last century.[13] Meanwhile, sensing that they were 'more likely to achieve success with children whose minds were still impressionable', Plütschau and Ziegenbalg began spending their meagre resources on a new school, borrowing when they needed more food and coin.[14] It was an early personification of the idea of mission education in India: something that would proliferate and leave a greater impact in the Hindu world than preaching itself.[15]

Neither missionary was prepared for the country, though—in fact, they knew so little of India that Ziegenbalg believed Tamils to be a 'truly barbaric people'.[16] But, unlike with the Jesuits, the opinion evolved rapidly after interaction. Indeed, soon he was writing of 'Malabarians'[17] as 'generally good natur'd, ingenious, and very industrious', with the sole, tragic defect that they were not Christian.[18] Conversations commenced at once on religion, and Ziegenbalg enjoyed parleying with Hindus. Early in 1707, for example, he met a Brahmin and launched forth on whether Tamils believed in monotheism. When the visitor confirmed they did indeed believe in a single, universal power, Ziegenbalg questioned how, then, they could venerate legions of idol gods. Sure, 'verbally you own the Existence of One Supreme Being', but there were so many subordinate deities that 'you are at a loss [as] to whom you had best address your Vows or offer Bloody Sacrifices'. The Brahmin would do better instead, he advised, to 'break off the Cords of inveterate Errors' and accept the 'One only True God', who was of Christian outline. Ziegenbalg's friend, however, did not take the bait. 'God has created both Good and Evil; Vice and Vertue; Happiness and Misery,' he answered sagely. Nothing could happen outside his will, so 'if we . . . are mistaken in point of Religion', this too was part of the divine plan. 'For who are we,' the Brahmin smiled, 'to resist the Will of God'? In other words, even if Hindus had it wrong, it was the almighty's considered desire that they should wallow in those wrongs.[19] Christians might be convinced of their truth; but considering that god chose not to directly brief Hindus, the latter viewed his self-proclaimed mouthpieces with courteous indifference.[20]

Next, as Ziegenbalg explained creation, original sin and Jesus's suffering, the Brahmin listened with genuine interest but refused to admit that this was the only way of knowing divinity. 'I believe all you say of God's Dealings,' replied the brown man to the German. But this was how he appeared to 'you White Europeans'. Among 'us Black Malabarians', in contrast, the supreme being made itself known in other forms. 'Revelations he made of himself in this Land are as firmly believ'd here to be true, as you believe those made in your Country: For as Christ in Europe was made Man; so here our God Wichtnu [Vishnu] was born among us,' suggested the (evidently Vaishnava) Brahmin. Ziegenbalg was by all means free to seek salvation through the Bible, but his discussant would serve his own god; he was arguing, in essence, for the idea of tolerance, highlighting that familiar Indian method of making space for ideological diversity. There was room for them to agree to disagree, for divine truth was not a one-way street. After all, finished the Brahmin, 'to save you one way, and us another, is one of the Pastimes and Diversions of Almighty God'.[21] Just as different castes and tribes in India chose from a panoply of sects, deities and styles of worship—ranging from ascetic renunciation to boisterous, ecstatic bhakti—Christians were welcome to do what they pleased. But they were expected to operate within a competitive spiritual marketplace, not attempt to capture or overturn it.

If Ziegenbalg was startled by this laissez faire attitude to religion, he was by no means the first to encounter it in India. Only decades before, the traveller-physician Francois Bernier (1620–88), observing purity rituals among high-caste Hindus, told a group that their propensity to dip in water multiple times a day would be deadly in chilly Europe. Clearly, therefore, such customs could not have been mandated by any universal god, and were, instead, 'a system of human invention'. If the doctor meant this as a blinding display of logic, his Hindu conversationalists were not disarmed. They reminded the Frenchman that nobody had claimed 'our law is of universal application'. On the contrary, 'God intended it only for us,' in a specific context and, presumably, climate. 'We do not say,' the Hindus added, 'that yours is a false religion; it may be adapted to your wants' because, in the end, god had 'appointed many different ways of going to heaven'. In India, a multiplicity of beliefs was valid, while those of Europeans made sense in *their* situations (a principle in line with arguments made a thousand years ago by pagan intellectuals like Symmachus and Celsus).[22] Bernier pushed his case but, in the end, departed frustrated. 'I found it impossible to convince them that the Christian faith was designed for the whole earth, and theirs was mere fable and gross fabrication.'[23] It was an elementary problem of perception: To Christians, theirs was the only bona fide Religion; everything else was diabolical pretension or primitive paganism. That the world might house religions (plural) of varying formats—and, significantly, that Christianity was *not* unique—was tough to swallow even at a conceptual level.

Ziegenbalg was more committed a fighter than Bernier, however. He went into a 'Multitude of Heathens' once, charging

A Saiva Brahmin, by Pierre Sonnerat in his *Voyage aux Indes Orientales et à la Chine* (1782), courtesy of the Library of Congress, Rare Book and Special Collections Division.

them with witchcraft and honouring satanic images, shunning the true one who 'breathed into our Nostrils the Breath of Life'. But he too was disappointed. As with that Brahmin, those gathered argued that they were placed in these circumstances by god himself—surely to rectify this was to challenge divine will?[24] One man asked Ziegenbalg if all Christians had been saved, that he had come to them: 'Pray Sir, would you not do better to exert your Charity first at home'?[25] Elsewhere, people responded with sarcasm, as occurred when a discussant inquired if he were guaranteed salvation in Christianity. Because why, he wondered, should he subject himself to the inconvenience of baptism, when 'I may be damned in yours, as well as in my own' religion?[26] Yet another raised a practical point around diversity practices in heaven: Were all languages of the world recognized? How did people of so many races communicate?[27] And when Ziegenbalg sent out a questionnaire asking why Hindus so disliked Christianity, a respondent castigated everything from Europeans' unseemly drinking habits to the trivia that white folk—in what discomposed a Mughal emperor too[28]—did not wash their bottoms.[29] Certainly, they agreed, the Bible (and Quran too) offered 'the possibility of salvation'.[30] But so did other alternatives. After all, Hindus themselves had many: One might bow to Siva at dawn, sacrifice to a goddess at dusk, revere the Vedas and with matching ease seek out sufis—all while acknowledging that each embodied the same higher principle.

Of course, Ziegenbalg's tirade against 'Graven Images' and 'Whoring Gods and Goddesses' who promoted 'Uncleanness and filthy Lusts',[31] did provoke annoyance also, and a reputation as the 'Christian Maker of Tranquebar' soon preceded him.[32] Once he caused outrage outside a temple by trotting about on a horse—customarily, even the elite dismounted near the shrine. Naturally, 'both Priests and People pealed me with Maledictions and Abusive words', while Ziegenbalg used the occasion for an unsolicited monologue on truth and falsehood.[33] So also when he tried to exit

Tranquebar—leased to the Danish by the Tanjore rajah—he was blocked from entering the latter's territory. This prince had reason to suspect missionaries: Years before, some of his staff had turned Catholic, causing scandal, and in 1701, complaints reached him of a stage performance that ended with Christians breaking Hindu images.[34] With Ziegenbalg, the stated explanation was that 'ever since you came to these Countries, you are . . . always scolding at our [temples], blaspheming our Gods, and cursing our Religious Ceremonies'.[35] While he was not himself taken into custody, his assistant Alagappa was allegedly imprisoned in Tanjore at one time for having 'revealed all the secrets of [Hindu] law and worship' to the missionary.[36] Books he printed acquired a notoriety of their own, meanwhile, with Brahmins (and Jesuits) objecting to their virulent anti-Hindu (and anti-Catholic) tone.[37] So, it was not the case that all 'natives' viewed the father with an open mind; some felt seriously attacked, to the extent that in 1712, a group of Brahmins, finding Ziegenbalg asleep in an inn, supposedly even toyed with the idea of making his repose permanent.[38] (And we will return, in due course, to the theme of violence in asserting the Hindu identity.)

Interestingly, while he was exasperating Hindus, the German's bosses in Europe were growing restless too. To start with, conversion was weak: From a servant acquired shortly after Ziegenbalg's arrival, six years later he counted only 117 lapsed Hindus.[39] But more worryingly, it seemed like the father was growing a tad sympathetic towards Hinduism, on an intellectual plane at least. It began innocently. Or as he reported,

> When at last I was entirely able to read their own books, and became aware that the very same philosophical disciplines as are discussed by scholars in Europe are quite methodically taught among them . . . I developed a very strong desire to be thoroughly instructed in their heathenism from their own writings.[40]

Within two years of opening, the Tranquebar mission had gathered 119 Tamil texts.[41] By 1714, Ziegenbalg owned over 600 in a total of fourteen languages.[42] These manuscripts, wide-ranging in subject, excited him. The *Tolkappiyam*, an ancient Tamil grammar, was 'the greatest book' but 'also the very hardest'; locals, he observed, 'rack their brains over it just as much as European philosophers do over the works of Aristotle'.[43] The *Tirukkural*, 'a book of morality in verse', was most 'edifying'[44]—an opinion shared by an earlier Jesuit, who instinctively speculated that its writer must have been under Christian influence.[45] The *Sivavakkiyam* taught 'good morality'; sadly, its followers, while ridiculing idol worship, applied the same sentiment to Christianity's claims of 'uniqueness'.[46] And, of course, there was the *Panchatantra*, 'similar to Aesop's Fables' and 'much used in schools'.[47]

In fact, amassing more literature than converts, the father would slowly dismantle part of his own prejudice. Or put another way, Ziegenbalg slid from learning '*about* India' to proposing that perhaps there was something to pick up '*from* India'.[48] That 'natives' were a thinking people, not fools flitting around malicious devils, also became clear through an 'interreligious dialogue' with Hindus.[49] Conducted through letters, it offered a variety of insights. To 'purify' their insides, one respondent stated, yogis had mastered the art of sucking water up the anus.[50] But more serious data too was received. There were, Ziegenbalg learnt, four Vaishnava sects and three pledged to Siva in these parts. But, his 'native' correspondent added, where 'religion is concerned, there is only one': an assertion of Hinduism's singularity; of that Brahminical consciousness discussed in this book's opening.[51] Equally, however, a second man grumbled that this feeling was not concrete, leaving Hindus fragmented in *real* terms—and susceptible to missionaries.[52] Monotheistic ideas were present, but without consensus: One writer pronounced god formless and beyond description;[53] another painted a verbal picture of Siva, giving divinity a shape.[54] Invariably, certain thinkers sought to defend Hinduism, knowing well Ziegenbalg's professional intent. Yes, some Hindu customs were regrettable, they agreed, but this hardly justified an assault on the entire religious architecture. For '[w]ere we to judge the Christian religion by the deeds of [some] Europeans, we [too] would hardly find any good in it'.[55] In fact, these interlocutors redefined missionary concepts. White men divided the world between Christians and heathens; to Hindus, on the other hand, heathens were those 'who live contrary to God', with bad habits and morals. And these existed in *all* religions.[56] Good did not reside exclusively with Christians, that is, apportioning bad alone to others; every culture held both in fractions.[57]

Despite his missionary urges, Ziegenbalg was fascinated. And so, like many before and after, he produced a book. Except that this upset his European superiors. For the *Genealogy of the South-Indian Gods* (1713) was a manual of Hindu deities, ranging from *gramadevata*s (village gods) who commanded 'devils' to grander powers such as Siva and Vishnu. On the face of it, it was an outsider's effort to grasp the layered, seemingly tangled mythologies of Hindu gods, structuring them into a family tree from the almighty.[58] Though offered—in keeping with most missionary productions—as a digest to arm future Christians for spiritual crusades in India, what is telling is the *Genealogy's* submission that Hindu thought had value. Admittedly, Ziegenbalg was not the first to suggest this: de Nobili, for instance, took a similar stance. Yes, he wrote, there was idol worship and 'fictitious tales'.[59] But buried within were parallels with Christian teachings.[60] Or more memorably, even if much 'reek[ed] of the dung pit', Hinduism had 'pearls'[61] by which white men too 'could benefit'.[62] Ziegenbalg agreed: As early as the year of his arrival, he argued against condemning all Hindus as demon-worshippers given how enough of them, it was patent, venerated the 'one Divine Being'.[63] Now in the *Genealogy*, he travelled further, adding that under a seeming pandemonium, 'these heathens still possess of traditions out of the Word of God'.[64] Christians had no monopoly on divine truths, that is; Hindus had means of accessing them as well, even if by 'the subtility of the devil' things were 'perverted and distorted' here.[65] While not equal to Christians, these people were yet not, the father felt, *as* awful in matters of faith as made out in European imagination.

It was a mature view. But at home, the church was looking neither for nuance nor a research paper on pagan theology. And so, when his thesis arrived in the post, it was denied publication. Missionaries, the German was warned, were sent out 'to extirpate heathenism', not 'to spread heathenish non-sense in Europe'.[66] 'Natives' might uphold the preposterous idea of multiple paths, but the father had to remember there was only one street; he had no business legitimizing Eastern errors. Ziegenbalg's subtle suggestion—that Christians had no new message to deliver, and that Hindus had *within* their traditions, strands aligned with the best of Biblical teachings—was a dangerous line. So much so that he himself appears to have applied for anticipatory bail in the book's preface. The *Genealogy* concerned itself, he loudly explained, with much 'heathen foolishness'. Writing the book was no 'delight', only 'punishment and [a] nuisance'.[67] That is, he deprecated his own work—and with good reason given the response it provoked. In any case, the manuscript was promptly shelved.[68] Missionaries, Ziegenbalg learnt, had better stick to prescribed goals, armoured in dogma; to allow pagan ideas to spark self-doubt was unwise. And if knowledge of local thinking were acquired, this must be deployed only—as we saw in previous cases—to ridicule their source, not reflect on Christianity and its limits. Indeed, after 1714, a chastened Ziegenbalg would largely cease writing on and studying Hinduism; he had strayed too far from the dictated path.[69]

Unfortunately, this did not end his woes. Plütschau had returned to Europe in 1711, leaving Ziegenbalg to carry on alone, and indeed die in Tranquebar eight years later. He did himself travel home once, marrying on this trip; if no German came out to India, he warned, he would seal the deal with a Tamil.[70] It was not, as such, a happy union: Two of three children born to the couple died, one in Ziegenbalg's lifetime, and there were many pressures born of financial constraints. His health too declined—for that long running stomach ailment, he was prescribed 'a steel cure which involved having to drink an infusion of iron files in water'.[71] To this ordeal was added stress from conflicts with higher-ups who never understood why a missionary needed money. His job, as they pictured it, was to live frugally, wandering about preaching to 'heathens'. Ziegenbalg, however, having encountered a rather more sophisticated society, pressed for funds to support his school, horses, buildings and to develop human resources. In February 1719, the father died a clearly harassed figure, and not long after, a 'bulky communication' arrived from Copenhagen with 'a complete condemnation' of his work. When a colleague opened it, he was 'scarcely able to read it for tears'.[72] Ziegenbalg had been sent out on a mission; by getting distracted, by ceasing to cork his mind from local influences and by telling his bosses what they did not wish to hear, he had ended up a failure.

In the story of modern Hinduism and its political awakening, however, Ziegenbalg had chanced on something powerful. A century after his death, when India came under colonial rule and prolonged evangelical stress, Hindus would again be rebuked for the 'wrongs' in their religion. Accused of practising a barbaric faith, they would be offered redemption in Christianity and European civilization. Given how white men had seized the land, making their prowess all too obvious, responding to these claims was not easy. It was no longer the case that a few passing missionaries were, by turns, amusing and irritating Hindus; having lost power, the latter now lived under Christian authority. Men of Ziegenbalg's vocation posed an even graver threat in these new conditions. And so, resistance was inevitable. But what is interesting is that in devising a response, many Hindus would take the same position as their priors who interacted with our eighteenth-century father. Sure, there were 'bad' features in their religion. However, offsetting these were enough that satisfied even Western parameters of 'good'. Popular, 'lower' Hinduism—visibly polytheistic and idolatrous—might, from the European perspective, deserve contempt. However, its 'higher' constructs could hold their own. Hindus, then, had no reason to convert, except in the sense of giving up 'embarrassing' traditions to underscore 'better' ones—an inner reorientation as opposed to a complete desertion. In doing so, they would partly also internalize a foreign gaze, of course. But under colonial domination, this was inescapable; this was a stung, defensive society, acting under a series of shocks and strains.[73]

Either way, the message foreshadowing the rise of modern Hinduism was this: White men might corner power in India. Where religion and identity were concerned, though, 'natives' could—and would—stubbornly continue to refuse instruction.

The proposition that Hinduism had higher and lower forms—the first resembling monotheism, the other 'messily' polytheistic—was neither new nor a European bifurcation.[74] In one Vedic text, thus, a sage is asked how many gods exist. He opens with 3306. But when pressed as to how many *really* exist, his answer changes: The number is pruned to thirty-three, then six, two, one and a half, and finally one.[75] A 1380 inscription makes a corresponding claim: God was the one Saivas worshipped as Siva, some philosophers in the abstract, others through ritual and Buddhists as the enlightened one.[76] Even masters of bhakti stressed this; as Purandara Dasa sang in the 1500s, '"My God", "Your God", don't talk like that. There is only one God.'[77] Muslim observers took note early on: An eleventh-century writer recorded that idols served the less-evolved by offering a physical anchor, but educated Hindus dwelt on a metaphysical god.⁷⁸ Among these latter, enough viewed popular practice with condescension even.⁷⁹ Just as girls played with dolls until mature enough for domestic life, a spiritual patriarch said to a Mughal prince, those 'unaware of the interior' fiddled with outer forms.⁸⁰ The gap with monotheisms elsewhere, however, is evident: In the West, principle and practice (largely) coincided. There was one god to whom prayers were addressed.⁸¹ In India, though, the principle sat atop a polytheistic infrastructure: God was one but worship was directed at many deities,⁸² drawn from a variety of cults, a few even competing for recognition as *the* god.⁸³ In fact, one of Ziegenbalg's informants argued that in time, all these would be 'transformed into the one divine Supreme Being who alone will then be God'.⁸⁴

In this multi-tiered system, there were gradations of orthodoxy. Philosophers and ascetics looked down on all forms of worship, irrespective of whether it celebrated mega beings like Vishnu or the village goddess of smallpox. Others discriminated differently; some of Ziegenbalg's contacts adored higher gods but decried the lower. Only the 'humble of the lowest castes' were fond of inferior deities, one said.⁸⁵ Another called them 'devils', to whom people made sacrifices from fear.⁸⁶ That is, where Christians demonized *all* Hindu deities, *some* Hindus branded *some* gods 'false' in matching terms.⁸⁷ Similarly, though Indians used images, this had come largely from outside the Vedic tradition; not all Brahmins, therefore, approved.⁸⁸ The most self-consciously 'authentic' among them eschewed temple service; priesthood was degrading.⁸⁹ Indeed, some thought laying eyes on temple-priests defiling,⁹⁰ and a key text equates them to butchers.⁹¹ Yet, these voices were a minority; as noted, Puranic Hinduism, cross-fertilized by so many sources, never had just one response to things. So, despite naysayers, most Brahmins adapted.⁹² Priests, facing purist disdain, retorted that 'the mere sight of the image of god was worth *more* than' prescriptions of the conservative.⁹³ But either way, in what would serve 'natives' well, their religious archive presented so many possibilities and interpretations that resources for every contingency were available.[94] If Europeans propped up monotheism, Hindus could sing along, even assert ownership, despite the surfeit of gods populating general imagination. If idolatry were rubbished, 'native' thinkers could nod in assent, simultaneously showing indulgence. White men saw in this hypocrisy and trickery, but to Hindus, this was entirely in keeping with their many-storeyed history and plural personalities.

It was Brahmins who typically provided narrative coherence for this diversity of thought and action, tailoring answers to the askers' expectations.[95] Unsurprisingly, they were showcased as the best candidates to explain Hinduism. This centrality of the Brahmin was widely admitted.[96] Even with Ziegenbalg, more than one Hindu interlocutor clarified that his inputs sprang from the correct sources—by which he meant Brahmin scholars. One writer apologized for a lag in correspondence; thanks to turbulent weather, the 'Piramanarkal' (Brahmins) had been staying home.[97] Another supplied information himself but felt it necessary to add the disclaimer that he had *not* asked Brahmins.[98] Indeed, dialogue with Brahmins opened up a less unkind view of Hinduism among some missionaries. Before our German, in 1651, for example, a book titled *The Open Door to Hitherto Concealed Heathenism* made its appearance in Europe. Described as the most 'capacious' study of Hinduism until then,[99] it was also an attempt to make sense of Hindu life from the inside.[100] European writing, as we know, often built on the strange and scandalous: externalities that highlighted 'monstrosity' to confirm Western superiority. Widow-burning, 'obscene' antics by nude sadhus and devils in temples, fit with ease negative categories already available to the Christian world.[101] But then, Jesuits like de Nobili triggered a crisis by showing how not all Hindu customs were outlandish and that the West 'could not command universal admiration'.[102] Now with *The Open Door*, Abraham Rogerius (1609–49) in Pulicat—granted the Dutch by Venkata II—went a notch further, enabled by his willingness to wed observation to 'native' guidance.[103] For helping the Dutchman comprehend Hindu culture was a Portuguese-speaking Brahmin fugitive from Goa (!) named Padmanabha.

This unlikely collaborator's antecedents notwithstanding, the result was a far more nuanced account of Hindu life. Gone were idols with cock's feet and fleshhook arms; instead, Rogerius soberly recorded that Vishnu was depicted with four arms, while Siva was cast as a lingam or as a man with 'two [eyes] in the natural place, and the third in the middle of the forehead'.[104] Practices like sati were noted but without shrillness: Families with accentuated notions of prestige might pressure widows to burn, but doing so was 'a crime that merits hell'.[105] There were festivals with chariot processions, but nobody in *The Open Door* rushes madly to throw themselves under wheels. So also the father formed an understanding of the country's sacred geography: The greater Tamil pilgrimage centres were at Srirangam, Madurai, Tirupati, Kanchipuram, etc., while the subcontinental map included shrines far in the north and west.[106] Indeed, Rogerius recognized Hinduism as a spectrum, including differences between the Brahminical orthodoxy and mass religion. Describing buffalo sacrifices, for example, he recorded how Brahmins abhorred these but 'dare not oppose it'.[107] Sectarian intricacies too were identified; Brahmins were not a uniform bloc—there were Vaishnavas (who projected Vishnu as supreme), Saivas (who argued for Siva), Saktas (for whom god was a goddess) and Smartas (who acknowledged all three and more as forms of divinity).[108] Subtler elements were not missed either, such as the 'ingenious' Puranic formula of linking temples to the great narrative via stories.[109] Why, the father grasped even caste in its insidious complexity: Parayars, he reported, were treated with contempt. And yet, with a group even lower, they *too* showed cruelty.[110] This was a society split into many parts vertically and sideways both: a source also of its religious heterogeneity.[111]

PLATE 24.

## SIGNS WORN BY BRAHMINS.

MAHA DEVA.

VISHNOO.

SOORYA.

GUNESH.

DEVEE.

HUNOOMAN.

[Sectarian] Signs worn by Brahmins, by S.C. Belnos (1851), from the Wellcome Collection.

In other words, as missionaries began to listen—if grudgingly only—to 'native' voices, even popular Hinduism looked less shocking. In the realm of ideas, meanwhile, a sense dawned that aspects of Hindu philosophy passed muster even against a Christian lens—something that in colonial times Hindus would, as we will see, turn to their advantage. Before Ziegenbalg, the Portuguese missionary John de Britto (1647–93), thus, concluded that 'natives' were not altogether hopeless. Because, '[s]uch as reflect seriously on the principal points of [their] doctrine . . . will soon be of opinion, that these idolaters were formerly acquainted with the mysteries of the christian [sic] religion'.[112] That is, buried under all species of difference was something relatable. So, if Francis Xavier reproached everything Hindu, better exposure now indicated that the system held its own logic, explaining also why Hindus felt little appetite for conversion. To be clear, Europeans still refused to admit parity between Hinduism and Christianity, given the rest of its 'idolatrous' baggage. For as de Nobili wrote, 'milk mixed with poison' still killed.[113] Nor was conversion abandoned. Yet, its method was reframed. Sure, some were willing to whisper, Hinduism was *perhaps* a step on god's ladder. But it was a poor, ramshackle one. The Bible, meanwhile, towered above. Conversion, that is, was positioned not as a choice between falsehood and truth—which failed on Hindus, with their infuriating relativism—but as a road to all milk, zero poison. Just as there were higher and lower paths within Hinduism, Christianity ranked above 'native' religion. And so, some hereon sought to persuade Hindus that their faith was adulterated; that for pure dairy, Jesus was the outlet. Or to quote our Italian Brahmin, Hinduism was like 'fragrant' balm in a 'dirty pot'. If they wanted the same item in its fitting receptacle, they must come to Christianity.[114]

By the eighteenth century, then, the attitude towards Hindus became a welter of contradictory feelings, ranging from violent opposition to compromise. While devil-talk continued, awareness emerged that what looked, at a glance, so certain to Western eyes was a pixelated image. But even as missionaries recalibrated, a fresh crop of men were watching. Europe, after all, was going through its own upheavals. The Protestant Reformation, combined with dynamics set off by the Renaissance, had led to a so-called Age of Enlightenment.[115] The grip of dogma slipped, and the 'discovery' of new countries sparked curiosity about its peoples and beliefs. Imperiling the church, murmurs arose that Christianity might not have all the answers—and, indeed, that there were religions (plural) in the world. And just as Protestants employed arguments against idolatry to discredit Catholics, Western rationalists, sceptics and scientists now calculated that Hindu philosophy might smash the orthodoxy in Europe. The Hindu scheme of time alone—*yuga*s, each lasting many millennia—cast doubt on Biblical claims that the world was under 10,000 years old, for instance. So, a reading of Hinduism, intended to buttress European preoccupations, gained intellectual currency. And just as de Nobili made his religion palatable to Hindus by stripping it of Western cultural accoutrements, Hindu ideas—cut from 'native' moorings—acquired a dim, functional legitimacy in European eyes. A quest would begin for 'authentic' Hinduism, separated from its complicated living culture. The latter was confusing; the former Westerners might understand, and indeed, even exploit for their own purposes.

Europe too, that is, was discovering 'higher' and 'lower' Hinduism. And in isolating the first, and seeking monotheism *outside* the Christian tradition, it would soon fix its attention on the Brahmins' most hallowed literature: the Vedas.

In September 1659, a great grandson of Emperor Akbar was paraded through the streets of Delhi. The people of the city were out in full force to see this prince, who was, undoubtedly, among the most extraordinary products of his dynasty. There were men at arms, and a great many others in attendance on forty-four-year-old Dara Shukoh. And yet, something was amiss. The crowd was restless and in tears. The prince himself was not in court attire but dirty rags. Where not long ago he owned 'pompously caparisoned' elephants, now he rode a 'miserable' beast, 'covered with filth'.[116] For what was underway was not a conventional state procession and the Dara the townsfolk saw no more the figure who lorded over his father's high council. This was, instead, a spectacle of defeat: The prince had lost the war of succession to his brother, Aurangzeb, who now sat on the Peacock Throne. Transfers of power with the Mughals tended, of course, to be bloody, contenders being blinded or poisoned, leaving no threats to whoever took the crown. But in *this* fratricidal war, the loser enjoyed much sympathy, so visible that day in the public's lamentations. Not long after that wretched elephant ride, therefore, a paranoid Aurangzeb would have Dara executed. But he also felt it necessary to justify this murder. Posing as a champion of faith, the new padshah claimed merely to be doing his duty; in destroying his sibling, he was only 'pluck[ing] out the thorn of apostasy' from the 'rose-garden' of Islam.[117] Decades later, a chronicler was more explicit in cataloguing Dara's sins. He had 'developed an inclination for the religion of the Hindus'; grown too fond of Brahmins; and worse, he declared their sacred books—the Vedas—to be the 'word of God revealed in heaven'.[118]

Portrait of Prince Dara Shukoh, Golconda painting (1686), from the Witsen Album, courtesy of the Rijksmuseum.

It was an exaggeration, for Aurangzeb was really after power and would have appropriated the nearest pretext to pulverize his brother. Yet, it was also true that Dara was reviewing Brahmin scripture.[119] In the same period when Catholic missionaries were coming around to guardedly studying Hinduism, as opposed to censuring it outright, the Muslim prince had been engrossed in his own intellectual exploits. These were varied: There was poetry, discussions featuring sufis, sanyasis and likely a Jesuit,[120] and a passion for books and critical inquiry. One of his writings, for instance, begins with the naughty line: 'Paradise is where no mullas are found.'[121] But even as he longed for a cleric-free society, Dara still believed in god. In fact, before succession politics abridged his life, he had been trying to find the world's original fount of monotheism. For with so many religions on offer—and several holy books claiming heavenly descent—divinity's first word surely existed somewhere. Identifying a Quranic line, which seemed to speak of a hidden book, Dara decided to locate it. And find it he did, with India's Brahmins and their Vedas. Many, of course, had known that Brahmins believed in one supreme being; now Dara crowned them custodians of that being's pristine wisdom as well. Recruiting scholars, dozens of Vedic manuscripts were examined and portions from the section known as the Upanishads translated into Persian. This 'distillation', the prince proclaimed on the project's conclusion, carried that elusive substance: 'pure, original monotheism'.[122] It was all very electrifying—until his enemies labelled the exercise heretical, that is, and made it a warrant for severing his head.[123]

With Europeans, the Vedas first entered consciousness when Dara's great grandfather was still an infant in the sixteenth century. Xavier had, in passing, mentioned a Brahmin who claimed that Hindus possessed the 'laws of God', preserved in 'books of sacred literature'.[124] But with his trademark contempt for all things pagan, our Jesuit showed no curiosity. It would take till the 1580s for a man called Agostinho de Azevedo to register more data: Brahmin scripture, he reported, included four Vedas, six Sastras, eighteen Puranas and twenty-eight Agamas.[125] When plagiarized in 1612 by Diogo do Couto, this (Saiva) outline of the Sanskrit corpus became more widely known.[126] Around the same period, in Kerala, Diogo Goncalves mentioned three Vedas in a report, but it was only with the 1651 arrival of Rogerius's *The Open Door* that their names appeared in print: Roggowedam (Rig Veda), Issourewedam (Yajur Veda), Samawedam (Sama Veda) and Adderawanawedam (Atharva Veda).[127] Meanwhile, de Nobili had already examined their contents: a not insignificant moment, for the Vedas were referred to in Tamil as *Marai*, or 'hidden' truths.[128] Luckily, one of the Italian's Brahmin converts quelled his scruples and un-hid the texts for him. But it was an anticlimax: The material seemed a 'disorderly congeries of various opinions' and a 'jumble where religious and civil precepts' were mixed up. Besides, it too featured multiple deities, not pure monotheism.[129] Nevertheless, de Nobili conceded that Hindus knew something of god in the same manner as Christians.[130] And that was that. In fact, a whole century later, Ziegenbalg, dismissing the Vedas as 'small books of law', drew most of his knowledge from other Tamil manuscripts.[131] One could learn everything about Hinduism even without these mysterious Sanskrit sources, whose value, to him, looked doubtful.[132]

By the time the Vedas physically reached Europe, then, more years would pass. It was French Jesuits who delivered manuscripts of 'irrefragable authority' to Paris. Writing in 1733, Jean Calmette (1693–1740) noted how difficult these were to obtain: Those Brahmins who had them would not sell,[133] and given how they didn't show these even to other Hindus, what were the chances foreigners could apply to borrow? In fact, missionaries were resoundingly scammed—one father parted with princely sums only to find himself encumbered with a pile of ancient-looking nonsense.[134] Bernier too complained that despite persistence, he was unable to obtain the Vedas even in Benares, the Hindus' holiest city.¹³⁵ While some thought the texts inaccessible due to Brahmin jealousy, most Brahmins also, in fact, lacked copies.¹³⁶ Ziegenbalg went to the extent of doubting the Vedas' very existence. Yes, his disputants were 'always speaking' of this 'Law, which you call God's Word'. But he was forced to propose that 'you have no such Law' because nobody ever produced it.¹³⁷ A less scathing writer ascribed this to other causes: Even Brahmins who held the material were ill equipped to decode it, the Sanskrit being archaic. Besides, to really comprehend meaning one required the aid of commentaries.¹³⁸ In the end, subterfuge was resorted to. The French fathers had a secret Brahmin convert who smuggled in the Vedas in the Telugu script.¹³⁹ And Calmette was elated, not from a scholarly spark, but because he believed these books offered missionaries 'weapons'. In other words, strains in Vedic thought that elevated monotheism could be used *against* Hindus; to best those Brahmins defending extant, idolatrous Hinduism, missionaries could brandish brown men's own conflicting ancestral Sanskrit writings.¹⁴⁰

It is ironic that an eighteenth-century Catholic was so anxious to assault Hinduism by stressing the cleavage between scriptural recommendations and actual practice. For this was exactly how the Roman church was assailed by Protestants from the sixteenth century onwards. One of the most stinging charges against Catholicism by Martin Luther had been that it screened off the Bible—in obscure Latin, with translations into vernaculars barred—from the masses. Ordinary Christians were fobbed off with the worship of saints, colourful processions and a camouflaged idolatry, while god's message circulated among the clerical few. Besides, for all its pretensions to holiness, even the text preserved by Rome was full of errors; in adjudicating the meaning and texture of every concept, the Catholic church had *corrupted* god's word.¹⁴¹ One zealot went so far as to equate Catholics with Muslims in wickedness.¹⁴² All the church really cared about, it was alleged, was preserving its institutional dominance. For Protestants, however, fidelity to god's (original, literal) word ranked higher than allegiance to a venal establishment. Which meant free access to the Bible by 'the mother in the house, the children in the street, [and] the common man in the market' in their own tongues.[143] Everything else was superfluous. Indeed, as Protestantism convulsed Europe, '[r]ood lofts were dismantled [in churches], elaborately wrought screens defaced, niches which had once housed statues were bricked in, [and] altars removed'.[144] Even murals depicting saints were painted over—because, to quote another critic, 'The BIBLE . . . the BIBLE only' was the true Christian religion.[145] All other cultural accretions were man-made, and hence, distracting and impure. Understandably, Catholics were furious, the two groups routinely accusing each other hereon of everything from sodomy to blasphemy.

In India, however, Christians of both denominations were united in attacking Brahmins along similar lines.[146] As far back as the 1540s, Xavier stamped this class 'evil to the very backbone'. Why? Because despite knowing there 'exists one God', they kept it 'secret'—a suspicion aired in Islamic courts too, which struggled to understand how Hindus could reconcile monotheistic ideas with its reverse in practice.[147] Ziegenbalg, similarly, disparaged Brahmins for persisting in idolatry even on recognizing the 'Falseness of [such] Gods'.[148] As for the Vedas, if they were *really* god's message, why hesitate to reveal them?[149] The answer could only be that either the books were rubbish or that Brahmin exceptionalism and control depended on a monopoly—much like the Catholic clergy. It helped that critiques of what Europeans termed 'priestcraft' existed locally also. Some of Ziegenbalg's informants, for example, accused Brahmins of telling 'lies', adding that Hindus could not filter truth from falsehood due to unfamiliarity with their texts. If at all fragments were revealed, it was to serve Brahmin interests only.[150] A thirteenth-century scholar, similarly, called the Vedas 'niggardly' for keeping their 'treasures' cloaked.[151] And Brahmin writers tangentially acknowledged the risks involved, including of losing followers to rivals. As the tenth-century

*Nyayasara* of Bhasarvajna puts it: Some Sudras—the lowest of the four caste-categories—when denied access to the Vedas, were won over by Jains, who freely peddled *their* texts.[152] So, in future, under colonial rule, while there was a so-called Protestantization of Hinduism, with an almost laboured intellectual emphasis on scripture above custom—and the enthroning of 'higher', philosophical Hinduism as more legitimate than the 'lower'—the fact is that arguments in favour could be deduced from *within* the tradition also. Hindus already possessed the impulse, that is, which would grow in a disproportionate spurt under Western influence.[153]

Paradoxically, meanwhile, the Vedas also appealed to the European enemies of Christianity. This was linked to an intellectual climate long in the making. By the mid-eighteenth century, a constituency had emerged in the West challenging religious orthodoxy. Post-Renaissance advances in science were a contributing factor alongside the Protestant levelling of the Catholic church's infallibility. Some at first attempted to align scientific knowledge with the Bible; a naturalist, for example, recommended that the line 'In the beginning God created heaven and earth' be read as 'In the beginning god created *the matter* of heaven and the earth.'[154] Others, however, proved outright sceptics. After all, even the ancients had had doubts about Biblical content. If god made all animals for humanity's sake, for instance, what led to the inclusion of crocodiles and snakes in his inventory? Historically, the church supplied allegorical masks for such awkwardness,[155] but with the Protestant insistence on a literal understanding of the Bible, the spectre of irreverence returned.[156] Examining scripture, some believed parts of it so 'badly written' that it would be cruel to lay its authorship at god's door.[157] Others, citing scientific explanations for lightning and earthquakes now sneered on hearing that this was heaven telling mankind off for its sins.[158] Corruption in the church too invigorated its critics: Several popes, for example, far from leading lives of selfless celibacy, had fathered children, promoted them and meddled in politics.[159]

The printing press widened this disenchantment; as a snarky critic warned, the pope had better abolish 'knowledge and printing', or the two would 'root him out'.[160] And by the eighteenth century, Rome looked besieged.

In this Age of Enlightenment, reason and rationality were leading virtues. And while there was a flash of atheism, many thinkers retained faith—except their god was no longer tethered to scripture.[161] The creator, they argued, was eternal, omniscient and omnipresent; it was *below* his majesty to interfere in human affairs, exhibiting miracles or emotions like anger. Indeed, as the universe's sovereign, he had little need of worship even;[162] he left the 'universe to its own devices' and was only the 'first cause of a self-perpetuating' world, which could be known via science.[163] Christian presumptions received rough treatment now. If god intended the Bible for all, why did he not bestow it upon every society?—a question 'natives' also posed. Why were missionaries resorting to violence if they served divine offices? No, Christianity failed the test of reason. At best, this religion—of human design, not divine revelation—was one among several; Biblical tales were mythology, not fact. Indeed, as knowledge flattened the supernatural, the Bible—read now by those mothers, children and market folk of Luther's hopes—was 'publicly mocked'.[164] The result was both transformation and crisis. For if the Reformation separated scripture from church, the Enlightenment severed god from Christianity. And where we are concerned, this led to an interesting byproduct: curiosity about ideas on god in *foreign* cultures. Did men elsewhere possess more reasonable thoughts on divinity? Could these help imagine a natural, universal religion more compelling than Christianity? In India, of course, such questions were being asked for generations: Akbar in the sixteenth century interrogated Islam's claims to primacy, for instance, given how 'truth inhabited every religion'.[165] And now, a hundred years after Prince Dara's quest, European brains were also wondering if pure, uncorrupted monotheism might be retrieved from India's Brahmins. After all, more sympathetic accounts of Hinduism were available now, so that deep in its evidently superstitious forest there seemed to glimmer great riches.

That Hindu ideas came in handy for intellectual iconoclasts in the West need not surprise us. Half a millennium before, a Muslim notable had already presented Brahmin philosophy as monotheism minus revelation and prophets—exactly the commodity Enlightenment leaders were fishing for.[166] More recently, Ziegenbalg believed 'natives' 'know from the *light of nature* that there is one god'—they had reached this conclusion without Biblical guidance.[167] Another man, translating contents from a Hindu text portrayed its god as 'subject neither to change nor anxiety'; one 'whose nature is indivisible' and above human qualities; 'the origin and the cause of all beings'; and 'support' of the universe.[168] This was all most inviting for proponents of reason. The philosopher Voltaire (1694–1778), for instance, was no admirer of Hinduism in its current configuration. Brahmins, he declared, 'maintain the populace in the most stupid idolatry'.[169] The religion was a 'tedious rubbish'[170] and rank 'stupidity'.[171] Yet, the man disliked the church more, writing that if Jesuits accused Indians of bowing to the devil, it was really 'they who served him'.[172] And in his anti-*Christian* polemics, Brahmin knowledge proved useful.[173] It was a matter of chronology: If Hindu texts predated the Bible, it confirmed that the latter was not the key

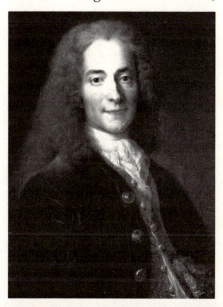

Voltaire as painted by Nicolas de Largillière, Wikimedia Commons.

to monotheism, nor divine revelation essential.[174] Indeed, where missionaries sought to 'prove' that Indians 'borrow'd' their loftier ideas from the Bible,[175] our Frenchman stressed the opposite: that it was 'our holy Christian religion' that was 'a miserable . . . copy' of the 'ancient Indian theology'.[176] Simply put, white intellectuals, dismissive of Hindu society in the *present*, began to romanticize its past (a formula Hindus would in time also amplify). And in the process, where missionaries hoped to smash Hinduism, Hindu texts were deployed in the West to try and dismantle Christianity instead.

The results were somewhat farcical, not least because Europeans actually knew little about what Sanskrit sources professed. In 1760, Voltaire was gifted the French translation of a mysterious Hindu text, the *Ezourvedam*. Designed as a dialogue between 'Biach' (Vyasa, assembler of the Vedas) and 'Chumantou' (Sumantu), in the *Ezourvedam* whenever the former dwells on superstitious ideas, the latter reviles it as falsehood. Voltaire was thrilled, describing this as 'the Gospel of the ancient bracmans' and 'the oldest book in the world'.[177] One can see why. For one, the *Ezourvedam* rubbishes prevailing (Puranic) ideas—Vishnu's avatars, Krishna's amours, Siva's lingam—and 'Biach' is told off by 'Chumantou' for his faith in idolatry. No license, thus, is allowed for elements in 'native' culture deemed disagreeable in the West. Chumantou also laments how the Vedas fell into worthless hands, perverting a pure understanding of god—akin to that familiar European charge against Catholics. To top this, the text recruits reason to invalidate irrational traditions. With a story where Vishnu incarnates as a dwarf to fell a king, Chumantou is outraged: God was above deception—a view aligned with Enlightenment convictions that divinity had neither emotions nor a desire to participate in this world. So, from Voltaire's perspective, this book looked ideally suited to European intellectuals' pet themes. It mattered little that he was warned that the *Ezourvedam* was untransparent; that its propositions were too convenient, even lazily providing a Hindu Adam ('Adimo').[178] The more dispassionate might have paused. But Voltaire's purpose was never to examine this material but to wield it against the church. And so, led by ideological certitude, he declared the *Ezourvedam* older than the Bible, thus placing Hindu monotheism centuries before the birth of Christ.[179]

It would take years, but eventually the *Ezourvedam* was exposed for what it was: a fabrication.[180] And one leading back to, of all people, our French Jesuits. When Calmette acquired the Vedas, he shrewdly saw in it utility. 'Ever since their *Vedam* . . . has been in our hands,' wrote the father, 'we have extracted texts suitable for convincing [Hindus] of the fundamental truths that ruin idolatry.' *À la* de Nobili, he thought these books held some good ideas amid largely bad ones, like 'gold dust on piles of dirt'.[181] The goal, though, was not to admire the good but call it to arms. For instance, the texts spoke of one god, while yet celebrating many more deities. Here, Calmette explained, the Brahmins' holiest works were already contradictory. And this, in turn, might cleave the way for the Bible; the Christians' book was the *real* Veda, it could be argued, not inconsistent Sanskrit literature. Next, having read parts of the Vedas, with a colleague, he created a text that missionaries could use when debating Hindus.[182] That is, just as de Nobili took on a Hindu avatar to market Christianity, this tool adopted the garb of a 'native' text to pierce 'native' beliefs.[183] So, what Voltaire used to 'bludgeon the Christian religion' in Europe was really an invention of Catholic priests in India; Calmette's 'weapon', intended to embarrass and challenge *Hindus*, was appropriated unknowingly by enemies of the Bible.[184] Understandably, after the *Ezourvedam* was discredited, Voltaire was charged with overzeal and 'giving this book an importance which it [did] not deserve'.[185] Luckily, he was dead by then.

But the misadventure is proof of a greater trend: a self-serving romance around the Vedas—in their impenetrable, mysterious language—among Enlightenment minds.[186] Of how the West used

Eastern cultures in its own quarrels, alternatively heaping compliments and contempt. For if missionaries cast their nets for converts in the East, these rivals were anxious for a fount of monotheism outside the Christian world. In a sense, it was the *idea* of the Vedas that gripped Europe, not its contents. Which is why manuscripts sent to Paris by Calmette sat untranslated for generations.[187] Or as a Jesuit scoffed, the Vedas were glorified because no one could be bothered to really read them.[188] When actually translated in the next century, missionaries would in fact encourage their colleagues to freely study the Vedas so they could 'emancipate' themselves from the fallacy that they contained a 'bright deposit of truth'.[189] But in the interim, Europe painted romantic images. John Holwell, an English surgeon, flaunted more spurious 'scripture' in the 1760s: The *Chartah Bhade Shastah*, he wrote, contained the Brahmins' monotheism. This held the 'originals' from which Christianity made its 'copies'.[190] That this *Shastah* has never been found (and was likely a mishmash of questionable provenance) is a different matter.[191] In the same period, an English captain, Alexander Dow, aired his finds too, claiming guidance from a 'learned Brahmin'.[192] Again, we read of an ancient, pure Hinduism, with a Vedic text, termed the *Bedang*, presented as its essence.[193] Amusingly, as news of these texts reached him, Voltaire discarded the *Ezourvedam*—the *Shastah* became his newest oldest book on earth, and the *Bedang* 'the most beautiful monument of all antiquity'.[194]

Simply stated, white thinkers in the West, disillusioned with religion at home, felt the need to idealize an alternative; to construct a counter with which to hem in Christianity. Hinduism—once dismissed as a demonic cult—was presented as just the item. Of course, given that in its popular form—with temples and idols—it was unfit for service, the approach was selective. Like our Mughal prince, who culled portions of the Vedas to 'find' his hidden book, Europeans too were picky. They preferred Hinduism's hazy antiquity—where they could fill in the blanks as suited them—to its living reality. Indeed, digging through the debris that was the Hindu present to revive its past acquired a certain glamour, and all kinds of theories were professed. Pierre Sonnerat (1748–1814), who first rubbished the *Ezourvedam*, declared India humankind's cradle, for example.[195] As to how its wisdom was contaminated: the land's riches, according to him, attracted invaders. In response, Brahmins veiled their ideas in 'ingenious allegories'.[196] While this did not dilute the 'fundamental tenet of the unity of the deity',[197] Hindu convictions were hereafter 'badly translated, or wrongly interpreted'.[198] The result was that the 'natives' grew ignorant, with a (Puranic) 'sequel' conflated with (Vedic) originals.[199] In the West, thus, Hinduism acquired a top-down reading: Just as Christians had scripture first, *then* division and (Catholic) corruption, there was a textual Hinduism, reduced to fragmented confusion. Authenticity lay in written material; if another Hinduism dominated in practice, this was perversion—a mirror construct of the emergence of Protestantism vis-à-vis Catholicism. And viewed this way, the conclusion was obvious: Hindus' 'true religion' resided in a 'faithful translation of the Vedams'.[200] Everything else was a weak, toxic appendage, and ought to be discarded to retrieve a purer nucleus—a premise that lingers on to this day.

Of course, this was historically unsound. Puranic Hinduism emerged not because of invasions but through an interaction between the Brahmins' religion, as it migrated with them across the subcontinent, with a variety of local systems. It was the Puranas—exactly the material dismissed now for irrationality, its carnal gods and temples—that was truly representative of Hindus at large. The Vedas, on the other hand, had remained the preserve of a small, select set of Brahmins and scholars. In Europe, it might have been the case that priests concealed scripture from the masses, and were called on, therefore, to democratize access. In India, however, Brahmins had largely adjusted *their* position to the demands of local societies, much like de Nobili assumed a 'native' appearance to transmit Christianity to Tamils. Hinduism was not a fixed set of ideas from one batch of texts but a hybrid culture of overlapping encounters. Europeans, however, came to believe that, as with the Bible, the Vedas alone were real Hinduism, and that all hopes of salvation must be pinned to it. Importing European dynamics into India, white men in effect expected ordinary Hindus—of so many castes, with so many histories, no one like the other—to subscribe purely to an orthodox, ancient Brahmin position, when historically this was a more complex engagement. But at this stage, little was known of India's past, and 'natives' of the present were viewed as hopeless. And so, as one commentator put it, given how Hindus had no means of redressing their situation—like Catholic laypeople who suffered for centuries under a diabolical papal regime—the West would supply 'conscientious . . . interpreter[s]'.[201]

In other words, foreigners would teach Indians 'authentic' Hinduism and where to find it. But this also begs the question: How did Hindus themselves perceive the Vedas traditionally?

In the ninth century CE, there lived in Tamil country a man we know as Nammalvar. He was a devotee of Vishnu, composing over 1000 verses in praise of the deity. His writing is packed with Puranic details—Vishnu's triumph over demons, his incarnations, his beauty and physical attributes—while also simultaneously declaring him god of gods, the almighty. It was all bhakti, devotion. Interestingly, in the succeeding centuries, Nammalvar's four collections were equated with the four Vedas, like them proclaimed timeless and eternal. Indeed, recitation of his poems became an integral part of temple ritual in these parts. Joint to the work of eleven other poet-saints, the complete corpus—of 4000 Vaishnava verses—are now known as the Tamil Veda. Or as Vishnu is shown to state in a later account, 'The Vedic (brahmins) who recite the [Sanskrit] Vedas . . .

do not understand what they chant, and are caught in delusion.' So, 'I shall render the Vedas in Tamil'.²⁰² Theologians in future would go to great pains to demonstrate how Nammalvar's bhakti was an encapsulation of Vedic principle; that, in fact, the point of the Vedas themselves was Vishnu's supremacy. Some would even brand the Tamil Vedas superior to the Sanskrit. For as rivers are 'cloudy and mixed' at the source, becoming 'clear[er] and drinkable' downstream, so also the Sanskrit texts were confusing, unlike their filtered Tamil alternative.²⁰³ As such this was not an unusual claim: In the same age, Saivas, positioning Siva as the highest divinity, said similar things. That is, sects competed to assert that they alone had comprehended the Vedas properly. Indeed, in one source, critics remark to Nammalvar: '*we* have not heard the Vedas utter [what you say]; this must be your imagination'.²⁰⁴

But what did the Vedas 'utter'? Compiled thousands of years ago in north and north-western India, the Vedas are not one thing but many.²⁰⁵ Their older portions are often called the *karma-kanda*, focused on sacrifice, rituals and invocations to ancient deities (most of whom would be overshadowed by Vishnu and Siva). The *vedanta*—the 'end' of the Vedas, both in a literal and metaphorical sense—meanwhile is the *jnana-kanda*, the repository of wisdom, containing the Upanishads. These are the pillars of Hindu philosophy. Thus we find, in even the oldest, highest Brahminical scripture, several layers reflecting different time periods and its motivations.²⁰⁶ This is also why, where Europeans were concerned, contradictory views emerged on the Vedas, depending on who read what. For as a colonial era authority put it, the Upanishads came from 'an entirely different state of the Hindu mind' than the more primitive previous sections.²⁰⁷ Missionaries, then, could underline prior parts of the Vedic corpus, with their many gods and ritualism, dismissing the Vedas as a polytheistic fruit salad. Others studying the Upanishads saw sophisticated ideas and pronounced monotheistic urges. As a nineteenth-century American philosopher wrote, these described

Vishnu's fish incarnation with four infants representing the Vedas. Print from the Raja Ravi Varma Press, courtesy of the Sandeep & Gitanjali Maini Foundation.

'the first inquisitive and contemplative access' to divinity. The Vedas here paved 'a loftier course through a purer stratum—free from particulars, simple, universal', offering a 'sensible account of God'.[208] So even if the Rig Veda's opening section invokes Agni (fire), Vayu (wind) and other deities, in the Upanishads, we find statements of a different variety: 'This Self is never born, nor does It die. It did not spring from anything, nor did anything spring from It. This Ancient One is unborn, eternal, everlasting.'[209]

But the Vedas' internal richness aside, history also impacted their place in Hinduism. Indeed, if Hindus outside philosophical circles were asked about their relationship with the Vedas, they would have shrugged, 'It's complicated.' Certainly, the texts commanded formal supremacy. In fact, a seventeenth-century poet construed it a special compliment to accredit a *Muslim* patron master of the Vedas.[210] But their direct presence in Hindus' lives was limited. In and of itself, this was not unusual. In Europe, the 'majority of medieval people' knew only 'rudiments' of their faith; religion was not 'a series of propositions to be believed but a series of practices to be undertaken'. If the Vedas were unknown to most Hindus—including many Brahmins—so too the Bible was 'alien to the great majority' of lay Christians.[211] And for the ordinary 'native' too, it was daily rituals of caste—how one dressed, what one ate— in parallel to temple-worship, that constituted religion. Yet, there was a difference. For while Christianity drew from a core book, Hindus possessed a wider, segmented archive. After all, Hinduism was an 'amoeba-like cluster of practices and beliefs',[212] stitching up countless groups, ideologies, gods and identities in various periods across vast geographies.[213] Each thread in this evolving web had a personality; each could inform and alter others while retaining its distinctness.[214] Of course, there were links but by design, it was not feasible for one book to authoritatively represent a bottom-up order like Hinduism. And in more real terms, the religion's outlines were fixed not so much by the Vedas but by the epics—the Mahabharata and Ramayana—along with orally transmitted Puranic tales. It is these that most Hindus identify with even today, the Vedas being primarily a restricted Brahmin concern.[215]

And yet, just as the stature of the Brahmin was generally acknowledged, the priority of his holy texts was also endorsed—even if few knew what lay in them. And in the process, Hindus formed a novel method of linking all kinds of other texts to the Vedas, much like Nammalvar's poetry 'became' the Tamil Veda. Historically speaking, his was the devotional expression of a human being at a specific moment. Yet, in theological terms, his writings were creatively interpreted as not just divine utterances but as completely Vedic; this way they were made palatable to the orthodox while simultaneously granting Tamil texts high status. This was part of a pattern: Different Hindu scriptures of varying origins could all claim Vedic inspiration. Thus, one text might anoint itself a 'restatement' of the Vedas; the epics could be described as their 'recapitulation' for mass consumption; another source might be styled a 'reflection' of their knowledge and so on.[216] Puranas representing competing sects, in fact, even claimed to be 'equal of the Vedas', demoting rivals.[217] In many cases, there might be little direct connection to the actual ancient scriptures; but even without a concrete communion, a nominal 'tip of the hat' was the norm.[218] For as Brahmins synthesized different beliefs into Hinduism, they did not supplant them, seeking just a 'legitimizing reference' to the Vedas.[219] Indeed, in complex cases, with trademark dexterity, they could even declare that these traditions stemmed from Vedas now 'lost'.[220] Either way, room and board for diverse texts was available, in which none surrendered their validity, while the Vedas occupied an honorary head office.

Predictably, there were schools that tested this. Some Saiva traditions, for example.[221] One text, the *Sivadharmottara* brands Vedic studies a 'waste'.[222] Another subordinates the Vedas; Saiva scriptures emerged from god's 'highest' face, the Vedas only from 'inferior faces'.[223] In the *Narada Sutras*, similarly, bhakti triumphs 'even the Vedas'.²²⁴ Nevertheless, implicit here is recognition of the texts as a gold standard. And in time, most sects, including several 'propounding *anti*-Vedic' ideas, were reconciled via 'statements of conformity'.²²⁵ Similarly, though the Vedas show little room for image worship, Vedic mantras became an essential component of temple ritual. So even if 'large segments of Hindus' had only thin links to them, to suggest that the Vedas did not matter to Hinduism would be 'as unhistorical as to argue that Aristotle was irrelevant to medieval Christianity since undoubtedly few European peasants were familiar with his work'.²²⁶ And yet their role in active religion was not the same as Western scripture.²²⁷ This was not because a 'native' analogue of the Catholic clergy cunningly veiled them but because different types of Hindus had different types of scriptures. White writers, though, were oblivious to such nuances. Instead of recognizing the numerous rivulets that together form the Hindu tradition, they assumed that a single fount came first, splintering over time into the seemingly muddy streams and puddles of 'idolatrous' Hinduism. In any case, the Hindu attitude vis-à-vis scripture would have scandalized them. For applied to the Western context, this was akin to saying that one could back a range of things—from idols to animal sacrifice—and remain Christian by acknowledging the Bible. Or rebrand pagan knowledge, adding with a wink that this was but an 'abridgement' of church-approved scripture.

Nevertheless, in Western eyes, 'pure' Hinduism gained a definite appearance: The Vedas were its Bible, and a certain kind of orthodox, scholarly Brahmin alone could speak for it. This latter point was all too obvious. Rogerius in his *Open Door*, for instance, complained that most present-day Brahmins had little grasp of the 'philosophy for which their ancestors were so famous'.²²⁸ In Goa, de Nobili dismissed its Brahmins as 'not genuine'. Why? Because, by his own reading of Sanskrit scripture, the truest claimants to that rank were those who 'exclusively pursue[d] learning and are versed in the books'.²²⁹ The temple Brahmin and others had compromised with popular religion, forfeiting all right to speak for Hinduism, that is. Naturally, there was no question of consulting non-Brahmins; or as Dow wrote, 'illiterate cast[e]s' and 'inferior tribes' would not do.[230] Focusing on Sanskrit, an emphasis on a literal interpretation of ancient texts, divorced from historical dynamics, would become all too normal with Europeans—this in a culture of orality, where even the Vedas were first an oral tradition.[231] For this way, foreigners could access Hinduism, without their foreignness feeling too grave a handicap.[232] It also offered the added advantage of fitting preconceived cultural ideas born of the Protestant approach to the Bible. It did not matter that this 'pure' Hinduism foreigners idealized never existed; to expect all Hindus to become rigid votaries of the Vedas was to construct something artificial. So much so that when in the nineteenth century, 'native' figures themselves attempted to raise up a scripturalist Hinduism, the majority ignored them, sticking to their temples and custom.[233] Hindus, in the past as today, that is, show no anxiety to gain direct access to the Vedas: Based on family, caste and regional traditions, faith remains available in a variety of formats, leaving scriptural concerns to Brahmins and philosophers.

Yet, however, it is worth remembering that there were always within Hinduism itself strands of thinking that coincided with European ideas. There were always ultraconservative Brahmins who too dismissed temples and mass Hinduism. To these purists also, the Vedas, and nothing but the Vedas, defined Hinduism. Which is why, late in the nineteenth century, as the Hindu religion was defined in a Protestant mould, a Brahmin writer would openly state that what was meant by (modern) Hinduism was 'Brahmanism'—this even as he admitted that down the ladder, observance of Brahminical norms was only 'fractional'.[234] There were other parallels too. Western ideas of the decline of Hinduism from its ancient purity found validation in the Brahmin concept of the kali yuga, the dark age of corruption. While this was a historical fiction to justify and enable adjustments and coping strategies in a plural society, it sat neatly with European speculations—of living Hinduism as the superstitious shadow of a pristine original Vedic system. The same applies to Sanskrit sources. These, while reflecting a Brahmin ideal, did not reflect uniform truths. As the scholar Audrey Truschke observes, 'Despite claims to encompass all knowable things in the world, many Sanskrit [works] do not match what people did in real life.'[235] Indeed, historically, Brahmin writings were often composed in *reaction* to preexisting tendencies on the ground—scriptural expostulations compensated for practical inadequacies, and served to help narrative catch up with reality.[236] Now however, a set of Sanskrit books was almost mechanically construed as the 'authentic' core of a shambolic religious system—and there were at least some Hindu authorities willing to operate on these terms, energized in their own conservatism by conditions of Western creation.

Of course, the majority of 'natives' might yet have ignored these unbalanced readings of their traditions. European debates around Hinduism would have been just that: noise on a distant, unfamiliar continent. Hindus, after all, rarely sought out an 'original' faith: Their religion was mixed, complicated and disputed even—but it was what it was; a living, organic, elastic entity. But then, political events began to make a difference: The advent of the white man's rule gave white men's ideas the muscle to remake reality. For by the time Voltaire sang his praises of the *Ezourvedam*, the English East India Company had triumphed at the Battle of Plassey (1757) in eastern India. Strangers were on the way to becoming the country's masters. And in their effort to understand the land, they would not only fall back on half-boiled theories but also infuse these with power and certainty. Indeed, by the 1860s, it would be entirely normal for British judges in India, citing white scholars of Hinduism along with Protestant-style Hindu reformers, to declare centuries old sects as 'contrary to . . . the ancient [and, thus, "real"] Hindu religion'.[237] Men could remark coolly that 'books which were written after the Vedas' lacked merit;[238] that no living sect 'at present' was genuinely

Hindu.[239] This is not to say that Hindus passively absorbed these Europeans notions, however. On the contrary, as we shall see, they resisted in myriad ways. But even in battling colonialism and its ideological filters—shaped by Christianity, Western contests, the Enlightenment and plain misreading—certain European filters were, nonetheless, coopted. Wedded to matching indigenous ideas, these would be recast as, in fact, Indian. It was in these circumstances that Hinduism's current avatar emerged—with one foot in tradition, the other in European sensibilities and confusion.

THREE

# GOVERNING THE GENTOOS

In 1804, the governor general of the English East India Company received a letter from a band of Hindu priests in coastal Orissa. News of Lord Wellesley's 'everlasting fame', they chorused in Sanskrit, had reached them, causing great delight. He was, after all, 'the unrivalled sun that [had] caused to bloom the lotus that is the English race', and 'numerous women' were singing his praises. The priests too were doing their bit, 'praying night and day' that Wellesley might protect them and their deity. Indeed, while under previous (Hindu) rulers these Brahmins faced 'obstruction even in the smallest matter', now 'we enjoy happiness'; the hope, therefore, was that their 'holy city may continue . . . for ever' under the Company Raj.[1] It was all intended to ingratiate themselves with the area's new masters, of course, though what the governor general made of the letter is not known. He is unlikely to have been surprised: Two years earlier, another Brahmin had already showered him with matching paeans. Wellesley, this man rhapsodised, surpassed 'all monarchs of sacred memory'. Restoring justice on earth, he had sent his enemies 'wander[ing] in terror'.[2] The trend, therefore, was clear, as all the old panegyrics heaped on Indian kings—Hindu and Muslim both—were trotted out now for the newest (Christian) power in the land.[3]

It had taken two centuries for the Company to achieve this status. Like the Portuguese before, ever since the English established trading posts in the country, they had been interacting with Hindus. But unlike the Portuguese, caution was their first principle: Or as Thomas Roe, royal envoy to Emperor Jahangir (Akbar's successor), famously urged, wisdom lay 'in quiet trade', and folly in seeking 'garrisons and land wars in India'.[4] Evidently in agreement, through the seventeenth century, English merchants usually treated local rulers—ranging from a petty rani in Kerala to Chhatrapati Shivaji, founder of the Maratha state—with watchful respect.[5] Hindu writers, meanwhile, recorded mixed reviews. A Telugu poet, on the founding of the Company's base in Madras, held that the region's ruler, fed up with Portuguese and Dutch quarrels, had simply planted the English in the middle for reprieve.[6] Another Sanskrit composition has two celestials touring India by sky. Hovering above the town, one of these *gandharva*s lists everything wrong with white folk: They gave Brahmins all the honour they might grass, so naturally, 'their villainy is inexpressible at the end of the tongue'. The other, however, was prepared to be lenient: The English did not 'unjustly extort', they 'never [spoke] false', they followed the law and traded in all kinds of 'curious' articles.[7] There was, then, good and bad both about these strangers—it was too soon to arrive at a categorical conclusion.[8]

The good must have prevailed at first, for many were drawn to the city. And by the time Madras next appeared in Sanskrit poetry late in the eighteenth century, it was a Hinduized place with gods, Brahmins and powerful brown men. Most of these last were *dubashe*s, or assistants, to the British;[9] and as white traders grew rich through exports, their Indian supporters pumped the commissions *they* earned into traditional channels of patronage. Besides sponsoring courtesans and poets, as one British grandee remarked, 'in this Country, Men who are fond of shewing their Wealth and Grandeur

Ravana by Pierre Sonnerat in his *Voyage aux Indes Orientales et à la Chine* (1782), courtesy of the Library of Congress, Rare Book and Special Collections Division.

have as yet found no better means of displaying Them than by the building of Temples'.[10] Company-sponsored wealth creation, that is, led to a boom in Hindu practice. Indeed, even though Indians and Europeans lived apart in white and black quarters, cultural exchange was inevitable—the violin was eased into 'classical' south Indian music,[11] while the British governor's processions featured dancing girls and 'country musick'.[12] In fact, the Company arbitrated caste disputes,[13] while its coins featured Hindu gods.[14] More intimate intercourse was also underway: '[o]ver half of marriages [recorded] at Madras' in 1700 were between white men and local women.[15] Only the odd orthodox voice protested—that same eighteenth-century poem has an anguished character ask how Hindus could kowtow to 'white-faced' foreigners. To this, his interlocutor sagely replies, that just as people lived under the wicked (but great) king Ravana of the Ramayana, so Madras carried on under English merchant-rajahs.[16]

As with Muslim conquerors long ago, Hindus were, in their own way, making sense of a foreign race. There was part rejection, yes, but also at first a strange, intrigued acceptance.

The transformation of the Company into what a critic lambasted as 'a state in the disguise of a merchant' was a process that lasted an age.[17] If in 1757, the victory of their troops against the nawab of Bengal netted 1,50,000 sq. miles of territory in eastern India, it would be 1849 before the Sikh empire in the north-west folded. Mysore in the south was crushed in 1799, while the Marathas of the Deccan—the subcontinent's final major force—were defeated in 1818. As for India's increasingly titular suzerains, the Mughals, the last of them would in 1858 be exiled on a bullock cart to Burma. The whole thing occurred in fits and spurts, but it was not as though Indian powers were naïve as to what was happening: Well before the subjugation of Bengal, a Maratha treatise warned of the perils of merchants acquiring too much nerve. Certainly, as a class they were 'ornaments' of the state and key to general enrichment.[18] However, added the *Ajnapatra* (1715), rajahs had better watch out for Portuguese, English, Dutch, French, Danish and other 'hat-wearers'. For,

> ... these are not like the other merchants. Each of them is subject to [foreign] kings, and it is by *their* command that these men come here. Can it be that kings do not covet territory? No, the hat-wearers certainly have designs to penetrate our provinces, swell their lands, and consecrate their own ideas [*svamat*]. Indeed, in various places they have already succeeded, and where territory has come into their obstinate grip, even death cannot part them from it. It is best to let them come and go, with no permanent base ... If they must be given land, let it be in the plains, far from the sea, where their guns and ships lie ... Let them build no forts and permanent structures. If they get on quietly on these terms, it is fine; if not, there is no need for them.[19]

In pre-1757 Bengal, in fact, its nawab (Mughal governor) appears to have been acting from corresponding motives when he objected to the Company fortifying its base at Calcutta.[20] And as they defied him, he took the place by force. Unfortunately, the British had a strong army in the south, which moved for revenge—since the 1740s, Anglo-French rivalries in *Europe* had set off proxy wars between their trading companies in the peninsula. Both augmented their forces and loaned them out as mercenaries in local political disputes.[21] Now, with a crisis in Bengal, British troops sailed up to save the day. While traditionally, the Company's victory is ascribed to the genius of Robert Clive (1725–74)—a rowdy schoolboy-turned-clerk-turned-commander—the fact is that he had plenty of support inside Bengal. For the nawab was an unpleasant man, prone, it is said, to drowning people for amusement.[22] In the space of under a year after his succession, he had alienated everyone from his own generals and ministers to the land's great bankers, the Jagat Seths.[23] So, Clive's arrival offered multiple interests an opportunity to rid themselves of an unpopular master. What everyone sought was a return to the way things were in the last nawab's day—and at the Battle of Plassey, therefore, much of the incumbent's own army stood aside, waiting for his reign to combust.[24]

Robert Clive, eighteenth-century mezzotint by C. Corbutt after Thomas Gainsborough, from the Wellcome Collection.

Soon afterwards, Clive and his fellow power brokers installed a more pliable nawab, but there was no returning to the earlier status quo. Boats full of treasure had left for Calcutta after Plassey, and British officers benefitted individually—Clive received not only over £200,000 in cash but also lands producing £27,000–30,000 per annum; instantly, this Shropshire man became one of the first white 'nabobs' flushing Britain with new money.[25] Having feasted on this yield, Company servants in Bengal had every incentive to keep meddling in its affairs.[26] They pressed the nawab for partisan policy and replaced him when he objected to English noses in unwanted places. Indeed, London too was upset: Spoils of war had birthed a proclivity for conflict, and in 1759, Company directors were complaining that their Bengal colleagues were so 'thoroughly possessed with military ideas', they seemed to forget 'your employers are merchants'.[27] But their protests went unheeded and by 1765, not only had the Company beat the

Mughal emperor in the field, they also forced him to relinquish to Calcutta the revenues of Bengal, Bihar and Orissa.[28] In eastern India, the British had now become what one observer would describe as merchant–sovereigns and sovereign–merchants. And it was this that would embolden them to jettison the relatively balanced compact seen in Madras for rank imperialism.[29]

It is often assumed, however, that the capture of the Indian subcontinent by 'the British' was an orderly enterprise promoted by the king's government and by every level of society.[30] The state was certainly embroiled in Company affairs, not only by claiming a portion of Bengal's income but also because as early as 1764, seventy elected parliamentarians were shareholders of the very corporate machine they would soon be asked to regulate.[31] The wealth it generated had social repercussions too—India-returns and their foreign loot upset economic and political balances in British society,[32] and there was intellectual angst that disproportionate luxury would deliver that nation to vice.[33] But many also voiced criticism about the obscenely long leash permitted the Company—it created a divided sovereignty between government and 'licensed bandits',[34] producing two standards and glaring immorality.[35] Multiple figures condemned the Company's expansionism: Adam Smith rebuked 'the plunderers of India' in his *Wealth of Nations* (1776),[36] while Edmund Burke logged those 'frauds and delusions' that let loose in Bengal a disgraceful 'tyranny'.[37] As early as 1772, even an ex-Company employee warned that British-ruled Indian territories would go 'from bad to worse', given that its protectors were really profit-miners.[38] In this phase, then, there was much discomfort around British conduct in the East—an element visible also in the unsettled postures Company men displayed in action.

The varying attitudes of individual governors general are proof: Where Warren Hastings made a warped effort—as we shall see—to rule in consonance with local norms in the 1770s and 1780s, his successor, Lord Cornwallis, preferred a disdaining aloofness, convinced that 'every native was irreversibly corrupt'.[39] Meanwhile, double-dealing *within* Company ranks rankled: In Madras, a governor was locked up by his own council when he sniffed out their clandestine financial arrangements with a nearby prince.[40] Another was notorious for routing bribes via his brother and dubash—an investigation, predictably, brought punishment only to the man with the darker skin.[41] Quarrels broke out between the Board of Control (created by parliament to moderate the Company) and the Company's directors,[42] and between the directors in turn and men on the ground.[43] Wellesley, for example, was an unapologetic imperialist: 'no greater blessing,' he wrote in 1801, could be 'conferred on . . . India than the extension of British authority'.[44] By the time angry superiors charged him with 'a pure and simple despotism', the man had conquered Mysore, bested the Marathas and seized control even of the Mughal emperor.[45] Wellesley's successor tried to rein things in but in vain: As a subordinate scoffed, he 'may as well set his chair on the sands of the sea and order the waves to stop'.[46] For by then, the British in India were, in another witness's view, 'no longer Merchants, but Sovereigns of a vast Empire'.[47] And this, in spite of unnerved directors in London.

Internal turmoil, thus, pervaded the British encounter with India, and inconsistencies defined policy in territories the Company swept up. For instance, in Bengal, with political competition pulped, the British got away with breathtakingly bad administrative innovations.[48] On the other hand, in Madras, officials were more circumspect, alert to the limits of their power. Strong local states existed here till the end of the eighteenth century, and Company servants knew privation and resistance. While secure Bengal had an over-strong army, Madras troops, in wars against Mysore, marched tens of miles on empty stomachs, sleeping without shelter.[49] If the Company were formidable in eastern India, that is, in the south and west, it was haunted by vulnerability, infecting its officers with a lifelong paranoia.[50] All this affected politics. In business matters too, the British were dependent on Indian bankers,[51] while as late as 1808, strategic intelligence was so shoddy that a commander wrote: 'beyond the Jumna [river] all is conjecture'.[52] Fear of revolt was eternal—precisely why the emasculated but symbolically potent emperor in Delhi was a concern. As Wellesley warned, 'the person and authority' of the padshah rendered him 'a dangerous instrument in the hands' of an antagonistic power.[53] So, dislodging the Marathas, the Company transferred him to its 'protection', fearful that he might become the figurehead its enemies needed to rally together.[54] All the proverbial glory linked with conquest, thus, barely masks the uncertainty and stress saturating the British experience in India.

What is interesting for our purposes, though, is that this caution at first also extended to Hindu institutions and cultural centres. When the Company snatched Orissa from the Marathas in 1803, Wellesley, for example, issued instructions to 'use every possible means to conciliate the inhabitants', paying 'particular attention' to the famous temple of Jagannath at Puri. While political interest in the region hinged on connecting Bengal to Madras on the map, for winning over the *people* and stabilizing the conquest, the governor general looked to the deity. British troops were, he wrote, to take 'every possible precaution to preserve the respect due to the pagoda' and honour the 'sanctity of the religious edifices' as well as the 'prejudices of the Brahmins'.[55] After all, from the thirteenth century onwards, Orissa's kings had legitimized their claims over the province through Jagannath; dynasties rose and fell, but they all bowed to the deity, who remained a constant.[56] The Mughals too had recognised the shrine's value: When once the gods absconded during a crisis, their imperial governor forcibly repatriated the idols—profits from the pilgrim economy were too lucrative even for a Muslim power to resist.[57] After the Marathas took the region, they also made rich grants to validate their rule; and with the area succumbing to the Company now, it was the turn of the British to continue the pattern.[58] Or as a report explained, '[i]n a political light [the temple's] value is incalculable.'[59] And prudence paid: Since

The Jagannath Temple in Puri, as depicted in William Urwick's *India Illustrated* (1891), courtesy of the Library of Congress.

Wellesley had respected 'native' sentiments, the temple's custodians responded with that grandiloquent Sanskrit letter quoted at the start of this chapter.

Tellingly, Puri was no exception. Already in the 1780s, the Company was involved in temple affairs in upper India.[60] As its authority spread out into the southern hinterland from Madras, here too white men became guardians of gods, managing festivals and religious endowments, British troops marching in Hindu processions. In 1789, we see, thus, an officer investigating the accounts of a Madras shrine,[61] and five years later, a second restoring sacred buildings in the vicinity.[62] In fact, by the 1830s, British civil servants would be watching over 7500 temples in just their peninsular territories.[63] Many made gifts to deities: A 'Clive', possibly son of Robert from Plassey, donated a *makara kandigai* (necklace) at Kanchipuram; the *Munro-gangalam* (vessel) at Tirupati was presented by the famous Thomas Munro. In Travancore, the Company agent offered a 'silver umbrella with emerald pendants' to the official state deity,[64] while in Madurai, a revenue collector placed 'valuable jewels' before its goddess.[65] Before long, local legends drew these officials into Puranic-style narratives. In the case of the Travancore man, when he once dealt unfairly with a temple, he was 'taken mysteriously ill and filled with such nameless dread', that he admitted its power.[66] In another story, when he scoffs at the menstruation rites of a female divinity, his wife is paralysed with bleeding.[67] The template in these tales is clear: The overbearing outsider is small fry when it comes to Hindu deities.[68] In a lopsided way, these accounts made room to reconcile with British dominion, as if proclaiming: 'If you respect our customs, we may yet accept your government'—something once done with Muslim powers.[69]

In a sense, as de Nobili in Madurai had Hinduized Christianity in the previous century, many Company men dressed their politics in Indian muslin at this juncture. Though some did genuinely respect Hindu culture, few were innocent of the imperial mission; that is, regard for 'native' sensibilities emerged from considerations of security. As Cornwallis had warned, 'disaffection in our native troops'—the backbone of 'our existence'—was to be avoided at all costs.[70] And mutiny in Vellore in 1806, a reaction to interference in matters of religion and identity, made the Company nervous. General sentiment also mattered: After the defeat of the Marathas in 1818, an officer recorded how 'the very minds of the inhabitants' were conquered but this was no guarantee 'these feelings will be permanent'.[71] An army could dominate, but not sustain conquest; so, the British would have to compensate by filling Hindu dynastic shoes as seamlessly as possible. Or as James Stuart wrote, by 'participating with natives of rank and influence' and 'avoiding interference with [their] customs and institutions' the Company could 'soften the odium naturally attendant upon the sway of strangers'.[72] After all, if even enervated figures like the Mughal emperor were 'magnets for disaffection', it was because of their cultural capital; in acting as they did, the British were coaxing a transfer of ownership for the same substance.[73] As such, this ought not to surprise us, because the Company was no monolithic, tidy enterprise with a single approach—it took different forms in different areas, under a host of leaders. At this point, there was no single, dominant strand of imperialism, only skittish variants attempting to establish what might keep 'native' energies sedated.

It was this pragmatism, then, that encouraged accommodation in the early nineteenth century. For example, on annexing Poona, seat of the Peshwas (premiers) of the Maratha state, in 1818, the Company was determined to project continuity. Little rituals—such as firing a gun morning and night—were sustained to avoid 'alarm attendant upon a translation from an old to a new state of things'.[74] The city's bankers were mollified; a ceremony for the rain gods was kept up; traditional punishments, such as blackening faces of convicts, continued and when an official arrived, he distributed presents to hundreds of holy men to show 'the Hindoos . . . [that] persons whom they respect are not intended to be neglected under the new Govt'.[75] Orders were given, similarly, to support temples, thereby demonstrating 'our anxiety to respect the religion of the country',[76] while in towns where the Company army committed wartime plunder and rape, ceremonial Hindu remedies were arranged to correct the resultant 'unfortunate impression'.[77] Still unsure, the British even offered the people a familiar focus of loyalty: a 'counterpoise to the remaining influence' of the defeated Peshwa state.[78] The Marathas had a king whose power was usurped by the Peshwas long ago.[79] While a proposal that the Company claim Peshwa-hood for itself was set aside,[80] a restoration, albeit in a small enclave, was orchestrated for the king. As with the Mughal emperor, the attempt here too was to mask the Company's alien origins by posing as custodians of 'legitimate' authority. Surely the British could not be *all* that strange and ignoble if they righted historical wrongs and pursued political justice for brown princes?

Internally, of course, the British infantilized the king—his delight on his renewal was compared to that of a schoolboy, which is precisely how his newest wardens treated him.[81] This tone is critical: The Company, even if it tolerated Hindu customs, rarely understood or endorsed them. And if it came to conflict between British authority and Hindu ideas, it was clear which would prevail.[82] The restored Maratha *chhatrapati* (king) was told as much: By no means was Company aid to be construed as reviving 'even in name' the Maratha imperium, for then 'the machine we are setting up will be liable to be turned against us'.[83] Since *they* had taken the king out of a gilded prison and given him a district, they retained the right to undo him—as would indeed occur when he assumed 'exaggerated notions of his consequence'.[84] So too, local nobles had their rank guaranteed by the Company, contingent, however, on obedience. When disbanding the old regime's army, similarly, the British supplied as many pensions as feasible—because 'deprived ... of every means of maintaining themselves', the ex-soldiers might feel a temptation to 'raise insurrections'.[85] As for the mass of Brahmins who had benefitted from the largesse of the fallen Peshwa, while the Company frowned at 'indiscriminate charities', they did continue a yearly contest where Sanskrit masters received prizes.[86] In other words, a foreign corporation was walking a tightrope between its imperial agendas and fitting the mould of a Hindu rajah. And if in Bengal an accident of history made the Company rulers, here there was a conscious—and cautious—building of empire, by alert white hands in a land with many shades of brown.[87]

Unsurprisingly, several Company officials in this period felt the need to explicate on just how this delicate venture should be managed—particularly if it were to prove more than a fleeting exploit. In the words of John Malcolm (1769–1833), in charge of central India after the fall of the Marathas, British survival depended on keeping Indian grievances from bubbling over. Indians had to feel a 'recurring sense' of benefit which, in turn, was dependent on the Company staying 'in good temper with [local] prejudices, their religion, and usages'.[88] Mountstuart Elphinstone (1779–1859), responsible for Maratha territories in the west, agreed—he offered Akbar as a model, for that Mughal emperor built cultural bridges, showed tolerance, delivered prosperity and reconciled Hindus to Muslim rule.[89] Allowing intrusion by European ideas and institutions was dangerous, for 'even just government will not be a blessing if at variance with the habits and character of the people'.[90] The British must speak to the 'natives' in *their* language, not expect them to lap up English ideals. Thomas Munro (1761–1827), therefore, warned white officers from Madras to avoid being 'fanatics in politics'. An emerging European tendency to 'suppose that no country can be saved without [Western] institutions', must be discarded, for the 'natives' already had 'their own to answer every useful object'.[91] Only such a middle path would permit British power to endure. Indians might accept foreign domination if those foreigners made an effort—or at least a show of it—to respect their modes and mores (a proposition the Portuguese in Goa had struggled with).[92]

Mountstuart Elphinstone as depicted in James Douglas's *Bombay and Western India* (1893), courtesy of the Rijksmuseum.

But then again, precisely because the Company had internal dissonances, there was opposition also to such proposals; there was always an equal number of men who rubbished all this prattle about accommodation. Why bother when the British owned hard power? India ought to be subjected to both Western morality and its institutions. Munro, for instance, was resisted by a superior who branded Indian legal institutions 'crude and barbarous', seeing no reason why a British government should uphold them. That is, if Indians paraded criminals with blackened faces, white men should teach them to abjure such methods. This opponent, in fact, felt European judges need not even learn local languages: Since quarrels always had the same triggers, any 'man who knew law could give justice to any society on earth'.[93] While Munro believed British rule 'should be gradually withdrawn',[94] others dismissed the notion as preposterous. Even the grant of a handsome pension by Elphinstone to the toppled Peshwa—a 'reasonable bargain', as he saw it, 'to purchase a quiet abdication'—invited disapproval.[95] But the real dispute was more fundamental: As the scholar Gauri Viswanathan puts it, some were 'resistant to replacing the rule of men with the rule of law', advocating instead paternalist government and a personal touch.[96] Impersonal, mechanical modes—particularly when the rulers were aliens—risked widening an already worrying cultural chasm. Elphinstone, for example, did not like brown people, but even so he felt a 'duty' towards them.[97] '[Y]ou must,' he lectured officers, 'take [them] along with you and give them a share in your feelings, which can be done by sharing theirs.'[98]

Empire, he seemed to be saying, was rarely a just affair. But with some effort, it could be made to look less unjust—and, thus, prevail. Of course, in theory this all sounded perfectly sensible; putting it into practice, however, particularly at the requisite scale, would prove a Himalayan challenge. And in the British failure to ultimately carry this forward—or bungle it up when they tried—lay a leading trigger for anti-colonial mobilization. Including among preceptors of what we now call Hindu nationalism.

Long before men like Elphinstone and Munro advocated a government of benevolence, there had been in Bengal a man who attempted to rule the 'natives' on this pattern. Warren Hastings (1732–1818) at five-foot-five was a small man with grand designs. Of humble origins, he arrived in India as a teenager, and like many such teenagers, his prime goal was to acquire a fortune. This he did, only to lose it and sail East again. Luckily, he was noticed in the right places, ending up by 1772 as governor of Bengal, soon also becoming the Company's first governor general. His place in imperial history is high; where Clive 'the mighty magician' took the British flag to the 'temple of victory' at Plassey, it was Hastings, we read, 'that gave it a foundation and its strength'.[99] And yet, the region he was to govern was in ruins. British policies and corruption had fractured the economy. The Company was in debt, moreover (Rs 10 million locally[100]), and where Clive had promised his bosses 'a clear yearly revenue of two millions sterling', the actual math was sobering.[101] Additionally, the land was drained to tip the British government also, which since 1767 demanded a share of the pickings.[102] Indians too, it must be admitted, participated in this despoliation—bankers and tax farmers made massive gains. Their job was to deliver a definite sum to the treasury, while pocketing any surplus; and this they toiled hard to extort. The result was that while individuals prospered, Bengal suffered.[103] As was reported less than a decade after the British takeover, this country, 'which flourished [even] under the most despotic' nawabi regime, had been steered to famine by its new, supposedly more civilised white rulers.[104]

When Hastings took over, his effort, then, was to clean up this mess, 'as wild as chaos itself'.[105] Reportedly, he became a one-man army, inspecting and correcting everything, to convert a muddy business venture into a public administration. In the process, the new governor alienated his own officers, many of whom did not share his sympathies, and were outraged when reforms chipped at their illicit operations.[106] Some of his official council blocked him, while a newspaper editor was jailed for scurrilous attacks, including an opinion suggesting Hastings had erectile dysfunction.[107] Meanwhile, with pervasive economic stress, control looked precarious; the last thing our man wanted was to be at odds with Bengal's people.[108] He certainly showed a warmer attitude towards them: Where some would learn to revile the Bengali as 'feeble', wielding 'falsehood, chicanery, perjury, [and] forgery' as his weapons,[109]

Warren Hastings, engraving by G.T. Stubbs after George Stubbs (1795), from the Harris Brisbane Dick Fund, 1917, The Metropolitan Museum of Art.

Hastings described a 'gentle, benevolent', 'faithful and affectionate' people.[110] To keep them happy, he aimed to fashion a system as Indian as possible—a view at variance with the writer Alexander Dow's, for instance, who had argued that such an approach would breed 'anarchy and confusion'.[111] So in the end, he chose compromise: While he would rule like 'an Indian and not as an alien', Hastings acknowledged the practical necessity that any administrative machinery he created must also be of a kind 'that English officials could operate and English opinions tolerate'.[112] And to engineer this hybrid—Indian enough to please its subjects but comprehensible to its (white) masters as well—this man from Gloucestershire set out to procure knowledge.

Understanding the 'natives', though, was a herculean mission. For while the goal of economic extraction was clear, confusion reigned when it came to summing up the millions of people at the giving end of the process; in Bengal, we first observe the sustained effect of colonialism on Hindu society, and of India on British minds.

Decades later, an official surveying local groups could still report no neat, unambiguous labels. In Bengal and Bihar, Muslims had 'recourse to the idols', while Hindus were 'addicted' to venerating Muslim divines—the opposite of what one might expect.[113] Identity was befuddling: A Brahmin rajah might have a Muslim son,[114] while a family raised boys as Hindu but girls for Islam.[115] Brahmins, romanticized by the likes of de Nobili and Voltaire as noble scholars— and disparaged by missionaries as wicked idol priests—could in general be neither: They worked as farmers and traders and a large number wielded arms, 'ignorant' of sectarian loyalties.[116] Indeed, these last ate meat and smoked tobacco, challenging bookish ideas of propriety,[117] and some groups carried Islamic influences even.[118] Nor was there geographical uniformity for a caste's status: If in Bengal, potters were ritually 'clean', in Bihar, they were not; 'barbers (*nai*), who in Bengal are so haughty', were 'reduced to the rank of impurity' next door.[119] Despite formal doctrines of equality, caste existed among Muslims too.[120] (Indeed, there had been Muslim kings in India who claimed descent from Hindu epic heroes.[121]) From the start then, the British were in for disorientation; they had to shape policy when they could barely grasp whom these were serving. The result was, as we have seen before, a skewed perception of reality— and of what the 'natives' expected and cherished. Except now it came backed by state power and gubernatorial righteousness. Where the Portuguese had ruled by the sword, the British, it seemed, would smother with (misaimed) affection.

And yet, Hastings's convictions notwithstanding, there was a peevish discomfort with Indians among most British. For Company servants had no resources—psychological included—for a serious immersion in Bengali society. Most of them tended to minimize interaction, relying on intermediaries instead, and acquiescing in what a Mughal writer called 'half-knowledge'—precisely why a later generation represented by Munro and his peers, urged better contact.[122] When the same Mughal critic asked why, unlike their

Indian priors, the British were allergic to open durbars with the public, for instance, the answer he received is revealing. They were not 'accustomed', his white discussant admitted, to meeting subjects face to face; instead, they worked better 'in the recess and silence of a closet', studying petitions.[123] In other words, the Company Raj was a detached reign of paper—a mark also of its nervousness, separating it from the society it governed.[124] Even after Hastings's efforts, in fact, it was patent that 'English Gentlemen . . . hate appearing in public audiences', and that they betrayed 'extreme uneasiness, impatience, and anger' with brown crowds.[125] Local rulers, the historian Jon Wilson notes, governed through familiarity, face to face;[126] now, in this reign of merchants, government was depersonalized. The world outside was so daunting to Bengal's new masters, that most chose to stay cloistered behind desks, inside cavernous offices where they felt more in control; it was 'natives' who were forced to navigate the new floor plan. 'A whole life,' the Mughal writer sighed, 'is needed to attend [the Company's] long, very long [bureaucratic] proceedings.'[127]

Indeed, within twenty years of British rule, brown voices had diagnosed its defects, chief among which—despite the stated surplus of good intentions—was an absence of meaningful dialogue with Indians. Previous rulers like the Mughals began as foreign conquerors too; but they, our critic argued, with a dose of wistful romanticism, settled among the people, Muslims mixing with Hindus 'like milk and sugar that have received a simmering'.[128] In contrast, white men 'shew for the company of the natives' an 'aversion', instead of 'love' and 'coalition'.[129] Strangers they were when they seized Bengal, and strangers they stayed afterwards too—and by definition, a stranger sought 'his own profit'.[130] So too the Mughal writer realized that it was the 'diversity of customs and institutions' that intimidated the Company; and in seeking to rule without unravelling this lay 'the origin of those troubles and those confusions that have been . . . the bane and ruin of the inhabitants'.[131] Worse still, the corporate

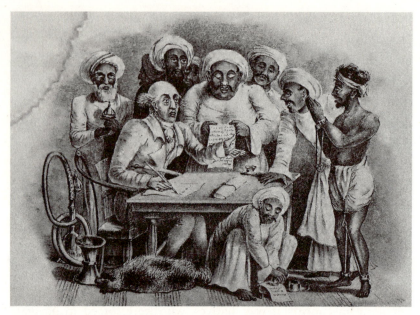

A British official in his *kutcherry* (office) as depicted in Fanny Parkes's *Wanderings of a Pilgrim* (1850).

A British official surrounded by petitioners as depicted in S.C. Belnos's *Twenty Four Plates Illustrative of Hindoo and European Manners in Bengal* (1832), courtesy of the Yale Center for British Art.

character of British authority puzzled Bengalis: Power was exercised not by a king or dynasty that might develop an emotional stake in the land but by a 'numerous body', with impermanent members seeking transient benefit. Bengal was like a house with no master, only parasitic tenants.[132] Governors came from a far-off island, and then left; there was no true commitment. A Hastings might make overtures, but under a successor, policy could (and did) tilt in a new direction.[133] So, in the end, a good part of British administration was improvisation: a shuffling about to balance commercial advantages with the moral pressure to govern; a contest between making money and trying to care about a people with whom these merchant–rajahs saw little in common.

Several of these defects surfaced in Hastings's effort—and those of his successors—to delineate 'Hindu law'. One the one hand, he was hostile to importing Western legal codes as urged in some quarters, thinking it safest to leave Indians to their traditional devices. But he sought to achieve this with a slate that was the opposite of blank. That is, even as the governor general avoided European codes, he could not help but cast a European *gaze* upon Indian society. After all, Hastings was a product of the Enlightenment. Hindus, he argued, were not 'sunk in the grossest brutality' when it came to faith. Their idolatry was, he sniffed, 'coarse', but textual 'precepts of their religion' ventured close to the 'refined mysteries' of the Bible.[134] In tune with this textualist approach, actual legal systems in Bengal were, to Hastings, not reflective of the great Hindu legal *tradition*, one that 'continued unchanged from the remotest antiquity'.[135] And so, as a well-meaning alien, he would aim for a 'renewal of the laws and forms established of old', which had been 'corrupted and distorted'—an attitude, as we saw in the previous chapter, Western intellectuals applied to Indian culture in general.[136] Hastings's ambition, that is, was to resurrect 'original principles', to help manage a complex reality.[137] In part also to keep lobbies urging anglicization at bay, he therefore transmitted the idea of a timeless

Hindu constitution 'buried under the weight of history', waiting to be reenergized by Europeans.[138] But in the end, the governor general would not retrieve anything; in fact, he invented a mongrel, 'native' in cosmetic terms, Western in shape and consequence. And far from clarifying things, its great culmination was a muddle, the damage scarring generations.

To start with, what was 'Hindu law'? The fact is that there was no unitary article of this name, everything being determined by context: region, caste, community, economic background, etc. There were Hindus, yes, but no single Hindu code. Thus, even twentieth-century Hindu gurus handling questions on, say, marriage, deferred to *desachara* (local custom).[139] And with reason. The ancient law code, the *Yajnavalkya-smriti*, for example, warns that fathers with unmarried post-pubescent daughters incur sin equivalent to foeticide.[140] But among Kerala's orthodox Namboodiri Brahmins, women traditionally remained 'unmarried without any social stigma' well into adulthood.[141] Why? Because *local* conditions, stemming from historical contingencies in *this* part of India, necessitated delays. So, where the *Yajnavalkya-smriti* might 'speak' to other Brahmins, in Kerala, it had no voice in this matter. And both practices were valid—only for different sets of people.[142] For Sanskrit books were never interpreted literally.[143] They were a 'theoretical source of law', while 'maxims and customs' were 'paramount'.[144] Indeed, the texts—blending law, religion, morality, ethics, and sociopolitical and cultural ideas—likely themselves began as compilations of maxims 'floating' about in diverse parts, so that the same authority might offer contradictory prescriptions.[145] To choose, Hindus simply placed the issue in context. What was law for a group or province might not fly in another; what was right for a litigant could be abhorrent for the one after—a natural state in a pluralistic society.[146] To illustrate, in the Deccan, drinking was tolerated with lower classes, but upper-caste men were penalized for their liquid transgressions. Status here fixed standards: A tipsy priest—who had a loftier role in society—was not judged on the same plane as a drunk farmhand.[147]

Given, however, that Hastings personified a world view in which 'genuine' Hindu ideas could only exist in ancient *sastra*s (normative texts), legal reality, like religion, was largely viewed as a distortion. This when really it was the sastras that led a rarefied life. They never represented Hindu society in full, being an 'ideologically driven' (Brahminical) 'blueprint for the proper management of society'.[148] With glorious inconsistency, they offered Brahmin-approved *options* for various concerns.[149] And if, as with many such writings, these works claimed to be universal and sacrosanct—a claim British minds, desperate to know India, would buy—it was largely just that: an assertion.[150] For most Hindus did not live by lawbooks in a language few could read.[151] As a French father related in 1714, there were 'neither codes nor digests' among Tamils, for instance. There were 'inviolable' customs, though, and if anyone showed a case as 'based on a custom . . . within the caste', that was adequate. Yes, in some cases, Brahmins were consulted, but custom 'prevails over the best arguments'.[152] Similarly, officials found female infanticide rampant among Rajputs up north, due to debilitating dowry practices. But so much for sastric authority, no amount of quoting condemnatory Sanskrit passages terminated the violence.[153] Again, when nineteenth-century officials hunting for a 'code' on succession and adoption sent questionnaires to five Rajput princes, four responded with conflicting answers—the fifth only spared everyone further confusion by ignoring the missive. Pressing on, by 1848, a book called *The Law of Adoption in Rajput States* did appear. Its author had to admit, however, that this did *not* resemble 'Hindu law'. Only in the 1870s was it conceded that Rajput customs were 'unwritten and uncertain'.[154] That is, the law was dynamic territory—as in Britain—not ideas inscribed in granite by long-dead sages awaiting European resuscitation.[155]

This, in fact, was the norm across the subcontinent. In the 1820s, an official surveying fifty-six castes in the Deccan concluded, thus, that they had 'no written documents or books to which they refer'. 'Ancient usage' dominated, and only in cases of 'extraordinary difficulty' were sastras introduced.[156] Indeed, local norms 'sanctioned many things in *opposition* to the Sastru [sic]'.[157] Even in Kerala, where Brahminical authority was strong, no one could tell 'where [Sastra] ends and local practice begins', the two being entwined in a peculiar knot.[158] Ideas from here could not simply be replicated in Bihar, for example.[159] In the realm of the (Brahmin) Peshwas of Poona too, while 'a conformity of the written law' was 'preferable', it was 'not considered necessary'.[160] Did this mean legal anarchy? No, for the system was robust enough for a judge in 1773 to sentence the Peshwa himself.[161] These native courts even took cognizance of marital rape, unrecognized in present-day India, where it is, ironically, seen as a Western concept.[162] Besides, as some Tamils said to that French missionary, if the law resided in books, 'only the learned' would know them; handed down orally, 'everyone is fully informed'. Indeed, the very fact that 'it is not necessary to write them down' was 'proof of their validity and authority'.[163] In other words, written laws were more a *colonizer's* need; locals knew their way and showed no great tenacity.[164] Looking in from the outside—and with much nervousness—the British sought 'order', while those living in India already possessed a familiar, evolving system; from their perch, they already had 'order'.

Previous imperial powers like the Mughals had trodden cautiously, in fact, preferring a hands-off approach.[165] For example, a seventeenth-century missionary travelling in Bengal discovered one day that a Muslim attendant had killed a peacock—a bird sacred to Hindus. While together they disposed of the evidence—by burying the feathers and making a quick meal of the flesh—the crime was soon detected. Dragged before a state functionary, the missionary offered the defence that as a 'follower of [the] Prophet', the Muslim accused had no cause to respect the Hindus' 'ridiculous precepts'. The answer he received is instructive. The Mughal officer endorsed

Islam's superiority. And yet, Hindus were promised they could 'live under their own laws and customs'. So, there would be punishment. While bribes to the official's wife softened things—from amputation to whipping—ultimately, a Muslim man, trying another Muslim, was led not by abstract principles or theory but by the region's Hindu conventions.[166] He even asked of the men: 'How . . . didst thou dare in a *Hindu* district to kill a living thing?'[167] The point was that elsewhere, where Muslims dominated, perhaps peacock murders could be forgiven, but in *this* region they were sin.[168] Indeed, it wasn't even the case that justice was dispensed at all times by the same authorities. For Indians 'lived in several penal jurisdictions': of king, village, caste, guild and so on—no one asserted a monopoly.[169] Legal matters were settled by a constellation, including local strongmen, caste unions and village panchayats, besides other scattered institutions.[170] In most matters, as a Company official later confirmed, Indians were 'ready to abide by what four impartial men may think right'.[171] And while Brahmins and texts were involved, they were only *a* factor, not *the* factor as many white men came to insist.[172]

Of course one must watch against romanticizing the existing system; it had flaws that will scandalize modern sensibilities.[173] Trials by ordeal, for instance—where parties stuck their hands into boiling oil and won if they were unscalded—could not have been terribly reliable in settling property disputes.[174] So also, as Ziegenbalg was told, the rich settled matters through fines, while the poor suffered full punishment.[175] And yet, a preference for arbitration and quick settlement kept things more efficient than the bureaucratic confusion the British installed. With his great desire to be accommodative, Hastings, for example, decided that in 'all suits regarding inheritance, marriage, caste, and other religious usages . . . the law of the Koran with respect to Mahometans [Muslims] and those of the [sastras] with respect to Gentoos [Hindus] shall be invariably adhered to'.[176] Superficially this was 'traditional'; except that 'Muslims in Bengal [being] Hindu converts . . . often continued to use local Hindu law',[177] and it was no aberration to find a Hindu judge in courts governed on Islamic principles either.[178] Hastings was even told that among Hindus, '[e]ach separate Tribe has its own distinct . . . Laws'.[179] And yet, to assuage colonial anxieties, he enshrined a strange cross-breed. Texts referred to by a minority of Hindus were repackaged as the 'law' of its totality; legal traditions limited to scholarly Brahmins were now deployed as the primary means to read 'Hindu law' in toto.[180] And if anyone was wrong, it was Hindus who had become 'universally ignorant of their canonical learning' and so 'lax' that Enlightened foreigners had to intervene.[181] Instead of dealing with Hindus in the present, that is, the white man yet again herded them into a synthetic 'classical' past.[182] Or to quote a future critic, 'no voices were heard unless they came from the tomb. It was as if a German were to administer English law from the resources of a library furnished with Fleta, Glanville, and Bracton, and terminating with Lord Coke'.[183]

This is not to say that eighteenth-century Hindu states did not make similar experiments. The Peshwa regime in Poona, for instance, tried repeatedly to persuade Brahmins—of various subcastes—to live by its own centralized sastric readings. One man, for example, who had become a Muslim, was re-Brahminized in 1772 by a caste council. The Peshwa's government, however, objected. Though resisted for years, it finally had its way, prevailing over local customary prerogatives. As the Marathas took territories in Malwa, here too the Peshwas launched a 'moral mission', aiming to 'revive' 'proper customs' for local Brahmins. One roll of instructions, thus, features forty-eight items on everything from appropriate clothing to acceptable jobs. Brahmins, it was ordered, thus, must cease doing menial labour; all boys must study the Vedas and so on.[184] Yet, these attempts had had limits and were somewhat different. The Peshwas—themselves Brahmins—had a special incentive in promoting orthodox norms, envisioning a 'rule by, for and of the

Brahmins'; their approach cannot be assumed as the norm for most Hindu rulers.[185] Besides, Brahmins themselves resisted centralized Peshwa-era innovations.[186] Riding roughshod over custom provoked violence too. Once when thieves apprehended in an area were tried at the Peshwa's capital, the local chief had state functionaries thrashed for trespassing on *his* magisterial rights.[187] Ultimately, that is, 'natives' engaged with a variety of stakeholders; and orthodox norms, even when promoted, were tempered by reality. Where local rulers had the cultural resources to negotiate this process, the Company, as an alien entity, flailed.[188]

To truly recognize law among Hindus, the British would have had to draw on invisible norms, that is. And this being tough, a monolithic, Western-style textual reading of 'tradition' became their standard. Indeed, with Hastings convinced that there were Brahmin 'professors' of an 'unchanged' law 'spread over the whole empire of Hindostan',[189] a Company servant was tasked with creating a digest. This would give both 'confidence to the people' and white judges guidance.[190] The result was Nathaniel B. Halhed's *A Code of Gentoo Laws* (1776). Its preparation was convoluted. Halhed knew Persian but was hopeless in Sanskrit. Eleven Brahmin 'lawyers' were summoned from 'every Part of Bengal', then, to translate into Persian 'Sentence by Sentence'

Nathaniel Brassey Halhed, Wikimedia Commons.

content 'from various Originals'.[191] Halhed then produced his *Code*, hoping to win 'the Affections of the Natives' and 'ensure Stability'.[192] Inadvertently, however, he admitted the limited resonance of the code: This was the first time 'Bramins have ever been persuaded to give up a Part of their own Consequence for the general Benefit of the whole Community.'[193] While neither man urged a rigid fidelity to texts yet—only providing, in English, an exemplar for white judges—in practice, things evolved differently. And what they set off would, within years, mutate into something unwieldy, frustrating even their countrymen. Or in the words of a future judge, assuming that predatory tribes, trader castes and cultivators could be guided by a single code was as foolish as suggesting their lives revolved around the Psalms of David.[194] In retrospect, as the Company grew in strength and awareness of Hindu realities, this seemed obvious. But in the eighteenth century, policy was often conjecture with a deceptive varnish.

Interestingly, 'natives' were able to adjust somewhat at first. For even as British judges unduly emphasized Sanskrit verse over custom, they relied on Brahmin pandits.[195] And pandits—Hindus living among Hindus—even if they 'tortured' texts to fit British standards, managed to bridge them with the people's ways. So far, 'no great harm was done'.[196] But then, in a post-Hastings age, British attitudes changed, undermining 'native' participation.[197] In the 1790s, a growing reluctance to depend on brown intermediaries saw a prominent judge learn Sanskrit. Convinced that pandits were deceiving him, he published a *Digest of Hindu Law* to prevent other white men from being 'led astray'.[198] That is, the way Hindus creatively reconciled text with practice—as was always done and which only men reared in a culture could do—looked, to an anxious foreign power, sinister. So, while some judges continued to depend on pandits, many began to interpret and apply 'Hindu law' themselves. Except this was more formulaic. If at all Brahmins were consulted, it was by posing abstract questions, without evidence or details of the specific case—like asking an English lawyer to opine on murder, without explaining if it was an act in self-defence or voluntary manslaughter.[199] Besides, lack of historical knowledge generated problems: For years, the courts merrily applied 'Hindu law' to Sikhs and Jains, because they had not yet worked out that these groups were not exactly Hindu.[200] And over time, the damage spread: In the 1810s, a Travancore officer, for example, unearthed texts. His intention too was to standardize law while maintaining a façade of 'tradition'; to construct a system Hindus would not think *completely* alien, but which aliens like him could grasp—and control.[201] All this when he was aware that the written sources he was building on were 'seldom consulted'.[202]

Eventually, then, 'Hindu law' became less about Hindus, more about white men and their apprehensions.[203] And critics lamented the problems this triggered: that Mughal writer related how, even in general administration, obsessed with 'Books and Memorandums', the Company routinely mistook 'the exterior and bark' for the 'pith'.[204] Or as the scholar Purushottam Agrawal put it, the British did not 'cut the cloth to fit the body' but 'cut the body to fit the cloth'.[205] By 1807, it was reported how the 'native who has a good cause always applies for a panchayat; while he who has a bad one, seeks the decision of a . . . [British] Judge' because the system was twisted enough to let the wrong party win.[206] So too in 1821, a London officer described 'Hindu law' as farce. The British had gone 'astray', legislating 'before they were acquainted with the real state' of things.[207] Far from reinstating order, the Company peddled anachronism: If Hindus objected to summoning women to court, for example, what was the point of putting up Sanskrit verses showing that 'in another part of India, two thousand years ago' women stood in the dock? 'How could we presume,' it was asked, 'to embody in a Code the various usages of so many millions of different rules and Castes?' As for fetishizing texts: 'did Socrates write . . . did our Saviour write?' To label Indians 'semi-barbarians' who could 'not even understand [their] own language and system' was not proof of their decline, but of British 'bigotry . . . pride, and . . . vanity'.[208] In fact, such frustrations were recycled as late as the 1870s: 'Hindu Law' was, a judge grumbled, a 'phantom', and court decrees 'grossly unjust'.[209] Another protested the 'grotesque absurdity' of applying Brahminical norms to people with little to do with them. But at 'this late day', he was compelled to stick to the travesty anyway.[210]

And so, Hastings's mongrel powered on even when exposed.[211] The man had been sincere in seeking to govern in accordance with 'native' ideas, but ultimately his legal framework offered not justice but a queer convenience—to the British at any rate.[212] In the century ahead, many officials continued stubbornly to compile guides to make sense of the mess, all along insisting they were honouring 'tradition'. Or in the words of one innovator, while 'Hindoo law' was 'unintelligible', the British had a 'duty' to identify 'beneficial' bits, and through 'undeviating application to cases', *manufacture* consistency. In so doing, they might 'cleanse the system of its aggregated corruptions', and 'defecate the impurity of the ages'.[213] Again, clumsy white men masqueraded as saviours to the brown; again, to borrow from our Mughal critic, they reduced 'natives' from a living, breathing people to 'pictures on a wall'.[214] Naturally, the latter too had responses. And not unlike general British uncertainty in this period, these too initially oscillated between profitable acquiescence and small subversions. It was as if all parties involved were still taking stock of one another. Only when the Company's attitude stiffened—as we will see—with sober voices being replaced by more hard-line, evangelical thinking, did Hindus turn militant in their opposition. Errors the Portuguese made in Goa the British would begin to commit at a more sophisticated, but no less offensive, scale. And with accommodation—plus the desire for it—fraying, Hindus would resort to a nationalism defined by the one thing their foreign rulers could never partake of with them: religion.[215]

In 1805, a Bombay judge called on the man fated to be the last Peshwa of the Marathas. Writing later, he described his host as 'the handsomest Hindu I have seen', albeit 'with more elegance than dignity'. In fact, added James Mackintosh, 'no lady's hands, fresh from the toilet and the bath, could be more clean than his uncovered feet'.[216] And yet, Bajirao II (1775–1851) was no effeminate nonentity. His capital was home to 1,00,000 people, making it smaller than London but greater than New York.[217] Poona hosted feared Arab guards, while an American led another body of troops. The Peshwa served Chinese tea at his court, where nearly 5000 clerks managed his business.[218] And yet, all the pomp and circumstance failed to mask Bajirao's vulnerability: The great Maratha satraps were against him, forcing him sometime before to quit his capital and seek British protection.[219] Evidently, he was unpopular with his people also—once asking that they turn 'joy' at his accession into payment of a happiness tax[220]—and apportioned his time between 'religious rites in public' and 'sensual enjoyment in private'.[221] But, as often happened, the white man's embrace proved more trying than unruly brown subordinates. So, by 1817, as those very satraps rallied against the Company for a clash, Bajirao joined in, now becoming 'a public enemy of the British government'.[222] Bloodshed followed and terrible battles were fought, until the Maratha effort floundered. Once again, the Peshwa fled Poona—this time fearing English guns.[223] As a song from the period rues, 'The Shrimant [Bajirao], brought up in the delicacies of the palace, is now roaming through forests.'[224] One presumes his feet lost some of their lustre.

Peshwa Bajirao II as depicted in an 1888 lithograph, from the Wellcome Collection.

Ultimately, after seven months on the run, the Peshwa surrendered. It was the end of the man and the institution he represented as he was exiled to a faraway village in the north. In prestige, Bajirao suffered: When he requested guns for ceremonial use, the British sent him two scrapyard pieces, one of which tended to backfire.[225] Materially, however, he received some consolation—his pension was substantial enough not only to allow great comforts but also for the ex-Peshwa to become creditor to his own captors, the Company.[226] He also led an eventful domestic life; married six times already, in exile he took five fresh wives.[227] And this way, Bajirao would spend decades in luxurious obscurity. Of course, he remained under surveillance. For the British still suspected the Peshwa of seeking to undermine them, now via seditious contacts in Nepal, next by tacitly backing rebels. No convincing proof emerged, but the Company forever viewed Bajirao with concern. For his part too, the man withheld all legitimacy from the British. Yes, on the face of it, there was cordiality: When an officer, with whom he got on went to bid farewell at the end of his posting, the Peshwa 'shed tears'. But then the fallen premier of the Marathas said something interesting: that he would pray to his Hindu gods for the white man to appear as a Brahmin in his next birth. For this way, he would gain a shot at salvation.[228] One might read an interesting subtext in this: that no matter how amiable a Company man was, no matter how he befriended 'natives', ultimately there was only one way the British could cease being strangers—they would need new bodies and brown skins. To become masters of the Hindus, even the best of men had to be born Hindu.

But while those disenfranchised by Company rule had reason to hate it, there were more than a few willing to work with the hat-wearers—much like those sky-faring gandharvas at the start of this chapter were divided in their views. Thus, ironically, British imperialism in India saw also the rise of a Brahmin collaborator class, serving and aiding the conqueror. In a sense, the Company here followed a pattern set by modernizing Indian states. As kingdoms transitioned from fragmented systems—where rulers shared power with warlords and diffused institutions—into centralized entities, bureaucracies became critical. In Kerala for example, the Travancore rajah crushed his warrior nobility by the mid-eighteenth century, importing Brahmins from Tamil country to run his government.[229] Pen-wielding mercenaries, they were loyal to the king, while their preeminent caste status offered protection.[230] Persian-speaking Telugu Brahmins, similarly, had served the Carnatic nawab,[231] and in the seventeenth century, the last Golconda sultan was the instrument of two Brahmins, leading an increasingly Brahmin secretariat.[232] As early as the sixteenth century, in fact, a Vijayanagara emperor had advocated this formula: to cultivate mobile Brahmin professionals in 'all departments' over hereditary strongmen, who, with their autonomous power bases, tested the centre.[233] For their part, while some Brahmins resented having to kowtow to questionable political masters,[234] the worldly-wise adapted. Even with Europeans, thus, men spoke of 'the Brahmin of so-and-so', which meant 'bookkeeper or representative',[235] and in mid-seventeenth-century Madras, we already find Brahmin officials wielding extraordinary influence.[236]

With the conquest or subordination of 'native' states, the Company now scaled up this trend. Maratha expansion in the seventeenth and eighteenth centuries had allowed Deccan Brahmins access to many parts of the subcontinent.[237] For instance, one family served Mughal governors in the south; later, a son became treasury master to Tipu in Mysore and after the sultan's fall, was appointed regent of that state by the British.[238] Even in areas which the Company trounced but did not annex, it placed trusted Brahmins in executive posts. Travancore, for instance, saw half-a-dozen British-backed Brahmins awarded its ministership by 1857—and the man who followed for the next fourteen years was nephew to one from the previous batch.[239] Though the people here spoke Malayalam, records were translated into Marathi—a language as foreign as English—

for these ministers' convenience.²⁴⁰ In Pudukkottai, the Company embedded so many outsiders, that fifty years later, imported Brahmins' 'paramount influence' remained a cause of 'universal complaint'.²⁴¹ That is, the 'foreigner' in these contexts was not only the white man but also his Brahmin aide; Company Raj also enabled a Brahmin Raj. In directly held territories in south India too, by the mid-nineteenth century, Brahmins supplied 'a majority of *sheristidar*s (head clerks) in the revenue offices'²⁴² and in a single district, one such ensconced seventy-four relatives in plum positions.²⁴³ Why, observing this mutually beneficial concord, a British officer declared the empire 'the wonder of the world'. For if the 'native soldiery' spilled its blood in battle, 'men of the priesthood' showed a matching clerical 'devotion'—all for 'a strange race sitting in the seat of the rulers'.²⁴⁴ The wonder would not last though: In time, Brahmins would become leading promoters of nationalism in India.

Either way, just as the Company had divergent voices within, Indian responses too were not uniform at this stage. The Bengali Brahmins who aided Halhed with his *Code* on 'Hindu law', are a case in point. In 1774, even as the *Code* was being prepared, Halhed composed a poem in which a 'care-worn Bramin' sits 'silent and sad' by the Ganga, tracing 'his country's progress to decay'. 'Weak man', thunders the river goddess; 'Rouse from this torpid lethargy of mind'. For the glorious British had destroyed the 'bigot zeal' of 'spoilers' like the Mughals. She next berates 'Ingrateful Hindus' for not recognizing the white man's 'tender hand' which 'Pours balm into your wounds'. These new rulers had restored 'your country's laws' and 'the slighted Vedas'; they had 'deliver'd [Hindus] from a tyrant's chain'. So, the Brahmin's duty was not to whine about India's decay but to show 'glad homage'.²⁴⁵ Almost as if in agreement, in their preface to the *Code*, the Brahmins expressed similar feelings. Of course, on the one hand, like their peers who had been debating Christian missionaries, they defended Hinduism. There was no one way to know god, for he 'appointed to each Tribe its own Faith'.²⁴⁶

And so, sometimes, he manifested in 'the Mosque, in counting the sacred Beads', sometimes 'in the Temple, at the Adoration of Idols'. This much stated, however, they validated the *Code*. In days of yore, it was announced, the Hindu religion was 'catholick and universal', till it was 'ravaged' by 'the Armies of Mahomedanism'—an early voicing of what is the cornerstone of Hindu nationalist history today. The 'Laws of Mahomed [became] the Standard of Judgment'—a historically unsound claim—breeding 'Terror and Confusion'. Until, that is, 'a Thought suggested itself to the Governor General', to rescue the 'Gentoo Religion'.[247] In other words, yes, the British were protectors of Hinduism itself.[248]

In fact, when Hastings later faced legal trouble in London, 112 Bengali Brahmins couriered a memorandum in his defence. Under him, it was recorded, they were 'richly blessed', as 'he endeavoured' for 'the promotion of our well-being and for the maintenance of our

Hindu priest, c. 1847, blessing the British flag. Courtesy of the British Library/Bridgeman Images.

honour'. Indeed, Hastings 'cherished us' like 'children'.[249] Pandits from Benares were equally warm: Hastings had not only brought fame to the government but delivered 'comfort' to its subjects. 'And all of us . . . offer our prayers for the prosperity of the . . . empire of the King and the Company, who are a veritable repository of never-failing kindness.'[250] Among some men at least, then, the British, despite foreign roots and Christian origins, were viewed as new rajahs; for just some time, the kind of policy men like Malcolm advocated looked like it might work. For worldly Brahmins too, this was not radical—they could come to terms with white men as they once had the Mughals. Their very presence in Company offices demonstrated a knack for survival. In a marble statue of Hastings, for example, we see the ex-governor general in a toga, posing like a Roman legislator. To his left, at a lower level, a Muslim maulvi pores over a Persian book. But to Hastings's right, stands a Brahmin. He has palm-leaf manuscripts in one hand, while the other is raised to his chin, as he gazes upon the ground, lost in thought. It is as if he cannot make up his mind, juxtaposed between a squatting Persian master and the faux-Roman conqueror. The context is new but also holds opportunity. And for better or worse, the Brahmin was in that spot—and he would have to live with it.[251]

One might argue that as beneficiaries of British rule, these Hindus had reason to air positive views. Besides, as Brahmins they might have been pleased by the attention the new dispensation gave their texts and traditions.[252] Hindus of *political* backgrounds—pressed by the Company's might—struggled, however. 'Hindu law', for instance, benefitted the Company in statecraft. Brahminical theory recognized kingship only for Kshatriyas—the second of the four 'classical' caste groups. But Indian princes were often descended from the peasantry; Kshatriyahood was *negotiated* and acquired. Armed with hardboiled textualism though, the British could declare Hindu rulers bogus: the issue of 'needy adventurers' and 'lucky farmers'. Toppling them was not, this way, unjust.[253] An early case comes from Tanjore. In the 1780s, a new rajah succeeded as per custom and precedent. But he was not submissive. Sensing opportunity, a rival claimant's faction demanded the man back his title with 'proof from the Shasters'.[254] Without irony, the governor general placed this Maratha case from Tamil country before north-Indian Brahmins, seeking 'accurately quoted' texts.[255] So, even if the rajah were backed by his 'chief people' and 'general opinion',[256] his status was made reliant on book-wielding Brahmins of a different province. Indeed, it was asked if his *own* backers could quote 'passages' and prove 'real knowledge' of Hindu law.[257] And soon, the British held the succession illegal, deposing the rajah; Tanjore pandits who disagreed were 'ignorant or corrupt'.[258] Simply put, the Company shrouded duplicity in malleable legalese to do as it pleased. As an amazed Englishman wrote, 'Brahmins may be induced to sanction any wish of the British'; it was possible to find in 'Hindu law' whatever suited the needs of power.[259]

The necessary—even natural—corollary to this attitude on the British side was its manipulation by Indians.[260] This comes across in the case of a rajah in Travancore in the opening decade of the nineteenth century. Hostile to British influence in his state, with a lopsided treaty forced on him, he supported rebels against the Company in 1809. The British won the day, and so the rajah faced punishment—so vindictive, in fact, that his wife was seized and put aside. Soon, the Company's representative tried to foist a new lady on the prince: sister of a minister loyal to them. However, the rajah declared the act illegal. On the face of it, he had a point: The sastras have rules he could hold against the annulment of his marriage. However, the fact is that his particular dynasty was matrilineal: a local custom with little reflection in texts. Marriage was *not* a sacred bond, nor was it indissoluble; polygamy and polyandry were permitted, and the rajah's *sister*, not wife, was queen. But faced with British pressure, and aware of the Company's half-knowledge about 'Hindu law', the rajah's advocates read it to his advantage.

They argued that he could never be separated from his wife, nor a new one imposed; it was 'forbidden' by law—this when the rajah's predecessor had multiple wives, and no such 'law' counted.[261] In the end, the rajah was reunited with his spouse.[262] The episode holds lessons. For, as the anthropologist Bernard Cohn observed, the conquest of India was as much a 'conquest of knowledge' as it was of land and goods.[263] And to pull on under colonial rule, Indians internalized even error, shrewdly learning to exploit it for their own purposes.[264]

In fact, Hastings's innovations too would unexpectedly come in handy for Hindus. As we saw, brown men possessed overlapping, plural identities: caste-based, sectarian, regional, linguistic, and, alongside these, the religious. While this last had long existed—and thanks to Islamic rule, Hindus were conscious in degrees of their separateness from Muslims—the legally enshrined colonial bifurcation of Indian society into two master groups now allowed it a more concrete life. That is, where Hindus had various forms of self-conception, sometimes in tension with one another, the government's approach empowered religion as an overarching, unifying principle. What was a fuzzy, incomplete feeling received hereon a definite impetus. Coupled in future with colonial censuses, Hindus would slowly begin to conceive of themselves in a new manner. The British intended enumerative exercises to help them 'see' India better; they ended up enabling Indians to see *themselves* in novel forms. With Hindus, thus, it was established almost overnight that they comprised a numerical majority, as against minorities like Muslims.[265] 'Before head counts of people were announced,' we read 'it was neither possible nor necessary for communities across the land to identify themselves with any degree of preciseness and to seek similarities or differences with others outside their immediate kin.'[266] Now, though, Hindu thinkers could focus more and more on what made them a single grouping; to construct unity despite diversity. History, knowledge and even the English language, would grow key to this, as the next chapter will show. So much so that if Portuguese persecution in Goa had been a local affair, it would eventually be perceived in national accounts as an attack on subcontinental Hindus as a whole—as a people.

The British, in other words, might have viewed Hindus, to borrow that line from our Mughal critic, like 'pictures on a wall'. The latter, however, subverting the same processes, would learn to portray themselves as a nation awakening after long.

FOUR

# 'AN INDIAN RENAISSANCE'

In the summer of 1826, the bishop of Calcutta arrived at the court of the rajah of Tanjore in southern India. Reginald Heber had already travelled a fair bit in the country by then, covering parts of upper India, and even calling on the Mughal emperor in Delhi. The latter, the bishop recalled, was dignified but all around this 'poor old prince' was decay and ruin as matched his actuality as a pensioned-off relic. There was, of course, no shortage of compensatory ceremony and valuable gifts were bestowed by the king. But the palace was filthy, with even the hall where the Mughals once sat in state 'full of lumber of all descriptions, broken palanquins and empty boxes'. The throne, in fact, was 'so covered with pigeons' dung that its ornaments were hardly discernible'.[1] It was a foreshadowing of the fate that awaited the descendants of Akbar the Great, who had once so amazed visiting Jesuits. A haughty governor general had already declined to appear before the emperor on the ground that protocol positioning the British as Mughal vassals was now outdated. Indeed, by 1835, the king's name would be scratched off Company coins as well. Two decades later, after the Great Rebellion (more on that in the next chapter), the last of the padshahs would be toppled officially, paving the way for Queen Victoria to name herself Kaiser-i-Hind, suzerain of India. What Heber saw in Delhi, then, were the last trickles of old wealth and 'native' majesty; behind appearances, the Mughal crown looked perfectly hollow.

In Tanjore, however, the bishop was pleasantly surprised. To begin with, there was a mission at work here with a thriving community of Christians: 1300 Tamils attended a service where he was present. But the visitor had also heard a good deal about the local Maratha rajah, noting with approval after an audience how 'I have seen many crowned heads,

Serfoji II of Tanjore (1800), courtesy of the National Museum of Denmark.

but not one whose deportment was more princely.'² This ruler, Heber reported, 'quotes Fourcroy, Lavoisier, Linnaeus, and Buffon fluently', and had 'a more accurate judgement of the poetical merits of Shakespeare than those so felicitously expressed by Lord Byron'. Why, he even 'emitted English poetry' of a 'very superior' variety, even as he was a 'good judge of a horse, and a cool, bold . . . shot at a tiger'.³ It was 'with the sincerest regret' that Heber took his leave, given that the place was 'so favored and so full of promise'—as he observed to a companion, 'instead of the usual danger of exaggerated reports and the expression of too sanguine hopes, the fault here was that enough had *not* been said' about Tanjore.⁴ An account of a second, informal meeting requested by Heber before resuming his travels, in fact, captures not only his animation but also a glimpse of the rajah's material and intellectual universe—a far cry from the rot so palpable in the house of the Mughals.

> The bishop paid a private visit to the rajah, who received us in his library—a noble room, with three rows of pillars, and handsomely furnished in the English style. On one side there are portraits of the Mahratta dynasty from Shahjee and Sivajee; ten book-cases, containing a very fair collection of French, English, German, Greek, and Latin books, and two others of Mahratta and Sanskrit manuscripts. In the adjoining room is an air-pump, an electrifying machine, an ivory skeleton,[5] astronomical instruments, and several other cases of books, many of which are on the subject of medicine, which was for some years [the rajah's] favorite study. He showed us his valuable collection of coins, paintings of flowers, and natural history, with each of which he seemed to have considerable acquaintance, particularly with the medicinal virtues of the plants in his *hortus siccus* . . . His stables contain several fine English horses, but that of which he is most justly proud, as the rarest curiosity of an Indian court, is an English printing-press, worked by native Christians, in which they struck off a sentence in Mahratta [sic] in the bishop's presence, in honor of his visit.[6]

Rajah Serfoji Bhonsle II of Tanjore (1777–1832) was used to glowing reviews, not least because it was rather startling for white men to encounter a Hindu prince surrounded by the outward appurtenances of European modernity. Heber's predecessor, for example, was certain that the rajah was not just 'a most accomplished Native Prince' but also represented something 'new in India'.[7] Where the Mughal emperor's throne, devastated as much by British contempt as by pigeons, served as an artefact of expired greatness, here was a seemingly virile mind, embracing the technological and material promise of the West, matching also many cultural benchmarks. When Viscount Valentia, a British aristocrat, visited Tanjore in 1804, for example, he was thrilled that the rajah spoke 'very good English', making this one of those rare occasions when 'I had been able to converse with a native prince' without interpreters. His palace was old but 'handsome', and the rajah himself was a man of such excellent manners that 'good nature beams from his countenance'. A tour of the premises, including its famous library, followed, and by the time he left, Valentia thought Serfoji an unusual Hindu who 'passes his life in a course of rational amusement and study', in contrast to 'the generality of Asiatic princes, who are either slaves to ambition, or sunk in the debauchery of the harem'.[8] Leaving aside the cliché of Eastern depravity, which came so naturally to even the kindest European voices, it was clear that on his Western visitors, Serfoji made a most uncommon impression.

This had much to do with the circumstances in which the rajah was installed in Tanjore—he was the very prince, described a few pages ago, who won the succession by convincing the British of a stronger claim under 'Hindu law'. Adopted in 1787 by the dying then-rajah, ten-year-old Serfoji was meant to bypass the rajah's brother.[9] But at the time, the Company quite justly judged the adoption 'irregular and deceptive', and put him aside.[10] However, soon the other candidate proved to be difficult, and here Serfoji's supporters sensed opportunity. 'I see you as my parents,' Serfoji declared to the British,[11] asking that they 'call me to Madras'.[12] His appeal was granted, and at the Company's southern headquarters, the boy was exposed to European education, picking up fluency in English and meeting everyone from Governor General Cornwallis to the sons of Tipu Sultan. While traditional lessons continued, they were joined to a curiosity about the West's intellectual and scientific advances, and a lifelong addiction to books. Meanwhile, his advocate, C.F. Schwartz (1726–98)—a missionary connected to the Tranquebar Mission started by Ziegenbalg, and who had been a friend of Serfoji's adoptive father—pushed his claim to the throne.[13] It was Schwartz who first raised the bogey of 'Hindu law' and the incumbent rajah's ineligibility according to those 'translation[s] . . . published in Bengal'.[14] The effort bore fruit—when the imperialist Lord Wellesley took charge, he deposed the ruler.[15] Lodging Serfoji in his stead, he next obtained a transfer of Tanjore territory to the Company. Serfoji, of course, was granted an abundant pension and he retained control of his fort palace—not a bad bargain for a boy whose right to power was dubious. In fact, his gratitude to Schwartz was such that decades after the missionary's death, he still referred to him as 'father'.[16] The deposed rajah, meanwhile, was exiled to a small town, where he died three years later, a parcel of regrets.

Observing the fate of maharajahs whose lands were 'assumed' by the British, a senior official would in time remark how 'the loss of much of their real power' tended to make Indian princes 'anxious to preserve forms that yet remain of royalty'.[17] This typically took the form of religious ceremony and acts of piety. Serfoji was no exception: One of his first deeds was to eject British troops garrisoned in the eleventh-century Siva temple in Tanjore, and having ritually purified it, to order renovations.[18] Tanjore was once the seat of the medieval Chola emperors, and then the Nayaka dynasty linked to Vijayanagara. Serfoji's Maratha ancestors came here as agents of an enemy sultan to assist the last of the Nayakas in a contest, only to quickly seize the kingdom for themselves.[19] Awkwardness about this less-than-gallant ascent to power was papered over with poetry: It was claimed that Siva called on the first Maratha rajah in a dream, confirming his right over Tanjore.[20] But another device to craft legitimacy was supporting the temple and its patronage networks, much like the British would do with Jagannath in Orissa. Serfoji, in fact, with power dissolved and his house a shell of what it was, literally inscribed on the walls of the structure a genealogy of the Marathas—a closing signature by a prince who understood he and his kind were fast becoming history.[21] In that sense, he was enacting a 'traditional' Hindu expression of kingship, anchored in religion and dynastic glory.

But Serfoji was no tragic soul, seeking consolation in empty ritualism and temple patronage. With the little authority left in him as master of a single fort-city, and the monetary resources the British allotted him, the rajah also inaugurated what has been called the 'Tanjore Renaissance' and the 'Tanjore Enlightenment'.[22] It was, to quote a scholar, 'a knowledge-making process that combined indigenous wisdom with all that was relevant and useful' in Western culture; it produced modern knowledge that yet remained 'rooted in tradition'.[23] That is, the rajah made a mark not as a political being but as an innovative intellectual. For example, on the one hand, Serfoji founded institutions for Vedic studies, meeting Brahmin ideals of kingly conduct. But on the other, he also established twenty-one schools offering free education of the European kind, albeit 'disengaged from Christian frames of reference'.[24] While years later, there would still be debates within the colonial establishment

Royal procession of Serfoji, c. 1800–1810, from the bequest of Edwin Binney, Los Angeles County Museum of Art (LACMA).

on whether vernacular or English education ought to receive official backing, Serfoji—a rajah 'with less power than an English nobleman'[25]—gave students instruction in five languages: Tamil (of the masses), Marathi (of his court), Telugu (a prestigious language from Vijayanagara's heyday), Persian (favourite of the Mughal order), and, of course, English (from India's new overlords).[26] One school, attached to an almshouse named after a beloved consort alone had fifteen teachers and 464 pupils, with a Vedic *pathasala* (academy) and temple functioning in parallel.[27] All at once, that is, this brown prince helmed a 'native' engagement with European modernity—a process, not imposed by the British from above, but pursued with a measure of autonomy.

These innovations were mastered by Serfoji in a period when Company authorities in Madras were hesitant to support public instruction—in setting up schools, the rajah was borrowing, in fact, from Christian missions, many of which separately received his support too. Yet, he was also moulding something new: Instead of using the usual highbrow term *sarva-vidya-kalanidhi-salai* ('house for the study of all sciences and arts'), the palace school was called the *nava-vidya-kalanidhi-salai* ('house of the study of *new* learning'), for example.[28] As with Christian mission institutions—and here perhaps can be traced his mentor Schwartz's influence—caste rules were relaxed; orphans and disabled children were admitted; and food and board provided to all in need of it.[29] Serfoji was equally conscious that in an impoverished country, knowledge for its own sake would not go far—the idea was to endow students with practical skills in gaining employment in Company offices, including by providing access to languages of power. Products of the Tanjore system would in time spread across southern India, achieving distinction—one of the rajah's aides, Subba Rao, was to not only become author of the first English play written by an Indian, but also tutor and then minister to the princes of Travancore: men who would themselves acquire reputations as enlightened, modern rulers.[30] Moreover, the rajah personally crafted textbooks, keeping them familiar to pupils in format, while also conveying new ideas absorbed from overseas. In its outer shell, this was Hindu learning, but the yolk inside had a Western flavour. Only an Indian well versed in European and 'native' ideas both could pull off something like this; only a Serfoji could Indianize the white man's knowledge and smoothly blend it with local culture.[31]

An example appears in Serfoji's adapted *kuravanji* play format, which, as the scholar Indira Viswanathan Peterson notes, was long popular in Tamil country for its 'heterogeneous characters, combined with its comic plot', and a fortune teller as its central figure.[32] The stories typically drew from mythology and folklore, and were consumed by a variety of audiences. In Serfoji's *Devendra Kuravanji*, however, there is a difference. In this Marathi text, the goddess Indrani meets with a fortune teller and asks her to speak of rivers, mountains and the numerous countries of the world. To an extent, all familiar. But then, she demands unusually: 'Tell me, what is the moon's orbit, and what planets revolve around the sun? What is the diameter of the Earthsphere?'[33] For this was a modern geography and astronomy class, and Indrani's interlocutor elucidates Copernican ideas, weaving a verbal picture of the globe. Besides, as one writer put it, kuravanjis usually featured temple towns: Tirupati, Chidambaram, Benares and Rameswaram.[34] With Serfoji, however, the listener encounters a new world: Delaware and Edinburgh, North Carolina and Ottawa, Jamaica and Nigeria, New York and Lisbon.[35] Instead of Puranic tales and concepts, the *Devendra Kuravanji* edified and educated in a new way, transmitting what the rajah had learnt in English to a wider audience in an Indian language. Indeed, as the fortune teller declares to Indrani, 'You know the cosmology of the Puranas. Listen! I shall now tell you a cosmography and geography different from that one.'[36] Both Indrani and her discussant were known to the listeners; it was what they spoke that was novel. Nor did this knowledge seem too intimidating or disruptive. For emerging from the mouths of established characters, they deftly sewed the unfamiliar into the familiar.

The rajah's contemporary and court poet, Vedanayakam Sastri, a student of Schwartz's, also produced several compositions of this nature. Sastri—a high-caste Christian who would fall out with British missionaries in time for refusing to renounce Hindu cultural markers and caste—authored a poem for Serfoji in which the Biblical narrative is enmeshed with the facts of science. Where the creation of man is discussed, Sastri tacks on a detailed account of the human body: muscles, blood vessels, a precise count of bones and more. Talking about Noah's Ark and its building, he first makes a detour to note 'ninety species of trees' around the Tamil countryside. There are lists of insects, the varieties of rice cultivated in the region and the types of fish in the water upon which the ark floats.[37] In receipt of a stipend from Serfoji, and himself an instructor at a mission school, Sastri was wedded to both his religion and modern education in a regional idiom. He was also, like his patron, a man with an eye on the future: When asked once about the contradiction between caste discrimination and the principle of equality, Sastri explained that change could not be forced, instead proposing something more incremental.[38] Serfoji was fond of him—on days when he was barred by custom from Hindu rites, Sastri would sing for him church songs and Tamil hymns.[39] It is likely, then, that the missionary strategy, exemplified by de Nobili and the like, of adapting Christianity to Hindu sensibilities, was here inverted to promote the cause of the rajah and his friends. Except that it was not religion they were selling but Western knowledge, as a means to adapt to a changing world.

While the rajah patronized everything from Sanskrit academies in Benares to missionary work in districts adjoining his seat, the hub of his intellectual pursuits was, of course, Tanjore. In fact, by the 1820s, there was such demand from every passing European to visit Serfoji's palace that he was forced to register a complaint about not wanting to make his home a 'Shew House'.[40] But public curiosity can be forgiven given the sheer activity underway in the fort. To its dispensary, for example, was attached a posse of experts: doctors who specialized in handling poison, eye diseases, urinary disorders and so on, their research and remedies catalogued in Tamil verse.[41] Art supplies and painting material were imported for the court painters, who invented a hybrid Anglo–Indian style and were soon in demand with Company officials.[42] Most significantly, in a city with a palace and a great temple, Serfoji emphasised a very different type of monument: the Sarasvati Mahal library. Originally under the Nayakas, its expanded shelves now featured 4500 books in Western languages, and ten times as many Indian manuscripts.[43] European music occupied thirty volumes, with local performers trained to play both the Indian veena and the piano.[44] White residents in and around Tanjore were overawed by the rajah's literary hoard, delighted when he allowed them to borrow. Even today, a visit takes us into a hall with cupboards stacked on cupboards, many filled with palm-leaf texts in Indian languages. That most of this was the collection of a single productive mind makes the experience only more astonishing. If the rajah believed himself, as a British official grumbled, to be 'the most interesting object in Hindoostan', one can forgive his immodesty.[45]

Notably, Serfoji was not a dilettante satisfying an idle curiosity—as his public education programme demonstrates, knowledge accumulated was intended for as wide a dissemination as possible. The printing press, Bishop Heber noticed, too was put to operation: While the rajah's hope to start a bilingual 'national gazette' never materialized, he did use it to publish a Marathi translation of *Aesop's Fables*, besides seven other texts.[46] And where his medical treatises stayed true to tradition by citing Hindu sages from Sanskrit books, their *actual* prescriptions were based on Serfoji's translations into Tamil of knowledge acquired from the latest European journals.[47] As early as 1800, in fact, the rajah commenced medical education, soon also taking lessons in anatomy with a British surgeon. When a human body made its way to him, despite the risk of corroding his caste status, he proceeded with his investigations. Intelligent as he was, Serfoji found a way to avoid scandal: Human beings, he announced, were 'wrought by the supreme being', so inquiries into their physical constitution were imbued with divine meaning.[48] Either way, as the historian Savithri Preetha Nair notes, decades before the first modern dissection by a Hindu was reported in British territory to overblown fanfare, here, in Tanjore, our prince set a precedent.[49] Serfoji also commissioned a wooden skeleton (for high-caste Hindus around him presumably, who saw touching real bone as taboo), besides obtaining a microscope and a host of other scientific gadgets—a mark of wide networks and also passionate interest.

So too the rajah put the talents of his court artists at work, on the one hand to produce portraits and material of a predictable type for distribution as gifts, and also to illustrate the natural world around him: fish, crabs, spiders, squid and prawns.[50] Botany was attended to: Plants were acquired from as far as China and America,[51] and he obtained not only more Sanskrit manuscripts but also seeds on a pilgrimage to Benares. The 'wonders' in Calcutta's botanical garden thrilled him; its 'significance,' he wrote to his son, 'cannot be praised in a simple letter'.[52] As Viswanathan Peterson states, 'While his European counterparts were collecting Asian exotica', Serfoji was focusing on Western technology and ideas, spending a fortune over three decades catalysing a small-scale Indian Enlightenment.[53] The most remarkable detail, however, is that he achieved this without causing injury to his position as a Hindu prince heading a social edifice of increasingly defensive orthodoxy. He maintained dozens of temples and built new ones, celebrating gods venerated in Tamil country, deities imported by his Maratha ancestors, and festivals sacred to his Muslim and Christian subjects.[54] In its outward manifestations and literary projects, his kingly identity stayed rooted in the land's cultural legacy,[55] and he was not above seeking good karma by feeding thousands of Brahmins or presenting cows, including to bemused white people.[56] Even his Marathi translation of *Aesop's Fables* featured woodcuts of his gods.[57] This meant that all at once, Serfoji was a 'good' Hindu, avoiding deracination. But equally he was at ease with the modern world, dominated by the West and its ideas.

It was this supposed contradiction that the British could never comprehend. Serfoji may have built a tower of glory to commemorate their victory over Napoleon, and he did refer fawningly to 'milk from the [Company's] breast' when they raised him from a middling 'Excellency' to a full 'Highness' in title.[58] But even so, no European was ever allowed entry into his temples, causing Valentia, for example, to wonder how someone 'with an excellent understanding' and rational sensibilities could yet remain 'a slave to Hindoo superstition'. That he could be 'more than indulgent' to Protestant missionaries and Catholics both, while holding on as a 'strict follower' of Brahmin ideologies was, to visitors, inexplicable.[59] To Serfoji, though, this was no paradox: Embracing knowledge, no matter its provenance, sat comfortably with 'native' ideals. To admire European advancements did not equal a wholesale purchase of European culture. He could operate both medieval shrines and study cadavers, just as he might use age-old poetic techniques to communicate fresh lessons. Indeed, long before Lord Macaulay notoriously wrote off India's languages and culture as incapable of grasping modern knowledge, the rajah's innovations revealed the fallacy of such sneering opinions.[60] On the contrary, Serfoji's example demonstrates how Indians were capable of identifying 'progress' without becoming anglicized inside out. Hindus could, this dispossessed rajah showed, engage with modernity on their own terms. One did not have to abandon the ground of one's forebears to walk in new gardens; one could build a bridge, flitting back and forth as needed—a selective appropriation of Western ideas that future nationalists would champion.

Photograph of the gateway and sculptured temple-tower of Tanjore (1903), Underwood & Underwood, courtesy of the Library of Congress.

It is tempting to imagine, then, if Serfoji might have achieved something path-breaking in India had he enjoyed greater power; whether the Tanjore model could, by the strength of its own brief success and originality, have been exported to other corners of the subcontinent. The British thought Hindus no good, believing their glories to have faded with the ancient past; and yet here was an exhibit who, even if at a modest scale, achieved greatness in the present. But sadly, little was carried forward: After the rajah died in 1832, the 'Tanjore Renaissance' wilted, with only paler versions following in other courts.[61] The political economy of the colonial system did not favour such experiments, while at a personal level, Serfoji's heir in Tanjore lacked energy and purpose. When in 1855 this man died without male progeny (despite a harem of twenty wives, seventeen of whom were acquired one desperate day[62]), the very Company which once deposed a sitting prince to consecrate an adoptee, denied his widows the right to nominate a successor.[63] The Maratha line in Tanjore, so far as the British were concerned, was extinct; it had become too expensive to maintain. An outrageous attempt was made to seize and auction the rajah's goods, but the royal dowagers fought this in a seven-year legal battle. And so, though his dynasty's rule ended, Serfoji's library survived.[64] The Sarasvati Mahal stands even now as a memorial to this extraordinary figure—prince, poet, botanist, scholar and an Enlightenment soul who remained, all the same, a committed Hindu.[65]

In 1806, less than a decade after his enthronement, Serfoji forwarded to the governor of Madras a complaint about transgressions by a Company official. F.W. Ellis (1777–1819), a magistrate posted not far from the rajah's seat, had used force to detain a palace peon in a police matter, leaving Serfoji 'disturbed in a very extraordinary manner'. His court and he, after all, enjoyed political immunity, and the rajah protested that he 'never would have signed any Treaty' were it known 'I might be considered to be personally amenable' to the Company's jurisdiction. The authorities moved at once to repair his feelings: London chastised Ellis for 'inexperience', while Madras would transfer him out of the district. Ellis did not appreciate the 'banishment',[66] but the real irony is that had he and Serfoji fraternized more, they would likely have got along: They had shared interests, attempted similar things and some of the former's writing coincided with the Tanjore rajah's experiments. For instance, just as Serfoji repurposed the kuravanji for geography lessons, Ellis also innovated, as seen in a Tamil text he produced, to promote the smallpox vaccine. In his *The Legend of the Cow-Pox*, thus, Ellis presents the Hindu lord of medicine in dialogue with the mother goddess, learning of a sixth element she has added to the cow's five (established) sacred products (*panchagavya*): 'pearls' (cowpox pustules!) to protect mankind from disease.[67] A scientific discussion follows on inoculation and vaccination, the aim being to inform its Tamil audience in a familiar cultural mode of advances in medicine.[68] This was a Serfoji-style literary creation—traditional shape, modern content—emerging surprisingly from the pen of an Englishman.

Ellis was what we today call an orientalist. In India, these were often officials moonlighting as savants, with a stated desire for unearthing and disseminating knowledge about the East in the West.[69] (Indeed, one scholar's formal day job included 'hunting' dacoits.[70]) While missionaries had for centuries been playing a similar role, their portrayals were inflected, as we saw, by religion. Eighteenth- and early-nineteenth-century orientalists, on the other hand, were keen not so much to Christianize India—*their* appetite to 'know' the country stemmed more from wanting to better *rule* it.[71] This, after all, was what Warren Hastings envisioned when propping up 'Hindu law'—to restore to Hindus their traditional legal systems, as he perceived it, inviting gratitude and legitimacy for his government. 'Every accumulation of knowledge' about those 'over whom we exercise dominion', he explained, was 'useful' in that it 'attracts and conciliates'. Showing an interest in local culture 'lessen[ed] the weight of the chain by which the natives are held in subjection'.[72] The chain itself was non-negotiable, but with the right sounds, Indians could be lulled into ignoring it. Or as the historian Richard Drayton notes, 'Service to the cause of Knowledge lent dignity to an enterprise which might have appeared otherwise as mere plunder and rapine.'[73] Officials, besides, had personal incentives in scholarship too. For this was a type of 'self-advertisement' for career advancement.[74] Simply put, though orientalists are often cast as noble figures working with 'few tools other than their enthusiasm',[75] they were and remained also instruments of colonial politics.[76]

Nevertheless, these men did break new ground and achieve a great deal; around the same time that Serfoji grew besotted with modern science, white officials launched a romance of sorts with *ancient* India and its mysteries. In the late eighteenth century, for instance, Sanskrit was assumed to be the 'grand Source of Indian Literature, the Parent of almost every dialect from the Persian Gulph [sic] to the China Seas'.[77] It was Ellis who amended prevailing wisdom by demonstrating that peninsular Indian languages 'form[ed] a distinct family'.[78] It was not a passing factoid: Future research would suggest that the Dravidian language group—as it is now called—once straddled the subcontinent, illuminating a historical era prior to the spread of Indo–Aryan culture.[79] Ellis's finding also reined in the idea that India could be known only through Sanskrit; there was a history to the land—and Hinduism—beyond the 'language of the gods'.[80] Similarly, while 'natives' had narratives of the past, registered in oral traditions, collective memory and in writing,[81] this new crop of white explorers began to stitch together diffused information, slowly developing a shared, scientifically analysed[82] and systematically presented *Indian* history—a commodity that would prove useful for nationalists in future. For example, starting in the 1780s, officials noted inscriptions in an indecipherable script. With one in Orissa, Brahmins knew it concerned Buddhists and viewed it, therefore, with 'shuddering and disgust'.[83] But it would be the 1830s, before James Prinsep (1799–1840)—whose official duties were at the government mint—joined inscriptional dots to decode Brahmi, ancestor to almost all Indian scripts.[84] Suddenly, the etchings came alive, reanimating a written system Indians had forgotten, and with it, fresh facets of the subcontinent's story.

But there was more. Thanks to Prinsep, a heap of inscriptions scattered around the country were confirmed as holding the words of one great figure: Emperor Ashoka. Brahmin and Buddhist traditions spoke, of course, of this third century BCE monarch,[85] but he was hardly common knowledge. Indeed, an 1808 book, the *Rajaboli* (*Story of Kings*), published by an Indian no less, made no mention of the man.[86] It was through British inquiries that Ashoka was recentered not just as one of India's most distinguished rulers, but as a global luminary, his influence as a patron of Buddhism felt as far as China. In time, a lion capital from one of his monumental pillars would inspire India's state emblem; his *chakra*, or wheel of righteousness, today sits at the centre of the country's flag. The Western 'discovery' of Ashoka, in fact, followed the equally momentous identification of his forebears. The celebrated William Jones (1746–94)—a Calcutta judge who was consulted during Serfoji's unusual succession,[87] and founded in 1784 the Asiatic Society where orientalist data was synthesized[88]—knew from Greek accounts of an ancient Indian city called Palimbothra. In India, he came across 'Pataliputra' in Sanskrit but locating the place proved a challenge—until, that is, a retired map-maker and surveyor reported that in the course of *his* work, he had heard the people of Patna, in Bihar, apply the term to their city.[89] One thing led to another, and by 1793, Jones was able to declare that the Indian king 'Sandracottus' who ruled from Palimbothra in Greek histories was likely Emperor Chandragupta, Ashoka's grandfather. For the first time, we read, 'Indian and Greco–Roman history could be synchronized', placing the country's past in a rational time frame and chronology.[90]

Jones, in fact, was to become the godfather of Orientalism in India, launching also a passion in the West for Sanskrit literature. On the one hand, as part of the British quest for 'Hindu law', he would translate the *Manusmriti* into English.[91] But what cemented his fame was poetry. It was through this Welshman that Europe acquired a fuller picture of 'the treasures' of Sanskrit.[92] Here, he 'discovered the Homers, Pindars, and Platos of the East', and in the poet Kalidasa he noted 'an oriental Shakespeare'.[93] His translation of the latter's *Abhijnanasakuntalam*

Sir William Jones, after a drawing by Arthur William Devis, courtesy of the Rijksmuseum.

as *Sacontala: Or The Fatal Ring* (1789) sparked a veritable craze in Europe: The philosopher Schlegel thought it represented 'the best idea of Indian poetry',[94] while Goethe wished to fly East, for 'Sakontala, Nala [the other protagonist], they have to be kissed'.[95] One writer went so far as to flatter a Prussian queen by comparing her with the play's heroine,[96] while Schopenhauer believed that as the revival of Greek literature had nourished the Renaissance, Sanskrit would catalyse something similar in the modern period.[97] Jones proclaimed the language itself to be 'more perfect than the Greek, more copious than the Latin, and more exquisitely refined than either'. Indeed, he noted how Sanskrit bore 'to both of [these European languages] a stronger affinity' than could 'possibly have been produced by accident'; they had 'sprung from some common source'.[98] It was another significant moment, for Jones had outlined what we identify now as the Indo–European language family. The spoken tongues of Europe, Persia and many in South Asia are descended, research confirms, from a common mother.[99] This again placed India's culture—once defined through monsters and paganism—in a temperate global history.

With religion too, there were advances. H.T. Colebrooke (1765–1837)—the son of a bankrupt former Company chairman—was able to see that the Vedic religion predated Buddhism, and that Hinduism as it later evolved was no resuscitation, but the novel Puranic system.[100] Despite its 'seeming polytheism', he confirmed too that its 'real doctrine' was not.[101] And he did this not on the basis of hearsay or secondary accounts, as with previous commentators, but by way of a study of Brahminical scripture. In fact, Colebrooke would, despite errors,[102] offer the first detailed account of Indian philosophy also, doing so through Sanskrit texts and commentaries. His admiration was, of course, not unqualified. Hindus were 'the most ancient nation of which we have valuable remains', argued Colebrooke, but it was also true that in their religion, 'the true and the false, the sublime and the puerile, wisdom and absurdity, [were] so intermixed, that, at every step, we have to smile at folly, while we admire . . . the philosophical truth'.[103] Though Christian critics at home accused Colebrooke of making a 'display of superstition' for even so circumscribed an airing of appreciation, it was nevertheless a scholarly leap compared to what had circulated so far.[104] And he persevered, writing on everything from the daily rituals of the ideal Brahmin, sectarian differences in Hinduism, on Jainism and caste,[105] to offering a lively zoological essay on 'A Species of Ox named Gayal'. For what it was worth, Colebrooke was also involved in the making of yet another digest of 'Hindu law'. While it added to his prestige, here, as might be expected, he had limited success; our Englishman's code was as confusing as prior attempts.[106]

While orientalists, thus, rearranged and organized Indian tradition and history, their approach was not, however, free of long congealed European biases. H.H. Wilson (1786–1860), who would publish everything from a Sanskrit dictionary to a translation of Kalidasa's *Meghaduta*, was convinced, for example, that there was no need to journey beyond Sanskrit to know India. Despite Ellis's findings in the south, Hindus, he declared, 'can be understood *only* through [its] medium'; 'it *alone* furnishes us with the master spring of all the actions and passions, their prejudices and errors, and enables us to appreciate their vices or their worth'.[107] While Sanskrit mattered, Wilson's statement is akin to arguing that Europe might only be unravelled via Latin, casting aside regional languages and their historical and religious material. Earlier, Halhed—Hastings's colleague who we met in the previous chapter—published *A Grammar of the Bengal Language* (1778). Bengali, he declared, was mauled by 'illiterate generation[s]' and Islamic influence. So, he excised 'words as are not natives of the country'—'unauthorized' terms from Persian—and offered a version 'derived from its parent the Shanscrit' alone.[108] While Bengali *is* descended from Sanskrit, over centuries it had formed a distinct identity; in 'purifying' it, Halhed 'set the clock back'.[109] He himself admitted that his version could not 'be expected of a distinct new entity: the 'native' who ceased assisting the West so as to *address* it.¹²⁸

Indeed, in what was an unforeseen byproduct of modern Orientalism, European researches contributed to a steady ballooning of Indian confidence. For one, the orientalist retrieval of past heroes and its celebration of brown men's accomplishments injected pride into Britain's colonized subjects. It sparked self-worth among 'natives', galvanizing what a twentieth-century historian called a 'patriotic spirit' and 'manly' feelings in an age of political enervation.¹²⁹ Thus, from the brown man's perch, Ashoka was not a historical curiosity but an Indian hero; Kalidasa's literary exploits were evidence of what Hindus had once achieved—and could, if they applied themselves, accomplish again. In the 'degraded' present too, there were British writers who posited strong prospects for Indians. James Tod (1782–1835), for instance, built up a glamorous image of Rajputs in India's north-western deserts as warriors, seeing in them a spirited people, rising throughout history to defend faith and freedom. He had his own goals in this—the man hoped to recruit Rajput states as British allies by providing them a measure of political autonomy.¹³⁰ But to quote the words of a late-nineteenth-century observer, the Scotsman's history also ended up making 'Hindoos proud of their ancestors'.¹³¹ The white man's researches, that is, accelerated the formation of modern identities and the Hindu self-image. So much so that if Hastings intended

Colin Mackenzie with his Indian associates, painting by Thomas Hickey (1816), Wikimedia Commons.

Western scholarly scrutiny to render chains of subjugation invisible, in only a few generations, 'natives' would appropriate such scrutiny to first loosen—and then break—their shackles. And just as Serfoji creatively wed modern ideas to tradition as a prince, his countrymen would strategically seize on orientalist learning to assert political individuality as a *people*.

Nothing illustrates this as well as the career of the Bhagavad Gita—a 700-verse meditation in the 1,00,000-verse epic Mahabharata between events of political negotiation and cataclysmic war. Lodged in a story of pan-Indian appeal, the Gita's teachings represent at one level the message of god; a dramatization, as the scholar W.J. Johnson put it, of the bond between man and the almighty.[132] A text that was always prized among Hindu philosophers, orientalists too began to celebrate the Gita. For one, Hastings, in promoting the 1785 English translation, wished to showcase the sophistication of Hindu thought, declaring the Gita's theology as 'accurately corresponding' with Christianity's fundamentals.[133] While his political goal was to resist lobbies at home urging anglicized government in India,[134] more generally, the text satisfied the Enlightenment-era trend too of 'finding' monotheism in the East.[135] Its translator, the 'Sanskrit-mad' Charles Wilkins (1749–1836),[136] thought the Gita to 'contain all the grand mysteries' of Hinduism, and proof of 'learned' Brahmins' loyalty to 'one God'.[137] In a Europe reeling from fabrications like the *Ezourvedam*, the Gita's credentials caused a sensation—indeed, Jones advised his peers to forget all that had preceded it.[138] In Germany, Schlegel viewed the text as a 'handbook of Hindu mysticism', while Humboldt thanked the heavens 'for having allowed him to live long enough' to soak in its wisdom.[139] While by 1869—as happened every now and then with Hindu material—a claim would appear that the Gita *actually* drew its ideas from the Bible,[140] the text received massive acclaim in the West as a window into uncorrupted Hindu spiritual thinking.

But even as orientalists valourized the Gita as part of their particular preoccupations, how did Hindus take to this? To begin with, it cannot be denied that British interest played a powerful role in popularizing the Gita among large sections of Hindus themselves. Until the eighteenth century, this was the preserve of a 'circumscribed and erudite' elite.[141] Why, even Gandhi first encountered the Gita not in its Sanskrit original or an Indian rendition, but in English.[142] The deity Krishna, who appears within as the supreme divinity, besides, is a serious figure; he in *popular* worship took an endearing, mischievous Puranic form, playing pranks and attracting legions of female admirers.[143] While this lovable Krishna has not been abandoned,[144] the Gita's new-found prominence enabled Hindus to hold their own against Christian criticism. Its success in Europe raised the text into a talisman for fighting charges of idolatry in India. So much so, that in the 200 years after Wilkins, over 1400 translations of the book have been published in dozens of local languages—a sign of its canonical centrality to modern Hinduism.[145] Today, the Gita enjoys global recognition as *the* book of all Hindus, or what an early-nineteenth-century brown intellectual considered the 'essence' of all their scripture.[146] Indeed some years ago, Britain's first Hindu prime minister was cheered in his ancestral homeland for having taken his parliamentary oath with a palm on a copy.[147] It is one of those ironies of history that this axiomatic stardom enjoyed by the text derives in good measure from the attention it received via a Shropshire-born civil servant.

Yet, this was not all. What British enthusiasm likely ignored was the context in which the Gita appears in the Mahabharata. 'Of the world's great scriptures,' a scholar writes, 'only the Gita is set on a battlefield',[148] at a moment where Arjuna, one of its heroes, is racked with guilt about going to war against his own kin. It is here that Krishna 'enlarges Arjuna's awareness beyond the personal and social values' that he 'holds sacred, compelling him to recognize why he must fight'.[149] This, in fact, would turn the Gita—so adored by orientalists—by the end of the next century into nationalist ammunition for Hindu elites *fighting* the Raj. As early as 1857, in fact—soon after the greatest armed anti-colonial uprising in India—a missionary warned of the Gita's threatening potential. Krishna's exhortation to dismiss 'unmanly weakness' and pick up arms could justify 'any leading mutineer'.[150] His fears were accurate. 'The Gita is the best answer,' a future revolutionary would proclaim, 'to those who shrink from . . . aggression as a lowering of morality.'[151] Indeed, by 1918, officials would be describing it as a 'text-book for the mental training of revolutionary recruits' in the country.[152] For besides all that the Gita offered the soul, it could also be read as a book of action,[153] making it the 'bible of the Indian national movement'.[154] Twentieth-century groups actively venerated it as a totem of Hindu nationalism, and as a text to surmount differences of sect and caste.[155] It was an amusing turn—translating the Gita, Wilkins had ascribed Brahmins' willingness to share it with foreigners to the gratitude 'natives' felt for British rule.[156] And here were 'natives' employing the same material not long after to show those foreigners the door.

In sum, the orientalist assembly of historical knowledge was an enterprise begun by a ruling race; its Indian appropriation, however, was about 'natives' reclaiming agency. Western inquiries into their past would allow Hindus to slowly attempt telling their own story, and in forms and ways that put them on the road to asserting nationality. After all, as the thinker Sudipta Kaviraj put it, 'To give itself a history is the most fundamental act of self-identification of a community.'[157] There was no disagreement that India had known greatness in the past. Had not Jones himself, after all, declared that no matter 'how degenerate and abased . . . the Hindus may now appear', 'they were [once] splendid in arts and arms, happy in government, wise in legislation, and eminent in various knowledge'?[158] The difference, however, lay in this: British voices saw in India's subsequent decline a justification for their own presence here, as saviours and uplifting, civilizing forces. 'Natives', however, would view foreign rule, in the scholar Monika Bhagat-Kennedy's words, as purely 'temporary tutelage'.[159] For them, as expressed in the writings of nineteenth-century thinkers, knowledge of the past—one that was 'arousing the enthusiasm of European scholars even today'[160]—was a force to 'accelerate' national progress; history was but a tool to 'teach the present' and shape a pathway to India's 'regeneration'.[161] That is, to quote a Bengali intellectual from the 1880s, the point of history was to make people 'complete beings'. 'A person who keeps thinking that his ancestors have not achieved anything of value will not achieve anything himself.'[162]

It was this emerging 'native' desire for present-day achievement that would unsettle the Raj. But for Hindus too, the journey ahead was long. Chanting praises of ancient glory helped prepare the ground, yes, and to lay a psychological foundation for articulating identity. Actively *building* on it, though, was a whole other process. And for many, empowerment lay in embracing yet more modern learning—much like with Serfoji—focused not only on history and literature but also science and technology.[163] These were the planks on which Europe had risen to power; this was how Britain, despite its 'sterile soil', rose to dominance in so many countries.[164] And so these must also, they argued, be the instruments with which India—and Hindu society—returned to its rightful place in the world.

Not long before Bishop Heber visited Serfoji in Tanjore, he travelled to Hinduism's most sacred city.[165] Benares was home to Brahmins from all over the land—107 groups by a later count—and kings vied to maintain almshouses and build pilgrim ghats along its riverbank.[166] The Company had conquered the area in the 1780s, and soon after, Jonathan Duncan, an associate of Hastings, was placed in charge. With well-meaning energy, the man set off 'improvements', ranging from taxes on new idols in a city evidently overflowing with gods, to building public toilets.[167] This effort to deliver 'order' was no success, though: In Heber's day, its roads were as cluttered as before, with cattle 'lazily' plodding alongside ascetics and streams of beggars.[168] And yet, 'in the midst of all this wretchedness' were mansions, and bazaars for diamonds, silks and foreign ware—for Benares was also a trading centre.[169] But what truly shook Heber—and not in a very welcome fashion—was the *vidyalaya* ('house of learning'), with 200 scholars engaged in Sanskrit studies. Walking into an astronomy lecture, the bishop observed a pandit at work: The South Pole, he was telling his class, was the perch of the tortoise Hindus reckoned bore the weight of the world. Heber likely rolled his eyes, for the Brahmin 'very slily' added that this is what 'our people' believed. It did little to mollify the intruder, who grew irritated that such anachronisms were being peddled at government expense. After all, the vidyalaya, also known as the Sanskrit College, worked under British authority; the pandit speaking of the mythical reptile was on the Company payroll.[170] It is no wonder that Serfoji left a superior impression: that Maratha prince, living off a political pension, represented something far more 'modern' to Western minds.

A view of Benares, by Thomas Daniell (1796), from the Wellcome Collection.

It is true that in the post-Enlightenment age, Puranic material was about as reliable in knowing the world as Greek mythology. The Puranas spoke of seven seas, for instance, but believed these to be of salt water, sugar cane juice, liquor, ghee, milk, curd and sweet water.[171] To teach this as established fact in the nineteenth century, understandably, rankled those who actually sailed the oceans and knew them to possess no flavour other than salty. But worse was the fact that if pandits taught outdated lessons, it was because the British subsidized this. Not long after taking charge in Benares, thus, Duncan proposed funding a 'Hindoo College' to preserve 'the Laws, Literature and Religion' of the land. This, he felt, offered twin benefits. By 'exceeding' earlier patrons 'in our attention' to Brahmins in this holiest of sacred sites, the Company would win popularity—a stance in line with trends seen in the previous chapter. The second advantage was that, besides helping collect 'complete treatises' in Sanskrit, such an institution would serve as a 'nursery of future doctors' of Hindu law, to 'assist' European judges.[172] Calcutta agreed: An 'Institution founded expressly to promote the study of Laws and Religion must be extremely flattering to [Hindu] prejudices.'[173] The idea, that is, was not so much the dissemination of good knowledge as making the Company look less forbidding. And if that was the 1790s, thirty years later, when Poona was taken from the Marathas, the same logic saw the establishment of a Sanskrit college there too.[174] It was only in the order of things, then, that Heber found pupils still learning about the world-bearing tortoise, even as Serfoji transmitted more updated lessons in Tanjore. Where a Hindu with agency and exposure explored Western ideas proactively, the Company, in its anxiety to fit in, seemed to side with obsolete learning.[175]

The orientalist justification for this was passionate. As Wilson wrote in 1836, the British had caused disruption in India. They had 'exterminated' Hindus' conventional patrons (rajahs and others) and 'usurped' power and wealth, untethering 'native literature' from its sources of shelter. Unless the Company were willing to restore the princes it had flattened, it could not afford a 'supercilious indifference' to Hindu learning. It was true that 'we cannot sympathize with their tastes', but that was irrelevant; by supporting what 'natives' ostensibly valued, the British would 'avoid reminding our subjects that we are still strangers'.[176] And he was not alone in adding to a sense of moral obligation paranoia around security. As early as the 1790s, a Company director thought it 'folly' to give brown men's intellects a modern polish, for armed with fresh ideas around liberty, they might conspire against the British.[177] Decades later, a governor general concurred that educating Indians was 'contrary to reason', because '[n]o intelligent people would submit to our government'.[178] From this perspective, speaking of sugar-water seas was safer, coming also with the advantage of reassuring the British that they were satisfying 'native' expectations. Besides, orientalist probing pointed to a fair deal that *was* good in Sanskrit. Hindus had compiled valuable material about 'the virtues of plants and drugs' and authored 'treatises on Astronomy and Mathematics'.[179] Referring to the *Bijaganita*, for example, a medieval tract on algebra, an official pronounced every 'scrap of Hindoo science' interesting.[180] Why, William Jones knew a Brahmin who himself ridiculed the Puranic fable of the seven seas, declaring the earth 'spheroidal', with salty oceans, based on a different Hindu school of astronomy.[181] Brown men, that is, only needed reminding of the best of their traditional ideas, not a potentially explosive cargo of imported intellectual goods.

Others in the Company, however, thought differently. In 1829, officials in Delhi argued that a dose of modern learning would inspire 'natives' to '*cease* to desire and seek independence'. It would turn their 'national character' 'Anglo-Indian', bringing the two sides closer, and *averting* risks of a 'reaction . . . on the English interest'.[182] Besides, did the Company not have a cultural responsibility to implant 'English principles', if only to make 'natives' smarter servants?[183] That is, the British, in the historian Gyan Prakash's memorable words, now began to conceive of a right to 'dominate in order to liberate' Indians from their 'civilizational shackles'.[184] Hindu prejudices needed not reinforcement, this argument decided, but dismantling. Intellectually, meanwhile, critics pointed to the limits of Sanskrit. Yes, there was good, but an immensity of the 'frivolous' also passed off for knowledge;[185] the 'Quixotism of fair dealing' was leading to the 'cultivation of Error'.[186] Who could reasonably endorse British patronage for 'superstitious' studies such as on astrology?[187] Evidence too supported a course correction. Within years of its founding the Benares College, for instance, became 'an object of [the people's] ridicule'. For far from 'an assemblage of learned Hindus', it seemed 'a band of pensioners supported by [government] charity'.[188] Orientalists countered by suggesting an 'engrafting' of Western ideas onto the better portions of 'native' learning,[189] and translating 'English works into Sanskrit'—a case of new wine, old bottles.[190] But this opened more complications. The Benares college principal would in time concoct scientific terminology in Sanskrit, thus.[191] Hydrogen became *jalakara*, 'maker of water', oxygen *pranapada*, 'that which gives breath'. Magnesia, meanwhile, was rather traumatizingly rendered as *adahyapatamulajanakasya pranapradaja*: 'that which is born from oxygen'.[192] Instead of a popular textbook, however, the attempt unsurprisingly ended in an unwieldy word-pickle.

Through the first half of the nineteenth century, then, the British oscillated between promoting 'traditional' learning and introducing Western ideas, struggling, unlike a Serfoji, to marry the two.[193] But there were technical questions too. Formally, from 1813, a modest sum was allocated for educating 'natives'.[194] On its utilization, however, competing viewpoints emerged. Some wanted 'schools for the elements of learning', others 'colleges for the higher branches'. 'Some would instruct teachers only, some would merely provide books, some would teach the English language, others . . . science through translations.' Besides there was friction on whether the 'wealthy' and 'learned' ought to be the focus, or the 'general community'.[195] The answers varied. In the 1820s, the governor of Madras recommended, for example, schools to maximize benefit; at barely Rs 50,000, his part of India could have 340 modern institutions,[196] oriented towards 'improvement of the country'.[197] Others, betraying British class influences, insisted on restricting colonial patronage to Hindu elites,[198] believing: 'light must touch the mountain tops before it could pierce to the levels and depths'.[199] Or as the governor general said in 1839—eighty years into British rule—time 'has *not* yet arrived' for mass education.[200] His successor agreed: White men ought to found colleges for 'the higher classes alone'.[201] These quarrels meant that action was often reversed. In Delhi, schools opened by an official were terminated.[202] In Madras, the governor's schools were abolished after his passing, with funds funnelled towards what would become a university.[203] Debate continued, with officials in the same province disagreeing.[204] So as with that word-salad of a textbook, the British architecture for education was also, until the 1850s, a patchwork of indecision.

But in all this, what exactly did 'natives' seek? A vocal section wanted schools and colleges both but in English. As far as elementary vernacular schooling went, they already had infrastructure (so that when the colonial state at last began to support primary education, they simply had to offer grants and streamline village pathasalas in many regions).[205] Or as Ziegenbalg had reported from Tranquebar as early as 1713, 'one can find, in all towns, places, and villages, schools in which the youth is informed in reading and writing'.[206] These were conducted in the homes of local grandees, in temples or under trees, imparting literacy, knowledge of the epics and arithmetic, with students departing after acquiring skills requisite to their caste vocations.[207] Madras in the 1820s, thus, had over 12,000 schools with 1,88,000 students.[208] In Bengal, in the next decade, a survey estimated one 'native' school per sixty-three children.[209] There were no rigid caste biases either: If in some parts, Brahmins ran the schools, in others, non-Brahmins took the lead. And in

A Hindu schoolmaster with his students, as depicted in *The Picture Scrap Book, or Happy Hours at Home* (c. 1860), from the University of Florida Digital Collections.

the classroom, students of diverse groups and religions studied together (the usual exception being 'untouchables', lowest in Hindu society).[210] So, to quote an 1830s traveller, 'The Hindoos are not literally an uneducated people.'[211] Which meant, as another writer affirmed, that the 'native mind although it is asleep is not dead'.[212] The dispute, then, was on how to arouse it, improving the quality and scope of lessons. If on the British side, powerful interests wished to use Sanskrit, impart Western ideas to elites through this medium and leave them to filter down, influential 'natives' wanted direct access to English.

Writing in the 1860s, for example—demonstrating how long the wrangle continued—a Hindu critic made clear that if India were to achieve 'regeneration, it cannot be . . . by means of Sanscrit tuition'. The latter offered 'romance', which orientalists certainly valued, but what Indians also needed was 'bread'. And for this English was essential.[213]

> The Hindoo mind is wedged in prejudices, and the Sanscrit 'cannot minister to a mind diseased.' The Hindoo patient wants food, and not poison. The benighted native wants to have the film removed from his eyes; but the Sanscrit surrounds him 'with a cloud instead, and ever-[en]during dark'. He wants to *advance*—which is the watchword of Europe; but the Sanscrit would keep him far in the rear of nations, and hold his mind in bondage to antiquated notions. The Sanscrit held some good some two or three thousand years ago; it is effete in the present day. The Sanscrit belongs to the age of the bow and arrow . . . The English belongs to the age of Armstrongs, Railways, and Electric Telegraphs. To cultivate the Sanscrit would be to doom ourselves to seek a grain of truth from a bushel of chaff—to perpetuate the reign of error, and to ignore those high achievements of the human intellect which have changed the face of the world . . . Surely, we do not want to uphold the geography [featuring] . . . Seas of Butter; but to know the use of the mariner's compass . . . We do not want dreamy speculations; but practical energy and matter-of-fact knowledge. We want to be men of the nineteenth century, and to be admitted into the comity of civilized nations. Unquestionably, it is through the agency of the English that this object can ever be hoped to be accomplished.[214]

While there was some romanticization of English here, the fact is that many 'natives' equated mastery over it to progress. Under colonial rule, this was to a degree natural; and Hindus had some experience seizing on new languages anyway, as with Persian under Islamic rule. About forty years before, thus, a Hindu intellectual in Bengal,[215] protested the inauguration of yet another Sanskrit college. Sanskrit, he groaned, took 'a lifetime' to learn, and was a 'lamentable check on the diffusion of knowledge'. It offered metaphysics, literature and grammar—which excited orientalists—but India had 'numerous professors' for these already; it did not require the British to furnish more.[216] Instead of being fed 'what was known two thousand years ago', he sought 'mathematics, natural philosophy, chemistry, anatomy' and other 'useful sciences'. *These* were the subjects that had elevated the 'nations of Europe'—*this* is what 'natives' must now have.[217] There was conviction here. Not long after, Swathi Tirunal (1813–46), Travancore's rajah and a pupil of one of Serfoji's ex-aides, proclaimed English books a 'barrier against many prejudices and false notions'.[218] Earlier, in 1816, a judge was 'struck with the enthusiasm' for 'western literature and science',[219] while twenty years thereafter, in Madras, 70,000 men signed a petition for the revival of the English schools established by that dead governor. 'We seek not education which depends on charity,' it was also clarified, for they would *pay* for English.[220] One entrepreneur who opened English schools in Bengal, in fact, was actively chased by boys shouting: 'Me poor boy, have pity on me, take me in,'[221] while another traveller observed that to master English, Brahmins would even pick up the Bible.[222] Why, in the Company-sponsored Sanskrit colleges too, pressure resulted in the inauguration of English sections, their popularity surpassing those of the original, founding classes.[223]

The orientalists dismissed this as stemming from purely pecuniary motivations. Indians picked up English but without imbibing seriously Western ideas. They had 'no taste for our literature, no participation in our sentiments, no impression of our principles', and, instead, remained 'in all essential respects of character . . . [at] a level with the rest of their countrymen'.[224] Their love of the ruling class's language was precipitated merely by hopes of employment. Was it wise, then, to invest in a selfish, 'promiscuous crowd of English smatterers', unlikely to serve as the 'regenerators of their country'?[225] On the face of it, there was truth to the charge. As early as 1626, trading centres had 'olive-coloured Indian foot-boys' who 'prettily prattle[d] English' as they assisted English merchants.[226] In the 1780s, schools Serfoji's mentor, Schwartz, set up grew attractive to job-seeking Brahmins.[227] In Madras city, a single road featured a rumoured 100 boards advertising English training,[228] and it was not uncommon for Company retirees to augment their income running language centres.[229] And yet, this was an incomplete picture: As the scholar Parimala Rao shows, most jobs available to Indians did not require English and the higher vacancies that did were barred. Even when the latter were opened, not many went for them: Of 900 boys who graduated from English schools between 1824 and 1836 in Bombay, less than 100 sought government positions.[230] The jibe that English education produced an army of clerks was incorrect; it would generate 'political leaders, professional men, and intellectuals'—not unlike Serfoji.[231] And most significantly, many *did* wish to regenerate their country; indeed by the 1840s, we find, as the next chapter will show, clear articulations of nationalist thought in India. And this was addressed directly to the colonial power, in its own mother tongue.[232]

Indeed, if in Calcutta the Company set up a Sanskrit college, the city's first *English* college was born of a union of brown intellectuals, businesspersons and dissenting white men. And where the state's entire budget for education was Rs 1,00,000, this contingent raised over Rs 1,13,000, almost wholly from 'native' benefactors.[233] A concerted effort by Hindus—the institution was even branded 'Hindu College'—to promote Western learning, it would be said that 'English Education was in a manner forced upon the British Government' by their actions. In 1827, a decade into its founding, the college offered classes on 'natural and experimental philosophy, chemistry, mathematics, algebra', with 'Milton and Shakespeare' on the side.[234] Where years later a governor would still lament the absurdity of having 'Natives rehearse Shakespeare',[235] the fact was that by 1831, Hindu College students displayed excellent 'command of the English language'—and, through it, 'familiarity with its literature and science'—exceeding 'schools in Europe'.[236] Orientalists, though, remained hostile. In Madras, an official wondered what the point was of introducing a fraction of 'native' society to 'the beauties of Shakespeare, of Milton and with the learning of Bacon' when the rest languished in 'hereditary ignorance'. The former would only grow 'isolated' from their countrymen.[237] A counter to this position, as voiced in the 1830s by Macaulay, was market economics: 'I know that your Sanskrit . . . books do not sell.' But 'English books . . . *do* sell. I know that you cannot find a single person at your Colleges who will learn Sanskrit . . . without being paid' stipends. But those 'who learn English are willing to pay' themselves.[238] Popular demand was its own answer.[239]

The transition from Sanskrit to English was most pointedly expressed in the mid-1830s, when the governor general ordered that state funding hereon be reserved for only modern education in English, and that 'artificial patronage' for 'Oriental learning' be gradually withdrawn.[240] Macaulay endorsed the move. In his mind, English was to Indians what Greek and Latin had been to Europeans some centuries ago: a potion for renaissance.[241] But how would knowledge touch the masses? In what are (in)famous words in India, Macaulay advocated the creation of a section of 'natives' who 'may be interpreters between us and the millions whom we govern'. A 'class of persons Indian in blood and colour, but English in tastes, in opinions, in morals and in intellect'. It was this set—keen on Western ideas and English—that would translate modern learning for the people, in their vernacular languages.[242] The British, it was clear to him, had little capacity to educate Indians—getting caught up in which language was best suited was a waste of time. 'What we now want are necessaries,' wrote Macaulay. 'We must provide the people with something to say, before we trouble ourselves about the style which they say it in. Does it matter in what grammar a man talks nonsense?'[243] In fact, Macaulay lambasted orientalist peddling of antiquated Sanskrit as sheer irresponsibility. Would Indians progress by learning 'how they are to purify themselves after touching an Ass, or what texts of the Vedas they are to repeat to expiate the crime of killing a goat'?[244] No, the British must offer fresh ideas, or *nava vidya*, as Serfoji would have preferred. And for this they needed 'native' intermediaries, which, in a sense, was precisely what the Tanjore rajah had also been.

Incidentally, such a class was on the rise—English-speaking 'natives', transmitting new-found knowledge via local languages.[245] Master Ramachandra (1821–80), for instance, taught at the government college in Delhi, offering Western science in Urdu as well as original mathematical research that expanded on ideas *within* Indian traditions.[246] Later in the century, B.P. Modak (1847–1906), a Deccan schoolmaster, authored a chemistry textbook in Marathi; though 'adulterated' with English terms, he would publish dozens more.[247] In this he was given the lead by B.S. Jambhekar (1812–46), a Bombay professor, who, despite his early death, achieved much: At seventeen, he translated Lord Brougham's *A Discourse on the Objects, Advantages, and Pleasures of Science*, later advocating for 'useful arts and sciences' in the press.[248] In 1843, Dadoba Pandurang (1814–82), also in Bombay published his *Dharmavivechan*, combining 'with Western rationalism India's own religious dissent'. His Marathi grammar would be of marked utility to translators.[249] Princes made contributions too. The Travancore rajah mentioned before, Swathi Tirunal, set up an observatory and English school in his capital; his successors would establish 'scores' of Malayalam-language institutions next.[250] One of these heirs, Rajah Uthram Tirunal (1814–60), was an amateur physician too, who delighted in parading his English-speaking daughter before guests. For educating daughters was even more novel than teaching sons.[251] Admittedly, these figures were few and scattered (and had

Dadoba Pandurang (1882) © Illustrated London News/Mary Evans Picture Library.

their own class and caste biases),[252] but they nonetheless shared a goal: to 'transfer,' as the iconic Bengali educator Iswar Chandra Vidyasagar (1820–91) preferred, 'the philosophy of the West into a native dress'.[253]

Indeed, if anyone feared that these men would be deracinated brown sahibs, tending to mimic the West mindlessly, they need not have worried. For while the likes of Jambhekar were consciously modern, they aspired to an *Indian* modernity. In Calcutta, for example, Akshay Kumar Datta (1820–66), was a reputed Bengali textbook-writer, 'Indianising European science'.[254] Covering everything from volcanoes to walruses in his work,[255] he also edited a journal that made science familiar to brown audiences. Yes, on the face of it he acknowledged Europe's superiority: There was no doubt that white men had pulled off technological miracles. Similarly, Hindus' current debilitation troubled him. They laboured, for instance, under the misconception that whatever was traditional was best.[256] Custom, as we saw in the Introduction, declared overseas travel polluting. Datta, however, wanted 'natives' to open themselves to the world, and to abandon outdated observances. Except, in urging them to do this, he did not simply suggest following in Europe's footsteps. Instead, culling from Greek sources down to the Sanskrit epics, he argued that the Hindus' *own* ancestors had been seafarers.[257] Significantly, Datta was not blind to the context in which European science—which he so esteemed—came to India; he could see his country's political prostration. Or as he explained, the British conquest was achieved by 'lowly instincts'; white men showed 'greed', 'self-love and tremendous malice'.[258] That is, even as Europe's technical achievements were conceded, admiration was selective.[259] Accepting the value of Western learning was not tantamount to legitimizing colonial *rule*. Besides, the whole point of embracing foreign ideas was to revitalize 'native' society—and a revitalized society would, it was a given, no longer require foreign superintendence.[260]

This Indian propensity for selecting and accepting only those elements of the encounter with the West as pleased them, was noticed by another cast of men. With the government reluctant for decades to back elementary education, especially in the vernaculars, missionaries had slid into that space. In the south, a German father, for instance, starting in 1820, established 107 schools in a space of fifteen years, catering to nearly 3000 students.[261] Soon after, colleagues opened 500 more in the area, bringing 38,000 students under instruction in total.[262] In Bengal, similarly, missionaries through the Calcutta School Society ran over 200 schools by 1835, teaching some 5000 boys.[263] Of course, the education they supplied was interlaced with religious propaganda, schools being perceived as 'evangelistic agencies'.[264] The very act of learning English, one man wrote in 1840, was calculated to leave students 'tenfold less the child[ren] of Pantheism, idolatry, and superstition than before'.[265] Another reported his method of 'giving [pupils] English phrases and sentences' to learn. Only, the sentences 'might be arranged as to teach them whatever sentiments the instructor should choose'. The hope was that some would form an attachment to the Bible, and after conversion, 'be made the instruments of pulling down their own religion, and of erecting in its ruins the standards of the Cross'.[266] In fact, as late as the 1870s, Madras authorities found 'offensive' allusions, targeting Hinduism and Islam, in textbooks used by Christian organizations. Even a geography book urged the 'people of India' to accept the message of Christ 'and endeavour to spread it'.[267]

And yet, despite the occasional conversion, most students proved adept at digesting only parts of the academic fare. Missionaries often found that children would memorize lessons, to pass exams. But hopes that they would *understand* them were disappointed. As a scholar suggests, 'the [mere] memorizing of texts' was perhaps 'an instinctive defence against a body and form of knowledge that looked hostile to everything that was meaningful in the child's environment'.[268] So too, instructors hoped that a scientific curriculum would demolish their pupils' faith in their gods; except those pupils were not so malleable. On the contrary, according to a frustrated master 'no books would detain their attention for any considerable time except the accounts of their own gods, and traditions'.[269] With very young children, many parents did not worry about conversion—'the missionary may teach,' it was noted, 'as much Christianity as he pleases' without objection, because there was confidence that it would *not* leave a mark.[270] But even at higher levels, as early as the first decades of the nineteenth century, a man of faith complained that despite exposure to science, students felt no pressure to embrace the gospel. Yes, some of the more 'preposterous errors' and 'revolting usages' of Hinduism might be abandoned but not anything further.[271] Indeed, one critic complained, Hindus mastering 'European languages, writings, and arts and sciences' showed a distinct tendency to 'father them on some of their own ancient sages'.[272] And by the end of the century, though 'Hinduism [had] been simultaneously assailed by western education and by Christianity', instead of breaching it, Hindus were using new-found skills to actually 'defend their religion'.[273]

For missionaries, then, the religious and educational went hand in hand; most of their 'native' wards, however, separated the strands, accepting education minus direct religious baggage. Hindus, that is, desired Enlightenment, but rejected the offer of *Christian* Enlightenment.[274] And this did not always require the invention at the hands of fabled sages everything modern science had delivered. It could be done simply by accepting that in life, different things served different purposes. Or as one Hindu educator put it, traditional accounts that spoke of seas of nectar were intended for the 'praise of God'; *vigyan*, or science, was a different commodity.[275] The two occupied separate compartments, and one could continue to value the Puranas as religious tradition, while accepting contradictory scientific information in other respects.[276] This should not, as such, be surprising. After all, science hardly upheld every tenet of Christianity;

yet, Christianity survived, and as we shall see in the next chapter, even enjoyed a resurgence in nineteenth-century Britain. Indeed, missionaries co-opted science to their cause, confidently publishing texts with headings like 'Botanical Objections to Hinduism' and 'Anatomical Objections to Hinduism', as if the Bible were exempt from similar criticism.[277] By the end of the nineteenth century, in fact, Hindus would actively consume works by Western thinkers who marshalled science and reason in attacking Christian scripture. Or as a Madurai-based missionary complained in 1888, in 'abusing our religion', Hindus 'find ammunition enough in the infidel tracts of [Charles] Bradlaugh and [Robert] Ingersoll, which they freely use'.[278] Here again access to English was put to 'native' uses.

Ultimately, whether it was with education or Orientalism, the ways in which Hindus responded did not meet their original promoters' assumptions. Writing in 1817, for instance, a missionary lamented that Indians accepted the Bible cheerfully, but not quite in fulfilment of Christian hopes. Instead, some took it out of 'curiosity', others to barter it 'in the markets' and some for use as 'wrapping paper' even.[279] The man probably felt a sense of crisis, but Hindus too were not as nonchalant as they appeared. For into the nineteenth century, with British power secure, missionary voices grew louder than ever before. Christian fathers were in the streets, running schools, printing books and mounting, no matter their own feelings of inadequacy, a more aggressive challenge than ever against Hinduism. Orientalism also—even as it recrafted 'native' ideas of self—assumed a missionary quality. Wilson, one of the leading Sanskritists of the age, was transparent when he admitted in 1840 that in studying Hinduism, one goal was to 'overturn their [Hindus'] errors'.[280] F. Max Müller (1823–1900), the celebrated Vedic expert, wrote of the Vedas as 'the root' of Hinduism.[281] But while superior to living, Puranic traditions, this was, he added nonetheless, 'childish and crude'[282]—to show Hindus 'what that root is, is, I feel sure, the only way of uprooting all that has sprung from it during the last 3000 years'.[283] Many nodded in agreement. Or as a colleague wrote to Müller, 'Your work will form a new era in the efforts for the conversion of India . . . by enabling us to compare that early false religion [of the Vedas] with the true.'[284]

Which brings us to the third element in the remaking of Hinduism in the nineteenth century, next to Orientalism and modern education: spectacular conflict with missionaries.

FIVE

# FOR GOD AND COUNTRY

In April 1853, a luxuriously produced copy of the Bible was placed before Lord Dalhousie for his signature and inscription. It was intended as a present for a high-born Indian, for whom the governor general entertained a 'great fancy'.[1] 'This Holy Book,' the white man wrote to the brown, was 'an inheritance richer . . . than all earthly kingdoms'—a uniquely snotty remark to make to an adolescent who had just been deprived of his kingdom, its riches—including the Koh-i-Noor diamond—and even the company of his mother.[2] And yet, the gift was fitted to the occasion: A few weeks prior, Duleep Singh (1838–93), the deposed maharajah of Lahore and leader of the Sikhs, had converted to the Christian faith. It was a public relations coup for evangelical missions in India, who for decades afterwards advertised the submission of the son of the Lion of Punjab—Ranjeet Singh—before the one true god. Tales abounded about how exactly the maharajah was converted. When he was evicted from Lahore after the annexation of his state, a graduate from a Christian mission school was chosen as one of his attendants. Bhajan Lal, though Brahmin by birth, entertained Protestant sympathies, and one day,

Maharajah Duleep Singh, as depicted in William Butler's *The Land of the Veda* (1895), courtesy of the Library of Congress.

Duleep Singh saw among his things the Bible. 'What is this?' asked the prince. When told it was the book of Christianity, the maharajah evidently requested that a chapter be read. 'Strangely enough,' the story went, 'it was the chapter in Acts containing the account of the conversion of Saul.' And with that began the Sikh ex-monarch's transfer into the arms of Christ.[3]

It was an event of great consequence. In Calcutta, the British archdeacon expressed hopes that Duleep Singh's 'conversion may have an important influence on our missionary prospects' in India.[4] Sympathetic press outlets declared that the Company must now march against 'ignorance, superstition, moral debasement and misery'—all placeholders for 'native' religions—and spread Christianity. It would, they argued, be a victory to 'eclipse [even] the glories of Plassy' (sic).[5] The *Oriental Christian Spectator* proclaimed that this gain of the prince—'no inappropriate specimen of his nation'—would open up 'remarkable opportunities' to win followers among Sikhs specifically.[6] Even the president of the Board of Control in London, expressed his hopes for 'a civilized and Christian empire', and was 'much satisfied' when he learnt about the maharajah.[7] Of course, the path to this moment had been paved carefully. When Duleep Singh first expressed a desire to discard, as would be later stated, the 'mummery, immorality and covetousness' of his ancestral religion,[8] the official line was that 'no improper influence' should be used to 'induce His Highness to abjure his original faith'.[9] Dalhousie meditated on the subject for two whole years, and only when the maharajah's guardian confirmed that the boy was determined to switch religions was baptism arranged. The great worry, naturally, was that any official enthusiasm on the British side might provoke 'native' animosities.[10] The governor general was keen but could not be *seen* as keen.

This fear was warranted, because 'native' anxieties were indeed inflamed. The deposed rajah of Coorg in southern India, whose daughter also converted in British custody,[11] wryly remarked that Duleep Singh must have been of 'wonderful precocity' given how he went from a nine-year-old who had never 'heard the word Christianity' to forming 'uninfluenced convictions' as a ward of the Company.¹² Decades later, the prince himself, even after returning to Sikhism, continued to regard his conversion as a free choice but hinted that he was placed in circumstances likely to encourage this turn. He was, on the one hand, separated from his only surviving parent—censured in the press as the Jezebel of Punjab¹³—who was prohibited from corresponding with him; when they met after twelve years, she was blind and shattered. On the other, during the years he spent under Company control, he was given no instruction in his own religion, and few of his countrymen from Lahore were permitted contact.¹⁴ Indeed, when he left his old capital, not a single copy of the holy book of the Sikhs, the Guru Granth Sahib, was packed.¹⁵ He was given no knowledge of 'the history of his country and family, and had,' as a pamphlet he sponsored argued, 'been taught to look to the British Government as his paymaster as well as his sole protector and guardian'.¹⁶ His interest in Christianity, while born of genuine curiosity, was at first only so serious that having vowed he would no longer play on Sundays, he did the exact opposite. When asked, the teenager sheepishly said that he 'forgot' his recently stated, very solemn convictions.¹⁷

In this situation, the influence of his superintendent, John Login, consciously or not, was key. For the fact is that this devout Christian and his family were all the society the maharajah was permitted for years, inclining him perhaps to imitate them in lifestyle as well as in faith.¹⁸ The first time he broke caste taboos, for instance, in front of his retinue was when he sipped from a glass used—and, thus, according to local beliefs, ritually defiled—by Mrs Login.¹⁹ And the government also privately began to prod the prince towards a more radical break from his past. As a Company higher-up wrote to Login in 1851:

> It is his Lordship's [Dalhousie's] earnest hope that the boy's spontaneous wish may prove to be rooted and stable, and that

he may imbibe with eagerness and perseverance that knowledge of Christian truth which he has thus early and unexpectedly sought. To that end our best and faithful exertions should now be steadily directed. We should content ourselves with the consciousness that we are laboring for good, and with the hope that it will in the end be fully and permanently secured. But in the meantime, his Lordship enjoins upon all concerned that they abstain from trumpeting abroad either the nature of their labours or anticipations of their issue.[20]

Dalhousie was as motivated by political goals as he was by religiosity. It was 'a remarkable historical incident,' he wrote, 'and if ever the finger of God wrote upon the wall, it did in the sight of this boy'.[21] The transformation of the maharajah 'from darkness to light'[22] was 'in every way gratifying' to the governor general's own evangelical sympathies.[23] But importantly, since Duleep Singh was ex-king of the Sikhs, his relinquishing their religion held strategic implications: 'we could desire nothing better for it destroys [the maharajah's] possible influence for ever' over that mass of warlike people.[24] There was no chance now of Duleep Singh's restoration; he was severed from his land, his subjects and culture. And in this, Dalhousie saw the prelude to something greater. Ranjeet Singh's son was 'the *first* Indian prince of the many who have succumbed to our power . . . that has adopted the faith of the stranger. Who shall say,' he wondered, 'to what it may not lead? God prosper the seed and multiply it.'[25] This desire for Christianizing India, expressed from the highest levels, stood at an alarming distance from the caution advocated by Elphinstone, Munro and Malcolm earlier in the century. In their time, when British power looked less certain, 'native prejudices' were handled with care. Dalhousie, in the 1850s, however, was restless, brusque even.[26] Imperial authority was, to all appearances, tightly embedded and in a position therefore to promote its own ideological programme. To view the Company merely as a utilitarian entity transacting power and commerce was for small minds. Instead, the governor general conceived of the British empire as a means to disseminate the holy word also. By so doing the Company would serve a taller purpose; with a little less self-doubt, it might achieve nobility even.[27]

Dalhousie, of course, did his best to push this vision until his term ended in 1856. And then the country responded: Within a year of his departure, India erupted in revolt.[28]

About twenty years before the Great Rebellion, Daniel Wilson, the bishop of Calcutta, stood on the deck of a boat on the Sutlej. Ranjeet Singh reigned in Punjab on the river's west, while the Company's territories ended on the eastern side. It was a border agreed to in 1809, and the British had relatively imperfect information on the lie of the land in Sikh country. But this did not prevent the bishop from making a dramatic gesture. As he sailed downriver, Wilson gazed at Ranjeet Singh's realm and crowed: 'I take possession of this land in the name of my Lord and Master, Jesus Christ.'[29] His companions might have been puzzled, because the Company seemed unlikely to pick a quarrel with the Lion of Punjab; the Sikh kingdom would implode only in the decade *after* Ranjeet Singh's death in 1839. But to Wilson's biographer, the bishop's remark portended what was to come. Given the 'speedy' nature by which the British took the region thereafter—exploiting infighting in the Sikh court in the 1840s—he saw proof of 'how faith has power with God'.[30] To seize these lands was Britain's destiny; 'Christian England' only had to wish it, and the world would be delivered by heavenly design. The Sikhs had looked formidable, but it was their white neighbours across the Sutlej who were backed by divinity. Empire was no longer about men doing politics. It became a holy mission entrusted to the British, and it was the Company's duty to spread the Christian message—even if whole kingdoms fell in the course of this august pursuit. After all these were 'native' states. They did not realize that Christian power subjected them for their own best interests.[31]

For all the talk of destiny in the story around Bishop Wilson, though, official attitudes towards Christianizing India featured much ambivalence and hesitation. Formally, as early as 1698, the charter parliament granted the Company for its trade in India, required it to support Protestant fathers and to 'instruct the Gentoos' in faith. But as Ziegenbalg experienced with the Danish in Tranquebar, Company men—fixated on profits—were not enthusiastic about complicating commerce with religion. Where they were mandated to have a clergyman aboard every ship of 500 tonnes and above, they simply built their ships below that size; when asked to impart lessons to 'natives', they interpreted this as meaning those Indians who worked for them, rather than Hindus at large.[32] Groups at home were nettled by the indifference. The SPCK—Society for the Promotion of Christian Knowledge—lobbied London and presented proselytism as offering political bonuses also. Making (Protestant) Christianity part of the export merchandise to India, they argued, would prevent Britain's rivals, the (Catholic) French, from seducing Hindus into unholy alliances.[33] In an argument that would be much repeated, it was claimed that turning 'natives' into Christians would cement British power; rulers and the ruled would become one.[34] After Bengal, with its millions of souls, became Company territory, calls for letting missionaries in to 'save' them grew. This was also linked to shifts in public sentiment, including a reaction to the Enlightenment and its elevation of reason over faith. British losses—its embarrassing expulsion from America in the 1770s, for instance—led to murmurs that god was punishing its people for being tepid Christians.[35] Britain, one bishop sermonized, had a 'duty' to convert all who lived under its sway.[36] Power and wealth could scarcely be ends in themselves; that would only birth sin.[37] What the country needed was purpose. 'Civilizing' its eastern subjects fit the bill—and the Bible, carried not far behind the Company's guns, offered the apparatus.

This sense of preordination pervaded even those not prone to religious conquest. Into the early nineteenth century, claims began to appear that there was something providential to the British subjugation of India. As one journal rhapsodized: 'What can be more astonishing, than that a handful of Europeans, impelled not by the love of conquest, but by circumstances over which they had no control, should have risen . . . from the situation of mere adventurers, carrying on a petty trade . . . to the lordship of the greatest, the most populous, and the most extensive empire, upon the face of the whole earth?'[38] Central to this was the growing myth of British superiority: The white man's character surpassed that of the brown; his religion was more exalted than the latter's archaic superstition; British values were shaping up the age, while Indians languished in the past, helpless at navigating the present.[39] Coinciding with the

Indian Christians at prayer, as depicted in M. Le Baron Henrion's *Histoire Générale des Missions Catholiques* (1846).

Industrial Revolution and material and technological developments in Europe, important minds bought into this self-image of the West as natural leaders, showering gifts of liberty and progress upon darker parts of the world. Where missionaries specifically were concerned, all this change was a confirmation of the need for revitalized religion. Revolution in France triggered fears of a similar upheaval in Britain, for example, and to maintain stability, a return to faith was advocated.[40] Inventions and 'improvements' were a mark of achievement, but whether they were used for good or bad depended on values—which also were anchored in religion.[41] As a new middle class began to emerge, upsetting older norms in British society and its settled elite, demonstrable piety became a currency for social mobility. And what better way to show 'good' (bourgeois) values than by supporting projects to 'save' ignorant 'heathens' in faraway places?[42] Even as the British were remaking India, then, India would catalyse a fresh impression of Britishness.[43]

Among the earliest figures to urge diffusing Christianity in the subcontinent was Charles Grant (1746–1823), a Company servant and future director. Personal tragedy had made him a man of faith and a committed mouthpiece for extending the benefit to Britain's Indian subjects. As early as 1784, Grant aired his belief that no matter how much 'good' the British did—by way of law, stability and so on—if Indians' *moral* standards were poor, it would lead nowhere.[44] Three years later, in association with friends, he proposed government support for Christian missionaries. Dismissing the so-called higher precepts of 'Hindooism'—Grant was evidently the first to use this term[45]—he argued that the whole religion was 'an infinity of absurdities'. On this was heaped a selection of other stereotypes: that India's tyrannical rulers loved anarchy and that its people were 'universally and wholly corrupt'. In this state of affairs, if the British had to govern, they would have to necessarily push a 'Reformation of the morals'. Indeed, 'good Government' required the people to possess qualities only Christianity could supply; in their current state, they were 'lamentably destitute' of even such basics as honesty and justice.[46] For all his passion in wanting to deliver Hindus from themselves, though, Grant's proposal did not fly. In 1790, Lord Cornwallis, then governor general, reiterated the longstanding policy that the Company's security rested on 'native troops'; to meddle in their religion would jeopardize security.[47] His successor also, while wishing 'eternal welfare' upon Indians, warned that proactive support to missionary work would 'excite alarm'.[48] In the larger scheme of things, then, politics prevailed over faith; Company men were Christians but not Christian (or unpragmatic) enough to let faith dictate matters of state.[49]

But Grant was not defeated. In fact, over the next two decades, he would, in coordination with allies, wage a propaganda battle in Britain to push the missionary cause. Even as orientalists sang of the glories of ancient India, its philosophies and (Sanskrit) literature, this parallel crop of men were producing material that was 'awful in its ethnocentric bigotry', casting Hindus as a class of infant-murdering, wife-burning debauchees, in desperate need of reform.[50] Grant's volley in his *Observations on the State of Society among the Asiatic Subjects of Great Britain* (1792) was ripe with hostility.[51] Reminding the Company that it owed its successes to god, and demanding its 'warmest gratitude',[52] Grant comprehensively denounced all things Hindu. The average Hindu was congenitally defective, his character displaying the worst of human tendencies: servility, cunning, obsequiousness, abusiveness, slander, selfishness, malice, virulence, barbarity, etc. These were people who sold their children into slavery for cash—it did not matter that such things occurred during famines, which the Company failed to alleviate[53]—and whose wives, for all their feigned modesty, lacked 'purity'.[54] If anything, India and its Hindus existed to prove the West's superiority. Thus, in Europe, there was a surplus of men of good character; in India, meanwhile, not a single exhibit of 'real veracity and integrity' could be located. Where in the West, deception aroused shock, in India, it was a routine trait. William Jones and his ilk, preoccupied with crumbling manuscripts, were naïve—the violence of the most 'obvious and popular tenets' of living Hinduism laughed, tauntingly, in their faces.[55] To support his polemic, Grant also threw in quotations from accounts by white men from the previous 100 years, including Company mandarins—unimpeachable evidence, apparently, to back his catalogue of hereditary Hindu sins.[56] Through all this, his principal thrust was simple: India *needed* the British, even if neither party was yet persuaded of this.

Grant's attack was a veritable chutney of old stereotypes that had long been circulating (as seen in Chapter 1) and of contemporary evangelical concerns. But while he did damage, his views were not swallowed willingly. The Company, as before, had to balance 'the world of domestic politics' in Britain along with 'the world of British India'.[57] London was not against missionary activities in principle, in 1752, for instance, authorizing their men in India to give financial aid to Protestant fathers. But they left the execution of such orders to local discretion—and officers on the ground harboured reservations.[58] Which is why, even as Grant was decrying Hinduism in Britain, his countrymen in India were—as we saw—sponsoring temple festivals, giving gifts to deities, mimicking rajahs, peddling 'Hindu law' and otherwise attempting to construct a bargain with 'natives'. Where Grant and his supporters wished for their Christian world to refashion the Hindu, Company officialdom saw in this a hazardous collision of values, political institutions and religion. They had barely managed to get comfortable in the country, and here was a proposal to try and seize not just land but the minds and emotions of its people, through spiritual crusades. Put off by their reluctance, Grant escalated the battle to Parliament next. In 1793, his friend, William Wilberforce—celebrated for his campaign against slavery, and who proclaimed Hinduism a 'grand abomination'—moved a resolution in the House of Commons. Declaring it Britain's 'bounden duty' to facilitate 'religious and moral improvement', his hope was to have these goals listed in the Company's charter, now up for renewal. But the leadership at India House—the Company's headquarters—objected. Besides, Europe was unsettled after the French Revolution, and some feared that spreading Christian ideas in India risked also transmitting notions of liberty: a threat to British power. So, in the end, the charter was renewed without the so-called 'pious clause'. As Wilberforce said, 'My clauses thrown out . . . and our territories in Hindostan, twenty millions of people included, are left in the undisturbed and peaceable possession . . . of Brama [the Hindu deity].'[59]

But it was not a complete loss, and with time, the missionary cause would thrive, setting the tone for the Victorian age with all its cultural judgement and self-righteous stiffness. To begin with, Britain was urbanizing, with an expanding working class. This segment was as attractive to evangelical Christians as 'heathens',[60] evangelicalism being a response to 'the emergence of modern urban society'; a novel form of faith for novel times, where spiritual authority was no longer the preserve of the church.[61] Printing and the ease with which texts could now circulate, backed by rising literacy, democratized religious practice. The Religious Tract Society, for example, in the fifty years since its founding in 1799 'produced nearly half a billion tracts, broadsheets, and handbills'.[62] Evangelical Christianity conceived of each individual as a means for spiritual and social rejuvenation. One did not need to be a priest or a churchman; one could be a pensioner distributing tracts in taverns, or a cart driver dropping pamphlets on the road—faith would piggyback on secular life.[63] Nor was religion about listening to sermons; it had become a *movement* led by charismatic men of diverse origins, inviting people to participate. For instance, among the first missionaries sent to India by the Baptist Missionary Society (BMS, established 1792) was William Carey, a shoemaker.[64] Some, in fact, lampooned evangelicals precisely for allowing 'every inspired cobbler, or fanatical tailor' to presume he had 'a kind of apostolic right to assist in the spiritual siege'.[65] One critic went so far as to even call BMS men 'detachments of maniacs'.[66] This did not deter evangelicals from building, innovating and blending radical methods with conservative ideas; change threatened the establishment but to them, offered opportunity.[67] Religion, as it emerged from rarefied spaces into a world where all rules were up for debate, saw also the rise of a 'religious public': a large segment of laypeople interested in faith, and keen to serve. And if Company and Parliament rebuffed their agenda, evangelicals cultivated this very class with a near-entrepreneurial drive, to swell their clout.

To be clear, the Company *did* let a fair amount of missionary activity pass. When Carey arrived in India, he attached himself to an indigo planter with evangelical sympathies. While local authorities knew exactly who the new man was and why he was in Bengal, on paper, they classed Carey as merely an indigo maker.[68] In 1800, he learnt he could preach even in Calcutta, so long as he avoided Government House.[69] In the peninsula, governed from Madras, European missionaries had become a fixture over previous centuries, so official attitudes were relatively relaxed. In 1806, thus, agents of the London Missionary Society (LMS, established 1795) reported how they had received every support from the administration.[70] Officials too were torn between the contradictions of their position: A future governor general wondered how 'we who pay the Brahmins' could deny Protestants.[71] But given that vending faith was a lower priority than trading goods and keeping order, much depended on individual officers' attitudes. U-turns occurred repeatedly. In the 1790s, thus, paranoia about French ascendancy in Europe caused the Bengal authorities to view BMS missionaries—some of whom espoused republican politics[72]—with suspicion.[73] In 1806, at Vellore, mutiny by 'native' troops made the Company more guarded. The British had standardized soldiers' uniforms, including turbans, moustaches, etc. But as was later noted, while nothing 'could appear more trivial to the public interests than the length of the hair on the upper lip of a sepoy, yet to the individual himself the shape and fashion of the whisker is a badge of his caste, and an article of his religion'. By interfering, rumours gained ground—not helped by missionary peregrinations in the region—that the redesigned uniforms were a scheme for mass conversion.[74] Again, evangelicals found themselves at the receiving end of opprobrium. While cordiality was soon reestablished with local authorities, in general these self-appointed white saviours continued to operate in a climate of uncertainty.[75]

In Britain, meanwhile, something of a public feud began—a pamphlet war of recriminations and verbal jousts.[76] In 1807, despite Grant's best efforts from inside the Company system as a director, his associates issued orders stating that, while not hostile to missionaries, they had no desire to 'add the influence of our authority' to religious work in India.[77] One critic attacked these spiritual salesman as 'madmen' preaching a 'puritanical rant of the most vulgar kind'.[78] Of course, it was also convenient to blame every kind of anti-British sentiment among Indians on them, but missionaries supplied adequate cause for this. Some material from the BMS press, for example, was so foul in its censure of Hindu gods and Islam that even Grant was embarrassed.[79] But as renewal of the Company's charter approached in 1813, the evangelical party saw a fresh window. The last time, twenty years ago, they were a nascent force; now, gains had been made. Using all its organizational muscle, the movement was able to excite public support for the 'pious clause'. Meetings were held, thousands of circulars issued and petitions swapped across the country in a signature campaign. India *had* to be 'saved'.[80] Parliamentarians also, observing the growth of the 'religious public', for political self-interest felt they had to be mollified.[81] Government, meanwhile, though still suspicious of freelance missionaries, was warming to the idea of setting up an official outpost of the Church of England in India, if for nothing else, to escape the allegation of being lazy Christians.[82] So when in the summer of 1813, 908 petitions signed by hundreds of thousands reached Parliament—'the greatest number of petitions ever presented' till then—the direction of the wind was clear.[83] And the missionary camp won: The Company's latest charter featured a clause on 'religious and moral improvement'. The British were, from now on required to afford, officially, 'sufficient facilities' in India to all who wished to aid this cause.[84]

How did this turnaround occur? An important contributor was missionary publications, which ranged from standalone travel accounts 'revealing' the depth of misery in India, to exchanges in increasingly popular evangelical journals on Britain's duty to export religious enlightenment. It was just the kind of emotional fodder to sway the public. Claudius Buchanan, a Company chaplain who also served at the College of Fort William in Calcutta, established to train young officers,[85] for instance, published *Christian Researches* in 1811. Ostensibly a travelogue, it offered a colourful (and coloured) picture of India. The author 'knew', thus, that he was approaching the Jagannath temple at Puri because human bones were strewn around this 'Valley of Death'. The deity was the 'Moloch of Hindostan' (a child-sacrifice craving pagan god in the Bible); temple sculptures were 'indecent'; when devotees sang, it was not the 'tuneful' Hallelujah but a 'hissing', and pilgrims voluntarily threw themselves to be crushed under the deity's chariot. Buchanan's point was clear: to 'know the state of the people, look at the state of the temple.' And if this significant one was a carnival of sin, imagine, he urged readers, the habits of those that congregated here.[86] They, not missionaries, were the madmen. Next, Buchanan spoke of sati, listing precise numbers of women burnt near Calcutta, evoking righteous disgust by adding how these crimes occurred to the background music of drums and cymbals. Nobody could halt this, for the Company 'acquiesced in its propriety'.[87] In the name of security, the British literally watched women burn. This was contrasted with Tanjore—Serfoji's seat—where there were 'native' Christians. Here, happily,

Buchanan saw 'becoming dress, humane affections, and rational discourse'. There were 'no skulls, no self-torture, no self-murder, no dogs and vultures tearing human flesh!' 'Christian virtues' had transformed the 'feeble-minded Hindoo': evidence of the 'excellence and benign influence' of the Englishman's faith.[88] In Bengal, under Company rule, that is, error prevailed; in the south, meanwhile, under the nose of a Christian-friendly *Indian* prince, 'natives' were saved.[89] What more substantiation was necessary to support the evangelical camp?[90]

Such writing was oriented towards a broad goal: a change in Company policy, making full use of the power of shame. Jagannath was, after all, under British protection. A table showed sums 'the English Government' dispensed, including for the maintenance of dancing girls. 'How much I wish,' Buchanan thundered, that the Company bosses in London 'could have attended the wheels of Juggernaut' and seen what they condoned.[91] The appeal of this

A woman committing sati, engraving by Bernard Picart (c. 1730), from the Wellcome Collection.

kind of literature is clear: It entertained and shocked, but most importantly, underlined the belief that the British—with the Bible—were obliged to lift up the world. Its popularity was also not in doubt: Within two years, in the run-up to the renewal of the Company's charter, Buchanan's book went into a dozen reprints.[92] Even a quarter-century later, *Christian Researches* was inspiring young men to join the missionary cause.[93] The author too was aware that he was catering to demand. In 1805, his previous work, besides arguing for shining the Church of England's light on India, spoke of civilizing 'natives' as a matter of honour; of raising *'our* just and generous principles' against *'their* base and illiberal maxims'.[94] The appendices to this volume included pages on supposedly normal local customs. Hindus, it was stated, fed children to sharks and crocodiles; drowned their sickly relatives; performed bloody rites and so on.[95] Equally, the much-discussed issue of security—the sternest argument against missionary fervour—was dismissed. In Buchanan's view, even in 'ten centuries the Hindoos will not be as wise as the English'; raising their moral stature would 'never injure the [Company's] interests'. In other words, Christianizing India was not equated with liberating India; vassals of Britain they were, and as such they would continue—only now in the good books of god.[96] They themselves wanted it this way: Referring (selectively) to Serfoji, Buchanan wrote how he positively wished for his 'wicked subjects' to be turned into 'honest and industrious men'. All with the aid of pious souls from the West.[97]

But what stirred public interest was also the counterarguments. This contest between opposing groups on the India question constituted its own brand of what we see in televised news debates in India today; what is called 'infotainment'. For instance, Buchanan's 1805 book provoked a rejoinder in *A Vindication of the Hindoos* (1808), by an unnamed Bengal officer.[98] Offering an 'impartial' survey, the author argued that Hindus had no need for Christian tutelage. They were a quite 'correct and moral people'; if there was superstition, this would recede without 'rash' foreign interjections.[99] Where Buchanan exaggerated the worst of popular practice, this critic cited sublime passages from Sanskrit texts like the Gita and the orientalists' favourite sastras. Page after page extracted content meant to appeal to Christian sensibilities, at times elevating Hindu ideas over Christianity. Many values evangelicals cherished were also shown to be internal to 'native' traditions, thus. Additionally, quotations from Mughal sources in praise of the Hindu 'character' were carried, as if saying that this last set of conquerors recognized in Hindus virtues, not vice—and that the British must follow precedent. Moreover, the 'Bengal Officer' warned that missionaries would attract only low castes; the church would grow associated with degradation, not moral upliftment.[100] As for practices such as sati, the wild numbers circulated by missionaries were based on lazy data; it was *not* a pan-Indian, mass practice, and to apply what happened in fairly narrow circles to the totality of Hindu culture was mischief.[101] This did not, of course, end the debate: Buchanan's votaries eviscerated the *Vindication*. A review in the *Christian Observer*, for instance, expressed amusement that its author held Hindu and Christian ideas to be on an equal footing; that he could not see how Christianity alone, 'of all religions', was designed to ensure the 'happiness of the [greatest] mass of the people'.[102] Put simply, Christian ideas were not, and could never be, up for debate. They set the terms against which cultures elsewhere would be interrogated.[103] Or in the acid words of the historian John Pemble, the British were determined to 'civilize others, not to civilize themselves'.[104]

What is instructive here, though, is that even in defending Hindus, friendly white men resorted to cliché and familiar tropes. Indomaniacs romanticized the country, focusing on texts and ideas; those peddling Indophobia picked on the most outrageous, 'exotic' aspects of practice to make their case.[105] In this lay the beginnings of what would guide most future understandings of Hinduism. This was either a spiritual, otherworldly, philosophical faith, pinned to writings in Sanskrit; or it was, at the other extreme, a wild raft of superstitious, devil-worshipping cults. The spectrum of ideas and practice, and their constant negotiations and intertwined coexistence, was lost amid these stark posts.[106] Hinduism, as it was imagined now, had no history, it could not be dynamic and it could not have evolved, or be subject to diversity. It was either this or that—both wickets being fixed by white disputants. Indeed, it might be argued that this was not even wholly about India but a debate on *Britain*: its ideology as an emerging imperial state, and its struggle to refigure contradictions born of change, technology and religious ferment. But given that the British were in power, their narratives of the world would gnaw at Indians also. William Jones had, romantically, observed how the 'greatest singularity of the Hindoo religion' was that it did not persecute 'those of a contrary persuasion'. All views were 'acceptable to the Supreme Being' and each 'adapted to the country where it is established'—a line Hindus took with Ziegenbalg also, as we saw.[107] But now, itself faced with harassment, Hinduism would acquire a new, defensive avatar. To regain agency, brown men—especially those exposed to the colonial state—would also place their religion in the white man's prism. It was like playing ball on a Christian field; Christianity laid the ground on which Hindus constructed their defence. Hinduism would, in key respects, be Christianized, internalizing that distinction between what was 'good' within and what 'bad'. Debates would begin among 'natives' on 'true' Hinduism and mass 'corruption'. They too would jettison the amorphous spectrum, reimagining faith as a defensible monolith; as a fortified, Protestant Hinduism.

Interestingly, however, the 1813 victory in Parliament for the missionary lobby was incomplete. For the new clause still upheld 'the authority of the local Governments' in filtering European access to India. In effect, that is, missionaries would continue to require permission and licences to operate; the subcontinent's gates had *not* been thrown open to all.[108] So too the 'natives' right to 'free exercise of their religion' was affirmed, hinting again that government was not keen to meddle in these matters from the perch of official policy.[109] Indeed, evangelical groups were soon to find that there was barely an improvement from earlier: As the historian Penelope Carson has shown, licences could be denied, and in some cases, they specified provinces, preventing access to others. Permission was contingent on what the government deemed good behaviour, and so, could be withdrawn. Similarly, while there was now an official Church of England bishop in Calcutta, the first occupant of that post was himself cold to evangelical societies—in his view, they trampled on his turf.[110] Of course, the authorities did partner with missions in areas like education but remained on guard to ensure that textbooks produced via such projects did not bear naughty Christian content. And in Madras, when evangelical publications lashed out at local culture, they were promptly censored.[111] As late as 1834, when the bishop of Calcutta—now someone well-disposed to evangelicals— argued for lighter civilian oversight over spiritual traffic in India, the governor general demurred. Referring to his predecessors' 'wise policy', he spoke of 'danger' if government lost control over 'indiscreet or over-zealous' religious professionals.[112] The bishop—the very man who would theatrically 'claim' the Punjab from a boat—was not pleased. This official church representative too began to doubt the British state's moral fidelity.[113]

The propaganda war, therefore, continued even after 1813. This, interestingly, had its peculiar economics, demonstrating how much Indian affairs were dictated by domestic events in Britain. The associations and societies involved in the evangelical cause functioned in one market. By the middle of the nineteenth century, several boasted high revenues: the BMS at £25,000 and the LMS at £75,000, for instance.[114] But they also competed for attention from the same pool of public interest.[115] Tales from India, with tragic widows, pagan customs, blood sacrifices and more were a way to hook interest.[116] Illustrations began to appear in missionary publications, to sustain the reader's animation. For instance, an 1816 issue of the Church Missionary Society (CMS, established 1799) periodical featured a fakir's image. A servant of the true god, the text declared, was 'so affected by the folly and superstition' of this mendicant that he had a drawing made so 'we Christians may see what a sad state the Heathen are in, and do all we can to open their eyes, and to turn them from darkness to light, and from the power of Satan unto God'.[117] The next year, a picture of Jagannath appeared, with a note on its 'monstrous' nature; this feature promised to, next time, also show an engraving of the chariot before which 'deluded' idolaters committed ritual suicide.[118] By Christmas 1817, a depiction of human sacrifice, complete with chopped head, and a trail of blood, made it to print, with an account of the 'indecent mirth and filthy singing' that accompanied this rite. And, of course, the point of these pictures—and the expectation by way of returns—was clarified: Good Christians must 'make great efforts . . . to teach [these people] better'.[119] Given that the CMS journal was a market leader—printing 4,00,000 copies annually by 1824—its hold on British imagination cannot be overstated.[120] The India debate was being arbitrated, that is, not by experts or on terms of sobriety, but by a press with religious bones to pick and zeal to market.

Of course, while missionaries may truly have been revolted by some ugly practices[121]—human sacrifice did happen now and then,[122] and if sati figures were exaggerated,[123] that sati occurred cannot be denied, including of infant 'widows'[124]—in constructing Hinduism for their British audience, they betrayed 'the relish of a voyeur'.[125] And this for reasons not wholly spiritual. As the scholar Geoffrey Oddie has shown, a large portion of the evangelical readership was lower class. It was therefore assumed that along with simple language, the focus of missionary journals must be on lurid externalities rather than complex (read boring) theological questions.[126] Missionary writings were not an exercise in academic comparison but a venture to expand the 'religious public': the

HUMAN SACRIFICE TO THE GODDESS JUGUDDHATREE.

CHRISTIAN FRIENDS—

Some of you may be ready to ask, "Why has that poor man been beheaded?" Read the following dreadful account, which is as true as it is dreadful, and you will understand why he was murdered.

The Female Figure which you see is that of a Heathen Goddess, whom the Hindoos call Juguddhatree. She is represented, as you see, with four arms, and sitting on what they mean for a lion. In one hand she holds a conch, or shell; in another, a discus, or round piece of iron like a quoit; in another, a club; and in another, the flower of the water-lily. The image is painted yellow, and is dressed in red clothes.

The worship of this Goddess is very popular. Large sums of money are sometimes expended on these occasions; especially in illuminations, dances, singing, and the feasting of Brahmins. Nearly 150 singers and dancers are hired; and a number of men are placed as guards, by way of pomp, near the temple.

Much indecent mirth and filthy singing take place. Numbers of men dance stark-naked before the image—AND THINK THIS THE WAY TO HEAVEN! the holy Brahmins, so called, smiling with complacency on those works of MERIT, as the poor creatures consider them.

Bloody sacrifices and offerings are presented to this Goddess and other Deities of the deluded Hindoos. Sheep, goats, and other animals, are thus sacrificed. Near the temple is fixed an instrument for cutting off the head of the animal. The form of this instrument may be seen in the picture. The neck is laid on the sharp edge, and the sacrificer cuts off the head at one blow. The Hindoos are very ambitious of the honour of cutting off the head of the animal cleverly, at the time of these sacrifices. If it be not done at one blow, the man is driven away

*No.* VIII. *Christmas,* 1817.      [Watts, Printer, Crown Court, Temple Bar.

An image and description of human sacrifice from the CMS's *Missionary Papers* (1817).

economic and political backbone for evangelicalism. This, in fact, handicapped voices resisting the onslaught: *Their* focus on texts and ideas—as seen in the *Vindication*—could convince discerning readers but not the broader mass. Sense, after all, sells less than the sensational; a simplistic picture in black and white soared above verbose attempts at nuance.[127] Besides, editors, whose 'all consuming task was to encourage subscriptions', printed chiefly such reports as offered a cocktail of pity, disgust and horror to persuade readers to open their purses.[128] And once a set of themes began to 'work', they were recycled relentlessly, as in earlier centuries.[129] Jagannath, thus, was a recurring tale of perversion, with Buchanan cited repeatedly. Even wording was copied, growing ingrained: Three decades after *Christian Researches* appeared, Bishop Wilson also, when describing a visit to Puri, called it a 'valley of death'.[130] Of course, he had fresh censure to add, but he did not hesitate to credit Buchanan as the original fount of his feelings. So also with sati, statistics made little difference; it had set itself in public opinion as essential to Hinduism.[131] A subcontinent, with a formidable range of customs and beliefs, much debate and disagreement, was reduced, in this way, to an inventory of violent but arresting stereotypes. Again.

Ideologically slanted (and commercially profitable) writing on Hinduism continued, therefore, steadily nurturing condescension among the British. Some books, such as William Ward's *A View of the History, Literature, and Religion of the Hindoos* (1815), attempted to guilt those who were still suspicious of missionary narratives.[132] Let these apologists, Ward declared, 'assist the bramhuns . . . while the fire is seizing the limbs of the young and unfortunate Hindoo widow'. Or 'join the dance, stark naked . . . before the image of [the goddess]'.[133] The language of moral outrage worked: Ward's book too enjoyed multiple editions and wonderful sales. It hardly mattered that the author's estimate of 10,000 yearly satis in Bengal was based on assumptions and mathematical gymnastics; this when the actual record was 378 in the year of his book's printing.[134] Others used what they portrayed as reason to make a comparison. George Mundy in *Christianity and Hindooism Contrasted* (1827), thus, tried to demonstrate how the Bible projected a consistent idea of god; the sastras, however, were confused, with 'fictitious' deities. The Christian god was pure, while Hindu pretenders were 'addicted to every vice', requiring 'profane songs' and 'indecent dancing'—how could anyone with the thinnest claim to common sense not tell which faith was superior?[135] Then, lastly, there were translations like the French missionary Jean-Antoine Dubois's *Description of the Character, Manners, and Customs of the People of India* (1817). Allegedly plagiarized, this book, with detailed notes on caste and Brahmins, was even purchased and published by the Company to serve as an official manual. But despite a relatively calm tenor, Dubois too did not hesitate to suggest that there was ultimately little keeping 'natives' from cannibalism.[136] He urged non-intervention, that is, not because Hindu culture had merits but from fear that experiments to reform would make a bad product worse. For Hindus simply would not surrender their odious ancestral proclivities.[137]

But perhaps the most damaging of this literary surge was James Mill's three-volume *The History of British India* (1817)—a 'judging history' he published without once setting foot in the country it decried. This, in the historian Thomas Trautmann's words, would become 'the single most important source of British Indophobia' hereon.[138] Mill, entirely guided by existing European writings as research material, in a sense bookended what had begun in the age of Warren Hastings. The scholarly foundation of Mill's critique, in fact, was works which had come into circulation from that period—writings we know were garbled and full of limitations.[139] Unsurprisingly, with imperfect sources, Mill's conclusions too were deformed. For instance, his denunciation of 'Hindu law', which he used to demonstrate that Hinduism, even in its most authentic, original sources—so attractive to orientalists—was execrable. As proof he cited such prescriptions in Sanskrit like one throwing adulterous women to be torn apart by dogs.[140] This when, in *practice*, adultery in Maratha country, to give a single illustration, was addressed primarily through fines and imprisonment.[141] Nobody, that is, was shredded. Because, however, translations of ancient texts by white men were certified as 'law', they became Mill's truth. It was this 'reliable' information—which most Hindus would not have recognized—that the man used to lambast them, both in the past and present. He might as well have cited historical fiction. Instead, Mill—who had once trained to become a pastor[142]—was touted as a formidable expert and awarded a job at India House in 1819.[143] And, his *History*, which at one point likens the Hindu to 'the eunuch' for excelling in the 'qualities of a slave', became prescribed reading for trainee civil servants.[144] Even before they sailed out from Britain, that is, officers had reason to prejudge India. The Hindu world, as constructed by the West and its itinerant saviours, simply could not escape condemnation.[145]

In December 1836, John Poynder (1779–1849), a Company shareholder, delivered an impassioned oration before fellow owners of India stock in London. His topic was the pilgrim tax, levied on all who visited the greatest Hindu shrines in the subcontinent. It was a traditional impost, the British having inherited the system from 'native' rulers they displaced—at Puri from the Marathas, for example. Not surprisingly, this infuriated evangelicals. By now, this lobby was even stronger, having won a substantial triumph: The renewal of the Company's charter in 1833 removed all preconditions to work in India. Gates limiting missionary access were finally dismantled. So, the movement pressed other demands—such as shirking profits from idolatry. The numbers, Poynder contended, were shameful. Four shrines alone had, between 1812 and 1834, delivered a million pounds sterling, after all expenses, to the Company through pilgrim taxes.[146] Citing everyone from Buchanan and Grant to Mill and Ward, Poynder decried this as 'sin'.[147] Company men, of course, had a different point of view, and were loath to forfeit this surplus. Early gains from Jagannath alone, for instance, had funded infrastructure projects, including a military road.[148] But for missionaries, this balance sheet was troublesome. After all, whenever they railed against idolatry, Hindu interlocutors coolly pointed to shrines maintained by the Company; to the revenue the British smilingly amassed from their gods.[149] To mollify evangelicals, then, London in 1833 had also issued orders terminating the pilgrim tax and ending Company participation in temple affairs. But in what looked to critics like deceit, they left the timeline for implementation to men on the ground.[150] And three years later, their officers were conveniently vacillating.

Lord Auckland, then governor general, tried to position things in a manner that would pacify critics like Poynder. The Company, he explained, only protected Hindu institutions as the law preserves 'a prostitute from robbery or a brothel from burglary'. It was not endorsing idolatry, only doing its bare minimum by way of duty. As for profits, missionaries should be relieved that instead of enriching the 'Hindoo priesthood', the pilgrim tax subsidized 'useful' schemes.[151] But even if Auckland dismissed the fuss, there is no denying that many of his own subordinates were now on the missionary side. As the 'religious public' grew at home, men reared within began to populate Company ranks, carrying evangelical motives into the state machinery.[152] In fact, by 1834, one of Charles Grant's sons would be governor of Bombay: the place where Elphinstone had, in the previous decade, pushed a policy of conciliation.[153] James Thomason, who would govern the North-Western Provinces for ten years from 1843, was the son of a Company chaplain.[154] The father of Lord Macaulay—who sat on Auckland's council—actively supported the 1813 campaign for the 'pious clause', personally distributing 1,00,000 circulars.[155] General Henry Havelock, who would play a key military role during the Great Rebellion, was son-in-law to Joshua Marshman, a BMS colleague of Carey's.[156] Missionaries, in fact, actively began to locate sympathizers in government, adjusting strategies in India accordingly. The LMS, thus, chose Salem, in Tamil Nadu, for a new post because its British collector was known to be a devout evangelical Christian.[157] More generally, debates on India and evangelicalism had formed the backdrop during formative years for an increasing number of officers. Lord Dalhousie, for instance, who cheered Duleep Singh's conversion, was born one year after *Christian Researches* first appeared. The future governor general's Britain was very different from Warren Hastings's world; their perception of Indians too diverged.[158]

This accretion of internal pressure—with a comparable dilution of empathy for the Company's 'native' subjects—had been in the making for decades. As far back as 1802, when Carey and Buchanan taught at the College of Fort William, its students (future civil servants) were writing essays that spoke of 'thousands' of 'human victims' annually slaughtered in India for 'horrid deities' at 'polluted altars'.[159] In the 1810s, the British representative at the Travancore rani's court not only made her give grants to the CMS but also had missionaries appointed judges in her state. The man was only imitating his predecessor—an uncle of Macaulay's, who had used *his* influence to promote the LMS.[160] In 1822, the governor of Madras, similarly, complained that a sub-collector at Bellary not only showed 'prejudice' against 'natives' but also crossed a line by using state resources to distribute 'moral and religious tracts'. Worse, the man was unrepentant when accused of being a missionary in civilian clothing; instead, he cited scripture and divine authority for his actions.[161] Indeed, a future Madras governor himself would, less than twenty-five years after this, endorse employing the Bible as a school textbook.[162] So also, the use of Company officials and troops in organizing temple celebrations—requiring vast numbers of peasants to be commandeered—generated uneasiness.[163] Was it healthy to expect a white official, as at Surat, to propitiate annually a local river goddess with coconuts?[164] Increasingly, responses were in the negative. One man refused to show himself at a festival as it happened on a Sunday.[165] Another in 1838 resigned on the count that when joining the civil service, he had not signed up to 'assist in, and uphold, the idolatrous worship of India'.[166] In Dhaka, officials openly defied orders to let a case of sati proceed; it created a moral conundrum for the judge deciding the matter too, who observed that as a man he rejoiced at the officers' stand, but in his formal capacity he could not brook disobedience.[167] Even so, whatever superiors said, much remained contingent on who was on the ground. Sometimes a senior officer might aid missionaries, while a junior thwarted them.[168] If, as occurred in Peshawar in the early 1850s, one official was hostile to evangelicals, his successor might reverse the attitude, showing welcome.[169] Within Company ranks too, then, a war of principles was underway.[170]

In these circumstances, even Auckland—who disagreed with the 'spirit of fanaticism' that had crept into the British government—had to grudgingly acquiesce to change.[171] Tolerance for the Company acting as 'the dry nurse of Vishnu' was dwindling.[172] Under pressure at home, the directors were practically forced to reiterate their orders, and by 1840, the pilgrim tax was terminated in Bengal.[173] Bombay and Madras followed suit.[174] In the latter presidency, over the coming years, the state withdrew from the religious space: Small village shrines were handed over to priests, larger ones to local committees, major pilgrim centres to influential community leaders and so on.[175] This general policy, however, upset Indians: In 1831, towards the end of his life, Serfoji took it as an affront that white officials were absenting themselves from Tanjore's festivals—after all, these religious events were pregnant with political symbolism also.[176] Other old practices too were dying: The firing of salutes by British troops at Hindu events, their placing of ritual offerings (like those coconuts at Surat) before regional gods and so on. Everything that, earlier in the century, was construed as a small price to pay for power was now considered wicked.[177] Or as one Company man remarked to a subordinate, 'every act' they were obliged to perform in connection with Hindu temples made them liable, as *Christians*, to the charge of idolatry.[178] The British no longer felt any incentive to fit the 'native's' world; it was the 'native' who had to reconcile to rescripted rules. Auckland was distressed: Allowing 'mistrust' to emerge about the Company's pledge of 'toleration' was unwise.[179] But by Dalhousie's era, even at the top there was little room for such sensitivities. Not only did this governor general support evangelicals, he was also viewed as endorsing them when he granted converts the right of inheritance in their original families. Hindus filed thousands of petitions in protest.[180] One went so far as to ask: 'If the eldest son of the King of England becomes a Catholic, will he be allowed to inherit the throne?'[181] But there was no answer because India's rulers were no longer listening.

Understandably, wrath towards missionaries was on the ascendant in Hindu circles, especially among high-caste groups. As early as 1800, when the BMS acquired its first convert—a carpenter—a crowd of 2000 reportedly gathered in objection.[182] In the south, Catholics were not as much of a fear—de Nobili's strategies were still in place—but Protestants, backed by power and 'more aggressive' in tone, looked a threat.[183] The conversion of Brahmins was advertised with grating triumphalism: As Carey remarked, 'What great thing is it to have a Carpenter and a distiller reject their cast [sic]?'[184] It was the cream they

The BMS's first convert, as depicted in George Smith's *The Life of William Carey* (1885).

craved. Zeal showed, and not always tastefully: One BMS proponent was compared, by his own colleague, to a hawk eyeing its prey, when he identified potential targets for preaching.[185] Another actually went insane on finally procuring two converts after years of toil.[186] Missionaries also evinced a devious delight in their scholarly pursuits: The BMS project of translating the Ramayana was combined with joy that 'Satan' was to 'be shot in his own bow'; sales of these 'destructive fables' would 'supply a fund for circulating the oracles of Truth'.[187] (A Hindu, meanwhile, reciprocated by describing the BMS's Hindi-language Bible as 'milk in a vessel of dog's skin'.[188]) Remarkably, even at this late date, dislike for Protestant reverends stemmed from the insistence that Christianity was the *only* path to god. The whole of the Hindu world was built on plurality. The Christian picture of things, however, seemed totalitarian. So, over a century and a half after Ziegenbalg was told off in the south, a northern Hindu critic would also question this presumption. Nobody, it was confirmed, objected to Christ, whose teachings were 'nectar for the soul'. 'But that *only* Christ was the saviour' was hubris.[189] Missionaries would not—could not—give way. And their unyielding stance triggered Indian restlessness. A CMS man in Benares—holiest of Hindu sites—noticed this in the 1840s. Ten years ago, preachers were laughed at; told 'no one will believe you', he reported. Now, however, Hindus admitted: 'You have already conquered our bodies, and you are in a fair way of conquering our minds also.'[190] It sounds like a compliment, but the fact is that the missionary had become a threat.[191]

Naturally, many on the 'native' side now prepared to resist. This could take the form of jeering and tearing up of pamphlets, as in 1836, in Nagapatam in Tamil country.[192] Or, as occurred in Travancore when that evangelical British agent retired, the Christians he had installed in high places were sacked.[193] One text even constructed a Puranic-style narrative in which hell faces a serious depopulation due to Hindus' devotion to their gods; it is to restore 'cosmic balance' that a false avatar, Jesus, arrives to hoodwink people—and resupply hell with waylaid souls.[194] But a key means was the public disputation. Charles Leupolt, that Benares-based CMS missionary, noted how bazaars, streets and riverbanks were all fields for toil.[195] Predictably, arguments flew back and forth. Once, for instance, Leupolt got into a debate on god's nature. According to a Hindu school of belief, the supreme exists in all beings and things; for Leupolt, however, this was equal to cutting god into pieces. There was, he stressed, a distinction between god and his creation. But his Hindu discussant brushed this off. The sun, he declared, was only one; and yet, it could be reflected in a thousand vessels. This did not mean there were a thousand suns, only that the same power manifested in myriad ways.[196] Leupolt was not convinced. If god were present in all beings, every thief could blame his thievery on divine play.[197] There was something very immodest and shameful, he believed, in the Hindu claim that god existed in all of them. His memoirs also speak of other obstacles. Once a fakir appeared, anxious to convert, only to be dragged away. Another time, Leupolt was talking to a crowd, until interrupted by a monkey dressed in the British soldier's uniform, sent in by miscreants. Even Hindus amenable to becoming 'disciples', insisted they should not be branded Christians or made to renounce caste.[198] This might have been an option for de Nobili two centuries ago but not for the CMS man; so, sympathetic candidates also turned away.[199]

Soon, Hindu–missionary debates, in fact, became grand spectacles, watched by heaps of people. Bombay was the scene of many such events. The *Oriental Christian Spectator* reported one from 1830, between a 'native' supporter of John Wilson—a Scottish evangelical—and Brahmins, held over several days, with a hundred listeners. As 'the onion and musk are known by their odour', vented the Indian convert, so Vishnu's avatars could be separated from Christ. This time the argument we witnessed in Benares was inverted: The Hindu side accused *Christians* of dividing the

A Christian missionary preaching at a Hindu festival from the CMS's *Missionary Papers* (1851).

almighty into three—as the father, the son and the holy spirit. To this, the convert brought up the analogy of the sun! There was the sun, its light and heat, and yet, it was all one. Wilson stepped in to highlight the absurdity of the incarnations: One of them arrived to retrieve the Vedas, lost when the god of creation was asleep. But how could god, who was omnipresent, not know the hiding place? Could god sleep? When, another time, the Hindu party repeated their proposition that there were many paths to salvation, Wilson disagreed. There was one god and he could only have created a single set of laws—this was no buffet.[200] To which a Brahmin demanded: 'why did God not give [these laws] to us'; did god make a mistake or had he *intended* for Hindus to be distinct? Clearly the debate was heading nowhere, and by the fourth day, only thirty men stayed listening.[201] One thing was obvious, however: Wilson and his aide had mastered Puranic material, skilfully summoning evidence from within Hindu traditions. In excoriating the use of idols, thus, they confidently quoted Sanskrit critiques of the practice.²⁰² Besides, the entire exchange was held in the region's Marathi language, which these men had painstakingly learnt.²⁰³ The Hindus realized they would have to match this rigour.²⁰⁴

A worthy opponent appeared the next year, and a six-day debate followed. In fact, after the public performance, Morobhat Dandekar, the Brahmin speaker, printed his arguments in his *Hindudharmasthapana* (*The Foundations of Hinduism*, 1832). Dandekar thought it puzzling that missionaries complained so much about idolatry—as if Hindus held the images themselves to be gods—when, in fact, it was a means to make divinity accessible. Their very fundamental understanding of the religion, in other words, was flawed. On avatars, Dandekar cited the tripartite Christian idea of god. 'If . . . these three Divinities occasion no bewilderment of [the] mind,' how, he asked, 'can the worship of Rama . . . and other gods occasion . . . bewilderment'?²⁰⁵ Moreover, as Hindus collected in temples, Christians gathered regularly 'to take a piece of bread . . . muttering a few words to eat it up . . . drink spirits . . . [and] pour water on the head'.²⁰⁶ In principle, then, temple worship was similar to attending church. On Christ, while Dandekar thought it estimable that he suffered pain on a cross for humankind, Hindu gods achieved those precise results without 'submitting to a reproachful death'.²⁰⁷ That is, to argue that Jesus was superior because he bled, and that Hindu avatars, on account of merrier lives, were inferior was silly; they just did their job better.²⁰⁸ But more to the point, why did god *let* Christ suffer? 'What! Had he no other ways of saving the world?' It was Christianity which, by arguing that god's hands were tied, brought an 'indelible stain' on his greatness.²⁰⁹ Hinduism was more logical. It perceived the almighty as a 'shopkeeper', who 'with a view of bringing all the customers' to his counter took diverse forms.²¹⁰ But then again, Dandekar finished, it was 'the way of all men to expose the faults of others . . . never to look at their own'—and Christian missionaries were particularly susceptible to this defect.²¹¹

Naturally, Wilson felt this written charge had to be addressed, publishing *An Exposure of the Hindu Religion* (1832). It followed the standard approach: There were false religions and only one that was true; Hindu ideas, such as that the earth rested on a tortoise, were puerile; the Puranas were puddles of confusion; its deities had promiscuous tastes and so on.[212] To this, Narayan Rao, a friend of Dandekar's, issued his *Svadeshadharmabhimani* (*Espouser of His Country's Faith*, 1834).[213] His effort was to demonstrate that the Bible 'even on its own terms' was a mess.[214] Why did god rest after creation; was he lazy? He made man in his own image; did that mean god looked human, suggesting that Christians too, effectively, had an idol in mind? Why did he not create Eve as he did Adam—why steal a rib?[215] In what was becoming a tedious pattern, Wilson returned fire with *A Second Exposure of the Hindu Religion* (1834). Sanskrit too was deployed. John Muir, a civil servant with evangelical leanings, produced the *Matapariksa* (*An Examination of Religions*, 1839), which provoked three responses from pandits over six years.[216] One of these soberly reasoned with Muir; another, citing Valtaya, Hiyuma and Pena—Voltaire, Hume and Thomas Paine!—was incandescent, casting aspersions on Jesus, adding that the real spiritual journey was from Christianity *to* Hinduism.[217] But a transition to print did not terminate public disputations: As late as 1857, Bombay witnessed a clash between a Hindu thinker, Vishnubawa Brahmachari, and missionaries. Conducted before 2000 spectators, their verbal tourney lasted months.[218] Wit helped. When told that his intellect equalled that of an ant against an elephant, the Brahmin smiled: '[A]n ant can creep into the trunk of an elephant and cause [its] death.'[219] In this instance, the Hindus claimed victory, for after a point, the missionaries did not return.[220]

Unexpected reversals of this type could afflict Hindus also, though. Among the critics of Muir's Sanskrit treatise was a man called Nilakantha Goreh (1825–95). He began his spiritual life as a staunch Brahmin—evidently, he refused to study at the Government Sanskrit College in Benares because this entailed dealing with Europeans.[221] So too, he gave up the worship of Siva for Vishnu, because the latter, he believed, better fit the exacting standards of the scriptural corpus and Hindu theological principles. In fact, Goreh attacked Siva's character, not unlike missionaries, inviting worry that he might one day defect.[222] Yet, the young man's first opinion of missionaries was decidedly poor: 'He heard [them], only to despise, or to show his superior knowledge and skill,' we are told.[223] Why, he was only twenty when he produced his rejoinder to Muir's *Matapariksa*—the 'sharpest' of the three that appeared.[224] Since Sanskrit had a small audience, he next composed prose in Hindi, poking fun at Christianity.[225] He actively went out to argue with a CMS missionary hoping to 'compel them either to leave the country or to confine themselves to the instruction of the Christians'.[226] Except that by 1848, following engagement with the CMS, it was Goreh who became Christian. This of course came as a shock to his Hindu kin and the community in Benares.[227] When his wife was baptized—dying days after—they blamed it on trauma from being forced to venerate the Bible.[228] But the real concern was that Goreh, a Sanskrit scholar, would become a dangerous instrument in the missionary camp. And indeed, the man would eventually publish *A Rational Refutation of the Hindu Philosophical Systems* (1862).[229] Coming from an ex-Brahmin, the attack was sharp; it seemed almost a betrayal.[230]

Though missionary gains in numbers remained modest, high-profile cases like this one boosted morale. If Goreh, a Brahmin, were won in the north, in the same period, the son of a rajah of Cochin in the south also converted. Jacob Rama Varma (1814–56), as he would be known, was a Vaishnava, who impressed his royal father by becoming, early in life, a fine scholar of Sanskrit and the Puranas. During a course of study in English at a mission school, however, he developed an interest in Christianity. His teacher was a CMS missionary and both agreed that image worship was crude. From this initial point of conjunction, Varma soon found himself listening to sermons. A lucky escape from death convinced him of Christ's power, and a little later, when unwell, he vowed that if he survived, he would convert. And so, in 1835, the rajah's boy went Christian.[231] To Hindus, of course, such cases were worrying: The jibe that people converted for money, to escape their inferior station or from other opportunistic motives did not explain high-status converts.[232] If, that is, men already possessed of social, cultural and material capital *still* opted to exit their parental faith, Christianity clearly offered something meaningful.[233] Or worse, there was a gap in Hindu ideas and a point of weakness. But high-caste harvests were not easy for Protestants to accommodate either. While as late as 1870, a missionary would speak of the 'thrill' of converting Brahmins,[234] this meant having to look away from ingrained Hindu legacies. Many Brahmin converts, thus, thought of themselves as *Brahmin* Christians; conversion did not mean throwing out 'caste dignity'.[235] After all, as one scholar observes, just as race did not miraculously vanish when the brown man joined the white missionary's church, so too caste could never recede by fiat.[236] Where Catholics like de Nobili embraced this—transformed it into opportunity even—modern evangelicals struggled.[237]

Jacob Rama Varma, courtesy of the University of Tübingen.

In 1841, the editor of *Bombay Gazette* was compelled to resign. His crime was simple: allowing outrageous Indian opinions to be aired in his newspaper. It began innocuously, with the man inviting 'natives' to express views on matters that would 'benefit the Indian people'.[238] One mid-twenties critic, Bhaskar Pandurang (1816–47)—brother of the teacher Dadoba Pandurang, mentioned in the last chapter—took up the offer, and from July-end to October, sent in eight letters. Signing them 'A Hindoo', these are counted among the earliest critiques of British imperialism by an Indian; indeed, in his very first letter, our 'Hindoo' hoped to 'methodically' make his case.[239] Conquest, he began, was a fact of history; he would not begrudge the British that they had seized India by the rules of power. But what then? Unless conquered people were invested in the new order, resistance was natural. And yet, instead of conciliating Indians, 'You keep yourselves quite aloof' and 'conduct yourselves with such haughtiness and pride as if you were quite a distinct and superior order of beings'. Racism, that is, would not do. India 'gained nothing' from British rule, Pandurang added, the white man's claims of bringing the land peace being 'humbug'. 'Natives', for example, were asked to be grateful that the Company had ended the predations of mercenary armies and dangerous tribes. And yet 'your trading system' had 'more effectually emptied our purses in a few years than the predatory excursions of these tribes could do in some five or six hundred years'.[240] 'You plunder us on all sides', he went on, and 'pompously' point to 'petty things' like public infrastructure. Sure, the British might not oppress like 'Barbarians', but this was because they didn't need to; 'under the garb of law and justice' they possessed fancier tools of extraction.[241] Oppression was still the primary feature of empire, and no quantity of gloss and sophistry could mask this.

Where religion was concerned, Pandurang believed things laughable. The Mughals too sneered at Hinduism, but they did not push Hindus away from office and respect. Besides, when someone converted, there were tangible benefits. But what did the Company offer? 'Can you point out a single instance of a Native who has embraced' Christianity and was subsequently 'nominated to a high civil appointment' or 'treated on equal terms with his white skined [sic] Brethren?'[242] British dislike of sati was touching, and certainly it was bad to burn widows, but expressions of 'common humanity vanish away in the mighty vortex of your *political* cruelty'.[243] This was also why good rajahs were pushed off their thrones, for the British had a shady incentive in propping up the 'weak and imbecil [sic]' as exemplars of 'native' character.[244] To civilize 'natives' that is, those 'natives' would constantly have to be projected as uncivilized. In any case, how was the Indian character to improve? 'You have taken away our money . . . made us wholly dependent on your bounty', filling the gap with unsolicited lectures on morality.[245] Writers, with 'the pomposity of words' and a 'show of erudition'—a reference probably to Mill—urged Hindus to be grateful for the empire,[246] but British rule was a 'bitter curse'; government by a 'race of demons'.[247] As Christians, the Company might presume they would get away with this, in the guarantee of 'final beatitude thro' the medium of your Saviour, Jesus Christ'. But it was fallacy: 'How could you dare hope that all your enormous crimes . . . will be pardoned in Heaven?' In fact, the British were mocking god. But then again, 'the most treacherous are always the most prosperous'.[248] Perhaps greed in the present was worth the risk of eternal damnation.[249]

Pandurang's criticism of Company rule, in fact, marks the context within which the religious entanglements between Hindus and missionaries were occurring. It was symptomatic of a new dynamic in India: the *political* fight between 'native' and colonizer. Talk of faith did not, that is, emerge in a vacuum, and debates around it were merely an outlet for a veritable basket of grievances. Evidence of this appears in interesting ways. In 1828, for instance, a missionary found that in north Indian villages, at the annual enactment of the Ramayana, the epic's villains were dressed like the governor general and Company troops.²⁵⁰ So too, press records reveal brown voices articulating resistance. Leupolt in Benares was alive to the threat. Government, by permitting 'natives' Western education were, he wrote, 'nourishing vipers'. Indians were devouring texts to 'expand their minds, and fill their heads with knowledge', not least of which was the language of political rights. And given that these ideas were penetrating 'native' skulls without a simultaneous Christianization of the soul, it could only have heinous consequences: 'Indians [awakened] could in one night destroy all the English throughout the length and breadth of the country.'²⁵¹ He was not wrong: Dandekar's debates with Wilson, for example, were cheered in the 'native' press. In 1823, *The Brahmunical Magazine* warned that if missionaries wished their religion to be viewed warmly, 'you [too] should not throw offensive reflections upon the religion of others'.²⁵² One brown intellectual, in arguing for his countrymen to absorb modern education, similarly asked: 'Is it not owing to the power which knowledge has given to the people of so small . . . a country as England' that they could seize India? 'Why is it thought the most extravagant dream to suppose [then] that *India* should ever conquer England?'²⁵³ In the next year, as the Company's charter was up for renewal, the *Bombay Native Observer* similarly called for a 'total' renovation of British policy; in its extant form, it 'implanted sorrow, misery, and aversion'. Brown men, simply put, were starting to speak up.²⁵⁴

While argued effectively—and sharply—the sentiments Pandurang expressed in English for the benefit of an equally English audience were not unprecedented, however. In fact, they had been building up. As early as 1809, when the *dewan* (minister) of Travancore attempted to box the Company out of Kerala, his proclamation to the people made matching points. The British were welcomed as friends, but they betrayed that trust with 'ingratitude and treachery'. When terms of treaties no longer suited them, he claimed, they revised it using craft and threats, until whole kingdoms were extinguished. Warning that if given further room, they would 'put their own guards in the palaces', 'destroy the royal seal', 'suppress the Brahmanical communities', impose 'exorbitant' taxes, 'put up crosses and Christian flags' and do all that was 'unjust and unlawful', the dewan appealed to Travancore's people to fight.[255] His pitch, simply, was that the Company threatened not just one or two isolated aspects of life but an entire order. And the people responded—an inquiry after the revolt revealed a 'deep rooted' hostility, and a desire for the 'subversion of [the Company's] power'.[256] And this, in an area not even under direct British rule—unlike Bengal, that is, this coastal state remained under a rajah, and *yet*, its people hated the Company. Indeed, the 'most respectable men in the Country, and the mass of the people' had answered the dewan's call from 'a sense of duty'.[257] But what is telling is the dewan's use of the language of justice. Just as British officials and missionaries enlisted moral jargon to back their claims, Hindus here brought forth *their* readings of principle to attack the enemy. To this, of course, were added points of public interest, such as taxes, but the glue binding them was emotion. And emotional union—or at least a simulation of it—with Indians was the Company's perennial infirmity.

In the end, as is well known, the country saw widespread rebellion in 1857. The British would later infantilize 'natives' by dismissing the revolt as provoked by the supply of cartridges greased with animal fat—of cows and pigs—thereby upsetting Hindu and Muslim 'prejudices'. Large parts of the Bengal army mutinied, launching a year-long military resistance.[258] Viewed this way, the rebellion was carnage by an irrational people lashing out over a triviality. But the fact is that the cartridges were merely the match that lit the fire; powder had been accumulating for years. It was feared, thus, that the Company, via the cartridges, use of which entailed loss of caste, was seeking to turn entire regiments Christian.[259] The increasingly visible nexus between the state and missionaries gave credence to rumours. After all, could white men attack Indian religions in the streets without official backing?²⁶⁰ Indeed, evangelicals waved Christian texts at Hindu festivals, including before men attending to the deities.²⁶¹ British love of beef also soured things—by the mid-nineteenth century, an estimated 3,50,000 cows were being slaughtered yearly in India to satiate the white man's palate.²⁶² So, once violence began, righteous judgement was reversed. When English officers demanded the soldiers' loyalty, the reply was: 'You Banchats [sister-fuckers]! have *you* been faithful to the King of Oude [Awadh]?', whose lands had been seized.²⁶³ Economic woes featured too: Every annexation of Indian territory caused disruptions; each time the British 'extinguished a court', it 'narrowed the areas of Indian employment'.²⁶⁴ Company soldiers were drawn, after all, from the rural mass that bore the brunt of British policies.²⁶⁵ Religion gave these grievances moral force, to back which the rebels sought political legitimation from dispossessed 'native' icons, like the Mughal emperor. Indian ideology, frames of thinking and ethnicity were summoned in resisting the Company, bringing together everyone from Brahmins to the 'untouchables' and tribal groups.²⁶⁶ And the realization that 'natives' were capable of such a combination—even if imperfectly—horrified India's foreign masters.²⁶⁷ The danger men like Munro and Malcolm had warned about all those years ago, finally came to pass.²⁶⁸

This is not to suggest that religion played a simply instrumental role. For many, fear of their culture, way of life and identity being

A Hindu soldier of the East India Company, c. 1790–1800, courtesy of the Rijksmuseum.

trampled on was real. And faith was an expression of all that mattered. In Awadh, after its annexation, one rumour announced that the Company was readying to send a hundred missionaries to convert their freshly acquired subjects.[269] When the rebellion failed, and a group of soldiers, on their way to execution, was interrogated, they too said: 'The slaughter of the English was required by our religion.'[270] Even those who did not join the mobilization gave it tacit support: Company policemen remarked to one witness that though ordered to challenge the rebels, they would not do so. 'All black men are one,' and it was 'a matter of religion'.[271] In the south, missionaries heard '[t]errifying rumours' that the rebellion was against Christians, whose religion would be 'exterminated'.[272] Faith became a means here to articulate a variety of concerns. As the historian Rudrangshu Mukherjee writes, religion was 'the source of solidarity and fraternity . . . something that was imbricated with their entire life', informing the ordinary peasant-soldier's view of the world.[273] A proclamation issued by a Mughal prince reflects this. Identifying the common threat—the Company and Christianity—it cast Hindus and Muslims both as defending the correct way of things. Noting the Company's tax policies, the exclusion of Indians from 'posts of dignity', the destruction of Indian industry and so on, the document presented 1857 not as a rebellion but a 'holy war'.[274] In fact, after the collapse of the resistance, when Queen Victoria issued her well-known proclamation of 1858, declaring the end of Company rule for direct government by the British crown, she guaranteed religious non-interference. But even then, a rebel leader declared:

> In the Proclamation it is written, that the Christian religion is true, but no other creed will suffer oppression, and that the laws will be observed towards all. What has the administration of justice to do with the truth or falsehood of a religion? That religion is true which acknowledges one God . . . Where there are three Gods in a religion [Christianity], neither Mussulmans nor Hindoos—nay,

not even Jews, Sun-worshippers, or Fire-worshippers can believe it true. To eat pigs and drink wine, to bite greased cartridges . . . to destroy Hindoo and Mussulman temples on pretence of making roads, to build churches, to send clergymen into the streets . . . to institute English schools . . . while the places of worship of Hindoos and Mussulmans are . . . entirely neglected; with all this, how can the people believe that religion will not be interfered with? The rebellion began with religion, and for it, millions of men have been killed. Let not our subjects be deceived; thousands were deprived of their religion . . . and thousands [preferred to be] hanged rather than abandon their religion.[275]

Hindus and Muslims were one in this—they had been wronged. And the villain of the piece, of course, was the white man. The Company had conquered and betrayed; it had violated treaties and the spirit of justice; it had toppled 'native' founts of authority, while failing to fit the mould and, finally, by allowing missionaries and their cultural project to intrude into India, they had attacked a powerful element of the Indian identity. A leading evangelical had, a few decades before, glibly remarked that no concerted anti-British effort was possible in India, for 'Hindoos resemble an immense number of particles of sand, which are incapable of forming a solid mass. There is no bond of union among them, nor any principle capable of effecting it.'[276] And yet, less than fifty years later, the British empire received its worst, most threatening paroxysm. The Great Rebellion was chaotic, fragmented and had its internal dissonances and problems. Yet, even in the *attempt* to give it an overarching goal, there was danger. Or as verses composed in one rebel leader's camp showed, the emerging Indian sentiment was clear:

We are the masters, Hindustan is ours.
It is the holy country of the people dearer to heaven.
This is in our ownership and Hi[n]dustan is ours.

The massacre of the English during the Great Rebellion, by Gustave Doré (1857), The Print and Drawing Club Fund, the Carter H. Harrison Fund, the Alfred E. Hamill Fund and the purchase account from sale of duplicates, The Art Institute of Chicago.

> The Firangis [British] coming from distant land[s] used deceit;
> Plundered our dear country with both hands.
> Today the martyrs have called upon you, o countrymen:
> Break the chain of slavery and rain fire.
> Hindu, Muslim and Sikh are our brothers.
> This is the flag of freedom to which we salute.[277]

But jolted as the British officialdom were, what impact did events of that blood-soaked year have on missionaries? Evidently nothing that inspired circumspection. Many, in fact, remained steadfast in their convictions, even identifying god's hand in the floundering of the revolt. Or as was declared at a meeting in southern India in 1858, if anything, it was now time to double down and bring yet more pressure on government to promote the Christian cause. 'The system hitherto,' its official statement announced, without any hint of irony, 'has been deference to idolatry and indifference to Christianity. We plead for a reversal of this system.'[278]

And so, the battle—inaugurated in the age of Charles Grant—raged on, unresolved.[279] As for the Hindus, a sense of crisis was clear, to resolve which, answers would need to be found.

SIX

# 'NATIVE LUTHERS'

In the town of Bhagalpur, Bihar, in January 1809 an Englishman had a quarrel with a 'native' of standing. The Company's district collector was waiting 'among some bricks' by the roadside when the Indian passed that way in a palanquin. Provoked that the brown man did not descend and do him salaam, Frederick Hamilton used an 'epithet of abuse', spewing expletives even as a servant in the Indian's retinue vouched that his master simply did not see him. Hamilton was not placated. Mounting his horse, he chased after the palanquin, getting its occupant to climb out and prostrate himself. His 'indecorous' verbal emissions did not cease, though, providing a background score to these happenings. Soon, the whole town heard of the Indian's 'public indignity'. Complaining later to the governor general about the 'degradation' that resulted, the latter asked if this were the standard 'natives' should expect from the British. Sure, in the age of the Mughals, men were expected to grovel to show 'external respect' to their superiors. But was not the Company 'milder' than the regime they replaced? Did they not claim to have introduced an 'enlightened and more liberal policy' as rulers?[1] The

Raja Ram Mohun Roy, as depicted in Jean-Jacques Chabrélie's *L'Inde Francaise, ou Collection de Dessins* (1827).

appeal worked: Hamilton was rebuked, despite influence in the British establishment, and told to learn to behave. As for the 'native', he had won a small but significant triumph, of both principle and self-respect.

The man in the palanquin—Ram Mohun Roy—would go on to become one of the most striking Indians of the century. Born in the 1770s,[2] he belonged to a house of Brahmins who swapped religious and philosophical pursuits for worldly prosperity through bureaucratic service. On his paternal side, his ancestors had served the Mughal state and their *nawabi* representatives, mastering Persian and Arabic in the process—languages Roy also learnt. His mother's family, however, remained wardens of faith, officiating as priests to the goddess Kali. And so, chiefly through maternal influence, it is believed, Roy absorbed Sanskrit and explored the Brahmins' sacred texts also. Added with his own later study of English, this polymath quality would allow the Bengali to cultivate not only erudition but also a new vision for Hindu society. Besides, he was rich. By his late twenties, aided by an inheritance, Roy was a moneylender, whose debtors included Company officials. In his forties, he owned several homes in Calcutta, not to speak of estates that turned in handsome rents. He also worked with more than one civil servant—and so well that one of them continued to engage him despite orders not to do so.[3] And to crown it all, towards the end of his life, he would be granted the title 'rajah' by the Mughal padshah, as whose envoy Roy sailed to Britain, bedazzling a fresh cast of persons.[4]

Given his antecedents, talent and social standing, one can see why Roy felt confident enough to demand action against his maltreatment by Hamilton. In fact, he was used to standing up for himself. He would later recall that already in his teens, he was asking difficult questions of his family on custom and faith.[5] From the opening years of the nineteenth century, Roy's scholarly inquiries would steadily upset everyone—from Muslim clerics, missionaries of the BMS, orthodox Hindus to even his mother (who, in her vehemence, instigated a grandson to sue him for half his property).[6] But while he occasionally needed bodyguards, his convictions won the man respect among intellectuals (including orientalists like H.H. Wilson) and young 'natives'. By the time of his death, in 1833, he would be known even in America; he became, we read, 'the first global Indian'.[7] When Roy arrived in Britain in 1831—statuesque, turbaned and in Mughal robes—crowds gathered to peer at him, resulting in 'police intervention' in at least one town. In London, even as the exactions of fashionable society left Roy physically depleted, he became likely the first Indian to sit in the royal pavilion with the British monarch.[8] The press, besides, was transfixed; soon, newspapers circulated talk of a romantic entanglement with an Englishwoman. Some also believed the Brahmin had fathered a child in Bristol.[9]

But a supposed mixed-race family aside, what is more fascinating is Roy's intellectual journey. He belonged, on the one hand, to a class of Anglophone Indians who did not view British rule as a disaster. When younger, Roy claimed, he felt 'aversion' to the Company, but mature reflection convinced him that British authority would aid the 'amelioration of the natives'; the 'foreign yoke' could translate into an instrument for regeneration.[10] On the other hand, he worked to also defend Hinduism from missionaries. This was not, however, the furious stance of other anti-evangelical figures. Unlike many of them, Roy admitted that there was indeed much in Hinduism that was woeful, and sati, as with foreign critics, topped his list. He judged religion by an ethical yardstick: All that passed his test was welcome; what did not, had to be excreted.[11] And, sati, a 'barbarous and inhuman practice', this husband of two wrote, failed here; it was simply glorified murder.[12] Over time, Roy also creatively reinterpreted scripture, constructing a Hindu rhetoric for reform, while calling out missionary hypocrisy. Indeed, when white men hit Hindus with the charge of idolatry, Roy accepted it but also returned the favour by highlighting corruptions in the Christian religion.[13]

Orientalists lamented Hinduism's decline from ancient glory; Roy sniffed about Christianity's loss of original purity.[14] He was also more than capable of delivering the occasional punch: Encountering racist nonsense about 'Asiatic effeminacy' once, he reminded his interlocutors that Jesus was an 'Asiatic'.[15]

But Roy was not in the business of pitting one faith against the other; all religions, he seemed to suggest, suffered from insincere custodians. To him, religion was not to be conceived of as a defence of dogma but as a celebration of ethical conduct; and to do this, mankind needed no intermediaries. These ideas first appeared in 1803–04 in his Persian exposition, the *Tuhfat-ul-Muwahhidin*.[16] Around the world, Roy observed, humans acknowledged 'One Eternal Being'; and god, in turn, subjected all of humanity to the same rules, emotions, physical limits, joys and so on. If then, rival religious traditions claimed to better represent god or exclusively offer means to serve him, they were only peddling man-made inventions; *institutionalized* faith had no divine authority. The proof lay in how religious regulations were so divergent. For instance, Brahmins claimed god's authority to use idols; Muslims denied idols, insisting *this* was god's real wish. 'Now,' asked Roy, 'are these contradictory precepts ... consistent with the wisdom and mercy of the ... disinterested Creator', or were they purely 'fabrications' by mortals? God only made uniform laws; it was men who 'invent[ed] doctrines' that fostered 'disunion'. It did not matter if the parties in question were Hindus or non-Hindus: They were governed, Roy held, by worldly prejudices. And unlike him, most of society was too 'blind and deaf' to admit this.[17] It seemed a radical take on the idea of religion itself; so radical, in fact, that Roy himself appears to have softened his tone somewhat in future.[18]

Even so, the *Tuhfat* is surprisingly aligned with European Enlightenment thought.[19] Some have tried to demarcate a Western intellectual genealogy for its ideas—surely, Roy knew at least fragments of Enlightenment philosophy to express something so tantalizingly similar? But the fact remains that at this stage, his exposure to European writing and English was limited; what is more probable is that these ideas emerged from his Persianate education.[20] Besides, India's bhakti saints from the early-modern period, like Kabir and Nanak, also articulated similar ideas: Their teachings may well have influenced Roy.[21] But if in the *Tuhfat* he also targeted Islam—and possibly got into trouble[22]—its basic tenets would inform his approach chiefly to Christianity and Hinduism. The existence of these rival religions, in and of itself, does not appear to have caused Roy grief: They were, he believed, the functional product of geography, cultural peculiarities and historical dynamics. But for this reason precisely, they could not be unnaturally forced into other regions.[23] As for core precepts, these were ultimately the same, drawing from natural laws and guided by reason. This had two results: Missionaries found fault with Roy for denying Christianity its universal ambitions, while Hindu conservatives resented his questioning entrenched 'native' customs. They saw, for instance, the 1829 British ban on sati as an assault on Hinduism; Roy, however, not only invited state intervention but also energetically campaigned against sati. Because, to him, this was not Hinduism: God did not ask to burn women. Men did.[24] And like Protestant minds that advocated a return to 'pure' scripture and its uncontaminated ideas, Roy would—from within Hindu society—seek to set off a Reformation of sorts. This was, in his mind, the only way Hindus could navigate modernity.

Roy's reform agenda for Hinduism began in the mid-1810s, through a set of tracts in Bengali (later translated into English)—a very missionary technique, making full use of the power of the printing press.[25] The choice of language is telling: Unlike Persian, which catered to elites, Roy hoped Bengali would filter downwards. In fact, he printed hundreds of copies of his writings at his own expense and had them freely distributed in the hope of reaching as wide a readership as possible.[26] He was not, that is, appealing to

Brahmins and intellectuals only but a larger audience—a successful strategy that helped centre his ideas in reframing Hinduism more generally in the nineteenth century. Here, however, European influences are visible in the form of prevailing orientalist wisdom that 'true' Hinduism could be located only in its ancient, authentic Sanskrit texts. And that all customs not 'imperatively enjoined' by such sources were open to reform.[27] This is clear from the fact that where his 1803–04 *Tuhfat* came from a time when Roy had minimal interaction with Europeans, by now, a decade later, he was in fluent contact with orientalists and missionaries.[28] So a textualist attitude towards religion, preferred by dominant outsiders—and in line with his Brahmin roots—sat easily with Roy. And through him and his successors, it would slowly become natural for many other Hindus also. Just as evangelicals in Britain nurtured a 'religious public', that is, reformers like Roy were cultivating one in India: a class that in time would also glaze their Hindu identity with nationalism.[29]

To start with, Roy argued that the reigning brand of Hinduism was a travesty: a view that was manifestly growing among a set of Indians, given that an English-speaking Brahmin from the south aired similar thoughts in the same period.[30] And so, Roy wrote in 1816, his endeavour was 'to convince my countrymen of the true meaning of our sacred books', while proving in tandem to British appraisers that 'superstitious practices which deform' living Hinduism were inconsistent with its 'spirit'.[31] The goal, then, was twofold: to teach Hindus that their religion, *as it existed*, was not actually their religion; and to persuade Europeans—as exemplified by James Mill and William Ward, whose notorious works appeared in the same years—that they had misjudged Hinduism. This was, patently, a top-down reading of faith: a marriage of a Western conception of what any religion ought to look like (such as the emphasis on scripture) with the slant of a Brahmin synthesizing European and 'native' ideas.[32] Except that in this case, what was a fluid system, which in its ability to absorb all manner of cults and beliefs had plural origins, hastened its move towards regimentation, with a one-source pedigree—and this time not in writings by foreigners. It was not, to be clear, the 'invention' of a new faith. For 'communities constantly renew themselves . . . and creative individuals can . . . make a critical contribution'.[33] The process, besides, was afoot ever since Hindus encountered Islam. But for all that, Hinduism had stayed an amorphous system, until colonialism and evangelical perils inspired some Hindus to espouse a firmer outline. Modern Hinduism was not, then, as some argue, a synthetic British construct. It was nevertheless a fresh incarnation, necessitated by political and social crises—somewhat like Vishnu assuming different forms to address problems in various ages.

Indeed, reformers could find justification for Hinduism's rebranding *within* the Hindu tradition; as we saw in the Introduction, this was a constantly transforming, responsive universe. Or in the words of a later writer, 'As knowledge grows, our theology develops.'[34] So, even if the terms were set by foreigners, sufficiently 'native' roots could be located for adopting and indigenizing those very terms. The Sanskrit corpus, as we know, is capacious enough that, with a bit of flexibility, evidence for everything might be discovered in it.[35] Roy knew this: In his tracts, he cited Vedic verses to set Hinduism in its new frame—as a uniform, non-idolatrous monotheism. Belief in the 'unity of God [was the] real Hindooism' of 'our ancestors', he would assert—a line that also lumped together all Hindus everywhere as one 'us', descended from a single set of spiritual progenitors.[36] Doing so, however, involved a bias in curation: The quotations Roy chose, thus, were not from the oldest part of the Vedas. Those, with hymns to many deities, rubbed against his goal of a rational Hinduism. (In fact, in London, seeing a scholar study these, he told him not to 'waste his time'.[37]) What Roy preferred was the Upanishads—philosophical ruminations, themselves diverse, and which had received orientalist praise[38]—from which he harvested lines to manufacture a tidy profile for Hinduism. Of course, he made errors and his knowledge of the

Vedas was incomplete. But few could tell.[39] Bengal had hardly any Vedic experts, and it took a Tamil Brahmin to spot flaws in Roy's postulations.[40] And in any case, this selective reading of scripture—embracing some bits, excising others—was never just a spiritual matter; it was political. Or as Roy acknowledged, '[T]he present system of [Hindus'] religion' was not 'well calculated to promote their political interest'; so, 'some change' was imperative.[41] And given that few showed any urgency, he had personified himself as a torchbearer for renovation. It is also not, therefore, a minor detail that Roy was perhaps the first Hindu to appropriate 'Hinduism' as a term and label in his writings. And by this he meant his own version of it.[42]

Ironically, this was the missionary method too: to pick and choose whatever pushed pet ideas, though in their case, it was to excoriate Hinduism. But more directly, Roy, like Protestants, placed scripture over 'custom and accumulated tradition'. Even his Bengali versions of Vedic extracts, which in translation were infused with his own messaging, mirrored Protestant efforts to vernacularize the Bible.[43] So also, having accepted the premise of Hinduism's decline from unparalleled purity, Roy had to explain how this happened. And here, he parked blame with Brahmins—another missionary theme, directly descended from the Protestant battering of Catholic 'priestcraft' in Europe.[44] For instance, just as Francis Xavier, the sixteenth-century Jesuit, accused Brahmins of veiling monotheism from the masses, Roy argued that Hinduism's loftiest ideas, 'concealed within the dark curtain of the Sungscrit language', never reached its beneficiaries thanks to Brahmin cunning.[45] Where Xavier charged this class with exploiting gullible 'natives' for gifts, Roy too declared that Brahmins pushed the 'absurdity of idolatry' for selfish 'comforts and fortune', hiding what really mattered: 'knowledge of their scriptures'.[46] And finally, he attacked Puranic Hinduism and its gods, in a tone reminiscent of James Mill and missionary pamphlets. Krishna, he declared, committed unholy acts with women; Siva's (phallic) icon was so 'indecent', it was 'impossible' to describe 'in language fit to meet the public eye'; Kali was singularly unladylike, with her taste for 'wine, criminal intercourse, and licentious songs'.[47] Declaring himself 'unwilling to stain' his pages with more 'stories of immorality', Roy prayed: 'May God speedily purify the minds of my countrymen from the corruptness' which enslaved them, and 'lead their hearts to that pure morality' of (designated parts of) the Vedas.[48]

Roy was clear on what his religion was not. But what *was* 'pure', distilled Hinduism? The Upanishads, he announced, saw 'polytheism with contempt'.[49] Given, however, that he could not ignore the many Vedic deities, Roy added that idolatry was *tolerated* as a 'last provision for those... incapable of raising their minds'. Sadly, the 'generality of the Hindoo community' existed in 'defiance of their sacred books', in this infantile state.[50] As we have noted before, it would have startled most Hindus to find that they must tailor religious life according to texts; that they must dismiss gods in temples as so many rocks. And yet the legitimacy Roy's ideas gained suggests that enough Hindus did welcome his interpretation.[51] In other words, he was filling a genuinely felt gap; Hinduism's extant avatar opened it to attack, and as national feelings grew, room for such criticism had to be eliminated. Besides, much of what Roy said was familiar. 'The greater religious systems of Hinduism,' after all, were 'always... accompanied by individuals or groups who challenged them.'[52] The perception of image worship as a subordinate practice came from the ninth-century philosopher, Sankara; Roy's anti-idol stance was anticipated 600 years before in the south by Basava; Brahminical ritualism, which Roy disparaged, was attacked in western India as far back as the fourteenth century by thinkers like Namdev.[53] Even his critics did not squirm at the idea of a single supreme being, for they too recognized it; what they denied was Roy's view that Puranic Hinduism—with its temples, gods and myths—was false; that one could slice Hinduism into religious ideas (good) and religious practice (bad).[54] So, despite innovation, there was much that would have been recognizable to Hindus in Roy's hybrid vision. That is, even if the brackets within which Hinduism was being placed betrayed Protestant influences, the paternity of the substance inside seemed justifiably Indian.[55]

And yet, there was a difference from older intellectual stances. While India had never faced a deficit of ideas, these were often scattered. They had rarely been lined up so neatly, with single-minded purpose. After all, earlier philosophers, even as they planted in the Indian mind notions fitting Roy's project, also upheld elements that sat poorly with him. Basava lampooned idolatry but challenged claims of Vedic supremacy too: Roy's veneration of the Upanishads would not have appealed to this medieval forebear. Namdev and the bhakti poets believed in a devotional culture, often focused on a humanized god, not just divinity in the abstract—this too would have made Roy fret.[56] Sankara's prescriptions on finding the formless god were for the 'ascetic and [Brahmin] intellectual', while our nineteenth-century man urged it on Hindus in toto; here again was dissonance.[57] So even if these ideas had swirled about, it was the combination of colonialism, modernity and the Christian threat that helped chisel them into a uniform, formal Hinduism. Similarly, while those earlier figures mattered, it is open to debate if they ever saw themselves as 'reformers'.[58] This is also why Roy's work seems such a direct corollary to the missionary project. White men berated Hindus and advertised their faith as purer; Roy modified this to sell Hindus not Christianity but a deep-cleansed, scripturalist Hinduism that could withstand Western censure. Evangelicals dreamt of transforming brown men through the Bible; Roy intended to do the same, but with Vedic passages.[59] Both thought Hindus deluded and competed, with proportionate condescension, to 'save' them. And yet Roy's political genius lay in erecting a serious obstacle in the missionary's path: a new 'ancient' Hindu alternative to Christianity, which rendered conversion theoretically—as well as theologically—redundant.[60]

This did tragically, however, circumscribe what it meant to be Hindu. Hinduism historically featured jostling, exchange and a good deal of negotiation, with Brahmins subsuming all kinds of practices. While this had its politics and was hardly neat, even in the nineteenth century, Hindus lived a fascinatingly rich life, with 'higher' and 'lower' aspects entwined. A memoir by a Deccan writer, born just before Roy's death, captures this reality. The man came of the Kasar caste of smiths. His prosperous family lived in a Brahmin area and viewed vegetarianism as ritually purer; yet they continued to eat meat, speaking in code of fish as 'water beans', mutton as 'red vegetables'. They bowed at Brahmin-led temples, but Brahmins likewise participated in their goddess rites featuring flesh and liquor; vegetarian values evaporated at such moments. The writer's father diligently read the (Marathi-language) Gita, and through it engaged with Hindu philosophy; meanwhile, an uncle paid visits to the shrine of a Muslim sufi. The women of the household prayed to serpents but also made vows on Muharram; and in general, the family engaged as much with the so-called inferior gods and shepherd priests as with Brahminical rites. 'My life,' the author concluded, 'was marked by the grossest inconsistencies' and 'contradictory doctrines'—inconsistent, that is, from the new viewpoint.[61] But that was precisely it: To Hindus, variety had been normal; their religious world was, as one scholar put it, like a Venn diagram of overlapping experiences.[62] This was not proof of decay, as missionaries, orientalists and Roy believed, but an organic reflection of history.[63] By the nineteenth century, however, new norms prevailed, demanding consistency. But in what might have vexed Roy, our kasar memoirist, instead of pledging himself to reformed Hinduism, hopped the fence to Christianity.

Roy's final years were spent away from home, in Britain, where he became a star. Meanwhile in India, the ideas he voiced would gain a robust intellectual life.[64] But if he was described as a 'native' Martin Luther, Roy never achieved Luther's practical success. His followers gathered in a group called the Brahmo Samaj, which upheld the

'Eternal Unsearchable and Immutable Being' and pledged itself against 'graven image[s]'.[65] This was, however, too unemotional a faith to persuade more than a few; instead, Brahmoism stayed a tiny sect, while worship of Siva, Kali and Vishnu continued predominant.[66] Indeed, Roy was unable to convince his mother even: While he forsook Puranic Hinduism, the lady defiantly clung on, spending her last days serving Jagannath at Puri.[67] Where Roy endured, then, was in identifying a formula to ennoble Hinduism in modern, Western eyes—the English-speaking intelligentsia especially found his Upanishads-based framing attractive. Moreover, he blunted the Christian threat to Hinduism. Between 1820 and 1823, Roy published much on Christianity, reiterating his stance from the *Tuhfat*. Jesus's moral teachings, he pronounced, deserved praise; all beyond that, such as miracles, was nonsense. (Besides, Roy warned, Hindus had a stockpile of these: Christ's walk on water paled next to Agastya, who drank an ocean, only to restore it via the bladder.)[68] Missionaries retorted by arguing—like Roy's Hindu critics—that he could not coolly delink ethical precepts from the remainder of a religious package. The real fear, though, went beyond this: for by subjecting Christian scripture to analysis, to sustained interrogation by reason, and interpreting it on *his* terms, this brown man reversed what Europeans did to 'native' religious literature.[69] Roy's strategy, that is, allowed Hinduism to hold its own in a changed, unequal world—and in key respects, to turn the tables.[70]

In fact, Roy's lowering of Christ as just another spiritual guru like Confucius in China,[71] would help claim not equality but superiority for Hinduism: for *this* faith was not dependent on human mediation.[72] So too, unlike Christianity, which, visualizing god, ascribes human features to him, the Upanishads' transcendent divinity rose above petty conceptions. And this confirmed that Hindus owned the rational truth.[73] The very stick with which missionaries beat 'native' religions was pointed the other way; to good Hindus, *Christianity* looked 'Heathenish', and to convert from the Puranic religion to the cult of Christ was tantamount to replacing 'one set of polytheistical sentiments' with another.[74] In time, this would popularize a boilerplate argument that is recycled even now: that the West might surpass India materially, but in spiritual affairs, India rules.[75] As for Hinduism's contemporary degradation, it was irrelevant: All nations had 'the ignorant and the enlightened'; it was the latter who embodied their culture's values.[76] Bankim Chandra Chatterjee, a late-nineteenth-century writer, thus, admitted 'the duty of every Hindu, actively to assail' the 'absurdities' which 'subvert[ed]' Hinduism.[77] But criticism from white men was laughable. After all, if a Hindu travelled to Europe, he too might see in the Catholic veneration of saints a polytheism—by standards applied in India, this should prompt him to at once declare Christianity idolatrous.[78] No, what mattered was principles. And here, even if the Hindus erred, Hindu*ism* was good. To argue otherwise was risky: for Christianity too must then bear responsibility for 'all the wars, all the massacres, all the murders that have been committed in its name'.[79] Yet again, then, the colonizer was shown his drawbacks, in a mirror of his own making—now seized on by 'natives'.[80]

That said, Chatterjee—whose *Bande Mataram* (1882), banned by the colonial state, later became India's national song and slogan—would journey a step further than Roy. For, even while confirming his belief in a paramount divinity, he questioned the near-totalitarian obsession with monotheism:

> ... what is the high ground which monotheism is believed to occupy ... ? Why is a pure monotheism ... a rational worship, and polytheism mere stupidity ... What evidence is there, that God is One and cannot be many? That the government of the Universe unlike that of society, is carried on by a single Personal Being ... If you come to the question of evidence ... there is probably as little in favour of monotheism as of polytheism ... You may point to the unity of design apparent in nature, as indicative of

a single Designer ... Will you infer from the unity of design apparent in a building that it was the work of a sole architect, who had no masons or labourers to co-operate with him?[81]

Memorial to Ram Mohun Roy at Arnos Vale Cemetery, Wikimedia Commons.

That is, the Western frame itself was flawed—and, Chatterjee seemed to suggest, Indians would do better to free themselves from operating within its limits. Today, we might describe this as intellectual decolonization; a smashing of that mirror. But back then, the writer was evidently ahead of his time. For in the nineteenth century, many Hindus continued to give purchase to the colonizer's perception of the world. And so, Roy's strategy lived on, growing powerful: an aspect that might have provided him a sense of achievement. As it happens, however, the postscript to the Bengali's tale is more amusing. A few years after he died, Roy's body was exhumed and reinterred in a cemetery in Bristol. Except that here, his well-wishers deposited him under a canopy designed to look like an Indian temple. In other words, Roy—the Brahmin laid to rest in Christian soil; the 'native' who had railed against idolatry—became, in death, enshrined like a Hindu deity.[82]

Somewhere around 1840, a teenager in Kathiawar, in western India, had a crisis of faith. The son of a Brahmin revenue collector and banker, he was raised in good comfort, much like Roy. Unlike the Bengali reformer, though, this young man had no knowledge of English—he studied Sanskrit texts and his vernacular tongue and was slowly being introduced also to the ritual prescriptions for men of his caste. One night during Sivaratri—the annual festival to Siva—our protagonist was asked to join a ceremonial vigil at the local temple. No one was supposed to sleep, and with his father being quite rigid about religious rites, he expected very much to have to stick both to the letter and spirit of the proceedings. Except, however, that within hours, daddy dozed right off. The teenager decided to do better, perhaps due to the vigour and determination of the young. Except that his reward was not magnified devotion but doubt. For at one point 'in the middle of the night', a mouse appeared and 'began to take liberties' with the mighty Lord of Destruction. The image of Siva showed him astride his bull, Nandi, trident in hand; and yet, the deity seemed powerless as the mouse 'ate away all the offerings that lay piled before' him. This, it is said, shook the watching Brahmin boy: What was the point of venerating a god who seemed helpless before a trespassing rodent? Was Siva even present in the idol or was this a 'piece of clay'?[83] In any case, as dawn approached, the teenager found himself in distress—his faith had suffered a crack, right down the middle.[84]

It is possible the story of the mouse is a bit of gloss in the official narrative around Dayananda Saraswati (1824–83), but it is meant to reflect the early seeding of scepticism in him—and the belief that temple-based Hinduism was inadequate. As such, the experience was not unique: The son of the Cochin rajah too, mentioned in the previous chapter, was triggered when a priest absconded with a family deity's jewels—surely, god could not have been present in the shrine, if his goods were so easily purloined?[85] In that case, though, the boy moved to Christianity, assuming the name Jacob; his younger contemporary in Kathiawar, on the other hand, became a reformer within Hinduism—yet another 'Luther of India'.[86] Of course, the transition was not instant, taking years after that latenight epiphany. Dayananda, the story goes, yearned for answers, and began to study under a guru. But then his family, fearing his increasing disinterest in worldly matters, ambushed him with an antidote: a woman. Frustratingly, the trick failed, and Dayananda, aged twenty-two, took drastic steps: The night before his wedding, he ran away. Whatever possessions he carried with him were stolen (by a band of mendicants, as it happened, who argued he had no need of earthly possessions in a spiritual quest). His father, at one point, even tracked him down and gave him a thrashing. But Dayananda fled a second time—now with success. He would never see his kin

Siva's Bull from the James Fergusson Collection of Photographs of Indian Architecture, Boston Public Library via Digital Commonwealth.

again; and by the time he returned to Kathiawar as a famous man, bonds of blood had entirely dissolved. He was a renunciant, and to this day, the identity of his family remains unsettled.[87]

Dayananda's life arc could not be more different from Roy's. Where the Bengali moved easily in urban and colonial spaces, our wandering Brahmin from the other side of India was a more traditional Hindu ascetic: a sanyasi.[88] Unlike Roy, who preferred to appear in rich robes, for decades Dayananda wore a loincloth; only in the 1870s, on the advice of Roy's intellectual heirs in Calcutta, did he give up this state of déshabillé to make himself presentable to cosmopolitan audiences.[89] So too where Roy's intellectual evolution had a genteel quality, Dayananda's was rough and uneasy, featuring all kinds of unhappy experiments with beef-eating pandits and grand but disappointing monks.[90] Both travelled: The Bengali, in service of the Company, went as far as Bhutan up north and Madras in the peninsula; the Kathiawari, meanwhile, roamed barefoot through western and upper India, doing yoga in its jungles, and climbing Himalayan slopes in search of fabled, mountain-dwelling ascetics.[91] Roy read a fair deal about Western science; Dayananda learnt from cutting experience. Once, for example, as he walked by a river, he found a corpse afloat. Pulling it ashore, Dayananda opened up the cadaver. 'I . . . examined the heart and compared it with descriptions in the [Sanskrit] books. I did the same with the head and the neck.' Sadly, he reports, 'there was not the slightest similarity between the text and the corpse'. The episode shattered all vestiges of unquestioning faith in received knowledge. When Dayananda resumed his journey, the books were bobbing alongside the mangled body.[92]

All along, though, the would-be hermit was hungry for spiritual answers. He consumed tantric texts only to dismiss them as 'disgusting literature', with 'obscenities', the worship of 'indecent images' and rites featuring 'liquors, fish, and all kinds of animal food'.[93] Ironically, he himself grew addicted to bhang—a cannabis-based drink—which, by his own admission, took time to shake off; the initial hope was that transportation into a different plane might aid his quest.[94] Idolatry he was already against, and his travels confirmed his view that Hindus in general were attached to outer forms as opposed to inner substance. Even ascetics let him down, some with their performative quirks: One, for example, had loud conferences with unknown beings in the dead of the night.[95] Finally, after a decade and a half of wandering, during which time he learnt what he could, where he could, Dayananda found a guru. In Mathura, a temple-town linked to the deity Krishna, there lived a blind sanyasi who hated idol worship.[96] Even as, all around him, pilgrims adored images of the romantic, cowherd god, this man promoted a more austere Vedic religion. When they met, the story goes, the guru asked Dayananda to head down to the river and first eject 'all the nonsense' he had learnt in his thirty-six years.[97] Then began the teaching, and at a standard, we read, that surpassed lessons even the philosopher Sankara received a thousand years ago, from *his* guru.[98] In fact, the old man played a central role in turning Dayananda away from a personal quest for answers, into a preacher addressing the world.[99] And after some years, when the disciple was ready, the blind elder outlined his mission: to 'devote everything' to propagating 'the Vedic religion'.[100] To become what admirers—in a rather missionary tone—described as a 'soldier of Light', ready 'to fight untruth and the false gods'.[101]

This narrative neatly accounts for Dayananda's espousal of a Hinduism anchored in the Vedas, and there is no reason to disbelieve it. But what is interesting is that this view emerged not from any direct exposure to the British or familiarity with orientalist scholarship; it came from a deep and genuine disillusionment with the world as it was, and Puranic Hinduism's inadequacy to supply solutions. This is linked to a larger phenomenon: that 'traditional' Hinduism too was a dynamic space, not a frozen monolith; it had figures within clamouring for change, even if they did not transact in English. Thus, for example, contemporary to Dayananda, was the Tamil Saiva saint Ramalinga (1823–74). He was not concerned with a uniform, purified Hinduism; instead, his focus was modernising Saivism. In this, he borrowed from past Saiva figures, composing, for example, erotic devotional poetry to Siva (a big no-no for anglicized Hindus).[102] So also, he challenged established Saiva institutions and endorsed a more accessible faith, not in a Western jargon but using Indian precedents and concepts. For him, Tamil, the common man's tongue, was preferable to elite Sanskrit. Indeed, he even invented new forms of temple ceremony, thus countering the idea that ritual and tradition are unchanging. To be clear, there were, of course, Roy-like Saiva reformers too, deploying Protestant techniques and who internalized a 'textual fundamentalism';[103] Ramalinga, on the other hand, worked with a different set of instruments. Unburdened by the obsession with looking 'rational', this meant he could even make claims of direct revelation from Siva and of miracles: anathema to reformers of the Westernized variety. But for all that, Ramalinga's work was also reform—born, though, with little foreign stimulus.[104]

So also, in Orissa, there emerged the Mahima Dharma, described by the end of the nineteenth century as a cult of 'Hindu dissenters'. Its founder, Mahima Swami, first arrived in the region in the 1820s but became a prominent teacher only three-and-a-half decades later. Supported by two others, including a poet, he travelled across the region, winning followers among tribes and low-caste groups— sections disenfranchised by prevailing Brahminical high culture. Over time, the movement spread not just in Orissa but also into Bengal in the east, Telugu country in the south and Assam in the north-east. Revealingly, here too we meet miracles: that poet and co-founder of the movement was blind, we are told, until restored his vision by Mahima Swami. But having seen how much suffering marred humanity, he opted for blindness again. What is interesting is that the Mahima Dharma did not—at least in theory—recognize caste, ritual discrimination (except for treating Brahmins as unrighteous), tribal blood rites and image worship. Indeed, in 1881, five years after its founder's death, a group of fifteen marched into the great temple at Puri, evidently to destroy its idols, none of this under missionary instigation. The keystones of this sect were simply ethical living, non-violence and good conduct, drawn from regional bhakti traditions as well as Buddhism; it was a message similar to Roy's, except it had bubbled up from below. In time, of course, a Vedic ancestry too would be 'discovered' when Mahima Swami's successors, without irony, began to Sanskritize and bridge his ideas with Brahminical Hinduism. But either way, the Mahima Dharma also was born not out of dialogue with the West, but as a movement within the Hindu world.[105]

Dayananda, in part, represents something similar, except that as time passed, he did not hesitate to borrow from Roy's school of reform. That is, he was able to reorient his localized, bottom-up campaign with tools that appeared in direct correspondence with colonialism and Christian evangelicalism. The process took time: When Dayananda first debated Brahmins on idolatry, their exchanges were held in Sanskrit—something that reveals the narrow audience he had in mind.[106] So too it was in orthodox circles that his reputation as an iconoclast grew: One pandit, in fact, would meet Dayananda only with a screen hung between them because it was inauspicious to behold an apostate.[107] But slowly he learnt Hindi to reach a wider section of north Indian society in their mother tongue, while also picking up skills that made missionaries such a force in the religious market. He began, for example, printing pamphlets to spread his message.[108] He also evinced curiosity about English, seeking texts from abroad, and asking 'a Bengali to teach . . . and to read to him Max Müller's translation of the Veda'.[109] Schools—a missionary favourite—were set up to raise a platoon of preachers for Dayananda's reformed Hinduism.[110] Despite many hiccups along the way, what we observe here is a 'traditional' ascetic very consciously attempting to enter new spaces, using technology, experimenting (and failing) and even learning from the competition. Dayananda, that is, unlike many non-cosmopolitan Hindu religious leaders, brought an added quality to the equation: an entrepreneurial eye to widen his venture beyond implicit limits.

Interestingly, in this too there is a partial precedent. If Dayananda trekked up from Kathiawar to the Gangetic belt, a generation before there was a Brahmin who did the reverse, settling in western India after his own spiritual peregrinations. This founder of the Swaminarayan sect, Sahajanand Swami (1781–1830), was, in fact, Roy's contemporary and was even compared to him as a reformer.[111] He preached a form of monotheism, but pivoted not on a formless being but Krishna. Individuals from all castes were welcomed, even if caste itself was never repudiated. And, like Dayananda, Sahajanand too was alert to changes in the world, and the opportunities these presented. For instance, he cultivated the Company's government to help establish his sect, which for years faced persecution. In certain Swaminarayan texts, thus, the Company *gavendra* (governor) is cast as a protector.[112] His reform programme also sat well with the British: Though sati was unusual in Kathiawar, Sahajanand was a vocal critic. Hearing of him, in fact, the bishop of Calcutta briefly believed he was 'an appointed instrument to prepare the way for the Gospel': a Hindu clearing the rot for Christians to comprehensively redraw the picture.[113] While that did not happen, to British writers, Sahajanand—who was seen by his followers as a living god, maintained in pomp and who travelled with a veritable army—was exactly the type of reformer they preferred. He was not radical like Roy, nor did he coopt a Western conceptual language, which always held risks for British authority. Instead, he sold reform in small, diplomatic, 'native'-looking doses. But for our purposes, Sahajanand matters for one more reason: that even as he built up a 'traditional' Hindu sect, he maneuvered it through a very modern, shifting landscape.[114]

Dayananda, however, did not approve of the Swaminarayan veneration of Krishna.[115] For the core of *his* Hinduism—*Arya Dharma*, faith of the Aryans—was the Vedas, as with Roy, and a shapeless, formless divinity. This is not surprising: When with his parents, Dayananda had already studied the Yajur Veda, in keeping with family convention.[116] His rule was simple: 'Whatever was not to be found in the Vedas... [was] false and useless; whatever was found in the Vedas,' on the contrary, was 'beyond the reach of controversy.'[117] That is, the only area where Dayananda was unyieldingly dogmatic was Vedic infallibility.[118] But where his Bengali prior built on the (chronologically later) Upanishads, Dayananda preferred the Samhitas: the oldest section, with its hymns. The Upanishads were acceptable, of course, so long as they did not contradict earlier parts; and if one admitted they were *not* divine revelation but appendices of human authorship. But what, then, of deities catalogued in the Samhitas? To Dayananda, these were not gods, just aspects of the almighty—an interpretation critics attacked as sophistry, to conceal polytheistic values.[119] Or as one acerbic writer quipped, Dayananda was a 'heretical fool' who read 'the Vedas according to the figments of his own imagination'.[120] Additionally, he viewed most other scriptural sources as 'false': the Puranas provoked Dayananda's 'contempt', for example.[121] Because they represented decline. An explanation was conjured via a marriage of history with dramatic license. Five thousand years ago, Dayananda claimed, all humanity subscribed to the Vedas, and India was paramount in the world. Indeed, in the epic war of the Mahabharata, every king—including of America!—sent troops.[122] But after this cataclysm, decay set in. War bred disunion, the truth of the Vedas was 'perverted' and Brahmins became 'false spiritual guides'—all at the cost of real Hinduism, hereafter eclipsed by the Puranas.[123]

In this last point one can identify Protestant influences: Indeed, in Dayananda's *Satyarth Prakash*, a Hindi text produced in the mid-1870s and then expanded some years later, the term *poplila* (or 'popery' in its English translation) appears repeatedly, borrowing from Protestant polemics against the Catholic church.[124] Similarly, like Roy, his tirade against Puranic Hinduism aligns with missionary views: Worshipping Siva through the lingam, he argued, was 'an act of barbarians'; the Vaishnavas' claims of divine incarnations were not only nonsense but an insult to intelligence. For example, if the divine boar Varaha—one of Vishnu's avatars—lifted the earth on its tusks, what

Photograph of a Sadhu, c. 1920, reading the Bible, from an album by W.K. Norton of the Pilgrims Mission, Benares, courtesy of the Yale University Library.

exactly was the beast standing on? The 'breast of the popish author' of this fable?[125] Understandably, incandescent Hindus branded Dayananda 'a Christian in disguise'.[126] But then, he castigated Christianity too, as well as Jainism and Islam. If Jesus could multiply bread, 'Why did he not make sweet pudding for himself out of earth, water, [and] stones' instead of wandering 'in his starvation to the fruit of fig trees?' Islam railed against temple images but in turning to Mecca and its Kaaba, Dayananda declared, it endorsed 'a great idol'. As for Jains, their teachers were plain old 'sinners'; Dayananda, in fact, blamed this class for spreading idolatry in India.[127] By the 1870s, in other words, the man who earlier worked in a relatively slim professional space, engaging with Sanskrit pandits, grew cognizant of a wider religious public. He realized also that besides restoring 'pure' Hinduism *among* Hindus, he would have to also preserve it actively from encroachment by *non*-Hindus.[128]

For Dayananda, this transition had much to do with a visit to Calcutta earlier in that decade. In fact, his biographer notes that until his arrival here, no evidence exists that he 'even thought about Hinduism in "national" terms or in . . . comparison with other religions'.[129] What made all the difference was an encounter with Roy's successors at the Brahmo Samaj. It was in Calcutta too that Dayananda read the *Brahmo Dharma* (1848), a Samaj guidebook, the influence of which is pronounced in his own *Satyarth Prakash*.[130] Put

Swami Dayananda Saraswati, Wikimedia Commons.

simply, the very idea of packaging his ideology in book form may have been inspired by the English-speaking reformers in Bengal. The world of the 'traditional' Hindu connected with Roy's, growing stronger for it. Soon Dayananda was doing lecture tours in cities; after Calcutta, in 1874, he went to Bombay, where his own venture, the Arya Samaj, was founded. 'His long and mostly fruitless efforts' in pilgrim towns in upper India had, we discover, taught Dayananda 'that the regeneration of Hinduism would not be effected through pandits and the brahmins: they had too big a stake in the status quo'. Instead, urban elites—men walking in Roy's footsteps—were more receptive to new ideas and fresh interpretations of old ones.[131] It was another issue that these figures did not entirely agree with Dayananda. But as one senior personage explained, 'What does it matter' if there was partial discordance? So long as enough points did 'accord with our principles', cooperation was justified.[132] And so, Dayananda—a sturdy, six-foot-tall sanyasi who once lived near-naked in forests—won legitimacy among India's coat-wearing, English-speaking, armchair intellectuals.

In fact, Dayananda had an advantage over Roy when it came to winning supporters. He was at a glance a Hindu ascetic: This endowed him with a degree of general reverence wherever he went—an appeal a worldly, cosmopolitan figure like Roy could never command. Secondly, he travelled extensively and had lived among the people—again a different setting from Roy and his lordly existence. But most critically, Dayananda's openness to learning from the urban reformist set, and *blending* it with his own mission, brought him long-awaited success. His idea of Hinduism was sculpted originally with his blind guru in 'traditional' settings, but he adopted strategies of the 'modern' city reformers in marketing that idea. That is, if Roy united Eastern and Western principles, Dayananda did so with impulses *within* India among different classes. This may be why the orthodoxy saw him as particularly menacing. As early as 1869, in Benares, after a debate with orthodox pandits, he was attacked.[133] As his fame grew, so did risks: In Poona in the next decade, after Dayananda delivered lectures, his hosts held a procession with their guest perched on an elephant. A rival party responded with a march 'honoring a donkey as a mock saint'—in the end, stones were hurled and things nearly escalated into a riot.[134] Apparently, there were also attempts to murder him, and his death in 1883 after a painful illness is ascribed to poison; in hagiographies, Dayananda understandingly forgives his treacherous cook.[135] His wicked enemies, we are informed, even weaponized lust—they sent him a woman once, hoping to mince his reputation for celibacy, post coitus. Except when the lady arrived, she observed 'a mystic light' all around her target and instead of disrobing, was reduced to 'shedding tears of penitence'.[136] It wasn't a miracle, à la Ramalinga, but it came close. Dayananda too, that is, did not occupy the world of the purely 'rational'. Enough was invested in emotion also.[137]

Understandably, then, Dayananda did not always pass tests of reason. One Hindu critic would declare 'Dayanandism' a 'sham' based on a mischievous interpretation of the Vedas.[138] A Christian noted, similarly, that if 'Dayanandis' were challenged with points countering their preceptor's claims, these were craftily played down as metaphorical. For example, Vedic animal sacrifice—how could this be symbolic when there were rules on 'slaughtering . . . distribution of the various parts, the method of cooking and the way of eating' the animal?[139] One man even branded Dayananda a 'dangerous *enemy* of the Veda'.[140] But the sanyasi was unmoved: Past interpretations of the great scriptures were simply flawed; he, meanwhile, had cracked the code to reach the right conclusions. In fact, as he became aware of Western technology, Dayananda pinned these also to his favourite texts: a step that permitted him to scorn foreign advances, while nevertheless appropriating them for Hindus. Or as Müller wrote, 'Steam-engines, railways, and steam-boats, all were shown to have been known, at least in their germs, to the poets of the Vedas'.[141] He was not exaggerating. The *Satyarth Prakash* tells, for example, of guns in ancient India; that all the 'sciences and arts' in 'the whole world' had 'their original start' in Vedic minds.[142] Future writers would put this down to an inferiority complex,[143] but for what it was worth, Dayananda lashed out at Müller too, decrying him as a hopeless scholar;[144] as an imposter whose real design was to subject Hindus to the Bible.[145] Stubbornly dismissing all criticism, then, Dayananda clung to his view that the Vedas were the source of everything. Or as he said to a missionary once: 'I do not believe there is a single error in any of the Vedas.' And 'if you show me one I will maintain that it is the interpolation of a clever scoundrel'.[146]

All along, boosted by growing success, in the second half of the 1870s, Dayananda developed a political project: a renaissance backed by India's Hindu princes. This was a proposal his guru had also entertained, and with good reason. After all, even if the British ruled 60 per cent of the country, the rest was under the control of 'native' royalty. And properly directed, these men—who owned resources and social capital—could do much to propel Dayananda's vision. In 1877, he went to a durbar hosted by the governor general to proclaim Queen Victoria empress of India; most of the land's princes had gathered here, opening the possibility of wooing them as a class.[147] Nothing came of it. Next, in 1881, Dayananda landed in Udaipur, whose ruler was one of India's highest-ranking Hindu princes. For six months he stayed here and certainly made an impression, even if not all his prescriptions worked: Dayananda expected the maharajah to go monogamous, while the latter startled his visitor by suggesting he head a Saiva institution—and, more gently, cease attacking image worship.[148] Still, Dayananda was quite optimistic when he went to Jodhpur next. Evidently, this state was full of Vaishnava 'fanatics' and the sanyasi warned: 'The more stubborn the perversity of a people, the stronger should be the remedies employed to uproot it.'[149] Except, however, that its prince was uninterested. He hosted his visitor and treated him well but showed little further resolve.[150] Dayananda even sent the maharajah letters of admonishment, with no effect. In fact, Arya Samaj accounts insist that the primary obstacle was a royal concubine; or in a more vivid rendering, a 'base bitch'.[151] Interestingly, the same lady—Nanhi Jaan—is accused of plotting the poisoning that allegedly killed Dayananda soon afterwards.[152]

But if rousing princes—a proposition Hindu nationalists would again consider a half-century later—failed, Dayananda had success galvanizing ordinary people towards action. That is, he began identifying causes with the potential to unite Hindus, otherwise fragmented into castes and sects.[153] The cow offered itself here as an option: castes, middling and high, all held the animal sacred, and Dayananda urged them to proactively protect it.[154] Reverence for the cow also had the benefit of separating not only the beef-eating British but also Muslims from Hindus. Dayananda's views first appeared in an economic shape. Deploying arithmetic, he argued that 'the milk of one milch-cow' could 'support 25,730 persons' in the great scheme of things. So too, 'three yokes of oxen' raised '48,000 lbs of corn', feeding thousands. On the other hand, if the cow were *eaten*, it could only 'appease . . . 80 carnivorous persons'.[155] In short, cow slaughter was bad economics: a line addressed to men of reason. But in 1882, Dayananda also highlighted the cow's emotional appeal, founding the Gaurakshini Sabha ('Cow-Protection Association'), members of which turned public squares into pulpits. Understandably, this provoked violence with Muslims,[156] while also serving as a means to coerce 'bad' Hindus—beef-eating low castes—into turning 'good' by accepting Brahminical values.[157] And after 1888, when a British court held that the cow did not fall under the category of 'an object held sacred', and was *not* protected by law,[158] its protection was transformed into a nationalist issue. Indeed, in 1893, the colonial state was surprised to find massive numbers of peasants signing cow-protection petitions.[159] That is, men from various linguistic and caste communities began to visibly constitute a united Hindu front under the banner of the divine bovine. Or as the governor general recorded, the cow 'supplied the whole of the disloyal elements . . . with a popular backing which they could not have obtained from any other source'.[160] In fact, by 1907, Dayananda's organization would be branded seditious, suspected by hyper-paranoid officials of plotting the overthrow of the British.[161]

Funnily enough, when Dayananda died, it was believed that the Arya Samaj he founded would fade into obscurity along with its pet causes. Or as Müller wrote in an obituary:

> India is in a process of religious fermentation, and new cells are constantly thrown out, while old ones burst and disappear. For a time this kind of liberal orthodoxy started by Dayananda may last; but the mere contact with Western thought, and more particularly with Western scholarship, will eventually extinguish

it. It is different with [Roy's] Brahma-Samaj . . . They do not fear the West; on the contrary they welcome it; and though that movement too may change its name and character, there is every prospect that it will in the end lead to a complete regeneration in the religious life of India.[162]

But the sanyasi belied his British critic's prophecy. For it was the *Brahmo* Samaj that faded, all but vanishing by the next century.[163] Meanwhile, the Arya Samaj, which already had nearly seventy-nine branches at the time of its founder's death, firmly planted itself in India. Today, it runs thousands of schools, hospitals, colleges and orphanages, with large international wings. The anglicized gentlemen's Hinduism exemplified by Roy's disciples, with its god of reason, did not flourish.[164] Instead, Dayananda's message—despite feuds between his moderate and radical followers—found welcome with millions. On the one hand, it crafted a middle-class Hinduism, especially in Punjab and upper India. Or as a commentator put it, it was the faith of the 'minor civil servants, schoolmasters, local pleaders, medical practitioners, and other active citizens'.[165] On the other, it positioned itself as 'an effective competitor to [Christian] missions', 'dogging the missionary movement, copying its organizations . . . and countering its strategies at every turn'.[166] Indeed, within a few years, Hindu reform receded as Samaj workers instead channelled energy towards puncturing the hopes of *rival* faiths; it became a defensive enterprise, evincing a 'patriotic antagonism' towards competitors.[167] Or as Gandhi would wryly note: 'The Arya Samaj preacher is never so happy as when he is reviling other religions.'[168] Most significantly, *shuddhi* (purification) schemes were developed, to re-convert those who departed Hinduism for Christianity or Islam. In 1913, 9000 persons, thus, were reclaimed in Jammu; in 1923, 15,000 in Rajputana followed.[169] Just as Francis Xavier some centuries before converted villages en masse in the south, now in the north converts were recouped—also en masse.

The Holy Cow personified as World Mother, chromolithograph from the Raja Ravi Varma Press, Wellcome Collection.

The Arya Samaj, that is, was transformed into an organism nobody had seen in India before: a Hindu evangelical movement.[170] And a uniform Hindu identity was no longer an intellectual argument alone; it was acquiring muscle to remake reality.[171] Viewed another way, where Roy set the stage with a theoretical basis for defending Hinduism, Dayananda went a step further: He became the grandfather of a mass-based Hindu *nationalism*. There was only one problem, though, blocking the rise of this new politicized Hindu identity. And the name of that problem was caste. For if Hindus were internally a divided people—where Brahmins ran even from the 'polluting' shadows of their lowborn countrymen—how could they unite in the face of external foes like the missionary? Furthermore, the lowborn were now discovering their own power and voice, rejecting the pretensions of their self-appointed superiors. So much so, that Hinduism—under siege from the outside—looked like it might also crumble from within.

When in 1875 Dayananda came lecturing to Poona, among the men he met was a middle-aged radical called Jotirao Phule.[172] Born in 1827 to a greengrocer, Phule came from the Mali caste of gardeners. It was one of the area's middling communities: not so high as to assert elite status but not so low as to be condemned to untouchability. Additionally, his family was prosperous: Phule's grandfather had served as official florist to the Peshwa's household before the Company takeover, and in this capacity owned a gift of tax-free land. His maternal family, similarly, were headmen in a nearby village. Among his peers, then, Phule belonged to what might be described as the cream.[173] Even so, little suggested this Mali boy would one day become a public icon; that long before Gandhi made the term familiar, *he* would be addressed as *mahatma* (great soul). Like most children, Phule went to a vernacular school, acquiring basic literacy and arithmetic skills. As his next logical step, he joined his father's trade and would have remained there until it was time for his own issue to someday follow. Except that Phule's road took an unusual turn. For in his teens, he went back to school—this time, at a Christian mission that taught English. It was a life-defining experience. And within a short span, it transformed this latest recruit into one of modern India's great anti-caste ideologues. Indeed, by the time Phule died in 1890, many viewed him as the 'father of Indian social revolution'.[174] Which is not to say he was universally admired among all Hindus: One Brahmin likened him, in sarcasm, to a 'jewel'—among the mean and lowborn, that is.[175]

Phule's life, in fact, exemplifies one of those little discussed consequences of colonialism in India: the political mobilization of subordinate castes, which successfully utilized British rule to bargain for just treatment from their traditional superiors.[176] It is proof of how missionary activities too, even as they incensed Hindu elites, offered marginalized sections of brown society a toolkit for self-assertion and agency.[177] Plain numbers demonstrate the impact: In 1819, the BMS alone had 7000 students in their schools, and the LMS, 4000; in the 1820s, it was estimated that a total of almost 40,000 students were under instruction in evangelical institutions.[178] To be clear, neither mission schools nor British officials actively intended to alter power dynamics within Hindu society. Governor Elphinstone, for example, argued *against* encouraging English education among low castes.[179] As rulers, white men preferred courting elite Hindus exclusively, seeing in them ideal consumers of Western learning. For missionaries, meanwhile, schools were an instrument for conversion, not a charitable scheme to produce local reformers. English education was only the 'preparing of a mine ... which shall one day explode and tear up the whole [of Hinduism] from its lowest depths'.[180] Exposing 'natives' to Western science came with the expectation that they would 'lose confidence in [their] own religion', allowing for the missionary to flush out the debris and point to the true faith. Schools even helped promote the Bible; added with other textbooks, 'no Hindoo would ever scent persecution'.[181] But as often happens, the results of such plans did not match their sponsors' calculations. For if some 'natives' converted—causing serious social tremors[182]—most simply picked up ideas from their teachers, refashioning these to alter arrangements within the Hindu world. Phule, though no enemy of conversion,[183] was one such beneficiary. He learnt from missionaries but adapted their strategies to his own anti-caste activism.[184]

As with many others, it was reading that made Phule the man he would become. Having joined the mission school, he partook of its usual academic menu. But English meant that literature of another type was also accessible, especially given that this period saw the germination of Indian nationalism. In 1848, certain English-speaking Brahmins gave Phule and his friends a copy of Thomas Paine's *Rights of Man* (1791), hoping to fire up hostility towards the British. Our reader, however, saw in Paine 'potential for radicalism of a very different kind'.[185] To begin with, he was inspired not only to think about men but also the prerogatives of women. And he was, first and foremost, a doer. Unlike many high-caste reformers who made fine propositions in public but failed to enact these in domestic settings, Phule began at home. His wife, Savitribai (1831–97), had entered his life as an illiterate child bride. Not only did Phule share school lessons now, his support for her individuality was such that in time, she would emerge as a poet and activist in her own right.[186] Savitribai eventually attended a mission institution, qualifying to teach as well—one of her poems, in fact, celebrates the emancipatory power of 'Mother English'.[187] Unsurprisingly, the first venture Phule and she launched in 1848, inspired by missionaries,[188] was a girls' school. But what made it historic was their declaration that they would open up education to all classes, including 'untouchables' (Dalits). And of course, such boldness came at a price: Within a year, Phule's scandalized family threw the couple out.[189]

Their experience with promoting education among marginalized groups would, however, go a long way in shaping Phule's future ideology. That first school they established, for instance, did not last, because most Hindu students refused to sit at an equality with Dalits. So, a little later when the Phules made a second effort, they had to separate ritually 'polluted' pupils into an exclusive institution, instead of mixing them with the 'clean'.[190] The affair was instructive of how deeply set caste was among Hindus. But compromise did not end their ostracization. In 1856, Savitribai's brother was still berating her for tutoring Dalits. Our lady, not one to give up before 'idiots'—and in full possession of the courage of her convictions—insisted that she and her husband were doing 'God's own work'.[191] Here again we see the appropriation of missionary language, with different goals. But brave words aside, life was difficult. If in 1852 they were lauded by the British for their 'labours in the cause of education',[192] harassment was also in perennial pursuit. Much of this was aimed at Savitribai—a childless, educated woman who rejected domesticity—and she was often pelted with stones and dung as she walked to work. Remarkably, she did not recoil: Savitribai simply began, it is said, to carry an extra pair of clothes whenever she stepped out.[193] With time, she got bolder. In 1868, thus, while at her maternal home, she heard of a couple—a Brahmin man and a Dalit girl—who were about to be murdered for an inter-caste romantic

Jotiba Phule, Wikimedia Commons.

dalliance. 'I rushed to the spot and scared' the mob away, she wrote, warning the irate folk of 'grave consequences'.[194]

The consequences she referred to was punishment under British law, which by now superseded customary, caste-based punishment. This was to become a key plank for the Phules: the window colonialism opened for change, not least by way of criminal law which did not discriminate between castes. In fact, Phule would be accused of showing a little too much *rajabhakti* (uncritical loyalty) to the British; of being a missionary in Hindu clothing.[195] One can sense why. While at one point he harboured anti-colonial feelings, by his own admission, his perspective soon shifted.[196] Political freedom as urged by (mostly) high-caste thinkers lost its appeal; instead, *social* liberation seemed more urgent. The chains Phule wished to throw off were caste, superstition and Hinduism itself—by which he meant the 'selfish counterfeit faith' of the Brahmins.[197] This, in fact, set him apart from most reformers of the time. Their articulation of change accommodated modern values within the Hindu fold. By design, they did not repudiate Hinduism. Phule, though, felt no such emotional allegiance. Instead, he used rational elements of the missionary critique to examine his culture. Colonialism, to him, had divested Hindu elites of power; lower orders, contrastingly, found *hope* in British rule.[198] So too if men like Dayananda, while acknowledging its flaws, never rejected caste itself, Phule was allergic to the very principle. It came from two different ways of viewing the world. Caste was foundational to Hindus because their society was 'order-oriented rather than justice-oriented'. That is, Hinduism's diversity made finding equilibrium between the many its main priority, not equality.[199] Phule, though, was drawn to a bolder idea—to him, deliverance lay in modern egalitarianism, not inherited hierarchy.

This comes through in his act of dedicating his famous 1873 polemic, *Gulamgiri* ('Slavery'), to the 'Good People of the United States' for abolishing 'Negro Slavery' (sic).[200] His determination to educate Dalits also stemmed from the same ideals. Indeed, Phule parted ways with some associates because the latter evidently held basic literacy adequate for Dalits. Phule, however, urged *education*, not tokenism.²⁰¹ His appeals to the British were also framed in words of justice and humanity. In his *Brahmanache Kasab* (*Priestcraft Exposed*, 1869), for example, he asks how Queen Victoria, who presided over the termination of slavery in the British empire, was blind to the suffering of her low-caste Hindu subjects.²⁰² In schools he founded, children recited: 'Tell Grandma we are a happy nation, but [millions] are without education.'²⁰³ This thrust on (Western) learning as a pathway to social awakening appears in most of his publications. In an 1855 play, thus, a peasant couple are hoodwinked by a cunning Brahmin peddling hocus-pocus and threatening grave consequences on their unborn child. Joining emotional blackmail with gaslighting, he swindles them. But then enters a missionary, bringing light and common sense. Rapidly, he breaks the peasants' faith in stone gods, and exposes the Brahmin as a charlatan. Yet, in the end, the man and his wife decide to remedy their ignorance not by converting but by enrolling in one of Phule's night schools; education is recognized as their passport to wisdom.²⁰⁴ In 1882, Phule would also feature among those rare nineteenth-century voices endorsing compulsory primary education.²⁰⁵

But appeals to the public required more than just a rationalistic argument if they were to excite action; they needed emotional stimulants. Which meant Phule had to also tell a *story* with heroes and villains. Where nationalists pointed to the British as the bad men, our reformer found his antagonists in Brahmins. To him, in fact, this class was the personification of all that was evil in Hindu society. As such, this position has a history. Tamil Saiva saints, for example, did not hesitate to take a similar stand in medieval times.²⁰⁶ In the Maharashtra region itself, there was a 'tradition of tension' with Brahmins, who, under the Peshwas, had been a ruling class until 1818.²⁰⁷ Besides, there was the memory of bhakti poets like Tukaram, incidentally also a grocer. 'He who refuses to touch

[Dalits],' this seventeenth-century thinker sang, 'has a polluted mind . . . a man is only as chaste as his own belief.'[208] So, as with Dayananda and Roy, Phule's vision too might be linked with existing traditions of dissent within Hinduism.[209] Like those men, he too enlisted a novel reading of history for his cause. Factually speaking, for example, many segments of Hindu society, including kings and landed elites, were invested in caste.[210] Thus, well before the Peshwas, non-Brahmin Maratha kings of the province actively sustained this system.[211] Phule, however, hoped to unite all non-Brahmin groups under a common label—Sudras (the lowest of the four-fold hierarchy in Sanskrit scripture), leaving only Brahmins beyond the pale. So, in *his* writings, caste is the devious offspring of priestcraft, born to chain Hindus under a selfish elite. This, of course, was a stance missionaries took; they also believed that Brahmins—in reality a diverse, fragmented class, with internal dissonances—*imposed* all that was ugly in Hinduism with totalitarian power.[212] Phule embraced and then expanded on this (admittedly simplistic) theory.

Critically, in the process he would redefine the idea of being 'native'. Simply stated, the entire lot of people now subject to the British could not claim this tag. It applied, he argued, only to non-Brahmins. Or to cite Savitribai, Sudras alone were India's true 'natives'.[213] In giving this idea legs, Phule—whose writings reveal his eclectic reading, with references to everyone from George Washington to Darwin—seized on prevailing (Western) scholarly notions of an ancient Aryan invasion of the country. This, he claimed, proved 'beyond a shadow of doubt that the Brahmans' had come as 'conquerors' to India; they were a 'race', 'highly cunning, arrogant, and bigoted'. Proof was located in the Brahmins' own texts—Vedic references, thus, of wars between gods and demons were 'the distorted reflection'[214] of conflict between Aryans (Brahmins) and India's natives (Sudras). The victors' faith spread through violence that would shame even Nero. Indeed,

Phule declared, the Brahmins' ancestors did not hesitate to order 'wholesale extermination' even.[215] Over thousands of years they then subjugated the Sudras psychologically, foisting *khote grantha* (false books) on them,[216] as well as a religion that prostrated them from birth to death, with unnecessary ceremonies, pilgrimages and expensive donations.[217] Brahminism, 'like the coils of a serpent', ensnared Hindus;[218] all of Hindu history emerged from an original race war.[219] In fact, Phule looked warmly at the arrival of Islamic power in India: By smashing temples and Brahmin control, Muslims *nearly* liberated Sudras from bondage.[220] While that did not yield lasting results, in the present, there was opportunity again to find freedom via the British—also despatched by god.[221] Indeed, Hindus had reason to be grateful for foreign rule; if, Phule declared, they had learnt humaneness despite living in the toxic world of caste, it was thanks to white men.[222]

Infuriating conservatives, Phule also attacked Puranic Hinduism in a pungently satirical tone. The Vedas hold a verse suggesting Brahmins are superior to all because they sprang from the head of the creator, Brahma; Sudras, on the other hand, emerged from his feet. But Phule had some questions: Was Brahma's head also a uterus? Did he menstruate? When the Brahmin infant was born, did the creator breastfeed it?[223] On Vishnu's avatars: Narasimha, the man-lion emerged from a pillar, but who cut the umbilical cord?[224] Parasurama, another incarnation, was said to be immortal. But had anyone seen him lately? Phule promptly wrote an open letter—dated 1 August 1872—demanding that the Puranic hero present himself in six months.[225] Ravana had ten heads with as many mouths; it was 'miraculous' that he got through life with a single rectum.[226] Essentially, then, tales recorded in Sanskrit were rubbish; *Aesop's Fables* were a thousand times better.[227] As for everyday ritual practices, the less said the better. Brahmins 'purify themselves by drinking the urine of the cow'—a reference to how a small quantity of the said substance is sprinkled with other products of the animal to sanctify persons and places. And yet, if offered clean water by a Sudra, they deemed it impure.[228] In what is equally interesting, while Phule attacked the 'higher' Hindu gods, he presented folk deities like Khandoba—venerated chiefly by non-Brahmins—as historical heroes, deified for resisting Aryans during those early days of conflict.[229] That is, at a time when most Hindu intellectuals played down the 'inferior' deities, Phule positioned them as emblems of respect and resistance. Predictably, his critics rolled their eyes: That snarky Brahmin critic cited before announced, for instance, that our grocer's son was so towering a man of ideas, he exceeded Gibbon in achievement.[230]

Importantly, this set Phule apart from other subaltern reformers of the day. In Travancore, for example, Narayana Guru (1856–1928) rose as spiritual leader to the Ezhavas: a populous but 'polluting' community. Like Dayananda, he too wandered a great deal in his early years, meditating in caves and debating with sanyasis, till he arrived at his most famous maxim: that there is only one caste (humanity), one religion and one god.[231] In 1888, he set up a Siva shrine for Ezhavas—an act of defiance, considering that temple consecration for 'higher' deities was the Brahmins' preserve. He established, that is, 'counter temples' for low-caste groups.[232] Like Phule, the guru was blunt—when in the 1920s, Gandhi asked him if Hinduism offered means for spiritual liberation, he nodded, adding though that people needed worldly liberty too.[233] Yet, unlike Phule, Guru's reforms entailed a degree of Sanskritization, including adopting the habits of high-caste Hindus; it was not a total defiance of Brahminical authority. Thus, speaking of toddy-tapping, a vocation associated with Ezhavas, he proclaimed: 'The tapper's body stinks, his clothes stink, his house stinks, whatever he touches stinks.' Ezhavas must give up this impure profession; those who demurred were to be treated like a 'diseased limb'.[234] Blood sacrifices and rites with alcohol for 'evil gods' were replaced, similarly, by conscious association with 'civilized gods'.[235] He also urged learning of the Vedas and Hindu philosophy, and, himself a Sanskrit scholar, taught these.[236] So in some respects, Guru's reform lay in rejecting Brahminism as a social practice, while democratizing Brahminical Hinduism.[237] In time, tales of miraculous powers coalesced around him too, besides.[238]

This was not Phule's style; nobody could transform him into a conventional guru.[239] Indeed, his fierce anti-Brahminism meant that he lost several friends over the years.[240] And the hostility of his pen was linked to a living, visible reality of Brahmin dominance. Brahmins—with their history in the literate professions—had embraced Western education, going on to then populate most of the colonial bureaucracy. Or as Phule wrote, there was a monopoly even in the villages, where Brahmin accountants possessed more clout than non-Brahmin headmen.[241] Historically this was a reversal of things: Before centralized, bureaucratic political systems emerged, those headmen had been stronger. So much so that one Sanskrit poet even complained how in 'every village a Sudra acts like master [sic]' with Brahmins timidly serving as clerks.[242] In nineteenth-century India, however, not only did the British 'view men and things through Brahmin spectacles', they also outsourced governance to Brahmin minions.[243] The latter were nepotistic and corrupt in turn, doing all they could to prevent rival castes from entering the fray.[244] Similarly, the government erred in pumping resources into higher education, where Brahmins dominated. (In fact, in Madras it would be found in the last decade of Phule's life, that of 1346 graduates, almost nine hundred were Brahmins.[245]) Even in schools, Brahmin teachers could not sympathize with non-Brahmin pupils.[246] Urging for an expansion of village schools, Phule advised, therefore, to do 'away with all Brahmin school-masters!'[247] The Sudras, after all, Phule concluded, 'are the life and sinews of the country'; the British would do well to recognize this. And as if offering an incentive, he added that if their 'hearts and minds' were 'made happy', the British could count on 'their loyalty'.[248] In other words, to obtain social justice, Phule was willing to subordinate political liberty.

One might see in Phule's tone a tendency to vilify Brahmins beyond reason. But fiery language aside—where he called them 'pen-wielding butchers', for instance[249]—Phule was not wrong in alleging a Brahmin territoriality in sharing space with others. Part of his own legend tells how his education was first cut short by a Brahmin accountant in his father's shop; the latter feared that the boy, if properly schooled, would deprive him of his job.[250] So too the response of Brahmin intellectuals to ideas of social justice reveal insecurity. Phule's younger contemporary, B.G. Tilak (1856–1920), later to become a leading nationalist, resisted all that Phule urged. Educating girls risked 'castrating' Hinduism;[251] doing so in English was worse—it would have a 'dewomanising' influence.[252] Saddled with too much knowledge, educated women would become 'a dead weight on their husbands', forgetting their duty as 'helpmates'.[253] So also, Tilak was against educating all castes, seeing in it the threat of cultural 'destruction'; the shattering of 'reverence' towards Brahmins and orthodox Hinduism.[254] What was the purpose, besides, of teaching peasants mathematics and geography? It offered no advantages in 'practical life'. These were people for whom education was 'unsuited'; men should only be granted learning, Tilak explained, 'befitting their rank and station'.[255] To him, all this talk of the 'doctrine of the equality of mankind' was really a handle for dividing Hindu society.[256] Put simply, internal hierarchies, as presented by custom, must not be questioned. To do so was to succumb to anti-national, Western influences: an ironic claim, given the number of Brahmins who 'oiled the wheels of colonialism', drawing salaries for it.[257]

This is not to say no Brahmins supported Phule. In fact, when he founded his Satyashodhak ('Truth-Seeking') Samaj in 1873, three were involved.[258] This was one of several organizations that sprouted in western India in the last decades of the nineteenth century. The Paramahansa Mandali twenty-four years prior, with matching vigour of intention, had prayed, for example, for a 'fusion of castes', an end to image worship, and for women's rights.[259] It was, however, a secret society, and after its existence leaked, was dissolved. But even if in private, the Mandali had flirted with boldness: Its members hosted a meal once where men of several castes dined together: so violent an assault on custom, that attendees wore veils.[260] Phule's contemporary, G.H. Deshmukh (1823–92), also shared his views, even if he wasn't as blunt. Brahminhood, he argued—as did Dayananda—came from action, not birth. There was proof, Deshmukh added, in the scriptures for this. Brahmins, even if they were once noble, could not, he added, escape charges of corruption in the present. As for British rule: Hindu society was in a lamentable state; god had sent the English as a wake-up call.[261] Interestingly, he too criticized India's colonial rulers for vesting too much faith in one class of people. Except where Phule, in making that charge, meant Brahmins, Deshmukh was highlighting disparities between white officials (in higher posts) and 'natives' (languishing below).[262] But Deshmukh's more sober tone still invited much criticism. Which perhaps explains why Phule dispensed with coyness and took on tradition more openly. Interestingly, he came to Brahmin reformers' defence when they were threatened by conservatives: this is why Phule and his supporters were among those protecting Dayananda during his Poona visit.[263] But for all that, he never found Brahmin reformers sincere. As a biographer put it, they 'believed in social evolution'; Phule wanted a blazing 'revolution'.[264]

By the time he died, Phule was in a difficult way,[265] having also suffered a stroke in 1889. While he had run several solid businesses,[266] his social projects had slowly drained him of capital. His lack of diplomacy alienated powerful interests—as late as the 1920s, a proposal to erect a statue of Phule in Poona generated resistance from Brahmin nationalists.[267] Towards the end, his friends were writing to a Maratha prince—who Phule wooed, as Dayananda had the Rajputs—to support him.[268] It was a sad end for a man of such fearlessness. But nonetheless, he left a colossal footprint: Already from the 1870s, sections of his own Mali community had stopped using Brahmins' services.[269] Moreover, he defined for his followers what he believed was the true religion; principles by which Hindus should live after throwing off Brahminism. There was to be, for instance, no idol worship; good morals were critical, including women's equality; caste distinctions had to die, for division of a single species was unnatural; the Vedas were not to be viewed as special, for if god had meant it for everyone, he would not have put it in an obscure language; no sacred text was error-free; men and women must never surrender reason; the ancient past should never be romanticized, for men have always been flawed and in general, ethical conduct must be the measure of a godly life. Phule also paid homage to Islam and Christianity for their tenets of equality—ultimately the foundation of any decent society. This, to him, sat in sharp contrast to Brahminical thought, where some were *bhudeva*s ('gods on earth') and the rest inferior.[270]

A memorial to Jotiba and Savitribai Phule in Pune (Poona), Wikimedia Commons.

But the strongest thrust for Phule remained education. Or as a poem by his wife, Savitribai, who died seven years after him, tending to plague victims, goes:

> Arise my untouchable brothers
> Wake up
> To break the chains of tradition!
> Wake up
> For education . . .![271]

As the twentieth century approached, Hinduism and Hindus were in a state of flux. Many felt that pressure for change, both to resist colonialism and to forge a nation. But 'Hindu reformers and publicists disagreed with each other on the constituents of reformed Hinduism.'[272] On the one hand, thanks to men like Roy, there was an intellectual, philosophical picture, particularly useful when framing Hinduism as a coherent world religion before Western audiences. It was this Hinduism, for instance, that the monk Swami Vivekananda (1863–1902) highlighted at the 1893 World's Parliament of Religions in Chicago to great applause. Then there was emergent Hindu nationalism, as represented in its early form by Dayananda's followers, actively rousing men to action in service of the cow and in opposition to Muslims and missionaries. Here, we find a more aggressive Hinduism, unafraid to soil its hands, and dismissive of intellectual views as defined on Western terms. But there was also contradiction in efforts to unify Hindus, as appears in Phule's anti-caste activism. This spotlighted cleavages *within* Hindu society. Viewed from this prism, Roy's romanticized Hinduism was a façade; the reality was less beautiful. Nationalism too, this school of thought would suggest, was a mischievous effort to subdue the low castes; an overplaying of the British threat to nip internal revolution. And as the Hindu identity consolidated itself, successors of Phule like B.R. Ambedkar—who would give India its post-colonial constitution—were ever present to point to its paradoxes.[273]

But what of the great mass of ordinary Hindus? Many found Roy's presentation attractive, even if, without irony, they continued to patronize temples and Puranic beliefs. With Dayananda, they saw practical value in a muscular identity, even if violence was discomfiting. As for Phule: caste was simply too entrenched. For the most part, Hindus would, therefore, pay this mahatma homilies, cordially ignoring his scalding radicalism. The advent of a nationalized Hindu identity, then, was riddled with inconsistences. So, in the end it would take another generation before a Hindu ideologue identified a means to transcend these; to draw a vision of 'Hinduness' to surmount its most gaping infirmities. And as much as this man was in favour of Luther-like reform, he was also a champion of direct action. To some, then, he is the father of Hindu resurgence; others see in him a dangerous prophet of violence.

SEVEN

# DRAWING BLOOD

In the last week of July 1908, the city of Bombay exploded in a frenzy. The 'native town,' the *Bombay Gazette* reported, was 'seething with anger.' Millworkers—the backbone of the region's booming cotton industry—struck work, raining stones on the police as they advanced through the streets in the thousands. 'It is a marvel,' the newspaper announced, that 'the officers escaped alive'.[1] Firing was resorted to and by the end, fifteen men were killed and many dozen more wounded, including boys as young as thirteen.[2] Some of the chaos leaked into the districts. In Nagpur, a mob attacked a European academic;[3] outside the temple-town of Pandharpur, a female missionary was lynched and left for dead by a crowd of forty.[4] In what prompted even greater anxiety in Bombay, the loyalty of the 'native' component of the police was in doubt. They shared, after all, an ethnic background with the rioting millworkers and seemed to have acted with a strange lethargy in the crisis.[5] Pro-government newspapers, though, gave events a different spin: It was third-party 'emissaries' who actively inflamed the men of the mills, most of whom had no clue why they were agitating. All responsibility was laid with a mischievous 'imported agency', unreflective of the broader, submissive public.[6] The British were firmly in charge, these voices insisted, and there was no reason for alarm—an assertion, which in its very necessity, betrayed the opposite.

The events of that week were triggered by a stubborn enemy of India's rulers. On the night of 22 July, B.G. Tilak—a 'well-known author', an ex-professor of mathematics and 'sometime member of the Bombay Legislative Council'—was sentenced to six years in prison on charges of sedition.[7] As a police report subsequently put it, this Brahmin had 'steadily been growing in popularity', and many viewed him 'as a man actuated wholly by his desire to ameliorate the condition of Indians'. Wherever he gave addresses, 'he gained adherents', but even in general, his reputation was high, 'especially amongst the working classes'. He was much admired in western India, and 'in countless houses pictures of him are hung on the wall'.[8] Given that Tilak was also 'the ablest and most dangerous of the [anti-British] party in this country', the goal when taking him to trial was to deal as 'shrewd a blow' as possible, and 'show to all waverers the strength of Government'.[9] Except that the ploy backfired. Tilak's conviction only generated 'sympathy on the part of the people'; even the capitalist class, otherwise 'perfectly satisfied with British rule', 'sympathise[d] with Tilak in his fall.'[10] Ultimately, then, while the violence in Bombay was stemmed, the affair nevertheless compounded imperial fears of an increasingly aggressive Indian nationalism.

It was, in fact, an exhortation to force—at least as the state saw it—that put Tilak on the wrong side of colonial law. For decades this *lokamanya* ('revered of the people') had edited a bold Marathi-language weekly called *Kesari*. In the summer of 1908, two articles opened for the British a window to prosecute. The first ('The Country's Misfortune') appeared in response to the killing of two white women with a bomb by revolutionaries in Bengal. Tilak condemned the loss of life but declared in his editorial that it was British 'obstinacy and perversity' that instigated young men—'solicitous for the advancement of their country'—to pick up bombs. Indians sought *swarajya*, self-government. And since the imperial power did not acknowledge this perfectly legitimate claim, instead taking to 'oppressive Russian methods', the people too were 'compelled' to respond in the fashion of Russian revolutionaries. The Bengal case was tragic. But, Tilak believed, it was critical to address the core ailment—colonial rule—rather than just its bloody rashes.[11] Incidentally, this was not the first time the *Kesari* had advocated aggressive 'Russian methods of agitation'. In 1907, for example, Tilak wrote that 'it is necessary for thousands of young men to risk their lives' for India; that no matter the Raj's might, 'the British themselves know . . . how unsound the foundation of their power . . . is'.[12] Violent action by brown persons, while generally lamentable was not, to him, politically inexplicable.[13]

The second article, meanwhile, had the title 'These Remedies Are Not Lasting'. This one argued against equating Bengal's revolutionaries with European anarchists, as the officialdom was wont to do. In white lands, the editorial claimed, it was 'hatred felt for selfish millionaires' that galvanized men. In Bengal, however, the root of violence was noble: 'an excess of patriotism'. Indians were adopting anarchist methods, yes, but it was better to equate them with brave Russians standing up to tsarist tyranny. The article also offered the analogy of a caged parrot. Typically, such pets were treated with affection; they received sugar and treats to compensate for the loss of freedom. But with India, the British had 'not only closed the door . . . [but also] commenced to pluck the wings and break the [bird's] leg'. As a nation, Indians were 'castrated'. Was it any surprise, then, that pushed to the limits of suffering, hot-blooded youth were seduced by the bomb? The item itself, unlike ordinary arms, did not require big factories or assembly lines; it could be produced easily. And if the 'policy of repression' continued, more and more men would take to making explosives in their kitchens.

The only way to prevent this, the *Kesari* counselled, was to grant Indians the rights they demanded. Revolutionaries were 'turnheaded', sure, but it was conditions of British invention that precipitated such cranial rotation. And so, common sense demanded that to avoid more pain and gore, the state must remedy its own behaviour.[14]

After his trial, Tilak, predictably, forfeited personal liberty but soared in public esteem. His courtroom

Bal Gangadhar Tilak (1897) © Illustrated London News/Mary Evans Picture Library.

address—lasting, in the words of the frustrated prosecutor a 'maddening' twenty-one hours[15]—did not sway the predominantly white jury. But while the accused was no orator, his punchy lines, trumpeted by the press, found their mark. Indeed, grumbled an official, the whole performance 'was made not so much to the jury as to the gallery'.[16] At the start, Tilak decried how the entire case rested on defective English translations of his Marathi writings. The subtext was clear: The legal system remained laughably foreign to the subject race on which it forced its 'justice'. Next, citing press freedoms, he added that so long as Indians admired fancy Western ideas quietly, things were fine. But 'as soon as we begin to imitate them you call it seditious'.[17] Weaving (perhaps deliberately) an excruciatingly dilated argument about his journalism being misunderstood, Tilak did not, however, abandon his stance. Bomb-throwing was criminal. 'But in condemning it,' he confirmed, 'we must also condemn the repressive measures of [the] Government.'[18] It is no surprise, then, that to the prosecution, whichever way it was viewed, Tilak's 'doctrine [was] subversive', relaying to Indians that if patriotism were the cause, even bloodshed was admissible.[19]

When the verdict was announced, hours before his fifty-second birthday, Bombay, as we saw, went up in flames. For a week, the British struggled, spared further stress only by the fact that the rioting public was disorganized and incapable of escalation. London, meanwhile, worried about long-term repercussions: 'mischief... will be done by this sentence', the secretary of state predicted, though it was too late to retreat; 'the milk is now spilled'.[20] In September, Tilak was deported to Burma where he would stay locked up for half a decade. In 1909, when asked by a friend to accept certain terms for an early release, he declined this 'undoing' of his life's work; to accept conditions would be to 'live as a dead man'.[21] Instead, in a memorial to London, he highlighted procedural flaws in his trial, branding it 'unlawful'.[22] In subsequent petitions too, such as in 1912, while his language mellowed, the British saw 'neither expression of penitence nor promise of future good behaviour'.[23] Indeed, Tilak had told an official that on release, he planned to 'recommence his preaching and teaching'; that 'no foreigner has a right to rule India',[24] So when at last in 1914, he was set free, having served his full term, the authorities still viewed the lokamanya as an accredited 'enemy of the British Government'.[25] And with good reason: If earlier he were a rising star, now after exile he 'appeared to his followers as little less than the reincarnation of a deity'.[26] In fact, by 1918, Tilak was being nervously described as 'probably the most powerful man in India',[27] having even won international approbation from the likes of Lenin.[28]

Unfortunately for the Maratha hero, age played spoilsport just as he arrived at the peak of his influence. Tilak died in 1920, and leadership of the nationalist movement was transferred from the lokamanya into the hands of a certain mahatma. Gandhi had returned to India after years abroad in 1915, preaching passive resistance and nonviolence—neither of which propositions amused Tilak. When at a gathering the new entrant piously proposed that Indian politics should be based on truth, the veteran snorted: 'My friend! Truth has no place in politics.'[29] Tilak was a student of philosophy, but in the realm of men, he championed pragmatic action. Or as he wrote in a commentary on the sacred Gita—composed, revealingly enough, when in prison—while saintliness had much to commend it, if required one must not hesitate to 'take out a thorn by a thorn'—or seek an eye for an eye.[30] 'Tilak . . . considers that everything is fair in politics,' protested the mahatma, who envisioned a more idealistic public discourse of 'honesty, fairplay and charity'. In return, Tilak reminded Gandhi that he was in 'a game of worldly people and not of sadhus (saints)'. This was not to suggest the younger man's principles were foolish; only that between their divergent styles 'one is more suited to this world'.[31] Or as Tilak simplified for a crowd in a speech some years prior, 'There is only one medicine for [the deliverance of] all people. That medicine is power; take it into your possession.'[32]

Centuries before Tilak, there lived in the Maharashtra region a Brahmin sage called Ramdas (1608–81). He had wisdom to impart on god and matters of the soul, but what most appealed to later-day nationalists were his political lessons. 'Meet boldness with boldness,' he advised, and 'villainy by villainy'.[33] One can see why this animated Tilak's generation. Indeed, in the colonial era, many in this part of India drew parallels between their own time and the age of Ramdas. If today they were fighting British imperialism, back then, it was Mughal power that had threatened their ancestors. Where in the present foreigners from overseas imperilled Hindu society, in the past, it was an invading northern empire that pressed it. The Mughal conquest had, in fact, aggravated everything from famine to political instability. In response—and in a tone Tilak would echo—Ramdas promoted the cult of power. 'In this tumultuous world, what can the weak do?'³⁴ No, the 'god-hating dogs' must be '*driven* from the land'. He commanded the Marathas to unite, spread their authority and bring order.³⁵ Patent here, however, was also a fusing of politics with religion: The enemy represented Islamic might, whereas resistance was Hindu—defined by Ramdas, in tune with his own background, in an orthodox mould.³⁶

But if Ramdas offered an intellectual frame for militant Hinduism, the real icon—the man who manifested it in action—was the contemporary Maratha king, Chhatrapati Shivaji (1630–80). In fact, claims would later be made, to supply modern perceptions of the past a tidier wellspring, that Ramdas was the latter's guru: an idea dismissed by scholars who argue that more likely, it was Shivaji's deeds that fertilized Ramdas's mind.³⁷ But either way, the seventeenth century saw something heady surface in Maharashtra, both intellectually and politically, generating powerful influences for future anti-colonialists. To start with, there was plain political resistance. By the time Shivaji was born, the old Islamic state his family served had crumbled,³⁸ and the area was torn between the Mughals and a neighbouring sultanate. Both were foreign, albeit in different degrees, and their resultant deficit in legitimacy—added to his phenomenal daring—allowed Shivaji to carve out an autonomous realm.³⁹ In 1659, the sultanate ordered its most feared general to crush the upstart Maratha, but in a sensational turn, Shivaji took Afzal Khan's head. Here, we encounter the triumph of the underdog against established might. Shivaji had till then been dismissed as an irritating rebel, as small fry; and *yet*, he felled the dreaded Khan. Or as would be stated in a eulogy—and arouse men like Tilak in the age of bombs and the Raj:

> Even a single ant
> Can kill an elephant
> By crawling into its trunk.
> So no one should consider
> Any enemy too small.⁴⁰

From now, Shivaji's career would pick up. And save for a few reversals, he successfully founded a Maratha kingdom in the Deccan—which, in the following century, would sweep up much of the subcontinent from Mughal control. But kingship is more than bald power; it requires an ideological foundation. Given that the region was governed by Muslim dynasties from as far back as the fourteenth century, society had largely grown used to Islamic sovereignty. Shivaji was seen as a parvenu; indeed, many leading *Marathas* refused to recognize him.[41] In any case, as a non-Muslim, he could not appropriate the sultanate model,[42] so the would-be king fell back on Hindu traditions, claiming space on fresh terms. In 1674, he organized a grand 'classical' coronation rite—of the like not seen for centuries—turning the proverbial table.[43] For from the Sanskritic perspective, it was *Islamic* rule that was illegitimate; in this reading, Shivaji was no rebel, but an idealized Kshatriya monarch, *restoring* order after a long eclipse. This countering of Islamic power structures with a Sanskritic one also accommodated his newness. And Shivaji ceased operating on an ideological ground set by rivals, instead reimagining the very basis of politics. Or, as a chronicle has him proclaim: 'My aim is to found a Maharashtra Empire. Our religion has been overthrown, gods and Brahmans are troubled, the *Mlechchhas* [barbarians] are supreme.' He would 'remove this [improper] state of things'.[44]

Thus, for instance, in one of the oldest Maratha ballads from this period, we find Islamic power delegitimized by highlighting the fanaticism and bigotry of Afzal Khan. When he is on his way to Shivaji before their fateful meeting, he plunders and despoils major temples: proof of why, ultimately, Islamic rule can never truly serve order in the Hindu sense.[45] In contrast, Shivaji is positioned as an instrument of the divine—through him, it is the gods who are at work.[46] That the region had long suffered from the decline of the sultanates and the many-generational war with the Mughals, also reinforced such claims. This said, Muslims as a people were not Shivaji's enemies: Indeed, in a court epic, a sultan is styled *dharmatma* (saintly), and a Muslim general who fought the Mughals in an earlier age, is likened to Hindu deities.[47] Why, Shivaji's father himself is believed to have been named, as mentioned in the Introduction, after a Muslim pir.[48] But as the founder of a new *political* entity and a consciously Hindu kingship, Islamic *power* was undesirable; the new space he was creating was 'accessible to all', sure, but would be 'governed by Hindus'[49]—a development which in due course offered Hindu nationalists a genealogy for their creed.[50] More broadly, for Tilak's generation, Shivaji's example could be marshalled for resistance to the British. The Raj called them seditious, but they denied unwelcome foreigners the ground to call them anything at all. Just as Shivaji refused to recognize norms set by Islamic authority in Maharashtra, Tilak would deny the British any berth in India.[51]

This overlap between a politically alert Hinduism and nationalism was particularly pronounced in Tilak's early career. The Indian National Congress—the chief colonial-era nationalist outfit, and to this day, one of the country's principal political parties—was established in 1885, mainly as a body of English-educated Indians. Their idea was to agitate, most politely, for greater representation for 'natives' in the country's administration. Five years later, Tilak—a prominent journalist, already hostile to the Raj—joined it.[52] But from the start, he perceived the organization as too moderate, not to speak of divorced from the masses. Yes, it was true that despite its diplomatic tone, the Congress faced British suspicion—to assuage the latter, its 1886 president had even to declare it India's 'good fortune' to suffer the Raj's 'civilizing rule'.[53] But for Tilak, a fear of imperial sensitivities was untenable. Congress, to him, looked like an elite talking shop; to grow fiercer, he urged a sustained outreach to ordinary people, in forms and an idiom they could identify with. That is, if Congress hoped for better 'native' representation in power, it would itself first have to better represent India's non-English-speaking classes. Tilak's plan to achieve this was to moor modern political freedoms and institutions in 'native' cultural ideas. And the way he would do this—to the discomfiture of many of his peers—was by injecting religion into nationalism.[54] Or as was argued, 'Why shouldn't we convert the large religious festivals into mass political rallies?' By so doing, the cause would escape narrow, anglicized confines for 'the humblest cottages'.[55] And Congress—lampooned by a British viceroy as akin to an adolescents' debating society—would be able to answer the gibe with a bite.[56]

In other words, Tilak was, to quote an admirer, 'trying to bring politics from the cloudland of words and general theories to the solid earth of reality'.[57] Instead of huffing along on British terms—submitting petitions, seeking seats in legal bodies and councils and attempting a politics of persuasion—Indians could, with a little effort, he felt, *force* a better bargain. The Congress in its moderate avatar was, he would sneer, like 'a seasonal activity', comparable to 'the croaking of frogs in the rains'.[58] So, in Maharashtra at any rate, he began to attempt transforming those croaks into something resembling a growl by developing festivals. His first was focused on the elephant-headed Ganapati, venerated as much by Brahmins as by non-Brahmins. This made the deity a compelling candidate to construct 'harmony amongst various sections of the Hindu community'.[59] Where individuals worshipped diverse gods in diverse ways and spaces, here was an opportunity to combine under one umbrella, 'with one heart and one sense of pride'.[60] What was mostly a private worship, thus, was turned from 1893 into a public celebration.[61] Different localities—housing specific castes—were encouraged to install a Ganapati, all these converging ten days later in a colourful procession. By its second edition, Poona alone had a hundred Ganapatis, with bands of musicians, acrobats, dancers and thousands of spectators.[62] Some grumbled it was undignified to turn faith into a spectacle. But for Tilak, 'demonstration and éclat [were] essential to the awakening of the masses'.[63] That is, this was not about god but kindling public energy; fun and play was a vehicle for 'imparting [political] knowledge'.⁶⁴ And he was vindicated: The festival was a success. By 1905, seventy-two towns, including a few outside the Deccan, would import the idea of Ganapati gatherings.⁶⁵

The second event Tilak launched was an annual commemoration of Shivaji: a hero on whom too 'all the different castes of Maharashtra could focus their loyalty'.⁶⁶ To begin with, the king's *samadhi* (memorial) in a faraway fort languished in neglect, as the dominion of 'kites and crows, vultures and dogs'.⁶⁷ A decade ago, the British had allocated a maintenance grant but hopes of raising a shrine were disappointed. Through his paper, Tilak invited public donations and by the end of 1895, 60,000 people had subscribed.⁶⁸ Shivaji, of course, had already been seized on by others: Phule, who we met in the previous chapter, presented him as a peasant leader, a man of the masses and an embodiment of justice, for instance. In the 1870s, Vasudev Balwant Phadke (1845–83), a clerk-turned-militant activist, had set off an armed revolt.⁶⁹ At the time, the press compared his agenda to Shivaji's.⁷⁰ Tilak, however, transformed the king into a totem for mass mobilization, including by shaming his countrymen. It was, he wrote, appalling that Maharashtra had 'forgotten the great man who laid the foundation of our empire, who upheld our self respect as Hindus'.⁷¹ They *owed* his memory reverence. Again, there were critics who believed Shivaji 'would not have liked' extravagance; that no human should be 'worshipped like God'.⁷² But Tilak would not yield: 'hero worship' was a key fount of 'nationality, social order, and religion'.⁷³ Or as a supporter's letter published in the *Kesari* explained, Shivaji was to Maharashtra 'what George Washington was to the United States of America'—a symbol of who his people were, and what they must fight for.⁷⁴ And here again, Tilak could claim a win: By 1907, brown students even as far as Tokyo were organizing Shivaji celebrations.⁷⁵

To nobody's surprise, the British resented both of Tilak's marquee enterprises. As early as 1896, it was observed that the objective of the

Chhatrapati Shivaji Maharaj in a print from the Raja Ravi Varma Press, courtesy of the Sandeep & Gitanjali Maini Foundation.

Shivaji festival 'is obviously to arouse if it exists or create, if it does not, a nationalist feeling among the Mahrattas'.[76] A decade later, it was even clearer that Ganapati celebrations served as an 'occasion of demonstrations against the British' while the 'cult of Shivaji' was 'an incitement to the expulsion of English rule'.[77] In the Marathi press, it was freely proclaimed how, as Shivaji delivered Maharashtra from Mughal oppression, rebuilding the samadhi would 'rouse the spirit of a future patriot to restore independence to his country.'[78] 'Shivaji's present popularity,' another journal explained, was predicated on the 'supposition that the Indians of the present day are suffering from the same evils ... as their ancestors suffered in the times of Shivaji'.[79] At the festivals itself, poets paraded zeal to stir up their audience, comprising everyone from peasants and teachers to shopkeepers. 'Fools, what is the use of your being men?' asked one. 'Of what use are your big moustaches?' India was 'called *Hindu*stan'; '[h]ow is it that the English rule here?' Describing the British as cow-killing butchers, listeners were told to not fear 'slaughtering the wicked'.[80] The mood was electric and inspired all kinds of markets—the society artist Raja Ravi Varma, for example, had an instant hit on his hands when he mass-produced prints of Shivaji's portrait.[81] The king, from a faceless outline in traditional tales, made his entry into thousands of Maharashtra homes this way, enveloped in history but also political sentiment.

These events, in fact, resulted in Tilak's first encounter with anti-sedition laws. In 1897, the Shivaji festival was pointedly arranged ten days before Queen Victoria's jubilee.[82] And speeches made on the occasion looked to the Raj like pure incitement. One figure endorsed the use of every option in regaining 'lost independence'; a second referenced the French Revolution, adding how committing murder in service of an ideal was justified, a principle that 'applied to Maharashtra'.[83] Another topic covered was Shivaji's killing of Afzal Khan at what was formally a diplomatic meeting between the two. There was a debate as to who struck first and was liable, therefore, to the charge of treachery.[84] One speaker argued that even if Shivaji were guilty, it was fine; the Maratha hero abandoned 'a minor duty' for 'accomplishing a major one'.[85] Tilak went further. 'If thieves enter our house and we have not sufficient strength to drive them out, we should without hesitation shut them up and burn them alive.' That is, morality was contingent on context; Shivaji killed out of higher motives. Finally, Tilak thundered: 'God has not conferred upon the foreigners the grant inscribed on a copper-plate of the Kingdom of Hindusthan.' Urging all to 'consider the actions of great men' in conceiving resistance, he called on them to escape the shackles of mere legality. For this, the Gita was pointed to—that religious text of orientalist delight, where a central figure from the Mahabharata, facing cousins and loved ones on the opposite side of the battlefield, is counselled by the divine Krishna to cast aside his scruples and do his duty.[86] It was difficult, and would not pass elementary moral exams, but what needed to be done had to be done.[87] Or in more contemporary language: no gain without pain.

This might all have passed for strong rhetoric, were it not for the fact that days later, two men enacted these lessons. W.C. Rand, an officer notorious for a rather harsh policy during a recent epidemic—and castigated in print by Tilak as 'sullen and tyrannical'[88]—was shot dead. The brothers Damodar and Balakrishna Chapekar were responsible. These men had for long flirted with violence, having until recently run a crew trained in martial skills. Claiming inspiration from the Gita, Shivaji and Americans, they harassed missionaries and even defaced in Bombay a statue of that 'fiend', Victoria.[89] In their mind, everything British was suspect, whether it was English education (which sneakily made brown men effeminate and anti-Hindu) or cricket.[90] 'Native' reformers were reviled with a passion: the Chapekars once assaulted with a metal pipe (from behind, it might be noted) the editor of a progressive journal.[91] To them, even Tilak was not bold enough, though he was 'better' than the Congress's moderates.[92] For his part, while the lokamanya knew the brothers—having recommended one for a job the previous year[93]—whether he was embroiled in Rand's murder is debatable.[94] A paper that suggested this had to apologize, for example.[95] But the British certainly held Tilak morally accountable. In 1897, in what was described in the 'native' press as a 'national calamity', he was jailed, spending twelve months behind bars.[96] The Chapekars, in the meantime, were hanged.[97] Tellingly, in Damodar's final hours, it was Tilak's copy of the Gita that kept him company.[98]

In fact, decades later, officials remained part-amused and part-flummoxed that the man, who through 'grandiose phrases' stressed direct action, showed horror when 'misguided students' actually did what he preached.[99] In the government's eyes, he was likely 'the chief conspirator, against the existence of the British' in India.[100] They could never find convincing proof, though, of Tilak's links to revolutionaries: Indeed, after the 1908 sedition case, one dejected bureaucrat complained how the man might have been neutralized, '[h]ad we been able to connect Tilak with the bomb or gun running business even indirectly'.[101] But that he was a formidable symbol was obvious. In Kolhapur, thus, a school was founded with hopes of producing boys 'of the stamp of Tilak'.[102] In 1909, when another British officer was killed in Nasik, the assassin admitted that the *Kesari* had influenced his thinking.[103] A fellow conspirator was an organizer of the city's Shivaji festival.[104] The next year, in a sedition case in faraway Punjab, several accused were apprehended carrying images of Tilak.[105] Why, when that Pandharpur missionary was attacked after his own conviction in 1908, it was to shouts of 'Shivaji ki Jai' ('Victory to Shivaji') and 'Tilak Maharaj ki Jai' ('Victory to Tilak').[106] The closest the authorities came to pinning the *lokamanya* was when a revolutionary, Hoti Lal Verma, claimed Tilak aided him with money and an introduction to men 'who knew how to make bombs'.[107] But there was no clinching proof—at any rate, by then this 'Father of Indian Unrest' was already incarcerated, serving out his second sentence in Burma.[108]

There are, however, complications to this tale of audacious courage. India, it was manifest—with its variety of identities, castes and languages—could never be a case study in homogeneity. How then to foster nationalism? Where Tilak was concerned, the solution lay in tethering the proposition to Hinduism; to cultivate a *Hindu* nationalism. Moderate Congressmen's views that everyone living in India was automatically part of an Indian nation was not convincing. Or as he explained, to view 'Hindus, Muslims, Sikhs, Parsis' and others as a unity was wrong; to claim 'their nationality has become one' was simplistic.[109] No mere 'aggregation of people' residing together constituted 'a nation'. For the genuine article one needed 'such bonds as a common language, a common religion, and a common history'.[110] The harsh truth to be faced, then, was that the 'majority of our society' was Hindu. And though internally diverse, Hindus all shared a palpable 'feeling of *Hindutva* (Hinduness)'.[111] This, therefore, must be the glue with which to activate nationalism. The Victorian tenet was that India was a dispersed 'assemblage of beings'.[112] But for Tilak, the great bulk of those beings converged under that great tent called Hinduism. By 'forgetting all the minor differences', it would be possible to secure them into a 'mighty Hindu nation'.[113] And naturally, 'the prosperity which we want must come about by means of a Hindu state'.[114] After all, as Tilak explained, the very name 'Hindustan' for India originated in the fact that this was the Hindu homeland. Contradictions within did not matter; 'pride in the Hindu religion' could convert most Indians into a forceful bloc.[115]

To frame this Hindu nationalism, however, Hinduism needed a clearer shape. Who exactly was Hindu? To begin with, internal caste and other differences were no impediment; as Tilak argued, among Christians too there were Protestants and Catholics. There might even be sectarian persecution, and yet, they were of one religion.[116] So too, Hinduism was 'made up of different parts co-related to each other as so many sons and daughters'; and all families had their squabbles.[117] In fact, to count as Hindu, one had to satisfy only a few requirements: acknowledge Vedic supremacy; accept that there are multiple paths to god; and that god did not open only one door to mankind through a single prophet or messenger but appeared in a host of forms.[118] It is striking how much of this matched what Hindus had always stated in their encounters with missionaries like Ziegenbalg. But Tilak's articulation that different peoples worshipped god in different ways was tailored also to accommodate Hinduism's *domestic* variety.[119] Interestingly, he did not romanticize Vedic revivalism of the Arya Samaj type; in fact, wrote the lokamanya, Hinduism had survived the ages precisely by being open to change, sometimes even incorporating features from rival traditions.[120] For this reason, he declared himself a friend of reform, subject however to the condition that it uphold Hindutva. Luther was offered as a model—the German called for transformation, yes, but remained a devout Christian. 'Native' Luthers too, then, were legitimate only if they worked within the limits of Hindu nationalist interests.[121] Viewed this way, one can recognize why Tilak was no champion of radicals like Phule, excoriating as they did Hinduism from top to bottom, in a missionary tone.[122]

That said, Tilak's Hindutva or Hinduness was largely still an academic portrait. As late as 1911, for instance, in swathes of upper India, census officials would find that 'a quarter of the persons classed as Hindus denied' both 'supremacy of the brahmans and the authority of the Vedas'. Even with cow worship, two-fifths ate beef.[123] So in terms of *practical* mobilization, Hinduness was reinforced by emphasizing not what Hindus were but what they were *not*: Christian and Muslim.[124] Where the Congress's moderates framed nationalism as political resistance, for Tilak it also involved addressing a cultural collision. In a 1901 article ('Wake Up or Die'), he declared, for instance, how modern science had shattered Christianity's claims; yet thanks to financial might and the fact of the British empire, missionaries had mushroomed even in India's villages. Charitable aid during calamities too was suspect. In the last drought, claimed Tilak, American donations alleviated pain but also helped missionaries amass for potential conversion 25,000 orphans. When 'this money is used to destroy our religion, how can we not object?'[125] Pandita Ramabai (1858–1922), a Brahmin female convert (and Sanskrit scholar), was similarly targeted for evangelical work; in a crude offensive, Tilak recommended she discard *pandita* (feminine for pandit) and restyle herself *reveranda*: a play on 'reverend' which evidently also punned in Marathi on 'randa', or whore.[126] Anti-Christian feeling entered Tilak's political speeches too. Hindus, he protested in 1907, were suspect even when they aired basic criticism of the Raj; missionaries, though, held full freedom of speech to attack Hinduism at its most sacred sites.[127]

But that was not all. Besides Christianity, the Hindu nation was also besieged by Islam. At one level, it appears that the conservative Brahmin in Tilak was not fond of interfaith overlaps—what looked happily syncretic from one gaze resembled adulteration from another. Muharram in Maharashtra, for instance, drew enthusiastic Hindu engagement—the latter made vows and even joined in processions.[128] While moderate politicians were charmed by this display of interreligious harmony,[129] as early as 1891, Tilak dismissed the festival.[130] In 1893, after Hindu–Muslim riots in the province—linked to cow-protection societies inspired by the Arya Samaj—Tilak went further.[131] In the *Mahratta*, his English paper, Bombay's chief mosque was construed as a nest of goons.[132] Citing Maratha opposition to Islamic kingdoms, another piece warned how 'the people' had 'sufficient capacity and intelligence to *make the Mahomedans* respect [their] rights'.[133] Patent here is the idea that Hindus were 'the people'; others might be tolerated, provided they accepted Hindu priority. In fact, one supposed motivation for the Ganapati festivities—in addition to organising against the British—was Tilak's determination to 'supplant the Mohurram'; of making a demonstration of Hindus' Hinduness.[134] And though he denied this charge of one-upmanship, Tilak could not help but add that Hindu presence in Muharram was 'because *we* saw God in all beings'. But *they*, Muslims, took this for granted.[135] In 1894, in fact, our man struggled to disguise his delight when reporting that if most Muharram *doli*s (palanquins) were hitherto offered by Hindus—100 of 150—the number had now dropped to twenty-five.[136] Hindus were owning their separateness, and openly too.[137]

Indeed, at its core the tension was this: Though Hindus were numerically stronger, a history of Islamic rule, combined with Hinduism's many-faced, flexible and splintered nature evidently gave Islamic culture a wide berth. Muslims, with their history of power and status, seemed to Tilak and his compatriots, as wielding disproportionate influence, especially when they were— as British censuses revealed—a minority of the population. How, then, could they pretend to equal claims with Hindus? Indeed, the British 'under the guise of religious tolerance were failing to keep the Mussalmans in check'; secretly the Raj *favoured* Muslims, he insisted.[138] As a result, flexing Hinduness became critical, while highlighting the fundamental irreconcilability of the Islamic and Hindu identities. During the Ganapati celebrations, for example, quarrels recurred about processions playing music near mosques, offending Muslims. In 1894, thus, the magistrate in Poona decreed that 'music must cease' in such spaces. Tilak, however, argued that the 'streets are public' and that all enjoyed 'equal rights . . . to use any street—both silently and otherwise'.[139] One official later alleged that personally, Tilak did not 'regard the right to play music as important'. But he shrewdly identified in it an occasion for Hindu assertion; a platform for castes to identify with that broad heading of *being Hindu* against a rival Other. So, it was 'not that Tilak adopted a particular method but that he aimed at a particular result'.[140] And the goal in mind was Hindu consolidation—step one towards Hindu nationalism.

This comes through in the Ganapati songs also. One, seeking to wean Hindus off Muharram, goes:

> Oh! why have you abandoned today the Hindu religion?
> How have you forgotten Ganapati, Shiva and Maruti?
> What have you gained by worshipping the *tabuts* [during Muharram]?
> What boon has Allah conferred upon you
> That you have become Mussalmans today?
> Do not be friendly to a religion which is alien
> Do not give up your religion and be fallen.
> Do not at all venerate the *tabuts*,
> The cow is our mother, do not forget her.[141]

Moreover, as with Christianity, in criticizing the British, dislike of Islam too slipped into Tilak's rhetoric. Referring to the Raj's demilitarizing of India, he complained, for example, how 'even a savage race like the Muhammadans did not disarm the Hindus'.[142] In an 1895 letter in the *Kesari*, we read: 'Would [Shivaji] not have burned with indignation at seeing Hindu temples demolished by Moslem fanatics?'[143] Other newspapers picked up this trend, comparing British rule with 'fanatical persecution' under Islamic powers.[144] Or in a critic's words, Tilak 'grafted a new hatred of British rule on to the old hatred of Mohammedan domination'.[145] In time, Hindu nationalists would expand this approach, so that in addition to foreign foes, Hindus were asked to beware of the (supposed) enemy within. Even with Shivaji—who could be positioned as more than just a parochial Hindu icon—Muslims were uncomfortable. Festival processions, for example, featured idols of Shivaji's favourite goddess Bhavani; Hinduness was conspicuous.[146] Tilak did not deny that 'the country can prosper only if Hindus and Muslims get along.'[147] There had, he also agreed, been good men like Akbar, and plenty of examples where Muslims patronized Hindus and vice versa.[148] But this did not erase the basic truth that from the first Islamic raids into the land nearly a thousand years ago, Hindus had suffered much torment from Muslims.[149] Indeed, Hindus had well before the British arrived, begun to resist; after all, Tilak observed, by the eighteenth century, the Marathas were masters of India. It was by defeating *them*—not the Mughals—that the Raj embedded itself.[150] The underlying message was this: If India were seized from Hindus, its proprietorship must also return in time to Hindus exclusively.[151]

Not long before his death in August 1920, in one of his final public speeches, Tilak was shocked by a physical assault. He was offering his opinion on whether compulsory primary education ought to be mandated only for boys or also for girls. The lokamanya's view was that, given poor resources, the focus should be on boys.[152] On the face of it, he was being pragmatic, but in fact, his position on social reform around women's rights had been consistently negative for decades. In 1886, for instance, he quipped how 'it was not with the help of girls who went to school' that Shivaji founded the Maratha state.[153] Five years later, he was among opponents of a bill upping the age of consummation of marriage for girls from ten to twelve. Progressive Hindus saw in this an urgent step in combating child marriage; an 1889 case where a ten-year-old died after intercourse with a husband of thirty, had shocked public opinion. Tilak, however, argued that a 'few examples' were being exaggerated to condemn Hindus; to accept British legislation would do violence to 'our traditions'.[154] He did not disagree that early consummation was unhealthy; British interference, however, was worse. When the bill passed anyway, an irate Tilak declared it 'an attack on our national character'; Hindus who enabled it were 'enemies' of their own.[155] Indeed, he compared the government's action to 'Muhamadans

[who] forced the Hindus to grow beards', i.e., forced conversion on them.[156] Back then, however, he was a rising star. In 1920, on the other hand, the crowd's mood was shifting. Even as the lokamanya laid out his position, on his home turf in Poona no less, 'tomatoes and eggs' were hurled, and he was 'driven off the stage'.[157]

It is something of an irony. At a pan-Indian level, Tilak had in fact mellowed over the years, gaining wider acceptability. That is, as he graduated from provincial celebrity to subcontinental fame, the man went from being a polarizing politician to projecting a statesmanlike image. His desire to energize Hindus remained, but in the fight against the British, Muslim cooperation, he realized, was unavoidable. So, Shivaji's appeal was expanded: Just as Nelson and Napoleon were heroes to the British and French nations, Tilak explained, Shivaji stood for *all* Indians.[158] Indeed, the Maratha king never hated Muslims; what he fought was 'tyrannical power', which *happened* in his lifetime to be Islamic.[159] In 1916, thus, he dismissed Muslim fears about a Hindu-dominated future. Stressing a shared Indian identity, he argued that if in Canada, with its French and English factions, an arrangement could be found, there was no reason why Muslims and Hindus could not manage in India. If Hindus won power, they would 'afterwards duly consult our Muhammadan brethren'.[160] Tilak was prepared to recognize all who exerted themselves for 'the good of India' as 'not alien'. Hindus were intrinsically Indian, of course, yet 'I don't call Muhammedans aliens' either.[161] Increasingly, in fact, the lokamanya looked rather moderate.[162] This is amusing given how his backers once attacked a liberal as 'the dirt of the gutter' and a 'eunuch'.[163] Tilak himself had previously decried moderation as 'unmanly'.[164] But to borrow from one of his lawyers, if he was 'communalistic' once, with experience Tilak acquired a 'greater National outlook'.[165] He had begun an inveterate Hindu nationalist but necessity blunted his sharp edges.

However, with social reform, his position was less elastic: The Hindu religion and *rashtra* (nation) were 'more important than

Portraits of Tilak by N.V. Virkar, Collection of Christopher Pinney.

social reforms'.¹⁶⁶ And here—especially when it came to questions of caste inequality—Hindutva looked fragile. Tilak was always alert to the risk of caste scuttling Hindu consolidation.¹⁶⁷ It was all effective to point to enemies at the door, but what of the fact that the house too was divided? For example, tension between Brahmins and non-Brahmins, so powerfully exemplified by Phule.¹⁶⁸ One point of friction was Brahmin domination of the bureaucratic job market. As we saw, Brahmins had emerged across India as suppliers of administrative talent. Even the British were served by legions of twice-born clerks,* so that despite being a minority among Hindus, Brahmins wielded extraordinary clout. In 1888, thus, in provinces attached to Madras and Bombay, out of 625 senior posts, 413 were with Brahmins. If in these parts they constituted less than 5 per cent of Hindu males, they yet controlled not less than 60 per cent of offices.¹⁶⁹ As non-Brahmins demanded a share, Brahmins felt threatened. Or as Tilak once sarcastically asked in response, did non-Brahmins intend 'to handle the plough or hold the grocer's . . . scales in the Legislative Councils'?¹⁷⁰ Where, as a nationalist, he would urge Indians to refuse service in the British army until given parity with white soldiers,¹⁷¹ as a Brahmin he was incandescent with the recruitment of 'untouchable' Dalits. Higher castes were the 'soul of the nation'; '[w]hat use are Mahars and Berads in the army? Their vocation is thieving.'¹⁷² That is, in equations *between* Hindus, the lokamanya's calls for equality appeared to go on vacation. Here, every now and then, a jealous Brahminness eclipsed his grand project of Hinduness.¹⁷³

So even as Tilak rose to influence in India at large, in Maharashtra itself, non-Brahmin leaders viewed Tilakite nationalism with suspicion. Indeed, some of Phule's followers decried the anti-British movement itself as a ruse for Brahmins to replace white men as rulers. One violent 1920s tract would, in talking of 'Brahmin imperialism', even malign Tilak as a 'preceptor of dogs'.¹⁷⁴ Yet, these caste tensions were not invented. As far back as a century ago, the British had

---

* Brahmins were often called twice-born. The first was biological birth; the second a spiritual rebirth after *upanayana*, a rite of passage.

noted Brahmin contempt for non-Brahmins; the former evidently thought the latter 'little better than monkies' (sic) when it came to literate vocations.[175] There was an air, quite pronounced in the region, where Brahmins had been a ruling class under the Peshwas, that *they* were society's most natural leaders. And the British too felt paranoia on this point. In 1879, the governor of Bombay warned, for instance, how local Brahmins 'esteem it their charter' to 'rule over the minds of Hindoos'. As the Peshwas demolished Mughal authority, this class was certain 'the British [too] shall be made to retire'; 'never have I known in India,' he added, 'a national and political ambition, so continuous, so enduring, so far reaching'.[176] It sounded alarmist, but the feeling lingered: Thirty years later, it was said again that of 'known enemies of Government' in the region, 80 per cent were Brahmins.[177] In leading political resistance too, whether it was Tilak on the more pugilistic side, or figures in the Congress's moderate wing, Brahmins were at the forefront in Maharashtra.[178] By 1910, in fact, the Bombay government would diversify its hiring practices to avoid overreliance on this set. For with the rise of Brahmin-designed nationalism, the Raj, it was feared, could no longer safely count on this class's loyal service.[179]

Tilak's first instinct was to deny the problem. Brahmin and non-Brahmin were fake categories to him: a sleight of hand to impede Hindu integration. To some extent, he had a point. In Maharashtra alone, Brahmins were hardly a unity: Under the Peshwas, it was a sub-caste called Chitpavans who profited from official patronage, while others like the Deshasthas resented them.[180] In any case, even if Brahmins controlled desk jobs, he argued, the military, land, trade, etc. were governed by others.[181] But 'non-Brahmin' was equally spurious a label: It included farmers, Dalits, potters, landowners and all manner of peoples, from all kinds of castes which had their own rivalries.[182] In making a dislike of Brahmins their sole uniting principle, non-Brahmin leaders were succumbing to British machinations, letting the colonial state divide and prevail.

In the south, for instance, there were even men who believed that 'Indian Brahmins are more alien to us' than whites; that only the Raj could 'hold the scales even between creed and class'.[183] This vexed the lokamanya: The British often justified their rule with the claim that Indians were like squabbling children; that if they left, India would sink into disorder. And here were brown men bolstering this position.[184] It was, at its core, a betrayal. Additionally, to suggest that caste must vanish and that social reform should precede political independence was, for Tilak, a suicidal view. After all, no inequities of Indian magnitude afflicted Ireland—but did the British leave the Irish alone?[185] India, in other words, could not wait for a perfect time—where women went to school and low castes were emancipated—to boot out the Raj. And the more Hindus argued among themselves, the less likely was the prospect of freedom for them all.

Non-Brahmin leaders, however, inverted the argument, asking: freedom for whom and what? Sayajirao Gaekwad III (1863–1939), the maharajah of Baroda, was a nationalist, for example.[186] But he disagreed with Tilak on reform. In his view, '[n]ational advancement *includes* social progress.'[187] To suggest that India must first obtain freedom, and that inconvenient topics like caste ought to be shelved till then was rubbish. True patriotism, lay in protecting 'with might' all that was of value but also in discarding 'unhesitatingly' elements of decay.[188] The point of political independence was not to go back to a pre-British age of social inequality or leave the structures of power within Hindu society untouched by modernity. Tilak clashed also with the Kolhapur maharajah, descended from Shivaji. It began with a feud over ritual: Brahmins had denied the prince Vedic rites (permitted to Kshatriyas), admitting only lower Puranic options (open to women and Sudras).[189] Shahu II (1874–1922) saw this as an affront.[190] And for all his talk of uniting Hindus, Tilak sided with the mulish orthodox party.[191] Where the lokamanya wished the ruler to 'take a proper pride in Hindutwa',[192] Shahu, tepid even to Tilak's

Maharajah Shahu II of Kolhapur and Maharajah Sayajirao Gaekwad III of Baroda, Wikimedia Commons.

effort to renovate his ancestor's samadhi,[193] saw this programme as Brahmin-oriented. So instead, he responded by clipping Brahmin influence: From 1902, half of all government appointments in Kolhapur were reserved for non-Brahmins.[194] In Baroda, Sayajirao—who too was denied Kshatriya rank—enacted similar measures.[195] It was a stance that made the loudest (Brahmin) promoters of Hindu unity restless. To critics, though, it seemed like Hindu consolidationists wanted nationalism, but without surrendering caste prerogatives.[196] Hindus must resist Muslims and Christians as a bloc; but *intra*-Hindu dissonances were (conveniently) to be tucked away.[197] It was in this context that Tilak was assaulted with eggs and vegetables.

In the immediate aftermath of the lokamanya's death, then, it looked like Hindutva was coming apart. Indeed, non-Brahmin radicals turned Tilak's playbook against him. By the middle of the new decade, they too organized festivals, with the difference that images of Phule and Shahu were paraded alongside Shivaji's. Clashes occurred, not between Muslims and Hindus; it was the non-

Brahmin at the conservative Brahmin's throat. Songs, meanwhile, were sung of Brahmin treachery; of why Hindu interests were *not* identical to narrow Brahmin interests.[198] And where Tilak promoted a monolithic division between Hindus and Muslims, these leaders manufactured a rigid boundary between non-Brahmins and Brahmins. The issue was frothing up elsewhere too. In Mysore, when its maharajah proposed to counter Brahmin dominance in his civil services, his premier resigned.[199] In Madras, one critic had years before sneered that if the British reigned in India, 'the Brahman rules it'.[200] Another leader, E.V. Ramaswami Naicker (1879–1973), would sourly state: 'If you have to choose between killing a Brahmin or a snake, spare the snake.'[201] So much so that in the early 1930s, the *Kesari*'s editor warned that Brahmins, who had contributed so much to the anti-colonial movement, would be compelled to exit the battle, the implication being this would injure the national cause.[202] But the broader point—which disturbs Hindu nationalism to this day—remained: that seams of Hindu unity, loose to begin with, risked coming undone in the face of domestic caste dissension.

Tilak need not have worried, though. For despite all this public warring—between the ideas of secular nationalism and Hindu majoritarianism, Brahmins and non-Brahmins—the pursuit of Hinduness sustained itself. Indeed, Tilak's opponents appropriated this concept too, just as they took his strategies of mobilization. A leading non-Brahmin, thus, called on Hindus to 'protect our Hindutva' and work for a 'Hindu Empire'; he rejected Brahminism, yes, but saw the broader Hindu label as valid.[203] Phule too—accused not too long ago of a Christian slant—was reincarnated in non-Brahmin propaganda as a *Hindu* hero; he had, it was now claimed, rescued Hinduism from Brahminism.[204] Missionaries branded Brahmins peddlers of an evil priestcraft; that argument was deployed now by non-Brahmins to rally all the *other* castes *as Hindus*, under *their* leadership. Naturally, this Hindutva was unlike Tilak's. Writing in 1891, the latter declared caste 'the basis of the Hindu nation'.[205]

Hindus had to rise above diversity to forge nationalism, but their essential variety was not, to him, illegitimate. Thus, a Brahmin would always remain a Brahmin, and other castes in their prescribed slots—and like parts of a machine they would combine to address common threats. The 1920s non-Brahmins accepted only one category, though: that of Hindus without distinctions. To be part of the Hindu nation, they argued—marrying Phule's anti-casteism with Tilakite cultural nationalism—caste must be rejected and equality embraced. Hinduness could not be trotted in and out selectively; it must demolish internal biases as vigorously as it fought external foes.

Brahmins were welcome to participate, of course, but after renouncing caste. Or as a polemicist declared: 'Reject the Brahmin who sees himself as a Brahmin; accept only he who merges with the rest of us *as a Hindu*.'[206]

Despite debate and disagreements, that is, Hinduness—Hindutva—was here to stay. And not long after Tilak exited the stage, it would acquire its greatest, most formidable exponent.

N.V. Virkar's photograph of Tilak's body before cremation, Collection of Christopher Pinney.

A little after 6.30 on the morning of 8 July 1910, a young man plunged into French waters at Marseilles. Vinayak Damodar Savarkar (1883–1966) was a prisoner onboard the SS *Morea*, on his way to standing trial in India. With two 'native constables' waiting just outside, he had gone into the toilet to accomplish his morning business. Until he quickly shot the door bolt and propelled himself to personal liberty via a porthole. Years later, stories would be told of bullets zipping around his head during this bold escape. Some said Savarkar swam for days to reach land and get ashore.[207] In fact, however, it took barely a few minutes before he was on the quay. The prisoner was quickly apprehended too, though the details are sketchy. A French gendarme said he chased Savarkar for 'about 400 metres' before catching up; and then walked another ten to hand him to the puffing constables. The latter, however, reported that the Frenchman had appeared from the left just as they were closing in from the right, and that moments after the gendarme gripped the escapee, they took over. All along, Savarkar, hoping to seek political asylum, pleaded with the French officer to transfer him to local authorities. Unfortunately, his detainer did not understand anything he was saying, and the prisoner was marched back to his ship—and to the bleak prospects of a windowless cabin.

Causing a nuisance to his captors, though, Savarkar's thwarted escape became an international controversy. Or as the French ambassador in London argued, 'As the prisoner had reached French soil . . . questions of international law were involved.'[208] That is, from the moment he got out of the water, his British–Indian keepers no longer enjoyed legal rights to pursue, arrest or cart him back to a foreign vessel. And till this question of jurisdiction were settled, Savarkar should not, it was demanded, be tried. In Britain, these French assertions prompted irritation, but they did seem to hold water. The home secretary—one Winston Churchill—agreed that London must submit 'to the law of nations', even if this entailed the 'petty annoyance of a criminal escaping' justice.[209] But his India colleagues were indignant: Savarkar was accused of waging war against the king-emperor, abetment to murder, sedition and worse. He was the 'head of a widespread conspiracy' that threatened British rule in the subcontinent—and must not, therefore, be handed freedom, gift-wrapped in technicalities.[210] Besides, the French had been informed in advance of Savarkar's passing through Marseilles, even providing additional security; it was this very arrangement that prevented his escape. But Paris would not budge, so in October, the matter was transferred to The Hague for arbitration. And here, Britain's view prevailed.[211] International law would not save this future face of Hindu nationalism.

Savarkar was born the second of four children into a (Chitpavan) Brahmin family not far from Nasik. Though they still owned a good stretch of land, their inherited memories were of lost greatness from the age of the Peshwas, when their ancestors led troops and lorded about in mansions.[212] As a boy, Savarkar studied in one of India's new, and keenly sought-after, English schools, while also, through his father, picking up traditional education in Sanskrit and Marathi. He was precocious, wilful and intelligent, and into adolescence, began soaking in ideas from the nationalist press, including Tilak's *Kesari*. But there were jolts too: When he was nine, his mother died, and by his teens, his father followed, succumbing to the plague of the 1890s.[213] In the same phase, Savarkar grew more radical. Towards the end of his days, he would recall how the execution of the Chapekars—who killed that British officer in Poona

V.D. Savarkar's photograph in his 1910 arrest record, from the British Library, File IOR/L/PJ/6/1069 6A.

in 1897—'stirred' him.²¹⁴ In a poem written around then we read: 'That you left your work undone, do not be upset. Further we will take your work.'²¹⁵ Indeed, early on, the British too noted how Savarkar was a 'firebrand' who held 'somewhat the same opinion' as the Chapekars.²¹⁶ A professor of his would similarly worry that while his 'patriotism was intense', it could do with an infusion of 'cold reason'.²¹⁷ In Nasik, thus, Savarkar had participated with enthusiasm in the Shivaji and Ganapati festivals, clashing with Muslim boys at school, and once vandalizing a mosque.²¹⁸ And by the age of twenty-two, the government would ban two ballads he composed on Shivaji, which were 'on everyone's lips' around his home town.²¹⁹

By now in Poona for higher studies, Savarkar had enrolled in Fergusson College, of which Tilak was a founder.²²⁰ Here, he began giving speeches, assisting the lokamanya in political activities (such as orchestrating a bonfire of British goods during a protest) and set up a secret society called Abhinav Bharat.²²¹ It was a loose network of aspiring revolutionaries—including one of Tilak's sons—whose goals broadly coincided, even if most of them lived diffused across Maharashtra. Thanks to this, while still at university, the colonial government began surveilling Savarkar. His nearness to Tilak—to whom he would soon dedicate his first book²²²—was reason enough, as was the lokamanya's interest in the boy. Tilak, in fact, helped Savarkar move to London next. An acquaintance, Shyamji Krishna Varma (1857–1930)—member of Dayananda's Arya Samaj, ex-minister to various rajahs, a man of means, a Sanskritist and, significantly, a patron of militant nationalism—had established scholarships for Indians to study abroad. One of these, named fittingly enough after Shivaji, was awarded to Savarkar; in recommending him for it, Tilak portrayed his disciple as a 'spirited young man', 'very enthusiastic' in the nationalist cause.²²³ Of course, when in 1906 Savarkar set sail for England, his declared intention was to train as a barrister. As it happened in the end though, he was never admitted to the bar; indeed, his advocacy of anti-colonial violence meant that even his earlier Indian degree would presently be nullified.[224]

Only four years after departure from Bombay—where he left a young wife and child—Savarkar landed in jail. It was not inevitable. At first, his nationalism in London seemed to wear a more intellectual garb: Between 1906 and 1910, 'he completed three books, a number of newspaper articles, a series of essays, and [several] newsletters'.[225] In fact, within weeks of arrival, he had translated into Marathi a set of Giuseppe Mazzini's writings, seeing in the Italian revolutionary the same impulses that had animated Ramdas.[226] Interestingly, Mazzini had for long attracted Indian minds, including Gandhi's.[227] But given Savarkar's reputation, his book was banned at once for preaching 'sedition under the guise of teaching historical lessons'.[228] Undeterred, he launched a new project: a revisionist tome on the Great Rebellion of 1857, published in 1909. Already in a pamphlet, Savarkar had presented that eruption not as a mutiny—a formulation preferred by the British—but as a war of independence. 'We take up your cry, we revere your flag, we are determined to continue that fiery mission', he wrote, pledging that in ten years, India would 'avenge' its martyrs' blood.[229] His book was an amplification of this theme, with the British seeing in it 'the grossest perversion of facts' and a 'savage hatred' for white rule.[230] So, again, his work was banned, this time before publication. But proscription was ineffective: Savarkar's latest was smuggled into India, via Europe, disguised amusingly in some cases as the Bible.[231] Jawaharlal Nehru—the country's future prime minister—thought it a 'brilliant' text, marred only by 'prolixity' and some 'want of balance'.[232]

But even as he articulated his own form of Tilakite nationalism in print, Savarkar was also more actively following in the wake of the Chapekars.[233] In London, he lived at India House—a club-cum-hostel set up by Varma and described by British intelligence as an 'anarchical society'.[234] When Varma departed for Paris, fearing prosecution for his anti-British operations, our barrister-in-training became its 'presiding deity',[235] hereafter also 'tailed nonstop' by the police.[236] The place was not for the meek or guarded, however: When a younger (vegetarian) Gandhi visited and showed reluctance to partake of animal food, Savarkar snorted, '[T]his is just boiled fish . . . we want people who are ready to eat the British alive.'[237] It was the prelude to a titanic clash, of men and ideas both, ending in the mahatma's murder by Savarkar's followers in 1948. Guns too soon appeared at India House. In 1909, a man called Madanlal Dhingra (1883–1909), described as one of Savarkar's 'closest aides', and supposedly in his thraldom, shot dead a British official who had been part of the political department at home.[238] In court, he declared: '[I]f it is patriotic in an Englishman to fight against the Germans if they were to occupy this country,' it was 'patriotic in my case to fight against the English'.[239] Gandhi proclaimed the act cowardly; Dhingra was intoxicated by hopeless ideas and equally 'worthless writings'.[240] The teachings of Savarkar—who made a pilgrimage to his friend before he was hanged—were, in Gandhi's opinion, 'injurious' to true nationalism.[241] Savarkar, however, upheld Tilak's interpretation of the Gita: to fight, as the old cliché goes, fire with fire.[242]

While the lokamanya might have approved, like with him this attitude nevertheless proved injurious to Savarkar's *personal* interests. As Dhingra's brothers darkly noted, the 'real culprits' behind their sibling were 'in the background'.[243] The British did not need any persuasion on this point: India House was closed. But it was another violent event that invited the full fury of the state upon Savarkar. A member of Abhinav Bharat Society killed an official in Nasik (a case alluded to in the previous section of this chapter). And it turned out that his gun was one of twenty couriered from London by Savarkar, who had also circulated a bomb-making manual.[244] Even as many of his friends were rounded up, their leader fled to Paris. But he didn't stay—whether from guilt at having abandoned his post when men like Dhingra went bravely to the gallows,[245] or because he calculated that a trial in England was unlikely to hurt, given that evidence was circumstantial,[246] Savarkar returned to London. He was arrested—posing defiantly in his police photograph—and a series of charges were slapped. But he had blundered. The British had no intention of trying Savarkar here; branding years-old speeches he gave in *India* seditious, they shipped this 'ablest of the Indian revolutionaries'[247] off to the colony, and into the jaws of a draconian legal system. Conviction now was certain. It was in this doomed situation that Savarkar squeezed himself out of that porthole in Marseilles.

His trial, which followed, had some parallels with Tilak's. For instance, the defence here also argued that his speeches looked seditious chiefly due to incompetent translation.[248] Savarkar professed innocence while refusing to acknowledge the court's authority; 'in England . . . one can expect to get justice,' he announced, but not in India.[249] When the verdict came, his sentence added up to half a century in prison, effectively meaning that the next time the twenty-six-year-old could walk free, he would be approaching eighty. Moreover, he would not spend this term on the mainland, but on the Andaman Islands, in a jail notorious for its tortures.[250] Packed into a vessel with every class of criminal, sleeping with his face by a make-do chamber pot, Savarkar reached his new home in 1911.[251] At first, Ramdas's teachings inspired stoicism. 'Your food may be delicious, yet it must turn into vomit and shit,' the sage had said. 'You might drink the water of the sacred Ganga, but this too must pass ultimately as piss.'[252] So Savarkar accepted his fate. But he did not budge on his views: Two years later, it was noted—in another parallel with Tilak—that he showed no 'regret or repentance'.[253] And yet, there was a difference. The lokamanya spent his time in Mandalay reading and writing. Savarkar, on the other hand, had to endure hard labour, yoked like an ox for hours every day to an oil mill.[254] He thought more than once of suicide but desisted—he would not give the British, he wrote later, the satisfaction of his 'dying like a dog'.[255]

In the end, Savarkar spent over a decade in the Andamans, where slowly his revolutionary urges wilted.[256] In the beginning, he refused work: What logic was there, he asked, in imposing physical chores like coir-pounding on men of cerebral frames?[257] For his intransigence, in 1914, he was punished with seven days of standing handcuffed; when he continued to resist, he was put in chains for months.[258] But others were also striking, so by 1915, the prison administration relaxed its grip; library access was granted too, where the shelves, funnily enough, held Mazzini's titles. However, despite material improvements, the ex-revolutionary's health was shattered. As, it is patent, was his spirit. In 1913, for example, he complained about not being permitted to go outside like ordinary prisoners. 'I have 50 years staring me in the face! How can I pull up moral energy enough to pass them'?[259] While he did not disown his deeds, he promised he was now a convert to constitutionalism, 'ready to serve the government'.[260] The next year, he seconded this with a more supplicant petition, offering himself to the British effort during the First World War.[261] Two more memorials were posted, but it was 1921 before Savarkar, at last, expressed *regret* for being 'caught up in the whirlwinds of political passions'; he was 'a mere boy' in 1910, who had now learnt his lesson.[262] His admirers claim this was a 'tactical ruse to secure a release and thereafter plan a future strategy'.[263] Detractors, however, sneer that Savarkar's appeals for clemency show how, despite loud rhetoric, when it came to *real* courage, his account was in a deficit.[264] It is an unkind stance. But such attacks on Savarkar have much to do with aversion for the ideology he would now make his life's mission.[265]

This next chapter of Savarkar's story begins in 1924. By this time, much had changed in India's political environment and the British decided to release their high-profile captive.[266] First, he had to sign a degrading statement—described in the press as 'shocking'[267]— accepting that his trial and sentence were fair, and forswearing 'methods of violence'.[268] There were other terms too: Savarkar was to remain within the limits of Ratnagiri district, south of Bombay, and play no part in politics—conditions that were withdrawn only in 1937. That he chafed against these is clear: In March 1925, he published an article on Hindu–Muslim violence in the north-west, attacking Gandhi.[269] (Who incidentally had publicly urged his release.[270]) On being questioned, Savarkar insisted the piece was not political but a type of cultural criticism.[271] To officials, it was obvious that his speeches and writings were 'almost incitements to violence', cloaked in 'social reform propaganda'.[272] But he was shrewd: Evidently he printed much under the names of his brothers when they contained problematic content, or through pseudonyms.[273] After all, what he admitted as his, was *still* susceptible to proscription. When he began a column in the *Kesari* describing his time in the Andamans, the government ordered it stopped. When these articles were compiled in a 1927 book and translated into English, it was banned.[274] An anonymously published *Life of Barrister Savarkar* (1926) met the same fate.[275] Curiously enough, however, the British never rearrested him, though quite aware of his stunts. For Savarkar was a sharp critic of Gandhi also, and in this regard, the colonial government saw in him a useful instrument.[276]

Either way, unlike his (by now departed) guru Tilak, Savarkar could not directly re-enter the political stage or freely opine on national issues. But if, in his own words, politics was the sword, 'social reforms' were the shield.[277] As a revolutionary, he had wielded the first, so now he directed his energies to a cause that would seal his place in history: Hindutva. For many, it remains a puzzle that Savarkar should become a proponent of Hindu nationalism. Yes, as a teenager, he got into scuffles with Muslims, but as a man, his patriotism looked inclusive. In his book on 1857, for instance, he urged a concord between Hindus and their Muslim countrymen. In Shivaji's day, when Islamic rule troubled Hindus, a 'feeling of hatred' was 'just'; today, however, he explained, it would be 'foolish'.[278] If in that 1909 book he quoted Ramdas in its early

Savarkar in a studio photograph from the 1930s, Collection of Christopher Pinney.

pages, at its close was a couplet by the final Mughal emperor.²⁷⁹ Hindus and Muslims, despite an imperfect history, were to the younger Savarkar 'brothers by blood' and 'children of the same mother'; a 'natural comradeship' united them, and the rebellion was its proof.²⁸⁰ Indeed, the 'Revolution of 1857' was a 'test to see how far India had come towards unity, independence, and popular power'; it marked the country's maturity and readiness for political evolution.²⁸¹ The message was clear, then: Savarkar of his twenties believed in a nationalism that welcomed *all* Indians. India belonged to 'whoever is born there'.²⁸² As a stance, it even matched Gandhi's and that of Congress moderates.²⁸³

Savarkar in his forties was a different man, however; and Hindus, in his mind, were not just the largest of all communities with a stake in the nation but sole claimants to its title deed. This argument appeared first in his *Essentials of Hindutva*, smuggled out of prison in 1923, and today, a century later, 'the de facto bible of militant and exclusionary Hindu nationalism'.²⁸⁴ To start with, Savarkar clarified that Hindu*ness* was not synonymous with Hindu*ism*; one could shun the Vedas and yet be Hindu.²⁸⁵ Indeed, in defining Hindutva, his terms were disarmingly simple: India must be one's fatherland, or the home of one's ancestors, but it must equally be one's 'holyland': the country of one's faith and all it held sacred. By this measure, Saivas, Vaishnavas, Jains, Buddhists, Sikhs and so on were invariably Hindu, even if only the first two recognised Hindu*ism*. Muslims and Christians, however, were barred. Yes, India was their homeland, and they shared blood with brown men; but their 'holylands' were in 'Arabia or Palestine'. This meant '[t]heir love is divided'.²⁸⁶ There was a context to this framing: After the First World War when the Ottoman sultan (also the caliph of Islam) was toppled, Muslim leaders in India organized an anti-British agitation for the caliphate's restoration. Gandhi lent it full support, in the hopes of securing Hindu–Muslim relations. But for Savarkar, this was proof that Muslims would always have allegiances outside of India; that loyalties to foreign institutions 'would always pose a political threat to Hindu sovereignty'.[287] Or as he later declared, Muslims and Christians 'had no permanent interest' here. If 'driven away they could go to other countries where their brethren lived.' But Hindus had nowhere '*except* India'.[288] They alone, to quote the scholar Janaki Bakhle, possessed an 'undivided, monogamous love' for their homeland.[289]

Savarkar's 150-page effort to delineate Hindus as a modern political unit was, conceptually, a triumph. For in *Essentials*, he achieved something far more powerful and practical than Tilak's Hindutva. The lokamanya, ultimately, presented the idea in religious terms such as loyalty to the Vedas.[290] But this begged the question: What *was* Hinduism? Was it Brahminism compressed into Sanskrit manuscripts? Was it temple culture, which sat at odds with Dayananda's 'true' faith? Or was it the distilled philosophy men like Ram Mohun Roy advertised to the West? And what of the contradictory customs that had no basis in any texts, existing unshakeably in the realm of habit only? With Hinduism itself not amenable to easy or uniform definition, any Hindutva constructed on its back would be—and was—contested. But Savarkar, skirting these issues, anchored his ideas in history: If philosophy, he once wrote, tended to make one question life's purpose, history felt empowering in pulling *through* life.[291] And *his* Hindutva was designed to empower, built not on faith therefore but on a shared past. It did not matter if you were Brahmin or non-Brahmin; it made no difference if you worshipped tribal deities with blood or poured sanctified milk over Brahminical gods. You might even fight one another in terms of caste and theology.[292] But so long as you shared blood as well as a sacred attachment to India—not Mecca or Rome—you were Hindu: heirs to a single heritage and one personality.[293] Or as the scholar Christophe Jaffrelot puts it, he borrowed a degree of openness from territorial or political nationalism (allowing most, though not all, membership of the nation), while utilizing cultural nationalism (to strategically exclude a few).²⁹⁴ It was a theoretical masterstroke, placing Hinduness in its current mould.²⁹⁵

To enable this, Savarkar naturally purveyed the past not as a scholar but as an ideologue. And where that shared past, so essential to his formulation, did not exist, it was made to exist. History, in his books, that is, appears not in its own context or on its own terms but as raw fodder to support a predetermined position (which in and of itself was not new; Phule too subordinated academic exactness to constructing a community of resistance).²⁹⁶ This he defended by pointing to the colonial state's own self-serving scholarship. Even in his 1909 book, Savarkar protested the 'wicked and partial spirit' in which writers painted 1857. His own goal was to demonstrate the rebellion's 'real spirit'.²⁹⁷ Consequently, complex motivations were reduced to simplistic emotions. In his translation of Mazzini's writings too, he admitted that the intent was not to see it 'as History' but to leave readers 'thrilled and inspired' to imitate the Italian.²⁹⁸ In *Essentials*, therefore, Savarkar does not offer a dispassionate analysis, instead doing what his rivals seemed to do: conscripting the past to tell a story. History here was about rearranging events to address present-day contingencies. To this end, he did not hesitate to make 'an occasional excursion into the borderland of conjecture' either.²⁹⁹ Thus, the birth of the Hindu nation was placed in the age of the Ramayana, and throughout history, in all situations, Savarkar perceived Hindus 'acting and thinking *as Hindus for Hindus and Hindusthan*'.³⁰⁰ Other identities and triggers were secondary. After all, the nation, he decided, must 'be the master and not the slave of its own history'.³⁰¹ And so, he would tell the story Hindus *needed* to hear to enthrone Hindutva and seize power.³⁰²

One consequence of this approach was that to Savarkar, all of Indian history was a prolonged battle for Hindu self-determination. Everything was viewed through the lens of a Hindu nation. For instance, in what was also a dig at Gandhi, he noted how in ancient times, the 'opiate' of non-violence had proved 'disastrous to the national virility'.³⁰³ What actually served Hindus was action. To a degree, Savarkar's conclusions were rooted in general fact: It was, he argued, 'furious conflict' with Muslims that made Hindus 'intensely conscious' of their nationality.³⁰⁴ As we saw in the Introduction, exposure to Islam did catalyse the making of a Hindu identity. However, this was neither 'intense' nor national. But that to Savarkar made little difference—an embryonic truth was enough to jump to conclusions.³⁰⁵ In a 1925 book on the Marathas, similarly, Savarkar made grand claims. '[D]istrict after district, and town after town,' we read, 'rejoiced' to see their flag.³⁰⁶ If this sat poorly with the truth, given how Hindus (outside Maharashtra) had resisted Maratha expansion, it was dismissed as 'strange'.³⁰⁷ Later in the text, Savarkar switches gears to claim that those challenging the Marathas did so because they too were seeking to head 'Hindudom'; this was not internal conflict but only a 'trial of strength' over leadership. Besides, if the Marathas were cruel to fellow Hindus, it was only because their accomplishments granted them a 'right to expect' submission.³⁰⁸ After all, 'for the sake of Italian unity Garibaldi, Victor Emmanuel and others' too fought 'not only with the foreigners' but also other Italians. If history 'absolves them', it must also the Marathas who revivified the nation.³⁰⁹ While India's leading professional historian of the day understandably dismissed Savarkar's work as a 'chauvinistic brag',³¹⁰ its emotional appeal was nevertheless remarkable.³¹¹

But, of course, as the lokamanya had also learnt, even the best intellectual exercises could not miraculously remake the world. And Savarkar, travelling where his guru hesitated to go, viewed caste as the greatest *practical* hurdle to Hindu consolidation. He transformed himself therefore into what those non-Brahmin intellectuals sought: a Brahmin who identified purely as Hindu. Only months after his release, he declared, thus: 'We must forget these [caste based] differences . . . we are all Hindus . . . the only common denominator.'³¹² What mattered was not separate caste groupings but a united ethnic identity.³¹³ Tilak had identified Christianity as one of the great threats facing Hindus, but he could not offer a workable response to the attractions conversion offered, given his own commitment to caste.[314] Savarkar, though, was direct: Only embracing Hinduness on equal terms with their lower-caste fellows could 'crush the designs of foreigners'.[315] The nation was sacred; caste 'dismembered' it.[316] Equally, he asked subordinate castes not to 'threaten to leave'; Hinduism was not the 'exclusive preserve of upper castes'.[317] In Ratnagiri, in fact, Savarkar scandalized the orthodoxy. Where even Brahmins subgroups would not dine together, he organized feasts where all castes ate as one. Between 1930 and 1935, 150 such exhibitions of commensality were staged.[318] While elsewhere in Maharashtra men worked anxiously to accommodate modern values within frames of scripture,[319] Savarkar declared he would not let archaic texts 'become fetters in my feet'; outdated sacred writings must simply be 'discarded'. That is, instead of performing intellectual acrobatics to locate modern ideas in obscure corners of the past, he was happy to move on.[320] The conservative backlash was instant; one petition demanded that the British rein in Savarkar and his 'immoral and irreligious preachings'.[321] Unbothered, in 1929, he established a temple where all castes worshipped together.[322] In actualizing Hindu*ness*, that is, unlike Tilak, his heir was prepared to bulldoze through even fundamental attributes of everyday Hindu*ism* like caste.[323]

And yet, despite his effort, social reform at best promised long-term results. In a more immediate sense, therefore, mobilization, à la Tilak, was achieved by maintaining the spectre of a shared enemy. Or as Savarkar wrote, 'Nothing can weld peoples into a nation and nations into a state as the pressure of a common foe. Hatred separates as well as unites.'[324] So, inevitably talk of Hindu *sangathan* (union) meant those deemed not Hindu came under attack. And Muslims, the largest (and politically most vocal) minority, were Savarkar's chief target. Ironically, as late as 1925, in his book on the Marathas, he assured Muslims that in critiquing Islamic rule, he was not railing against them as a community. That would be 'ridiculous'.[325] But twelve years later, his stance hardened. Coinciding with the lifting of the limitations placed on him, in 1937 he likened the British to 'foreign dacoits' but also warned Hindus to beware of a 'thief' in their midst.[326] In the 1940s, in a provocative interview with an American, who asked how Muslims might be treated under Hindu rule, Savarkar coolly replied: 'As a minority, in the position of your Negroes.'[327] 1937 also saw him become head of the Hindu Mahasabha—a cultural body founded in 1915.[328] While Savarkar saw the Mahasabha as 'an enlarged and more comprehensive edition of the Arya Samaj',[329] under him, it would no longer remain a religious society. It became, instead, a political party for Hindus, 'in all its social, political and cultural aspects'. And hereon, the Mahasabha would fight not only the secular nationalism of the Congress (whose members Savarkar likened to eunuchs) but also Muslims.[330]

This shift in Savarkar's approach towards Muslims—from a willingness to engage to certified dislike—seems to have multiple roots. One spark was supposedly personal. His prison memoirs put out that most warders he dealt with in the Andamans were Muslim. South Indians among them were supposedly not fanatical, but instigated by peers from the north, they too exhibited cruelty.[331] Given this division along religious lines—Muslims in authority, Hindus under watch—petty matters generated hatred. Thus, (Hindu) prisoners' food, inadequate to start with, was often filched by corrupt (Muslim) warders. Muslim inmates were allowed breaks to pray five times a day, but Hindus were denied the privilege, on grounds that it was not essential to their faith. For Savarkar, this was confirmation that the two groups could never live as brothers.[332] Muslims, from infancy, he added, were reared to believe that converting non-Muslims was a religious duty; Hindus, meanwhile, belonged to a tradition that acknowledged multiple ways. Which effectively meant that Muslims did all the feasting, while Hindus ended repeatedly on the menu. Indeed, in prison jailers too pressed conversion, he alleged, and many succumbed, if only for better treatment.³³³ In these circumstances, whatever their old virtues, Hindus would have to get tough, according to Savarkar. Tolerance was weakness, no matter how it was romanticized, when surrounded by intolerant faiths.³³⁴ Indeed, jail was the laboratory where he experimented first with organizing Hindus *as Hindus*, to survive in a hostile environment.³³⁵

To this might be added a more general preoccupation of this period: an anxiety about keeping up Hindus' numerical strength. After all, identity in twentieth-century India was also a game of numbers.³³⁶ This consciousness of Hindus—divided into sects and castes—as being a single 'majority' was itself a product of colonial censuses, which enumerated Indians and solidified what, earlier, were more vague labels.³³⁷ Coupled with concerns about conversion, which as we saw, had a controversy-ridden history, by the twentieth century, there was fear that Christians and Muslims were drawing away critical human capital, particularly from low-caste segments. In 1911, for example, it was found that in the last decade alone, in just one province, 40,000 Hindus had crossed over to Islam, and 1,20,000 to the church.³³⁸ The necessity of maintaining a majority vexed not just self-declared Hindu nationalists or organizations such as the Arya Samaj but also men like Gandhi: When in the 1930s, the British proposed granting lower-caste Hindus separate electorates, the mahatma saw this as designed to 'vivisect and disrupt' Hinduism.³³⁹ Indeed, colonial voices did ask that if Hinduism were formally defined along Brahminical lines, surely those not subscribing to Brahminism belonged elsewhere?³⁴⁰ Savarkar's Hindutva and reform efforts were a means to resist this; Hindutva had nothing to do with Brahmins.³⁴¹ And he was catering to widespread paranoia. In 1936, for example, when the Travancore maharajah granted Dalits temple entry, it was chiefly to prevent conversion and neutralize the missionary threat.³⁴² And Savarkar had for long viewed Christian proselytization as a device to make Hindus 'ashamed', deprive them of 'national feeling' and strengthen foreign rule.³⁴³

The attitude of organizations like the Muslim League, founded in 1906, exacerbated things.[344] Censuses showed that despite their self-image as a ruling elite in upper India especially, Muslims did not possess strength in numbers. So, to hold their own, and maintain a measure of political power, some argued that they constituted a separate *nation*. That is, if they were just a fragmented community among others, Muslims would be a 'perpetual minority'; asserting status as a *nation*, helped duck this 'logic of numbers', and claim parity with Hindus.[345] In a 1906 address to the viceroy, in fact, a delegation of Muslim grandees specifically required that the community be viewed 'not merely' on the basis of 'numerical strength' but also its 'political importance'; memories of power had 'not faded' from their minds.[346] India, in other words, housed not one but two peoples. Of course, like with the Hindu identity, this too had contradictions: Malabar's matrilineal Muslims venerated the Quran, as did Muslims in Bhopal; but in colour, dress, food and language, they were strangers.[347] Cultural distinctions, in fact, made some Muslims look unIslamic even: As late as 1943, a report expressed annoyance with Kashmir in the north. A 'true ... religious leadership' was absent, it complained, and 'counterfeit' preceptors 'legalised for [Kashmiris] everything that drives [a] coach and four through [mainstream] Islam'. It would take great effort to 'convert them into true Muslims'.[348] That is, like those Hindus who stressed a single identity, the League too built its position on the myth of a monolithic Muslim category. Claims of separate nationhood depended on it. Congress under Gandhi, meanwhile, denied both these claims, insisting that the only nation in the country, open to all, was a united *Indian* one.

Savarkar, however, refused to allow territorial nationalism, also dismissing Congress's efforts to brand Hindutva an illegitimate religious supremacism. Addressing the Mahasabha in 1937, he noted that all nationalism was ultimately 'a parochial conception'. If Congress's logic were allowed, should men not see the earth as their motherland and humanity as the true nation? Congress ought, then, to stress universal brotherhood—why had it cut out those living south of the Himalayas as 'Indians'? In any case, if Congress could do this, it had no right to tell Hindus off for imagining the nation via the conceptual frontiers of Hindutva. Similarly, to call Hindu nationalism reactionary did not, in his view, stick. For, by that measure, why fight the Raj, 'our brothers in Humanity'? Was that also not a reaction to British rule? No, the fact was that every nation defined itself in distinction to another, and Hindutva defended the 'fundamental rights of a particular nation'; Congress and he just drew boundaries differently.[349] The latter, in fact, erred in elevating territoriality. In the past, he wrote, England was a 'clear-cut territorial unit'. But in fraught times, Catholics showed divided loyalties; these Englishmen cared more for alien Rome 'than their Protestant English Sovereigns'. It was proof that territorial allegiance by itself could never forge a nation.[350] This is why, to Savarkar, nationalism had necessarily to be reinforced with culture. And when it came to this, Muslims had their 'faces . . . ever turned towards Mecca'; to a Hindu, on the other hand, 'India is all in all of his National being.' Only Hindus were committed to the country.[351] Which meant also that their interests were *the* national interest.

On the ground, then, the politician in Savarkar urged practical action to sustain a majority. In a universe of missionary faiths, he called on Hindus to cultivate missionary qualities—or viewed another way, to become what their enemies were. In prison, he claimed already to have run a programme, inspired by the Arya Samaj, to reconvert those who went over to Islam. On his release, this became a key plank for Hindutva. For '[e]ven if a man is a thief,' it was declared, 'a Hindu thief is less dangerous . . . than a Muslim'. For unlike the latter, a Hindu would 'merely thieve' not 'destroy temples, [or] smash idols'.[352] 'If the Moslems increase in population,' he wrote similarly in 1938, 'the centre of political power is bound to be shifted in their favour' [sic].[353] At the time of the Bengal Famine of the

1940s, alleging that Muslims were buying converts 'like vegetables', dispensing grain for allegiance,[354] he asked Hindu groups to 'rescue, feed, clothe and shelter Hindu sufferers alone'; that is, to behave as deviously as Muslims did (supposedly).[355] Savarkar grew even more acidic as the League's claims to represent a Muslim nation acquired political wings. Indeed earlier too, in his younger days, tolerance for Muslims had been, in the end, conditional. Or as his 1909 book observes, if the two communities worked together during the Great Rebellion, it was because Hindus had already broken Islamic power, redressing 'national shame'. Brotherhood emerged *because* Muslims no longer ruled India.[356] The League's efforts to assert itself, then, looked to him like a strategy to resurrect an unnatural dynamic. And this, inevitably, was prejudicial to Hindu priority in their holyland.

Savarkar in a studio photograph from the 1930s, Collection of Christopher Pinney.

But, Savarkar added, Hindus had only themselves to blame. Historically, the 'Hindu mind' was too 'tolerant', which to him was another word for 'shameless or callous'.[357] So, 'no evidence can generally be found . . . to show if anyone was yearning to avenge the Muslims atrocities and their religious victory'.[358] After 1857, Hindus again 'began to pamper the Muslims by respecting their whims', till the latter grew 'swollen-headed'.[359] That is, to resist the Raj, nationalists placed a premium on interfaith harmony; and Muslims, exploited this.[360] The Congress, he warned, was letting the League blackmail it.[361] Hindus did not demand 'an inch more for [themselves] than what is due . . . in relation to their population proportions'. They would even let non-Hindus live in peace. But Muslims sought 'to browbeat the Hindus into yielding... more than what is due to them'.³⁶² Even the press's equating of Congress and the League as India's main parties irritated Savarkar. For it served to 'insinuate and inculcate the idea that Hindus and Moslems... stood on equal footing'. Nothing, in his opinion, could be more ridiculous.³⁶³ As the League began demanding a separate state—Pakistan—his umbrage was magnified. 'If anybody says that Wales should exercise self-determination and fall out of Great Britain, he would be shot dead.'³⁶⁴ But Congress, he declared, instead of taking a tough line with the League, went out to attack the *Mahasabha* for frightening Muslims. 'Get looted,' it seemed to him to say, 'but don't report; get stabbed, but don't shriek; get repressed as Hindus but don't organize to resist it as Hindus; or else you will be damned as traitors to the cause of our Indian nationalism'.³⁶⁵

For all his eloquence, however, the Mahasabha neither succeeded in building an organizational base, nor in wooing many Hindus.³⁶⁶ Not least because Congress also, behind a veneer of high-minded impartiality, often acted like a Hindu party, sans the divisive language. Most Hindu interests, then, backed Gandhi's entity instead of betting on a more extreme party.³⁶⁷ Worse, when during the Second World War, Gandhi launched the Quit India agitation—triggering, in the British viceroy's words, 'the most serious rebellion since that of 1857'³⁶⁸—Savarkar, who once wrote a book *on* 1857, quietly compromised with the Raj. The British had thrown Congress leaders in jail and were scouting for brown allies; Savarkar now became one of these allies. Brandishing 'responsive cooperation'—an idea Tilak crafted to allow occasional understandings with the colonial government—Savarkar saw a window for the Mahasabha to swell in stature. All forms of justification were arrayed to support this move, which has caused embarrassment since.³⁶⁹ So too the fascination Savarkar and his supporters felt for Nazi Germany backfired. 'It is absurd to call [Hindus merely] a community in India,' he declared once. 'The Germans are the nation in Germany and the Jews a Community.'[370] Another Mahasabha man wished Hindus to '[m]ake Savarkar your Fuehrer'.[371] At a youth conference held alongside the party's 1938 session, one resolution even read: 'Muslims to be Treated like Jews.'[372] Germany and Italy, Savarkar noted, had 'grown so powerful' at the 'touch of the Nazi or Fascist wand'; this showed that these ideologies were 'congenial tonics' for those nations.[373] And as if to elucidate what this might mean in India, in 1944, his secretary suggested keeping Muslims in 'internment camps' until 'security of their good conduct is guaranteed.' 'This,' he wrote, 'is Savarkarism.'[374]

In 1947—almost 200 years after Clive's victory at the Battle of Plassey—the British were ejected from the subcontinent. But they left a visible, festering legacy, for the country was divided. The Muslim League got Pakistan, and what remained, under Congress, would fashion itself as a secular republic. But this partition was marked by bloodshed, and resultant Hindu–Muslim strife. Hindu nationalists never forgave Congress for letting the League win. In 1948, Gandhi was murdered: an event some Mahasabha units celebrated with sweets.[375] In fact, twelve years prior, an official had mused how it was not difficult to visualize Savarkar liquidating the mahatma.[376] As it happened, the assassin was a Chitpavan Brahmin by the name of Nathuram Godse (1910–49). And Godse, a tailor, was part of Savarkar's circle, having met the latter first when he was nineteen.[377] But even as he made use of his mentor's speeches in drafting his court statement,[378] Godse distanced Savarkar from his violence. In fact, he proclaimed it 'an insult to my intelligence' to be suspected of being someone's 'tool'.[379] Not everyone was convinced, though. Savarkar—who had retired from active politics in 1944, suffered a heart attack, lost his teeth, and even found himself cornered in the Mahasabha after his flirtation with the Raj[380]—was arrested but declined knowledge of, or participation in, the plot.[381] While he was acquitted for want of proof, an odour of suspicion lingered over the man's name nonetheless.[382] As it still does, all these decades later.

Retreating to Bombay, Savarkar died in the political wilderness. Indeed, just as he was under British surveillance in his twenties, he spent his last years watched by the Indian government.[383] After a meeting with him some years before, the penultimate British viceroy had written: 'I thought [Savarkar] an unpleasant, intolerant little man, full of communal bitterness.'[384] And at the end of his career—which had seen guns and plots, prison, and an unrealized mission to give Hindu nationalism wide political appeal—what seemed to remain was indeed bitterness. This comes across in Savarkar's final major offering, a yarn around six 'glorious epochs' in Indian history. Between its fanciful interpretations of the past, there is much frustration, as Savarkar vents on how Hindus *ought* to have behaved; of what he saw as lost opportunities.[385] When, for example, foreigners invaded from the north-west in ancient times, southern Hindus, he claimed, had a 'national duty' to rush to upper India—this, when there was no national sentiment anywhere in that era.[386] Christianity in Kerala, similarly, which spread peacefully, was to Savarkar an 'infiltration' that converted 'millions . . . at the point of the bayonet'; an argument built on pure imagination.[387] Islamic conquerors raped women, but Hindus, with 'perverted' ideas of 'chivalry', compounded it by acting honourably with Muslim women. Suppose, Savarkar wondered, 'Hindus also . . . decided to pay the Muslim "fair sex" in the same coin'—Muslims 'could not have thrived so audaciously'.[388]

But on the whole, the book reads as frustration with his own times: how Hindus actually behaved in supporting Congress, versus what they should have done—backed him.[389] The problem this father of Hindutva confronted was that while there were Hindus, most were not the type he *wished* them to be; the kind of people for whom he had (re)written whole histories. He hoped Hindus would do as Muslims did in this 'millennial' war, becoming a mirror image of their supposed civilizational enemies.[390] Sadly, the bulk of them didn't seem interested: Hindus' innate diversity stood in the way of crafting one identity, one vision and one purpose. So, from Savarkar's perspective, even after the British left the country, when Indians ruled themselves, the story had not ended. And under the decades-long dominance of Congress, which (formally at least) stayed wedded to religious neutrality, Hindutva—already facing a crisis after's Gandhi's murder—retreated into the shadows.

And yet, he need not have worried. For the power of an idea is that it can germinate and flourish long after its original agents are dead. And proof of Hindutva's resilience came less than four decades after Savarkar's death. In 2003, the president of the Indian republic unveiled a fresh portrait in Parliament. And there, in what is often called the temple of Indian democracy, today hangs, next to a picture of Gandhi, the image of the man who allegedly inspired his murder.

1970 V.D. Savarkar commemorative stamp, Wikimedia Commons.

Life did not give Savarkar all he had hoped for. But Hindutva, it turned out, was biding its time. And not too long after he was enshrined in the house of the people, having won power, it would begin a process—now well underway—of remaking the Indian state in its own image.

# EPILOGUE

## WHAT IS HINDUISM?

In June 1889, a man called W.H. Findlay produced a crisp defence of missionary activity in India. Writing in the *Harvest Field*, he challenged the increasingly prevalent view that evangelical work, in education particularly, was a failure. After all, the argument went, far from converting in large quantities, brown men were subverting Western formulas of thinking for 'attempts to revive Hinduism'. What we might today call evidence of 'native' agency triggered laments in Findlay's colleagues. But he himself proposed a different view; movements to reform Hinduism were, in his mind, proof of Christianity's *success* in the land. Yes, as 'Hindus begin to awaken', it was 'natural, and indeed proper, that they should first resort to the religion of their fathers'; that the initial 'result of the operation of the spirit of Christianity' must 'almost necessarily be a revival of Hinduism'. But this defensive instinct would, Findlay believed, run aground. And when Hindus, following childish attempts to build with borrowed tools what Christianity alone could guarantee, realized this, they would 'accept what we offer'. The modern rebranding of Hinduism, in other words, was not an event in its own right but merely a step to 'the complete and general triumph of Christianity'. It was a temporary case of 'Christian wine in Hindu bottles'; in the next stage, those 'bottles [would] burst'. Indeed, the very fact that through 'our schools and colleges' missionaries had stirred Hindus to re-envision their religion was a victory. Or as the man explained:

> The task the revivers of Hinduism have set themselves is to make it satisfy new ideals which they have accepted from Christianity. They are not supporting Hinduism as their fathers believed it . . . they are trying to imagine it to be, or to frame out of it, a worthy rival of Christianity . . . So ignorant have Hindus, in general, been in the past, of what their conglomerate religion is, that they can easily persuade themselves that what they now call Hinduism is the old genuine belief of their fathers, which in our descriptions we grossly malign. But this error of theirs is of very secondary importance. Our triumph is that the Hindus who have, at last, begun to value religion, have a high, a Christian ideal of what a religion should be.[1]

Its blind wishfulness aside, there is some truth to Findlay's assertion. As we have seen, dialogue with missionaries that began in the sixteenth century first provoked puzzled amusement and some petty irritation on the Hindu side. But the advent of European power in the land rendered Christianity a concern. Even if the number of converts was never alarmingly high,[2] the joining of the Bible with white political authority represented a challenge to 'native' ways of thinking, organizing society, and defining faith and divinity. All along, Western ideas that presented religion as a fixed, consistent affair—with a book, core principles, a mania for monotheism—played on colonized minds. And so, in adapting to survive, Hindu intellectuals reframed their beliefs. Figures like Ram Mohun Roy represent this impulse: a desire to synthesize a dominant idea of what 'religion' ought to look like, with matching bits in the Hindu tradition. This meant that some elements of the Hindu past were espoused, others branded adulteration; some ideas of god exaggerated but a plurality of living traditions denied. After all, as the social theorist Ashis Nandy observes, '[T]he ultimate violence which colonialism does to its victims' is that 'it creates a culture in which the ruled are constantly tempted to fight their rulers within the psychological limits set by the latter.'[3] And Findlay had a point when he noted that Christianity's triumph lay in determining exactly these psychological terms for colonized Hindus.

And yet, this triumph was hardly total or unqualified, for Indians never ceased to resist. Even in a politically enervated state, even with the terms of engagement set by another, the colonized mind found strategies to assert itself; to try and shape matters to its own advantage. At an intellectual level, after all, Roy, while he accepted a new structure for Hinduism, used the same process to critique Christianity as well. As the scholar Eric Sharpe wrote, one characteristic of modernity is that 'sacred scriptures, whatever their origin' could be 'read by those for whom they were initially not intended'. Holy texts, in alien hands, could be examined 'not in the light of [their] 'original' religious, liturgical, philosophical or social setting' but against 'entirely different presuppositions'.[4] The Vedas and Puranas were subjected to this process first, and Europeans 'discovered' in them whatever they desired: from Voltaire's undefiled monotheism, to the 'shameful' gods and polytheism that so agitated missionaries. Each party made use of these 'discoveries' to bolster their views and positions; they utilised Hinduism and India to develop *their* sense of self and *their* identities vis-à-vis others. 'Native' thinkers like Roy, however, reversed the gaze. And they too drew from the West what they felt essential to reconstructing and defending *their* positions under colonialism, while rejecting all that did not fit this need. It was a case of selective appropriation to meet contingencies of the age. And what brown men seized, it can be argued, was not Christian wine for Hindu bottles, but Christian bottles for Hindu wine.[5]

It is this acquisition of a new shape, with its tendency to mimic the Christian pattern, that often sparks the argument that modern Hinduism is 'invented'; that in squeezing a diversity of beliefs and sects uncomfortably into those Christian frames, what was manufactured was synthetic yarn.[6] While there is no doubt that colonialism and exposure to the West dramatically altered Hinduism—indeed, even gave it its current name—the suggestion that this is 'invention', and by extension lacks legitimacy, is somewhat simplistic. It assumes, for one, that Hinduism could never reincarnate itself; that it could only have one appearance—fluid, loose, amorphous—that defies attempts to place it within solid brackets, like water on a sieve.[7] However, we know that long before Europeans arrived on the scene, Hindu intellectuals had already started to delineate a separate identity *as Hindus*. One impetus came from Islamic rule. Or as the historian Muzaffar Alam notes, 'By the fourteenth century the term Hindu had significantly begun to denote a religious culture to encompass all such cults and traditions as originated and developed within the geographical limits' of India. Muslim accounts bunched together many types of traditions, ranging from the Brahminical to those antithetical to it, under the label 'Hindu'.[8] By this yardstick, Hinduism's 'invention' began not in the colonial era but several centuries before, in the reign of sultans. European rule, it would appear, only ripened what already existed in a foetal shape, its conception the product of a different set of encounters.[9]

Viewed against the long arc of history, though, 'invention' still grants too much power to those on the outside, while denying those supposedly being 'invented' any autonomy. In pre-Islamic India, sects and groups we now lump as Hindu—Saivas, Vaishnavas, Saktas, each representing a spectrum—had something in common when contrasted with Jains and Buddhists.[10] Already, that is, seeds of unity existed, alongside that Brahminical drive for it discussed at the start of this book. However, *assertion* of such unity became necessary only when the context presented itself. After all, Hinduism was never shaped by a book as much as by the currents of history.[11] And faced with Islamic rule, motivations grew to fasten these religious ideas under a shared canopy. To supply an analogy, five brown persons in a room—each a shade different from the other—might not view themselves as a single organism. Indeed, they might violently disagree with one another. But the entry of a white person shifts something; the brown grow cognizant of their common features. If the new entrant is also threatening in some respect, that shared brownness becomes a means to mount joint action. Inner contradictions might remain—not to speak of the fact that white and brown could cheerfully consort too—but a new dynamic is born.[12] With Islamic power, even if it was Muslim commentators who initially lumped diverse non-Muslims into the 'Hindu' category, the latter appropriated the tag, owning it for themselves—because they recognized value here.[13] Hindus, that is, asserted Hinduness as an overarching principle precisely because they confronted an identity separate—and occasionally hostile—to theirs.[14]

This consciousness of a Hinduness grew with time, though it was neither linear nor the same everywhere, always.[15] And it certainly wasn't as categorically defined or total as Savarkar would suggest. Yet *something* was underway. It is often noted, for example, that in seventeenth-century Mughal miniatures, Muslim nobility appear with their upper coat tied on the right side. Non-Muslims, however, tie the *jama* to the left.[16] The latter came from a variety of distinct castes: Rajputs, Brahmin, Kayasthas. Some were vegetarian, others were not; some offered hereditary scribal service, others were wedded to the sword. None of these would intermarry or even dine together. And yet court convention viewed them as a group. As the historian Gijs Kruijtzer notes, only with the Maratha hero Chhatrapati Shivaji do we find the jama tied to the right—quite possibly in deliberate defiance.[17] Aided by the fact that they shared gods and religious practices—that they had enough in common to transcend caste differences—Hinduness is implicit. This is not to say that Hindus and Muslims were monoliths; on the Islamic side, for instance, a whole empire in the Deccan imploded due to ethnic conflict between Persian immigrants and local Muslims.[18] There was, that is, no want of dissension. But in specific contexts, religious identity allowed for networks of solidarity, and for political and social mobilization.[19] Nor was this just an elite affair. The poet–saint Kabir—a weaver—in his fifteenth-century writings actively identifies Muslims and Hindus as separate types.[20] Which suggests there was a recognizable Hinduness long in the air; colonial pressures only roused this into fortifying itself a certain way.[21]

In this, borrowing a structure or certain strategies from the West was a critical innovation, but it was not 'invention'. Instead, it was an instrument of *re*-invention. Dayananda Saraswati, for instance, had been long on the path of reform, with little exposure to Western thought.[22] A visit to Calcutta opened his eyes to new strategies and tools, but the desire to reform appeared from within. Communities in general are not concrete blocs; they are 'social formations continuously engaged in self-recreation'.[23] Identities shift and transform; all of Hinduism's history, we know, is marked by adaptation. Indeed, there had once been several versions of Christianity as well. Eventually, some readings gained precedence, and internal coherence was constructed.[24] As with Hindus, there were 'large bodies of Christians who did not believe all the same things and who had relatively little to do with each other'.[25] Yet, just as Rajputs and Brahmins possessed caste identities but also shared a Hinduness, different varieties of Christians also could claim a shared Christianity. And this could be selectively drawn on, in times of nervousness especially. Thomas Roe, Britain's envoy to the Mughals, for example, met at Emperor Jahangir's court an Italian Jesuit. The latter requested that despite a 'vast difference' in their view of religion—Catholic and Protestant—they must avoid displaying this. For it would hinder conversion.[26] In *this* setting, that is, unity was urged; in Europe, on the other hand, sectarian prejudices looked incompatible. Indeed, among India's Hindus and Muslims, 'Europeans came to feel more like members of a [more singular] Christian community than they would have felt' at home.[27]

In other words, the white figure entering that room full of brown people was reminded also of his own whiteness in that moment.[28] And just as the latter evolved their sense of self and its strategies of self-preservation to address the new environment, so did he. De Nobili, as we have seen, was a committed Catholic. Yet, the Catholicism he administered among the Tamils looked little like its main fount in Rome: the acquisition of the Brahmin's sacred thread, the embrace of Hindu customs and caste, rebranding the Bible as a Veda—these generated controversy in Europe. But de Nobili was a white man in a country where brown men still prevailed; so, he adapted his religion to their terms. At that time, it was he who repackaged his wine, transferring Christianity to Hindu bottles. As the tables turned, however, and foreigners mastered the land, grafting onto it their own ideas—as evidenced, for instance, by 'Hindu law'—it was Hindus who were pressed to reinvent themselves. New institutions and novel conceptions of the world came into play, and they responded—as all societies do. Where religion is concerned, Europe pictured it as a specific type of box with specific contents. 'Native' minds hitherto experienced religion as a network of beliefs, yes; but living under colonial pressures now, many endorsed the box, populating it with chosen strands from their traditions.[29] And if de Nobili's Christianity, despite innovations—tolerating even the odd goat sacrifice—was still Christianity, Hinduism's latest avatar is also Hinduism, in a fresh garb.[30]

Indeed, where Hindus are concerned, the acquisition of new clothes for older bodies—even if they were of foreign design— appears in other contexts too, making this a familiar shift. The

Brahma, engraved by de Marlet, from The Stapleton Collection/Bridgeman Images. As with the deity's several heads and faces, Hinduism too features a new, different face in the modern age.

Travancore rajahs, for example, defined themselves as not sovereigns but vassals of the deity, Sri Padmanabhaswamy (Vishnu). Their kingdom 'belonged' to him, and they were only his custodians—a very Vaishnava, Hindu and Brahminical definition of their political selves. Yet, even as they served this role, they also operated in a world organized around other principles. In the eighteenth century, with the aura of the Mughals still alive, the same rajahs, thus, found value in Persianate culture. In their 'original' form, they were exclusively a deity's vassals; now they sought titles from a Muslim emperor.[31] In temple processions, the rajahs appeared bare-chested in line with Hindu ritual tradition; in court, they wore the jama as in Islamic durbars. While diplomatic correspondence was conducted in Persian, with the ascent of the British, these Malayalam speakers began to learn English,[32] also acquiring the white man's clothes by the mid-nineteenth century.[33] The rajahs were still Hindu, but in each of these contexts, altered their appearance. Hinduism's draping of new clothes too—its refashioning from Hinduness to a modern *ism*—is a product of such change. And, while looks convey much, they must not be overstated. To see the body, one must look past the cloth. Hinduism, we might conclude, then, is only 'invented' insofar as all religious categories are invented—and reinvented.[34]

Of course, this process was never uncontested, not only by critics outside but also those within. While external influences played their part, nineteenth-century reformers of Hinduism, it is widely acknowledged, advertised it through an idealized Brahminical frame—so idealized in its stubborn, exclusive exalting of the ('pure', ancient) Vedic over the (living, breathing) Puranic, that many *Brahmins* were aggrieved.[35] While purists always existed among Hindus,[36] appeal for a 'return to the Vedas' stemmed here from the political validation it contained. The Vedas' philosophical segments, after all, enjoyed European (orientalist) approval even as the rest of Hindu culture was lambasted. In a time when colonized Hindus sought self-respect as well as a shield against missionaries, a Veda-oriented presentation of religion served multiple purposes. In the process, though, Hindus themselves denigrated other aspects of their religious system. Yes, the orthodox Brahmin had always looked down on certain traditions—'inferior' deities, blood rites and popular religion more generally. However, as the scholar Günther-Dietz Sontheimer wrote, there had in the past been a 'continuum' between different 'currents of religion'. The Brahmin of older ages 'could not and would not abolish folk religion', only stamping it as lower in rank. But his modern reformist successor not only viewed these segments of Hinduism with contempt, he also actively railed against it, often in language echoing the missionary.[37]

But Hinduism's equation with a purely Brahminical reading of it was enabled by another factor too. Even in pre-colonial times, Brahmin presence in administration and courtly spaces was on the ascendant. In Hindu states especially, a template of Brahminized ritual and practice was rising already.[38] This meant that in the modern period, Brahmins were primed to slide into positions of dominance in the public sphere: They were at the forefront of engagements with white men, in the press, literate professions, state offices, political movements, universities and more. In emergent national spaces, their voices acquired a force exceeding their real numbers among Hindus. And naturally, their framing of religion gained potency. So much so that Phule and his school of thought would see in modern Hinduism not a response to the West—given how they viewed colonialism as *liberating* many sections from 'native' power structures—but a strategy to entrench Brahmin control.[39] Others did not go quite as far as Phule in denouncing Brahminical Hinduism, instead preferring an internal form of selective appropriation. Thus, in Kerala, Narayana Guru rejected caste and social practices linked to Brahminical thought but not its philosophical content. Instead, asking his fellow travellers to give up 'unclean' rites and 'lower' gods, this sage, himself born in a marginalized caste, invested in modern Hinduism. Brahminical ideas, that is, were seized—and amended—by non-Brahmins, just as Hindus had appropriated those Christian bottles.

Caste, however, remained a problem in answering the question: Who is a Hindu? Historically, the term, while including many we now locate under the label, excluded others. As the historian Divya Cherian shows for eighteenth-century Marwar, the Hindu identity was here positioned not only in contrast to Muslims but also Dalits ('untouchables'). Indeed, what divided Hindu from non-Hindu was untouchability, not faith, Muslims being cast with 'polluting' groups.[40] Other pre-colonial usages of the term 'Hindu' also appear restricted to high-caste people.[41] Why, on the cusp of the twentieth century too, Hindu officials were scandalized at classifying Dalits as Hindu in decadal censuses; they saw them as 'them', not 'us'.[42] In 1891, the editor of (the fittingly named) *The Hindu* similarly lamented from Madras how Hindus did not view castes like the Parayars as 'part of their community'.[43] Even in 1916, in Chhattisgarh, to call someone a Hindu 'convey[ed] primarily that he is not a Chamar' (a Dalit caste),[44] and many of Dayananda's successors too were aghast at the Arya Samaj's inclusion of Dalits in its reform programme.[45] So it is not surprising that as late as the 1950s, the political theorist Kancha Ilaiah, growing up Dalit, saw Muslims, Christians and Brahmins as *all* 'different from us'. That the Brahmin and he belonged in a single tent was news.[46] The historical Hindu, put another way, represented some specific (privileged, dominant) sections of Indian society, not the whole.[47]

The 'modern project of Hindu political monotheism', however, 'induct[s] the privileged and the pariah into a universal, congregational plane of Hindu identity'.[48] This had something to do with religious belief, but a lot with politics. After all, as discussed in the previous chapter, with the British enumerating communities, size began to matter. In fixing who had the strongest claim on the state's resources—and with the rise of nationalism, on the country itself—value emerged in the idea of asserting 'majority'.[49] Acquiring

Dalits' numerical loyalties was critical, not least as missionaries tended to woo them to strengthen 'minorities'. While Dalit groups in the past did occasionally negotiate for higher status within the Hindu order,[50] it was an inconvenient fact that many in the modern period obtained this outside it. As a south Indian official confirmed, for example, moving to Christianity opened avenues to employment otherwise sealed from low castes.[51] In the north, a convert declared: 'I have become a christian [sic] and am one of the Sahibs; I shall do no more *bigar* [conventional caste-based menial service].'[52] It was to counter this trend that modern Hinduism also saw movements to supply Dalits a dignified space inside the Hindu box, whether it was Savarkar's anti-caste activism or Gandhi's. The mahatma, in fact, even remarked to Ambedkar, the foremost Dalit leader and intellectual of the twentieth century: 'You cannot escape the situation that you are Hindus in spite of your statement to the contrary.'[53] Ambedkar was, understandably, not impressed.[54]

So, while modern Hinduism has a much longer lineage than is usually acknowledged, and while the Hindu identity itself is older than previously thought, it also incorporates groups that existed until relatively recently on its peripheries. In this, it creatively borrows missionary strategies. The Arya Samaj, for example, pursued Dalits despite the risk of violence from orthodox Hindus horrified by the idea.[55] The threat of rival religions was amplified to justify change. Or as one leader remarked: 'The Christian missionary with his millions is at the door. Mahommedan Mullahs are . . . rushing to the scene. The Arya Samaj mission alone can save the situation by taking [Dalits] into the bosom of the Vedic church.'[56] Dalits, meanwhile, who accepted their Hinduness were expected to amend several existing practices, particularly those that provoked high-caste disgust or featured Muslim influences. In the words of a 1928 pamphlet, '[T]hose of you who circumcise, who marry and bury by Muslim rites, are perpetrating a great sin.'[57] These efforts, in great measure, have delivered success: As the scholar Joel Lee shows, Dalits gave up old names (Rahim for Ram Das), old gods (though these are worshipped in some secret pockets) and replaced prior ceremonies with high-caste rites.[58] In Maharashtra, Savarkar's anti-caste reforms also witnessed 'untouchables' being vested with the Brahmin's sacred thread and taught Sanskrit mantras, with the instruction: 'Take these holy threads and stop bickering.'[59]

For Hindu nationalists, in fact, this last word is key. For if there is one thing that endangers the bottle of modern Hindu political assertion, besides the missionary, it is internal, caste-based 'bickering'. Or as a recent verse addressed to Hindus goes,

> The chest is not higher than the shoulder
> No caste is bigger than religion.
> If the shoulder is lost, what will you do with your chest?
> If the religion is lost, what will you do with your caste?[60]

The very fact that a century after Savarkar vivified Hindutva, Hindus must still be reminded of this reveals certain fragilities.

This book began with the tale of a maharajah, and now it ends with the travels of another. Four years after Madho Singh of Jaipur journeyed to Edward VII's coronation in London, a man called Bijay Chand Mahtab, maharajah of Burdwan, set out on a tour of Europe. Foreign travel was still a radical thing for Hindu princes, so much so that on the day of this one's departure, his ADC was either abducted by his relations or himself absconded from fear. Indeed, one of the maharajah's peers warned that it was wholly un-Hindu for him to sail; he didn't even possess the excuse of it being a 'Coronation or Jubilee year' in England to justify the adventure.[61] But Mahtab was young and determined, and went anyway. And the trip delivered as expected. It took the Bengali to Italy, France, the Netherlands, Ireland, Germany,

Belgium, and of course, Britain. There was much that amused the man: electrification in small European towns, encounters with boisterous American tourists, a gift from the pope of His Holiness's signed (and, of course, blessed) photograph, the presence of exclusively handsome people in Italy, the absence of manly sturdiness in the French, the sight of a live volcano and the prodigious book-binding budget of the British Library. Why, he even got to see a whale on the trip, describing it with fitting princely restraint as a 'novel experience'.[62]

But it was in the vicinity of Mount Vesuvius in Naples that Mahtab felt compelled to remark on local religion, becoming that rare thing: a brown man, in his travelogue, describing a foreign people and their strange ways. 'The most noticeable fact of all,' the maharajah sniffed, 'was the immense number of churches I saw.' 'Every street has a Saint of its own and in every convenient and possible nook and corner . . . one notices shrines.' The Neapolitans were sunk in superstition. If they wanted rain, '[y]ou find the Madonna of such and such a Church taken out amidst bonfires and fireworks to bring rain'. And if this did not produce a downpour, 'the people are told . . . that this particular Madonna has lost her spiritual power, and such and such a Madonna of such and such [other] place must be sought for.' The result was '[a]nother procession, more offerings and fire-works' by people who 'meekly submit to all the ceremonies imposed on them by the Church of Rome'. For Mahtab this was all a 'rude shock': The 'spiritual guides' of the Christians, instead of 'enlightening the flocks, instead of teaching them the Truth of Religion, in their bigotry, [were] teach[ing] the people a form of idolatry'. In fact, he added, 'one may well wonder whether this be Christianity or Paganism!'—so 'revolting' overall that the Hindu was almost tempted to raise the issue with the pope himself.[63]

Given how Europe's encounter with India began, one cannot help but chuckle. Things had, one might even say, come a full circle. But then again, this is the way of the world. And perhaps god does work in mysterious ways.

# ACKNOWLEDGEMENTS

I have been thinking about the themes in this book for over a decade. I first attempted a study of the modern Hindu identity as a twenty-one-year-old postgraduate student. That dissertation earned me a flattering grade, but in the years that have passed since, my comprehension of the subject has, as it must, evolved. In some respects, it has shifted substantially. I cannot claim that my store of knowledge is perfect even now—I don't think anyone would be bold enough to say this when it comes to Hinduism. But I have made a sincere effort here to answer questions that have played on my mind. There will be other ways to address the birth of modern Hinduism; *Gods, Guns and Missionaries* marks the path I have pursued. I hope it will stand up to scrutiny. The book may not satisfy everyone—I am not sure it has entirely satisfied me, for there is so much more to explore—and it has its limitations. But hopefully it will inspire some thought and contribute to ideas around Hinduism.

In writing this book, I have benefited from the kindness of many scholars, friends and readers. The chapter featuring Serfoji of Tanjore owes much to Indira Viswanathan Peterson, who sent me drafts of her forthcoming biography of the rajah. Father Jomy Joy helped me contextualize the Nasrani Christians of Kerala. Savita Damle kindly went over my Marathi translations to confirm I had not misunderstood the original texts. I must also thank Govind Krishnan V. and Rahul Sagar—in Govind's case, an offhand remark, and with Rahul, a tweet, helped me add interesting details to the book. When I was unable to gain access to a rare nineteenth-century text by Vishnubawa Brahmachari, Suresh Gokhale saved the day with a scanned copy. I also thank Prof. Richard Fox Young and Prof. Daniel Jeyaraj for pointing me to Ziegenbalg's letters. In London, Ranvijay Singh Hada made time to look up material for me. And Prof. Christopher Pinney was very kind in sharing his collection of pictures of Tilak and Savarkar for this book.

Among institutions, archives and image repositories, I must thank the British Library, London; the National Archives of India, New Delhi; the National Library of Scotland, Edinburgh; the Gokhale Institute of Politics and Economics, Pune; the Bhandarkar Oriental Research Institute, Pune; the New York Public Library; the Asiatic Society of Mumbai; the Sandeep and Gitanjali Maini Foundation, Bengaluru; the Library of Congress, Washington, D.C.; the Harvard Art Museums, Cambridge, Massachusetts; the Digital Commonwealth, Massachusetts; the Wellcome Collection, London; Hamburger Kulturgut Digital; the Rijksmuseum, Amsterdam; the Metropolitan Museum of Art, New York; the Yale Center for British Art and the Yale University Library, New Haven; the National Museum of Denmark, Copenhagen; the Los Angeles County Museum of Art; the University of Florida Digital Collections; Bridgeman Images; the Mary Evans Picture Library; the University of Tübingen; the Art Institute of Chicago; Archive.org and Wikimedia Commons.

I am particularly thankful to friends who have contributed in various ways to this book. Over the last two years, I have had the most enriching exchanges with Vinay Varanasi on Hinduism, discussing ritual, theology, history, custom and much else.

Prof. P. Vijayakumar patiently read through an early draft of this book in 2020. Later, Smitha Nandakishoran, Sharik Laliwala and Keerthik Sasidharan went through all or parts of my manuscript, and I thank them for the meticulous attention they devoted to the text. There is one more person I must mention, but they do not wish to be named. Nonetheless, thanks, M, for the granularity with which you read the book. If it weren't for these readers, this project could not have taken its final, publishable shape. At a personal level, my friends Shrayana Bhattacharya and Uzair Siddici have been part of the years-long process of finishing this book, boosting my confidence when I was tired or frustrated, and generally just being there for me in times of self-doubt.

This book would not have been possible without David Godwin, who championed it from the start—thanks to Chiki Sarkar for playing matchmaker and introducing us. My thanks also to Aparna Kumar, who gave me very useful inputs as the book neared completion. My editors at Penguin, Manasi Subramaniam in New Delhi, and Stuart Proffitt, with his colleague Vartika Rastogi, in London, have been a pleasure to work with. I am grateful also to Manali Das, who endured countless emails from me during the copyediting process as I changed my mind on everything, from image dimensions to font size, and to her colleague Yash Daiv. Thank you to Devaki Khanna for proofreading the book. For the beautiful cover of this book, I thank Ahlawat Gunjan. Thanks also to his colleagues Neeraj Nath and Aakriti Khurana. And for my photograph on the jacket, I am obliged to Ashish Sharma.

This is my fifth book, and in some respects, I am familiar now with the routine. Yet, this has also been an unusually demanding, draining enterprise. Most of the writing occurred alongside minor but constant irritations around my health. I could not have finished the book were it not for my family. I dedicate this book to my mother, Pushpa, who has been my strongest source of assurance and common sense. But in equal measure, I owe thanks to my sister Indrani, my brother-in-law Kurt (in whose beautiful home I wrote the final parts of the book) and my cousin Biju G. It is my name on the cover, but in different ways this is their production too.

It is nine years now since I published my first book. If I have lasted this long, it is because there has been an audience for my work. In closing, therefore, I thank my readers. For everything.

# NOTES

## Introduction: A Brief History of Hinduism

1. Lynn Zastoupil, *Rammohun Roy and the Making of Victorian Britain* (New York: Macmillan, 2010), p. 1. We will see more of Roy in Chapter 6.
2. Pudma Jung Bahadur Rana, *Life of Maharaja Sir Jung Bahadur of Nepal*, ed. Abhay Charan Mukerji (Allahabad: Pioneer Press, 1909), p. 121. Half a century later, a successor also travelled with cows. See *Daily News* (London), 9 May 1908.
3. Fatesinghrao Gaekwad, *Sayajirao of Baroda: The Prince and the Man* (Bombay: Popular Prakashan Ltd, 1997 ed.), p. 119.
4. Vibhuti Sachdev, 'Negotiating Modernity in the Princely State of Jaipur', p. 173, in *South Asian Studies* 28, 2 (2012): 171–81. Earlier, temple dancers from southern India had performed in Europe in 1838. Whether they took cows is not known.
5. Shivnarayan Saxena, *Jaipur Naresh Ki England Yatra* (Jaipur: Jail Press, 1922), p. 13.
6. Ibid., p. 16.
7. *Times of India*, 13 September 1902, in its report following the maharajah's return. The ritual was an old one. In 1689, John Ovington, an English chaplain, witnessed a similar ceremony in Surat. The gilded coconuts used were not, however, enjoyed by the sea, for boys jumped into the water and collected them. See J. Ovington, *A Voyage to Suratt in the Year 1689* (London: Jacob Tonson, 1696), p. 133.

8   Saxena, *Jaipur Naresh Ki England Yatra*, pp. 20–21. The preparations, even at the time, captured attention in Britain, with newspapers detailing the number of kitchens on the ship, the exact tonnage of the luggage and so on. See *East Anglian Daily Times*, 19 June 1902.
9   Saxena, *Jaipur Naresh Ki England Yatra*, p. 39.
10  It wasn't just maharajahs. More ordinary travellers were also keen to stress that they did not violate any customs abroad. See Pothum Janakummah Ragaviah, *Pictures of England* (Madras: Gantz Brothers, 1876), p. 2, for example.
11  Saxena, *Jaipur Naresh Ki England Yatra*, p. 61.
12  Ibid.
13  Sachdev, 'Negotiating Modernity', p. 172.
14  *St James's Gazette*, 23 June 1902.
15  Susan Bayly, *Saints, Goddesses and Kings: Muslims and Christians in South Indian Society, 1700–1900* (Cambridge: Cambridge University Press, 1989), pp. 66–67. The last known instance of this ritual being performed for a caste upgrade was in 1790 in Khaspur, Assam.
16  In other versions, a gold vessel called the Padmagarbha (lotus-womb), replaced the cow. See D.D. Kosambi, *An Introduction to the Study of Indian History* (Bombay: Popular Prakashan, 1975 ed.), p. 318. The cow ceremony was lampooned early on. In the thirteenth-century *Basavapurana*, Basava is shown criticizing the caste upgrade of a tanner. See Velcheru Narayana Rao and Gene H. Roghair (trans.), *Siva's Warriors: The Basava Purana of Palkuriki Somanatha* (New Jersey: Princeton University Press, 1990), p. 232. On a related note, there is also the (unverified) story of two envoys sent by the Brahmin ruler—the Peshwa—of Poona to England. On their return from that 'polluted' country, they were made to pass through a gold *yoni* (representation of the vagina) and restored to their caste following what was also presumably a ritual rebirth. See James Forbes, *Oriental Memoirs: A Narrative of Seventeen Years Residence in India* (London: Richard Bentley, 1834), p. 240.
17  In Travancore, thus, the head and neck of the golden cow went to the head priest, the front legs and trunk to his juniors, and whatever remained to temples. See R.P. Raja, *Swathi Thirunal: Through Trails of History* (Thiruvananthapuram: R.P. Raja, 2021), p. 696.
18  I use the term 'national' not in the sense of modern nationalism but Brahminical ideology that attempted to construct narrative unity for India. In this, I follow Ainslie T. Embree's essay 'Brahmanical Ideology and Regional Identities', in Embree (Mark Juergensmeyer ed.), *Imagining India: Essays on Indian History* (Delhi: Oxford University Press, 1989), pp. 9–27.
19  The word 'Hindu' is an anachronism for this period, but I use it to avoid confusion.

20  For a neat essay on the idea of the kali yuga, see Heinrich von Stietencron, *Hindu Myth, Hindu History: Religion, Art, and Politics* (Ranikhet: Permanent Black, 2005), pp. 31–49.

21  For a history of the Vedic people (who themselves were no monolith) prior to this move, see Hermann Kulke and Dietmar Rothermund, *A History of India* (Fourth Edition) (London: Routledge, 2004), pp. 31–50.

22  Aloka Parasher, 'A Study of Attitudes towards Mlecchas and Other Outsiders in Northern India (c. A.D. 600)', Unpublished PhD dissertation, School of Oriental and African Studies, London (1978), pp. 64–65. See also Romila Thapar, 'The Image of the Barbarian in Early India', in *Comparative Studies in Society and History* 13, 4 (1971): 408–36 for a summary of the Brahmin usage of the term *mlechha* for groups they encountered, and how, as these were integrated, the appellation could be withdrawn.

23  Parasher, 'Mlecchas', p. 136. See also P.P. Narayanan Nambudiri, *Aryans in South India* (New Delhi: Inter-India Publications, 1992), p. 44. A Brahmin tradition in Bengal also has the community's ancestors visit the region to perform Vedic rites, but when they returned to their homeland, they were treated as outcastes. See Swati Datta, *Migrant Brahmanas in Northern India: Their Settlement and General Impact (C.A.D. 475–1030)* (Delhi: Motilal Banarsidass, 1989), p. 84. Their descendants came to be known as the Radhiya and Varendra Brahmins of Bengal. Similarly, as late as the nineteenth century, it was reported that people who died in Patna, Bihar, were cremated on the other side of the river—the river being the boundary between an original Aryan land and a *mleccha-desa*. See Bholanauth Chunder, *The Travels of a Hindoo to Various Parts of Bengal and Upper India*, Vol. 1 (London: N. Trubner & Co., 1869), p. 120. Scottish surgeon and surveyor Francis Buchanan-Hamilton found immigrant Brahmins in Bihar stating that it was 'such an impure country, that, whoever dies in it becomes an ass'. See Buchanan, *An Account of the Districts of Bihar and Patna in 1811–12* (Patna: The Bihar and Orissa Research Society, 1939), p. 321.

24  See, for example, a seventh-century text cited in Audrey Truschke, *The Language of History: Sanskrit Narratives of Muslim Pasts* (Gurugram: Penguin Allen Lane, 2021), p. 31, and Alexis Sanderson, 'The Saiva Age: The Rise and Dominance of Saivism During the Early Medieval Period', p. 42, in Shingo Einoo ed., *Genesis and Development of Tantrism* (Tokyo: Institute of Oriental Culture, 2009), pp. 41–350, where we read how any land where the four-fold system of caste is established becomes pure for Vedic sacrifices.

25  Even in the modern era, not all parts of India were suitable for these rituals. There is an oral tradition in Kerala that the kingdom of Travancore was not ritually pure for Vedic sacrifices (*yaagam*s), since it lay south of the Periyar river. Its maharajahs had to conquer territory for the privilege of doing a yaagam. In 1788, the maharajah travelled to Aluva, next to the Periyar, thus, to conduct one. See P. Shungoonny Menon, *A History of Travancore from*

*the Earliest Times* (Madras: Higginbotham & Co., 1878), pp. 210–11. On the Vedas and their evolution, see Frits Staal, *Discovering the Vedas: Origins, Mantras, Rituals, Insights* (Gurugram: Penguin Random House, 2008).

26   V.D. Savarkar, *Hindu Rashtra Darshan: A Collection of the Presidential Speeches Delivered from the Hindu Mahasabha Platform* (Bombay: Laxman Ganesh Khare, 1949), p. 38. He refers to this process as one of 'colonization and conquest'. This, of course, is an exaggeration based on now-debunked racial theories about the Aryans. As Kosambi puts it, the expansion of Brahminical culture 'spread . . . a new way of living', rather than a conquest by large numbers of people. See Kosambi, *An Introduction*, pp. 113–14.

27   Parasher, 'Mlecchas', p. 25. See also Patrick Olivelle, 'Social and literary History of Dharmasastra', p. 19 in Olivelle and Donald R. Davis eds., *The Oxford History of Hinduism: Hindu Law: A New History of Dharmasastra* (Oxford: Oxford University Press, 2018), pp. 15–29, where we read that Brahminical claims were less a reflection of reality, more an attempt to 'shape' it. Importantly, non-Brahmin sources, such as Emperor Ashoka's inscriptions, are 'completely silent' on the four *varna*s (social classes), though the term 'Brahmin' is used.

28   As Sanderson, 'The Saiva Age', p. 115 notes, even those who supported Buddhists and others maintained Brahminical ideas on order, which served kings well. And as Dutch indologist Johannes Bronkhorst observes, much of Brahminism's success comes from its transformation into a 'socio-political ideology' as opposed to a religion. See Bronkhorst, *How the Brahmins Won: From Alexander to the Guptas* (Leiden: Brill, 2016), pp. 3–4.

29   Bronkhorst quotes inscriptions from around India, thus, between the first and tenth centuries CE where Brahmins are granted land for rites to protect the king, bring victory and so on. See Johannes Bronkhorst, *Buddhism in the Shadow of Brahmanism* (Leiden: Brill, 2011), pp. 80–84. It has also been noted that even early Vedic literature primarily focuses on concerns of priests and male warriors, again suggesting the importance of this equation. See Jan Gonda, *Aspects of Early Visnuism* (Delhi: Motilal Banarsidass, 1969), p. 6. For a relatively late example from the sixteenth century where a newly constituted ruler obtains divine origins and Kshatriya rank from Brahmins, see K.L. Barua, *Early History of Kamarupa: From the Earliest Times to the End of the Sixteenth Century* (Shillong: K.L. Barua, 1933), pp. 287–88.

30   The *Manusmriti* quoted in Patrick Olivelle, 'Orality, Memory, and Power: Vedic Scriptures and Brahmanical Hegemony in India', p. 218, in Vincent L. Wimbush ed., *Theorizing Scriptures: New Critical Orientations to a Cultural Phenomenon* (New Brunswick: Rutgers University Press, 2008), pp. 214–19. Interestingly, the Mahabharata declares that many Kshatriyas were *reduced* to Sudra status because they had no Brahmins among them—the presence of Brahmins was critical to Kshatriyahood. See Bronkhorst, *Buddhism*, pp. 32–33. For another affirmation, see Patrick Olivelle (trans. & ed.), *Dharmasutras:*

*The Law Codes of Apastamba, Gautama, Baudhayana, and Vasistha* (Oxford: Oxford University Press, 1999), p. 97: 'Brahmins united with Ksatriyas uphold the gods, ancestors, and human beings.' See also Bhikhu Parekh, 'Some Reflections on the Hindu Tradition of Political Thought', p. 23, in Thomas Pantham and Kenneth L. Deutsch eds., *Political Thought in Modern India* (New Delhi: SAGE Publications, 1986), pp. 17–31, where we read how 'almost the entire Hindu tradition of political thought was based on the unquestioned assumption of a close alliance between the two highest castes'.

31  Romila Thapar, *The Penguin History of Early India: From the Origins to AD 1300* (London: Penguin Books, 2002 ed.), pp. 146–50. See also Kulke and Rothermund, *History of India*, p. 44, and Velcheru Narayana Rao, 'Coconut and Honey: Sanskrit and Telugu in Medieval Andhra', pp. 25–26, in *Social Scientist* 23, 10–12 (1995): 'This dialectic of mutual construction—Brahmins conferring the status of Ksatriyahood on kings and the Ksatriyas making Brahmins powerful by their patronage—is predominantly the story of Brahmin ideology in premodern India.'

32  I do not digress here into other philosophies such as of the Carvakas and Ajivikas.

33  See Patrick Olivelle, *Ashoka: Portrait of a Philosopher King* (Gurugram: HarperCollins India, 2023), pp. 242–43.

34  Thapar, *Early India*, p. 62, p. 181, p. 190, pp. 193–202; and Olivelle, *Ashoka*, pp. 293–94. See also ibid., p. 159, pp. 240–41. The Brahmin–Sramana issue is complex. I do not delve into it, but for some complexities, overlaps and issues, see Nathan McGovern, *The Snake and the Mongoose: The Emergence of Identity in Early Indian Religion* (New York: Oxford University Press, 2019). It is also interesting that the eleven disciples of the principal Jain *tirthankara* (teacher) Mahavira are supposed to have been Brahmins—a hint of Jainism's claims to superiority over the disciples' original tradition.

35  On Hinduism as a missionary faith, see Arvind Sharma, *Hinduism as a Missionary Religion* (Albany: State University of New York Press, 2011).

36  Mahapadma Nanda, who usurped the Magadhan throne in the fourth century BCE, is described in later Sanskrit texts as 'destroyer of all Kshatriyas'. See Kulke and Rothermund, *History of India*, p. 59.

37  As Sharma notes, the *Manusmriti* refers to Yavanas (Greeks), Sakas (Indo-Scythians) and other alien groups as 'Kshatriyas (who) have gradually sunk in this world to the condition of Sudras' by the 'omission of the sacred rites' and for 'not consulting' Brahmins. This opened the door for the recognition and placement of foreign groups into the Brahmin world view, albeit at an inferior level. See Sharma, *Hinduism as a Missionary Religion*, p. 82.

38  See Thapar, *Early India*, p. 131, and Kulke and Rothermund, *History of India*, p. 48. See also Johannes Bronkhorst, *Greater Magadha: Studies in the Culture of Early India* (Leiden: Brill, 2007), pp. 16–28 for Sramanic influences in the Upanishads. Already in the Atharva Veda—the youngest of the four—we

find Vedic deities sharing spaces with 'folk' gods. See Vasudeva S. Agrawala, *Ancient Indian Folk Cults* (Varanasi: Prithivi Prakashan, 1970), pp. 3–7.

39  On this, see Suvira Jaiswal, 'Semitising Hinduism: Changing Paradigms of Brahmanical Integration', p. 21, in *Social Scientist* 19, 12 (1991): 20–32, and Jan Gonda, *Visnuism and Sivaism: A Comparison* (Delhi: Munshiram Manoharlal, 1970), p. 95. In parallel, new groups when encountered were also thrown into the Sudra category, allowing space within the Brahmin world view, but at an inferior level.

40  It is also interesting that in subsequent tales in the Puranic texts, Vishnu (and his avatars) and Siva are shown as triumphing in various ways over Indra—a version of Indra very different from the triumphant Vedic Indra.

41  This is leaving aside a possible Greek connection with Dionysus, discussed by Alain Danielou in *Gods of Love and Ecstasy: The Traditions of Shiva and Dionysus* (Rochester: Inner Traditions, 1992 ed.), who sees more than coincidence in the shared phallic iconography, emphasis on mountain abodes and so on.

42  Laurie L. Patton, 'The Transparent Text: Puranic Trends in the Brhaddevata', p. 3, in Wendy Doniger ed., *Purana Perennis: Reciprocity and Transformation in Hindu and Jaina Texts* (Albany: State University of New York Press, 1993), pp. 3–30. See also Suvira Jaiswal, *The Origin and Development of Vaisnavism: Vaisnavism from 200 BC to AD 500* (New Delhi: Munshiram Manoharlal, 1980 ed.), p. 51, where she observes how in the Vedas, Vishnu was 'a deity of the fourth rank'. Jaiswal adds that the new Vishnu was himself a composite of other gods such as Narayana and Krishna–Vasudeva.

43  Burton Stein, *A History of India* (Oxford: Wiley Blackwell, 2010 ed.), p. 57.

44  Kulke and Rothermund, *History of India*, p. 47. Indeed, the other marriages of the Pandavas with the so-called demons (like Hidimbi), Nagas (like Ulupi) and Yadavas (like Subhadra) also indicate non-Aryan alliances.

45  On the shift from the Vedic religion to Puranic Hinduism, Louis Renou wrote:

> The Vedic contribution to [present day] Hinduism, especially Hindu cult-practice and speculation, is not a large one; Vedic influence on mythology is rather stronger, though here also there has been a profound regeneration. Religious terminology is almost completely transformed between the Vedas and the Epics or the Puranas a fact which has not been sufficiently emphasized; the old terms have disappeared or have so changed in meaning that they are hardly recognizable; a new terminology comes into being. Even in those cases where continuity has been suggested, as for Rudra-Siva, the differences are really far more striking than similarities.

Renou quoted in Asko Parpola, *The Roots of Hinduism: The Early Aryans and the Indus Civilization* (New Delhi: Oxford University Press), p. 4. Or as Bibek Debroy puts it, the 'general understanding and practise of *dharma*' as we know it today 'is based much more on the Puranas than on the Vedas'.

See Debroy (trans.), *Shiva Purana*, Vol. 1 (Gurugram: Penguin Books, 2023), p. xvi.

46  Kunal Chakrabarti, 'The Gupta Kingdom', p. 56, in Kunal Chakrabarti and Kanad Sinha eds., *State, Power and Legitimacy: the Gupta Kingdom* (Delhi: Primus Books, 2019), pp. 43–64. See also F.E. Pargiter, *Ancient Indian Historical Tradition* (London: Oxford University Press, 1922), pp. 74–77, where he refers to this process in more political terms, as 'tampering' with knowledge in a way that reshaped it 'according to Brahmanic ideas'.

47  On the caste identity of the Guptas, see Ashvini Agrawal, *Rise and Fall of the Imperial Guptas* (Delhi: Motilal Banarsidass Publishers, 1989), pp. 82–84.

48  The Chellur (Perumchellur) settlement of Namboodiri Brahmins in Kerala, at present-day Taliparamba, for example, was in existence at the dawn of the Christian era. See Kesavan Veluthat, *Brahman Settlements in Kerala: Historical Studies* (Calicut: Sandhya Publications, 1978), p. 3. In the south, the Pallava kings in this period were also influenced by Brahminical culture, helping its spread.

49  As Jaiswal observes, Vaishnavas (followers of Vishnu) emerged from the Bhagavata and Pancharatra traditions, which in the *Kurmapurana* are considered non-Vedic. Over time, the former accepted Brahminical supremacy, while the latter seem to have stayed away. See Jaiswal, *Vaisnavism*, p. 46. See also Gonda, *Visnuism and Sivaism*, pp. 90–95.

50  See Anita Raina Thapan, 'Ganapati: The Making of a Brahmanical Deity', in *Studies in History* 10, 1 (1994): 1–22 for an account of the transformation of Danti—'the Toothed one'—from outside the Brahminical pantheon into a central figure in that pantheon. See also S.M. Michael, 'The Origin of the Ganapati Cult', in *Asian Folklore Studies* 42, 1 (1983): 91–116, with regard to the transformation of the deity from a negative figure in early texts into a positive force. On Ganapati's brother, see Richard D. Mann, *The Rise of Mahasena: The Transformation of Skanda-Karttikeya in North India from the Kusana to Gupta Empires* (Leiden: Brill, 2012).

51  Jaiswal, *Vaisnavism*, p. 82. The *Bhagavatapurana* lists the fourteen incarnations additional to the ten well-known ones. In Tamil Nadu also it appears that the '63 Nayanars', or saints of the Saiva tradition, feature many 'of doubtful historicity' and were possibly 'fictitious' and 'added to make up the number sixty-three which was directly borrowed' from the Jain idea of sixty-three illustrious beings. See R. Champakalakshmi, 'Ideology and the State under the Early Medieval Pallavas and Colas: Puranic Religion and Bhakti', p. 128 at https://toyo-bunko.repo.nii.ac.jp/record/6690/files/MASR05-29.pdf

52  Jaiswal, *Vaisnavism*, pp. 131–33.

53  Kunal Chakrabarti, *Religious Process: The Puranas and the Making of a Regional Tradition* (New Delhi: Oxford University Press, 2001), pp. 149–54. Interestingly, in the *Saurapurana*, Saivas cast Vaishnavas as having been sent

by the gods to a beautiful Saiva land to lead its people astray. See Gonda, *Visnuism and Sivaism*, p. 100.

54 P. Ragaviah, 'Refutations of Mr Newnham's Charges against the Hindoos', in Kirkpatrick Papers, IOR MSS EUR F228/20.

55 Adheesh A. Sathaye, *Crossing the Lines of Caste: Visvamitra and the Construction of Brahmin Power in Hindu Mythology* (New York: Oxford University Press, 2015), pp. 154–60 gives the example of the Nagar Brahmins, whose legends appear in a thirteenth-century addition to the *Skandapurana*. This gave their town of Vadnagar a gloss. A Ramayana story about a king who desired to go to heaven with his body intact was modified; where in the original, he went directly, in this retelling, he first purifies himself at Vadnagar.

56 Wendy Doniger, 'The Scrapbook of Undeserved Salvation: The Kedara Khanda of the Skanda Purana', pp. 59–60, in Doniger ed., *Purana Perennis*, pp. 59–84. Doniger is not alone in this: Centuries before, the *Narayansabdanirukti* also observed that 'fabricated texts on the greatness of sacred centers, which concern modern temples and other sites, are being composed and attributed precisely to the Skanda Purana'. Quoted in Elaine M. Fisher, *Hindu Pluralism: Religion and the Public Sphere in Early Modern South India* (Oakland: University of California Press, 2017), p. 127. The Puranas themselves would be graded in descending order as *satv*ic (pure), *raja*sic (passionate) and *tama*sic (dark), with the *Skandapurana* in the last category.

57 P. Sundaram Pillai, *Some Early Sovereigns of Travancore* (Madras: Addison & Co., 1894), p. 24.

58 Ibid., p. 7. See also David Dean Shulman, *Tamil Temple Myths: Sacrifice and Divine Marriage in the South Indian Saiva Tradition* (Princeton: Princeton University Press, 1980), pp. 37–39.

59 B.K. Chaturvedi, *Bhavishya Purana* (New Delhi: Diamond Books, 2006), p. 56.

60 See McKim Marriott, 'Little Communities in an Indigenous Civilization', pp. 197–201, in Marriott ed., *Village India: Studies in the Little Community* (Chicago: University of Chicago Press, 1955), where he conceptualizes this process as a 'parochialisation' of the pan-Indian Brahminical tradition, and of the 'universalisation' of local traditions into the pan-Indian.

61 Or as a colonial-era pandit shrewdly observed, 'Nothing is written with no basis.' Gopalacharya quoted in Ramchandra Chintaman Dhere (Anne Feldhaus trans.), *The Rise of a Folk God: Vitthal of Pandharpur* (Ranikhet: Permanent Black, 2011), p. 20.

62 See also Velcheru Narayana Rao, 'Purana as Brahmanic Ideology', p. 88 in Doniger ed., *Purana Perennis*, pp. 85–100, where he observes: 'All civilizations make their own past to make sense of the present,' as well as Chakrabarti, *Religious Process*, p. 96. This is not to say that the Vedic tradition disappeared. To quote Hermann W. Tull, '"Vedic" or "Puranic"

or even "tribal" are not separable entities, but rather, are akin to strands that converge and diverge, historically and geographically'. See Tull, 'F. Max Muller and A.B. Keith: "Twaddle", the "Stupid" Myth, and the Disease of Indology', p. 30, in *Numen* 38, 1 (1991): 27–58.

63 Ian Copland, Ian Mabbett, Asim Roy, Kate Brittlebank and Adam Bowles, *A History of State and Religion in India* (Abingdon: Routledge, 2012), pp. 62–63.

64 Vijay Nath, 'From 'Brahmanism' to 'Hinduism': Negotiating the Myth of the Great Tradition', p. 20, in *Social Scientist* 29, 3–4 (2001): 19–50. Even in an earlier period, there are traces of adaptation—it has been suggested that the *janeu*, or sacred thread, integral to Brahmins may have been borrowed. See Bronkhorst, *How the Brahmins Won*, pp. 31–32. Buddhists too used 'local deities to emplace themselves within a local society'. See Richard S. Cohen, 'Yaksini, Buddha: Local Deities and Local Buddhism at Ajanta', p. 377, in *History of Religions* 37, 4 (1998): 360–400.

65 M.G. Ranade (Ramabai Ranade ed.), *The Miscellaneous Writings of Mr Justice M.G. Ranade* (Bombay: Manoranjan Press, 1915), p. 206. Some of the puritanical ritualism associated with Brahmins might also have its origins here. To borrow a scholar's words from another context, minorities, to avoid being 'swallowed up' by the majority around them, develop 'a multitude of contradistinctive customs—such as purity laws'. See Jan Assmann, *Of God and Gods: Egypt, Israel, and the Rise of Monotheism* (Madison: University of Wisconsin Press, 2008), p. 101.

66 Julius Lipner, *Hindus: Their Religious Beliefs and Practices* (London: Routledge, 1998), p. 10.

67 Not that in earlier periods there was no resistance to this Puranic turn. Evidently, Brahmins who preferred the older Vedic tradition looked down on their fellows who adapted and embraced the Puranas. The latter were viewed as 'having fallen away from the highest brahmanic standard'. There was 'clear rivalry on the part of the Puranas with the Vedas'. See Pargiter, *Ancient Indian Historical Tradition*, pp. 29–30.

68 Nath, 'Myth of the Great Tradition', p. 32. Similarly, Bhils in central India claim descent from Siva's union with a forest lady. For narrative and political methods by which Boyas became a part of Hindu society in Andhra territory, see P.S. Kanaka Durga and Y.A. Sudhakar Reddy, 'Kings, Temples and Legitimation of Autochthonous Communities: A Case Study of a South Indian Temple', in *Journal of the Economic and Social History of the Orient* 35, 2 (1992): 145–66.

69 See Chandan Baruah, 'Hinduisation of the Ahom Court in the Medieval Assam', in *Proceedings of the Indian History Congress* 65 (2004): 357–61. For a parallel in Cooch Behar, see Amiruzzaman Sheikh, 'The 16th Century Koch Kingdom: Evolving Patterns of Sanskritization', in *Proceedings of the Indian History Congress* 73 (2012): 249–54. The Koch were seen as mlecchas even in the seventeenth century.

70  See Chakrabarti, *Religious Process*, pp. 66–68, for more on the *Kalikapurana*. See also Karel Rijk van Kooij, *Worship of the Goddess According to the Kalikapurana, Part 1* (Leiden: E.J. Brill, 1972), pp. 8–9.

71  The feminine form of Vishnu, Mohini, originally appears in two verses in the Mahabharata, with the story of Siva's desire and the birth of Hari-Hara-Suta ('son of Hari and Hara') coming as a product of the Puranas. The European referred to is Bartholomaus Ziegenbalg in Ziegenbalg (J. Thomas Philipps trans.), *Thirty Four Conferences between the Danish Missionaries and the Malabarian Bramans (or Heathen Priests) in the East Indies* (London: H. Clements, 1719), p. 105.

72  See Dhere, *The Rise of a Folk God* for a study on Vitthal's evolution, and specifically p. 189 for the Jain claim. Jain traditions also exist where characters in the Mahabharata eventually become Jains; where Sita, wife of Rama in the Ramayana, becomes a Jain nun at the end of her life, etc. See R. Umamaheshwari, *Reading History with the Tamil Jainas: A Study on Identity, Memory and Marginalisation* (New Delhi: Springer, 2017), p. 128, and Velcheru Narayana Rao, David Shulman and Sanjay Subrahmanyam, *Textures of Time: Writing History in South India 1600–1800* (New York: Other Press, 2003), p. 15.

73  Badri Narayan, *Fascinating Hindutva: Saffron Politics and Dalit Mobilisation* (New Delhi: SAGE Publications, 2009), p. 21. As late as the nineteenth century, it was admitted that many castes 'originally . . . were not Hindus'. See Gajanan Krishna Bhatavadekar, *Report on the Census of the Baroda Territories, 1881* (Bombay: Education Society Press, 1883), p. 92.

74  See S.K. Pillai, 'The Sacred Palmyra Grove', in *India International Centre Quarterly* 24, 1 (1997): 76–84. In Aranmula also a low-caste group was slowly ejected along with their blood rites. See Rich Freeman, 'The Literature of Hinduism in Malayalam', pp. 163–64, in Gavin Flood ed., *The Blackwell Companion to Hinduism* (Oxford: Blackwell Publishing, 2003), pp. 159–81. Violence also was in play. Brahmin legends themselves hint at painful encounters. As Thapar notes in *Early India*, p. 56, the Mahabharata speaks of the clearing of the Khandava forest by fire to establish a settlement, describing forest-people as demons. In Kerala, Brahmin tradition notes that a first immigration failed, while the second one succeeded. Reference to 36,000 arms-bearing Brahmins, even if an exaggeration, hints at more than diplomacy in play. See Veluthat, *Brahman Settlements*, p. 4, and Nambudiri, *Aryans in South India*, p. 145. In the same region, the *Sri Vallabha Kshetra Mahatmyam* tells of a 'demon' who prevented Brahmins from living in a region and had to be killed by a Vishnu avatar—a reference possibly to a tribal ruler. See V. Raghavan Nambyar, 'Annals and Antiquities of Tiruvalla', pp. 87–89, in *Kerala Society Papers*, Vol. 1, Series 2 (Thiruvananthapuram: Government of Kerala, 1997 ed.), pp. 57–94.

75  Among Namboodiris, for example, the Brahmins are divided as Othulla and Othillatha, based on who was permitted Vedic knowledge. On food,

Saraswat Brahmins ate fish, while meat was consumed by Brahmins living in the Himalayan foothills.

76  Burial, for instance, is followed by Aradhya Brahmins in Andhra. See Nambudiri, *Aryans in South India*, p. 75.

77  These Brahmins of Payyannur were later deemed degraded, though their own logic for accepting matriliny is not that it was a concession to local customs, but that Parasurama—the Vishnu avatar who created Kerala—urged it to expiate his sin of matricide. See Veluthat, *Brahman Settlements*, p. 22. On adapting local customs the 'colonists', a twentieth-century retelling explains, 'conciliated the natives by . . . adopting some of their usages and practices, while, wherever they went, they diffused around them a halo of higher civilization'. See C. Achyuta Menon, *The Cochin State Manual* (Ernakulam: Government of Cochin), p. 32. See also the Malayalam *Keralolpatti* in Herman Gundert ed., *Keralolpatti: The Origin of Malabar* (Mangalore: Basel Mission Press, 1868); A. Aiyappan, *The Personality of Kerala* (Trivandrum: University of Kerala, 1982), p. 155; and L.K. Ananthakrishna Iyer, *The Cochin Tribes and Castes*, Vol. 2 (Madras: Government of Cochin), p. 39.

78  Nath, 'Myth of the Great Tradition', p. 26. See also Jwala Prasad Mishra, *Jati Bhaskar* (Bombay: Sri Venkateswar Steam Press, 1926), p. 135. In a different retelling, they were fishermen graduated to Brahmin status. See Madhav M. Deshpande, 'Panca Gauda and Panca Dravida: Contested Borders of a Traditional Classification', p. 37, in *Studia Orientalia* 108 (2010): 29–58. See also ibid., pp. 38–39 for another variant in which these Brahmins were created from fourteen dead bodies.

79  Nath, 'Myth of the Great Tradition', p. 26; Rosalind O'Hanlon, 'Performance in a World of Paper: Puranic Histories and Social Communication in Early Modern India', in *Past & Present* 219 (2013): 87–126; Bhatavadekar, *Census of Baroda*, p. 150; and Jogendranath Nath Bhattacharya, *Hindu Castes and Sects: An Exposition of the Origins of the Hindu Caste System and the Bearing of the Sects Towards Each Other and Towards Other Religious Systems* (Calcutta: Thacker, Spink and Co., 1896), p. 87. See also Deshpande, 'Panca Gauda', p. 39. In the version recorded by O'Hanlon, male semen falls on a pile of asses' bones.

80  Kosambi, *An Introduction*, p. 318. We see an instance of this also in a story where Rama, of the Ramayana, encounters tribal folk in need of priests and creates a class of Brahmins. See Mishra, *Jati Bhaskar*, p. 167. Bhatavadekar, *Census of Baroda*, p. 146, speaks of Gujarati Brahmins of tribal descent, raised to Brahminhood by Rama. For Brahmins among the medieval Boya tribe of Telugu country, see R.N. Nandi, 'The Boyas: Transformation of a Tribe into a Caste', pp. 99–102, in *Proceedings of the Indian History Congress* 1 (1968): 94–103.

81  Chaturvedi, *Bhavishya Purana*, p. 41. See also Abraham Eraly, *The First Spring: The Golden Age of India* (New Delhi: Viking, 2011), p. 287. The term 'Maga'

for Iranians continued to be used even in the seventeenth century. See Audrey Truschke, 'Contested History: Brahmanical Memories of Relations with the Mughals', p. 440, in *Journal of the Economic and Social History of the Orient* 58 (2015): 419–52. See also Johannes Bronkhorst, 'The Magas' in *Brahmavidya: The Adyar Library Bulletin* 78–79 (2014–15): 459–86. Interestingly, in a Buddhist text, the Magas are described as mlecchas from the West. See Bronkhorst, *How the Brahmins Won*, p. 125. See also Bronkhorst, *Buddhism*, pp. 56–59 for a note on how Southeast Asians were also likely accepted as Brahmins. And see Yamunacharya's *Agamapramanya* quoted in J.A.B. van Buitenen, 'On the Archaism of the Bhagavata Purana', pp. 28–29, in Milton Singer ed., *Krishna: Myths, Rites, and Attitudes* (Chicago: The University of Chicago Press, 1968), pp. 23–40, which has arguments against Bhagavatas by Smarta Brahmins. Here, the Smarta complains that 'crooks' and Sudras, by appropriating Brahmin marks and symbols, were claiming Brahmin status.

82  Reference is to the Shenoys. See Madhav M. Deshpande, 'Ksatriyas in the Kali Age? Gagabhatta & His Opponents', pp. 96–97, in *Indo-Iranian Journal* 53, 2 (2010): 95–120.

83  There was only one varna, that is, of Brahmins. But within this varna—or caste category—many *jati*s, sub-castes, existed. The same is true of non-Brahmin groups also, and often politically ascendant jatis might claim a higher varna status.

84  In Bastar, thus, a fifteenth-century king brought Brahmins from Orissa 'to spread settled agriculture' while even the Sangam poetry of Arisil Kizhar praises a Chera king for transforming his kingdom 'which abounded in thick forests' by bringing in Brahmins. See Nandini Sundar, *Subalterns and Sovereigns: An Anthropological History of Bastar, 1854–1996* (Delhi: Oxford University Press, 1997), p. 13, and Nambudiri, *Aryans in South India*, p. 126. This transition from primitive agriculture to advanced, organized systems was not, however, always peaceful or welcomed by locals. See, for example, Rajan Gurukkal, 'Non-Brahmana Resistance to the Expansion of Brahmadeyas: The Early Pandya Experience', in *Proceedings of the Indian History Congress* 45 (1984): 161–63. See also Thapar, *Early India*, pp. 56–57 on ancient references to conflict with forest chiefs and peoples. Note, however, that competing groups like the Jains also followed this formula, building tanks, canals and other investments in rural areas to entrench themselves. See Umamaheshwari, *Reading History*, p. 91. For an interesting but matching situation in Bengal, where Islam spread thanks to Muslim holy men who cleared forests and helped establish agriculture and cultivation, see Richard M. Eaton, *The Rise of Islam and the Bengal Frontier, 1204–1760* (Berkeley: University of California Press, 1993), pp. 208–19.

85  Dilip Menon, *Caste, Nationalism and Communism in South India: Malabar, 1900–1948* (New Delhi: Foundation Books, 1994), p. 46. See also Yasuchi Uchimayada, '"The Grove Is Our Temple": Contested Representations of

Kaavu in Kerala, South India', in Laura Rival ed., *The Social Life of Trees: Anthropological Perspectives on Tree Symbolism* (Abingdon: Routledge, 2020), pp. 177–96 and A. Krishna Poduval, 'The Kurichas of the Wynaad', p. 365 in *The Malabar Quarterly Review* 2, 4 (1903): 359–73. See also Chakrabarti, *Religious Process*, p. 87, pp. 178–79 for examples from Bengal, Uttar Pradesh, Jharkhand and Chhattisgarh, and Hermann Kulke, *Kings and Cults: State Formation and Legitimation in India and Southeast Asia* (New Delhi: Manohar, 1993), pp. 6–9 for Orissa.

86  Interesting reversals could also occur as when a tribe in Bastar abandoned 'higher' Puranic gods when they migrated to a new region and took up local tribal ones. See Sundar, *Subalterns and Sovereigns*, pp. 47–49. See also Kulke, *Kings and Cults*, pp. 26–27, for an Orissan case of 'retribalization'. For an 'outsider' god's arrival in Kullu in Himachal Pradesh, see reference in Daniela Berti, 'Ritual Kingship, Divine Bureaucracy and Electoral Politics in Kullu', p. 45, in *European Bulletin of Himalayan Research* 29–30 (2006): 39–61. In Bastar again, for the dynamics of a 'higher' goddess being tribalized, or a tribal goddess being Hinduized, see Alfred Gell, 'Exalting the King and Obstructing the State', in *Journal of the Royal Anthropological Institute* 3, 3 (1997): 433–50. Goddesses who normally are vegetarian could also on certain occasions receive sacrifices and meat, all signalling historical dynamics. See an instance in C.J. Fuller, *The Camphor Flame: Popular Hinduism and Society in India* (Princeton: Princeton University Press, 2004 [1992]), p. 83.

87  A.K. Ramanujan, *Speaking of Siva* (Middlesex: Penguin Books, 1985 ed.), p. 24.

88  Buchanan, surveying Bihar for the East India Company in the early nineteenth century, noted a similar pattern, where Brahmins preferred to describe a local goddess, Patanesvari (goddess of Patna), as Siva's wife. See Buchanan, *Bihar*, p. 362.

89  Ines G. Zupanov, *Disputed Mission: Jesuit Experiments and Brahmanical Knowledge in Seventeenth-Century India* (New Delhi: Oxford University Press, 1999), p. 19. The Kallar god's role in the wedding is also described in William Harman, *The Sacred Marriage of a Hindu Goddess* (New Delhi: Motilal Banarsidass, 1992 ed.), pp. 77–83. On the androgynous goddess, see Harman, 'How the Fearsome Fish-Eyed Queen Minatci Became a Perfectly Ordinary Goddess', pp. 40–42, in Elisabeth Bernard and Beverly Moon eds., *Goddesses Who Rule* (New York: Oxford University Press, 2000), pp. 33–50.

90  For the festival as also a demonstration of resistance to economic inequalities, see Sayant Vijay, Anupama Nayar C.V. and Anandhu S., 'Kunde Habba: The Profane and the Sacred', in *Economic and Political Weekly* 58, 14 (2023): 65–66.

91  See Sanjay Subrahmanyam, 'Warfare and state finance in Wodeyar Mysore, 1724–25: A missionary perspective', p. 218, in *Indian Economic and Social History Review* 26, 2 (1989): 203–33. Even in the nineteenth century, a

British official found a 'rooted aversion to Brahminical influence' in the region. See extract from the administration report for Mysore and Coorg (1864–65) in *Further Papers Relating to the Transfer of the Province of Mysore to Native Rule* (London: House of Commons, 1881), p. 164.
92  Nath, 'Myth of the Great Tradition', p. 30.
93  See Brian K. Smith, *Reflections on Resemblance, Ritual, and Religion* (Delhi: Motilal Banarsidass, 1998), p. 29.
94  Parasher, 'Mlechhas', p. 28
95  Hanuman of the Ramayana, thus, has multiple places of 'birth'. There is Anjaneri in Maharashtra, Anjanadri to the south in Telugu country and another location in Karnataka of the same name. As a somewhat frustrated missionary voice would later state, 'Every district has its peculiar superstitions and its tutelary divinity; and with them the people have modified different features of the general mythology.' See James Hough, *The History of Christianity in India: From the Commencement of the Christian Era*, Vol. 1 (London: Seeley, Burnside & Seeley; Hatchard & Son; Nisbet & Co., 1845), p. 18.
96  K. Ishwaran, *Speaking of Basava: Lingayat Religion and Culture in South Asia* (Boulder: Westview, 1992), p. 212.
97  Rao, 'Purana as Brahmanic Ideology', p. 97. Chakrabarti, *Religious Process*, pp. 116–22, also notes that in Bengal, an accomplished Brahmin was not one well-versed in the Vedas but in the Puranas. Indeed, when kings sought Vedic knowledge, experts had sometimes to be imported from outside.
98  Sir Alfred C. Lyall, *Asiatic Studies: Religious and Social* (London: John Murray, 1882), p. 8.
99  Friedhelm Hardy, for example, argues that the *Bhagavatapurana*, which spread out through India with its intense devotionalism for Krishna, was a Sanskritized version of what originated in the poetry of the Tamil Vaishnava saints, itself, inspired by stories received from the North. See Hardy, *Viraha-Bhakti: The Early History of Krsna Devotion in South India* (Delhi: Oxford University Press, 1983).
100  See Bronkhorst, *How the Brahmins Won*, p. 111 and Bronkhorst, *Buddhism*, p. 66, where he calls this process as a Brahmin 'colonisation' of the past. See also Shulman, *Tamil Temple Myths*, p. 9, where he speaks of the 'unifying, synthesizing, fertilizing force' that was Brahminism.
101  As Copland et al., *History of State and Religion*, p. 66 note,

> . . . with their legends, their lists of past kings mingling real people with mythical figures, and their associations with notable sacred sites, the Puranas provided 'cosmological charters', certifying, for each community, its unique place in the universe; in this way, people's loyalties to local gods and shrines became slowly linked to a wider explanatory framework, which was, at once, coherent and all encompassing, and which bound them together to an extent well beyond the capacity of the political or 'national' institutions of those times.

102 See Chakrabarti, *Religious Process*, pp. 134–40. See also Samira Sheikh, *Forging a Region: Sultans, Traders and Pilgrims in Gujarat 1200–1500* (New Delhi: Oxford University Press, 2010), p. 142, for a story related to the Jain absorption of local deities; and Balkrishna Govind Gokhale, 'Bhakti in Early Buddhism', in Jayant Lele ed., *Tradition and Modernity in Bhakti Movements* (Leiden: E.J. Brill, 1981), pp. 16–28 for an essay on how Buddhism became a religion of the laity with pilgrimages and other activities.

103 Thapar, *Early India*, p. 275.

104 Compare for instance the *Brihaddharmapurana* and the *Padmapurana*. His critics who saw him as a 'crypto-Buddhist' included Ramanuja of the eleventh century. See Thapar, *Early India*, p. 349, where she notes how Sankara's practical techniques with its monasteries etc. were influenced by Sramanic groups. See also Natalia Isayeva, *Shankara and Indian Philosophy* (Albany: SUNY, 1993), p. 10, and Govind Chandra Pande, *Life and Thought of Sankaracarya* (Delhi: Motilal Banarsidass, 2011 ed. [1994]), pp. 255–70.

105 To be clear, Sankara did allow image worship, but as an intermediate technique.

106 As Richard Davis tells, Sramanic religions first began to make figures of their founders and other divinities around the first century CE, within a century of which we find images of Hindu gods appearing (though references to images used in worship evidently appear in older sources such as Panini's *Ashtadhyayi* and Patanjali's *Mahabhasya* several centuries BCE). By the fifth century CE, Sanskrit texts spoke of practical and ceremonial elements around image consecration. See Richard H. Davis, *Lives of Indian Images* (Princeton: Princeton University Press, 1997), p. 26 and John E. Cort, *Framing the Jina: Narratives of Icons and Idols in Jain History* (Oxford: Oxford University Press, 2010), p. 53. See also Copland et al., *State and Religion*, pp. 62–63; Hardy, *Viraha-Bhakti*, pp. 31–32; Kulke, *Kings and Cults*, p. 98 (for examples of how aniconic tribal gods became mainstream Hindu gods); Dhere, *The Rise of a Folk God*, p. 46 (for an example from Maharashtra where the old aniconic image is still worshipped alongside a new carved one); and Shulman, *Tamil Temple Myths*, pp. 47–48. Note that bhakti was not purely a Hindu phenomenon. For a Jain parallel, see John E. Cort, 'Bhakti in the Early Jain Tradition: Understanding Devotional Religion in South Asia', in *History of Religions* 42, 1 (2002): 59–86.

107 See Gil Ben-Herut, *Siva's Saints: The Origins of Devotion in Kannada according to Harihara's Ragalegalu* (New York: Oxford University Press, 2018), pp. 80–81 for the thirteenth-century story of a Siva devotee who kills those who get in his way and threatens to kill himself if the deity does not accept his offerings. For bhakti literature in which god is a lover, see examples from A.K. Ramanujan, Velcheru Narayana Rao and David Shulman, *When God Is a Customer: Telugu Courtesan Songs by Ksetrayya and Others* (Berkeley: University of California Press, 1994). On Tamil bhakti, see Sekkizhaar

(G. Vanmikanathan ed. & trans.), *Periya Puranam: A Tamil Classic on the great Saiva Saints of South India* (Madras: Sri Ramakrishna Math, 2015 ed.).

108   Kerala's Chengannur Mahadeva temple, thus, has a menstruating goddess.

109   A.K. Ramanujan, *Hymns for the Drowning: Poems for Visnu by Nammalvar* (Delhi: Penguin, 1993 ed.), p. 106. Indeed, temple construction became attractive to kings, and royalty claimed in inscriptions to have erected many shrines, even when they might not have. See an example in Padma Kaimal, 'Early Cōḻa Kings and "Early Cōḻa Temples": Art and the Evolution of Kingship', p. 54 in *Artibus Asiae* 56, 1/2 (1996): 33–66.

110   For the link between temple culture and bhakti, see Kesavan Veluthat, 'The Temple-Base of the Bhakti Movement in South India', in *Proceedings of the Indian History Congress* 40 (1979): 185–94.

111   For a history of temple culture and its meanings and evolution, see Arjun Appadurai, *Worship and Conflict Under Colonial Rule: A South Indian Case* (Cambridge: Cambridge University Press), pp. 1–80. See also Davis, *Lives*, pp. 28–37. Interestingly, temple Brahmins were generally deemed inferior, and Puranic stories suggest that orthodox Brahmins reconciled to the idea of temples reluctantly. See Bronkhorst, *How the Brahmins Won*, pp. 135–36. See also Stietencron, *Hindu Myth*, pp. 56–61, and B.D. Chattopadhyaya, 'Political Processes and Structure of Polity in Early Medieval India: Problems of Perspective', p. 9, *Social Scientist* 13, 6 (1985): 3–34.

112   Manu V. Devadevan, *A Prehistory of Hinduism* (Berlin: De Gruyter Open, 2016), p. 19. This does not mean there was no laity for different groups—only that this did not necessarily define their identities.

113   See S.R. Goyal, 'Unification of the Ganga Valley', pp. 264–66, in Chakrabarti and Sinha eds., *State, Power and Legitimacy*, pp. 258–91.

114   See Sanderson, 'The Saiva Age', pp. 70–72, p. 108, and Bronkhurst, *Buddhism*, p. 64.

115   H. Sarkar, *An Architectural Survey of Temples of Kerala* (New Delhi: Archaeological Survey of India, 1978), p. 19.

116   See Burton Stein, 'All the King's Mana: Perspectives on Kingship in Medieval South India', pp. 147–48, in J.F. Richards ed. *Kingship and Authority in South Asia* (Delhi: Oxford University Press, 1998 ed.), pp. 133–90. In parallel, persecution could also be switched: Mahendravarman, the seventh-century Pallava king, is said to have transferred the violent attentions of the state from Saivas to Jains when moving from Jainism to Saivism. See John E. Cort ed., *Open Boundaries: Jain Communities and Culture in Indian History* (Albany: State University of New York Press, 1998), p. 215.

117   Sanderson, 'The Saiva Age', p. 115 thus cites a royal inscription where the ruler is a Buddhist who yet 'ensured that members of the caste-classes and disciplines observed their prescribed roles'. Bronkhurst, *Buddhism*, pp. 41–42 also notes that kings were not obliged to accept the 'whole package' when it came to religion, choosing whatever 'services' suited them. Stein in 'All

the King's Mana', pp. 156–57 adds that Jainism's decline may have been because kings found the Brahmin alternative more politically advantageous. A more concrete example comes from Nepal where King Jayasthiti Malla in the fourteenth century, aided by Brahmins from India, established caste among the Newars. See Stephen Michael Greenwold, 'Kingship and Caste', pp. 55–56, in *European Journal of Sociology* 16, 1 (Observer's Analysis of Caste and Clientele) (1975): 49–75.

118   See Kesavan Veluthat, 'The Temple-Base of the Bhakti Movement' for more on this in the context of the Pallava dynasty. See also Geoffrey A. Oddie, *Hindu and Christian in South-East India* (London Studies on South Asia) (London: Curzon Press, 1991) for numbers from an 1818 report that show three major Tamil temples together employing 1173 persons, including priests, dancers, musicians, potters, lamplighters, cow-keepers, security staff, suppliers, etc.

119   See Diana L. Eck, *India: A Sacred Geography* (New York: Harmony Books, 2012).

120   Richard H. Davis, *The Bhagavad Gita: A Biography* (Princeton: Princeton University Press, 2015), p. 2.

121   In a similar sense, tradition ascribes the 'rediscovery' of lost holy spots in Braj (associated with the deity Krishna) in upper India to Vallabhacharya, who came from Andhra in the south and whose followers in the Pushtimarga school of bhakti are now spread primarily in western India. See Charlotte Vaudeville, 'Braj, Lost and Found', in *Indo-Iranian Journal* 18, 3–4 (1976): 195–213. Geography placed barriers in the formation of a homogenized religion, and yet it was possible for such barriers to be surmounted.

122   And in time this would also be used to assert India's right to political unity. See, for example, K.M. Panikkar, *Indian Nationalism: Its Origin, History, and Ideals* (London: The Faith Press, 1920), p. 8. See also Rabindranath Tagore, *Nationalism* (San Francisco: The Book Club of California, 1817), p. 137, where he describes Hinduism as 'a United States of a social federation'.

123   Indira Viswanathan Peterson, *Poems to Siva: The Hymns of the Tamil Saints* (Princeton: Princeton University Press, 1989), p. 4. Pali and Prakrit, as Viswanathan Peterson points out, were used by Buddhists and Jains, but in the broad category of Hindus, it was Tamil that first produced religious literature outside Sanskrit.

124   Devadevan, *Prehistory*, pp. 40–41.

125   Devadevan's research shows at least 170 temples to have been constructed in eight *taluk*s of Karnataka between 1000 and 1200 CE, out of its total of 240-odd taluks.

126   Ramanujan, *Speaking of Siva*, p. 19.

127   Ibid., p. 25

128   Ibid., pp. 53–54. The Hindi scholar Hazariprasad Dwivedi described it as the *bhakti andolan*. 'Andolan' means both 'movement' as in bhakti movement as well as 'protest'. Of course, the matter is more complicated. See John

Stratton Hawley, Christian Lee Novetzke and Swapna Sharma eds., *Bhakti and Power: Debating India's Religion of the Heart* (Seattle: University of Washington Press, 2019).

129 This is why it is odd to refer to bhakti as one 'movement'. See John Stratton Hawley, *A Storm of Songs: India and the Idea of the Bhakti Movement* (Cambridge: Harvard University Press, 2015). Or to cite another scholar, 'Bhakti can range from sober respect and veneration that upholds socioreligious hierarchies and distinctions to fervent emotional enthusiasm that breaks down all such hierarchies and distinctions in a radical soteriological egalitarianism. Bhakti is not one single thing.' See Cort, 'Bhakti in the Early Jain Tradition', p. 62. See also Christian Lee Novetzke, *Religion and Public Memory: A Cultural History of Saint Namdev in India* (New York: Columbia University Press, 2008), p. 44 for another example of rivalry between bhakti groups; and Krishna Sharma, *Bhakti and the Bhakti Movement: A New Perspective: A Study in the History of Ideas* (New Delhi: Munshiram Manoharlal Publishers, 1987).

130 Sekkizhaar, *Periya Puranam*, p. 41, p. 173, pp. 530–31.

131 J.S.M. Hooper, *Hymns of the Alvars* (Calcutta: Association Press, 1929), p. 12, p. 24.

132 Reference is to Sambandhar and Tirumangai. See Sekkizhaar, *Periya Puranam*, p. 263, and Hooper, *Hymns*, p. 17.

133 See Ranjeeta Dutta, 'The Politics of Religious Identity: A Muslim Goddess in the Srivaishnava Community of South India', p. 164, in *Studies in History* 19, 2 (2003): 157–84. The Saiva persecutor is a Chola ruler, while the Jain-turned-Vaishnava is a Hoysala king. In the sixteenth century, Krishnadevaraya of Vijayanagara, in his *Amuktamalyada*, also relates the story of Yamunacharya who successfully gets a Pandya king in Tamil country to renounce Saivism and become a Vaishnava. See Velcheru Narayana Rao, David Shulman and Sanjay Subrahmanyam, 'A New Imperial Idiom in the Sixteenth Century: Krishnadevaraya and His Political Theory of Vijayanagara', p. 76, in Sheldon Pollock ed., *Forms of Knowledge in Early Modern Asia: Explorations in the Intellectual History of India and Tibet, 1500–1800* (Durham & London: Duke University Press, 2011), pp. 69–111.

134 M.N. Srinivas, *The Remembered Village* (Berkeley: University of California Press, 1976), p. 296. In the nineteenth century, similarly, visiting Mathura, a Hindu writer observed how the one Siva temple in that predominantly Vaishnava city gave the impression of a 'foreigner holding a passport' to stay, with 'no right, title or [further] interest' there. See Bholanauth Chunder, *The Travels of a Hindoo to Various Parts of Bengal and Upper India*, Vol. 2 (London: N. Trubner & Co., 1869), p. 30. See also Gonda, *Visnuism and Sivaism*, p. 94.

135 Ben-Herut, *Siva's Saints*, pp. 156–57. It probably did not help that in Buddhist iconography, Hindu gods could be treated as inferiors. Chakrabarti, *Religious*

*Process*, p. 141 notes that images show 'Marici trampling Siva, Indra holding the umbrella for Aparajita, and Avalokitesvara riding on the shoulders of Visnu'. See also Gonda, *Visnuism and Sivaism*, pp. 96–98 for stories that seek to reconcile Vishnu and Siva.

136 Viswanathan-Peterson, *Poems to Siva*, p. 10. See also Noboru Karashima ed., *A Concise History of South India: Issues and Interpretations* (New Delhi: Oxford University Press, 2014), pp. 69–92, as also Sekkizhaar's *Periya Puranam*, where Buddhists and Jains are treated as liars and peddlers of falsehoods.

137 Quoted in Truschke, *Language of History*, p. 128. Segregating Hindus this way—despite internal inconsistencies—from Jains and Buddhists is not a new trend: in the seventeenth-century *Dabistan-i-Mazahib* of the Mughal court, as Irfan Habib tells, the author was 'hard put to describe what the beliefs of a Hindu are and ultimately he takes shelter in a very convenient position but the only position—Hindus are those who have been arguing with each other within the same framework of argument over the centuries'. Of course, in this text, Jains, given their debates with Brahmins, are classed as Hindus, and it is the Muslim who is outside because they do not 'share any basic terminology with the others'. See Satish Chandra, J.S. Grewal and Irfan Habib, 'Akbar and His Age: A Symposium', p. 68 in *Social Scientist* 20, 9/10 (1992): 61–72.

138 See stories of Jommayya in Ben-Herut, *Siva's Saints*, p. 172 from Harihara's thirteenth-century *Ragalegalu*, and of Sankaradasimayya in ibid., pp. 190–91. Saiva–Vaishnava animosity also appears marked in the poetry of the sixteenth-century Appayya Dikshitar. See N. Ramesan, *Sri Appayya Dikshita* (Hyderabad: Srimad Appayya Dikshitendra Granthavali Prakasana Samithi, 1972), pp. 68–69, for example. See also ibid., pp. 65–66 for how Appayya's work extolling Saivism was partly a reaction to state patronage under the final emperors of Vijayanagara for Vaishnavism. For more on Appayya, see also Jonathan Duquette, *Defending God in Sixteenth-Century India: The Saiva Oeuvre of Appaya Diksita* (Oxford: Oxford University Press, 2021).

139 Reference is to the *Palnatu Virula Katha*. See Cynthia Talbot, *Precolonial India in Practice: Society, Region, and Identity in Medieval Andhra* (Oxford: Oxford University Press, 2001), pp. 70–71.

140 Fisher, *Hindu Pluralism*, p. 19.

141 Copland et al., *State and Religion*, p. 160. A similar event occurred in Haridwar in 1760, leaving reportedly 18,000 people dead. See Mountstuart Elphinstone, *The History of India*, Vol. 1 (London: John Murray, 1843), p. 116. Orthodox Brahminical dislike of Virasaivas is clear from the seventeenth-century *Visvaguna Darasana*, in which one of the characters berates 'infidel tyrants . . . whose bosoms are embraced by the Lingam and are impure by reproaching the Vede and religion'. See Caveli Venkata Ramasswami (trans.), *Viswaguna Darsana; Or, Mirror of Mundane Qualities, Translated from the Sanscrit of Venkatachari* (Calcutta, 1825), p. 52.

142 See Catherine Clementin-Ojha, 'The anti-Vaisnava policies of the maharaja of Jaipur in the 1860s' at https://www.academia.edu/15178148/The_anti_Vai%E1%B9%A3%E1%B9%87ava_policies_of_the_maharaja_of_Jaipur_in_the_1860s.

143 See Dhere, *The Rise of a Folk God*, pp. 60–66 for a fascinating overview of the Tirupati deity's past. According to the *Venkatachala Itihasamala*, by Ramanuja's disciple Anantarya, it was Ramanuja, who during the dispute, placed weapons and emblems of Siva and Vishnu, following which the deity chose Vaishnava marks. Sripati's *Srikarabhasya*, meanwhile, makes the case for Siva. See also V.N. Srinivasa Rao, *Tirupati Sri Venkatesvara-Balaji: Origin, Significance & History of the Shrine* (Madras: Umadevan & Co., 1949), pp. 132–53.

144 Of course, Buddhists and Jains also took over places: as Thapar notes in *Early India*, p. 48, in Amaravati, a megalithic site was repurposed by Buddhists for a stupa. In Mathura, both Hindus and Buddhists claimed a Jain site. See Paul Dundas, *The Jains* (London: Routledge, 1992), p. 114. See also ibid., p. 126, where Dundas refers to recent efforts in Karnataka at a pilgrimage site, to replace a Hindu image with a Jain one.

145 Sarkar, *Architectural Survey*, p. 54. See also V. Nagam Aiya, *The Travancore State Manual*, Vol. 1 (Trivandrum: Government of Travancore, 1906), p. 296.

146 Carl W. Ernst, 'Admiring the Works of the Ancients: The Ellora Temples as Viewed by Indo-Muslim Authors', p. 114, in David Gilmartin and Bruce B. Lawrence eds., *Beyond Turk and Hindu: Rethinking Religious Identities in Islamicate South Asia* (Gainsville: University Press of Florida, 2000), pp. 98–120. See also Olivelle, *Ashoka*, p. 272 for another case where even in a grant made by that emperor to a group called the Ajivikas, their name was scratched out later and replaced with their own by Buddhists.

147 Copland et al., *State and Religion*, pp. 182–83.

148 Today this Buddha sits at a junction in Mavelikara town, watching over traffic.

149 M.G.S. Narayanan, *Perumals of Kerala: Brahmin Oligarchy and Ritual Monarchy* (Thrissur: Cosmobooks, 2018 ed.), p. 342. At Kiliroor, elsewhere in Kerala, meanwhile, a Buddha is worshipped as Vishnu. See P.K. Padmanabha Panikkar, 'Pallivanar in Kiliroor', p. 331, in *Kerala Society Papers*, Vol. 1, Series 6, pp. 331–32.

150 See Shantinath Dibbar, 'The Construction, Destrucion and Renovation of Jaina Basadis: A Historical Perspective', p. 72, in Julia A.B. Hegewald ed., *The Jaina Heritage: Distinction, Decline and Resilience* (New Delhi: Samskriti, 2011), pp. 63–76. In so significant a site to Hindus as Sringeri too, local memory recalls a time when Jains lived in the area. See Leela Prasad, *Poetics of Conduct: Oral Narrative and Moral Being in a South Indian Town* (New York: Columbia University Press, 2007), pp. 33–34. Talbot also observes

that in Andhra, not only did temple practice in the late medieval period bear Buddhist traces, but it is also likely that several temples were housed in Buddhist structures. See Talbot, *Precolonial India*, p. 91.

151  See Gil Ben-Herut, 'Literary Genres and Textual Representations of Early Virasaiva History: Revisiting Ekanta Ramayya's Self-Beheading', in *International Journal of Hindu Studies* 16, 2 (2012): 129–87.

152  Ben-Herut, *Siva's Saints*, p. 200, pp. 210–14. The 8000 figure remains alive in popular memory of the Tamil Jains. See Umamaheshwari, *Reading History*, p. 100, p. 104, pp. 117–18.

153  Sharma, *Hinduism as a Missionary Religion*, p. 86. Reference is to Tirumangai Alvar. As late as the eighteenth century, Brahmins objected to Jain temples. See a case from Pune in Balkrishna Govind Gokhale, *Poona: In the Eighteenth Century: An Urban History* (Delhi: Oxford University Press, 1988), p. 161.

154  Periyalvar quoted in Kamil Zvelebil, *The Smile of Murugan: On Tamil Literature of South India* (Leiden: E.J. Brill, 1973), p. 196. See also Dundas, *The Jains*, pp. 127–29, and Indira Viswanathan Peterson, 'Sramanas Against the Tamil Way: Jains as Others in Tamil Saiva Literature', in Cort ed., *Open Boundaries*, pp. 163–86.

155  K.V. Subramania Aiyar cited in Edgar Thurston and K. Rangachari, *Castes and Tribes of Southern India*, Vol. 2 (Madras: Government Press, 1909), p. 438. Of course, indications also exist that Jains plotted against Saivas. See an account in Shulman, *Tamil Temple Myths*, p. 129. In another story, a Jain causes an image of Siva to burst into pieces, and townspeople transfer their loyalties to Jainism. See Umamaheshwari, *Reading History*, p. 126.

156  In Tamil Nadu, for example, out of a total population of seventy-two million in 2011, Jains numbered just over 89,000. Jains constitute less than 0.5 per cent of the total Indian population today. For a study of how the Jains fared in Tamil Nadu, see Umamaheshwari, *Reading History*.

157  Ben-Herut, *Siva's Saints*, makes this point through multiple examples from the Virasaiva tradition. See for example pp. 95–101.

158  See Rao and Roghair, *Siva's Warriors*, p. 37, pp. 233–35. One also finds a similar story in the Maharashtrian saint Jnaneshwar's hagiography where he makes a buffalo recite the Vedas. See C.A. Kincaid, *Tales of the Saints of Pandharpur* (Bombay: Humphrey Milford Oxford University Press, 1919), pp. 14–15.

159  Reference is to Harihara's *Ragelegalu*. See Ben-Herut, *Siva's Saints*.

160  Rao and Roghair, *Siva's Warriors*, pp. 16–17. See also Elaine M. Fisher, 'Remaking South Indian Saivism: Greater Saiva Advaita and the legacy of the Saktivisistadvaita Virasaiva Tradition', in *International Journal of Hindu Studies* 21, 3 (2017): 319–44.

161  See P.C. Alexander, 'Palli Bana Perumal', in *Proceedings of the Indian History Congress* 10 (1947): 159–63. For an account of the Buddhist temples set up by the king, see also Kottarathil Sankunni (Sreekumari Ramachandran trans.),

*Aitihihyamaala: The Great Legends of Kerala*, Vol. 2 (Kozhikode: Mathrubhumi Books, 2010), pp. 138–39. See also T. Madhava Menon (trans.), *Keralolpathi by Gundert: Translation into English* (Thiruvananthapuram: International School of Dravidian Linguistics, 2003), p. 21, p. 100 for a theory that he converted to Christianity.

162 See Menon, *Keralolpathi*, p. 64.

163 Sebastian R. Prange, *Monsoon Islam: Trade and Faith on the Medieval Malabar Coast* (Cambridge: Cambridge University Press, 2018), pp. 1–2.

164 Two of these, Travancore and Cochin, existed as autonomous states until 1949.

165 Prange, *Monsoon Islam*, p. 10102, p. 108. See also Zainuddin Makhdoom (M.K. Rowlandson trans.), *Tohfut-ul-Mujahideen: An Historical Work in the Arabic Language* (London: Oriental Translation Fund, 1833), pp. 49–51.

166 Further up on the coast also there were Muslim trading communities. A 926 CE inscription tells that the Rashtrakuta emperor Krishna II appointed a Muslim called Madhumati (Muhammad), son of Sahiyarahara (Shahryar), governor of an enclave. See Finbarr B. Flood, *Objects of Translation: Material Culture and Medieval 'Hindu–Muslim' Encounter* (Princeton, Princeton University Press, 2009), p. 21, p. 23. These coastal, south-Indian Hindus also served local kings: Ibn Batuta claimed there were 20,000 Muslim soldiers in the Hoysala army in Karnataka and when the sultans of Delhi took Tamil territory, here too the Hindu ruler had Muslim soldiers. See Peter Jackson, *The Delhi Sultanate: A Political and Military History* (Cambridge: Cambridge University Press, 1999), pp. 193–94. For Kerala Muslims casting the region as a legitimate 'abode of Islam', see Mahmood Kooria, 'An Abode of Islam Under a Hindu King: Circuitous Imagination of Kingdoms among Muslims of Sixteenth Century Malabar', in *Journal of Indian Ocean World Studies* 1 (2017): 89–109.

167 Davis, *Lives*, pp. 93–96. Reference is to the goddess Manat of Arabia, one of whose idols escaped Muhammad's iconoclasm in Mecca and was, it is claimed, enshrined in Somnath ('Su-Manat'). Apparently, some Hindus would later claim connections with Mecca; that just as an imprint of Vishnu's foot existed in Gaya in India, another did at Mecca. See a nineteenth-century account in J.C. Murray Aynsley, *Our Visit to Hindostan, Kashmir, and Ladakh* (London: W.H. Allen & Co., 1879), pp. 154–55.

168 Flood, *Objects of Translation*, pp. 27–32.

169 So much that Sicilian idols were couriered here once for sale by their capturer. Ibid., p. 27. See also Yohanan Friedman, 'Medieval Muslim Views of Indian Religions', in *Journal of the American Oriental Society* 95, 2 (1975): 214–21 for a tradition in which it was believed that pre-Islamic idolatry in Arabia came from India.

170 See Davis, *Lives*, pp. 201–02 for Governor General Ellensborough's attempt to 'restore' the gates of Somnath. For Somnath's subsequent place in Indian

imagination, see Romila Thapar, *Somanatha: The Many Voices of a History* (New Delhi: Penguin, 2008 ed.).

171 Sudipta Kaviraj, *The Imaginary Institution of India: Politics and Ideas* (New York, Columbia University Press, 2010), p. 54. See also Basile Leclere, 'Ambivalent Representations of Muslims in Medieval Indian Theatre', in *Studies in History* 27, 2 (2011): 155–95.

172 The *Kalacakratantra* quoted in Trushcke, *Language of History*, p. 11.

173 Thapar, 'The Barbarian in Early India', p. 435.

174 Cynthia Talbot, 'Inscribing the Other, Inscribing the Self: Hindu-Muslim Identities in Pre-Colonial India', pp. 698–99, in *Comparative Studies in Society and History* 37, 4 (1995): 692–722. It was, as Tagore would put it, however, a 'feeble' unity, always faced with the pressure of managing diversity. See Tagore, *Nationalism*, p. 136.

175 Truschke, *Language of History*, p. 8 citing Leonard van der Kuijp.

176 Habibullah quoted in Sheldon Pollock, 'Ramayana and Political imagination in India', p. 286, in *The Journal of Asian Studies* 52, 2 (1993): 261–97. Emphasis added.

177 See Truschke, *Language of History*, pp. 25–26. Reference is to Jayanayaka's *Prithvirajavijaya*.

178 See ibid., pp. 202–05 for a translated excerpt from the *Prithvirajavijaya*.

179 Cynthia Talbot, *The Last Hindu Emperor: Prithviraj Chauhan and the Indian Past, 1200–2000* (Cambridge: Cambridge University Press, 2016), pp. 43–45. Reference is to the *Taj al-Maasir*.

180 See Manu S. Pillai, *Rebel Sultans: The Deccan from Khilji to Shivaji* (New Delhi: Juggernaut, 2018), pp. 57–58.

181 Quoted in Talbot, 'Inscribing the Other', p. 697.

182 This point is also made by Copland et al., *History of State and Religion*, p. 161.

183 Often material from demolished Hindu temples was reused for mosques. For cases in Bengal, see Eaton, *Bengal Frontier*, pp. 37–38, p. 42. In Delhi at the Qutb Minar, similarly, one can still see pillars that originally belonged to temples.

184 See Copland et al., *History of State and Religion*, p. 98. He was not wrong. As Benjamin B. Cohen shows in his study of Hyderabad, under a topsoil of Islamic rule, subordinate Hindu dynasties survived all the way from the medieval period till the mid-twentieth century. See Cohen, *Kingship and Colonialism in India's Deccan, 1850–1948* (New York: Palgrave Macmillan, 2007). See also Wolseley Haig, *The Cambridge History of India, Vol. III: Turks and Afghans* (Cambridge: Cambridge University Press, 1928), p. 4, where he notes that even with the first Islamic campaigns in Sindh, this was treated 'not [as] a holy war for the propagation of the faith, but a mere war of conquest'.

185 In Delhi, by the reign of Muhammad bin Tughluq in the fourteenth century, the king showed favour to Jains, and at the installation of his successor,

Brahmins had the honour of paying obeisance in person. Even in the previous century, sultans adopted several Hindu practices and though formally no new temples were to be built, this was not the case. However, it was possible to flip to intolerance if a specific ruler were ill-disposed. See Jackson, *Delhi Sultanate*, pp. 280–95. On Jain memories of these sultans, see Steven M. Vose, 'Jain Memory of the Tughluq Sultans: Alternative Sources for the Historiography of Sultanate India', in *Journal of the Royal Asiatic Society*, Series 3 (2021): 1–25.

186 Richard M. Eaton, 'Temple Desecration and Indo-Muslim States', p. 297, in *Journal of Islamic Studies* 11, 3 (2003): 283–319.

187 Caleb Simmons, *Devotional Sovereignty: Kingship and Religion* in India (New Delhi: Oxford University Press, 2020), pp. 65–76. As Simmons writes, Tipu could all at once be 'Muslim, have a Hindu guru, patronize Hindu temples, and wage holy war' against Hindu kings.

188 See James Laine and S.S. Bahulkar (trans.), *The Epic of Shivaji: Kavindra Paramananda's Sivabharata* (New Delhi, Orient Longman, 2001), p. 45.

189 While the *Sivabharata* (ibid., p. 56) simply states that Shahaji Bhonsle was named after a holy man, other Maratha sources are explicit in naming Shah Sharif of Ahmednagar as the *pir* in question. See, for example, V.S. Wakaskar ed., *Shri Shivchhatrapatinchi 91 Kalami Bakhar* (Pune: Venus Prakashan, 2018 ed.), p. 2; for the Chitnis bakhar (chronicles), see Malhar Ramrao Chitnis (S.R.V. Herwadkar ed.), *Shri Shivachhatrapatinche Saptaprakarnatmak Charitra* (Pune: Venus Prakashan, 2000 ed.), p. 13; and for the Shedgaonkar bakhar, see Vinayak Lakshman Bhave, *Shrimant Maharaj Bhonsle Yanchi Bakhar* (Thana: Vinayak Laxman Bhawe, 1917), pp. 7–8. See also Lennart Bes, *The Heirs of Vijayanagara: Court Politics in Early Modern South India* (Leiden: Leiden University Press, 2022), p. 74. This was not an isolated incident. The son of a fourteenth-century Rajput king was unable to have children. Going to a Muslim sufi called Shaikh Burhan, he received divine blessings. His descendants, born of his son, Shaikha, have ever since been called Shekhawats. See *Rajasthan District Gazetteers: Sikar* (Jaipur: Directorate of District Gazetteers, 1974), pp. 24–25.

190 Pushkar Sohoni, 'Vernacular as a Space: Writing in the Deccan', pp. 263–65, in *South Asian History and Culture* 7, 3 (2016): 258–70. He is generally called Muntoji Bahmani.

191 See Tony K. Stewart, 'Alternate Structures of Authority: Satya Pir on the Frontiers of Bengal', in Gilmartin and Lawrence eds., *Beyond Turk and Hindu*, and Eaton, *Bengal Frontier*, pp. 280–81.

192 Devadevan, *Prehistory*, pp. 147–54.

193 Phillip B. Wagoner citing the *Prataparudra Caritramu* in 'Harihara, Bukka and the Sultan: The Delhi Sultanate in the Political Imagination of Vijayanagara', pp. 308–09, in Gilmartin and Lawrence eds., *Beyond Turk and Hindu*, pp. 300–26.

194 Dhere, *The Rise of a Folk God*, p. 193. Khandoba also has a Lingayat wife, a Dhangar (shepherd) wife, and a Muslim wife, among others.
195 Copland et al., *History of State and Religion*, p. 87. See also ibid., p. 74, where we read:

> It seems fairly clear that, traditionally in India, people readily transferred or distributed their allegiance between different sects, seeing no logical inconsistency in approaching different gods for different purposes, and that this apparently syncretic style of religious behaviour encouraged a relaxed attitude of what others did as well.

196 Muzaffar Alam and Sanjay Subrahmanyam, *Indo-Persian Travels in the Age of Discoveries: 1400–1800* (Cambridge: Cambridge University Press, 2007), p. 140.
197 Charlotte Vaudeville, *Kabir* (London: Oxford University Press, 1974), p. 8, p. 32.
198 This is the Atharva Veda, though the manuscript is now lost. See M. Athar Ali, 'Translations of Sanskrit Works at Akbar's Court', in *Social Scientist* 20, 9–10 (1992): 38–45. For a history of translation of Indian writings into Persian, see Carl W. Ernst, 'Muslim Studies of Hinduism? A Reconsideration of Arabic and Persian Translations from Indian Languages', in *Iranian Studies* 36, 2 (2003): 173–95. On Akbar's innovations and his motivations, see Audrey Truschke, *Culture of Encounters: Sanskrit at the Mughal Court* (Gurgaon: Penguin Random House India, 2016), pp. 14–19.
199 Truschke, *Culture of Encounters*, p. 39. See also Shandip Saha, 'Muslims as Devotees and Outsiders', p. 335, in Vasudha Dalmia and Munis D. Faruqui eds., *Religious Interactions in Mughal India* (New Delhi: Oxford University Press, 2014), pp. 319–41. For criticism of Akbar by conservative Muslims, see George S.A. Ranking trans., Al-Badaoni, *A History of India: Muntakhabu-T-Tawarikh*, Vol. 2 (New Delhi: Atlantic Publishers, 1990), pp. 264–65. His great-grandson Dara Shukoh, similarly, would be likened to Rama and Indra. See Supriya Gandhi, *The Emperor Who Never Was: Dara Shukoh in Mughal India* (Cambridge: The Belknap Press of Harvard University, 2020), p. 136.
200 Flood, *Objects of Translation*, p. 43. Emphasis added.
201 See N.K. Wagle, 'Hindu-Muslim interactions in medieval Maharashtra', p. 145, pp. 135–36, in Gunther-Dietz Sontheimer and Hermann Kulke eds., *Hinduism Reconsidered* (New Delhi: Manohar, 2001 ed.), pp. 134–52. Another story has Islam originate from a Brahmin called Moosal Maha Moonee (a play on the term 'Musalman'). See Richard Fox Young, 'Empire and Misinformation: Christianity and Colonial Knowledge from a South Indian Hindu Perspective (ca. 1804)', p. 73, in Richard Fox Young ed., *India and the Indianness of Christianity: Essays on Understanding* (Grand Rapids, Michigan: William B. Eerdmans Publishing Company) (2009), pp. 59–81. On the Coromandel coast, a Tamil Purana, meanwhile, seized on the metaphor of the four Vedas to describe the Torah, the Book of David,

the Gospel and the Quran. See Vasudha Narayanan, 'Religious Vocabulary and Regional Identity: A Study of the Tamil Cirappuranam', pp. 77–81, in Gilmartin and Lawrence eds., *Beyond Turk and Hindu*, pp. 74–97. In seventeenth-century Bengal, a Muslim text, the *Nabibamsa*, cast Vishnu, Siva and other Hindu deities as prophets of god, succeeded in time by the Prophet. See Eaton, *Bengal Frontier*, pp. 285–90. This business of claiming Western religions as 'originally' Hindu has seen modern proponents too: P.N. Oak (1917–2007) claimed that the Vatican and even Westminster Abbey were originally Hindu temples.

202  James Laine, *Shivaji: Hindu King in Islamic India* (New York: Oxford University Press, 2003), p. 43. It may be tempting to demarcate the Hindu–Muslim encounter along political clashes at kingly levels and syncretic experiences below. But even this is simplistic. For there were sultans too who admired Hindu culture. One in Bijapur styled himself son of the Hindu gods Ganapati and Sarasvati, not unlike those medieval kings who supported Brahmins and Buddhists alike. See Pillai, *Rebel Sultans*, p. 132. Even Mahmud Begada (1459–1511), a Gujarat sultan who sacked Somnath, is in Sanskrit poetry lionised as Vishnu-like; the goddess Sarasvati abandons heaven to reside in his superior country. See Aparna Kapadia, *In Praise of Kings: Rajputs, Sultans and Poets in Fifteenth-Century Gujarat* (Cambridge: Cambridge University Press, 2018), p. 105, pp. 122–23. Interestingly, the term *turuska* (Turk) associated with Muslims, was applied to *Hindus* who defied norms: King Harsha in twelfth-century Kashmir was branded as such for his iconoclasm. And when in the fifteenth century a Muslim promoted Brahmins, he was eulogized as descended from Hindu heroes! See Truschke, *Language of History*, pp. 90–94. See also Satoshi Ogura, 'Incompatible Outsiders or Believers of a Darsana? Representations of Muslims by Three Brahmans of Sahamirid Kasmir', in *Rivista degli studi orientali*, New Series 88, 1/4 (2015): 179–211, and Wagle, 'Hindu-Muslim interactions', pp. 137–39. The term 'sultan' too, to a degree, lost religious connotations: Vijayanagara's kings were styled *hinduraya suratrana*, 'sultans among Hindu kings'. See Pillai, *Rebel Sultans*, p. 80.

203  Sheikh, *Forging a Region*, p. 111 cites a twelfth-century text where the Chalukya king's Chudasama enemy is described as a demon born of a mleccha mother. 'He takes away the cows of the sages . . . kills Brahmans, spoils sacrifices . . . and demands money and taxes of the ascetics.' See also Divya Cherian, *Merchants of Virtue: Hindus, Muslims, and Untouchables in Eighteenth-Century South Asia* (Oakland: University of California Press, 2023), where we find the term 'Hindu' used to not just demarcate certain castes from Muslims, but also from lower-caste groups.

204  This continued even in the eighteenth century when, Martanda Varma of Travancore, for instance, attacked temples and seized their treasures, and in 1802 when the Maratha (Holkar) ruler of Indore plundered temple towns in

Rajasthan, with deities in Nathdwara even going into temporary exile. See Mark de Lannoy, *The Kulasekhara Perumals of Travancore: History and State Formation in Travancore from 1671 to 1758* (Leiden: CNWS, 1997), p. 55, p. 113, p. 115, pp. 125–26, and R.K. Saxena, *Maratha Relations with the Major States of Rajputana (1761–1818 AD)* (New Delhi: S. Chand & Co.), pp. 147–48. On the Muslim side, meanwhile, an invading army not only plundered Hindus but also local Muslims in the areas under attack. See Jackson, *Delhi Sultanate*, p. 208.

205  See the Hindu–Muslim dialogue in Eleanor Zelliot, 'Medieval Encounter between Hindu and Muslim: Eknath's Drama-Poem Hindu Turk Samvad', in Fred W. Clothey ed., *Images of Man: Religion and Historical Process in South Asia* (Madras: New Era Publications, 1982), pp. 171–95. See also Eleanor Zelliot, 'Chokhamela and Eknath: Two Bhakti Modes of Legitimacy for Modern Change', p. 149, in Lele ed., *Tradition and Modernity*, pp. 136–56. Kabir also clearly identified Hindus as a community. See Purushottam Agrawal, *Kabir, Kabir: The Life and Work of the Early Modern Poet Philosopher* (Chennai: Westland Publications, 2021), pp. 86–87. Malik Muhammad Jayasi makes a similar distinction in the sixteenth century. See Purushottam Agrawal, *Padmavat: An Epic Love Story* (New Delhi: Rupa Publications, 2018), p. 25. So also we find in the Mughal court a division between Hindus and Muslims. See Ernst, 'Muslim Studies', pp. 180–82.

206  We will in chapters ahead see more on Brahmins and their links not just with Muslim powers but also, in time, the British. On Persian, this was soon Indianized, of course, and became the language of diplomatic correspondence and transregional communication even among Hindu powers until the nineteenth century.

207  See for instance Jaiswal, 'Semitising Hinduism', p. 24. See also Eaton, *Bengal Frontier*, p. 38 for how at first ordinary people denied legitimacy to Islamic power, even after having lived under it for decades.

208  This comes across in the *Rajaramacarita*. In it we read: 'How will men find peace in this ghastly Kali Yuga/That is bringing on the victory of the great Mughals (mlecchas)/Everywhere the Mughal king destroys class boundaries (*varnadharmavighatin*)/Every field of dharma has been destroyed by that bad-souled man.' Quoted in Truschke, *Language of History*, p. 156.

209  This is visible also in the increasing usage of the term 'Hindu'—hitherto a generic expression for Indians—as a signifier of religious identity. Recorded first in the ninth century, it occurs sparsely thereafter. But between the sixteenth and eighteenth centuries, in Bengal alone variants of 'Hindu' appear forty-eight times in sectarian texts. For a history of the term 'Hindu' and its evolving meanings, see Audrey Truschke, 'Hindu: A History', in *Comparative Studies in Society and History* 65, 2 (2023): 246–71. See also Copland et al., pp. 139–40. In time, Hindu kings would consciously label

themselves as Hindu. See Truschke, *Language of History*, p. 45, and Cynthia Talbot, 'The Story of Prataparudra: Hindu Historiography on the Deccan Fronier', pp. 283–84, in Gilmartin and Lawrence eds., pp. 282–99.

210 Muzaffar Alam, 'Competition and Co-Existence: Indo-Islamic Interaction in Medieval North India', p. 49, in *Itinerario* 13, 1 (1989): 37–60.

211 Prange, *Monsoon Islam*, p. 131, p. 192.

212 Ogura, 'Incompatible Outsiders', pp. 190–97. This appears in Srivara's *Rajatarangini*.

213 The *Gita Ranaji Pratapasimhaji Ro* quoted in Ira Mukhoty, *Akbar: The Great Mughal* (New Delhi: Aleph Book Company, 2020), p. 208. These can be read as 'epics of resistance'. See Aziz Ahmad in 'Epic and Counter-Epic in Medieval India', in *Journal of the American Oriental Society* 83, 4 (1963): 470–76. In the *Ranmallachanda*, celebrating a Gujarat king, the portrayal of a Muslim foe similarly reveals awareness of religious variance. See Kapadia, *In Praise of Kings*, p. 65, p. 71.

214 Gijs Kruijtzer, *Xenophobia in Seventeenth-Century India* (Leiden: Leiden University Press, 2009), p. 130.

215 Phillip B. Wagoner, *Tidings of the King: A Translation and Ethnohistorical Analysis of the Rayavacakamu* (Honolulu, University of Hawaii Press, 1993), p. 53. See also Kruijtzer, *Xenophobia*, p. 266 for poetry by a Golconda sultan in the early modern period where he identifies Muslims and Hindus as separate.

216 Quoted in David N. Lorenzen, 'Who Invented Hinduism?', p. 651, in *Comparative Studies in Society and History* 41, 4 (1999): 630–59. Sanjay Subrahmanyam cites a similar eighteenth-century poem by Gogulapati Kurmanatha Kavi. See Subrahmanyam, *Courtly Encounters: Translating Courtliness and Violence in Early Modern Eurasia* (London: Harvard University Press, 2012), p. 34. For parallel complaints against Hindu assertion by Muslims, see Eaton, *Bengal Frontier*, p. 53, pp. 89–90.

217 Shireen Moosvi, 'The Mughal Encounter with Vedanta: Recovering the Biography of 'Jadrup''', p. 17, in *Social Scientist* 30, 7–8 (2002): 13–23.

218 Wheeler M. Thackston trans., *The Jahangirnama: Memoirs of Jahangir, Emperor of India* (New York: Oxford University Press, 1999), p. 313.

219 For details of Jahangir's temple patronage, see Tarapada Mukherjee and Irfan Habib, 'The Mughal Administration and the Temples of Vrindavan during the Reigns of Jahangir and Shahjahan', in *Proceedings of the Indian History Congress* 49 (1988): 287–300.

220 *The Jahangirnama*, p. 153. He also demolished the seat of a yogi and threw out another idol nearby. See also ibid., p. 349 where the emperor is horrified that a certain set of Muslims, who had converted from Hinduism, continued to intermarry with Hindus. Taking daughters from Hindus was 'well and good', but 'giving them to Hindus' was, in his mind, scandalous.

221 Moosvi, 'The Mughal Encounter', p. 18. See also Mir Dulfiqar Ardestani (David Shea and Anthony Troyer eds.), *The Dabistan, or School of Manners*,

Vol. 2 (Paris: Oriental Translation Fund of Great Britain and Ireland, 1843), pp. 144–45.
222  Bartholomeus Ziegenbalg quoted in Urs App, *The Birth of Orientalism* (Philadelphia: University of Pennsylvania Press, 2010), p. 100.
223  On this see, Brian K. Pennington, *Was Hinduism Invented?: Britons, Indians, and the Colonial Construction of Religion* (New York: Oxford University Press, 2005), p. 172.
224  To avoid entangling the reader in too many knots, I do not here venture into the debate on 'religion' itself as a concept which might or might not be translatable universally and across cultures. In any case, to quote one scholar, Indian thinkers in the nineteenth century did show an 'implicit understanding of religion as a universally applicable concept'. See Arvind-Pal S. Mandair, *Religion and the Specter of the West: Sikhism, India, Postcoloniality, and the Politics of Translation* (New York: Columbia University Press, 2009), p. 53. See also Pennington, *Was Hinduism Invented?*, p. 15, p. 178, where 'religion' is represented as a 'flexible and polyvalent' and 'elastic' concept.
225  Henry Rice, *Native Life in India: Being Sketches of the Social and Religious Characteristics of the Hindus* (Oakland: Pacific Press Publishing Company, 1891), p. 134.
226  I borrow this phrase 'domination of strangers' from Jon E. Wilson.

## One: Monsters and Missionaries

1  Sir Edward Maclagan, *The Jesuits and the Great Mogul* (London: Burns Oates & Washbourne 1932), p. 25.
2  J.S. Hoyland trans. and S.N. Banerjee ed., *The Commentary of Father Monserrate SJ.: On His Journey to the Court of Akbar* (London: Humphrey Milford Oxford University Press, 1922), p. 2. Akbar had earlier invited a Christian father called Julian Pereira from Bengal. Some Portuguese officials also supplied information but not to the depth Akbar desired. See also Agnieszka Kuczkiewicz-Fras, 'Akbar the Great (1542–1605) and Christianity. Between religion and politics', in *Orientalia Christiana Cracoviensia* 3 (2011): 75–89. He may, of course, have had motivations of a less religious nature too, as did the Portuguese. See João Vicente Melo, *Jesuit and English Experiences at the Mughal Court, c. 1580–1615* (Cham, Switzerland: Palgrave Macmillan, 2022), p. 3, p. 11, p. 20, p. 25.
3  *Father Monserrate*, p. 28.
4  Ibid., p. 38.
5  Ibid., p. 37.
6  *Muntakhabu-T-Tawarikh*, p. 267. The prince was Murad. In 1595, when another Jesuit mission was on the way to court, they met the prince, who arranged money and assistance. For all his early instruction in Christianity, the prince showed little interest as an adult. See Maclagan, *The Jesuits and the Great Mogul*, p. 52.

7   *The Jahangirnama*, p. 40.
8   R. Nath, *Calligraphic Art in Mughal Architecture (1526–1658 A.D.)* (Calcutta: Iran Society, 1979), pp. 19–20.
9   Abraham Eraly, *The Mughal Throne: The Saga of India's Great Emperors* (London: Weidenfeld & Nicolson, 2003), p. 196.
10  Truschke, 'Hindu: A History', p. 259. See a Vaishnava inscription that expresses similar feelings about Akbar in Gopal N. Bahura, 'Sri Govinda Gatha Service rendered to Govinda by the rulers of Amera and Jayapura', p. 201, in Margaret H. Case ed., *Govindadeva: A Dialogue in Stone* (New Delhi: IGNCA, 1996), pp. 195–213. For an early-nineteenth-century text that shares this memory, see Partha Chatterjee, 'History and the Nationalization of Hinduism', p. 109, in Vasudha Dalmia and Heinrich von Stietencron eds., *Representing Hinduism: The Construction of Religious Traditions and National Identity* (New Delhi: SAGE Publications, 1995), pp. 103–28.
11  *Father Monserrate*, p. 197.
12  Ibid., p. 142.
13  Maclagan, *The Jesuits and the Great Mogul*, p. 32.
14  *Father Monserrate*, pp. 62–63.
15  Melo, *Jesuit and English Experiences*, p. 28.
16  Maclagan, *The Jesuits and the Great Mogul*, p. 31. In fact, Akbar, even in 1595, would not concede this point, as the third Jesuit mission found.
17  This was in deference to Jains who persuaded the emperor to ban animal slaughter for some days each year.
18  *Father Monserrate*, p. 191. See also Mela, *Jesuit and English Experiences*, p. 35. About his son Jahangir also a Jesuit would state that he was 'not a Moor, nor Gentile, nor Christian, because unlike the faithful he does not adhere firmly to any creed'. See Jorge Flores, *The Mughal Padshah: A Jesuit Treatise on Emperor Jahangir's Court and Household* (Leiden: Brill, 2016), p. 94.
19  *Father Monserrate*, p. 171.
20  Ibid., p. 184.
21  Maclagan, *The Jesuits and the Great Mogul*, p. 38. Jesuits in Japan also deemed its people 'white'.
22  *Father Monserrate*, p. 177.
23  Ibid., p. 120
24  Ibid., p. 37. We should note here, however, that this is what the Jesuits reported home; it is possible that while expressing these thoughts before the emperor, their language was less impassioned. That controversial ideas were expressed is not in doubt. Years later, when the third mission complained that the emperor was not taking them seriously, Akbar reminded them that 'he had at least done this much for the Fathers that, whereas under former rulers they could not have dared to affirm the divinity of Christ, they could now do so with perfect safety'. See Maclagan, *The Jesuits and the Great Mogul*, p. 57.

25  *Father Monserrate*, p. 45.
26  On the glorification of martyrdom in the Christian world, see Catherine Nixey, *The Darkening Age: The Christian Destruction of the Classical World* (New York: Mariner, 2019), pp. 60–67.
27  *Father Monserrate*, p. 195. This was not specific to Akbar. Decades later, the traveller Thomas Coryate could publicly call the Prophet an imposter, noting that in Mughal India, 'a Christian may speake much more freely than he can in any other Mahometan Country in the World'. Quoted in Nandini Das, *Courting India: England, Mughal India and the Origins of Empire* (London: Bloomsbury, 2023), p. 90.
28  Quoted in Mukhoty, *Akbar*, p. 305.
29  *Father Monserrate*, p. 9. In 1748, the famous *dubash* (translator or interpreter) Ananda Ranga Pillai also confirmed to the French governor in southern India how besides Tamil Hindus who were 'observers of auspicious times and omens', the 'Muhammadans and even the English do as Brahman astrologers tell them'.
30  *Father Monserrate*, p. 17.
31  Ibid., p. 22.
32  Ibid., pp. 23–24. The ancestor of the Mughal emperor, Babur, was also offended by these rock sculptures decades before because of the exposed genitalia. See Annette Susannah Beveridge (trans.) and Dilip Hiro (ed.), *Babur Nama: Journal of Emperor Babur* (Gurugram: Penguin Random House India, 2006), pp. 313–14.
33  *Father Monserrate*, p. 27.
34  Ignatius of Loyola quoted in John Correia-Afonso, *Jesuit Letters and Indian History: A Study of the Nature and Development of the Jesuit Letters from India (1542–1773) and of Their Value for Indian Historiography* (Bombay: Indian Historical Research Institute, 1955), p. 14.
35  Antonio Possevino quoted in Grant Boswell, 'Letter Writing among the Jesuits: Antonio Possevino's Advice in the "Bibliotheca Selecta" (1593)', p. 254, in *Huntington Library Quarterly* 66, 3–4 (2003): 247–62.
36  Correia-Afonso, *Jesuit Letters*, p. 16. Voltaire wrote as late as 1756: 'People are busier sending us goods from the coasts of Malabar than truths. A particular case is often portrayed as a general custom.' Quoted in App, *The Birth of Orientalism*, p. 42.
37  Sir Henry Yule and Henri Cordier eds., *The Book of Ser Marco Polo, the Venetian concerning the Kingdoms and Marvels of the East*, Vol. 2 (London: John Murray, 1903), p. 345.
38  Partha Mitter, *Much Maligned Monsters: A History of European Reactions to Indian Art* (Oxford: Clarendon Press, 1977), pp. 3–5.
39  Ibid., p. 10.
40  Richard Fletcher, *The Conversion of Europe: From Paganism to Christianity, 371–1386 AD* (London: Fontana Press, 1998), pp. 254–55.

41  Ibid., pp. 51–52.
42  *De Correctione Rusticorum* quoted in ibid., p. 53. See also J.N. Hillgarth ed., *Christianity and Paganism, 350–750: The Conversion of Western Europe* (Philadelphia: University of Pennsylvania Press, 1986), p. 58, and Nixey, *The Darkening Age*, pp. 18–19.
43  John E. Rotelle and Maria Boulding eds., *The Works of Saint Augustine: A Translation for the 21st Century: Exposition of the Psalms 73–98* (New York: New City Press, 2002), p. 414.
44  Robert Bartlett, 'From Paganism to Christianity in Medieval Europe', pp. 67–68, in Nora Berend ed., *Christianization and the Rise of Christian Monarchy: Scandinavia, Central Europe and Rus' c. 900–1200* (New York: Cambridge University Press, 2007), pp. 47–72.
45  I use the word 'now' because before sustained intercourse with Indians, European writers maintained a positive, romanticized picture of the country and its Brahmins, inheriting these views from 1000-year-old Greek accounts. See note 180.
46  Arthur Coke Burnell ed., *The Voyage of John Huyghen van Linschoten to the East Indies*, Vol. 1 (London: Hakluyt Society, 1885), pp. 223–24. He would secretly copy Portuguese nautical charts and maps, thus enabling the Dutch and others to also enter the Indian Ocean trade.
47  Ibid., p. 296. The comparison with the pope's tiara was also a Protestant taking potshots at Catholicism.
48  Diana L. Eck, *Darsan: Seeing the Divine Image in India* (New York: Columbia University Press, 1998), p. 41.
49  The 1703 publishers of Philip Baldaeus's 1672 travel diary acknowledged as much when they wrote that existing accounts on India were 'very defective' because their authors added 'fabulous' claims to 'please the Reader, than to pursue the strict Rules of Truth'; 'hearsay' was their chief source. See Baldaeus, *A True and Exact Description of the Most Celebrated East-India Coasts of Malabar and Coromandel, As also of the Isle of Ceylon*, Vol. 3 (London: Awnsham & John Churchill, 1703 ed.), p. 563. On a good study of a recycling of another dubious story in a later period and its consequences, see Partha Chatterjee, *The Black Hole of Empire: History of a Global Practice of Power* (Princeton: Princeton University Press, 2012).
50  John Winter Jones trans. and George Percy Badger ed., *The Travels of Ludovico di Varthema in Egypt, Syria, Arabia Deserta and Arabia Felix, in Persia, India, and Ethiopia, A.D. 1503 to 1508* (London: Hakluyt Society, 1863), p. 137.
51  Ibid. For an interesting perspective that Varthema might have actually seen an image of the goddess Bhadrakali, see Manmadhan Ullatil, 'The Devil of Calicut: A Misconception' at https://historicalleys.blogspot.com/2022/12/the-devil-of-calicut-misconception.html.
52  Mandelslo wrote:

> The Figure under which they represent him [i.e. god, or rather the devil] is dreadful to look on. The Head, out of which grows four Horns, is adorn'd with a triple Crown, after the fashion of a Tiara. The countenance is horribly deformed, having coming out of the Mouth two great Teeth, like the Tusks of a Boar, and the Chin set out with a great ugly Beard . . . Under the Navil, between the two Thighs, there comes out of the Belly another Head, much more ghastly than the former, having two Horns upon it, and thrusting out of the Mouth a filthy Tongue of extraordinary bigness. Instead of Feet it hath Paws, and behind, a Cows-tail.

See 'The Travels of John Albert de Mandelso', in John Davies trans., Adam Olearius, *The Voyages and Travells of the Ambassadors sent by Frederick Duke of Holstein* (London: John Starkey, 1669), p. 52.

53  Mitter, *Much Maligned Monsters*, pp. 17–18.
54  On this, see also Jyotsna G. Singh, *Colonial Narratives/Cultural Dialogues: 'Discoveries' of India in the Language of Colonialism* (London: Routledge, 1996), chapter one.
55  Henry Yule trans., *Cathay and the Way Thither: Bring a Collection of Medieval Notices of China*, Vol. 1 (London: Hakluyt Society, 1866), p. 79.
56  Ibid.
57  The ban was through the sixty-four *anacharam*s, or peculiar customs, established either by Parasurama, the mythical figure, or Sankaracharya, the eighth-century philosopher for Namboodiri Brahmins. For non-Brahmin high-caste groups, matriliny precluded the centrality of the husband—and thus sati—anyway. See the list of anacharams in V. Nagam Aiya, *The Travancore State Manual*, Vol. 2 (Trivandrum: Government of Travancore, 1906), pp. 267–71.
58  See Uma Maheshwari ed., *Mathilakam Rekhakal*, Vol. 1 (Thiruvananthapuram: Sri Uthradom Tirunal Marthanda Varma Literary and Charitable Trust, 2018), p. 248.
59  Yule and Cordier, *The Book of Ser Marco Polo*, p. 341.
60  The fact that sati stones were erected to commemorate women who burned themselves is a sign that it was not an everyday affair. Its occurrence was rare enough for individual satis to be memorialized. So too the process, where, as one traveller put it, there was 'the Country Musick . . . a great many Maids and Women, singing and dancing before the Widow' alongside a 'company of Men, Women, and Children' in a procession, suggests that it was a special enough occurrence to be celebrated in this extremely public manner. We also find Henry Lord in *A Display of Two Forraigne Sects in the East Indies* (London, 1630), p. 68 noting that sati was performed by 'persons of greater worth' though its 'examples be more rare now'. Colonial officials like H.T. Colebrooke in the 1790s also spoke of its rareness. See H.T. Colebrooke, *Essays on the Religion and Philosophy of the Hindus* (London: Williams &

Norgate, 1858 ed.), p. 75. See also Jorg Fisch, 'Dying for the Dead: Sati in Universal Context', p. 303, in *Journal of World History* 16, 3 (2005): 293–325 for an analysis of numbers during the British era, noting an average of 581 cases out of a total population of about 50 million in just one province, and an all-Indian average of one case for every 1000 widows.

61  Yule, *Cathay and the Way Thither*, p. 83.
62  'The Travels of Nicolo Conti in the East in the Early Part of the Fifteenth Century', p. 28, in R.H. Major ed., *India in the Fifteenth Century: Being a Collection of Narratives of Voyages to India* (London: Hakluyt Society, 1857).
63  *The Voyage of John Huyghen van Linschoten*, p. 295.
64  Sanjay Subrahmanyam, *Europe's India: Words, People, Empires, 1500–1800* (Cambridge: Harvard University Press, 2017), p. 30.
65  See Kulke, *Kings and Cults*, pp. 71–72 where, for Puri, he observes that even under supposedly civilized British control, the frenzy and excitement during the procession caused deaths. These were *accidents*, because of the sheer number gathered, even if in 'rare cases' people consciously sacrificed themselves.
66  Kate Teltscher, *India Inscribed: European and British Writing on India 1600–1800* (Delhi: Oxford University Press, 1995), p. 28. Or to quote anthropologist Talal Asad on a related note, 'Europe did not simply expand overseas; it made itself through that expansion.' See Asad, 'Muslims and European Identity: Can Europe Represent Islam?' p. 220, in Anthony Pagden ed., *The Idea of Europe: From Antiquity to the European Union* (Cambridge: Cambridge University Press, 2002), pp. 209–27.
67  *The Voyage of John Huyghen van Linschoten*, pp. 250–51.
68  Nicholas Withington in William Foster ed., *Early Travels in India: 1583–1619* (London: Humphrey Milford Oxford University Press, 1921), p. 221.
69  Ovington, *A Voyage to Suratt*, p. 343. Often, of course, the other extreme was also offered, i.e., the idea of the Hindu widow as so dutiful to her husband that she preferred to kill herself than live without him—an angle that was, evidently, intended as a comparison with European wives and as a lesson in wifely fidelity.
70  Teltscher, *India Inscribed*, p. 53.
71  Pompa Banerjee, *Burning Women: Widows, Witches, and Early Modern European Travelers in India* (New York: Palgrave Macmillan, 2003), pp. 146–73. Interestingly, in the eighteenth century, when a missionary asked a Tamil Hindu about sati in the region, his response was that in kingly settings, women were burned so that *after* the king's death, if they should commit sexual transgressions, it would not embarrass the royal family. See the Second Letter in Daniel Jeyaraj and Richard Fox Young eds., *Hindu–Christian Epistolary Self Disclosures: 'Malabarian Correspondence' between German Pietiest Missionaries and South Indian Hindus (1712–1714)* (Wiesbaden: Harrasowitz Verlag, 2013), p. 108.

72  Subrahmanyam, *Europe's India*, p. 23. Pietro della Valle and Francois Bernier both speak of trying to dissuade sati-elects.

73  L. Besse, *Father Beschi of the Society of Jesus: His Times and His Writings* (Trichinopoloy: St Joseph's Industrial School Press, 1918), p. 26. The event is supposed to have happened in 1710 when the rajah of Ramnad died. See also Kruijtzer, *Xenophobia*, pp. 225–26, for a 1665 instance when an Englishman actually witnesses a sati but relates it without exaggeration.

74  Ovington, *A Voyage to Suratt*, pp. 211–12.

75  Captain Cope, *A New History of the East-Indies: With Brief Observations of the Religion, Customs, Manners and Trade of the Residents* (London: H. Owen, 1758), p. 239.

76  W.H. Moreland and P. Geyl trans., *Jahangir's India: The Remonstrantie of Francisco Pelsaert* (Cambridge: W. Heffer & Sons, 1925), p. 72.

77  Cope, *A New History*, p. 303.

78  Father Tachard quoted in John Lockman, *Travels of the Jesuits into Various Parts of the World* (London: T. Piety, 1762), pp. 168–69.

79  Samuel Purchas, *Relations of the World and the Religions observed in all Ages and Places discovered, from the Creation into the Present* (London: Henrie Fetherstone, 1614), p. 486. English traveller and historian Sir Thomas Herbert also noted this 'tradition'. See also Baldaeus, *A True and Exact Description*, p. 832, where Baldaeus, 'for Modesties sake' describes this custom in Latin—a traditional technique when touching on potentially delicate subjects.

80  Amusingly, British historians and writers would later use similar stereotypes about their early colonial rivals in India—the Portuguese—and their women, who escaped the 'vigilance of their husbands' by drugging the latter and admitting paramours to their beds. See William Wilson Hunter, *A History of British India*, Vol. 1 (London, New York & Bombay: Longmans, Green & Co., 1899), pp. 156–57.

81  Ovington, *A Voyage to Suratt*, p. 362.

82  Cope, *A New History*, pp. 240–41. Penis rings, to *prevent* sex with women, not titillate them, were noted by the occasional Arab traveller too. Abu Zaid, for example, spoke of this in the tenth century. See K.A. Nilakanta Sastri, *Foreign Notices of South India: From Megasthenes to Ma Huan* (Madras: University of Madras, 1939), p. 125.

83  John Fryer, *A New Account of East-India and Persian: In Eight Letters* (London, 1698), p. 179.

84  The Afghan ruler Ahmad Shah Abdali in the eighteenth century was horrified when an Indian ally brought an army of sadhus to the battlefield. An account from the time poses the question: 'How could the Kaffirs [infidels] have so much liberty as to walk with their things and buttocks exposed before the Moslems?' Quoted in Ira Mukhoty, *The Lion and the Lily: The Rise and Fall of Awadh* (New Delhi: Aleph Book Company, 2024), p. 35.

Sadhus would in the colonial future also serve as agents of anti-British sentiment. As was written: 'With absolute freedom to go where they will, with access to all quarters, with fellow initiates in every town their powers of underground propaganda may be very great, and their power for evil serious.' Quoted in Kim A. Wagner, *The Great Fear of 1857: Rumours, Conspiracies and the Making of the Indian Uprising* (Oxford: Peter Lang, 2010), p. xix.

85   Nineteenth-century British accounts were more sober, stating that there were perfectly decent sadhus just as there were offensive ones—there was no one standard for the whole lot. See Elphinstone, *A History of India*, Vol. 1, p. 118.

86   Ines G. Zupanov, *Missionary Tropics: The Catholic Frontier in India (16th-17th Centuries)* (Ann Arbor: The University of Michigan Press, 2005), pp. 179–80.

87   Ibid.

88   Ines G. Zupanov, 'Lust, Marriage and Free Will: Jesuit Critique of Paganism in South India (Seventeenth Century)', p. 206, in *Studies in History* 16, 2 (2000): 199–220.

89   A whiff of these stereotypes—and their long life—appears even in Karl Marx's nineteenth-century summarization of Hinduism, for instance, as 'at once a religion of sensualist exuberance, and a religion of self-torturing asceticism; a religion of the Lingam and the Juggernaut; the religion of the Monk, and of the Bayadere [temple dancer]'. Quoted in Trevor Ling, *Karl Marx and Religion: In Europe and India* (London: The Macmillan Press Ltd., 1920), pp. 70–71.

90   See the eighteenth-century cases of Umi Kostin, who mixed powdered glass and made *bhakri* for her husband and father-in-law and Gangi Pardesin, who mixed poison in a sweet potato dish in N.K. Wagle, 'Women in the Kotwal's Papers, Pune, 1767–1791', p. 19, in Anne Feldhaus ed., *Images of Women in Maharashtrian Society* (Albany: State University of New York Press, 1998), pp. 15–60.

91   Zupanov, *Missionary Tropics*, p. 16. Thomas Trautmann in *Aryans and British India* (Berkeley & Los Angeles: University of California Press, 1997), pp. 19–20 shows how even into the twentieth century, the cliché of climate creating an 'enervating' situation in India continued, for instance in the writings of Henry Kissinger. Indians were not immune either. In a speech in 1913, the technocrat minister M. Visvesvaraya of Mysore State repeated the myth when he said, 'In our warm climate we have not got the same incentive to exertion and we may never be able to attain the same level of prosperity as Western people.' See M. Visvesvaraya, *Speeches by Sir M. Vivesvaraya, Dewan of Mysore, 1910–11 to 1916–17* (Bangalore: Government Press, 1917), p. 85.

92   Besse, *Father Beschi*, p. 31. See also Eaton, *Bengal Frontier*, p. 168 for similar views among the Mughals earlier.

93   E.G. Ravenstein ed., *A Journal of the First Voyage of Vasco da Gama 1497–1499* (New Delhi: Asian Educational Services, 1998 ed.), pp. 54–55.

94  Joan-Pau Rubiés, *Travel and Ethnology in the Renaissance: South India through European Eyes, 1250–1625* (Cambridge: Cambridge University Press, 2004), p. 166. See also *A Journal of the First Voyage*, p. 49, which confidently declares that 'The city of Calecut is inhabited by Christians', whose local, Hindu habits were interpreted as 'a sign that they are Christians'.

95  M.N. Pearson, *The Portuguese in India (The New Cambridge History of India)* (Cambridge: Cambridge University Press, 1987), p. 75.

96  See Jorge Flores and Giuseppe Marcocci, 'Killing Images: Iconoclasm and the Art of Political Insult in Sixteenth and Seventeenth Century Portuguese India', in *Itinerario* 42, 3 (2018): 461–89. King Sebastian even flirted with the idea of sailing to India himself 'to lead his troops against the infidels'. See Dauril Alden, *The Making of an Enterprise: The Society of Jesus in Portugal, Its Empire, and Beyond: 1540–1750* (Stanford: Stanford University Press, 1996), p. 84.

97  Kaviraj, *Imaginary Institution of India*, p. 55. On royal messianism combined with mercantilism in King Manuel's reign in Portugal, see Sanjay Subrahmanyam, *The Portuguese Empire in Asia, 1500-1700: A Political and Economic History* (Chichester: John Wiley & Sons, 2012), pp. 53–54.

98  Pearson, *The Portuguese in India*, p. 74. See also Philip E. Steinberg, *The Social Construction of the Ocean* (Cambridge: Cambridge University Press, 2001), p. 47. The Mughals and other big powers had business interests, of course, but the sea was not thought of as a militarized space that required land powers to project power. Or as Reddy observes, 'The Mughal state was so disinterested with the sea that by the mid-seventeenth century [Emperor] Aurangzeb finally outsourced his naval needs.' See Srinivas Reddy, 'Disrupting Mughal Imperialism: Piracy and Plunder on the Indian Ocean', p. 130, in *Asian Review of World Histories*, Vol. 8 (2020): 128–42.

99  As a Portuguese viceroy himself declared, 'Nothing else preserves peace and friendship with the kings and lords of India than having them believe ... that our only interest is the sea.' See Angela Barreto Xavier, *Religion and Empire in Portuguese India: Conversion, Resistance, and the Making of Goa* (Albany: State University of New York, 2022), p. 47.

100 Sanjay Subrahmanyam, *Courtly Encounters: Translating Courtliness and Violence in Early Modern Eurasia* (Cambridge: Harvard University Press, 2012), pp. 13–14. See also Rubiés, *Travel and Ethnology*, pp. 186–87. That an Indian ruler made such a proposal should not be surprising. Even among the Mughals, Emperor Jahangir allowed the conversion of his nephews (sons of Akbar's son Daniyal). These princes took Portuguese names: Tahmurs became Dom Filipe, Baisunghar became Dom Carlos and Hoshang became Dom Henrique. To the aggravation of the Jesuits, once relations with the Portuguese soured, the princes apostatized and became Muslims again. See Flores, *The Mughal Padshah*, p. 17, p. 92.

101 Or as an eighteenth-century commentator put it, 'The first Portuguese conquerors . . . robbed, preached, massacred; and converted the Indians.' See Jean Deloche (ed.) and G.S. Cheema (trans.), *Soldier of Misfortune: The Memoirs of the Comte de Modave*, Vol. 1 (New Delhi: Manohar Publishers, 2024), p. 95.
102 Pearson, *The Portuguese in India*, p. 16.
103 Duarte Nunez quoted in Alexander Henn, *Hindu–Catholic Encounters in Goa: Religion, Colonialism, and Modernity* (Bloomington & Indianapolis: Indiana University Press, 2014), p. 41.
104 Reference is to the temple at Divar Island. See Anant Kakba Priolkar, *The Goa Inquisition: Being a Quatercentenary Commemoration Study of the Inquisition in India* (New Delhi: Voice of India, 1961), p. 65.
105 Rowena Robinson, 'Sixteenth Century Conversions to Christianity in Goa', p. 299, in Rowena Robinson and Sathianathan Clarke eds., *Religious Conversion in India: Modes, Motivations, and Meanings* (New Delhi: Oxford University Press, 2003), pp. 291–322, and Ananya Chakravarti, *The Empire of Apostles: Religion, Accomodatio, and the Imagination of Empire in Early Modern Brazil and India* (New Delhi: Oxford University Press, 2018), p. 45. This is not surprising: in Kerala, where the Portuguese demanded the expulsion of Arab traders, the Hindu rajah of Calicut refused. However, the only local *Muslim* royal house on the coast aligned with them. From their perspective, this was a form of insurance against Calicut's dominance. Thus, domestic politics in Kerala guided how the Portuguese were received. See Mahmood Kooria, 'An Abode of Islam', p. 94.
106 Priolkar, *The Goa Inquisition*, pp. 68–69. See also Xavier, *Religion and Empire*, p. 46, pp. 70–71, which notes that by 1541 in Tiswadi, a taluka in the district of North Goa, alone, 300 temples were destroyed. For another 300 in the mid 1560s, see ibid., p. 253.
107 Henn, *Hindu-Catholic Encounters*, p. 42. See also Baldaeus, *A True and Exact Description*, p. 646.
108 Henn, *Hindu-Catholic Encounters*, pp. 42–43.
109 It would officially last from 1560 until 1812.
110 Pearson, *The Portuguese in India*, pp. 117–18. To be clear, some converted willingly also. Priolkar, *Goa Inquisition*, p. 56 notes a 1567 instance where a Brahmin, unable to marry his lower-caste lover, converted with her to Christianity. See also Robinson, 'Sixteenth Century Conversions', p. 302, and for persecution, pp. 305–06.
111 On the density and variety of gods in Goa, see Angelo Barreto Xavier and Ines G. Zupanov, *Catholic Orientalism: Portuguese Empire, Indian Knowledge (16th-18th Centuries)* (New Delhi: Oxford University Press, 2015), pp. 73–74.
112 Davis, *Lives of Indian Images*, p. 16.
113 Kulke, *Kings and Cults*, pp. 34–35.

114  Norbert Peabody, *Hindu Kingship and Polity in Precolonial India* (New Delhi: Foundation Books, 2006), pp. 53–54.
115  Richard M. Eaton, *Temple Desecration and Muslim States in Medieval India* (Gurugram: Hope India, 2004), p. 35.
116  Davis, *Lives of Indian Images*, pp. 65–67. Reference is to the Balakrishna from Udayagiri brought to Hampi by Emperor Krishnadevaraya, and to Vitthal of Pandharpur—this latter was returned.
117  See the inscription from Kulottunga Chola I's reign quoted in Burton Stein, *Peasant State and Society in Medieval South India* (Delhi: Oxford University Press, 1980), p. 174.
118  Thus, during feuds with priests of the famous Padmanabhaswamy Temple, the Travancore rajahs were not above burning down its gate and attacking them. Expiatory gifts were later made. See A. Gopalakrishna Menon, *History of Sri Padmanabsvami Temple Till 1758* (Thiruvananthapuram: Menon & Co., 1996), p. 22, p. 122, p. 128, p. 138. Even the conquest of territories under rival Hindu rulers involved temple desecration: in the eighteenth century, Martanda Varma of Travancore burned 'churches, pagodas, and palaces' in a rival's state, while his troops in one case were beaten up with brooms by priests when they attempted to appropriate its property. See Mark de Lannoy, *The Kulasekhara Perumals of Travancore*, p. 55, p. 123, p. 126.
119  Or as a scholar puts it in the context of another part of the world, there can be an 'intrasystemic' Other (as in the case of Hindus clashing) and 'extrasystemic' ones (Hindus versus Muslims) where the Other operates within a 'different construction of reality'. To intrasystemic rivals, these were still gods; to the extrasystemic, they were 'mere pieces of wood or stone'. See Assman, *Of God and Gods*, p. 31.
120  Davis, *Lives of Indian Images*, p. 129.
121  The *Vimanarcanakalpa* quoted in ibid., pp. 127–28. Even when idols were destroyed, they could be 'found'. As Jahangir once observed sardonically, Brahmins conveniently 'dreamed' of the locations of hidden images—planted there in advance—and consecrated these in place of what was destroyed. See *Jahangirnama*, p. 375.
122  Xavier and Zupanov, *Catholic Orientalism*, p. 126.
123  Henn, *Hindu-Catholic Encounters*, p. 61, and Xavier, *Religion and Empire*, p. 136. See also Chakravarti, *Empire of Apostles*, p. 184.
124  Priolkar, *Goa Inquisition*, p. 86. For some of the amounts involved, see Xavier, *Religion and Empire*, p. 275.
125  Chakravarti, *Empire of Apostles*, p. 186. See also Xavier, *Religion and Empire*, pp. 255–56, and Pratima Kamat, *Farar Far: Local Resistance to Colonial Hegemony in Goa, 1510–1912* (Panaji: Institute Menezes Braganza, 1999), p. 54.
126  Cornelius Heda, the artist, quoted in Kruijtzer, *Xenophobia*, p. 28. (Heda was Dutch, and his remarks might be tinted with anti-Portuguese and

Protestant prejudice.) Meanwhile, Hindu attitudes only made Jesuits more paranoid. Alarmed at the ease with which locals created gods, even a Portuguese grandee's statue caused fear that some might 'adore it'. See Flores and Marcocci, 'Killing Images', p. 465. See also Alden, *The Making of an Enterprise*, p. 77, where he notes that in general, Jesuits did not hesitate to use 'force to expedite conversions', pointing to Brazil and Japan as well where 'compulsory conversions' occurred.

127 Anthony D'Costa, *The Christianisation of the Goa Islands: 1510–1567* (Bombay: A. D'Costa, 1965), p. 5.

128 Henn, *Hindu–Catholic Encounters*, pp. 51–52; Pearson, *The Portuguese in India*, p. 120; D'Costa, *The Christianisation of the Goa Islands*, p. 34; and Kamat, *Farar Far*, pp. 43–44.

129 Chakravarti, *Empire of Apostles*, p. 184. See also Xavier, *Religion and Empire*, p. 222.

130 D'Costa, *The Christianisation of the Goa Islands*, p. 72, and Xavier, *Religion and Empire*, p. 231.

131 Henn, *Hindu–Catholic Encounters*, p. 48.

132 See also Xavier, *Religion and Empire*, p. 27.

133 See also ibid., p. 253, where we find that the Portuguese reputation for demolishing temples and mosques was such that in a treaty with a Muslim prince, a promise *not* to do this or force conversions featured as a clause.

134 P. Podipara quoted in Prema A. Kurien, *Ethnic Church Meets Megachurch: Indian American Christianity in Motion* (New York: New York University Press, 2017), p. 243.

135 For a succinct history, see ibid., pp. 37–52.

136 Susan Bayly highlights an old hagiography of St Thomas where he is supposed to have come to Taxila in the north-west of India. From there, it travelled to southern India and was 'simply . . . transformed to fit the local sacral landscape'. See Bayly, *Saints, Goddesses and Kings*, p. 244. Frykenberg, meanwhile, notes how when St Thomas Christians were confronted with lack of clear evidence about St Thomas's coming to Malabar, they pointed out that there was no evidence for St Peter having come to Rome either.

137 Yule, *Cathay and the Way Thither*, p. 81.

138 Bayly, *Saints, Goddesses and Kings*, p. 257. They are also described as being 'in a state of considerable prosperity' at the time of the Portuguese arrival. See Stephen Neill, *A History of Christianity in India: The Beginnings to AD 1707* (Cambridge: Cambridge University Press, 1984), p. 195.

139 Michael Geddes, *The History of the Church of Malabar: From the Time of Its Being First Discover'd by the Portuguezes in the Year 1501* (London: Sam, Smith & Benj. Walford, 1694), p. 2.

140 See George Menachery, *The St Thomas Christian Encyclopaedia*, Vol. 2 (Trichur: St Thomas Christian Encyclopaedia of India, 1982), p. 203, p. 214. See also Bayly, *Saints, Goddesses and Kings*, p. 277.

141  They did seek a friendly alliance, only for de Gama, when presented a staff, to misunderstand the gesture as a mark of submission. Note, however, that as early as 1329, Pope John XXII had created a Catholic diocese in Quilon in Malabar, with the traveller Jordanus Catalani as its bishop, after John of Montecorvino informed Rome of the existence of a Christian community in the region. At this time, relations with St Thomas Christians were friendly. On the Christians seeking Portuguese protection, especially in 1523, see Robert Eric Frykenberg, 'Christians in India: An Historical Overview of their Complex Origins', p. 40, in Robert Eric Frykenberg ed., *Christians and Missionaries in India: Cross-Cultural Communication since 1500* (Grand Rapids: William B. Eerdmans Publishing Company, London: Routledge, 2003), pp. 33–61.

142  Bayly, *Saints, Goddesses and Kings*, p. 266. Things also got heated because the Church of the East, meanwhile, was split after a schism, with one section entering into communion with Rome. This internal strife may have encouraged the Portuguese to claim the Nasranis for the pro-Rome faction. See also Neill, *Christianity in India*, pp. 196–97, where we read that already by the 1510s and 1520s, due to the insistence of certain Portuguese priests that Nasranis abandon all aspects alien to Catholics, there was ill-feeling.

143  Geddes, *Church of Malabar*, pp. 94–95.

144  Archbishop Alexio de Menezes quoted in ibid, Appendix: 'The Publication and Calling of the Synod'.

145  Bayly, *Saints, Goddesses and Kings*, pp. 252–53. One special privilege the St Thomas Christians enjoyed was that only their 'touch' could purify oil and ghee used in Hindu temples and high-caste households. These customs continued into the twentieth century. See Aiya, *The Travancore State Manual*, Vol. 2, p. 123, where we also read that some Nasrani women dressed like Brahmin women, as a mark of descent from Brahmin converts made by St Thomas.

146  Xavier and Zupanov, *Catholic Orientalism*, p. 135.

147  Decree XIV in Geddes, *Church of Malabar*, p. 154.

148  Decree XVI in ibid., p. 172. Most of these books were lost forever. See J.P.M. van der Ploeg, *The Christians of St Thomas in South India and Their Syriac Manuscripts* (Bangalore: Dharmaram Publishers, 1983), pp. 19–20.

149  See Neill, *Christianity in India*, pp. 316–19. Known as Ahatallah, the man's antecedents are complicated, but for the Nasranis, the idea that they had been sent a bishop from the Church of the East was a catalyst.

150  This was through the famous Coonan Cross Oath of 3 January 1653. See Frykenberg, 'Christians in India', p. 42. See also James Puliurumpil, *Glimpses of Syro-Malabar History* (Kottayam: Oriental Institute of Religious Studies, 2019), pp. 85–101. Under pressure from British missionaries in the nineteenth century, where they tried to draw Nasranis close to the Protestant

Church of England, there would be a reaffirmation of links with Antioch by Nasranis resisting this. See van der Ploeg, *The Christians of St Thomas*, p. 35.

151 See for example Susan Viswanathan, *Wisdom of Community: Essays on History, Social Transformation, and Culture* (New Delhi: Bloomsbury India, 2022), p. 39, and Corinne G. Dempsey, *Kerala Christian Sainthood: Collisions of Culture and Worldview in South India* (Oxford: Oxford University Press, 2001), pp. 55–56.

152 Claudius Buchanan, *Christian Researches in Asia* (Boston: Samuel T. Armstrong, 1811), p. 89. On a scholarly evaluation of the privileged 'dominant caste' status of Nasranis in Kerala, see Sonja Thomas, 'Syrian Christians and Dominant-Caste Hindus', in Chad M. Bauman and Michelle Voss Roberts eds., *The Routledge Handbook of Hindu–Christian Relations* (Abingdon: Routledge, 2021), pp. 69–78.

153 Chakravarti, *Empire of Apostles*, p. 7.

154 Robinson, 'Sixteenth Century Conversions', pp. 300–01.

155 Xavier, *Religion and Empire*, p. 10. See also Kamat, *Farar Far*, pp. 46–48.

156 Quoted in Robinson, 'Sixteenth Century Conversions', pp. 306–07. See also D'Costa, *The Christianisation of the Goa Islands*, p. 45. See also Xavier, *Religion and Empire*, p. 226, pp. 231–32, pp. 240–41, where we find that lower-caste groups (branded 'untouchable' and ritually 'polluting') often converted for better treatment in their new identity; this threatened high-caste groups (Brahmins, landed elites) who in turn converted to preserve their social dominance. The result was that the same hierarchies reappeared, now *within* the Christian fold. See also ibid., p. 227. See also R.F. Young and G.P.V. Somaratna, *The Buddhist–Christian Controversies of Nineteenth-Century Ceylon* (Vienna: De Nobili Research Library, 1996), p. 39, where in the context of Sri Lanka, we read how European powers there, while not as forceful as in Goa, put in place 'a system of inducements . . . that favored baptism and the acculturation of the colonial mentality'.

157 Maria Jose Ferro quoted in Xavier, *Religion and Empire*, p. 91. Or as occurred in a French-ruled enclave in 1746, where Hindus protesting the desecration of a temple said, when coerced into dispersing: 'Why do you strike us? Cannot people meet, and deliberate when their religion is at stake . . . Why do you come, and beat us? You had better kill us all.' See J. Fredrick Price and K. Rangachari eds., *The Private Diary of Anand Ranga Pillai, Dubash to Joseph Francois Dupleix*, Vol. 1 (Madras: Government Press, 1904), p. 333.

158 D'Costa, *The Christianisation of the Goa Islands*, pp. 59–62. Conversion to Christianity, that is; Islam and Judaism were banned as options. See ibid., p. 64. See also Xavier, *Religion and Empire*, p. 80, pp. 84–85.

159 Robinson, 'Sixteenth Century Conversions', pp. 309–10.

160 On this massacre, see A.X. D'Souza, 'Martyrs of Cuncolim', in Charles G. Herbermann, Edward A. Pace, Conde B. Pallen, Thomas J. Shahan and John J. Wynne eds., *The Catholic Encyclopedia: An International Work of*

*Reference on the Constitution, Doctrine, Discipline, and History of the Catholic Church*, Vol. 4 (New York: Robert Appleton Company, 1908), pp. 568–69. See also Xavier, *Religion and Empire*, p. 264, and ibid., p. 268, p. 273 for other instances of violence.

161 Paul Axelrod and Michelle A. Fuerch, 'Flight of the Deities: Hindu Resistance in Portuguese Goa', p. 392 in *Modern Asian Studies* 30, 2 (1996): 387–421.

162 Robinson, 'Sixteenth Century Conversions', p. 306. Though not all were always permitted back into the fold. See, for example, Sudha V. Desai, *Social Life in Maharashtra under the Peshwas* (Bombay: Popular Prakashan, 1980), p. 102.

163 Axelrod and Fuerch, 'Flight of the Deities', p. 395 and Kamat, *Farar Far*, pp. 65–66.

164 Quoted in ibid., p. 412. In 1667 also the Portuguese viceroy would order the expulsion of Hindus from Bardez in North Goa because 'their presence affected the loyalty of the Christians to their religion'. See P.S. Pissurlencar (T.V. Parvate trans.), *Portuguese Mahratta Relations* (Bombay: Maharashtra State Board for Literature and Culture, 1983), p. 47. Similar complaints were made even in the 1630s, suggesting that Hindus showed resilience. As late as 1736, the Inquisition published an edict banning certain customs and rituals for converts, suggesting that these 'Hindu' customs had tended to continue. See Rowena Robinson, 'Taboo or Veiled Consent? Goan Inquisitorial Edict of 1736', p. 2423, in *Economic and Political Weekly* 35, 27 (2000): 2423–31.

165 Xavier, *Religion and Empire*, pp. 75–76. See also ibid., p. 141, where a Portuguese father himself criticized these home invasions, accusing the Jesuits leading them of doing 'terrible things, both night and day'.

166 Ibid., pp. 255–56. See also Kamat, *Farar Far*, pp. 50–51.

167 At Diu in Gujarat, as early as the 1590s, when the Portuguese attempted to take a hard-line religious position, the governor replied that if enacted, 'everyone would leave and then there would be no trade here'. Quoted in M.N. Pearson, *Merchants and Rulers in Gujarat: The Response to the Portuguese in the Sixteenth Century* (Berkeley: University of California Press, 1976), p. 104. Another cause for the return of tolerance was that at sea Portuguese dominance was challenged by the Dutch, and on land by the Hindu Marathas by the end of the seventeenth century, making stability within Goa expedient. See Xavier, *Religion and Empire*, p. 276.

168 As early as 1630, the Goan authorities, already facing declining income, suggested permitting Hindu weddings again on payment of a sum. This would make about 3000 cruzados a year. 'That such a trifling sum could, even as a proposal, dictate such a major policy change,' Pearson observes, 'is indicative indeed of the Portuguese government's financial straits'. See Pearson, *The Portuguese in India*, p. 134. See also D'Costa, *The Christianisation of the Goa Islands*, p. 68, p. 71, and Xavier, *Religion and Empire*, pp. 95–96 for criticism

of the hardline policy within the Portuguese camp. See also ibid., p. 228 for how mass desertions by peasants led to economic problems for the Goa government, which also therefore saw some rules relaxed, and p. 275. In Kerala too, Portuguese power was 'strongest in the coastal regions' with Nasranis, not in the interiors. See van der Ploeg, *The Christians of St Thomas* (Bangalore: Dharmaram, 1983), p. 18.

169 Henn, *Hindu–Catholic Encounters*, p. 13. Of course, some of this was because certain churches stood at the same spot as Hindu sites; so, if people made offerings once to a goddess, the replacement of the building with a church led them to continue doing so, now to the Virgin. See Xavier, *Religion and Empire*, p. 153. On the relaxation of earlier rules, Priolkar, *Goa Inquisition*, p. 29 adds that local dressing habits, taboos around pork and beef consumption, and other such 'petty Gentile and Mahomedan superstitions' were now allowed for converts. See also Robinson, 'Negotiating Traditions', pp. 41–42, p. 45, p. 49.

170 Kamat, *Farar Far*, p. 56, pp. 70–71.

171 Xavier, *Religion and Empire*, p. 121. See also Xavier and Zupanov, *Catholic Orientalism*, p. 281 for another set of figures from the 1730s for Goa more generally: 25,000 Hindus to 175,000 Christians.

172 Henry James Coleridge, *The Life and Letters of St Francis Xavier*, Vol. 1 (London: Burnes & Oates, 1874), pp. 68–69.

173 Ibid., p. 151. The Paravar, of course, also used their newfound Christian identity to claim a more prestigious position for their caste community within the broader Tamil context. See Rowena Robinson, 'Negotiating Traditions: Popular Christianity in India', pp. 34–35, *in Asian Journal of Social Science* 37, 1 (2009): 29–54.

174 Coleridge, *Life and Letters*, p. 231. The problem of polygamy and conversion continued even into the nineteenth century. See P. Sanal Mohan, *Modernity of Slavery: Struggles against Caste Inequality in Colonial Kerala* (New Delhi: Oxford University Press, 2015), pp. 76–82.

175 This practice of new converts being asked to break images of their old gods continued even into the twentieth century. See Joel Lee, *Deceptive Majority: Dalits, Hinduism, and Underground Religion* (Cambridge: Cambridge University Press, 2021), p. 47.

176 Coleridge, *Life and Letters*, pp. 279–82. Xavier also had bigger fish to fry. For the missionary enterprise was not divorced from Portuguese geopolitical ambitions. In the Sri Lankan kingdom of Kotte, a rajah put to death a son who wished to convert. Naturally, wrote Xavier, a miracle followed: 'The persons present at his execution declare that they saw a cross of fire in the heavens', and even the earth 'opened in the form of a cross' (pp. 282–83). While it was described as a tale of heroic faith, what Xavier obscured was that all this emerged from Portuguese interventions in the kingdom. Its ruler, under pressure from a rival, sent an embassy to Lisbon for military

aid. It was also hinted broadly that the rajah might become a Christian, but when four fathers landed up, he reneged. Watching this, meanwhile, a son whom the ruler intended to deny the throne, saw an opening and went to the Portuguese to be baptised—it was this opportunist whose death generated divine fireworks. In the end, the rajah was assassinated, a grandson rose to power, and not long thereafter, having become Christian, the puppet ruler 'willed' away his realm to Portugal. See Subrahmanyam, *The Portuguese Empire*, p. 139, and Zoltán Biedermann, *(Dis)connected Empire: Imperial Portugal, Sri Lankan Diplomacy, and the Making of a Habsburg Conquest in Asia* (Oxford: Oxford University Press, 2018), pp. 109–10.

177 Coleridge, *Life and Letters*, p. 153.

178 Ibid., pp. 157–59. In this context, it is important to remember that even the Nasranis came to hate the Jesuits. As we read, they may yet have accepted the pope if he sent a 'true bishop' instead of placing them at the mercy of Jesuits and the Portuguese. See Neill, *Christianity in India*, p. 320.

179 Coleridge, *Life and Letters*, p. 159. D'Costa, *The Christianisation of the Goa Islands*, p. 117 notes a 1545 memorandum by another figure on Goa affairs where we read: 'There is in this land a caste called Sinai Brahmins, very opposed to the Faith, and not only do they themselves not become Christians, but . . . prevent others also from doing so . . . They are wholly detrimental to the State . . .' See another similar remark in Xavier, *Religion and Empire*, p. 89.

180 This might also be linked to the fact that, until direct exposure in the early modern period, many Europeans had a romanticized idea of Brahmins from Alexander lore as a 'people safeguarding Christian principles in the East'; as an ideal for Christians. On actually meeting Brahmins, the picture changed. See Raf Gelders, 'Genealogy of Colonial Discourse: Hindu Traditions and the Limits of European Representation', pp. 571–72, in *Comparative Studies in Society and History* 51, 3 (2009): 563–89. Equally, however, some early Christian accounts were also critical of Brahmins already in the third century CE. See Thomas Hahn, 'The Indian Tradition in Western Medieval Intellectual History', p. 217, in Joan-Pau Rubiés ed., *Medieval Ethnographies: European Perceptions of the World Beyond* (Abingdon: Routledge, 2009), pp. 209–30. Material for appreciation and criticism, that is, were both available.

181 Duarte Barbosa (Mansel Longworth Dames trans.), *The Book of Duarte Barbosa: An Account of the Countries Bordering on the Indian Ocean and Their Inhabitants, written by Duarte Barbosa and Completed About the Year 1518 A.D.*, Vol. 1 (London: Hakluyt Society, 1918), pp. 115–16.

182 *The Voyage of John Huyghen van Linschoten*, p. 252. See also Xavier and Zupanov, *Catholic Orientalism*, pp. 130–31.

183 Of course, monotheistic ideas existed among some of these pagans also, especially among the Romans and Greeks, though what this meant exactly

is debated. See, for example, Stephen Mitchell and Peter Van Nuffelen eds., *One God: Pagan Monotheism in the Roman Empire* (Cambridge: Cambridge University Press, 2010), and essays in Polymnia Athanassiadi and Michael Frede eds., *Pagan Monotheism in Late Antiquity* (Oxford: Clarendon Press, 1999).

184  An opinion repeated in the seventeenth century by Paulo da Trindade, a Franciscan missionary. See Xavier and Zupanov, *Catholic Orientalism*, pp. 185–86. This phenomenon—of recognizing many gods as aspects of one great god—is these days characterized as Summodeism.

185  Quoted in Shulman, *Tamil Temple Myths*, p. 84. Another nineteenth century intellectual used the analogy of the forest; god was the forest while images of gods the trees. See Pennington, *Was Hinduism Invented?*, pp. 61–62. See also a discussion on the *Vishnudharmottara* and its apology for image worship in Phyllis Granoff, 'Reading between the lines: Colliding attitudes towards image worship in Indian religious texts', pp. 389–421, at https://books.openedition.org/editionsehess/17161?lang=en

186  Of course, this did not mean that many did believe the opposite. As a later critic would write,

> This decided taste for allegory, which is characteristic of the founders of the Hindu religion and polity, has proved the source of many errors in the case of a people who are invariably guided simply by the impressions of their senses, and who, accustomed to judge things only by their outward appearance, have taken literally that which was represented to them under symbols, and have thus come to adore the actual image itself instead of reality.

Abbe Dubois quoted in Swagato Ganguly, *Idolatry and the Colonial Idea of India: Visions of Horror, Allegories of Enlightenment* (New York: Routledge, 2018), pp. 17–18. Equally, Hindus could sometimes be surprised with Christian worship; in the late nineteenth century, a young Brahmin girl, witnessing Christians kneel before their chairs and pray, thought—in the absence of an image before them—that they were 'paying homage to the chairs'. See Meera Kosambi, *Pandita Ramabai: Life and Landmark Writings* (Abingdon: Routledge, 2016), p. 268.

187  This also meant that their earlier assumption that they alone had a proper religion, while others had only superstition and forms of witchcraft was now challenged; the Brahmins clearly presided over a belief system that had its own internal meanings like Christianity.

188  Brahmins would also, for instance, deny that the lingam through which Siva is worshipped is a phallic symbol. See Zupanov, 'Lust, Marriage and Free Will', p. 205, even though iconographic evidence clearly shows otherwise. For instance, the lingams at Vishnupad in Gaya or at Devipuram and Gudimallam in Andhra Pradesh. This may well have occurred as Brahmins,

as shown in the Introduction, accepted old forms but gave it new meanings that sat better with their own theological positions.

189 Brahmins were already part of European imagination, despite no actual interaction for about a millennium, thanks to ancient Greek accounts. See Gelders, 'Genealogy of Colonial Discourse'. Now with actual interaction underway, they were understandably a reference point for Europeans, just as the old romanticized Greek account of Brahmins and their religion was replaced by present-day travel reports.

190 In the 1560s, thus, Brahmins 'not essential to the economic order' were expelled, maintaining room for those on whom the government depended, and who could not be replaced with Christians (yet). See Xavier, *Religion and Empire*, p. 91.

191 For instance, local rajahs in Kerala who backed the Nasranis in their quarrel with the Catholics, shifted positions under Portuguese pressure. See Kurien, *Ethnic Church*, pp. 43–44.

192 Jarl Charpentier ed., *The Livro Da Seita Dos Indios Orientais of Father Jacobo Fenicio* (Uppasala: Almqvist & Wiksells, 1953), p. lix. The famous Philippus Baldaeus plagiarized large parts of this.

193 For an analysis of Fenicio's motives, see Zupanov, 'Lust, Marriage and Free Will'.

194 Jarl Charpentier, 'Preliminary Report on the "Livro da Seita dos Indios Orientais"', pp. 744–45, in *Bulletin of the School of Oriental Studies, University of London* (1923): 731–54. This included poetry by a low-caste saint in Kerala called Pakkanar, who sang against 'idols and false gods' and whose ideas seemed to correspond with Christian beliefs. See Ferroli, *The Jesuits in Malabar*, Vol. 1 (Bangalore: Bangalore Press, 1939), pp. 252–53.

195 A summary of some of its contents is available at L.V. Ramaswami Aiyar, 'An Old Portuguese Work on Kerala Beliefs', pp. 33–39, available at https://dutchinkerala.com/rb/reader.php?bookid=023 (accessed 14 October 2023).

196 Charpentier, 'Preliminary Report', p. 746.

197 During Akbar's campaign in Afghanistan, the Jesuits passed Mathura, believed to be the birthplace of Krishna, or 'Crustnu'. They referred to him as 'a restless and unruly boy, a petty thief and liar. He lived with a shepherd, and stole milk and cheese . . . and stole the clothes of some girls who were bathing in a river. He broke the pots and furniture of the neighbours . . . Beginning thus with childish mischief, he went on to steal eight wives from their husbands by force, and sixteen thousand by fraud and guile, as soon as he attained manhood'. See *Father Monserrate*, p. 92.

198 Even in the nineteenth century, tales around Krishna would be weaponized by missionaries, and anxious Hindu respondents would come up with innovative ways to reinterpret them. See, for instance, Vishnubawa Brahmachari, *Vedokta Dharmaprakash* (Mumbai: Indian Printing/Kashinath Balwant Ranade, 1867), p. 46, pp. 62–68.

199  Charpentier, 'Preliminary Report', pp. 746–48.
200  Geddes, *Church of Malabar*, p. 77. This nephew later seems to have become a travelling companion to Fenicio during preaching tours. A queen and her son were also, reportedly, keen to convert. See Ferroli, *The Jesuits in Malabar*, Vol. 1, p. 252.
201  James Hough, *The History of Christianity in India: From the Commencement of the Christian Era*, Vol. 1 (London: R.B. Seeley & W. Burnside, 1839), p. 382.
202  Pearson, *The Portuguese in India*, p. 10. In Europe too, Jesuits were active in courts and played roles that were not strictly religious. See, for example, Alden, *The Making of an Enterprise*, chapter four, where we read how Jesuits were accused of trying to turn monarchs into their puppets.
203  D. Ferroli, *The Jesuits in Malabar*, Vol. 2 (Bangalore: National Press 1951), pp. 1–2.
204  See Flores, *The Mughal Padshah*, p. 9.
205  Sanjay Subrahmanyam, *Penumbral Visions: Making Polities in Early Modern South India* (Ann Arbor: University of Michigan Press, 2001), p. 38. See also T.K. Velu Pillai, *The Travancore State Manual*, Vol. 2 (Trivandrum: Government of Travancore, 1940), p. 174.
206  Coleridge, *Life and Letters*, p. 191.
207  Zupanov, *Missionary Tropics*, p. 176. See the original in Diogo Goncalves (Josef Wicki ed.), *Historia Do Malavar* (Münster, Westfalen: Aschendorfersche Verlagsbuchhandlung, 1955). Goncalves clearly had impressive knowledge of local politics and culture. He reports, for instance, how the Travancore kings raised their status through the ceremony of the golden cow (p. 21), on the great Mamankam festival under the Calicut rajah (p. 43), legends associated with major temples, as well as their wealth—for instance, the Padmanabhaswamy temple in Trivandrum (pp. 44–46), the absence of widow-burning among locals (p. 66), the defences and resources of cities like Quilon and Suchindram (pp. 81–85), and the history of the Nasranis (pp. 91–93).
208  See G.T. Mackenzie, *Christianity in Travancore* (Trivandrum: Travancore Government Press, 1901), p. 15 for instances from the 1570s, when three churches were destroyed by a rani. See also D'Costa, *The Christianisation of the Goa Islands*, pp. 68–69, where we read how Ramaraya, regent of Vijayanagara, demolished a Portuguese church on the east coast, in 1559, and ibid., p. 120 for other tensions with the rajah of Cochin, an ally.
209  Henry Heras, *The Aravidu Dynasty of Vijayanagara*, Vol. 1 (Madras: B.G. Paul, 1927), p. 468. On the Mughal emperor Jahangir in the same period up north, we have a Jesuit write how he did not 'hinder' conversion either. See Flores, *The Mughal Padshah*, p. 104.
210  Manu S. Pillai, *Rebel Sultans*, p. 17, p. 74.
211  Vincent Cronin, *A Pearl to India: The Life of Roberto de Nobili* (London: Rupert Hart-Davis, 1959), p. 77. See also Melo, *Jesuit and English Experiences*, p. 21,

on how using missionaries as unofficial envoys also held incentives for the Portuguese.

212 Cronin, *A Pearl*, pp. 76–77. See also Joan-Pau Rubiés, *Travellers and Cosmographers: Studies in the History of Early Modern Travel and Ethnology* (Abingdon: Ashgate, 2007), p. 233.

213 Heras, *The Aravidu Dynasty*, p. 478.

214 Ibid., pp. 500–03. It appears also that the emperor's friend Father Coutinho died, and his successors were unable to match his influence. For Dutch grievances about Portuguese intrigues at the Vijayanagara court, see Kruijtzer, *Xenophobia*, pp. 55–56. Dutch Protestants would also in time raze Jesuit 'monasteries, college . . . churches and chapels', even converting one cathedral into a warehouse. See Delio Mendonca, 'Protestant and Jesuit Encounters in India in the Eighteenth and Nineteenth Centuries', p. 143, in Jorge Canizares-Esguerra, Robert Aleksander Maryks and R.P. Hsia eds., *Encounters between Jesuits and Protestants in Asia and the Americas* (Leiden & Boston: Brill, 2018), pp. 137–58.

215 Interestingly, almost at once the Portuguese central government sent a proposal to the Goan authorities that the old idea to plunder the Tirupati temple be reconsidered. See Rubiés, *Travel and Ethnology*, p. 328.

216 Cronin, *A Pearl*, p. 11. See also Anonymous, 'Robert de Nobili', in *The Irish Monthly* 9, 102 (1881), pp. 643–62.

217 Alberto Laerzio quoted in Richard M. Swiderski, *Lives between Cultures: A Study of Human Nature, Identity and Culture* (Juneau: The Denali Press, 1991), p. 10. See also Stietencron, *Hindu Myth*, p. 209, where de Nobili is quoted as stating the following as essential to missionaries: 'patrios abnegare mores, et inter Indos Indum esse', i.e., 'to set aside the customs of his homeland and to be an Indian among Indians'.

218 The book may be read here: https://eap.bl.uk/archive-file/EAP636-3-12 (accessed 12 June 2023). See also Henn, *Hindu–Catholic Encounters*, p. 70. Henn also talks of the 'Library Purana' (pp. 74–78), which borrowed Stephens's method but to create a work to refute Hindu ideas and show their inadequacies.

219 For more on the *Kristapurana*, see Annie Rachel George and Annapurna Rath, 'Translation, transformation and genre in the Kristapurana', in *Asia Pacific Translation and Intercultural Studies* 3, 3 (2016): 280–93. The quote is from Annie Rachel George and Annapurana Rath, '"Musk among Perfumes": Creative Christianity in Thomas Stephens's "Kristapurana"', p. 307, in *Church History and Religious Culture* 96, 3 (2016): 304–24. In Kerala, in the eighteenth century, the German Jesuit priest and missionary Johann Ernst Hanxleden, locally called Arnos Pathiri, would also compose the *Puthen Pana*, modelled on Hindu devotional poetry, to communicate the story of Jesus Christ. I would, however, qualify George and Rath's remark, in that Nasranis probably had the full Bible story in the Malayalam language long before the *Kristapurana* appeared.

220 Charpentier, *The Livro Da Seita*, p. lx.
221 Father Antonio Rubino quoted in Heras, *The Aravidu Dynasty*, p. 368. See also Rubiés, *Travellers and Cosmographers*, p. 220.
222 Cronin, *A Pearl*, p. 44. The association with lower-caste groups would continue to haunt missionaries in future too. In Kerala, in the nineteenth century, the London Missionary Society chiefly converted members of the Kuravar tribe, 'which gave Christianity the name of "Kurava Vetham", or the religion of the Kuravars'. See Dick Kooiman, *Conversion and Social Equality in India: The London Missionary Society in South Travancore in the 19th Century* (New Delhi: Manohar, 1989), p. 71.
223 Heras, *The Aravidu Dynasty*, p. 368.
224 Xavier, *Religion and Empire*, p. 60
225 Kurien, *Ethnic Church*, p. 39. See also a later remark in Richard Hall Kerr, *Report on the State of the Christians Inhabiting the Kingdoms of Cochin and Travancore* (London: H. Bryer, 1813), pp. 10–11 where we read how 'The Hindoos have . . . a much greater respect' for Nasranis as opposed to those who went over to the Catholics, 'which may be accounted for by their [the Nasranis'] not associating with the lower orders of people'.
226 See also a comment made in 1609 by another Jesuit along these lines in Rubiés, *Travellers and Cosmographers*, p. 220.
227 Father Peter Martin in John Lockman ed., *Travels of the Jesuits into Various Parts of the World*, Vol. 2 (London: T. Piety, 1762), p. 366.
228 Later French Jesuit used this term too: *Pranguinisme*, or Parangi-ism, which is how 'natives' viewed the Christian religion. See Xavier and Zupanov, *Catholic Orientalism*, p. 120.
229 Over two centuries later, missionaries would still get excited at the prospect of Brahmin conversions. See Y. Vincent Kumaradoss, *Robert Caldwell: A Scholar-Missionary in Colonial South India* (Delhi: ISPCK, 2007), p. 180.
230 In doing so, he was following in the footsteps of not only Alessandro Leni but also Matteo Ricci, who in China wore local dress and presented the Bible as the culmination of Confucian ideals.
231 Zupanov, *Disputed Mission*, p. 47. For a defence of de Nobili's position written in 1613, see *Report Concerning Certain Customs of the Indian Nation* in Anand Amaladass and Francis X. Clooney, *Preaching Wisdom to the Wise: Three Treatises by Roberto de Nobili, S.J.: Missionary, Scholar and Saint in 17th Century India* (Chennai: Satya Nilayam Publications, 2005), pp. 51–216.
232 For a list of some of his innovations, see Neill, *Christianity in India*, p. 289.
233 Father Fernandes quoted in Zupanov, *Disputed Mission*, p. 49.
234 Ibid., p. 63. Two centuries later, missionaries would continue to grapple with this question. See, for instance, Robert Caldwell, *Observations on the Kudumi* (Courtallam: The Times Press, 1867), for a similar debate on whether converts could keep the tuft of hair that high-caste Hindus sported. See also D. Dennis Hudson, 'The Life and Times of H.A. Krishna Pillai

(1827–1900): A Study in the Encounter of Tamil Sri Vaishnava Hinduism and Evangelical Protestant Christianity in Nineteenth Century Tirunelveli District', Unpublished PhD dissertation, Claremont Graduate University (1970), pp. 285–88 for other issues that caused conflict between converts and missionaries in a later period.

235 Zupanov, *Disputed Mission*, p. 64.
236 De Nobili to the pope in 1619 quoted in Cody C. Lorance, 'Cultural Relevance and Doctrinal Soundness: The Mission of Roberto de Nobili', p. 417, in *Missiology: An International Review* 33, 4 (2005): 415–24.
237 Zupanov, *Disputed Mission*, pp. 25–26.
238 And there was tension brewing between Rome, which wanted to play a more proactive role in controlling missionary work, and Portugal. See Xavier and Zupanov, *Catholic Orientalism*, p. 254.
239 Zupanov, *Disputed Mission*, pp. 68–69.
240 De Nobili, *Report*, p. 60, p. 65, p. 67, pp. 69–70, p. 73. He supported this argument by noting that priests could come, especially for secondary deities, from other castes as well. See ibid., pp. 110–15.
241 Ibid., p. 121. See also p. 141 and pp. 153–55, where he notes how his Brahmin converts had been attacked as apostates and for changing their faith, but nobody complained about their wearing threads.
242 Interestingly, as early as the 1540s, when a Kerala prince converted ('the king of Tanor'), he insisted, successfully, on retaining his sacred thread and other caste markers. See Xavier and Zupanov, *Catholic Orientalism*, p. 150.
243 Cronin, *A Pearl*, p. 74.
244 Ibid., pp. 50–51.
245 Zupanov, *Disputed Mission*, p. 65. This was, interestingly, not the first time such debates arose. Among the Nasranis, there is an epic that tells how in 293 CE, seventy-six families of persecuted Tamil Christians fled to Kerala. Some were 'led astray' by a Saiva, and a quarrel broke out after they began to venerate the products of the cow, like Hindus, as well as to smear their bodies with holy ash. See Frykenberg, 'Christians in India', pp. 35–36.
246 Quoted in Cronin, *A Pearl*, p. 57.
247 Zupanov, *Disputed Mission*, p. 72. As early as 1611 he announced in Madurai that converts could keep their caste. See David Mosse, *The Saint in the Banyan Tree: Christianity and Caste Society in India* (Berkeley: University of California Press, 2012), p. 8.
248 Zupanov, *Disputed Mission*, p. 94.
249 Ibid., p. 177.
250 De Nobili's 1619 defence to the pope quoted in Lorance, 'Cultural Relevance', p. 420.
251 As he wrote to Paul V in 1619, he had tried the conventional way 'to bring the heathens to Christ' but this had not worked because 'with a sort of barbarous stolidity', they refused the 'customs of the Portuguese' and to 'put

aside the badges of their ancestral nobility'. Quoted in Mosse, *Banyan Tree*, p. 7.
252 Zupanov, *Disputed Mission*, p. 110.
253 As he complained, even when he won in debates, they went away 'more confused than converted.' See Amaladass & Clooney, *Preaching Wisdom*, 46, and Mosse, *Banyan Tree*, p. 8. This resilience of the Brahmins, as Robert Cowan tells, was 'in sharp contrast to the learned Buddhists of Ming China and Japan, among whom the Jesuits found not insubstantial numbers of converts'. See Cowan, *The Indo–German Identification: Reconciling South Asian Origins and European Destinies, 1765–1885* (Rochester: Camden House, 2010), p. 19.
254 Mosse, *Banyan Tree*, p. 35.
255 Quoted in Neill, *Christianity in India*, p. 484.
256 See Robinson, 'Taboo or Veiled Consent?'
257 S.G. Tulpule quoted in George and Rath, 'Creative Christianity', p. 319. Two centuries later, in fact, missionaries would meet Hindus willing to embrace Christian ideas but without simultaneously embracing European culture, and practices such as eating beef. See, for example, an 1817 episode from Delhi in Homi K. Bhabha, 'Signs Taken for Wonders: Questions of Ambivalence and Authority under a Tree outside Delhi, May 1817', pp. 145–46, in *Critical Inquiry* 12, 1 (1985): 144–65.
258 Robinson, 'Taboo or Veiled Consent?'
259 Father Martin in Lockman, *Travels of the Jesuits*, p. 5. And in 2019, when a bishop appeared in saffron robes with a tilak, though it caused a furore among Hindu nationalists, it was in keeping with longstanding, indigenized Christian tradition. See 'Furore over Belgavi bishop's saffron robe', *Times of India*, 13 September 2019 at https://timesofindia.indiatimes.com/city/hubballi/furore-over-belagavi-bishops-saffron-robe/articleshow/71106070.cms (accessed 18 October 2023).
260 Joanne Punzo Waghorne, 'Chariots of the Gods: Riding the line between Hindu and Christian', p. 14, in Selva J. Raj and Corinne C. Dempsey eds., *Popular Christianity in India: Riting between the Lines* (New York: State University of New York Press, 2002), pp. 11–37.
261 John W. Kaye, *Christianity in India: An Historical Narrative* (London: Smith, Elder & Co., 1859), pp. 33–34.
262 Abraham Rogerius (Abraham Roger), *A Dissertation on the Religion and Manners of the Bramins*, p. 315, in Jean Frederic Bernard and Bernard Picart, *The Religious Ceremonies and Customs of the Several Nations of the Known World*, Vol. 3 (London: Nicholas Prevost, 1731), pp. 309–56.
263 Geoffrey A. Oddie, *Hindu and Christian in South-East India* (London: Curzon Press, 1991), p. 173. Later Protestant missionaries were also forced to deal with caste. Or as one wrote, 'The "[high] caste Christian" is resolved rather to die than partake of food cooked by one of lower caste, or take a

draught of the purest water from his hand; and this solely in order to retain his caste position with the heathen.' See Samuel Mateer, *The Gospel in South India: Or the Religious Life, Experience, and Character of the Hindu Christians* (London: The Religious Tract Society, 1880), p. 37. Of course, converts of low-caste origins also objected and sometimes carried the day. See, for instance, a 1745 instance in *The Private Diary of Anand Ranga Pillai*, Vol. 1, pp. 284–85.

264   Mosse, *Banyan Tree*, p. 2. Mosse also records how in 2009 the archbishop of Chennai acknowledged the 'injustice' the church's upholding of caste had done to 'thousands and thousands of our own people'.

265   Selva J. Raj, 'Transgressing Boundaries, Transcending Turner: The Pilgrimage Tradition at the Shrine of St John de Britto', pp. 87–90, in Raj and Dempsey eds. *Popular Christianity*, pp. 85–111.

266   Besse, *Father Beschi*, p. 37 and A. Muttusami Pillei, *Brief Sketch of the Life and Writings of Father C.J. Beschi or Vira-Mamuni* (Madras: J.B. Pharaoh, 1840), p. 8.

267   Upset Brahmins, tellingly, tried to resurrect the idea of the Christians as Parangis, with all its negative connotations. See Mosse, *Banyan Tree*, p. 37.

268   As an aside: it was possible to breach this clause of 'the sun and moon'. In nineteenth-century Gujarat, a prince resumed a grant made by a predecessor for 'as long as the sun and moon shall endure' by taking advantage of an eclipse. See *Journal of the East India Association, July 1867* (London: Macmillan & Co, 1867), p. 64. This amusing story came to my attention through a tweet by the scholar Rahul Sagar.

269   Quoted in Mosse, *Banyan Tree*, pp. 41–42. Like this 1801 grant, we see a very similar inscription in an older church established by C.J. Beschi in 1734 also at Elakurichi. See Pillei, *Brief Sketch*, p. 9.

270   Francis X. Clooney, 'Hindu-Jesuit Encounters', p. 82, in Bauman and Roberts eds., *The Routledge Handbook of Hindu-Christian Relations*, pp. 79–89.

271   See Sowmya Mani, 'Religious harmony at Vellaimariyal church in Illupur draws attention', *New Indian Express*, 14 April 2022, at https://www.newindianexpress.com/good-news/2022/apr/14/religious-harmony-at-vellaimariyal-church-in-illupur-draws-attention-2441908.html (accessed 22 June 2023).

272   See for instance David Mosse, 'Catholic Saints and the Hindu Village Pantheon in Rural Tamil Nadu, India', p. 307, in *Man* (New Series) 29, 2 (1993): 301–32. Evidently in ancient Rome also, in the early years of Christianity, it was quite normal for people to be Christian while retaining their old gods. See Nixey, *The Darkening Age*, pp. 22–23.

273   T.R.A. Thumbu Chetty quoted in Chandra Mallampalli, *Christians and Public Life in Colonial South India, 1863–1937: Contending with Marginality* (London: Routledge, 2004), pp. 56–57.

274  See for instance Abhishek Kumar Singh, 'The story of De Nobili—the Jesuit Priest who dressed up like a Brahmin to convert Hindus', in TFI Post, 15 December 2021 at https://tfipost.com/2021/12/the-story-of-de-nobili-the-jesuit-priest-who-dressed-up-like-a-brahmin-to-convert-hindus/ (accessed 17 October 2023).

275  In this regard, recall again the idea of ancient Brahminism as a missionary enterprise. See Arvind Sharma, 'Ancient Hinduism as a Missionary Religion', in *Numen* 39, 2 (1992): 175–92. In fact, just in the century before de Nobili, in Bengal Brahmins were wooing the Koch people by accepting their religious practices and deities, while simultaneously recasting those deities as forms of Hindu gods. See Eaton, *Bengal Frontier*, pp. 187–88.

276  Claudius Buchanan, *Memoir of the Expediency of an Ecclesiastical Establishment for British India* (Cambridge: Society of Inquiry on the Subject of Missions, 1811), p. 8.

277  Frykenberg, 'Christians in India', p. 41. Nasranis also appear to have been reluctant to style Mary the 'mother of god', opening them to the charge of being Nestorian heretics. See, for instance, van der Ploeg, *The Christians of St Thomas*, pp. 15–16.

278  Coleridge, *Life and Letters*, p. 147.

279  Ibid., p. 174.

280  Lockman, *Travels of the Jesuits*, p. xiv. As Rubiés notes, even Marco Polo, we read in one manuscript, used to heal the sick back home using soil he had brought back from Mylapore, from the supposed tomb of St Thomas, and on having lost goods once to thieves, he solicited the services of a Chinese idol for their restoration. See Rubiés, *Travel and Ethnology*, p. 65.

281  Protestants also saw the Nasranis as having been corrupted by the Portuguese. That is, 'while the Portuguese Roman Catholics had' earlier 'traced all the evils' of the Nasranis to their 'isolation from Rome', Protestants 'considered that if only the Roman elements' introduced by the Portuguese 'could be eliminated', the Nasranis would be 'a glorious exhibition of primitive purity'. See George Milne, *The Syrian Church in India* (London: William Blackwood & Sons, 1892), p. 283.

282  Besse, *Father Beschi*, pp. 84–85.

283  Ibid., p. 89. It was later also claimed that Protestants 'purchased' converts. 'In many of the small stations,' we are told, 'their efforts are directed rather to make the Catholics become Protestants than to win the heathens to Christianity.' See William Strickland, *The Jesuit in India: Addressed to All Who are Interested in the Foreign Missions* (London: Burns & Lambert, 1852), pp. 90–93. See also Gelders, 'Genealogy of Colonial Discourse', pp. 574–79 for how Protestants in Europe actively compared Catholic practices, which they criticized, with so-called idolatrous Indian ones and with Hindu reference points. So much so that one writer even described 'Deumo', the 'devil' worshipped in Calicut, as an agent of the Pope.

284   Besse, *Father Beschi*, p. 89. This is not entirely surprising given how even in Francis Xavier's time a colleague complained how . . .

> The people of this country who become Christians do so purely from temporal advantage . . . Slaves . . . seek baptism in order to secure their manumission . . . Others do so to get protection from tyrants, or for the sake of a turban, a shirt, or some other trifle they covet, or to escape being hanged, or to be able to associate with Christian women. The man who embraces the faith from honest conviction is regarded as a fool.

See Niccolo Lancilotto quoted in Cronin, *A Pearl*, p. 29. Interestingly, Europeans were aware that Catholic–Protestant sparring could affect their common interests in India. See Kruijtzer, *Xenophobia*, pp. 59–60, for example.

285   Daniel Jeyaraj, 'Indian Participation in Enabling, Sustaining and Promoting Christian Mission in India', p. 32, in Richard Fox Young ed., *India and the Indianness of Christianity: Essays on Understanding* (Grand Rapids: William B. Eerdmans Publishing Company, 2009), pp. 26–40.

286   Besse, *Father Beschi*, p. 105. Beschi's 1728 *Veda Vilakam* also dedicates much energy to fighting off Lutheran claims and justifying the worship of saints and other Catholic practices.

287   From the late 1750s, the Jesuits of the Society of Jesus were also expelled from various countries under European domination. This was partly because governments in emerging nation states of Europe began to view them as a rogue political network linked to the papal state, till in 1773 the pope suppressed the society. It was reinstated in 1814 but did not regain its earlier influence. On Catholic grievances in India in the nineteenth century, see Strickland, *The Jesuit in India*.

288   Lord Macaulay quoted in George Otto Trevelyan, *The Life and Letters of Lord Macaulay*, Vol. 1 (London: Longmans, Green & Co., 1876), p. 375. Still, even today India has the highest number of Jesuits in the world. See Francis X. Clooney, p. 80, in Bauman and Voss Roberts eds., *The Routledge Handbook*, pp. 79–89.

## Two: 'Heathens' and Hidden Truths

1   Ziegenbalg, *Thirty Four Conferences*, pp. 84–87.
2   Physical stature did often matter for missionaries wanting to make an impact. Alessandro Valignano of the sixteenth century, for instance, was tall enough to 'turn heads in Europe and draw large crowds in Japan'. See J.F. Moran, *The Japanese and the Jesuits: Alessandro Valignano in Sixteenth-Century Japan* (London: Routledge, 2004 ed.), p. 30.
3   D. Dennis Hudson, 'The First Protestant Mission to India: Its Social and Religious Development', p. 45, in *Sociological Bulletin* 42, 1–2 (1993): 37–63.

4   On conflicting birth dates, see Daniel Jeyaraj, *Bartholomaus Ziegenbalg: The Father of Modern Protestant Mission: An Indian Assessment* (New Delhi: The Indian Society for Promoting Christian Knowledge, 2006), p. 52.
5   Brijraj Singh, *The First Protestant Missionary to India: Bartholomaeus Ziegenbalg* (1683–1719) (New Delhi, Oxford University Press, 1999), pp. 13–15. For a somewhat outdated but detailed volume on the Tranquebar Mission as well as Ziegenbalg, see J. Ferdinand Fenger (Emil Francke trans.), *History of the Tranquebar Mission* (Tranquebar: Evangelical Lutheran Mission Press, 1863).
6   Singh, *The First Protestant*, p. 16. The Danish authorities evidently also asked the captain to delay their exit.
7   There were, of course, Protestants who came before them, but Ziegenbalg and Plütschau were the first *missionaries*. The earlier Protestant priests were chaplains and ministers for local Europeans.
8   Ziegenbalg and Plütschau were Pietists, whose movement was not popular with Danish Christians.
9   Julius Richter (Sydney H. Moore trans.), *A History of Missions in India* (New York: Fleming H. Revell Company, 1908), p. 104.
10  Bartholomaus Ziegenbalg, *Propagation of the Gospel in the East: Being an Account of the Success of Two Danish Missionaries Lately sent to the East-Indies for the Conversions of the Heathens in Malabar* (London: J. Downing, 1709), p. 26.
11  Ziegenbalg, *Propagation of the Gospel*, p. 30, and Jeyaraj and Young, *Malabarian Correspondence*, p. 48.
12  Singh, *The First Protestant*, p. 18.
13  Daniel Jeyaraj, 'Embodying Memories: Early Bible Translations in Tranquebar and Serampore' at http://hira.hope.ac.uk/1022/1/Essay%20Embodying%20Memories%20-%20Daniel%20Jeyaraj.pdf
14  Singh, *The First Protestant*, p. 18.
15  Of course, Jesuits in Goa also, in running establishments for orphans, focused on providing a Christian education. In the south, as early as 1567, Portuguese missionaries are believed to have established a school at Punnakayal.
16  Quoted in Will Sweetman and R. Ilakkuvan, *Bibliotheca Malabarica: Bartholomaus Ziegenbalg's Tamil Library* (Pondicherry: Institut Francais de Pondicherry, 2012), p. 3.
17  Malabarian here does not refer to Malabar (Kerala) on the west coast, but to Tamils on the east.
18  Ziegenbalg, *Thirty Four Conferences*, p. ii.
19  Ibid., pp. 6–7.
20  A century before Ziegenbalg, a Jesuit had similarly lamented: 'these blacks are deeply attached to their diabolical foundation' so that 'whilst they recognise our religion as good, they say that theirs is equally valid, that they can be saved with it, and thus with it they want to live'. Quoted in Rubiés, *Travellers and Cosmographers*, p. 218.

21 Ziegenbalg, *Thirty Four Conferences*, p. 14. Ironically, in the sixteenth century, a European, Guillaume Postel, also took much the same line. See Raf Gelders and S.N. Balagangadhara, 'Rethinking Orientalism: Colonialism and the Study of Indian Traditions', p. 114, in *History of Religions* 51, 2 (2011): 101–28. This Hindu conviction in multiple paths would irritate Christians and be viewed as an impediment to conversion even in the mid-nineteenth century. See H.H. Wilson, *Essays and Lectures Chiefly on the Religion of the Hindus*, Vol. 2 (London: Trubner & Co., 1862), p. 82. It was also noted by Islamic figures centuries before. See Alam, 'Competition and Co-Existence', p. 49.
22 See Assman, *Of God and Gods*, p. 56.
23 Francois Bernier (Archibald Constable trans. 1891, Vincent A. Smith ed.), *Travels in the Mogul Empire: A.D. 1656–1668* (London: Humphrey Milford Oxford University Press, 1916), pp. 327–28.
24 Ziegenbalg, *Thirty Four Conferences*, p. 39.
25 Ibid., pp. 42–44.
26 Ibid., p. 250. See also ibid., p. 252 where a Brahmin wryly remarks that death came for Hindus and Christians both, and nobody's grandfathers came back from the dead to explain the facts of who was damned and who was not.
27 Ibid., p. 291.
28 Shahjahan accused 'Franks' of three sins: infidelity in religion; the consumption of pork and thirdly that 'they do not wash those parts from which replete Nature expels the superfluous from the belly of the body'. Quoted in Sanjay Subrahmanyan, *Europe's India*, p. 286.
29 D. Dennis Hudson, *Protestant Origins in India: Tamil Evangelical Christians, 1706–1835* (Cambridge: William B. Eerdmans Publishing Company, 2000), p. 92. See also the original letter *Malabarian Correspondence*, Part 2, First Letter, pp. 87–88.
30 Seventeenth Letter in *Malabarian Correspondence*, Part 3, p. 258.
31 Ziegenbalg, *Thirty Four Conferences*, pp. 88–89.
32 Ibid., p. 155.
33 Ibid., p. 158.
34 Jeyaraj and Young, *Hindu–Christian Epistolary Self-Disclosures*, p. 44. See also James Hough, *The History of Christianity in India: From the Commencement of the Christian Era*, Vol. 2 (London: R.B. Seely & W. Burnside, 1839), pp. 434–37. The Tanjore rajah's hostility might have been a reason why the Danish Company was unhappy to see missionaries in Tranquebar.
35 Ziegenbalg, *Thirty Four Conferences*, p. 156.
36 App, *The Birth of Orientalism*, p. 91.
37 A Madurai Jesuit described the Bible printed by Ziegenbalg as 'black ink spilt on a beautifully drawn picture' and as so badly done, that reading the first line alone caused 'the reader's eyes [to] burn'. Quoted in Will Sweetman, 'The Prehistory of Orientalism: Colonialism and the Textual Basis for

Bartholomaus Ziegenbalg's Account of Hinduism', p. 29, in *New Zealand Journal of Asian Studies* 6, 2 (2004): 12–38.
38   Singh, *The First Protestant*, p. 22.
39   Hudson, 'The First Protestant Mission', p. 39. Fenger, *History of the Tranquebar Mission*, p. 35 mentions the first converts in 1707 as five slaves.
40   Quoted in Sweetman and Ilakkuvan, *Bibliotheca Malabarica*, pp. 4–5. The process had in fact begun early. Writing in 1706, Ziegenbalg described how his schoolmaster had 'often put such Philosophical Questions to me, as [they] really made me believe, that in searching their Notions, one might discover things very fit to entertain the Curiosity of many a learned Head in Europe'. See Ziegenbalg, *Propagation of the Gospel*, p. 30.
41   This collection was later published. See Sweetman and Ilakkuvan, *Bibliotheca Malabarica* for a full analysis.
42   Fenger, *History of the Tranquebar Mission*, p. 33. One of his methods of obtaining books for cheap was from the widows of Brahmins.
43   Sweetman and Ilakkuvan, *Bibliotheca Malabarica*, p. 47.
44   Ibid., p. 53.
45   Rubiés, *Travellers and Cosmographers*, p. 229, and Will Sweetman, 'The Absent Vedas', p. 786, in *Journal of the American Oriental Society* 139, 4 (2019): 781–803. Centuries later, in a parallel, a missionary would suggest that while there was 'much to admire' in Rama of the Ramayana—an incarnation of Vishnu—much of what was ascribed to him was likely borrowed from Christianity. See 'Report of J.P. Ellwood', in *The Church Missionary Intelligencer and Record*, Vol. 3 (New Series) (London: Church Missionary House, 1878), p. 305
46   Sweetman and Illakuvan, *Bibliotheca Malabarica*, p. 84.
47   Ibid., p. 72.
48   Jeyaraj and Young, *Hindu–Christian Epistolary Self-Disclosures*, p. 1.
49   Daniel Jeyaraj in Bartholomaus Ziegenbalg (Daniel Jeyaraj trans.) *Genealogy of the South Indian Deities: An English Translation of Bartholomaus Ziegenbalg's original German manuscript with a textual analysis and glossary* (London & New York: RoutledgeCurzon, 2005 ed.), p. 18. It has been suggested by App, *The Birth of Orientalism*, p. 91 that most of these letters were authored by Alagappa. Sweetman, however, differs, pointing out that this claim, following Ziegenbalg's death, was made by missionaries absent at the time, and in the context of their own inability to obtain local correspondents. See Sweetman and Ilakkuvan, *Bibliotheca Malabarica*, p. 8. On the background of these writers, who were mostly Saivas, see Jeyaraj and Young, *Hindu–Christian Epistolary Self-Disclosures*, p. 66. Several letters do, however, show their senders having first consulted Brahmins before formulating a response.
50   Second Letter in *Malabarian Correspondence*, Part 2, p. 103.
51   Third Letter in *Malabarian Correspondence*, p. 114.
52   Fortieth Letter in *Malabarian Correspondence*, Part 3, p. 294.

53   Third Letter in *Malabarian Correspondence*, Part 2, pp. 120–21.
54   Thirty-Eighth Letter in *Malabarian Correspondence*, Part 3, p. 292.
55   Twenty-Sixth Letter in *Malabarian Correspondence*, Part 2, p. 186.
56   Twenty-Sixth Letter in *Malabarian Correspondence*, Part 3, p. 274. See also Thirty-Third Letter in *Malabarian Correspondence*, Part 3, p. 286, and Ziegenbalg, *Thirty Four Conferences*, p. 15. Remarkably, Ziegenbalg's informants were aware of divisions within Christianity too; see Thirteenth Letter in *Malabarian Correspondence*, Part 2, p. 151.
57   A conclusion reached also by al-Biruni centuries before. See Yohanan Friedmann, 'Medieval Muslim Views of Indian Religions', p. 215, in *Journal of the American Oriental Society* 95, 2 (1975): 214–21.
58   The idea of a genealogy was evidently inspired by a Tamil text called *Tirikala Cakkaram* authored according to Ziegenbalg by Tirumular. See Sweetman and Ilakkuvan, *Bibliotheca Malabarica*, p. 120. See also Sweetman, 'Retracing Bartholomaeus Ziegenbalg's Path' at https://www.otago.ac.nz/religion/staff/articles/retracing.pdf.
59   De Nobili, *Report*, p, 78.
60   See ibid., p. 85, pp. 92–94.
61   Ibid., p. 101.
62   Ibid., p. 74.
63   Ziegenbalg, *Propagation of the Gospel*, p. 19. The same letter also refers to four books, presumably the Vedas, without naming them.
64   Indeed, within weeks of his arrival, he had stated in a preliminary report that while Hindus had hundreds of deities, they did recognize a single supreme god. See App, *The Birth of Orientalism*, p. 44.
65   Ziegenbalg's preface in Bartholomaus Ziegenbalg (G.J. Metzger trans.), *Genealogy of the South Indian Gods: A Manual of the Mythology and Religion of the People of Southern India* (Madras: Higginbotham & Co., 1869), p. xvii.
66   Publisher's Preface in ibid., p. xv.
67   Ziegenbalg (Daniel Jeyaraj trans.), *Genealogy*, p. 40.
68   Ziegenbalg's *Malabar Heathenism*, finished in 1711 was published only in 1926, and the *Genealogy* under his name in 1867. The latter was, however, published anonymously at the end of the eighteenth century in Berlin.
69   Sweetman, 'Prehistory of Orientalism', p. 17.
70   Singh, *The First Protestant*, p. 36.
71   Ibid., p. 39.
72   Richter, *History of Missions in India*, p. 110.
73   See also, in this context, Ashis Nandy quoted in the Epilogue.
74   I use 'monotheism' for ease of communication. For why this might not be the most precise term to depict Hindu beliefs, see Wendy Doniger, *On Hinduism* (New York: Oxford University Press, 2014), pp. 10–20. So also, scholars such as Julius Lipner instead of polytheism prefer 'polymorphic monotheism'.

75  Aditya Malik, 'Hinduism or Three-Thousand-Three-Hundred-and-Six Ways to Invoke a Construct', pp. 10–11, in Sontheimer and Kulke, *Hinduism Reconsidered*, pp. 10–31.
76  Fisher, *Hindu Pluralism*, p. 32. The Rig Veda also declares: 'The wise speak of what is One in many ways.'
77  So too Annamacharya sang: 'God is only one, the Supreme Being in only one/The Supreme Lord is only one, The Supreme is one.' See William Jackson, *Songs of Three Great South Indian Saints* (Delhi: Oxford University Press, 1998), p. 66, p. 129.
78  Aby Rayhan Muhammad ibn Ahmad al-Biruni (Edward C. Sachau trans.), *Alberuni's India: An Account of the Religion, Philosophy, Literature, Geography, Chronology, Astronomy, Customs, Laws and Astrology of India about A.D. 1030*, Vol. 1 (London: Kegan Paul, Trench, Trubner & Co., 1910), pp. 27–32. See also Friedmann, 'Medieval Muslim Views', p. 215. See also R. Nath and Faiyaz Gwaliari eds., *India: As Seen by Amir Khusrau in 1318 AD* (Jaipur: Historical Research Documentation Programme, 1981), pp. 51–57. Similar tensions about the use of images existed in the Christian world also. See, for example, Jas Elsner, 'Iconoclasm as Discourse: From Antiquity to Byzantium', in *The Art Bulletin* 94, 3 (2012): 368–94, and Charles Barber, 'From Image into Art: Art After Byzantine Iconoclasm', in *Gesta* 34, 1 (1995): 5–10.
79  As did Buddhists: the emperor Ashoka also frowned on popular religion. See Olivelle, *Ashoka*, p. 214.
80  Quoted in Gandhi, *The Emperor Who Never Was*, p. 168. See also Eck, *Darsan*, p. 45 where she quotes the *Jabala Upanishad*, which declares images as 'meant for . . . the ignorant'.
81  I use the term 'largely' because Catholics, in Jacques Barzun's words, showed a 'kind of polytheism' in worshipping saints: travellers relied on St Christopher, sailors on St Elmo and so on. See Barzun, *From Dawn to Decadence: 500 Years of Western Cultural Life: 1500 to the Present* (New York: HarperCollins, 2000), p. 22. It can also be argued that in addition to god, Christianity also has semi-divine beings in angels. See Michael Frede, 'Monotheism and Pagan Philosophy in Later Antiquity', pp. 43–44, in Athanassiadi and Frede eds., *Pagan Monotheism*, pp. 41–68.
82  The Brahmin Communist leader E.M.S. Namboodiripad would recall how in his childhood, they had to bow before the 'preceptor, then . . . Lord Ganapathy and then . . . Goddess Saraswathi . . . then . . . the gods and goddesses in our own Sanctum . . . and before the deities housed in the various parts of the family house . . . [after which came prostrations] in the name of several other temples . . . and finally, lest we should inadvertently skip any important god, a "compensatory prostration" before all the gods together!' See Namboodiripad (P.K. Nair trans.), *How I Became a Communist* (Trivandrum: Chinta Publishers, 1976), pp. 4–5.

83    People could also 'convert' on this basis. Between the thirteenth and fifteenth centuries, thus, sections of Gaud Saraswat Brahmins in Goa, following the sage Madhvacharya, began to recognize Vishnu as the supreme deity. See Frank F. Conlon, *A Caste in a Changing World: The Chitrapur Saraswat Brahmans, 1700–1935* (New Delhi: Manohar, 2024 [1977]), p. 21.

84    Thirty-Eighth Letter in *Malabarian Correspondence*, Part 2, pp. 202–04. Interestingly, in ancient Greece, too, the idea had emerged that there was one god (singular) and that gods (plural) were subordinates managing his dealings with mankind, just as an emperor had satraps to manage his empire. See A.J. Droge, 'Self-definition vis-à-vis the Graeco-Roman world', p. 241 in Margaret M. Mitchell and Frances M. Young eds., *The Cambridge History of Christianity: Origins to Constantine* (Cambridge: Cambridge University Press, 2006), pp. 230–44.

85    Eighth Letter in *Malabarian Correspondence*, Part 2, pp. 136–37. This could vary, however. In the Deccan, the last (Brahmin) Peshwa worshipped not just Siva and Vishnu on the occasion of the birth of a son but also local gods such as Khandoba, Mhasoba, Vetala, Munjya, Pir, etc. See Sudha V. Desai, *Social Life in Maharashtra under the Peshwas* (Bombay: Popular Prakashan, 1980), p. 103.

86    Twentieth Letter in *Malabarian Correspondence*, Part 2, p. 171.

87    Twenty-Sixth Letter, *Malabarian Correspondence*, Part 3, pp. 273–74. Reference is to gods such as Mariyamman, Ankalamman, Taruman, Perumal, Ellamman, Pitari, Viran, etc. The higher gods are Vishnu, Siva, Subramania, Ganapati etc. We have, long after Ziegenbalg also, Hindus stating this. In the early 1800s, for example, one would assert how blood was spilled only for 'infernal demon[s]' by the 'vulgar' See Ragaviah, 'Refutations' op. cit. Buchanan, *Bihar*, p. 361 also refers to 'people of rank' who 'pretend to reject the worship' of the lower gods. For an example of how such attitudes continue and inferior gods are dismissed by elite Hindus, see Fuller, *Camphor Flame*, pp. 97–98. All the same, scholars note that even the 'lower' gods and their rituals are joined in complex ways to the 'higher'. See, for example, Madeleine Biardeau, 'Brahmans and Meat-Eating Gods', in Alf Hiltebeitel ed., *Criminal Gods and Demon Devotees: Essays on the Guardians of Popular Hinduism* (Albany: SUNY Press, 1989), pp. 19–34. Amusingly, later Brahmins, noting blood sacrifices in the Old Testament, viewed the Christian god as comparable to 'one of the inferior Hindu deities'—this offered another reason *not* to convert. See Pennington, *Was Hinduism Invented?*, p. 71.

88    Richard H. Davis, 'Images and Temples', p. 349, in Olivelle and Davis eds., *Hindu Law*, pp. 347–70. However, this does not mean, simplistically, that image-worship was a subaltern tradition appropriated by elites. See Gilles Tarabout, 'Theology as History: Divine images, Imagination and Rituals in India', in Phyllis Granoff and Koichi Shinohara eds., *Images in Asian*

*Religions: Texts and Contexts* (Vancouver: University of British Columbia Press, 2004), pp. 56–84. See also Granoff, 'Reading between the lines', op. cit., and Suvira Jaiswal, 'Origin of Image Worship and Its Rituals', in *Proceedings of the Indian History Congress* 28 (1966): 58–64.

89. For a discussion see, Declan Quigley, 'Kings and 'Contrapriests', in *International Journal of Hindu Studies* 1, 3 (1997): 565–80; J.C. Heesterman, 'Priesthood and the Brahmin', in *Contributions to Indian Sociology* 5, 1 (1971): 43–47; and P.V. Kane, *History of Dharmasastra*, Vol. 2 (Part 1), pp. 109–10, and (Part 2) (Poona: Bhandarkar Oriental Research Institute, 1941), p. 707. See also de Nobili, *Report*, pp. 114–17; and Swami Vivekananda, *The Complete Works of Swami Vivekananda*, Vol. 4 (Calcutta: Advaita Ashrama, 1958 ed.), p. 164, where we read how temple priests were seen as 'making merchandise of sacred things'.

90. Julius J. Lipner, *Hindu images and their Worship with special reference to Vaisnavism: A Philosophical-Theological Inquiry* (Abingdon: Routledge, 2017), p. 27, citing Yamnuacharya's *Agamapramanya*.

91. Ibid., p. 43 citing the *Manusmriti*. See also Davis, 'Images and Temples', p. 351. In fact, within the Brahmin fold, vestiges held of this conundrum: the higher classes of Namboodiri Brahmins in Kerala even in the twentieth century were occupied with Vedic studies and philosophy; priests were only a notch above *jatimatra* (namesake) Brahmins. See V. Nagam Aiya, *Travancore State Manual*, Vol. 2, pp. 249–50. See also David Smith, *The Dance of Siva: Religion, Art, and Poetry in South India* (Cambridge: Cambridge University Press, 1996), p. 58. Interestingly, de Nobili also recorded that among Brahmins the 'truly authentic' were those 'whose constant activity . . . consists in nothing else than in the teaching of the sciences'. See de Nobili, *Report*, 60, pp. 66–67.

92. See Lipner, *Hindu Images*, pp. 25–33 for a detailed discussion. See also Marko Geslani, 'From yajna to puja', pp. 104–05, in Knut A. Jacobsen ed., *Routledge Handbook of South Asian Religions* (Abingdon: Routledge, 2021), pp. 97–110. It is important to note that this was again a two-way street and temple culture also drew from Vedic ideas. Besides, as Diana Eck notes, even if Vedic poets did not worship images, they 'were image-makers in another sense; they created vivid images of the gods in their poetry'. See Eck, *Darsan*, p. 33. See also de Nobili, *Report*, p. 78, where he notes that while the Puranas were popular, many Brahmins and 'idolaters' themselves frowned on them.

93. Heinrich von Stietencron, 'Orthodox Attitudes towards Temple Service and Image Worship in Ancient India', p. 132, in *Central Asiatic Journal* 21, 2 (1977): 126–38. Emphasis added. Pilgrimage also aggravated Vedic purists. See Knut A. Jacobsen, *Pilgrimage in the Hindu Tradition: Salvific Space* (Abingdon: Routledge, 2013). See also Granoff, 'Reading between the lines'.

94. For instance, in Vedic texts alone where there are references to the consumption of meat, including beef, the same texts also elsewhere prohibit

it. See Edwin Bryant, 'Strategies of Vedic Subversion: The Emergence of Vegetarianism in Post-Vedic India', pp. 195–96, in Paul Waldau and Kimberly Patton eds., *A Communion of Subjects: Animals in Religion, Science, and Ethics* (New York: Columbia University Press, 2006), pp. 194–203.

95  For example, Brahmins assisted the Mughal prince Dara Shukoh in producing a Persian work celebrating the Hindu Upanishads as a fount of monotheism. But those sections of the same sources that risked compromising this goal were played down or phrased innovatively to avoid weakening his argument. See Gandhi, *The Emperor Who Never Was*, pp. 209–10. See also Ernst, 'Muslim Studies', pp. 183–87.

96  As early as the fourteenth century, a Muslim critic in calling on Muslim kings to 'overthrew infidelity' in India urged them to 'slaughter its leaders, who . . . are the Brahmans.' Diya al-Din Barani quoted in Friedmann, 'Medieval Muslim Views', p. 214. In the eighteenth, a French father wrote, similarly: 'Nothing is here more contrary to (our Christian) religion than the caste of brahmins. It is they who seduce India and make all these peoples hate the name of Christian.' Quoted in App, *Birth of Orientalism*, p. 374.

97  First Letter in *Malabarian Correspondence*, Part 2, p. 84. See also ibid., p. 90.

98  Third Letter in ibid., p. 112. This is, of course, not to suggest that Ziegenbalg only spoke to Brahmins; many of his correspondents were non-Brahmin.

99  A. Leslie Willson, 'Rogerius' 'Open Deure': A Herder Source', p. 17, in *Monatshefte* 48, 1 (1956): 17–24. Remember that though Ziegenbalg wrote in the early eighteenth century, he was not published for decades afterwards; hence Rogerius's work remained a key resource until the late eighteenth century.

100  Many of the father's findings were anticipated by de Nobili. But the Italian's 1613 *Report* was never published. On the *Open Door* itself, as Rubiés writes, it seemed not to throw open idolatry's doors to missionaries wielding the gospel but to unlock esoteric ideas behind *image-worship* to a European audience. See Rubiés, *Travel and Ethnology*, p. 309.

101  Rubiés, *Travel and Ethnology*, p. 311.

102  Ibid., p. 325. As de Nobili wrote, it was unreasonable to suggest it was 'impossible for wise men among the non-Christians to produce anything like a sound doctrine, such that even Christians could benefit by it'. See de Nobili, *Report*, p. 74, p. 101.

103  So much so that its less than broad-minded editor and French translator were 'somewhat mocking' when they published it. See Sanjay Subrahmanyam, 'Monsieur Picart and the Gentiles of India', p. 201, in Lynn Hunt, Margaret Jacob and Wijnand Mijnhardt eds., *Bernard Picart and the First Global Vision of Religion* (Los Angeles: The Getty Research Institute, 2010), pp. 197–214. Or as Rubiés tells, Rogerius provided for the first time 'a full empirical narrative largely free from any immediate polemical intent'. See Rubiés, *Travellers and Cosmographers*, p. 241. Indeed, it was so exhaustive, including

in deploying Indian words, that Sanjay Subrahmanyam believes *The Open Door* would have been practically 'impenetrable' to much of its audience. See Subrahmanyam, *Europe's India*, p. 120. Subrahmanyam however cautions against being too generous to Rogerius; he is hardly 'dispassionate or sympathetic'. See Subrahmanyam, 'Forcing the Doors of Heathendom: Ethnography, Violence, and the Dutch East India Company', p. 143, in Charles H. Parker and Jerry H. Bentley eds., *Between the Middle Ages and Modernity: Individual and Community in the Early Modern World* (Plymouth: Rowman & Littlefield Publishers, 2007), pp. 131–54.

104   Rogerius, *A Dissertation*, p. 346. [See also William Caland ed. *Abraham Rogerius, De Open-Deure tot het Verborgen Heydendom* ('s Gravenhage: Martins Nijhoff, 1915), p. 118]. The father described the phallic lingam in some detail, causing anxiety to a translator who refused to repeat its 'immodest shape'. See ibid., p. 339. [Caland, p. 93].

105   Ibid., p. 333 [Caland, pp. 73–74]. This is not, of course, to say women were not forced; only that 'natives' had a moral position on forced sati. See Second Letter in *Malabarian Correspondence*, Part 2, pp. 108–09, where it is also acknowledged that sometimes, women were indeed forced.

106   Ibid., p. 345 [Caland, pp. 113–14], ibid., p. 358 [Caland, pp. 151–53]. Holy days transcended provincial limits too: such as Sivaratri ('Tsevaeratre'), Shravana Pournima ('Trasvanala Pondema'), Mahanavami ('Maherna Houmi'), etc. ibid., pp. 348–49 [Caland, pp. 129–30].

107   Ibid., p. 354 [Caland, pp. 144–45]. Again, we must remember that this was all based on Padmanabha's view; there were also Brahmins who *participated*, albeit not directly, in buffalo sacrifices. See for example Biardeau, 'Brahmans and Meat-Eating Gods', p. 24.

108   Rogerius was conscious that what he was describing was specific to Brahmins. See Will Sweetman, *Mapping Hinduism: 'Hinduism' and the study of Indian religions, 1600–1776* (Halle: Franckesche Stiftungen zu Halle, 2003), p. 97. Rogerius, *Dissertation*, p. 316 [Caland, pp. 13–14]. So too, while he does not state it in so many words, he noticed interesting subtleties in epic poetry. In describing the Ramayana, for example, Rogerius observed how the villainous Ravana's power is enhanced with boons from Siva, while it is Vishnu's incarnation that defeats him. See Rogerius, *Dissertation*, pp. 339–40 [Caland, pp. 96–99]. On the sects, de Nobili also makes similar points. See de Nobili, *Report* in Amaladass and Clooney, pp. 92–93.

109   Or as he wrote, 'The Bramins are very ingenious in heightening the fame and reputation' of their shrines using a 'fruitful imagination'. The idol of Vishnu at Srirangam, for example, belonged to Rama, they said. After Ravana's fall, Rama gave it for installation in Lanka. The recipient was on the way, when suddenly he had to 'make water' in Srirangam. In the middle of a Vaishnava affair, Siva's son now appears and volunteers to hold the idol

for thirty minutes. But, thanks to divine machinations, the transporter takes hours to urinate, so Siva's son drops the idol, consecrating it at that spot. What Rogerius records here is not just a local Purana but also an origin myth reflecting rivalries between Saivas and Vaisnavas, whose gods subverted each other's designs. Ibid., p. 345 [Caland, p. 115]. Of course, other versions of the story also exist, without Siva's intervention or the story of Ravana's brother having a full bladder. One states that the river goddess Kaveri was promised by Vishnu that he would come to reside by her, which is why he was reconciled to his image dropping in Srirangam. See also G.S. Ghurye, *Gods and Men* (Bombay: Popular Book Depot, 1962), pp. 110–11. Either way, this basic plot of one god's doings necessitating another god's actions appears more generally also. In Kerala is worshipped Vettakkorumakan, a son born to Siva and the goddess Parvati, when they were living as hunters in the forest. He was originally a local forest god, absorbed into the Puranic system, but what is interesting is that his mythology talks of how this son of Siva grew into an unruly young man, troubling Brahmins and sages during their sacrifices. It took Vishnu to appear before him with a magnificent *churika* (golden short sword), which he offered the boy if he would promise never to put it down. Vettakkorumakan then moved his bow and arrow to his left hand (making it impossible to use it again) and took the churika in the right hand. He was, in a way, disciplined, thus, and became hereafter a protector of sacrifices.

110 Rogerius, *Dissertation*, p. 315 [Caland, p. 8].
111 For an English translation of parts of Rogerius's dissertation, see also A.V. Williams Jackson, *History of India, Vol. 9: Historic Accounts of India by Foreign Travellers Classic, Oriental, and Occidental* (London: The Grolier Society, 1907), Chapter VIII.
112 *An Historical Dissertation on the Gods of the East Indians*, pp. 391–95, in Bernard and Picart, *Religious Ceremonies*, pp. 357–97. I rely on Sanjay Subrahmanyam's ascription of the authorship of the text to John de Britto in *Europe's India*, p. 126. What is interesting is that where Ziegenbalg would get his information from Saivas, de Britto obtained information from Saktas, crediting Parashakti, or the goddess, as supreme.
113 De Nobili, 'Inquiry into the Meaning of "God"', pp. 316–17, in Amaladass and Clooney eds., *Preaching Wisdom*, pp. 303–21.
114 De Nobili, 'The Dialogue on Eternal Life', p. 258, in ibid., pp. 223–302.
115 While the term 'Enlightenment' is used here and ahead to convey a broader point, this too was no singular affair, and it is now generally acknowledged that there were many Enlightenments (plural) occurring, with their own internal quarrels and dissonances.
116 Bernier, *Travels in the Mogul Empire*, p. 98.
117 Quoted in Gandhi, *The Emperor Who Never Was*, p. 219.
118 Ibid., pp. 238–39.

119 The equation of Hindu sacred texts with the Western idea of scripture is not unproblematic. See James Laine, 'The Notion of "Scripture" in Modern Indian Thought', in *Annals of the Bhandarkar Oriental Research Institute* 64, 1/4 (1983): 165–79. But I use the term in its generic understanding as 'sacred texts' and for ease of narrative and communication of the broader point.
120 Gandhi, *The Emperor Who Never Was*, pp. 184–85.
121 Ibid., p. 153.
122 Ibid., p. 207.
123 Before the Mughals, in the time of the Lodi sultans of Delhi, we read of a Brahmin who was put to death for suggesting that Hindus and Muslims worshipped the same god and both religions were 'equally good'. See Alexander Dow (trans.), *The History of Hindostan*, Vol. 2 (London: A. Wilson, 1803 ed.), p. 153. With Dara, some even believed he was likely to turn Christian. See Deloche and G.S. Cheema, *Soldier of Misfortune*, p. 231.
124 Coleridge, *The Life and Letters of Francis Xavier*, Vol. 1, pp. 159–62.
125 Subrahmanyam, *Europe's India*, pp. 94–95.
126 App, *Birth of Orientalism*, p. 83. Saivas have twenty-eight Agamas; Vaishnavas have 108.
127 Ibid., p. 330.
128 Except for the Atharva Veda, which de Nobili believed was lost.
129 See the section on the Vedas in de Nobili's *Report*, pp. 97–102. It is possible that de Nobili read the *samhitas*, or that part of the Vedas with hymns to various deities, as opposed to the later Upanishads, which deal with more metaphysical subjects.
130 Ibid., and Zupanov, *Disputed Mission*, p. 116.
131 App, *Birth of Orientalism*, p. 105.
132 Even de Azevedo who first reported on the Vedas, linked them to *Tamil* books. See Sweetman, 'The Absent Vedas', p. 786.
133 Ziegenbalg in 1706 also noted this difficulty. See Ziegenbalg, *Propagation of the Gospel*, p. 19.
134 App, *Birth of Orientalism*, p. 375. Father Pons in Pondicherry was the victim of this scam in 1726.
135 Bernier, *Travels in the Mogul Empire*, p. 336. This reluctance continued down into the late nineteenth century. Richard Garbe in the 1880s recorded that pandits in Benares were uncomfortable showing Europeans their texts. See Kaushik Bagchi, 'An Orientalist in the Orient: Richard Garbe's Indian Journey, 1885–1886', p. 311, in *Journal of World History* 14, 3 (2003): 281–325.
136 See Sweetman, 'Absent Vedas'. This is not surprising, especially considering, as we saw in the Introduction, that many Brahmin subcastes were actively denied access to the Vedas.
137 Ziegenbalg, *Thirty Four Conferences*, pp. 138–39. Even de Nobili, who did access these texts, was at first told that the fourth, the Atharva Veda, was

lost, prompting him to pass off Christian teachings in its place. See Zupanov, *Disputed Mission*, pp. 115–16.
138   *Lettres Edifiantes et Curieuses, Ecrites Par Des Missionnaires de La Compagnie de Jesus*, Vol. 13, p. 374. See also Al-biruni, *Alberuni's India*, p. 125, where he too noted, centuries prior, that though many knew the Vedas, few understood its meaning.
139   *Lettres Edifiantes*, p. 394.
140   Ibid. He claimed, of course, that he had all the Vedas. But the fourth, the Atharva Veda, which came into his hands was not actually that Veda but as Sweetman finds, merely an 'assortment of tantric and magical texts'. See Sweetman, 'The Absent Vedas', p. 797. See also App, *Birth of Orientalism*, p. 374.
141   Peter Harrison, *The Bible, Protestantism, and the Rise of Natural Science* (Cambridge: Cambridge University Press, 1998), pp. 93–96. See also Alexandra Walsham, 'Unclasping the Book? Post-Reformation English Catholicism and the Vernacular Bible', in *Journal of British Studies* 42, 2 (2003): 141–66.
142   John Redwood, *Reason, Ridicule and Religion: The Age of Enlightenment in England 1660–1750* (London: Thames and Hudson, 1996 [1976]), p. 47.
143   Martin Luther quoted in Jonathan Sheehan, *The Enlightenment Bible: Translation, Scholarship, Culture* (Princeton and Oxford: Princeton University Press, 2005), pp. 11–12.
144   Harrison, *The Bible, Protestantism, and the Rise of Natural Science*, pp. 116–17.
145   Quoted in Liam Jerrold Fraser, *Atheism, Fundamentalism and the Protestant Reformation: Uncovering the Secret Sympathy* (Cambridge: Cambridge University Press, 2018), p. 30.
146   As Alden writes in *The Making of an Enterprise*, p. 77: 'In Europe, Jesuits were intimately identified with the forces of Catholic orthodoxy; abroad they became revolutionaries.'
147   Coleridge, *Life and Letters*, Vol. 1, pp. 159–62. On the Mughals, see Truschke, *Culture of Encounters*, p. 34.
148   Ziegenbalg, *Thirty Four Conferences*, p. 52, p. 88, p. 132. See also Al-biruni, *Alberuni's India*, p. 122, where in the eleventh century, this Muslim writer also laments 'priestly tricks' to keep the 'uneducated' in 'thraldom'.
149   Ziegenbalg, *Thirty Four Conferences*, p. 125. The local response to Ziegenbalg was that Brahma—the lord of creation—had 'ordered those who introduced the Vetam into the world' to restrict access to Brahmins, for they alone possessed the 'habits' and 'purity' for the responsibility. See Second Letter in *Malabarian Correspondence*, Part 2, p. 98.
150   Sixth Letter in *Malabarian Correspondence*, Part 2, p. 133. See also Second Letter, *Malabarian Correspondence*, Part 2, p. 98 for a similar letter but less resentful, Twenty-Seventh Letter in *Malabarian Correspondence*, Part 2, pp. 187–88, and Ziegenbalg, *Thirty Four Conferences*, p. 125.

151 Jnaneshwar (M.R. Yardi trans.), *Shri Jnanadeva's Bhavartha Dipika: Popularly known as Jnaneshwari* (Pune: Bharatiya Vidya Bhavan, 2011 [1991]), pp. 349–50. Jnaneshwar adds that the Vedas took the form of another text known as the Gita precisely because they were 'afraid of being called miserly'.

152 Quoted in Sheldon Pollock, 'Deep Orientalism? Notes on Sanskrit and Power Beyond the Raj', p. 126, in Carol A. Breckenridge and Peter van der Veer eds., *Orientalism and the Postcolonial Predicament* (Philadelphia: University of Pennsylvania Press, 1993), pp. 76–133.

153 This somewhat nuances Timalsina's view that Hinduism in the colonial period 'discovered itself in the image of the faith of the colonizers'. See Sthaneshwar Timalsina, 'Reason, Dharma, and the Discovery of Faith: Insights from the modes of classical Hinduism', p. 94, in Jacobsen ed., *Routledge Handbook*, pp. 83–96. It certainly did but only because it could identify matching trends *within* tradition.

154 Louis Chatellier, 'Christianity and the rise of science, 1660–1815', p. 259, in Stewart J. Brown and Timothy Tackett eds., *The Cambridge History of Christianity: Enlightenment, Reawakening and Revolution 1660–1815* (Cambridge: Cambridge University Press, 2006), pp. 251–64. See also Harrison, pp. 136–41, and Redwood, *Reason, Ridicule and Religion*, p. 15.

155 Harrison, *The Bible, Protestantism, and the Rise of Natural Science*, p. 20, p. 24. See also ibid., p. 108.

156 Margaret C. Jacob, 'The Enlightenment critique of Christianity', p. 268, in Brown and Tackett eds., *The Cambridge History of Christianity*, pp. 265–81.

157 Redwood, *Reason, Ridicule and Religion*, p. 64.

158 Ibid., p. 45.

159 C.J. Betts, *Early Deism in France: From the so-called 'deistes' of Lyon (1564) to Voltaire's 'Lettres philosophiques' (1734)* (The Hague: Martinus Nijhoff Publishers, 1984), p. 139.

160 John Foxe quoted in Harrison, *The Bible, Protestantism, and the Rise of Natural Science*, p. 118.

161 As one scholar notes, even less militant figures 'conceded the pre-eminence of reason' and 'were prepared to test revelation, as well as its evidences in miracle and prophecy, by the standards which reason suggested.' See Gerald R. Cragg, *Reason and Authority in the Eighteenth Century* (Cambridge: Cambridge University Press, 1964), p. 32.

162 Betts, *Early Deism in France*, p. 122, p. 139, p. 160.

163 Redwood, *Reason, Ridicule and Religion*, p. 12, p. 30.

164 Fraser, *Atheism, Fundamentalism and the Protestant Reformation*, pp. 32–33. See also ibid., p. 77.

165 See Harbans Mukhia, 'A Rationality Immersed in Religiosity: Reason and Religiosity in Abu'l Fazl's Oeuvre', in *The Medieval History Journal* 23, 1 (2020): 50–73.

166   Reference is to Ibn Hazm in the eleventh century. See Jacques Waardenburg, 'The Medieval Period: 650–1500', p. 26, in Waardenburg ed., *Muslim Perceptions of Other Religions: A Historical Survey* (New York: Oxford University Press, 1999), pp. 18–69. See also ibid., pp. 34–35
167   Ziegenbalg (Jeyaraj trans.), *Genealogy*, p. 48. Emphasis added.
168   Quoted in App, *Birth of Orientalism*, p. 40.
169   Quoted in ibid.
170   Raymond Schwab (Gene Patterson-Black and Victor Reinking trans.), *The Oriental Renaissance: Europe's Rediscovery of India and the East, 1680–1880* (New York: Columbia University Press, 1984), p. 153.
171   App, *Birth of Orientalism*, p. 39. Voltaire was capable of flip flops. At one point, he thought sati evidence of Indians having been 'an invincible, warrior nation' where 'even the women' sacrificed themselves. Quoted in Cowan, *The Indo-German Identification*, p. 39.
172   See Francois-Marie Arouet, *Oeuvres Completes De Voltaire*, Vol. 4 (Paris: Chez Furne, 1836), p. 786. In fact, as early as 1745, Urs App tells, Voltaire rejected Biblical authority, commandeering Eastern histories.
173   Quoted in App, *Birth of Orientalism*, p. 40. He was, that is, not dispassionately studying India but making 'use of India'. See D.S. Hawley quoted in Halbfass, *India and Europe*, p. 58.
174   Or to quote Wilhelm Halbfass, 'In his polemics against Christianity, it was vitally important for Voltaire to have chronological arguments' to bolster his position. See Halbfass, *India and Europe*, p. 57.
175   Their creator, Brahma, was Abraham; his consort, goddess Sarasvati, Sarah, for instance. 'Vati' being 'madam', apparently, making her 'Madam Sarah'. See 'A Letter from Father Bouchet a Jesuit Missionary to Maduras, and Superior of the new Mission of Carnata, to Monf. Huet, Bishop of Avranches' in Bernard and Picart, *Religious Ceremonies*, pp. 397–407. As early as 1553, in fact, we find a stray attempt to link Brahmins to the Abrahamic religions. See App, p. 30.
176   '*Il m'a paru evident que notre sainte religion chrestienne est uniquement fondee rur l'antique religion de Brama. Notre chute des anges qui a produit le diable, et le diable qui a produit la damnation du genre humain, et la mort de Dieu pour une pomme, ne sont qu'une miserable et froide copie de l'ancienne theologie indienne. J'ose assurer que votre majeste trouvera la chose demontree.*' See Francois-Marie Arouet, *Ouevres completes de Voltaire*, Vol. 52, *Correspondance Avec Le Roi De Prusse* (Tome Troisieme) (Paris: P. Dupont, 1824), p. 351. Some Brahmins played along, except that instead of allowing foreign inspiration for their ideas, it was Judaism and Islam that, they claimed, were 'heresies from what is contained in the Bedas' (Vedas). Alexander Dow trans., *The History of Hindostan*, Vol 1 (London: Vernor and Hood, Cuthell and Martin, J. Walker, Wynne and Scholey, John Debrett, Blacks and Parry, T. Kay and J. Asperne, 1803 ed.), pp. iv–v.

177  Ludo Rocher ed., *Ezourvedam: A French Veda of the Eighteenth Century* (Amsterdam & Philadelphia: John Benjamins Publishing Company, 1984), pp. 4–6.
178  App, *Birth of Orientalism*, p. 47.
179  Rocher, *Ezourvedam*, p. 6.
180  It was published in 1778 and thus open to wider scrutiny.
181  Quoted in App, *Birth of Orientalism*, p. 376.
182  Rocher, *Ezourvedam*. The full text is at pp. 105–206.
183  The French fathers had some experience in this direction: by the 1730s, they already had in circulation a Sanskrit polemic, the *Punarjanmaksepa*, to deflate the Hindu doctrine of reincarnation. See Gerard Colas and Usha Colas-Chauhan, 'An 18th Century Jesuit "Refutation of Metempsychosis" in Sanskrit', in *Religions* 8, 192 (2017) at https://www.mdpi.com/2077-1444/8/9/192.
184  Schwab, *Oriental Renaissance*, p. 155. See also S.N. Balagangadhara, *'The Heathen in His Blindness': Asia, the West & the Dynamic of Religion* (Leiden: Brill, 1994), p. 122, where we read: 'To Voltaire, this document showed the subtlety and the sublime nature of Indian thought–refuting and criticising the grossness of Christianity. To the Christian priests who created it, [the *Ezourvedam*] showed the subtlety and sublime nature of Christianity—refuting and criticising the grossness of heathendom.'
185  Pierre Sonnerat (Francis Magnus trans.), *A Voyage to the East-Indies and China; Performed by Order of Lewis XV, between the years 1774 and 1781*, Vol. 1 (Calcutta: Stuart and Cooper, 1788), p. 104. While this aborted infatuation, the text continued to circulate for decades, until scholars agreed it was a product of deceit. Even the translator was unknown: some thought it was Pierre Martin of Pondicherry, a Jesuit who disguised himself as a Hindu to join a 'Brahminical University' in 1699. See E.W. Grinfield, *The Jesuits: An Historical Sketch* (London: Seeleys, 1853), p. 200. Decades later, some laid the *Ezourvedam* at de Nobili's grave, while others like the indologist Max Müller, felt it was one of the latter's Indian converts who wrote it. One 1830s volume even announced, with breathtaking confidence, that de Nobili (who died in 1656) personally sent the *Ezourvedam* to Voltaire (who was born in 1694). See Rocher, *Ezourvedam*, pp. 34–35.
186  Sweetman, 'The Absent Vedas', pp. 787–88 explains exactly how. See also K. Meenakshi, 'The Siddhas of Tamil Nadu: A Voice of Dissent', in R. Champakalakshmi and S. Gopal eds., *Tradition, Dissent and Ideology: Essays in Honour of Romila Thapar* (Delhi: Oxford University Press, 1996), pp. 111–34.
187  The 'West' in these contexts represents elite intellectuals rather than society in toto, of course.
188  Sweetman, 'The Absent Vedas', p. 800. The story of the *Zend Avesta* of the Zoroastrians is similar. Zoroaster was famous in Europe through the writings of Pliny the Elder of the first century CE (besides through

speculation that he was Noah's son Ham in the Hebrew Bible). But even in the eighteenth century, his teachings were not directly available. In 1754, Abraham Hyacinthe Anquetil-Duperron learning Avestan, copied it from Parsis (Indian Zoroastrians of Persian descent). After ten years of translation, in 1771, the *Zend Avesta* was published. It did not live up to Western expectations, and Duperron was accused of not really knowing Avestan. Decades would pass before he was vindicated, but the episode reflects how European intellectuals had preconceived notions to which they could stick stubbornly.

189   See William Arthur, *A Mission to the Mysore: with Scenes and Facts Illustrative of India, Its People, and its Religion* (London: Partridge & Oakey, 1847), p. 445. Max Muller, who translated the Rig Veda, also stated in 1875 that it belonged to a 'primitive and rude state of society'. In his autobiography, he again noted how Europeans had 'expected too much' from the Vedas.

190   John Zephaniah Holwell, *Interesting Historical Events Relative to the Provinces of Bengal, and the Empire of Indostan*, Part 2 (London: T. Becket & P.A. De Hondt, 1767), p. 28. As Holwell argued, there were certain unrevealed, 'primitive truths' which 'impressed the human heart' during creation. While later tainted, these included the notion of a universal god; the immortality of the soul; and so on. See John Zephaniah Holwell, *Interesting Historical Events Relative to the Provinces of Bengal, and the Empire of Indostan*, Part 3 (London: T. Becket & P.A. De Hondt, 1771), pp. 4–5.

191   App, *Birth of Orientalism*, pp. 297–323. Some scholars did believe that he may have had a text, perhaps in Hindustani, not Sanskrit, on which he based his *Chartah Bhade Sastah*. However, Howell was also notorious for writing the *A Genuine Narrative of the Deplorable Deaths of the English Gentlemen, and Others, who were Suffocated in the Black Hole in Fort-William, at Calcutta, in the Kingdom of Bengal; in the Night succeeding the 20th Day of June, 1756* (London: A. Millar, 1758), a highly exaggerated account where he claimed that of 146 English prisoners held by the Nawab of Bengal in a small room after a military victory, 123 died of suffocation. Subsequent research has shown that this was almost entirely invented by Holwell, and that less than twenty died.

192   Dow, *The History of Hindostan*, p. xxii. Unlike others who derived knowledge from 'the unlearned part of the Brahmins', he argued, his find was authentic (ibid., p. xxxvii).

193   Ibid., p. xlix. For a sustained study of Holwell and Dow, see Jessica Patterson, *Religion, Enlightenment and Empire: British Interpretations of Hinduism in the Eighteenth Century* (Cambridge: Cambridge University Press, 2022). Note also that Hindus have the Vedanga, which refers to six disciplines, not to any one book.

194   See App, *Birth of Orientalism*, p. 72, p. 74.

195   Sonnerat, *Voyage*, p. iv and Stietencron, *Hindu Myth*, p. 212.

196  Sonnerat, *Voyage*, p. 1. For example, when Siva was revered in 'the instrument of re-production of the human species', it was not an obscenity as much as a symbol of the power of creation (ibid., p. 144). Sonnerat, like those before him, was influenced more by Hinduism in south India than the north: for instance, he places Ayodhya, home of Rama in the Ramayana, in Siam where flourished the kingdom of Ayyuthaya. He even analysed the Puranas and the chief gods of the Sanskrit pantheon to come up with his own theories: Siva was the oldest, Vishnu emerging much later (ibid., p. 71). Similarly, stories about incarnations and battles conveyed clashes between sects (ibid., p. 79). The matter was never, Sonnerat laments, settled, and sectarian feuds raged, till foreign armies penetrated the land. This obliged Saivas and Vaisnavas to 'suspend their religious quarrels; but without reconciling them,' which was why even in the eighteenth century, each side treated the other with contempt. He had clearly picked up these ideas from those he was speaking to and seems to echo their views.
197  Ibid., p. 80.
198  Ibid., p. 85.
199  Ibid., p. 81.
200  Ibid. Or as Ziegenbalg had written, Hindus began well but ended up 'deviating'; they did not worship Satan, but Satan 'misled' them. See Ziegenbalg (Jeyaraj trans.), *Genealogy*, p. 48.
201  Rudolph von Roth quoted in Hermann Tull, 'F. Max Muller and A.B. Keith', p. 31. Haberman summarizes the general messaging as follows: 'You Hindus were once great . . . but that was past. You are now corrupt, lost . . . We are here to help you . . . You are not capable of representing yourself, for in your present state you are blind.' See David L. Haberman, 'On Trial: The Love of the Sixteen Thousand Gopees', p. 55, in *History of Religions* 33, 1 (1993): 44–70. That Enlightenment minds had such confidence is not surprising. After all, Montesquieu thought it perfectly reasonable to state that liberty 'was intended for the genius of European races, and slavery for that of the Asiatics'. The latter were congenitally in need of outside assistance and light.
202  Quoted in Vasudha Narayanan, *The Vernacular Veda: Revelation, Recitation, and Ritual* (Columbia: University of South Carolina Press, 1994), p. 33.
203  Ibid., p. 27.
204  Quoted in ibid., p. 24. Emphasis added. See also ibid., p. 26.
205  As R.C. Dwivedi writes,

> The mood of prayer in the mantras is hardly reflected in the ritualistic explanations of the Brahmanas [another section of the Vedas] or these in turn hardly form the symbolism of the Aranyakas [yet another portion] or the mysticism of the Upanisads. There is no real thematic unity and continuity in the evolution of Vedic literature.

See R.C. Dwivedi, 'Concept of the Sastra', p. 44, in *Indologica Taurinensia* 13 (1985–86): 43–60.

206  Though formally there are exactly 108 Upanishads, in reality over 200 have been catalogued, some of these composed as late as medieval times. See

Thomas B. Coburn, '"Scripture" in India: Towards a Typology of the Word in Hindu Life', p. 445, in *Journal of the American Academy of Religion* 52, 3 (1984): 435–59.

207 H.H. Wilson (trans.), *Rig-Veda-Sanhita: A Collection of Ancient Hindu Hymns Constituting the First Ashtaka, or Book, of the Rig-Veda; the Oldest Authority for the Religious and Social Institutions of the Hindus*, Vol. 1 (London: W.H. Allen & Co., 1850), p. ix.

208 Henry David Thoreau (Bradford Torrey ed.), *The Writings of Henry David Thoreau*, Vol. 2 (Boston & New York: Houghton Mifflin & Co., 1906), pp. 3–4.

209 Katha Upanishad translated in Swami Paramananda, *The Upanishads: Translated and Commented*, Vol. 1 (Boston: The Vedanta Centre, 1919), p. 59. Indeed, the later Upanishads even critique the ritualism that marks the earlier segment of the Vedas. See Staal, *The Vedas*, p. 177.

210 Gandhi, *The Emperor Who Never Was*, p. 136.

211 Fraser, *Atheism, Fundamentalism and the Protestant Reformation*, p. 19, pp. 31–32.

212 See 'Introduction', p. 2, in Laurie Patton ed., *Authority, Anxiety, and Canon: Essays in Vedic Interpretation* (Albany: State University of New York Press, 1994), pp. 1–18.

213 This extends even to sectarian groups. As Fisher tells, Vaishnava and Saiva 'sectarianism, as it emerged in the late-medieval and early modern period, was not a fragmentation of original unity but a synthesis of originally discrete religions that gradually came to be situated under the umbrella of a unified Hindu religion'. See Fisher, *Hindu Pluralism*, p. 31. See also Cherian, *Merchants of Virtue*, pp. 19–20.

214 In this I follow Kaviraj's analogy of Indian society as a big circle, with many autonomous smaller circles within it. See Sudipta Kaviraj, *The Imaginary Institution of India: Politics and Ideas* (New York: Columbia University Press, 2010), pp. 14–15.

215 On this, see again Debroy, *Shiva Purana*, Vol. 1, p. xvi, where he notes how 'general understanding and practise of *dharma*' by Hindus 'is based much more on the Puranas than on the Vedas'. In politics too, whether it was Gandhi or Hindu nationalist parties, a principal point of reference is Rama of the Ramayana, rather than talk of the Vedas or orthodox religious scripture.

216 See Smith, *Reflections on Resemblance*, p. 29.

217 See McComas Taylor, 'What Enables Canonical Literature to Function as "True"? The Case of the Hindu Puranas', p. 311, in *International Journal of Hindu Studies* 12, 3 (2008): 309–28.

218 Louise Renou quoted in Borayin Larios, *Embodying the Vedas: Traditional Vedic Schools of Contemporary Maharashtra* (Berlin: Dr Gruyter, 2017), p. vii. See also Dwivedi, 'Concept of the Sastra'.

219 See Smith, *Reflections*, pp. 13–14. See also Laine, 'The Notion of "Scripture"', p. 167.

220 As an example, the Dharmasastras base their prescriptions theoretically on the Vedas, but with regard to practices that do not appear in them, cite 'Vedic texts that are now lost'. Reference to the Vedas was often 'a strategic exegetical device than a historical claim'. See David Brick and Donald R. Davis, 'Dharma in Classical Hinduism', pp. 76–77, in Jacobsen ed., *Routledge Handbook,* pp. 72–82. See also C. Sankararama Sastri, *Fictions in the Development of the Hindu Law Texts* (Adyar: Vasanta Press, 1926) and Fisher, *Hindu Pluralism,* Chapter 2 for the 'vedicizing' of traditions in specific periods. For criticism of the 'lost Vedas' strategy by Hindu thinkers, see Doniger, *On Hinduism,* pp. 48–49.

221 See Fisher, 'Remaking South Indian Saivism', pp. 323–24. In the seventeenth-century *Visvaguna Darsana* by the Brahmin Venkatadhvarin, one grievance against Virasaivas is also that they 'reproach the Veda'. See Venkata Ramasswami, p. 52.

222 Fisher, *Hindu Pluralism,* pp. 32–36. See also Sanderson, 'The Saiva Age', p. 289, where we read how early Saiva texts 'boldly' (even if mostly theoretically) declared caste differentiation an unnatural 'fabrication'.

223 See Richard H. Davis, *Ritual in an Oscillating Universe: Worshipping Siva in Medieval India* (Princeton: Princeton University Press, 1991), pp. 29–30. See also Kamil V. Zvelebil, *The Poets of the Powers: Magic, Freedom, and Renewal* (California: Integral, 1993), pp. 63–64, pp. 80–81, where we read of Sivavakkiyar who was not above 'repudiating the authority of the Vedas'. See p. 84 where we find Sivavakkiyar saying: 'In the Four Eternal Vedas/In the study and reading of scripts/In sacred ashes and in Holy Writs/And muttering of prayers/You will not find the Lord!' On p. 101 we have Pattinattar who too argues that god was 'beyond the reach of the four Vedas'. In a similar vein, some Saivas dismissed the Vedas as serving the worldly; for the truly spiritual, only Saiva texts would do. See H.W. Schomerus (Mary Law trans.), *Saiva Siddhanta: An Indian School of Mystical Thought* (Delhi: Motilal Banarsidass, 1979 ed. [1912]), pp. 18–19. See also ibid., pp. 6–7. See also Annette Wilke, 'Negotiating Tantra and Veda in the Parasurama-Kalpa Tradition', pp. 141–43, in Ute Husken and Frank Neubert eds., *Negotiating Rites* (New York: Oxford University Press, 2012), pp. 133–60.

224 Sutra 49 in V. Subrahmanya Sarma ed., *Narada's Aphorisms on Bhakti* (Mysore: The Adhyatma Prakasha Karyalaya, 1938). See also Sutra 61.

225 Doniger, *On Hinduism,* p. 48. Emphasis added. There were also, of course, texts in common to different sects. The Gita, certain Upanishads, etc. were accepted by most. See Renou, *Religions of Ancient India,* p. 92.

226 See Embree, *Imagining India,* p. 14. Temple ceremonies, for instance, often saw a blend of Vedic rites with ceremonies of mixed origins. So also, at great festivals it was customary for Sanskrit recitations to be arranged—even if most Hindus did not know the sacred language, the act of reciting

and hearing was itself important. See Coburn, '"Scripture" in India', p. 447, p. 454.
227 Or as Arvind Sharma writes, Hinduism's bond with the Vedas was 'debatable' and in 'constant negotiation'. See Sharma, 'The Hindus as a Textual Community: The Role of the Vedas', *India International Centre, Occasional Publication 40*, (2012): 18. Patrick Olivelle adds how 95 per cent of Hindus had no access to the Vedas. See Olivelle, 'Orality, Memory', p. 214. Aditya Malik also asks, 'If folk religion is where most of the practice occurs then isn't it the 'primary' feature of Hinduism' rather than texts? See Malik, 'Hinduism', p. 18.
228 Rogerius, *A Dissertation*, p. 321.
229 Quoted in Zupanov, *Disputed Mission*, p. 131.
230 Dow, *The History of Hindostan*, p. xxxvii. This was not exclusive to India: as S.J. Barnett, *The Enlightenment and Religion: The Myths of Modernity* (Manchester: Manchester University Press), pp. 62–64 argues, in Europe also, the history of the Enlightenment has focused excessively on the written, printed text of elite thinkers instead of digging deeper, ignoring those 'not represented in the historical record'.
231 There are Hindus, in fact, who still believe that reciting the Vedas from a book is improper. See Prasad, *Poetics of Conduct*, p. 142.
232 Or as is noted in de Nobili's case, pursuing Brahmin texts offered 'a reassuring sense of textual order that also claimed to represent reality. If there was no perfect fit between the two', they would 'bridge the gap between the real and the ideal.' See Zupanov, *Disputed Mission*, p. 25.
233 Ziegenbalg was told something similar. When debating idol-worship with Brahmins, some of them said that whatever their flaws, idols were worshipped for 'Ten thousand Years' by their ancestors and gave the people contentment. Why meddle with a working system? See Ziegenbalg, *Thirty Four Conferences*, p. 181.
234 V. Nagam Aiya, *Report on the Census of Travancore 1891*, Vol. 1 (Madras: Addison & Co., 1894), p. 327. In fact, as late as 1911, in large swathes of upper India, census officials would find that 'a quarter of the persons classed as Hindus denied' both 'supremacy of the brahmans and the authority of the Vedas'. See R.B. Bhagat, 'Census and the Construction of Communalism in India', p. 4354, in *Economic and Political Weekly* 36, 46–47 (2001): 4352–56.
235 Truschke, *Language of History*, p. xxxiv. In the parallel sense of lived reality, Leela Prasad's research around Sringeri—seat of a major Hindu *matha* that authoritatively interprets tradition—showed that far from this institution being 'unquestionably central in the normative worldview' of locals, the latter had 'plural sources . . . of the normative' that often deviated from the matha's ideas. See Prasad, *Poetics of Conduct*, p. 12.
236 See for instance Parasher, 'Mlecchas', p. 22, p. 25 and Thapar, *Early India*, 260–61. See also Wendy Doniger and Brian K. Smith eds., *The Laws of*

*Manu* (London: Penguin Books, 1991), where we read of how the famous text, the *Manusmriti*, emerged at a time when Brahmin claims to social superiority needed a solid theoretical framing, besides the resolving of contradictions.

237  Reference is to the famous Maharajas Libel Case of the 1860s. See Judgement of Sir Matthew Sausse in Appendix, p. 82, in Karsondas Mulji, *History of the Sect of Maharajas, or Vallabhacharyas, in Western India* (London: Trubner & Co., 1865). On the case itself, see Haberman, 'On Trial'.
238  Karsondas Mulji's testimony in *History of the Sect of Maharajas*, p. 20.
239  The orientalist John Wilson quoted in ibid., p. 30.

## Three: Governing the Gentoos

1  Letter from Puri's priests to Lord Wellesley in Surendranath Sen and Umesha Mishra eds., *Sanskrit Documents: Being Sanskrit Letters and Other Documents Preserved in the Oriental Collection at the National Archives of India* (Allahabad: Ganganatha Jha Research Institute and National Archives of India, 1951), pp. 90–92 (pp. 26–29 for the Sanskrit original).
2  Kashinath Pandit in *Sanskrit Documents*, p. 89 (Sanskrit original, p. 25).
3  Of course, when they thought the balance of power was about to switch, the priests sang a different tune. During an 1817 revolt against the Company, the priests 'openly proclaimed the fall of the English rule'. See G. Toynbee, *A Sketch of the History of Orissa: From 1803 to 1828* (Calcutta: Bengal Secretariat Press, 1873), p. 19.
4  Quoted in Dennis Judd, *The Lion and the Tiger: The Rise and Fall of the British Raj, 1600–1947* (Oxford: Oxford University Press, 2004), p. 15.
5  On the Company and its slow integration in this period into Asian political systems, see David Veevers, *The Origins of the British Empire in Asia, 1600–1750* (Cambridge: Cambridge University Press, 2020). This is not to say that the British did not get embroiled in skirmishes. For instance, when some got embroiled in local politics, the Company's officials berated their own: 'How you came in prison you knowe well. 'Twas not for defending the Companies goods; 'twas for going . . . and tossing balls, with a flagg that was knowne to bee the Englishes. It [the Indian ruler's response] was but as any other would doe . . . for marchants, while trading in a strainge country . . . may live quietly . . .' See William Foster, *The English Factories in India: 1661–64* (Oxford: Clarendon Press, 1923), p. 87.
6  This is Ankbhupala Damarla's *Ushaparinayam* of the seventeenth century. See Kruijtzer, *Xenophobia*, p. 109.
7  *Viswaguna Darsana*, p. 78. For a more recent translation of this segment, see Velcheru Narayana Rao, David Shulman and Sanjay Subrahmanyam, *Symbols of Substance: Court and State in Nayaka Period Tamilnadu* (Delhi: Oxford University Press, 1992), pp. 5–6.

8     Much later in Bengal as well, we find this ambivalence. See Pennington, *Was Hinduism Invented?*, pp. 148–49.

9     The term comes from 'du-bhashi', speaker of two languages. In Bengal, their counterparts were the 'banians'. As Peter Marshall, 'Masters and Banians in Eighteenth-Century Calcutta', p. 193, in Blair B. King and M.N. Pearson eds., *The Age of Partnership: Europeans in Asia before Dominion* (Honolulu: The University Press of Hawaii, 1979), pp. 191–214 tells, service with an Englishman for these Indian partners was lucrative, not from salaries but because of 'a whole range of profits'—arrangements with contractors, gifts from people seeking access and shares of their employers' illicit trade. A case in point is Krisna Kanta Nandy. See Somendra Chandra Nandy, *Life and Times of Cantoo Baboo: The Banian of Warren Hastings*, Vols 1 and 2 (Bombay: Allied Publishers, 1978, 1981). And dubashes could be very influential. As one remarks in an Indian text, 'Whatever I say, [my boss] will accept.' See Rao, Shulman and Subrahmanyam, *Textures of Time*, p. 27.

10    Henry Davison Love ed., *Vestiges of Old Madras, 1640–1800: From the East India Company's Records Preserved at Fort St. George and the Indian Office, and from Other Sources*, Vol. 2 (London: Government of India & John Murray, 1913), p. 503. See also an example in Hudson, 'Life and Times of H.A. Krishna Pillai', p. 192, and K. Subba Rao, *Revived Memories* (Madras: Ganesh & Co., 1933), p. 5. In Bengal, it was not temples but grand Durga Puja festivities that served a similar purpose, with one 1819 journal speaking of the 'emulative rivalry' between 'wealthy Natives'. Quoted in Rachel Fell McDermott, *Revelry, Rivalry, and Longing for the Goddesses of Bengal: The Fortunes of Hindu Festivals* (New York: Columbia University Press, 2011), p. 25. For an academic study of Madras's temples, see Joanne Punzo Waghorne, *Diaspora of the Gods: Modern Hindu Temples in an Urban Middle-Class World* (New York: Oxford University Press, 2004), pp. 35–74.

11    V. Raghavan ed., *The Sarva-Deva-Vilasa: Edited with Critical Introduction and Notes* (Madras: The Adyar Library and Research Centre, 1958), p. 52.

12    Thomas Salmon quoted in *Vestiges of Old Madras*, p. 75.

13    For a study, see Niels Brimnes, *Constructing the Colonial Encounter: Right and Left Hand Castes in Early Colonial South India* (Abingdon: Routledge, 2019 ed.). See also Kruijtzer, *Xenophobia*, chapter 3.

14    See John S. Deyell and R.E. Frykenberg, 'Sovereignty and the "SIKKA" under Company Raj: Minting Prerogative and Imperial Legitimacy in India', p. 13, in *Indian Economic and Social History Review* 19, 1 (1982): 1–25.

15    Veevers, *Origins*, 21. For a parallel with the Dutch in Masulipatam and their interactions with local Muslims, see Kruijtzer, *Xenophobia*, p. 38.

16    See Raghavan, *The Sarva-Deva-Vilasa*, p. 69 and Kanakalatha Mukund, *The View from Below: Indigenous Society, Temples and the Early Colonial State in Tamilnadu, 1700–1835* (Hyderabad: Orient Longman, 2005), pp. 187–89.

17 Edmund Burke, *The Speeches of Edmund Burke on the Impeachment of Warren Hastings* (London: George Bell & Sons, 1889), p. 23.

18 We get a sense of the importance of European merchants in Bengal based on the bullion they pumped into the local economy. See P.J. Marshall, *Bengal: The British Bridgehead, Eastern India 1740–1828 (The New Cambridge History of India)* (Cambridge: Cambridge University Press, 1987), pp. 64–66.

19 See Ramachandra Chintaman Dhere ed., *Ramachandra Amatya-Pranit Svarajyaneeti: Ajnapatra* (Pune: Padmagandha Prakashan, 2014 ed.), pp. 89–90. The term 'svamat' may also be translated in a broad sense as religion. A similar claim is made for the mid-eighteenth-century nawab of Bengal, Alivardi Khan, who is supposed to have warned that 'the hat-men wou'd possess themselves of all the shores of Hindia'. See *A Translation of the Seir Mutaqherin Or View of Modern Times: Being an History of India from the Year by Seid-Gholam-Hossein-Khan*, Vol. 2 (Calcutta & Madras: Cambray & Co., 1902), p. 163. See also Veevers, *Origins*, pp. 254–55. So too in 1742, the Travancore king Martanda Varma would tell the Dutch that as traders, they had no business interfering in political affairs. See de Lannoy, *The Kulasekhara Perumals of Travancore*, p. 110. In the early sixteenth century, the Zamorin of Calicut similarly warned the Quilon rajah that the Portuguese were 'a very bad race, and if he admitted them into his land they would rise up against him'. See Afonso de Albuquerque (Walter de Gray Birch ed.), *The Commentaries of the Great Afonso Dalboquerque* (London: Hakluyt Society, 1875), p. 9. This was acknowledged in Britain also: a character in Samuel Foote's play *The Nabob* remarks: 'Why, here are a body of merchants that beg to be admitted as friends, and take possession of a small spot in a country' only to 'cunningly encroach, and fortify by little by little, till at length, we growing too strong for the natives, we turn them out of their lands, and take possession of their money and jewels.' Quoted in Nick Robins, *The Corporation That Changed the World: How the East India Company Shaped the Modern Multinational* (London: Pluto Press, 2012), pp. 106–07. See also Kruijtzer, *Xenophobia*, p. 32 for a seventeenth-century European urging the Dutch to keep Indian states 'friendly through fear rather than by begging', and to prioritize military strength to cow down local powers.

20 Marshall, *Bengal*, pp. 75–76.

21 Thus, in the house of the nawab of Arcot, the regional Mughal representative, one successor was backed by the British and the other by the French.

22 William Dalrymple, *The Anarchy: The East India Company, Corporate Violence, and the Pillage of an Empire* (New Delhi: Bloomsbury Publishing, 2019), p. 82.

23 On the importance of bankers in eighteenth-century India, see C.A. Bayly, *Rulers, Townsmen and Bazaars: North Indian Society in the Age of British Expansion, 1770–1870* (New Delhi: Oxford University Press, 2012 ed.), pp. 204–08. See also ibid., p. 265, pp. 281–82 for their significance to the British.

24 Marshall, *Bengal*, p. 75, p. 79–80. See also pp. 63–64 for a sense of the Jagat Seths' power.
25 Michael Edwardes, *Warren Hastings: King of the Nabobs* (London: Hard-Davis, MacGibbon, 1976), p. 28. For exact figures of what others received, see Geoffrey Moorhouse, *India Britannica* (London: William Collins Sons & Co. Ltd, 1983), p. 48. Such gains continued for a long time: as late as 1843, Charles Napier, after the Battle of Hyderabad in the Sindh, personally gained £70,000. See Meadows Taylor, *A Student's Manual of the History of India* (London: Longmans, Green & Co., 1870), pp. 661–62.
26 This despite Clive's promise that the Company 'should not anyways interfere in the affairs of the Government, but leave that wholly to the Nawab . . . [and] return to Calcutta and attend solely to commerce, which was our proper sphere.' See Clive to the Calcutta Council, 30 June 1757 in A.C. Banerjee ed., *Indian Constitutional Documents, Vol. 1: 1757–1858* (Calcutta: A. Mukherjee & Co., 1945), p. 1.
27 Edwardes, *Warren Hastings*, p. 30. A few decades earlier we find a similar refrain when London reminded their India men that 'the Society whom you serve are a Company of Trading merchants and not Warriors'. Quoted in Jon Wilson, *India Conquered: Britain's Raj and the Chaos of Empire* (London: Simon & Schuster, 2016), p. 72. See also Veevers, *Origins*, p. 69 on London's disapproval of the construction of Fort St George in Madras. And in 1832 when a parliamentary committee asked if 'India has been conquered and administered in spite of instructions from England', the response they got was: 'To a considerable degree that is the truth.' See James Mill's testimony in *Minutes of Evidence Taken Before the Select Committee on the Affairs of the East India Company (VI: Political or Foreign)* (London: House of Commons, 1832), p. 9.
28 See the emperor's grant in *Indian Constitutional Documents*, Vol. 1, pp. 5–6. Most of Orissa, however, was in Maratha hands, so the transfer was nominal, until the British defeated the Marathas in 1803.
29 William Bolts, *Considerations on India Affairs; Particularly Respecting the Present State of Bengal and Its Dependencies* (London: J. Almon & F. Elmsly, 1772), p. vi. Ghulam Hussain wrote how this transfer took place in 'less time than would have been taken up for the sale of a jack-ass'. See *A Translation of the Seir Mutaqherin or View of Modern Times: Being an History of India from the Year by Seid-Gholam-Hossein-Khan*, Vol. 3 (Calcutta & Madras: Cambray & Co., 1902), p. 9. Company voices agreed: as Nathaniel Halhed would write, thanks to Clive 'we exchanged the pliability of mercantile negotiation for the steadiness of political independence'. See Halhed, *A Letter to Governor Johnstone on Indian Affairs* (London: S. Bladon, 1783), p. 39.
30 In parallel, in India, it is assumed that all British were part of the colonial state, with similar motives, whereas, as David Gilmour shows, they had a

whole spectrum of reasons to be in India. See Gilmour, *The British in India: Three Centuries of Ambition and Experience* (London: Allen Lane, 2018).

31  Richard Bourke, *Empire and Revolution: The Political Life of Edmund Burke* (Princeton: Princeton University Press, 2015), p. 338.

32  As Penelope Carson observes, it was not the fact that the nabobs 'bought' parliamentary seats that was scandalous, but that their Indian wealth allowed them to do so above the 'going rate'. See Carson, *The East India Company and Religion: 1698–1858* (Woodbridge: The Boydell Press, 2012), p. 18.

33  See David Spadafora, *The Idea of Progress in Eighteenth-Century Britain* (New Haven: Yale University Press, 1990), p. 14, pp. 215–17; John Marriott, *The Other Empire: Metropolis, India and Progress in the Colonial Imagination* (Manchester: Manchester University Press, 2003), pp. 19–20, p. 25; and George D. Bearce, *British Attitudes toward India, 1784–1858* (London: Oxford University Press, 1961), p. 19.

34  The expression was used by Denis Diderot, the French thinker.

35  As late as the second half of the nineteenth century, thus, Lord Dalhousie would record the 'perpetual disparagement of the power that rules India' by 'mischievous' minds in Britain, and the 'perpetual storm of attack, censure, contempt and calumny in the Parliament of England, and from the Press'. See *Indian Constitutional Documents*, Vol. 1, p. 279.

36  As Smith wrote, owning Company stock allowed 'even a man of small fortune' if not a 'share . . . in the plunder', at least a role in 'the appointment of the plunderers of India'. See *An Inquiry into the Nature and Causes of the Wealth of Nations* (Edinburgh: Adam & Charles Black, 1850 ed.), p. 338.

37  Burke's speech on Fox's India Bill in *Celebrated Speeches of Chatham, Burke, and Erskine* (Philadelphia: E. Claxton & Company, 1882), p. 208, p. 236. Burke did not think empire itself bad but objected to the Company's attitude.

38  Bolts, *Considerations*, p. viii, p. ix.

39  Moorhouse, *India Britannica*, p. 67, and Thomas R. Metcalf, *Ideologies of the Raj* (The New Cambridge History of India) (Cambridge: Cambridge University Press, 1995), p. 24. See also Gauri Viswanathan, *Masks of Conquest: Literary Study and British Rule in India* (New York, Columbia University Press, 1989), p. 11 and Gilmour, *The British*, p. 39. As Viswanathan observes, however, these flip-flops came from 'an unstable foundation of knowledge' about India. On Cornwallis's views, he described the dubashes of Madras as 'the most cruel instruments of rapine and extortion'. Quoted in Burton Stein, *Thomas Munro: The Origins of the Colonial State and His Vision of Empire* (Delhi: Oxford University Press, 1989), p. 38.

40  Bourke, *Empire and Revolution*, pp. 520–34. See also Edwardes, *Warren Hastings*, 87–88. See also *Copies of Papers Relative to the Restoration of the King of Tanjore, the Arrest of the Right. Hon. George Lord Pigot, and the Removal of his Lordship from the Government of Fort St. George, by sundry Members of the Council* (London: 1777).

41 See Mukund, *The View from Below*, pp. 148–50; Jim Phillips, 'Parliament and Southern India, 1781–3: The Secret Committee of Inquiry and the Prosecution of Sir Thomas Rumbold', in *Parliamentary History* 7, Part 1 (1988), pp. 81–97, and Philip Lawson and Jim Phillips, '"Our Execrable Banditti": Perceptions of Nabobs in Mid-Eighteenth Century Britain', p. 227, in *Albion: A Quarterly Journal Concerned with British Studies* 16, 3 (1984): 225–41. In Bengal in 1786 the Mughal writer Ghulam Hussain also reported how for anything that might cause 'ill renown', it is 'the Indians that are made use of' by Company officials. See *Seir Mutaqherin*, Vol. 3, p. 28. And when steps were taken to rein in corruption, many officers disliked it. As a young Colin Mackenzie wrote, the novel practice of sending out governors 'only distinguished for [their] uprightness' prevented 'our acquiring money'; 'the good old times when everything could be bought and sold here are now no longer'. See Tobias Wolffhardt (Jane Rafferty trans.), *Unearthing the Past to Forge the Future: Colin Mackenzie, the Early Colonial State and the Comprehensive Survey of India* (New York & Oxford: Berghahn, 2018), p. 56. For a similar remark by the young H.T. Colebrooke, see Rosane Rocher and Ludo Rocher, *The Making of Western Indology: Henry Thomas Colebrooke and the East India Company* (Abingdon: Routledge, 2012), p. 15. For a broader study of corruption in the British empire (and its changing meanings), see Mark Knights, *Trust and Distrust: Corruption in Office in Britain and its Empire, 1600–1850* (Oxford: Oxford University Press, 2021). Interestingly, as late as the 1940s, we find—in Sir Arthur Hope—a final case of high-level corruption.

42 See, for instance, the directors' complaint in 1816 in *Indian Constitutional Documents*, Vol. 1, pp. 165–66.

43 This was a longstanding issue. See, for example, Veevers, *Origins*, p. 51, for a 1634 lament. Such tensions affected the French in India too. See Amar Farooqui, *The Colonial Subjugation of India* (New Delhi: Aleph Book Company, 2022), pp. 30–31.

44 Montgomery Martin ed., *The Despatches, Minutes, and Correspondence of the Marquess Wellesley During His Administration in India*, Vol. 2 (London: W.H. Allen & Co., 1836), p. 607.

45 Quoted in Jack Harrington, *Sir John Malcolm and the Creation of British India* (New York: Palgrave Macmillan, 2010), p. 51. See also Martha McLaren, 'Writing and Making History: Thomas Munro, John Malcolm and Mountstuart Elphinstone: Three Scotsmen in the History and Historiography of British India', Unpublished PhD dissertation, Simon Fraser University (1992), p. 80 and Marshall, *Bengal*, p. 135, where we learn that Wellesley spent 42 per cent of his total expenditure as governor general on the army.

46 Charles Metcalfe quoted in Harrington, *John Malcolm*, p. 28.

47 John Malcolm quoted in ibid., p 24. See also pp. 57–58 for Harrington's discussion on the directors.

48 Its revenue policy, for example, rapidly impoverished the region. See Marshall, *Bengal*, pp. 144–45. A seminal study on this is Ranajit Guha's *A Rule of Property for Bengal: An Essay on the Idea of Permanent Settlement* (Ranikhet: Permanent Black & Orient Blackswan in association with Ashoka University, 2016 ed.).

49 McLaren, 'Writing and Making History', p. 51. Discontent with Bengal's overbearing attitude and lack of support to Madras comes across in Thomas Munro's letters from this period. See Stein, *Thomas Munro,* pp. 18–21.

50 This paranoia is repeatedly pointed out by Jon Wilson, Harrington and others. Another clue is that in Madras, the dubashes—wealthy and influential—were increasingly treated with suspicion, thought to wish to derail Company plans, etc., in a way not known with Bengal's banians. See Susan Neild-Basu, 'The Dubashes of Madras', in *Modern Asian Studies* 18, 1 (1984): 1–31.

51 C.A. Bayly, *Rulers, Townsmen*, pp. 281–82. See also Kenneth Ballhatchet, *Social Policy and Social Change in Western India: 1817–1830* (London: Oxford University Press, 1957), p. 7, p. 77 for how after the Company army took the Peshwa's capital, it was merchants among whom 'popularity' of the British was highest. See also Lakshmi Subramanian, 'Banias and the British: The Role of Indigenous Credit in the Process of Imperial Expansion in Western India in the Second Half of the Eighteenth Century', in *Modern Asian Studies* 21, 3 (1987): 473–510.

52 Quoted in C.A. Bayly, *Empire and Information: Intelligence Gathering and Social Communication in India, 1780-1870* (Cambridge: Cambridge University Press, 1996), p. 48.

53 Montgomery Martin ed., *The Despatches, Minutes, and Correspondence of the Marquess Wellesley During His Administration in India*, Vol. 4 (London: W.H. Allen & Co., 1837), p. 153.

54 This occurs with the Marathas also, where the king was a figurehead and the Peshwa the real ruler, who kept watch to avoid the king's becoming 'a potential focus for . . . disaffection'. See Andre Wink, *Land and Sovereignty in India: Agrarian Society and Politics under the Eighteenth-century Maratha Svarajya* (Cambridge, Cambridge University Press, 1986), p. 77. Clive recommended treating the titular nawab in Bengal also with dignity. See *Indian Constitutional Documents*, Vol. 1, pp. 7–8.

55 Wellesley in 'Correspondence between the Court of Directors and the India Board and the Supreme Government of India relative to Mahomedan and Hindoo Worship', p. 76, in *Parliamentary Papers*, Vol. 34 (1845).

56 Kulke, *Kings and Cults*, pp. 86–87.

57 Ibid., pp. 46–48. See also p. 54, where we read how even under Aurangzeb, when orders were issued for the temple's destruction, the local rajah and Mughal governor sent up a fake image. See also Simmons, *Devotional Sovereignty*, p. 66 about Tipu Sultan's patronage of the Sringeri Matha, continuing an older political tradition.

58  Indeed, when the Marathas, conceding Company victory over the region, asked for the temple alone to be returned, Wellesley refused. See Nancy Gardner Cassels, *Religion and Pilgrim Tax under the Company Raj* (Maryland: The Riverdale Company, 1988), p. 39.
59  Quoted in ibid., p. 45
60  Carson, *East India Company and Religion*, p. 15.
61  Chandra Mudaliar, *State and Religious Endowments in Madras* (Madras: University of Madras, 1976), p. 15.
62  Davis, *Lives of Indian Images*, p. 204.
63  Mudaliar, *State and Religious Endowments*, p. 32. See also Franklin A. Presler, *Religion Under Bureaucracy: Policy and Administration for Hindu Temples in South India* (Cambridge: Cambridge University Press, 1987). As late as 1946, the Privy Council in London had to adjudicate rival claims between Brahmin groups in the Tirupati Temple as to who had the right to open and conclude the daily worship. See the judgment at http://acharya.org/bk/bl/misc/pcr.pdf.
64  Aiya, *Travancore State Manual*, Vol. 1, p. 482. Reference is to John Munro.
65  W. Francis, *Madras District Gazetteers: Madura* (Madras: Government Press, 1907), p. 259. At Sringeri, seat of a major spiritual head of the Hindus, tax concessions granted by Hindu rulers, similarly, were continued by the Company well into the nineteenth century. See Prasad, *Poetics of Conduct*, p. 76.
66  See S.K. Pillai, 'The Sacred Palmyra Grove', p. 84.
67  This refers to the Chengannur Temple. See also Kottarathil Sankunni, *Aitihihyamaala*, Vol. 2, p. 352. Sankunni relates the story of John Munro and his wife in a sequence of other tales connected to the temple, showing how the foreigner became part of the general landscape.
68  With the Madurai officer, local lore tells how he was 'saved' by the goddess, thus explaining his reverence. It is another matter that he was accused of embezzlement and died by suicide in 1828.
69  See Padmanabha (V.S. Bhatnagar ed.), *Kanhadade Prabandha: India's Greatest Patriotic Saga of Medieval Times* (New Delhi: Aditya Prakashan, 1991), pp. 56–64 which presents Sultan Alauddin Khilji of Delhi doing battle against a Hindu prince, Kanhadade. The sultan's daughter, however, wishes to marry Kanhadade's son—to whom she was wed in six previous births. It is only due to sin on her part that she was born in a Muslim family (suggesting inferiority). See Ramya Sreenivasan, 'The 'Marriage' of 'Hindu' and 'Turak': Medieval Rajput Histories of Jalor', in *Medieval History Journal* 7, 1 (2004): 87–108. See also Richard H. Davis, 'A Muslim Princess in the Temples of Visnu', in *International Journal of Hindu Studies* 8, 1–3 (2004): 137–56, and Ranjeeta Dutta, 'The Politics of Religious Identity', pp. 157–84 for stories which cast a Muslim princess as consort to a Hindu deity, again asserting resistance against Islamic power via spiritual victory

for the Hindus. Another example is the story of the first Bahmani Sultan of the Deccan being foster son to a Brahmin. See Sumit Guha, 'Serving the barbarian to preserve the dharma: The ideology and training of a clerical elite in Peninsular India c. 1300–1800', pp. 515–16, in *Indian Economic Social History Review* 47, 4 (2010): 497–525. In the British period, for a story with parallels to the Travancore one, see also Thomas Munro and his encounter with a seventeenth century sage (!) at https://www.speakingtree.in/blog/sir-thomas-munro-and-the-story-of-mantralaya.

70 Charles Ross ed., *Correspondence of Charles, First Marquis Cornwallis*, Vol. 2 (London: John Murray, 1859), p. 19.

71 Quoted in Harrington, *John Malcolm*, p. 129. To quote Bayly, 'the Company's aim was stability not equity'. See C.A. Bayly, *Indian Society and the Making of the British Empire* (Cambridge: Cambridge University Press, 1988), p. 108.

72 Stuart's Minute, *Modification of the Judicial System in the Bengal Provinces* (Calcutta, 1815), p. 38.

73 Bayly, *Indian Society*, p. 110. See also Bayly, *Empire and Information*, p. 286.

74 Quoted in Ballhatchet, *Social Policy and Social Change*, p. 8.

75 Mountstuart Elphinstone quoted in ibid., p. 12. Elphinstone even went to Wai, to which prominent families fled on the British arrival and conciliated them.

76 Quoted in ibid., p. 28.

77 Quoted in ibid., p. 27. See also pp. 188–89, where we read how certain officers even took to wearing Indian clothes. This, however, invited disapproval, for fear that it might diminish 'British character' and allow those officers 'to do under its guise what they never would have thought of doing in the costume of their country'. (Those who did, such as William Fraser in Delhi, 'go native', evidently suffered in their careers, showing that this anxiety was real.)

78 Quoted in ibid., p. 16.

79 See Wink, *Land and Sovereignty*, p. 77, pp. 81–82 for more on the ceremonial observances maintained around the rajah by the Peshwa even when the king was for all practical purposes powerless.

80 Ballhatchet, *Social Policy and Social Change*, p. 66. It was Thomas Munro who made the suggestion, writing: 'The Company, acting as the Pundit Purdhan [sic, the other title of the Peshwa], would hold an office, which, as in the case of that of the Dewanee in Bengal [received from the Mughal emperor], would take from it none of its sovereign powers; and its governing the country under this ancient title, would, I believe, reconcile the Jageerdars [nobles] to the change of masters, and to induce them to employ their troops willingly at the call of the British Government.' Quoted in Stein, *Thomas Munro*, p. 233, p. 34.

81 Ballhatchet, *Social Policy and Social Change*, p. 18.

82  See ibid., pp. 59–60 for example, where he discusses how the Peshwa's subordinate lords were only allowed to retain enough land for a dignified maintenance.

83  Quoted in ibid., p. 19.

84  *Gazetteer of the Bombay Presidency, Volume XIX: Satara* (Bombay: Government Central Press, 1885), pp. 310–11. The British belief was that the rajah was in touch with Russia, though it turned out he had contacted only the Portuguese in Goa. In any case, 'Troops occupied his palace ... The Rajah was torn from his couch, placed in a litter, carried for a distance of eight miles, and deposited in a cow-shed', after which he was removed to Benares. Meanwhile, over £300,000 in treasure was confiscated. See Anonymous, *Indian Annexations: British Treatment of Native Princes* (London: Trubner & Co., 1863), p. 11.

85  Quoted in Ballhatchet, *Social Policy and Social Change*, p. 83. As it happened, in 1839, a rebellion was attempted in the ex-Peshwa's name, over two decades after his deposition. See S.P. Desai, 'A Little Known Rising Instigated by the Ex-Peshwa (1838–1839)', in *Proceedings of the Indian History Congress* 32 (1970): 63–68.

86  Ballhatchet, *Social Policy and Social Change*, pp. 85–86. Eight thousand Brahmins benefitted from the Peshwa's largesse. Many followed the Peshwa in exile—in 1837 there were 8000 people in the ex-Peshwa's camp, and by 1847 the number crossed 15,000. See Pratul C. Gupta, *The Last Peshwa and the English Commissioners: 1818–1851* (Calcutta: S.C. Sarkar & Sons, 1944), pp. 6–7. The *dakshina* given to Brahmins under the Peshwas were large: the Rs 16,354 in 1736 apparently went up to Rs 18,00,000 in 1758. In 1770, nearly 40,000 Brahmins received dakshina from the Peshwa. Cited in Madhav M. Deshpande, 'Pune: An Emerging Center of Education in Early Modern Maharashtra', p. 62, in *International Journal of Hindu Studies* 19, 1–2 (2015): 59–96.

87  And Indians often responded. In 1809, Hindus in Benares in a dispute with local Muslims called on the Company as 'the distributor of justice' that was 'acquainted with the Beyds (the Vedas), (the) Poorauns (Puranas)' and so on. See Copland et al., *History of State and Religion in India*, p. 167.

88  Quoted in Harrington, *John Malcolm*, pp. 129–30.

89  McLaren, 'Writing and Making History', p. 241.

90  Quoted in ibid., p. 278.

91  Quoted in Stein, *Thomas Munro*, p. 238. See also Munro, 'Southern India', pp. 233–34. All that was needed, he argued, was to 'ameliorate' what was well established. Quoted in Stein, *Thomas Munro*, p. 125. For his attack on the Bengal system, see ibid., p. 106. Indeed, all three men in the new areas under their supervision resisted reforms of the Bengal variety, preferring 'native' institutions or methods that came closest. See ibid., pp. 182–83 for a note on Munro's struggles, for instance. He, in fact, lobbied the Board of Control

where there were sympathetic figures like James Cumming to get them to thwart the Company officialdom. This sometimes included exchanges on even wording. As Munro wrote once:

> I think it necessary to caution you, that if it is expected that instructions are to be obeyed, the strongest and plainest of words must be used: for instance, the expressions, 'It is our wish'; 'It is our intention'; 'We propose'; do not, it is maintained here, convey orders, but merely recommendations. Unless the words 'We direct', 'We order', are employed, the measures to which they relate will be regarded as optional.

See ibid., p. 185. For Elphinstone's criticism of the Bengal system, see his *Report*, pp. 55–56. See also ibid., p. 98 where he urges removing abuses and 'reviving' the energy of native legal institutions instead of imposing half-baked British ones. Elphinstone also wrote: 'I am convinced the Maratha plan if cleaned of abuses & vigorously acted on will do very well for the people & and I should dread to see Judges' of the Bengal type. Quoted in Ballhatchet, *Social Policy and Social Change*, p. 105. Recognizing the complexity of the country, Munro also suggested that it was best to leave each province to 'act for itself' in ways that fitted its context. Quoted in Stein, *Thomas Munro*, p. 280.

92  These men were also influenced by Romanticism in this period in Europe. See Metcalf, *Ideologies*, pp. 24–25. Munro also believed that Indians should be appointed to the Company government's higher offices, deeming their exclusion unjust. See Munro's Minute dated 31 December 1824 in *The Asiatic Journal and Monthly Register*, Vol. 3 (New Series) (London: Parbury, Allen & Co., 1830), p. 59.

93  Reference is to Robert Fullerton of the Madras Council. See Bearce, *British Attitudes*, pp. 135–36.

94  Munro, 'Southern India', p. 237. Elphinstone shared these views. See Ballhatchet, *Social Policy and Social Change*, p. 250. See also Edward Colebrooke, *Memoir of the Honourable Mountstuart Elphinstone* (London: Parker, Son & Bourn, 1861), pp. 72–73 where Elphinstone is described in a conversation as stating that to educate natives was 'our high road back to Europe'. When asked why he insisted on it if that were the case, he replied that it was 'our duty'.

95  Quoted in Ballhatchet, *Social Policy and Social Change*, p. 43. See also ibid., p. 45, where Elphinstone urges supporting the old charities of the Peshwa, for otherwise the unhappiness would offer 'fine materials for an intriguing ex-Paishwah'.

96  Viswanathan, *Masks*, p. 32. Remarkably, similar views were expressed centuries before by some Portuguese minds in Goa as well. Instead of the tough style in vogue, one man suggested 'a light and soft yoke' and a 'liberal' administration. Even Christianity in Goa, he advised, 'amidst such diverse non-Christian sects' must be 'simple and plain and tolerant, without rigour or excessively narrow views'. See D'Costa, *The Christianisation of the Goa Islands*, p. 68.

97  Mountstuart Elphinstone, *Report on the Territories Conquered from the Paishwa* (Calcutta: Government Gazette Press, 1821), p. 60.

98  Quoted in Bearce, *British Attitudes*, p. 134. Long before, William Bolts had also warned that 'the most despicable reptiles will turn when trod upon'. See Bolts, *Considerations*, p. vii. Interestingly, compared to Elphinstone, Munro and Malcolm were even more openminded. For a declaration by Munro in favour of diversity, see McLaren, 'Writing and Making History', p. 207. When once asked if India would benefit from exposure to the West, he responded that if 'Hindoos' were backward in science and government, in other areas, they were the superiors. Indeed, 'if civilization is to become an article of trade between the two countries, I am convinced,' he finished, 'that this country [Britain] will gain by the import cargo.' Quoted in Stein, *Thomas Munro*, p. 162. Munro also lamented what British dominance would do to the Indian nation. Without leaders in positions of authority, even if they benefited from the security and peace, they would be 'debased' and lose 'national character' and self-respect. See ibid., p. 224. Malcolm agreed: The Company's role ought to be limited to 'useful public works', 'a moderate assessment of revenue', 'toleration' of religious practices, and to govern India 'with more attention to . . . the character and condition of [its] inhabitants, than to the wishes and prejudices of those of England'. For as a regime 'of strangers', British power could not 'endure but in the shape' suggested above. See John Malcolm, *The Political History of India: From 1784 to 1823*, Vol. 2 (London: John Murray, 1826), pp. 322–24.

99  *Memoirs of Warren Hastings*, p. 61. See also A. Merwyn Davies, *Warren Hastings: Maker of British India* (London: Ivor Nicholson & Watson, 1935) which in its very title expresses similar admiration for the man.

100 Robert Travers, *Ideology and Empire in Eighteenth-Century India: The British in Bengal* (Cambridge: Cambridge University Press, 2007), p. 102.

101 Bourke, *Empire and Revolution*, p. 334

102 Ibid., p. 557

103 The land revenue demand for Purnea district was raised by £260,000 in 1781 alone. Zamindars who could not deliver the amounts set by Hastings's government lost their licenses to those who could i.e., those willing to use force. See Amit Ray, *Representations of India, 1740–1840: The Creation of India in the Colonial Imagination* (London: Macmillan Press Ltd., 1998), p. 22

104 Richard Becher's 1769 note in *Indian Constitutional Documents*, Vol. 1, pp. 8–9.

105 Lionel James Trotter, *Warren Hastings: A Biography* (London: W.H. Allen & Co., 1878), p. 140.

106 Moorhouse, *India Britannica*, p. 56

107 Andrew Otis, *Hickey's Bengal Gazette: The Untold Story of India's First Newspaper* (Chennai: Tranquebar, 2018), p. 304.

108   Michael S. Dodson, *Orientalism, Empire and National Culture: India, 1770–1880* (New York: Palgrave Macmillan, 2007), p. 20. Bengal also financed Madras's and Bombay's political entanglements. See Wilson, *Domination*, p. 48, p. 54. See also Marshall, *Bengal*, p. 135, which tells how in the decade between 1761 and 1771, 44 per cent of Company expenditure in Bengal was on its military.
109   Macaulay, *Warren Hastings*, p. 21
110   Quoted in Dalrymple, *The Anarchy*, p. 239. Indeed, even in art, Hastings sought 'a sense of harmony between India and Britain', having William Hodges do a series of paintings. See Ashok Malhotra, *Making British Indian Fictions: 1772–1823* (New York: Palgrave Macmillan, 2012), p. 37. As late as 1812, Hastings would write that Indians were not 'sufficiently noticed', that they deserved to be 'participators in the same equal rights of society' with white men. See letter dated 2 December 1812 from Hastings to Lord Moira in Joshua Ehrlich, 'Straddling the Imperial Meridian: Warren Hastings as an Observer of Change in British India', p. 5, in *History of European Ideas* (2023), https://doi.org/10.1080/01916599.2023.2190746.
111   Alexander Dow, *The History of Hindostan: From the Death of Akbar to the Complete Settlement of the Empire under Aurungzebe* (London: T. Becket & P.A. de Hondt, 1772), p. cxliii.
112   A. Mervyn Davies, *Strange Destiny: A Biography of Warren Hastings* (New York: G.P. Putnam's Sons, 1935), pp. 71–72.
113   Reference is to Francis Buchanan-Hamilton. See Marshall, *Bengal*, p. 34; E. Daniel Potts, *British Baptist Missionaries in India, 1793–1837: The History of Serampore and Its Missions* (Cambridge: Cambridge University Press, 1967), p. 16 (on Muslims venerating Hindu gods); and Buchanan, *An Account of the Districts of Bihar and Patna in 1811–12* (Patna: The Bihar and Orissa Research Society, 1939), p. 307. On p. 365, he also refers to a Muslim figure worshipped by Hindus. Indeed, even in the 1880s, officials would see Hindus worship a stone with an Arabic inscription. See A. Cunningham and H.B.W. Garrick, *Report of Tours in North and South Bihar in 1880–81* (Calcutta: Office of the Superintendent of Government Printing, 1883), pp. 25–26. This criticism appears among the more orthodox elsewhere in India. On the Muslim side, Emperor Jahangir was upset in the seventeenth century to see Muslims 'traverse vast distances' to worship a Hindu goddess. See *Jahangirnama*, p. 374. See also Cherian, *Merchants of Virtue*, p. 73. Among Hindus, the saint Ramdas in Maharashtra, in the seventh *samas* of the fourteenth *dashak* of the *Dasbodh*, laments how Brahmins had forgotten their duties and were following Muslim pirs. See *Shree-Samartha Ramdas-Swami-Virchit Shree-Dasbodh* (Pune: Bhat & Co., 1945 [?]), p. 324 accessible at: https://archive.org/details/Shri.Dasbodh. of.Shri.Samartha.Ramdas.Marathi/page/n1/mode/2up.
114   Buchanan, *Bihar*, p. 306. Reference here is to Raja Mitrajit, but even in western India, the Brahmin Peshwa had a Muslim wife. Their descendants

were the nawabs of Banda. Purbiya chiefs also used to keep Muslim wives. See Dirk H.A. Kolff, *Naukar, Rajput and Sepoy: The Ethnohistory of the Military Labour Market in Hindustan, 1450–1850* (Cambridge: Cambridge University Press, 1990), p. 96.

115   Buchanan, *Bihar*, p. 328. In Gujarat, Hindus and Jains intermarried. See Bhatavadekar, *Census of Baroda*, p. 91.

116   Reference is to Bihar's Bhumihars. See Buchanan, *Bihar*, p. 325 and pp. 357–58. See also pp. 322–24 for other Brahmin occupations. See also Bayly, *Rulers, Townsmen, and Bazaars*, p. 21. Interestingly, a reference in the *Visvaguna Darsana* to Brahmins in Kashi who 'procure maintenance by arms and neglect the science' may refer to the same community. See Ramasswami, *Viswaguna Darsana*, p. 30. On actual military work by the Bhumihars, see Bayly, *Rulers, Townsmen*, p. 21. See also an overview of Brahmin professions in pre-British Bengal in Kumkum Chatterjee, 'Scribal Elites in Sultanate and Mughal Bengal', in *Indian Economic Social History Review* 47, 4 (2010): 445–72. There were Brahmins among the Pindaris—dreaded freelance horsemen—too. See Amar Farooqui, *Sindias and the Raj: Princely Gwalior c. 1800–1850* (Delhi: Primus Books, 2011), p. 25. In the south too, this trend appears: the sixteenth-century Brahmin poet-saint Purandaradasa's father was a merchant in Vijayanagara. In Kerala, among the Namboodiri Brahmins also there were 'Jatimatras' ('nominal Brahmins') who could be physicians or warriors. See Aiya, *Travancore State Manual*, Vol. 2, pp. 250–51. V. Raghavan Nambyar, 'Annals and Antiquities of Tiruvalla', p. 76 tells of Tamil Brahmins imported into Kerala specifically to serve as cloth merchants. In Maharashtra, the saints Tukaram and Ramdas wrote of how Brahmins would do any job if paid. See A.R. Kulkarni, 'Social and Economic Position of Brahmins in Maharashtra in the Age of Shivaji', pp. 66–67, in *Proceedings of the Indian History Congress* 26, Part 2 (1964): 66–75. See also Marshall, *Bengal*, p. 15. So also in Rajasthan and Kathiawar, the Paliwal Brahmins were traders and bankers, as were Nagar Brahmins in Gujarat. Sometimes Brahmins were punished for giving up priestly vocations in favour of 'more remunerative' careers. See, for example, Divya Cherian, 'Ordering Subjects: Merchants, the State, and Krishna Devotion in Eighteenth-Century Marwar', Unpublished PhD dissertation, Columbia University (2015), p. 92. In late-medieval Andhra, there was already a bifurcation between Brahmins who performed religious work and those who pursued secular professions. See Talbot, *Precolonial India*, p. 57. Nor was this a new phenomenon: the Jataka Tales compiled 1500 years before refer to Brahmin 'caravan-guards, farmers, animal-herders, hawkers, carpenters, snake charmers, carriage drivers, and wheelmakers'. See Upinder Singh, *Ancient India: Culture of Contradictions* (New Delhi: Aleph Book Company, 2021), p. 14. A fourteenth-century Sanskrit work, the *Parasaramadhava*, also states that in the kali yuga, 'Brahmins are entitled in particular to

practice agriculture' and that 'trades and crafts' belonged to all castes: formal concession, that is, for Brahmins taking up various vocations. Quoted in Theodore Benke, 'The Sudracarasiromani of Krsna Sesa: A 16th Century Manual of Dharma for Sudras', Unpublished PhD dissertation, University of Pennsylvania (2010), p. 273. In 1880s Gujarat, it would be noted that of 300-odd professions, Brahmins were active in '[n]o less than 115'. See Bhatavadekar, *Census of Baroda*, p. 148. In Maharashtra, we find Brahmins involved even in the slave trade and making large profits. See Desai, *Social Life in Maharashtra under the Peshwas*, p. 56.

117  Buchanan, *Bihar*, p. 353.
118  Reference is to the Pirali and Hussaini Brahmins. See Aparna Bhattacharya, *Religious Movements of Bengal and their Socio-Economic Ideas (1800–1850)* (Patna: Aparna Bhattacharya, 1981), pp. 126–27.
119  Buchanan, *Bihar*, pp. 339–40. In Kerala, a parallel exists in the temple-drummer caste of Marars. In central Kerala, they are deemed superior to Sudra castes such as the Nairs; in the southern Kerala, the order is reversed. In Maharashtra, the Chandraseniya Kayastha Prabhu's caste went up and down at different times. See Deshpande, 'Ksatriyas in the Kali Age?' pp. 95–120. In Nepal, castes could be raised from 'impure' to 'clean' status, similarly, by political leaders. See Greenwold, 'Kingship and Caste', pp. 65–67.
120  Buchanan, *Bihar*, p. 310. Muslims in Bengal also participated in goddess worship, often shared rites with Hindus, consulted Hindu astrologers and visited temples. For an account of many such overlaps, see Jafar Sharif (G.A. Herklots trans.), *Islam in India or the Qanun-i-Islam* (New Delhi: Oriental Books, 1972 ed.). See also Swapna Liddle, *The Broken Script: Delhi Under the East India Company and the Fall of the Mughal Dynasty, 1803–1857* (New Delhi: Speaking Tiger, 2022), p. 147 for the British trying to impose the purdah on Mughal princesses in Delhi, based on their 'imperfect understanding' of reality, when in fact 'seclusion of women within the royal family was not particularly strict'.
121  See Kapadia, *In Praise of Kings*, p. 9.
122  *Seir Mutaqherin*, Vol. 3, pp. 184–85.
123  Ibid., p. 198. Lord Bentinck, future governor general, would agree, writing:

> We do not, we cannot, associate with the natives. We cannot see them in their houses and with their families. We are necessarily very much confined to our houses by the heat; all our wants and business which could create a greater intercourse . . . is done for us, and we are in fact strangers in the land.

Quoted in John Rosselli, *Lord William Bentinck: The Making of a Liberal Imperialist* (London: Sussex University Press & Chatto & Windus, 1974), p. 146.

124  Colonial historians recognized this. As John Kaye wrote, in a country with so many races, religions and differences, a 'veil of ignorance and obscurity' separated ruler from the ruler. See Kaye, *A History of the Sepoy War in India: 1857–58*, Vol. 1 (London: W.H. Allen & Co., 1880, 9th ed.), p. 510.

125 *Seir Mutaqherin*, Vol. 3, p. 200. He also notes how 'now that the English seldom visit or see any of us . . . to obtain justice is become a very difficult business, a very operose article'. See ibid., p. 170, and pp. 182–83.
126 Jon Wilson, *The Domination of Strangers: Modern Governance in Eastern India, 1780–1835* (London: Palgrave Macmillan, 2008).
127 *Seir Mutaqherin*, Vol. 3, p. 200. This depersonalization is usually dated to the reign of Lord Cornwallis in the 1790s as governor general though Ghulam Hussain sees it as beginning well before. See also ibid., p. 159, p. 162.
128 Ibid., pp. 188–89, p. 158. Ghulam Hussain also refers to Hindus and Muslims as 'brothers of one mother'. Hastings agreed in a sense that the Mughals did not interfere much with their Hindu subjects. See Davies, *Strange Destiny*, p. 83.
129 *Seir Mutaqherin*, Vol. 3, p. 161.
130 Ibid., pp. 185–86
131 Ibid., pp. 184–85.
132 Ibid., p. 185. Decades later, the famous Company diplomat-administrator John Malcolm expressed similar views when he wrote: 'The power exercised by British rulers has none of that prejudice in its favour which often supports hereditary monarchies and national governments, even at a period of decline.' Quoted in Harrington, *John Malcolm*, p. 153.
133 Indeed, Hastings himself would later speak with disapproval of some of his successor's innovations. See Ehrlich, 'Straddling the Imperial Meridian'.
134 Davies, *Warren Hastings*, p. 102.
135 G.R. Gleig ed., *Memoirs of The Life of Warren Hastings, First Governor-General of Bengal*, Vol. 1 (London: Richard Bentley, 1841), pp. 400–01. Interestingly, even Hastings's great foe at home, Edmund Burke, agreed. Hindus, Burke believed, had 'a law accurately written' and 'great principles of jurisprudence'. See David P. Fidler and Jennifer M. Walsh eds., *Empire and Community: Edmund Burke's Writings and Speeches on International Relations* (Boulder, Colorado: Westview Pres, 1999), p. 229.
136 Davies, *Warren Hastings*, p. 79.
137 Gleig, *Memoirs*, pp. 400–01.
138 Neeladri Bhattacharya, 'Remaking Custom: The Discourse and Practice of Colonial Codification', p. 22, in Champakalakshmi and Gopal eds., *Tradition, Dissent and Ideology*, pp. 20–51. For the political context in which talk of this ancient constitution emerged, see Wilson, *Domination*, pp. 50–52.
139 Prasad, *Poetics of Conduct*, p. 114. Reference is to the Sringeri Matha. A similar pattern occurs among Jains also in adapting prescriptive ideas to local custom. See Cherian, *Merchants of Virtue*, p. 125.
140 Ludo Rocher (Donald R. Davis ed.), *Studies in Hindu Law and Dharmasastra* (London: Anthem Press, 2012), p. 91.
141 Aiya, *Travancore State Manual*, Vol. 2, p. 259.

142  Because the lawbooks, when cited, were 'entrenched in specific temporal, geographic, social and political environments'. See Deshpande, 'Ksatriyas in the Kali Age?', p. 104. See also Dodson, *Orientalism, Empire and National Culture*, p. 45, and Richard W. Lariviere, 'Justices and Panditas: Some Ironies in Contemporary Readings of the Hindu Legal Past', p. 759, in *Journal of Asian Studies* 48, 4 (1989): 757–69, where we read how the texts were, among a certain elite, 'statements of theory' if not 'descriptions of practice'. See also Lariviere, 'Dharmasastra, 'Real Law' and 'Apocryphal' Smrtis', pp. 621–22, in *Journal of Indian Philosophy* 32, 5–6 (2004): 611–27 for an example of how the texts themselves emerged in response to specific issues. The *Devalasmriti*, for example, was composed after Islamic invasions into India, for converts to regain Hindu status.

143  Which also comes across in how textual ideas, for example on widow remarriage, might make later commentators uncomfortable, when social attitudes towards women changed. The text would acquire new readings. See Richard Lariviere, 'Dharmasastra, 'Real Law' and 'Apocryphal' Smrtis', p. 617.

144  Rocher, *Studies in Hindu Law*, p. 56. They were a 'scholarly and scholastic tradition, not a practical legal' one. Davis in ibid., pp. 18–19. One is reminded here also of Singh's observations on how in the Mahabharata the official norm is 'frequently ignored and transgressed'. Indeed, in the *Arthasastra*, she adds, while lip service is paid to Brahminical ideas, in a clash with practicalities, it is the practical that prevails. See Upinder Singh, *Political Violence in Ancient India* (Cambridge: Harvard University Press, 2017), pp. 66–73, p. 122. Equally, we have a story, albeit unverified, from eighteenth-century Maharashtra where a leading noble of the Peshwa's court found his daughter widowed while she was still a child. Permission for remarriage—customarily disallowed among Brahmins—was granted by leading legal scholars in Poona and Benares, but such scholarly sanction did not ultimately prevail over local custom. See M.G. Ranade, *Rise of the Maratha Power* (Bombay: Punalekar & Co., 1900), pp. 310–12.

145  Rocher, *Studies in Hindu Law*, p. 54.

146  Ibid., p. 116. See also See Wendie Ellen Schneider, *Engines of Truth: Producing Veracity in the Victorian Courtroom* (New Haven: Yale University Press), pp. 111–12.

147  Sumit Guha, 'An Indian Penal Regime: Maharashtra in the Eighteenth Century', pp. 112–15, in *Past & Present*, No. 147 (1995): 101–26. See also instances cited in C.J. Abhang, 'Two Unpublished Letters of Hon. Justice Ramshastary Prabhune, a Judge of the Peshwa 18th Century', *Proceedings of the Indian History Congress* 60 (1999): 465–72; Arvind Sharma, *Modern Hindu Thought: An Introduction* (New Delhi: Oxford University Press, 2005), pp. 151–53; and Fatima Ahmad Imam, 'Institutionalizing Rajadharma: Strategies of Sovereignty in the Eighteenth-Century Jaipur', Unpublished PhD dissertation, University of Toronto (2008), p. 211, p. 248.

148 Patrick Olivelle, 'Social and Literary History of Dharmasastra', pp. 18–19, in Olivelle and Donald R. Davis eds., *Hindu Law*, pp. 15–29. At moments, and in certain places, the texts may have had force, but broadly they were, a second scholar notes, 'legal fiction', 'divorced from the practical administration of justice'. See Ludo Rocher quoted in Donald R. Davis, 'Introduction', p. 4, in ibid., pp. 1–14. See also Nandini Bhattacharyya Panda, *Appropriation and Invention of Tradition: The East India Company and Hindu Law in Early Colonial Bengal* (New Delhi: Oxford University Press, 2008), chapter one.

149 Lariviere and Davis both argue that the *Dharmasastras* were not promulgated by ancient sages, as believed, but reflect records of customs in different places, at different times, gathered into Sanskrit texts. Davis notes for example that the *Sankarasmriti* popular among Brahmins in Kerala was composed in the fifteenth century, centuries after its supposed author, Sankara, to give the text 'an authority not otherwise possible'.

150 Lariviere, 'Justices and Panditas', p. 762. Steele in 1827 also observed how 'different interpretations are given of original text-books by different commentators' and so different tenets were 'held as authorities in different provinces of India'. See Arthur Steele, *The Law and Custom of Hindoo Castes within the Dekhun Provinces Subject to the Presidency of Bombay* (London: W.H. Allen & Co, 1868 ed.), pp. vii–viii.

151 In Bengal thus, 'Most litigants appearing before British district courts did not quote dharmasastra texts.' See Wilson, *Domination*, p. 84.

152 Ludo Rocher, 'Father Bouchet's Letter on the Administration of Hindu Law', pp. 18–20, in Richard W. Lariviere ed., *Studies in Dharmasastra* (Calcutta: Firma KLM Pvt. Ltd., 1984), pp. 15–48. Moreover, even texts such as Gautama's *Dharmasutra* urge that the 'laws of countries, castes, and families', so long as they did not clash with the orthodox position, have full authority. See Rocher, *Studies in Hindu Law*, p. 51. Of course, as Davis notes, while conformity with Vedic ideas was ideal, it was 'not necessarily a fact of history', because 'the standards of real people' could supersede orthodox norms. See Donald Richard Davis, 'The Boundaries of Law: Tradition, "Custom," and Politics in Late Medieval Kerala', Unpublished PhD dissertation, University of Texas at Austin (2000), p. 45. Greenwold in 'Caste and Kingship', pp. 55–56 also observes how Jayasthiti Malla, a fourteenth-century king in Nepal, even when he tried to introduce law based actively on Hindu normative texts, made concessions to Buddhist influences and other local practices. This inconsistency between the written record and practice appears in economic matters also. Written sources prescribed that the king collect one sixth of the peasant's produce in tax. But in practice there was variation. See T.V. Mahalingam, *South Indian Polity* (Madras: University of Madras, 1955), pp. 165–66, and Burton Stein, *Peasant State and Society in Medieval South India* (Delhi: Oxford University Press, 1980), pp. 258–59.

153  See L.S. Vishwanath, 'Efforts of Colonial State to Suppress Female Infanticide: Use of Sacred Texts, Generation of Knowledge', in *Economic and Political Weekly* 33, 19 (1998): 1104–12, and Malavika Kasturi, 'Taming the "Dangerous" Rajput: Family, Marriage and Female Infanticide in Nineteenth-Century Colonial North India', in Harald Fischer-Tine and Michael Mann eds., *Colonialism as Civilizing Mission: Cultural Ideology in British India* (London: Anthem Press, 2004), pp. 117–40. See also Cherian, *Merchants of Virtue*, p. 116, where we read how in Marwar in Rajputana, while infanticide was outlawed, this was not stressed in the same manner as other strictures. In fact, 'saving animal lives was a much higher priority than saving female infants'.

154  See Robert W. Stern, *The Cat and the Lion: Jaipur State in the British Raj* (Ahmedabad: Allied Publishers, 1988), pp. 102–05. This is, of course, not to say that all custom, among all groups everywhere was unwritten; custom could be written down just as it might exist in an unwritten format.

155  Similar patterns existed among India's Muslims also, so that as one medieval writer put it, 'what time has sanctioned, they never relinquish' even if outside of scriptural principles. The *Tarikh-i-Tahiri* quoted in Gyanendra Pandey, *The Construction of Communalism in Colonial North India* (Delhi: Oxford University Press, 1990), pp. 85–86.

156  As a later writer would record, the attitude was: 'We observe our own rules. In a case where there is no rule we ask the pundits.' See John D. Mayne, *A Treatise on Hindu Law and Usage* (Madras: Higginbotham & Co., 1878), p. 10.

157  Steele, *Law and Custom*, pp. 122–23. Emphasis added. See also V.T. Gune's *The Judicial System of the Marathas* (Poona: Deccan College Post-Graduate & Research Institute, 1953) where too we read (for instance p. 69) how, while Sanskrit lawbooks were referred to as needed, 'The mediaeval society gave more importance to tradition and custom than to the written law', and how 'customs of the different castes were scrupulously observed' and that 'the state was not allowed to interfere'.

158  Donald R. Davis, 'Recovering the Indigenous Legal Traditions of India: Classical Hindu Law in Practice in Late Medieval Kerala', p. 162, in *Journal of Indian Philosophy* 27, 3 (1999): 159–213. Davis elsewhere also notes that because his study of Kerala depends on written texts, 'it seems inevitable' that they may not represent all people. See Davis, 'The Boundaries of Law', p. vi. He also agrees on p. 116 that while in Kerala, with its strong Brahminism, the sastras were 'powerful' their influence was not 'total'. Or to quote Nedumpally, 'Brahminical domination acted as an *external* force' while 'within the boundary [of] these [other] caste groups', they had their own rules. See Nedumpally, 'Ways of Knowing: Asaris, Nampoothiris and Colonialists in Twentieth Century Malabar, India', Unpublished PhD dissertation, Emory University (2012), p. 111.

159 Even in military matters, the British did tend to 'transfer theories from one micro-environment to the subcontinent as a whole'. See Randolf G.S. Cooper, *The Anglo–Maratha Campaigns and the Contest for India: The Struggle for Control of the South Asian Military Economy* (Cambridge: Cambridge University Press, 2003), p. 137.

160 Steele, *Law and Custom*, p. 126. Wagle, 'Kotwal's Papers', and Anne B. Waters in 'Family Disputes, Family Violence: Reconstructing Women's Experience from Eighteenth-Century Historical Records', pp. 3–14, in Feldhaus, *Images*, study the Kotwal records of the Peshwas. These demonstrate that while the sastras recommended ways of handling crimes, to quote Waters, there was 'flexibility and pragmatism'. See also Elphinstone, *Report*, p. 53, where he notes that 'the custom of the country' dominated, and the Sastras were 'sometimes consulted . . . in cases connected with Religion'. See also ibid., p. 81 for another such remark.

161 Reference is to the case of Raghunathrao Peshwa, sentenced by Ramshastri Prabhune. The Peshwa system expected conformity to Sastric texts in Brahmins, but much depended on other factors, including affluence. See also Balkrishna Govind Gokhale, *Poona in the Eighteenth Century: An Urban History* (Delhi: Oxford University Press, 1988), pp. 167–69 on how sectarian, caste-related, sexual crimes, and other issues were handled under the Peshwas. See also Elphinstone, *Report*, pp. 55–57, where he states that any notion of Maharashtra as 'a complete scene of anarchy and violence' was inaccurate.

162 See Wagle, 'Kotwal's Papers', p. 30 for an example, and Surendra Nath Sen, *Administrative System of the Marathas* (Delhi: LG Publishers, 2021 ed.), p. 248 for another case of rape, where the Brahmin victim of a Muslim rapist was re-inducted into her caste after certain rites. For more on maintenance of law and order and police duties at village level in the Peshwa's country, see Elphinstone, *Report*, pp. 47–50. Elphinstone also wrote how 'Hindu law', which was 'our own introduction' in Bengal generated 'dread'. See Elphinstone, *Report*, p. 56, p. 71, and also Ballhatchet, *Social Policy and Social Change*, p. 31.

163 Rocher, 'Bouchet's Letter', pp. 20–21. This also matches a report by a British writer in Maharashtra. Observing local peasants, he wrote:

> . . . they are fond of conversation, discuss the merits of agriculture, the characters of their neighbours, and everything that relates to the concerns of the community, and many of them are not without a tolerable knowledge of the leading events of the history of their country. On the whole, they are better informed than the lower classes of our own countrymen.

See Thomas Coats, 'Account of the Present State of the Township of Lony', pp. 204–05, in *Transactions of the Literary Society of Bombay*, Vol. 3 (London: Longman, Hurst, Rees, Orme, Brown, & John Murray, 1823), pp. 183–280.

164 This appears also in the context of British sponsorship of grammars for Indian languages. When one colonial officer asked people in Faizabad in north

India if they had a Hindustani dictionary, they with 'astonishment' asked why 'men had to consult vocabularies . . . for their own vernacular speech.' Quoted in David Lelyvelt, 'The Fate of Hindustani: Colonial Knowledge and the Project of a National Language', p. 195, in Breckenridge and van der Veers eds., *Orientalism and the Postcolonial Predicament*, pp. 189–214.

165 This point was noted by the Company's British critics also. See Bolts, *Considerations*, p. 20, for example. For Mughal practice in Gujarat where too Hindus were left free to handle their civil matters, and even minor criminal matters were settled locally without involvement of a state-appointed Muslim qazi, see Pearson, *Merchants and Rulers*, p. 152.

166 See Eaton, *Bengal Frontier*, pp. 179–82.

167 Ibid., p. 182.

168 This, of course, also stemmed from political considerations of stability. As was recorded in Kerala in 1673 by a Dutch commander, the people were 'not bound to observe any orders, commands, or whims and council decisions of the king which are not in conformity with their [own] laws, welfare, or privileges, and have not been approved in their own district and ratified at the meeting of their district assemblies.' Quoted in Manu S. Pillai, *The Ivory Throne: Chronicles of the House of Travancore* (Noida: HarperCollins Publishers, 2015), p. 251.

169 Guha, 'An Indian Penal Regime', p. 110.

170 See also Elphinstone, *Report*, p. 81 where he notes that panchayats were 'often conducted in the way of conversation, and nothing was written but the decision, and sometimes not even that.'

171 See Cumming, 'Internal Administration'. See also Rocher, 'Bouchet's Letter'. Here (p. 31) we read the Jesuit's record in the early eighteenth century on how every village head is 'the natural judge' aided by 'three or four of the most experienced villagers'. Respondents could appeal to higher bodies. Caste matters were decided by caste assemblies, and religious gurus settled sectarian disputes. See also a case cited in Sumit Guha, *History & Collective Memory in South Asia: 1200–2000* (Ranikhet: Permanent Black and Ashoka University, 2019), p. 85. Finally, in 1807, Thomas Munro also advocated the use of panchayats because these were 'as much the common law of India . . . as that by jury in England. No native thinks that justice is done where it is not adopted'. Quoted in McLaren, 'Writing and Making History', pp. 278–79.

172 Dodson, *Orientalism, Empire and National Culture*, p. 45. Hastings evidently recognized this. See Gleig, *Memoirs*, p. 402.

173 Or as Guha writes, 'Customary rights might all too often be but ancient abuses.' See Sumit Guha, 'Wrongs and Rights in the Maratha Country: Antiquity, Custom and Power in Eighteenth-century India', p. 26, in Michael R. Anderson and Sumit Guha eds., *Changing Concepts of Rights and Justice in South Asia* (New Delhi: Oxford University Press, 2000), pp. 14–29.

189  Gleig, *Memoirs*, p. 400.
190  Ibid., p. 402.
191  Nathaniel B. Halhed, *A Code of Gentoo Laws, Or, Ordinations of the Pundits from a Persian Translation, made from the Original Written in the Shanscrit Language* (London: 1776), p. x. He also notes, however, that he and Hastings had tried, and failed, to persuade the pandits to teach him Sanskrit (p. xxxvi). At this time, in fact, a lot of European sponsors of translations worked through Persian. In 1784, Hastings would commission a second Sanskrit work called the *Puranartha Prakasa*, which was translated into Persian two years later, and *then* into English by Halhed. Jonathan Duncan also obtained access to Puranic texts via Persian. See Carl W. Ernst, 'Muslim Studies', pp. 187–90 for more on British-era Persian translations of Hindu texts.
192  Halhed, *Code*, p. ix.
193  Ibid., p. xii. Personally too, Halhed was an Enlightenment man. He saw 'similitude' between Brahmin ideas and Abrahamic ones, adding how there was a 'wonderful Correspondence' between Hindu law and the Institutes of Moses. Indeed, even Bengal's dancing girls behaved like the 'Women of Israel' of Judaic lore. ibid., p. xxxvii, p. lx.
194  See J.H. Nelson, *A View of the Hindu Law as Administered by the High Court of Judicature at Madras* (Madras: Higginbotham & Co., 1877), pp. 27–28.
195  Mayne, *Treatise on Hindu Law*, p. 30.
196  Ibid., pp. 30–31.
197  Wilson, *Domination*, pp. 58–65. On different coping mechanisms by white judges, see ibid., pp. 86–90.
198  Metcalf, *Ideologies*, p. 23, and Dodson, *Orientalism, Empire and National Culture*, p. 56. See also Wilson, *Domination*, p. 83. (See however also Wilson, *Domination*, pp. 79–83 for an analysis of William Jones's attempt to create the *Digest* without sacrificing legal dynamism to rigid textualism.) As a judge in Bengal complained, in its 'pure and original state', Hindu law appeared straightforward. But the whole thing was so encumbered with commentaries and conflicting interpretations, that, combined with the 'venality' of pandits, it had become unsettled. Quoted in Lariviere, 'Justices and Panditas', p. 762. Steele echoed his views, noting how court Brahmins could be 'biased by sinister influence'; there was no way a white judge could decide how truthful they were being. Steele, *Law and Custom*, p. iii. In 1823, the governor of Bombay, for this very reason, grumbled that honesty and learning among pandits was 'not now common' and was becoming rarer still.
199  Rocher, 'British Orientalism', p. 238. See also Bayly, *Empire and Information*, pp. 6–7, where he speaks of the British fear of the 'wiles of the natives', and how 'colonial knowledge was derived ... from indigenous knowledge, albeit torn out of context and distorted by fear and prejudice'.
200  See Mayne, *Treatise on Hindu Law*, p. 36 and Umamaheshwari, *Reading History with the Tamil Jainas*, pp. 60–61.

201 The pattern continued in the Bombay Presidency: Steele in the 1820s responded to official desire for 'a book of information' to serve as a 'complete code of laws sanctioned by Government'. The intention was to identify rules 'binding on all Hindoos' and to separate them from those specific to castes or local in nature. See Steele, *Law and Custom*, p. xviii.

202 Letter dated 10 October 1811 from Col. John Munro to Chief Sec., Govt. of Madras, IOR/F/4/385/9798.

203 Such 'chaos' was visible with Muslims also. In the 1780s, in Benares when the British consulted local authorities as to how the Mughals punished forgery, they were told that it depended on the judge, the criminal's status and 'whether it was a season of scarcity or plenty; whether . . . forgeries were very prevalent', or not, and so on. See Radhika Singha, *A Despotism of Law: Crime and Justice in Early Colonial India* (New Delhi: Oxford University Press, 1998), pp. 11–12.

204 *Seir Mutaqherin*, Vol. 3, p. 29.

205 Agrawal, *Kabir, Kabir*, p. 130.

206 Quoted in Alexander J. Arbuthnot, *Major-General Sir Thomas Munro: Selections from his Minutes and Other Official Writings*, Vol. 2 (London: C. Kegan Paul & Co., 1881), p. 4. Of course, the idea of the panchayat as a 'traditional' institution went through its own mutations. See James Jaffe, *Ironies of Colonial Governance: Law, Custom and Justice in Colonial India* (Cambridge: Cambridge University Press, 2015).

207 In this, his views matched Thomas Munro's who wrote how the British tried 'to better the condition of the people, with hardly any knowledge of the means by which it was to be accomplished'. See Munro, 'On the Condition of Southern India', in *Asiatic Journal* 3 (New Series) (London: Parbury, Allen & Co., 1830), p. 233.

208 James Cumming, 'Internal Administration'. Malcolm shared similar views. By 'vexing and disturbing' local systems, and 'introducing principles of rule foreign to all their usages', the British risked rousing the 'restless and bold spirits of the country'. Quoted in Harrington, *John Malcolm*, p. 141.

209 Nelson, *A View of the Hindu Law*, p. 2, p. 15. In fact, even when customary law *was* given recognition, British authorities textualized it as against allowing fluidity. See, for instance, Bhattacharya, 'Remaking Custom'. Lord Dalhousie condensed the principle at play when he said: 'It is possible . . . to domestic[ate] primitive law: you can redeem it from barbarism without killing it down.'

210 See the judgment in *Kattama Nachiar vs. Dorasinga Tevar* in P.O. Sullivan and J.M.C. Mills ed., *Reports of Cases Decided in the High Court of Madras in 1870 and 1871* (Madras: Higginbotham & Co., 1872), p. 341. Others also noticed this. Rudolph & Rudolph, 'Barristers', pp. 33–34, quote Judge Julius Jolly: 'It is quite true that before the establishment of British rule in India, customary law used to be given more weight in deciding law suits than . . . any

other digest. Most quarrels did not come within the cognizance of the Courts at all, but were decided by private arbitration.' Rachel Sturman also points out how publication of Henry Maine's *Ancient Law* (1861) was an important milestone in the recognition of custom, as well as the 1868 *Collector of Madura vs. Mootoo Ramalinga Sathupathy* privy council ruling where it was held that 'under the Hindu system of law clear proof of usage will outweigh the written text'. See Sturman, *The Government of Social Life in Colonial India: Liberalism, Religious Law, and Women's Rights* (Cambridge: Cambridge University Press, 2012), p. 152. The British judge J.H. Nelson also posed the question:

> Has such a thing as 'Hindu Law' at any time existed in the world . . . For myself I have always been unable to bring myself to believe that the innumerable non-Muhammadan tribes and castes of India have at any time agreed to accept . . . an aggregate of positive laws.

See Nelson, *A View of the Hindu Law*, p. 2. See also pp. 12–13, where he notes the eclipsing of usage, and how white judges, basing their knowledge on translations, were expected to work 'Hindu law'. For another note on practical constraints faced by British judges in interpreting and applying Hindu law, see T. Goldstucker, *On the Deficiencies in the Present Administration of Hindu Law* (London: Trubner & Co., 1871). For a 'native' critique of the British judicial system in 1831, see Rammohun Roy, 'Questions and Answers on the Judicial System of India' in Bruce Carlisle Robertson ed., *The Essential Writings of Raja Rammohan Ray* (Delhi: Oxford University Press, 1999), pp. 197–225.

211 Some of this comes across in contemporary Indian writing. Soon after Hastings claimed he was governing India according to its traditions, Ghulam Hussain, the Mughal critic, wrote in 1786 that the British were *importing* customs from their country. See *Seir Mutaqherin*, Vol. 3, p. 162. However, not all such efforts were ill-designed.

212 In 1815, Charles Metcalfe admitted as much when he that stated that 'sufficient attention' was not paid to 'local usages'. Yes, a 'simple[r] and a more summary' style was 'better suited' to the land. But by then the system was too far gone and overthrowing it would be inconvenient. Besides, Indians were also at fault, he added, by 'labouring to deceive' judges. See letter dated 12 December 1815 from Charles Metcalfe, Resident at Delhi, to C.M. Ricketts, Secretary to the Governor General, pp. 36–37 in *Modification of the Judicial System*. A judge also advised that small cases be left to local officers and Indian authorities by which 'people would be driven to settle their little disputes among themselves; and the mischiefs attending the numerous petty Courts scattered over the country with their knots of law intriguing retainers would be avoided.' See James Stuart's Minute in ibid., p. 18. See also Nelson, *A View of the Hindu Law*, p. 15 for later criticism of how 'Hindu law' was continued simply because it was by then established.

213 Francis Workman Macnaghten, *Considerations on the Hindoo Law, as it is Current in Bengal* (Serampore: Baptist Mission Press, 1824), p. vi. One

is reminded here of a scholar's remark that 'Codification as a process of rewriting tradition was carried through not by self-assured imperial minds confident of their strategies and goals, but by minds troubled by self-doubt and anxieties', not least of which was the sense of impotence that dependence on native informants generated. See Neeladri Bhattacharya, 'Remaking Custom', p. 49.
214 *Seir Mutaqherin*, Vol. 3, pp. 191–92.
215 Or as Lord Curzon would eventually write in his trademark racist tone, 'the normal Asiatic would sooner be misgoverned by Asiatics than well governed by Europeans.'
216 Robert James Mackintosh ed., *Memoirs of the Life of James Mackintosh*, Vol. 1 (London: Edward Moxon, 1836), p. 285.
217 Gokhale, *Poona*, p. 40.
218 Ibid., p. 57, p. 65, p. 86.
219 As one writer sharply put it, the Marathas at this juncture 'bore less resemblance to a confederacy' and more 'to a sack of rabid ferrets'. See Ferdinand Mount, *The Tears of the Rajas: Mutiny, Money and Marriage in India 1805–1905* (London: Simon & Schuster, 2015), p. 185.
220 Govind Sakharam Sardesai, *New History of the Marathas: Sunset Over Maharashtra (1772–1848)*, Vol. 3 (Bombay: Phoenix Publications, 1948), p. 328.
221 Ibid., p. 327. See also ibid., p. 338 and p. 394 where we hear of the Peshwa suffering an 'unmentionable disease'.
222 Mount, *Tears of the Rajas*, p. 194.
223 As late as 1803, the Maratha infantry had been very potent, especially under the Scindias of Gwalior, and the quality of their artillery superior to that of the Company. But the latter was able to orchestrate defections and bring about a collapse in the military leadership, also cornering financial support. See Cooper, *The Anglo–Maratha Campaigns*.
224 Quoted in Sardesai, *New History*, Vol. 3, p. 496.
225 Mount, *Tears of the Rajas*, p. 216.
226 Ibid., p. 217.
227 Pratul C. Gupta, *Baji Rao II and the East India Company: 1796–1818* (Oxford: Humphrey Milford Oxford University Press, 1923), p. 203.
228 Recounted in Ursula Low, *Fifty Years with John Company: From the Letters of General Sir John Low of Clatto, Fife: 1822–1858* (London: John Murray, 1936), p. 1. For more on the Peshwa's life in exile, see Gupta, *Last Peshwa*. On the rebellion referred to see S.P. Desai, 'A Little Known Rising'.
229 So much so that K.M. Panikkar called Travancore 'a Tamilian conception' and the 'victory of Tamilian over Kerala culture'. See Panikkar, *A History of Kerala: 1498–1801* (Annamalainagar: The Annamalai University, 1960), pp. 258–59. See also Pillai, *Ivory Throne*, p. 252, p. 258, p. 311. 'Brahmin domination' (by this time of Tamil Brahmins) and 'hatred' on the part

of locals was acknowledged by Travancore's minister as late as 1937, and of thirty-seven department heads, twenty-three were Brahmins. See A. Sreedhara Menon, *Triumph and Tragedy in Travancore: Annals of Sir CP's Sixteen Years* (Kottayam: Current Books, 2001), p. 72, p. 86.

230 To quote Velcheru Narayana Rao, 'Here is a class of people, unlike any other class, who are unusually mobile, in a sense uninterested in acquiring roots in any locality, and therefore no threat to any local peasant or landowner.' Quoted in Rao, 'Coconut and Honey', p. 26.

231 Phillip B. Wagoner, 'Precolonial Intellectuals and the Production of Colonial Knowledge', pp. 796–97, in *Comparative Studies in Society and History* 45, 4 (2003): 783–814.

232 Pillai, *Rebel Sultans*, pp. 196–200. Even the Sikh emperor, Ranjit Singh, would give 'preferment' to Brahmins. See Susan Bayly, *Caste, Society and Politics in India*, p. 66. Then there were cases like that of the Peshwas in Pune—themselves Chitpavan Brahmins from Konkan—who having acquired power, cemented it by importing castemen from their ancestral region to constitute a socio-political and economic network. See Gokhale, *Poona*, p. 6, pp. 109–12.

233 Krishnadevaraya's *Amuktamalyada* quoted in Velcheru Narayana Rao, *Texts and Tradition in South India* (Ranikhet: Permanent Black in association with Ashoka University, 2016), pp. 116–17. See also Rao, Shulman and Subrahmanyam, 'A New Imperial Idiom', p. 83, p. 88. Additionally, bringing in a preferred sect through patronage, land grants and by introducing them into major temples, the emperor created a religious frame to back political goals. As Stoker observes, these 'institutions came to function as courtly outposts, rest stations, and targeted locations for strategic development', especially in conquered areas. While the Brahmins, thus, obtained platforms to propagate their beliefs, their monasteries served the imperial cause of stability. See Valerie Stoker, *Polemics and Patronage in the City of Victory: Vyasatirtha, Hindu Sectarianism, and the Sixteenth-Century Vijayanagara Court* (Oakland: University of California Press, 2016), pp. 8–9. In eighteenth-century Marwar, however, instead of Brahmins we find rulers making use of (also mobile) merchant castes to shore up power against hereditary kinsmen and chiefs. See Cherian, *Merchants of Virtue*.

234 See Ramasswami, *Viswaguna Darsana*, p. 49 for example. This was not a new state of affairs. In the *Lingapurana* also we read how in the kali yuga, kings were mostly Sudras, Brahmins 'behave like Sudras', Brahmins were dependent on Sudras, etc. The *Kurmapurana* complains how the twice-born would stand like supplicants before Sudras and wait on them. Quoted in Benke, 'The Sudracarasiromani', pp. 123–24.

235 Kruijtzer, *Xenophobia*, p. 232.

236 Ibid., pp. 112–13.

237  See David Washbrook, 'The Maratha Brahmin model in south India: An Afterword', in *Indian Economic and Social History Review* 47, 4 (2010): 597–615 for a brief study of the transition of Deccan Brahmins from religious to secular purposes under various rulers, including the Company. See also James William Ballantine Dykes, *Salem: An Indian Collectorate* (London: W.H. Allen & Co., 1853), p. 322 where we read how Maratha Brahmins were 'eager to swell the revenue of the English Government'.

238  Reference is to Dewan Purniah. See Nigel Hugh Mosman Chancellor, 'Mysore: The Making and Unmaking of a Model State, c. 1799–1834', Unpublished PhD dissertation, University of Cambridge (2002), pp. 121–22. See also Sebastian Joseph, 'A Service Elite Against the Peasants: Encounter and Collision (Mysore 1799–1831)', in *Proceedings of the Indian History Congress* 41 (1980): 670–81.

239  See Manu S. Pillai, *False Allies: India's Maharajahs in the Age of Ravi Varma* (New Delhi: Juggernaut, 2021), pp. 68–69.

240  Resident in Travancore to Acting Chief Sec., Madras, 15 March 1843, IOR/F/4/2047/93291.

241  Venkat Row, N. Thiagarajan ed.), *Manual of the Pudukkottai State* (Pudukkottai: Sri Brihadamba State Press, 1921), p. 105. Things were so altered by the Maratha Brahmins, in fact, that state papers in Pudukkottai too came to be kept in Marathi. In Mysore too Purniah introduced so many friends and relatives, that they became a powerful class, loyal only to themselves, triggering insurrection. See Chancellor, 'Mysore', for more and also T. Hawker, W. Morison, J.M. Macleod, & M. Cubbon, *Report on the Insurrection in Mysore (December 1833)* (Bangalore: Mysore Government Press, 1858). The imported Brahmins in Mysore had, the report recorded (p. 71), 'engrossed almost all offices of any importance' by the 1830s.

242  Washbrook, 'The Maratha Brahmin', p. 608.

243  Robert Eric Frykenberg, 'The Administration of Guntur District With Special Reference to Locals Influences on Revenue Policy: 1837–1848', PhD Thesis (1961), School of Oriental and African Studies, p. 263.

244  Ballantine Dykes, *Salem*, 324. In north India, similarly, elite Muslims held similar positions as late as the 1880s. See Avril Ann Powell, *Muslims & Missionaries in Pre-Mutiny India* (Surrey: Curzon Press, 1993), p. 58. On this point, see also Richard I. Cashman, *The Myth of the Lokamanya: Tilak and Mass Politics in Maharashtra* (Berkeley: University of California Press, 1975), p. 17 where he writes:

> An elite performs a highly useful function for a colonial power. From its numbers are drawn bureaucrats to help in the task of administration and to interpret colonial rule to indigenous society, providing a model of the type of behaviour which the rulers hope might be emulated by other groups of the society. In return the elite hopes that it may be recognized

as the legitimate spokesman of its society and may enjoy a continuing flow of benefits from the colonial power.

245 Nathaniel B. Halhed, 'The Bramin and the River Ganges', in Rosane Rocher, 'Alien and Emphatic: The Indian Poems of N.B. Halhed', pp. 217–19, in Blair B. King and M.N. Pearson eds., *The Age of Partnership: Europeans in Asia before Dominion* (Honolulu: The University Press of Hawaii, 1979), pp. 215–36. Halhed's overwrought claims were divorced from the facts, of course, for from Akbar's day, the Mughals had been keen consumers of Sanskrit—it was Dara Shukoh's Persian translation that granted Europeans access to the Upanishads for the first time, for example. See Truschke, *Culture of Encounters*, and Supriya Gandhi, *The Emperor Who Never Was*, for detailed discussions on patronage of Sanskrit at the Mughal court. See also Stephen Cross, 'Turning to the East: How the Upanishads reached the West', in *India International Centre Quarterly*, Vol. 25, Nos. 2–3 (1998): 123–29. Halhed, of course, in the context of Brahmins picking up linguistic innovations of the Mughals called them people 'whose ambition' had 'overpowered their principles', giving us a hint of what he would have made of more intellectual cooperation between the two. See his *Grammar*, p. xii.

246 Halhed, *Code*, p. 4.

247 Ibid.

248 Decades later, in 1825, another Brahmin with a history of Company employment, proclaimed also how Hindus had the British to thank for 'judiciously and unequivocally' reconciling 'conflicting interpretations' of their 'ancient laws'—a turn they themselves had not made in all these ages. Ramasswami, *Viswaguna Darsana*, 'Dedication', p. iii.

249 See 'Bengali Pandits of Benares on Warren Hastings', in Sen and Mishra eds., *Sanskrit Documents*, pp. 75–79 (pp. 11–16 for the Sanskrit original).

250 Ibid., pp. 66–67 (pp. 5–10 for the Sanskrit original). Another pandit, at the start of a 1783 work on the Puranas sponsored by the governor general praised Hastings as 'king of kings', representative of the gods, and even interpreted his name as *Hestina*, meaning 'the man who always clearly (*ha*) fulfils the wishes (*ista*) of all people.' Rosane Rocher, 'The Career of Radhakanta Tarkavagisa, an Eighteenth-Century Pandit in British Employ', p. 628, in *Journal of the American Oriental Society*, 109, 4 (1989): 627–33.

251 This marble statue of Hastings with the Brahmin and the maulvi are still visible in the Victoria Memorial in present-day Kolkata.

252 Ramasswami, *Viswaguna Darsana*, 'Dedication', p. iii. See also McLaren, 'Writing and Making History', p. 183 where Malcolm notes how the 'more intelligent' Brahmins 'differ little from Europeans' in ideas of justice, politics and finance. Dirks notes how 'what was useful for British rule also became available for the uses of many Indians who were recruited to participate in one way or another in the construction of colonial knowledge.' See Nicholas

Dirks, *Castes of Mind: Colonialism and the Making of Modern India* (Princeton: Princeton University Press, 2001), p. 14. See also Wilson, *Domination*, p. 99 for another instance of pandits taking a textualist approach.

253   Robert Needham Cust, *Pictures of Indian Life: Sketched with the Pen from 1852 to 1881* (London: Trubner & Co., 1881), p. 96. The rajahs of Pudukkottai were Kallars, or of 'robber caste'; the Holkars, Maratha rulers of Indore, were Dhangars, or shepherds; the Nayaka kings of the post-Vijayanagara successor states were Sudras; and even in states like Travancore, where the rajah claimed to be a Kshatriya, this claim was dubious.

254   Hugh Pearson, *Memoirs of the Life and Correspondence of the Reverend Christian Frederick Swartz*, Vol. 2 (London: J. Hatchard & Son, 1839), p. 263.

255   Minute by Governor General Cornwallis dated 17 May 1793 in Charles Cornwallis (Charles Ross ed.), *Correspondence of Charles, First Marquis Cornwallis*, Vol. 2 (London: John Murray, 1859), pp. 562–64. Furthermore, the pandits hired were to record opinions on how far 'the authority of custom' could hold 'when different from the ordination of the Shaster.'

256   Ibid.

257   Pearson, *Memoirs*, p. 266.

258   Ibid., p. 277. See also K.K. Rajayyan, *A History of British Diplomacy in Tanjore* (Mysore: Rao & Raghavan, 1969), pp. 104–05. Similarly, among Pahari Rajputs of the Himalayan foothills, while sati—widow burning—was valourized, implementation was infrequent. But in the nineteenth century, a rani would be barred from acting as regent because a rival faction convinced the British she had lost status by refusing to die with her husband in keeping with 'tradition'! See Arik Moran, *Kingship and Polity on the Himalayan Borderland: Rajput Identity during the Early Colonial Encounter* (Amsterdam: Amsterdam University Press, 2019), p. 107.

259   George, Viscount Valentia, *Voyages and Travels to India, Ceylon, The Red Sea, Abyssinia, and Egypt*, Vol. 1 (London: William Miller, 1809), p. 355. Such confusion vexed Muslims also: when Tipu Sultan's wives expressed a desire to be buried at the same place as their dead husband on the grounds of custom, the request was denied because some imagined pristine version of 'Muslim law' did not certify the practice. See Kate Brittlebank, *Tipu Sultan's Search for Legitimacy: Islam and Kingship in a Hindu Domain* (Delhi: Oxford University Press, 1997), p. 97.

260   For another example, see Pamela G. Price, *Kingship and political practice in colonial India* (Cambridge: Cambridge University Press, 1996), pp. 66–67. See also Price, 'Acting in public' for another case.

261   Vakils of the Travancore Rajah to the Governor General, in Political Proceedings, Fort William, 12 February 1810, in Minto Papers, MS 11582, National Library of Scotland.

262   It was late though; he died shortly after.

263  Cohn, *Colonialism and Its Forms*, p. 16.
264  Indeed, decades later, as Nairs in Kerala clamoured for 'reform' and the end of the matrilineal system (seen, after Victorian influences, as unnatural), some would pick up the sastras as a justification for making such a radical shift in local culture, and to bring things in line with pan-Indian—and more generically Hindu—patrilineal practices. See K.R. Krishna Menon's testimony in *Report of the Malabar Marriage Commission* (Madras: Lawrence Asylum Press, 1891), p. 46. See also p. 10 (where we read how matriliny had no 'code') and how the committee studying the subject could with difficulty find only one thirty-seven-year-old copy of a Sanskrit text—the *Keralamahatmyam*—which offered some textual certification for local practices. In this time, Nair marriage itself would be questioned, with some arguing that because it had no basis in the sastras, it was not marriage at all. Efforts to invent a basis did not cease, however. As was stated some years later, there were men taking 'considerable pains' to '[dive] into Sastraic lore to find a Sastraic origin' for matriliny. It was akin to striving 'to extract sunbeans out of [a] cucumber'. See *Report of the Nair Regulation Committee of Cochin* (Ernakulam: Cochin Government Press, 1920), p. cxv.
265  This, of course, is on the pan-Indian scale. In provinces such as Bengal, the census threw up surprises when it revealed that Muslims existed in far greater numbers than imagined. See Rafiuddin Ahmed, *The Bengal Muslims, 1871–1906: A Quest for Identity* (Delhi: Oxford University Press, 1981), p. 1.
266  Bhagat, 'Census and the Construction of Communalism', p. 4353.

## Four: 'An Indian Renaissance'

1  George Smith, *Bishop Heber: Poet and Chief Missionary to the East, Second Lord Bishop of Calcutta, 1783–1826* (London: John Murray, 1895), p. 229, p. 234.
2  J.W.B., *The Life and Writings of Bishop Heber: The Great Missionary to Calcutta, the Scholar, the Poet, and the Christian* (Boston: Albert Colby & Company, 1861), p. 305.
3  Heber quoted in Savithri Preetha Nair, *Raja Serfoji II: Science, Medicine and Enlightenment in Tanjore* (New Delhi: Routledge, 2012), p. 22.
4  J.W.B., *Life and Writings*, p. 308. Emphasis added.
5  The skeleton was really made of wood, of a kind and finish that gave it the *look* of ivory. See Nair, *Raja Serfoji*, p. 35. An actual ivory skeleton was made by Rajah Uthram Tirunal in Travancore decades later.
6  J.W.B., *Life and Writings*, pp. 307–08.
7  Thomas Middleton quoted in Nair, *Raja Serfoji*, p. 20.
8  George Annesley, *Voyages and Travels to India, Ceylon, the Red Sea, Abyssinia, and Egypt*, Vol. 1 (London: William Miller, 1809), pp. 358–61.
9  Rajayyan, *Tanjore*, p. 86.

10  Minute by Governor General Cornwallis dated 17 May 1793 in Charles Cornwallis (Charles Ross ed.), *Correspondence of Charles, First Marquis Cornwallis*, Vol. 2 (London: John Murray, 1859), p. 563.
11  Quoted in Nair, *Raja Serfoji*, p. 3.
12  Quoted in Indira Viswanathan Peterson, 'Tanjore Renaissance: King Serfoji and the Making of Modern South India', unpublished manuscript, chapter 1.
13  The Tanjore rajahs were not, originally, favourable to missionaries, as we know from Ziegenbalg's foiled attempts to enter their territory. Shahu I (r. 1684–1712) was called the 'Nero of Tanjore' and his successor Serfoji I (1712–28) too was hostile. However, Indian converts like Rajanayakan, a military man of the Parayar caste, managed to serve as proxies; by the end of the 1720s, there were 367 Protestants in the vicinity of Tanjore fort, and in the 1740s, Rajanayakan opened a school inside the city. See Hudson, *Protestant Origins*, pp. 45–47. A high-caste convert Aaron (Arumugham Pillai) became the first Protestant pastor in India, also ordained by the Tranquebar missionaries. He too enjoyed freedom of movement in Tanjore (ibid., pp. 30–31).
14  Pearson, *Memoirs*, 263. Schwartz had a personal dislike of the rajah: he had denied Schwartz's request for a mission school in 'a very idolatrous place', seeing the father 'as an enemy'. Jesse Page, *Schwartz of Tanjore* (London: Society for Promoting Christian Knowledge, 1921), pp. 131–32, p. 134.
15  One charge against Ameer Sing, the sitting rajah, was that he was of illegitimate birth. But earlier in the eighteenth century also, there had been a rajah whose mother was a 'sword wife'. The issue really was the rajah's hesitation in 1796 to transfer three districts to the Company. British troops surrounded the palace to force his pen—it was only because the Bengal authorities were embarrassed that status quo was restored afterwards. Rajayyan, *Tanjore*, pp. 101–03. See also Governor General John Shore's letter dated 5 July 1796 to Henry Dundas in Holden Furber ed., *The Private Record of an Indian Governor-Generalship: The Correspondence of Sir John Shore, Governor-General, with Henry Dundas, President of the Board of Control, 1793-1798* (Cambridge: Harvard University Press, 1933), pp. 102–03.
16  This was how Serfoji recalled Schwartz to Bishop Heber. See J.W.B, *Life and Writings*, p. 304. On Schwartz's death, Serfoji commissioned a marble sculpture showing him at the missionary's bedside in his final moments.
17  Minute by Thomas Munro dated 24 July 1821 in Thomas Munro (Alexander J. Arbuthnot ed.), *Major-General Sir Thomas Munro: Governor of Madras: Selections from his Minutes and Other Official Writings*, Vol. 2 (London: C. Kegan Paul & Co., 1881), p. 87.
18  Nair, *Raja Serfoji*, p. 18.
19  C.K. Srinivasan, *Maratha Rule in the Carnatic* (Annamalainagar: Annamalai University, 1944), p. 134.

20  Sanjay Subrahmanyam, *Penumbral Visions*, p. 147, where we read of this claim made in the *Bhosalavamsavali* by Venkatakavi. Ayyaval's *Sahendravilasa* also contains this. See Ayyaval (V. Raghavan ed.), *Sahendravilasa: A Poem on the Life of King Sahaji of Tanjore, 1684–1710* (Tanjore: T.M.S.S.M. Library, 1952), p. 6.
21  Nair, *Raja Serfoji*, p. 103. The Tanjore Marathas styled themselves Choladesadhipathi, Cholabhupathi and Cholasimhasanadhipathi (Lords of Chola country) and after a pilgrimage in 1801, Serfoji consecrated in the great temple 108 lingams brought from different parts of the region.
22  The terms come from Indira Viswanathan Peterson and Savithri Preetha Nair, respectively.
23  Nair, *Raja Serfoji*, p. xviii.
24  Indira Viswanathan Peterson, 'The schools of Serfoji II of Tanjore: Education and princely modernity in early nineteenth-century India', p. 18, p. 21, in Michael S. Dodson and Brian A. Hatcher eds., *Trans-Colonial Modernities in South Asia* (Abingdon: Routledge, 2012), pp. 15–44.
25  Heber quoted in Nair, *Raja Serfoji*, p. 22.
26  Viswanathan Peterson, 'The schools of Serfoji', p. 22.
27  Ibid.
28  Ibid.
29  Ibid., p. 26. As always, however, 'untouchables' were not permitted.
30  Soobrow, *Kishun Koovur: A Tragedy in Five Acts* (Trevandrum: Government Press, 1840). See also Savithri Preetha Nair, ' "Of real use to the people": The Tanjore printing press and the spread of useful knowledge', pp. 516–17, in *Indian Economic and Social History Review* 48, 4 (2011): 497–529. The Travancore rajahs taught by Subba Rao were Swathi Tirunal and Uthram Tirunal. For more, see Pillai, *False Allies*, chapter one. Serfoji also sent Rao to Tranquebar to study experiments with electricity. See Savithri Preetha Nair, 'Native Collecting and Natural Knowledge', p. 293, in *Journal of the Royal Asiatic Society* (Third Series) 15, 3 (2005): 279–302.
31  Some missionaries and white men did also try, of course, but their use of Indian languages was mechanical, limited and unidiomatic, drawing criticism.
32  Indira Viswanathan Peterson, 'Tanjore, Tranquebar, and Halle: European Science and German Missionary Education in the Lives of Two Indian Intellectuals in the Early Nineteenth Century', p. 109, in Robert Eric Frykenberg, *Christians and Missionaries*, pp. 93–126.
33  Ibid., p. 118.
34  Pradeep Chakravarthy, 'India's Best-Kept Secret: The Sarasvati Mahal', p. 13, in *the India International Centre Occasional Publication* 28 (2011).
35  See Serfoji (T.L. Thyagaraja Jatavallabhar ed.), *Devendra Kuravanji by Serfoji Rajah* (Tanjore: S. Gopalan, 1950). Australia though is missing from Serfoji's portrait of the world.

36  Quoted in Viswanathan Peterson, 'Tanjore, Tranquebar, and Halle', p. 118.
37  Ibid., p. 106.
38  Hudson, *Protestant Origins*, p. 131. See also Padma Rangarajan, *Imperial Babel: Translation, Exoticism, and the Long Nineteenth Century* (New York: Fordham University Press, 2014), p. 70.
39  Hudson, *Protestant Origins*, p. 135.
40  Nair, *Raja Serfoji*, p. 22.
41  Ibid., p. 40. For more on Serfoji's medical experiments, see Nair, 'Native Collecting', pp. 287–91.
42  Nair, *Raja Serfoji*, p. xxxii.
43  Viswanathan Peterson, *Tanjore Renaissance*, Introduction. A descendant of the rajah, Pratap Sinh Bhosle in *Contributions of Thanjavur Maratha Kings* (Chennai: Notion Press, 2017), p. ix, refers to as many as 50,000 manuscripts.
44  Viswanathan Peterson, *Tanjore Renaissance*, chapter four. For more on Serfoji's patronage of Western music see Takako Inoue, 'The Reception of Western Music in South India around 1800', research paper presented at the 'Orient on Orient: Images of Asia in Eurasian Countries' symposium (2010) at http://src-h.slav.hokudai.ac.jp/rp/publications/no13/13_2-3_Inoue_mono.pdf. See also Indira Viswanathan Peterson, 'King Serfoji II of Thanjavur and European Music', in *Journal of the Music Academy Madras* 84 (2013): 57–71.
45  Resident Blackburne, quoted in Nair, 'The Tanjore printing press', p. 525.
46  Nair, *Raja Serfoji*, p. 23, and Nair, 'The Tanjore printing press', p. 515. See also Stuart Blackburn, *Print, Folklore, and Nationalism in Colonial South India* (Delhi: Permanent Black, 2003), p. 73.
47  Viswanathan Peterson, *Tanjore Renaissance*, Introduction.
48  Nair, *Raja Serfoji*, p. 33.
49  Ibid., p. 30.
50  Ibid., p. 88.
51  Ibid., p. 75.
52  Ibid., p. 115. See also Nair, 'Native Collecting', pp. 298–301.
53  Viswanathan Peterson, *Tanjore Renaissance*, chapter four.
54  Viswanathan Peterson explains the significance of pilgrimage to the rajah's self-image and kingly legitimacy in 'The Sequence of King Sarabhendra's sacred places: Pilgrimage and Kingship in a Marathi text from 19th-century Thanjavur', in Anna Aurelia Esposito, Heike Oberlin, Karin Juliana Steiner, B.A. Viveka Rao eds., *In Her Right Hand She Held a Silver Knife with Small Bells* (Studies in Indian Culture and Literature) (Wiesbaden: Harrassowitz Verlag, 2015), pp. 275–81.
55  Viswanathan Peterson, *Tanjore Renaissance*, chapter three.
56  Nair, *Raja Serfoji*, p. 17.
57  Nair, 'The Tanjore printing press', p. 515.
58  Viswanathan Peterson, *Tanjore Renaissance*, chapter one.

59 Annesley, *Voyages*, p. 363.
60 Thomas Babington Macaulay's minute dated 02 February 1835 in Lynn Zastoupil and Martin Moir ed., *The Great Indian Education Debate: Documents Relating to the Orientalist-Anglicist Controversy, 1781–1843* (London & New York: Routledge, 2016), pp. 161–73.
61 In Travancore, for example. This was a problem even with other Serfoji-like figures earlier. In the context of Jai Singh of Jaipur in the early eighteenth century, for example, we read how despite personal achievements and scientific interests, he never established institutions to take them forward. See Deepak Kumar, *Science and the Raj: A Study of British India* (New Delhi: Oxford University Press, 1995), p. 30.
62 Letter dated 6 November 1855 from the Resident to the chief secretary, Fort St George, in William Hickey, *The Tanjore Mahratta Principality in Southern India: The Land of the Chola; The Eden of the South* (Madras: C. Foster & Co., 1874), pp. xxxix–xlvi.
63 This despite their own official supplying precedents. Resident Forbes quoted not just the *Digest of Hindu Law* published by H.T. Colebrooke in Bengal but also named specific Sanskrit authorities who saw daughters as heirs to their fathers.
64 Hickey, *Tanjore Mahratta Principality*, p. 156. Serfoji's son's widow, the Rani Kamatchi Bai, took the Company to court successfully. The British had lost no time in marching troops into the palace to seize not just valuables but also 'toys, squirts, pins and needles'. The governor general in 1856 refused to recognize a daughter as heir not least because 'perpetuating a titular principality at a great cost to the public revenue' was not agreeable (that Tanjore had surrendered territory in return for this pension was forgotten). See J.B. Norton, *Case of the Ranee of Tanjore* (London: Richardson & Co., 1861).
65 Or as one scholar puts in the context of Serfoji's *Devendra Kuravanji*, he was able to find a way to 'locating oneself in yet another world, while still carrying the older world and its forms of expression'. See Aprameya Manthena, 'Significance of the Kuravanji: In Conversation with Radhika Seshan' at https://www.sahapedia.org/significance-of-the-kuravanji-conversation-radhika-seshan.
66 Thomas R. Trautman, *Languages and Nations: The Dravidian Proof in Colonial Madras* (Berkeley & Los Angeles: University of California Press, 2006), pp. 99–100
67 The five products are milk, urine, dung, curd and ghee. The Tamil title of the work was *Aramavara Vilaccam*. See Emmanuel Frances, 'Tamil Original of Ellis' Legend of the Cowpox Found' at https://rcsi.hypotheses.org/488.
68 The complete English translation appears in Trautmann, *Languages and Nations*, Appendix A, pp. 231–41.
69 A limited definition but one that will suffice for our purposes here.

70  Reference is to John Leydon. See Trautmann, *Languages and Nations*, p. 88. Some of these men themselves wondered if they were scholars. H.H. Wilson would remark, for example: 'You see, I am not a scholar, I am a gentleman who likes Sanskrit, and that is all.'

71  This is not to say that none of them had Christian motives, as we will see below.

72  See letter dated 4 October 1784 from Warren Hastings to Nathaniel Smith in Charles Wilkins trans., *The Bhagvat-Geeta, or Dialogues of Kreeshna and Arjoon in Eighteen Lectures with Notes* (London: C. Nourse, 1785), pp. 5–13. A successor as governor general agreed: translation projects and Sanskrit studies were part of efforts to 'inspire confidence in minds where distrust was habitual'. See John Shore (S.C. Wilks ed.), *Memoirs of the Life, Writings, and Correspondence of Sir William Jones*, Vol. 2 (London: John W. Parker, 1835), p. 18. Not all were convinced, however. H.T. Colebrooke, in the same period, noted that Indians would 'remember the yoke as the heaviest that ever conquerors put upon the necks of conquered nations'. See Rocher and Rocher, *The Making of Western Indology*, p. 19.

73  Richard Drayton, 'Knowledge and Empire', p. 249, in P.J. Marshall and Alaine Low eds., *The Eighteenth Century* (Vol. 2 in *The Oxford History of the British Empire*), pp. 231–25. Even William Jones—among the most respected of the orientalists—was not immune. At home, he had a reputation as a republican, but where India was concerned, 'I shall certainly not,' he wrote, 'preach democracy to the Indians, who must and will be governed by absolute power.' Quoted in Michael J. Franklin, *Orientalist Jones: Sir William Jones, Poet, Lawyer, And Linguist (*New York: Oxford University Press, 2011), p. 4. Before him, Halhed also wrote that it was 'Natives of Europe who are to rule, and the Inhabitants of India who are to obey.' See Nathaniel B. Halhed, *A Grammar of the Bengal Language* (Hoogly, 1778), p. ii.

74  Muhammad Abdul Qayyum, 'A Critical Study of the Bengali Grammars of Carey, Halhed and Haughton', Unpublished PhD dissertation, School of Oriental and African Studies (1974), pp. 154–55. See also Rocher and Rocher, *The Making of Western Indology*, p. 18 for H.T. Colebrooke making a similar criticism.

75  Charles Allen, *Ashoka: The Search for India's Lost Emperor* (London: Abacus, 2012), p. xvi.

76  As Freitag writes: 'Not a single line written by any historian in imperial service, or even in the imperial context, can be properly understood without also understanding the sheer discrepancies in power relations that existed between the historian and his subjects, and which were perpetuated by the histories that were produced.' See Jason Freitag, *Serving Empire, Serving Nation: James Tod and the Rajputs of Rajasthan* (Leiden & Boston: Brill, 2009), p. 15.

77  Halhed, *A Grammar of the Bengal Language*, p. iii.
78  See Ellis's essay in A.D. Campbell, *A Grammar of the Teloogoo Language, Commonly Termed the Gentoo, Peculiar to the Hindoos Inhabiting the North Eastern Provinces of the Indian Peninsula* (Madras: College of Fort St. George, 1820), pp. 1–31. In 1807, another colleague had also begun to note a contrast between Sanskrit-centered narratives constructed in Bengal and contrary evidence visible in the peninsula. 'It is certain,' Colin Mackenzie wrote, 'that the Hindu languages of the south of India are not derived from the Sanscrit'. Quoted in Rama Sundara Mantena, *The Origins of Modern Historiography in India: Antiquarianism and Philology, 1780–1880* (New York: Palgrave Macmillan), p. 81. See also Trautmann, *Languages and Nations*, p. 177.
79  See Bhadriraju Krishnamurti, *The Dravidian Languages* (Cambridge: Cambridge University Press, 2003), pp. 1–43. The term 'Dravida' was already used in the medieval period for the languages of Kerala and southern Tamil in the *Lilatilakam*. But Kannada and Telugu, which are part of the family, were excluded. See David Shulman, *Tamil: A Biography* (Cambridge: Harvard University Press, 2016), p. 6. See also ibid., pp. 17–18 for Dravidian influences in Vedic texts. Dravidian languages also, of course, borrowed from Sanskrit.
80  This is not surprising given how so many missionaries acquired their ideas of Hinduism from Tamil sources.
81  For an argument against the notion that Indians had mythology but no historical consciousness, see Rao, Shulman and Subrahmanyam, *Textures of Time*. See also ibid., p. 5 specifically where we read how 'Each community writes history in the mode that is dominant in its own literary practice. By the same token, newly ascendant or powerful cultures may deny history to the communities they seek to dominate, and historicity to their texts.'
82  According, that is, to *Western* historiographical traditions that were formalizing history as a genre and subject with a universalized method and process.
83  Allen, *Ashoka*, pp. 108–09.
84  Trautmann, *Languages and Nations*, p. 64.
85  Nayanjot Lahiri, *Ashoka in Ancient India* (Cambridge: Harvard University Press, 2015), pp. 14–15.
86  David Kopf, *British Orientalism and the Bengal Renaissance: The Dynamics of Indian Modernization, 1773–1835* (Calcutta: Firma K.L. Mukhopadhyay, 1969), p. 124.
87  See Pearson, *Memoirs*, Vol. 2, p. 274, and Viswanathan Peterson, *Tanjore Renaissance*, chapter one.
88  Indians were not admitted until 1829. Even thereafter, it was not always easy for scholarly 'natives' to join European-run scholarly organizations. See Kumar, *Science and the Raj*, p. 56.
89  Allen, *Ashoka*, pp. 64–65.

90    Sushma Jansari, *Chandragupta Maurya: The Creation of a National Hero in India* (London: UCL Press, 2023), p. 70. See also Allen, *Ashoka*, pp. 67–68.

91    See William Jones, *Institutes of Hindu Law; Or Ordinances of Menu* (Calcutta: Government of Bengal, 1794). A 1799 marble statue of Jones by John Bacon, located in St Paul's Cathedral in London, shows the Orientalist posing with a large volume bearing the title *The Institutes of Menu*.

92    Jawaharlal Nehru, *The Discovery of India* (Calcutta: The Signet Press, 1946), p. 375.

93    Abu Taher Mojumder, *Sir William Jones and the East* (Dacca: Begum Zakia Sultana, 1978), p. 35. In one enraptured sequence we read how, if Clive looted material riches, 'Jones would pillage Indian knowledge', 'rifle Sanskrit culture' and destroy 'linguistic, cultural, and conceptual barriers' for a free flow of intellectual wealth. Why, he even had a role 'eradicating racial stereotypes'. See Franklin, *Orientalist Jones*, p. 42.

94    Quoted in Mojumder, *Sir William Jones*, p. 37.

95    Quoted in Franklin, *Orientalist Jones*, p. 252

96    Ibid., p. 271.

97    Quoted in Schwab, *The Oriental Renaissance*, p. 13. A decade before him, the French orientalist Anquetil-Duperron also wrote how 'We stand, in relation to Sanskrit, where Europe stood in relation to Greek at the time of the fall of Constantinople and Hebrew at the time of Luther's Reformation.'

98    William Jones, 'On the Hindus', p. 252, in Marshall, *The British Discovery of Hinduism*, pp. 246–61. See also William Jones, 'The Third Anniversary Discourse delivered 2 February 1786', p. 26, in John Shore ed., *The Works of Sir William Jones*, Vol. 1 (London: G.G. & J. Robinson, 1799), pp. 19–34. Funnily, in 1827, the philosopher Dugald Stewart would argue that Sanskrit was similar to Greek because it was *indeed* Greek that Brahmins overheard during Alexander's invasion, mixed thereafter with Indian words! See Trautmann, *Aryans and British India*, pp. 124–26.

99    Franklin, *Orientalist Jones*, p. 37. See also Trautman, *Languages and Nations*, pp. 14–15. Indeed, Jones, though not first to propose it, would refer to Sanskrit as a 'sister' of Latin and Greek. With Kalidas's *Abhijnanasakuntalam*, he first translated the text into Latin and *then* into English. See William Jones trans., *Sacontala: Or the Fatal Ring* (Calcutta: Trubner & Co., 1875 ed.), p. ii. Before Jones, in 1768, a Jesuit called Gaston-Laurent Coeurdoux noted similarities between Greek, Latin and Sanskrit, but his work was not published till decades later; and Halhed also, in his Bengali grammar from Hastings's time, spoke of a link between Sanskrit and Greek. See Trautman, *Languages and Nations*, pp. 18–19. And before them all, Sirajuddin Ali Khan Arzu wrote of the 'concord' that existed between Persian and Sanskrit, wondering why nobody had made the connection. See Abdul Azim, 'Khan-i Arzu's Observations on the Relationship of Sanskrit and Persian', in *Zeitschrift der Deutschen Morgenländischen Gesellschaft* 119, 2 (1969): 261–69.

100 Rocher and Rocher, *The Making of Western Indology*, p. 79. See also Colebroke, *Essays*, p. 289 where he notes that the Hindu religion spread out from north India towards the south.

101 Rocher and Rocher, *The Making of Western Indology*, p. 45. See also H.T. Colebrooke, *Essays on the Religion and Philosophy of the Hindus* (London: Williams & Norgate, 1858 ed.), p. 68.

102 As one scholar wrote: 'It is less important that Colebrooke made one mistake than that he furnished so many data that were accurate.' See Daniel H.H. Ingalls, 'On the Study of the Past', p. 193, in *Journal of the American Oriental Society* 80, 3 (1960): 191–97. Jones too made errors. In his time, he assumed the Brahmi script was Ethiopian, and that Ashoka was a Saiva king. See Allen, *Ashoka*, p. 41, p. 141.

103 Quoted in Rocher and Rocher, *The Making of Western Indology*, p. 23.

104 Ibid., p. 45, pp. 174–75. Holwell earlier also ran into pointed hatred: He had proposed that Hindus, far from being 'a race of stupid and gross Idolaters' with 'monstrous' images, had a religion with 'a most sublime rational source and foundation'. John Zephaniah Holwell, *Interesting Historical Events Relative to the Provinces of Bengal, and the Empire of Indostan*, Part 1 (London: T. Becket & P.A. De Hondt, 1767), p. 6, p. 10. This depiction of Hinduism was declared by a publication 'nonsense, rhapsody, and absurdity', besides an insult to intelligence; Hindu religion was at best a thin tissue of tolerable philosophy, and 'debased Christianity'. See P.J. Marshall, 'Introduction', pp. 38–39.

105 Early on Colebrooke noted that despite Sanskrit texts, caste was not as rigid as it seemed; 'almost every occupation, though regularly it be the profession of a particular class, is open to most other tribes'. Quoted in Rocher and Rocher, *The Making of Western Indology*, p. 42. See also ibid., p. 29.

106 Ibid., p. 37.

107 Horace Hayman Wilson, *A Dictionary, Sanscrit and English* (Calcutta: Hindoostanee Press, 1819), p. iv. Emphases added. Importantly, this view was encouraged by Brahmins. One official, for instance, found his pandit sneer at his desire to study the Kannada language; it was, the Brahmin said, 'an indignity . . . to be asked to speak' the vernacular. On the suggestion of bringing in a Kannada teacher, he 'laughed heartily' stating that 'he always thought the purpose of education was to gain polish not vulgarity'—the point being that true knowledge existed only in Sanskrit. See Geoffrey A. Oddie, *Imagined Hinduism: British Protestant Missionary Constructions of Hinduism, 1793–1900* (New Delhi: Sage, 2006), p. 131. That is, Orientalist prejudices often coincided with Brahminical ones.

108 Halhed, *A Grammar of the Bengal Language*, pp. xxi–xxii. See also p. 178 for further criticism of Islamic influence, and p. xix, where Halhed states that what makes his study distinct from earlier European writings about Bengali was his tracing its links with Sanskrit. For the implications of this

attitude, see Henry Schwarz, 'Laissez-Faire Linguistics: Grammar and the Codes of Empire', *Critical Inquiry* 23, 3 (1997): 509–35. See also Rosane Rocher, 'British Orientalism in the Eighteenth Century: The Dialectics of Knowledge and Government', p. 222, in Breckenridge and van der Veer, *Orientalism and the Postcolonial Predicament*, pp. 215–49, on this theme of rescuing in general.

109  Qayyum, 'A Critical Study', pp. 137–38.
110  Halhed, *A Grammar of the Bengal Language*, p. xx.
111  See Qayyum, 'A Critical Study', pp. 91–93, p. 96. See also pp. 106–08, p. 136, where we learn that the Sanskrit terms Halhed used were not acquired from original sources but from Brahmin informants.
112  This is not to say all white authorities behaved in the same way. William Carey, the missionary, in *his* Bengali grammar argued that Persian and other loanwords had enriched, not corrupted Bengali. See Carey, *A Grammar of the Bengalee Language* (Serampore: Mission Press, 1801), p. iii. Halhed may well have published his imperfect Bengali grammar to construct a reputation and further his career interests. See Qayyum, 'A Critical Study', pp. 151–55.
113  Franklin, *Orientalist Jones*, p. 268. In fact, Jones was to take a purist stand even on technicalities. In Bengal, Brahmins used the local script for Sanskrit, rarely learning the Devanagari of upper India. Instead of noting diversity and Sanskrit's adaptability (southerners preferring the Grantha script), Jones dismissed this as proof of Brahmin 'indolence'. Quoted in Rosane Rocher, 'Weaving Knowledge: Sir William Jones and Indian Pandits', p. 59, in Garland Cannon and Kevin R. Brine eds., *Objects of Enquiry: The Life, Contributions, and Influences of Sir William Jones (1746–1794)* (New York & London: New York University Press, 1995), pp. 51–82. See also the original in William Jones, 'A Dissertation on the Orthography of Asiatick Words in Roman Letters', p. 8, in *Asiatic Researches or, Transactions of the Society, Instituted in Bengal for Inquiring into the History and Antiquities, the Arts, Sciences, and Literature of Asia*, Vol 1. (London: J. Sewell, Vernor & Hood, J. Cuthell, J. Walker, H. Lea, Lackington, Allen & Co, Otridge & Son, R. Faulder, J Scatcheed, 1799), pp. 1–56. A British judge was essentially dictating the 'authentic' way to write the Hindus' sacred language. This derived from his belief that 'the languages of Indian were originally written' in Devanagari. See Jones, 'Third Anniversary Discourse', p. 27.
114  Similarly, in his 'Hymn to Durga,' Jones 'deliberately censors the sexual coupling of Shiva and Parvati as it may offend European sensibilities'. See Malhotra, *Making British Indian Fictions*, p. 71.
115  Rocher and Rocher, *The Making of Western Indology*, p. 106. See also ibid., p. 46 for his horror at Tantric worship and 'indecent' rites around the goddess.
116  John Leyden quoted in Trautmann, *Languages and Nations*, p. 40.
117  Ramanujan, Rao and Shulman, *When God Is a Customer*, p. 29.

118  Indeed, in the larger scheme of things, while the violent muscularity of the Raj draws notice, such intellectual schemes were 'as powerful' as 'military and economic imperialism.' Nicholas Dirks in Cohn, *Colonialism and its Forms*, p. ix. Orientalists, for example, did not hesitate to place Indian history within Christian frames of reference. Halhed's *Code*, besides seeking to give Europeans an idea of 'Hindu law', was also intended to demonstrate its 'wonderful Correspondence' with the Institutes of Moses. See Halhed, *Code*, p. lx. Jones, deploying complex calculations, citing parleys with a Brahmin, extracting lists from Sanskrit texts and connecting Puranic figures to Biblical ones also dragged Hindu narratives into the Christian scheme of things. See P.J. Marshall, 'Introduction', p. 36, in P.J. Marshall ed., *The British Discovery of Hinduism in the Eighteenth Century* (Cambridge: Cambridge University Press, 1970), pp. 1–44, and Jones, 'The Third Anniversary Discourse', p. 29. See also Trautmann, *Languages and Nations*, pp. 15–16, and Trautmann, *Aryans and British India*, p. 74 for Jones's role in making the study of Hinduism 'safe' for Protestant Christians.

119  Mantena, *The Origins of Modern Historiography*, p. 19.

120  See Preface in William Jones, *Sacontala*, p. i. See also Rocher, 'The Career of Radhakanta Tarkavagisa', p. 629, where we read how Jones helped pay his debts, and the man stayed in Company employment. Halhed's highly Sanskritized, artificial Bengali grammar was, similarly, influenced by an 'intelligent' Brahmin tutor, who seemingly shared his passion for the 'classical'. See Qayyum, pp. 77–90, pp. 136–39, p. 161, p. 177.

121  See Trautmann, *Aryans and British India*, pp. 91–92. See also Wilford's original note in *Asiatic Researches; Or, Transactions of the Society Instituted in Bengal for Inquiring into the History and Antiquities, the Arts, Sciences, and Literature of Asia*, Vol. 8 (London, 1808), pp. 245–66. Similarly, on the ground, those providing information to orientalists could manipulate material. See Dirks, *Castes of Mind*, p. 103. Even one like Colebrooke, when writing on Buddhism and Jainism, was dependent on (prejudiced) Brahmin sources. See Rocher and Rocher, *The Making of Western Indology*, p. 172.

122  Cohn, *Colonialism and Its Forms*, p. 83, and Clements Markham, *A Memoir on the Indian Surveys* (London: W.H. Allen & Co; Edward Stanford; Henry S. King & Co., 1871), p. 59.

123  As Mackenzie wrote, 'My own want of knowledge of the languages, has rather impeded my progress; but I have the advantage of able native assistants.' Quoted in Mantena, *The Origins of Modern Historiography*, p. 66. By the end of the first decade of the nineteenth century, in fact, Mackenzie had eleven assistants, including the Kavali brothers, a Jain, a Muslim, Christians and others. See Wolffhardt, *Unearthing the Past to Forge the Future*, p. 188.

124  Quoted in Mantena, *The Origins of Modern Historiography*, p. 104

125  Wolfhardt, *Unearthing the Past*, p. 190.

126 'The qualifications of Cavelly Venkata for such an office' were not appropriate, according to Prinsep. Indeed, no native could ever be 'equal to such a task'. Indians may be useful 'as auxiliaries' in 'a train of research' supervised by a white superior but any 'outlay of public money' to a project solely under 'native' direction was preposterous. See 'Report of the Committee of Papers on Cavelly Venkata Lachmia's proposed renewal of Col. Mackenzie's investigations' in James Prinsep ed., *The Journal of the Asiatic Society of Bengal*, Vol. 5 (Calcutta: Baptist Mission Press, 1836), pp. 512–13.

127 Mantena, *The Origins of Modern Historiography*, p. 82, pp. 106–07. This also highlights another dynamic with Orientalism. In discovering Ashoka's inscriptions, Alexander Cunningham is a prominent name. However, in the same period, an Indian called Bhagwanlal Indraji was also cataloguing inscriptions. 'His work is much less recognized that Cunningham's because the bulk of his early writings was in Gujarati,' not English. See Lahiri, *Ashoka in Ancient India*, p. 16.

128 See Ramasswami, *Viswaguna Darsana*. In 1828, Ramasswami published in English, the *Descriptive and Historical Sketches of Cities and Places in the Dekkan*, followed in the next year by *Biographical Sketches of the Dekkan Poets*. Both were intended for a Western readership—where, for instance, supernatural elements appear in his biographical snippets, he is apologetic about having to include them. See Cavelly Venkata Ramaswamie, *Biographical Sketches of Dekkan Poets, being Memoirs of the Lives of Several Eminent Bards, both Ancient and Modern, who have Flourished in Different Provinces of the Indian Peninsula* (Calcutta, 1829). For more on other 'pundit-publishers', see Blackburn, *Print, Folklore, and Nationalism*, pp. 96–111. Interestingly, in 1802, Borayya, one of Mackenzie's assistants, prepared for him an outline for a proposed history of south India. As Mantena, writes, if Borayya (who died soon after) had gone ahead, he would have produced a book at par with histories authored by colonial authorities in the late eighteenth and early nineteenth centuries; a new, Western-style history, created, however, by an Indian. See Mantena, *The Origins of Modern Historiography*, pp. 102–04.

129 Jadunath Sarkar, *India through the Ages: A Survey of the Growth of Indian Life and Thought* (Calcutta: M.C. Sarkar & Sons, 1928), p. 115.

130 On Tod's study and motivations, see Freitag, *Serving Empire, Serving Nation*, and Florence D'Souza: *Knowledge, Mediation and Empire: James Tod's Journeys among the Rajputs* (Manchester: Manchester University Press, 2015). Tod's superiors were not pleased, fearing he was too fond of Rajputs to do his duties as a Company representative. See also Norbert Peabody, 'Tod's *Rajast'han* and the Boundaries of Imperial Rule in Nineteenth Century India', *Modern Asian Studies* 30, 1 (1996): 185–220.

131 Harischandra quoted in Dalmia, *The Nationalization of Hindu Traditions*, p. 329. Tod feared this too: unless British power acted in a 'protecting' manner, Rajputs themselves 'may in time prove the most formidable opposers of

the power which raised them'. Quoted in Freitag, *Serving Empire, Serving Nation*, p. 19.
132 See W.J. Johnson trans., *The Bhagavad Gita* (Oxford: Oxford University Press, 1994), pp. vii–xix.
133 Letter dated 4 October 1784 from Hastings to Smith in Wilkins, *The Bhagvat-Geeta*, p. 10. There had earlier been a Portuguese abridgement of the Gita. While it was attributed to the Jesuit Fernao de Queyroz (d. 1688), mention of the Third Battle of Panipat (1761) in the text suggests it was authored by someone else not long before Wilkins. See Ethel M. Pope, *India in Portuguese Literature* (Bastora, Goa: Rangel, 1937), pp. 166–68.
134 See Ray, *Negotiating the Modern*, p. 41.
135 Before them, the Mughal emperor Akbar had commissioned a Persian translation of the Gita.
136 H.T. Colebrooke on Charles Wilkins quoted in F. Max Muller ed., *Biographical Essays* (London: Longmans, Green & Co., 1884), p. 237.
137 Wilkins, *The Bhagvat-Geeta*, p. 24.
138 Schwab, *The Oriental Renaissance*, p. 40.
139 Ibid., p. 161, p. 59.
140 See Eric Sharpe, *The Universal Gita: Western Images of the Bhagavad Gita* (Illinois: Open Court, 1985), pp. 49–50. See also C.A. Bayly, 'India, the Bhagavad Gita and the World', p. 9, in Shruti Kapila and Faisal Devji eds., *Political Thought in Action: The Bhagavad Gita and Modern India* (New York: Cambridge University Press, 2013), pp. 1–24. See also ibid., p. 10 where we find other European writers doing the opposite, that is, claiming that the idea of Christ was actually inspired by Krishna.
141 Richard H. Davis, *The Bhagavad Gita: A Biography* (Princeton: Princeton University Press), pp. 43–44, p. 74. See also Shruti Kapila and Faisal Devji's introduction, p. xi, in Devji and Kapila eds., *Political Thought in Action*. A nineteenth-century Hindu writer also credited the printing press for 'emancipating' 'Hindoo literature' in general from 'the mystification and falsification of the Brahmins'. See Chunder, *Travels of a Hindoo*, Vol. 1, p. 14.
142 This was, famously, Edwin Arnold's *The Song Celestial, or Bhagavad Gita* (1886). See M.K. Gandhi, *The Story of My Experiments with Truth* (Ahmedabad: Navjivan Press, 1927), p. 164. See also Sharpe, *The Universal Gita*, 68. For an expression by Gandhi of affection for the text, see ibid., p. 114.
143 As scholars such as Richard H. Davis, Edwin F. Bryant and others note, the *Bhagavata Purana* offers a more emotional, humanized form of the deity; where the former reveals Krishna as omnipotent and supreme, the Puranic Krishna appears as a friend, child, lover, prankster and more. Jones, incidentally, quite enjoyed this purana, describing it as 'by far the most entertaining book . . . that I have ever read' with great 'novelty and wildness'. See footnote in Marshall, *The British Discovery of Hinduism*, p. 205.

144 Missionaries, in fact, tended to focus on *this* Krishna to embarrass their Hindu disputants. See Nagappa Gowda, *The Bhagavadgita in the Nationalist Discourse* (New Delhi: Oxford University Press, 2011), p. 3. Perhaps for this reason, Indian figures such as Bankim Chandra Chattopadhyay attempted to construct a more serious Krishna devoid of play and pleasure. See Anustup Basu, *Hindutva as Political Monotheism* (Durham & London: Duke University Press), pp. 116–21 for a note on Chattopadhyay's *Krishnacharitra* (1888).

145 Winand Callewaert and Shilanand Hemraj cited in Davis, *The Bhagavad Gita*, p. 155.

146 Reference is to Ram Mohun Roy. Quoted in Sharpe, *The Universal Gita*, p. 12.

147 Reference is to Rishi Sunak.

148 Peter Heehs, *The Lives of Sri Aurobindo* (New York: Columbia University Press, 2008), p. 268.

149 Barbara Stoler Miller, *The Bhagavad-Gita: Krishna's Counsel in Time of War* (New York: Bantam Dell, 2004 [1986]), p. 8.

150 William Taylor, *A Catalogue Raisonne of Oriental Manuscripts in the Library of the (Late) College, Fort Saint George*, Vol. 1 (Madras: Fort St George Gazette Press, 1857), p. 12.

151 Aurobindo quoted in Heehs, *The Lives of Sri Aurobindo*, p. 157.

152 Aravind Ganachari, 'British Official View of "Bhagwat Gita" as "Text-Book for the Mental Training of Revolutionary Recruits"', p. 601, in *Proceedings of the Indian History Congress* 56 (1995): 601–10.

153 J.V. Naik, 'British Secret Official View of Tilak's "Gitarahasya" (M.S.)', p. 452, in *Proceedings of the Indian History Congress* 62 (2001): 450–55. See also Basu, *Hindutva as Political Monotheism*, pp. 113–14.

154 Sharpe, *The Universal Gita*, p. 6.

155 Akshaya Mukul, *Gita Press and the Making of Hindu India* (Noida: HarperCollins Publishers India, 2015), pp. 121–30. Wilkins himself speculated that the 'principal design' of the Gita was 'to unite all the prevailing modes of worship'. See Wilkins, *The Bhagvat-Geeta*, p. 24. So too over a century later Aurobindo, the philosopher, wrote how the Gita 'does not cleave asunder, but reconciles and unifies.' See Sri Aurobindo, *Essays on the Gita* (Pondicherry: Sri Aurobindo Ashram Publication Department, 1997 ed.), p. 8.

156 Wilkins, *The Bhagvat-Geeta*, pp. 23–24.

157 Kaviraj, *The Imaginary Institution of India*, p. 183.

158 Quoted in Monika Rani Bhagat-Kennedy, 'Imagining Bharat: Romance, Heroism, and Hindu Nationalism in the Bengali Novel, 1880–1920', Unpublished PhD dissertation, University of Pennsylvania (2016), p. 26.

159 Bhagat-Kennedy, 'Imagining Bharat', p. 9. On European attitudes, as Lushington wrote: 'The English are really of a superior race compared with

the Hindus; they know better than the inferior race itself what is suitable to it.' Quoted in Kumar, *Science and the Raj*, p. 57.
160 Tarinicharan Chattopadhyay quoted in Partha Chatterjee, *The Nation and Its Fragments: Colonial and Postcolonial Histories* (Princeton: Princeton University Press, 1993), pp. 97–98. In his 1850s *Charupath*, similarly, Akshay Kumar Dutta presents a 'dream vision' in which Valmiki (author of the Ramayana) is in dialogue with Kalidasa. 'The young generation of our race does not celebrate us as it celebrates poets from other races,' one says to the other. 'However, what is heartening is that the learned folk from other races have realized our stature and give us proper respect . . . therefore, some of the recent scholars from our part of the world have begun to show some interest in our work.' Quoted in Sumit Chakrabarti, *Local Selfhood, Global Turns: Akshay Kumar Dutta and Bengali Intellectual History in the Nineteenth Century* (Cambridge: Cambridge University Press, 2023), p. 197. That is, Western certification of India's historical greatness carried a legitimizing value.
161 Nundolal Dey, *Civilization in Ancient India* (Calcutta: New Arya Mission Press, 1903), p. 5. Though published in book form in 1903, the contents of Dey's text were originally carried in a newspaper between 1877 and 1878.
162 Bankim Chandra Chattopadhyay quoted in Bhagat-Kennedy, 'Imagining Bharat', p. 66. This idea of history as not an objective study in its own right but as a means to energize people's identities and self-worth remains a central principle for Hindu nationalism to this day.
163 These last two paragraphs owe much to Bhagat-Kennedy's summarization of these dynamics in Bengal.
164 The *Bombay Durpan* dated 24 August 1832 quoted in Deepak Kumar, 'The 'Culture' of Science and Colonial Culture, India 1820–1920', p. 199, in *The British Journal for the History of Science* 29, 2 (1996): 195–209.
165 For a succinct account of Benares's religious and political significance, see Vasudha Dalmia, *The Nationalization of Hindu Traditions: Bharatendu Harischandra and Nineteenth-Century Banaras* (Ranikhet: Permanent Black, 2010 ed.), pp. 50–59.
166 Maria Misra, *Vishnu's Crowded Temple: India since the Great Rebellion* (Yale University Press, 2009), p. 37. See also Dalmia, *Nationalization*, pp. 94–95.
167 Madhuri Desai, *Banaras Reconstructed: Architecture and Sacred Space in a Hindu Holy City* (Hyderabad: Orient Blackswan, 2017), pp. 154–55.
168 Reginald Heber, *Narrative of a Journey through the Upper Provinces of India, from Calcutta to Bombay, 1824–1825*, Vol. 1 (London: John Murray, 1828), pp. 373–75.
169 Ibid., p. 381.
170 Ibid., pp. 390–92.
171 Richard Fox Young, 'Receding from Antiquity: Hindu Responses to Science and Christianity on the Margins of Empire, 1800–1850', p. 186, in Frykenberg

ed., *Christians and Missionaries*, pp. 183–222. Even a generally sympathetic figure like Elphinstone could not help but state that Hindus had made 'less progress' in geography 'than in any other science'. See Elphinstone, *History of India*, Vol. 1, p. 258. For similar debates with Buddhists in Sri Lanka, see Young and Somaratna, *Buddhist-Christian Controversies*, pp. 92–93.

172 Letter dated 1 January 1792 from the Resident at Benares to the Governor General in Council in *Selections from Educational Records, Part I, 1781–1839* (Calcutta: Superintendent, Government Printing, 1920), pp. 10–11. Other sources, however, date this letter to 1791. This view would be repeated by William Adams in his survey of education in Bengal in the 1830s, when he wrote how Sanskrit schools, though a 'separate' class of institutions from other village schools, 'represented the cultivated intellect of the Hindu people', receiving respect also because of the 'hereditary sacredness' of Brahmins. See J. Long, *Adam's Report on Vernacular Education in Bengal and Behar: Submitted to Government in 1835, 1836, and 1838* (Calcutta: Home Secretariat Press, 1868), pp. 196–97. Hereafter 'Adams's *Report*'.

173 Quoted in Narain, *Jonathan Duncan*, p. 173. This was particularly because their enemies, the Marathas, had great influence over Benares, which, in its eighteenth-century shape, was largely Maratha-made. And on the face of it, the investment paid: many princes—Serfoji included—gave donations to the Benares college, though there was suspicion that this was to please British officials, not a sincere endorsement of their experiment. On Serfoji, see Nair, 'The Tanjore printing press', pp. 513–14. On British suspicion of other donors, see Dalmia, *Nationalization*, p. 100.

174 Parimala V. Rao, *Beyond Macaulay: Education in India, 1780–1860* (Abingdon: Routledge, 2020), p. 96. In parallel, to win Muslim support, madrasas and Arabic college were similarly established by the Company. However, the Company did innovate in these Sanskrit colleges, in that instead of the Vedas, the emphasis was on study of sastras, which would be of use to British courts etc. See Kumar, *Western India*, p. 51.

175 One of the early instructors at the college, interestingly, was Pandit Vidyananda, the same man who had supplied forged Puranic verses to Francis Wilford.

176 See H.H. Wilson, 'Education of the Natives of India', pp. 7–8, in *The Asiatic Journal and Monthly Register* (New Series), Vol. 19 (1836): 1–16.

177 Quoted in Syed Mahmood, *A History of English Education in India: Its Rise, Development, Progress, Present Condition and Prospects* (Aligarh: M.A.O. College, 1895), pp. 2–3.

178 Lord Ellenborough to the House of Commons, quoted in Charles Hay Cameron, *An Address to Parliament on the Duties of Great Britain to India, in Respect of the Education of the Natives, and their Official Employment* (London: Longman, Brown, Green & Longmans, 1853), p. 19.

179 Letter dated 3 June 1814 from the Court of Directors to the Governor General in Council in *Educational Records*, p. 24. See also Adams's *Report*, p. 198.
180 Edward Strachey, *Bija Ganita: or the Algebra of the Hindus* (London: W. Glendinning, 1813), p. 8.
181 See William Jones quoted in *Asiatick Researches, or Transactions of the Society Instituted in Bengal for Inquiring into the History and Antiquities, the Arts, Sciences, and Literature, of Asia*, Vol. 2 (London: J. Swan & Son, 1807 ed.), pp. 290–91. This is not to argue that these ideas were widely known; only that some in India held ideas and theories that aligned with Western scientific positions. Jai Singh, the maharajah of Jaipur in the first half of the eighteenth century, had also conducted his astronomical studies along the Copernican model. See Kumar, *Science and the Raj*, pp. 21–23. The *Jyotisa Siddhantas* 'rejected Puranic cosmology', so that some British figures like Lancelot Wilkinson also presented Copernican models as 'an extension of the astronomical Siddhantas'. See Christopher Minkowski, 'A Nineteenth Century Sanskrit Treatise on the Revolution of the Earth: Govinda Deva's *Bhumibhramana*', pp. 200–01, in SCIAMVS 5 (2004): 199–224.
182 See Liddle, *The Broken Script*, p. 208. Emphasis added. See also M.A. Laird, 'The Contribution of Christian Missionaries to Education in Bengal, 1793–1837', Unpublished PhD dissertation, University of London (1968), pp. 146–47, p. 164 for an 1817 speech by the governor general, who argued against the idea 'that to spread information among men is to render them less tractable and less submissive to authority'.
183 T.V. Ventakeswaran, 'Negotiating Secular School Textbooks in Colonial Madras Presidency', p. 149, in *Journal of Scientific Temper* 1, 3&4 (2013): 143–97. See also Robert Eric Frykenberg, 'Modern Education in South India, 1784–1854: Its Roots and Its Role as a Vehicle of Integration under Company Raj', p. 43, *The American Historical Review* 91, 1 (1986): 37–65, for an 1818 remark by the Company's directors who hoped to turn Brahmins especially into loyal British public servants.
184 Gyan Prakash, *Another Reason: Science and the Imagination of Modern India* (Princeton: Princeton University Press, 1999), p. 5. Or to quote Richard Drayton, 'Science and technics came to supplement Christianity as justification for imperial outreach.' See Drayton, 'Science, Medicine, and the British Empire', p. 265, in Robin W. Winks and Alaine Low eds., *The Oxford History of the British Empire: Historiography* (Vol. 5) (Oxford: Oxford University Press, 1999), pp. 264–76.
185 Quoted in Bhagwan Dayal, *The Development of Modern Indian Education* (Bombay: Orient Longmans, 1955), p. 180. This was not unheard-of criticism. Al-Biruni in the eleventh century observed: 'I can only compare their [Hindus'] mathematical and astronomical literature . . . to a mixture

of pearl shells and sour dates, or of pearls and dung, or of costly crystals and common pebbles.' See al-Biruni, *Alberuni's India*, Vol. 1, p. 25.

186 See letter dated 21 January 1835 from J.C.C. Sutherland to H.T. Prinsep in *The Great Indian Education Debate*, p. 138.

187 Michael S. Dodson, 'Re-Presented for the Pandits: James Ballantyne, "Useful Knowledge", and Sanskrit Scholarship in Benares College During the Mid-Nineteenth Century', pp. 265–66, in *Modern Asian Studies* 36, 2 (2002): 257–98. See also Adams's *Report*, p. 199, where Adams acknowledges this but remains optimistic.

188 T. Brooke's minute dated 1 January 1804 in *Educational Records*, p. 33. Blame was of course placed on the fact that there had been no European superintendence. It did not help that its head pandit pocketed stipends meant for students. See Dalmia, *Nationalization*, pp. 98–99.

189 Lord Auckland's minute dated 24 November 1839 in Pramod K. Nayar ed., *Colonial Education and India, 1781–1945: Commentaries, Reports, Policy Documents*, Vol. 1 (Abingdon: Routledge, 2020), p. 106, p. 109. See also letter dated 29 September 1830 from the Court of Directors to the Governor of Madras in *The Great Indian Education Debate*, pp. 125–27. The dilly-dallying frustrated British officials too. See Adams's *Report*, p. 261.

190 A. Troyer, 'Report on the Sanskrit College, Calcutta, 31st January 1835', in *Selections from Educational Records*, Vol. 1, pp. 40–41.

191 Michael S. Dodson, 'Translating Science, Translating Empire: The Power of Language in Colonial North India', p. 828, in *Comparative Studies in Society and History* 47, 4 (2005): 809–35.

192 Dodson, *Orientalism*, p. 138. Even translating into vernacular tongues was tough: a Hindi edition of the principal's *A Synopsis of Science* was 'harsh and unidiomatic'. See Dodson, 'Translating Science', p. 833. Finding vernaculars deficient in vocabulary, translators then relapsed into Sanskrit to invent jargon, leaving 'jejune', 'pedantic' products, which few of its intended beneficiaries could comprehend. See Hakim Ikhlef, 'Constructive Orientalism: Debates on Languages and Educational Policies in Colonial India, 1830–1880', p. 164, in Barnita Bagchi, Eckhardt Fuchs and Kate Rousmaniere eds., *Translational and Cross-Cultural Exchanges in (Post)Colonial Education* (New York: Berghahn, 2014), pp. 156–71. Similarly, some years earlier, a Sanskrit translation was commissioned of Robert Hooper's *The Anatomist's Vade-Mecum*. Many asked if it was worth it—given how a microscopic set of Hindus alone was proficient with Sanskrit—to which the retort was that this set was exactly the book's expected audience. See ibid., pp. 162–63. See also Charu Singh, 'Science in the vernacular? Translation, terminology and lexicography in the Hindu Scientific Glossary (1906)', p. 68, in *South Asian History and Culture* 13, 1 (2022): 63–86 and Adams's *Report*, p. 315.

193 And when a Pandit authored a work *Siddhantasiromaniprakasa* (1836) in which he accepted Copernican ideas, he faced a backlash from orthodox

Brahmins, who published their own rejoinders reinstating tradition over his modern proposition. See Young, 'Receding from Antiquity', pp. 197–205, in Frykenberg, *Christians and Missionaries*, pp. 183–222.

194 'It is . . . interesting to note that the British parliament thus required the East India Company to take responsibility for public education in India twenty years before the British government would do the same in Britain.' See Lynn Zastoupil & Martin Moir, 'Introduction', p. 7, in *The Great Indian Education Debate*, pp. 1–72.

195 Note dated 17 July 1823 by Holt Mackenzie in *Educational Records*, pp. 58–59. See also Ellenborough's views in Veena Naregal, *Language Politics, Elites, and the Public Sphere* (New Delhi: Permanent Black, 2001), pp. 142–43, where he endorses focussing on the elites.

196 Thomas Munro's minute dated 10 March 1826 in *Educational Records*, pp. 73–75. This modest figure reminds one of Gyan Prakash's line on the promotion of science being accompanied by 'a minimum of expense and maximum of ambition'. See Prakash, *Another Reason*, p. 13. The number of elementary schools in Bengal, albeit deemed imperfect and limited in scope, was also very high as late as the 1830s. See Adams's *Report*, 18–19. For his recommendations, matching Madras's, see pp. 2–3, p. 251, pp. 261–62.

197 Quoted in Rao, *Beyond Macaulay*, p. 128.

198 Krishna Kumar, *Political Agenda of Education: A Study of Colonialist and Nationalist Ideas* (New Delhi: SAGE Publications, 2005 [1991]), p. 17, p. 31. See also Rao, *Beyond Macaulay*, pp. 61–62, p. 72, pp. 82–89, p. 103, p. 182 and p. 210, and Frykenberg, 'Modern Education', p. 49, p. 55, pp. 58–59, p. 62, for how colonial officials often actively wished to limit education to the upper castes and classes, where earlier economic background in traditional schools had not been much of a factor, and a much wider segment of society participated, both as teachers and students.

199 George Norton in 1841, quoted in *Report of the Indian Education Commission* (Calcutta: Government Printing, 1883), p. 88.

200 Lord Auckland's minute dated 24 November 1839 in Pramod K. Nayar ed., *Colonial Education and India, 1781–1945: Commentaries, Reports, Policy Documents*, Vol. 1 (Abingdon: Routledge, 2020), p. 106, p. 109. Emphasis added. See also letter dated 29 September 1830 from the Court of Directors to the Governor of Madras in *The Great Indian Education Debate*, pp. 125–27. The dilly-dallying frustrated British officials too. See Adams's *Report*, p. 261.

201 Lord Ellenborough quoted in Naregal, *Language Politics*, pp. 142–43.

202 Rao, *Beyond Macaulay*, p. 85. See also Liddle, *The Broken Script*, p. 204.

203 See Rao, *Beyond Macaulay*, pp. 128–37. Convenience also played a role here. The Company had been so busy, as stated in 1815, 'repelling' enemies and 'securing . . . new possessions', they had 'little leisure' to study the needs of the people 'beneath our sway' in any serious manner. Lord Moira's minute dated

2 October 1815 in *Educational Records*, p. 25. Or as a Bengali intellectual sighed, 'coming from a distance of many thousand miles to govern a people whose language, literature, manners, customs, and ideas are almost entirely new and strange', the British 'cannot easily become so intimately acquainted with [the people's] real circumstances'. See Letter dated 11 December 1823 from Ram Mohun Roy to Lord Amherst in *The Great Indian Education Debate*, p. 111. Setting up a few 'traditional' colleges for Brahmins was just easier.

204  As happened between Mountstuart Elphinstone in Bombay and his council-member Francis Warden. See also Zastoupil and Moir, 'Introduction', p. 46 for a similar split in London. This also meant, however, that the colonial state showed a 'calculated ambivalence intended to give room for manoeuvre at all points'. See Naregal, *Language Politics*, p. 140.

205  Rao, *Beyond Macaulay*, pp. 37–40; Venkateswaran, 'Negotiating Secular School Textbooks', pp. 157–58. Rao (p. 38) also adds that for a 'grant' of as little as a rupee, the government could pass off a village school as a government-supported school when reporting to London.

206  Quoted in Jana Tschurenev, 'A Colonial Experiment in Education: Madras, 1789–1796', p. 108, in Bagchi, Fuchs, and Rousmaniere, *Translational and Cross-Cultural Exchanges*, pp. 105–22.

207  See Mary Hilton, 'A Transcultural Transaction: William Carey's Baptist Mission, the Monitorial Method and the Bengal Renaissance', p. 86, in Bagchi, Fuchs and Rousmaniere, *Translational and Cross-Cultural Exchanges*, pp. 85–104; Venkateswaran, 'Negotiating Secular School Textbooks', pp. 153–54; Rao, *Beyond Macaulay*, pp. 27–28. It had certain advantages, in that teachers were accountable to the local community, rather than some central bureaucratic order. On how this changed after British intervention, turning the teacher into something of an unhappy, underpaid bureaucrat, see Kumar, *Political Agenda of Education*, p. 50, pp. 75–85. The teachers were largely remunerated in kind, with students giving grain, flour, vegetables according to their means, and not with fixed salaries. See, for example, Liddle, *The Broken Script*, p. 199; Kumar, *Political Agenda of Education*, p. 78; and J.W. Massie, *Continental India: Travelling Sketches and Historical Recollections*, Vol. 2 (London: Thomas Ward & Co., 1840), pp. 387–88.

208  Frykenberg, 'Modern Education in South India', p. 44.

209  Adams's *Report*, pp. 18–19.

210  See Rao, *Beyond Macaulay*, pp. 15–26; Frykenberg, 'Modern Education in South India', pp. 44–46; Kumar, *Western India*, p. 53. Missionaries also confirmed this from their own schools. See Laird, 'The Contribution of Christian Missionaries', pp. 146–47. On how learning was imparted, see Kumar, *Political Agenda of Education*, pp. 74–75. On excluding 'untouchables', this would continue under the British also. See note 263 below.

211  Massie, *Continental India*, Vol. 2, p. 385. Emphasis added.

212　Adams's *Report*, p. 198.
213　Chunder, *Travels of a Hindoo*, Vol. 1 (1869), pp. 276–77.
214　Ibid., pp. 278–79.
215　Raja Ram Mohun Roy. We will meet him in Chapter 6 again.
216　Even in 1850, thus, Benares remained home to 193 private institutions, with almost 2000 scholars. See Dalmia, *Nationalization*, p. 97. For a similar 1817 list of eighty-three teachers and their hundreds of students, see William Ward, *A View of the History, Literature, and Mythology of the Hindoos*, Vol. 1 (Serampore: Serampore Mission Press, 1818), pp. 588–92. At Nadia in Bengal, officials found forty-six Sanskrit academies; similar patterns appeared in the west and south. See Rao, *Beyond Macaulay*, pp. 30–33.
217　Letter dated 11 December 1823 from Ram Mohun Roy to Lord Amherst in *Educational Records*, pp. 99–101. See also Mahmood, *A History of English Education in India*, pp. 28–29. This was by no means a purely Indian phenomenon. In 1838, the Ottoman Sultan Mahmud II remarked to medical students: 'You will study scientific medicine in French . . . my purpose in having you taught French is not to educate you in the French language; it is to teach you scientific medicine and little by little to take it into our language . . .; Quoted in Sumit Sarkar, 'Rammohun Roy and the Break with the Past', p. 57, in V.C. Joshi ed., *Rammohun Roy and the Process of Modernization in India* (Delhi: Vikas Publishing House, 1975), pp. 46–68.
218　Quoted in Subba Rao (Rahul Sagar ed.), *Krishna Kumari: The Tragedy of India* (London: Methuen Drama, 2024), p. 39.
219　Rao, *Beyond Macaulay*, p. 77.
220　Quoted in ibid., p. 135. See also ibid., p. 85 for figures from elsewhere showing how 'natives' did pay substantial sums for modern schools, and Massie, *Continental India*, Vol. 2, pp. 393–94, where he writes:

> So far, however, as I have discovered, the Hindoos . . . have evinced the strongest desire to attain, and a zeal in the pursuit which indicated a deep sense of the value of instruction. The educational philanthropist is not required, even in rural districts, to use stimulants to excite attention, or to beat up for scholars that his school may be filled.

Laird, 'The Contribution of Christian Missionaries', pp. 151–52 also notes ordinary villagers paying missionaries to establish schools. In the 1840s, another civil servant reported a similar clamour in his district. See Rao, *Beyond Macaulay*, p. 185.
221　Asok Sen, *Iswar Chandra Vidyasagar and His Elusive Milestones* (Calcutta: Riddhi-India, 1977), p. 14.
222　Massie, *Continental India*, Vol. 2, p. 401. See also Rao, *Beyond Macaulay*, p. 130 where we find an official reporting a popular Tamil proverb that went: 'not the Shastras but a knowledge of English.' This is not to say that English was accepted by everyone with unmeasurable delight. As always there were

orthodox sections in Hindu society that feared its advent. See Kumar, *Political Agenda of Education*, p. 63. Others were willing to accept English but moderated by a regard for one's own traditions and identity. As an 1852 Marathi article suggested, 'Students who learnt only English were likely to become shallow braggarts.' English *and* rootedness in one's own language were both essential like 'brick and mortar' in the building of a house. See Naregal, *Language Politics*, p. 136.

223 Modhumita Roy, '"Englishing" India: Reinstituting Class and Social Privilege', p. 98, in *Social Text* 39 (1994): 83–109; Rao, *Beyond Macaulay*, p. 84; Naregal, *Language Politics*, pp. 81–82. For similar patterns in colleges promoting Islamic learning in Arabic and Persian, see the case of the Delhi College in Liddle, *The Broken Script*, pp. 205–32. See also Sen, *Iswar Chandra Vidyasagar*, p. 35.

224 John Stuart Mill's draft 1836 letter in *The Great Indian Education Debate*, p. 232.

225 Letter dated July 1837 from the Resident in Nepal in ibid., p. 264.

226 Thomas Roe quoted in Roy, '"Englishing" India', p. 90.

227 Frykenberg, 'Modern Education', p. 41. See also Roy, '"Englishing" India', p. 92, p. 99. In this context, it was once written how 'A Bengalee School Boy cannot see what advantage is to be derived from a knowledge of the shape of the Earth, its dimensions revolutions etc.' because his primary goal was employment. Quoted in Laird, 'The Contribution of Christian Missionaries', p. 102.

228 Frykenberg, 'Modern Education', p. 46.

229 Rao, *Beyond Macaulay*, p. 55. See also Bruce Tiebout McCully, *English Education and the Origins of Indian Nationalism* (Gloucester Massachusetts: Peter Smith, 1966), pp. 91–100.

230 Rao, *Beyond Macaulay*, p. 149, p. 202, 239. Besides, there were even cases where students *gave up* English for Persian, seeing greater opportunity with the latter. See Laird, 'The Contribution of Christian Missionaries', p. 322. An 1830s petition from Hindus even argued that since the 'higher posts are given to the Europeans, the lower offices alone fall to the lot of the Bengallees', it was pointless to promote English. See Petition (1837–1838) from the Hindus of Bengal in *The Great Indian Education Debate*, p. 277.

231 Kumar, *Political Agenda of Education*, p. 25. B.G. Tilak, for example, a staunch nationalist who appears later in the century, saw no irony in setting up a school called the New English School in Pune. However, the cliché that colonial education churned out only clerks was embraced by some Indians also. See Sen, *Iswar Chandra Vidyasagar*, p. 48, for a late-nineteenth century writing in which the gods visiting Calcutta, find there only clerks.

232 On Indians being smatterers of English, Thomas Macaulay would counter that there were 'natives who are quite competent to discuss political or scientific questions with fluency and precision in the English language'.

Some, indeed, even exceeded the English in 'facility and correctness'. See Rao, *Beyond Macaulay*, p. 162.
233 Mahmood, *A History of English Education*, p. 25.
234 Ibid., pp. 25–26. When financial woes, caused by the loss of its endowment after the collapse of the company in which the money was invested, hit the Hindu College, the Company reluctantly offered aid. See Rao, *Beyond Macaulay*, pp. 77–78.
235 Quoted in Frykenberg, 'Modern Education', p. 56.
236 Committee of Public Instruction quoted in Charles E. Trevelyan, *On the Education of the People of India* (London: Longman, Orme, Brown, Green & Longmans, 1838), p. 108. Until government policy shifted in the mid-1830s in favour of English education, 'the Hindu College remained the greatest achievement in the domain of purely English education'. See McCully, *English Education*, p. 25.
237 Quoted in Rao, *Beyond Macaulay*, p. 141.
238 Lord Macaulay quoted in Michael John Whitfield, 'Dr John Tytler (1787–1837), Superintendent of the Native Medical Institution, Calcutta', p. 5, in *Journal of Medical Biography* (2019), pp. 1–6. See also Macaulay's Minute dated 2 February 1835 in *The Great Indian Education Debate*, p. 168.
239 Missionaries also often found themselves explaining to Indians that they lacked funds and could not cater to all the demand to open new schools. See Laird, 'The Contribution of Christian Missionaries', p. 151.
240 The governor general's resolution dated 7 March 1835 in *The Great Indian Education Debate*, pp. 194–96.
241 The Renaissance in Europe was catalysed by a renewed interest in ancient Latin and Greek works, not only of a philosophical nature—which generated fresh ways of thinking—but also pertaining to mathematics and science. As Macaulay wrote in his minute, if the British in this time had remained wedded to their Anglo–Saxon literature alone, ignoring a superior store of knowledge that came from these foreign high languages, they could not have progressed. India now, with English, was in the same position.
242 Macaulay's Minute dated 2 February 1835 in *The Great Indian Education Debate*, p. 171.
243 Quoted in John Clive, *Thomas Babington Macaulay: The Shaping of the Historian* (London: Secker & Walburg, 1973), p. 368. In 1833, in Parliament in London, Macaulay had also asked: 'Are we to keep the people of India in ignorance in order that we may keep them submissive?' See McCully, *English Education*, p. 64.
244 Macaulay's Minute dated 2 February 1835 in *The Great Indian Education Debate*, p. 170.
245 Indeed, when Macaulay pressed English, he also saw it as vernacular training, in that the meaning of English terms would have to be explained in local languages. See Rao, *Beyond Macaulay*, p. 169

246 Dhruv Raina, 'Mathematical Foundations of a Cultural Project or Ramchandra's Treatise "Through the Unsentimentalised Light of Mathematics"', p. 373, in *Historia Mathematica* 19 (1992): 371–84.
247 See Abhidha S. Dhumatkar, 'Forgotten Propagator of Science: Kolhapur's Balaji Prabhakar Modak', in *Economic and Political Weekly* 37, 48 (2002): 4807–816.
248 See Rosalind O'Hanlon, *Caste, Conflict, and Ideology: Mahatma Jotirao Phule and Low Caste Protest in Nineteenth-Century Western India* (Cambridge: Cambridge University Press, 1985), pp. 90–92. For some of Jambhekar's translations, see Ganesh Gangadhar Jambhekar ed., *Memoirs and Writings of Acharya Bal Gangadhar Shastri Jambhekar: Pioneer of the Renaissance in Western India and Father of Modern Maharashtra* (Poona: G.G. Jambhekar, 1950), pp. 62–64.
249 Rao, *Beyond Macaulay*, p. 199.
250 Aiya, *Travancore State Manual*, Vol. 1, pp. 488–89, p. 549. A European durbar physician here in 1860 published *Remarks on the Uses of Some Bazaar Medicines*, which listed treatments available for a variety of ailments using aloe, asafetida, nuts, cloves and other easily available ingredients, the book being printed in both English and Malayalam. See Edward J. Waring, *Remarks on the Uses of Some Bazaar Medicines, and on a Few of the Common Indigenous Plants of India, According to European Practice* (Trivandrum: Travancore Sircar Press, 1860).
251 Pillai, *False Allies*, pp. 33–35.
252 See, for instance, Naregal, *Language Politics*, p. 106, p. 141, pp. 173–74. In 1851, an official believed that Western education would cause 'caste, infant marriages, polygamy' etc. to 'melt away, like snow before fire'. See Rao, *Beyond Macaulay*, p. 203. In reality, however, educated 'natives' would find ways to hold on to many of these ideas, defending them in English. Or as Kumar notes in *Political Agenda of Education*, p. 46, Western knowledge could be deployed for 'the reconstruction of a traditional India'.
253 Iswar Chandra Vidyasagar quoted in Sen, *Iswar Chandra Vidyasagar*, p. 25. It was not easy: in Bombay, Jambhekar noted how in each class, English passages had to be explained to students in both Marathi and Gujarati (these being the chief language groups in the city). The reward lay in the students' keenness. See Rao, *Beyond Macaulay*, p. 111 and Naregal, *Language Politics*, p. 109. Translation of books was also not performed in a mechanical manner; elements that would 'apply only to Europe' and would be incomprehensible to Indian students were left out; instead, examples that would be more 'easily accessible' to the latter were used. See Naregal, *Language Politics*, pp. 120–21.
254 John Anderson quoted in Chakrabarti, *Local Selfhood*, p. 65.
255 Chakrabarti, *Local Selfhood*, p. 66. Naregal in *Language Politics*, pp. 134–35 also notes the Marathi paper *Dnyanaprasarak*, which in 1852 commended

the British for 'replacing a taste for ancient tales from the puranas' with 'knowledge about the efforts to men' who worked to improve society.
256 Chakrabarti, *Local Selfhood*, p. 194.
257 Ibid., p. 106. Indeed, Datta added that they anticipated key scientific principles: To give an example, Kanada, in the early centuries BCE, had 'propounded a theory of atoms'. The tragedy was that such innovations were not developed further. See Tapan Raychaudhuri, 'Europe in India's Xenology: The Nineteenth-Century Record', p. 164, in *Past & Present*, 137 (1992): 156–82. Datta's approach, understandably, upset missionaries who accused him of 'filching' from the West what he could not find at home. See Brian H. Hatcher, *Eclecticism and Modern Hindu Discourse* (New York: Oxford University Press, 1999), p. 114.
258 Chakrabarti, *Local Selfhood*, pp. 144–45. See also ibid., p. 199.
259 Indians who went abroad also showed this kind of selective admiration, on the one hand praising British liberty but not pretensions to racial superiority; technology but not parliamentary corruption, and so on. See, for instance, Charles Stewart (trans.), *Travels of Mirza Abu Taleb in Asia, Africa, and Europe during the Years 1799 to 1803* (New Delhi: Sona Publications, 1972 ed.), and Jehangeer Nowrojee & Hirjeebhoy Merwanjee, *Journal of a Residence of Two Years and a Half in Great Britain* (London: W.H. Allen & Co., 1841).
260 In fact, Lord Bentinck, the governor general who in 1835 sided with English education stated his 'entire dissent' from keeping Indians 'in ignorance. I cannot recognize the advantage of ignorance to the governors or the governed. If our rule is bad, as I believe it to be, let the natives have the means, through knowledge, to represent their grievances and to obtain redress.' See Letter 730 in C.H. Philips ed., *The Correspondence of Lord William Cavendish Bentinck: Governor-General of India, 1828–1835*, Vol. 2 (Oxford: Oxford University Press, 1977), p. 1286. See also Raychaudhuri, 'Europe in India's Xenology', p. 162. It is also not surprising that these Indian teachers fathered, quite literally, future nationalists. Gangadhar Tilak, who taught mathematics and in 1854 published an award-winning text on trigonometry, was the father of B.G. Tilak, a nationalist we will meet in the last chapter. See Vaibhav Purandare, *Tilak: The Empire's Biggest Enemy* (Gurugram: Vintage, 2024), pp. 3–4.
261 Frykenberg, 'Modern Education', p. 43.
262 Ibid.
263 Rao, *Beyond Macaulay*, p. 60. Importantly where the British hesitated to support the education of 'untouchables', missionaries refused to recognize caste divisions, opening their doors to all equally. In the mid-1850s, for example, in Maharashtra a Mahar boy was denied admission into a government school. In 1833, in Madras, a Parayar boy was similarly denied entry. See Eleanor Mae Zelliot, 'Dr Ambedkar and the Mahar Movement', Unpublished PhD dissertation. University of Pennsylvania (1970), pp. 47–48 and Rao, *Beyond Macaulay*, p. 131, pp. 61–62, p. 208.

264 I borrow the term from Laird, 'Contribution of Christian Missionaries', p. 81. Modern medicine was another means by which missionaries gained acceptability. Or as Strickland writes in *The Jesuit in India*, p. 127, it was as 'a physician of the body' that the missionary 'often first gains access to a Pagan house or village, where, as a Christian preacher, he would have had no hearers'.

265 Alexander Duff, *India and India Missions: Including Sketches of the Gigantic System of Hinduism* (Edinburgh, John Johnstone, 1840, second edition), p. 544. See also McCully, *English Education*, p. 39.

266 Quoted in Homi K. Bhabha, 'Signs Taken for Wonders: Questions of Ambivalence and Authority under a Tree outside Delhi, May 1817', p. 148, in *Critical Inquiry* 12, 1 (1985): 144–65.

267 Venkateswaran, 'Negotiating Secular School Textbooks', pp. 177–78. See also Laird, 'The Contribution of Christian Missionaries', p. 121, where we read how one missionary, on the founding of Hindu College in Calcutta, saw even this as god's work in favour of ultimately dismantling Hinduism.

268 Kumar, *Political Agenda*, p. 66. See also Pennington, *Was Hinduism Invented?*, pp. 158–59. One is reminded here also of Ranajit Guha, who wrote: 'Did education have nothing other than intellectual exertion and advancement of knowledge as its content? . . . Although colonialism and the many-sided thrust of liberal politics made it out to be so, there was more to education than was thus conceived. *It stood not only for enlightenment but also authority*'. Emphasis added.

269 Kumar, *Political Agenda*, p. 66.

270 Venkateswaran, 'Negotiating Secular School Textbooks', p. 161. In 1824, in Bombay, a bureaucrat put this down to the 'easy tolerant spirit of Hinduism' which did not mind the use of Christian texts for children's education. Quoted in Rao, *Beyond Macaulay*, p. 63.

271 Eustace Carey, *Memoir of William Carey* (Boston: Gould, Kendall & Lincoln, 1836), pp. 274–75.

272 See John Bentley, *A Historical View of the Hindu Astronomy* (Calcutta: Baptist Mission Press, 1823), p. 147.

273 Quoted in Venkateswaran, 'Negotiating Secular School Textbooks', pp. 171–72. See also ibid., p. 173 for another missionary noting that while some thought education would bring Hindus to Christianity, 'We believe that they are being prepared for occupying a position extremely antagonistic to it.' This is not to say there were no exceptions. A student of Hindu College once ate beef and threw the bones into a Brahmin's yard. See Laird, 'The Contribution of Christian Missionaries', p. 294.

274 See Laird, 'The Contribution of Christian Missionaries', pp. 106–08.

275 See Kumar, *Science and the Raj*, p. 61.

276 On the general idea of religion and science not being, as is popularly believed, in eternal combat, but having a much more complex relationship, see John

Hedley Brooke, *Science and Religion: Some Historical Perspectives* (Cambridge: Cambridge University Press, 2014 [1991]).

277  See Young, 'Receding from Antiquity', p. 194. See also *Report of the Fourth Decennial Indian Missionary Conference* (London: Christian Literature Society, 1903), p. 78, where we read how 'Science is the hand-maid of religion'.

278  See *The Missionary Herald: Containing the Proceedings of the American Board of Commissioners for Foreign Missions*, Vol. 84 (Boston: Stanley & Usher, 1888), p. 438. The reformer Dayananda Saraswati—who we will meet in a subsequent chapter—was also said to be 'similar to Ingersoll' in his treatment of the Bible. See F.L. Neeld, 'Hindu Puritan Reform—The Arya Somaj', p. 298, in Arthur T. Pierson ed., *The Missionary Review of the World*, Vol. 5 (New Series) (New York: Funk & Wagnalls Company, 1892), pp. 297–99.

279  Quoted in Homi K. Bhabha, *The Location of Culture* (London: Routledge, 1994), p. 92. Similar remarks appear in Strickland, *The Jesuit in India*, p. 89.

280  Wilson, *Essays and Lectures*, Vol. 2, p. 42.

281  Quoted in Nirad C. Chaudhuri, *Scholar Extraordinary: The Life of Professor Friedrich Max Muller* (London: Chatto & Windus, 1974), p. 325.

282  Quoted in Georgina Grenfell eds., *The Life and Letters of Friedrich Max Muller*, Vol. 1 (London: Longmans, Green & Co., 1902), p. 362. Indeed, Muller saw even the Upanishads—the Vedas' philosophical ruminations—as rich in 'poetical eloquence' but otherwise mostly 'rubbish' and 'meaningless jargon'. See Sharada Sugirtharajah, 'Max Muller and Textual Management: A Postcolonial Perspective', p. 40, in Rita D. Sherma and Arvind Sharma eds., *Hermeneutics and Hindu Thought: Toward a Fusion of Horizons* (London: Springer, 2008), pp. 33–44.

283  Quoted in Chaudhuri, *Scholar Extraordinary*, p. 325.

284  Letter dated 02 June 1860 from E.B. Pusey to Max Muller in *Life and Letters of Friedrich Max Muller*, Vol. 1, pp. 237–38. See also ibid., p. 236 for a similar letter from the bishop of Calcutta. In 1856, Muller wrote in fact of maybe going to India someday and to 'take part in a work, by means of which the old mischief of Indian priestcraft could be overthrown and the way opened for the entrance of simple Christian teaching.' Quoted in Chaudhuri, *Scholar Extraordinary*, p. 325. In later life, of course, Muller would be accused of being *anti*-Christian.

## Five: For God and Country

1  John Login quoted in Lena Login, *Sir John Login and Duleep Singh* (London: WH Allen & Co., 1890), p. 192.

2  *The Maharajah Duleep Singh and the Government: A Narrative* (London: Trubner & Co, 1884), p. 82.

3   Anonymous, *The Christian Treasury: Containing Contributions from Ministers and Members of Various Christian Denominations*, Vol. 33 (1877), p. 263. In actual fact, Bhajan Lal's statement dated 17 January 1851 shows that Duleep Singh first learnt of Christianity through a textbook called the *English Instructor* and began asking questions about Hindu customs, such as the benefits of bathing in the Ganga. It was thereafter—by which time the maharajah had started identifying 'nonsense' in his own culture—that he saw Bhajan Lal's Bible. In December 1850, he formally expressed a desire to 'embrace the Christian religion' because 'I have long doubted the truth of the one I was brought up in'. See Login, *John Login*, pp. 245–48 and p. 250.

4   Archdeacon John Pratt quoted in W.W.W. Humbley, *Journal of a Cavalry Officer: Including the Memorable Sikh Campaign, 1845–1846* (London: Longman, Brian, Green & Longmans, 1854), p. 213.

5   *Bombay Guardian*, 8 July 1853.

6   *The Oriental Christian Spectator* quoted in Humbley, *Journal*, p. 217.

7   Sir Charles Wood quoted in *Bombay Guardian*, 8 July 1853.

8   William Butler, 'Gentlemen of India', p. 33, in *The Ladies' Repository: A Monthly Periodical Devoted to Literature and Religion*, Vol. 31 (New Series Vol. 7) (1871).

9   Secretary, Government of India, to John Login on 17 February 1851, in Login, *John Login*, p. 262. As a publication Duleep Singh arranged later affirmed, 'the choice was his own', after he grew 'much impressed' with precepts of the Gospel. See *The Maharajah Duleep Singh*, p. 82.

10  It was in 1851 that Duleep Singh's desire was communicated to Lord Dalhousie, who recorded in March 1853 that his 'probation' had ended. See J.G.A. Baird ed., *Private Letters of the Marquess of Dalhousie* (Edinburgh & London: William Blackwood & Sons, 1910), p. 156, p. 248. Login, of course, knew as early as December 1850.

11  There was even briefly a plan to have this princess marry Duleep Singh.

12  Veer Rajinder Wuddair's letter dated 3 July 1856 in *Morning Post*, 4 July 1856.

13  *Gloucester Journal*, 13 February 1864. The British fear of Duleep Singh's mother was real. When someone spoke to Dalhousie about the maharajah's beautiful eyes, he wrote: 'Those "beautiful eyes", with which Duleep has taken captive the court [in England], are his mother's eyes—those with which she captivated and controlled the old Lion of the Punjab.'

14  *The Maharajah Duleep Singh*, p. 79, p. 81.

15  Login, *John Login*, p. 232.

16  *The Maharajah Duleep Singh*, p. 86.

17  Bhajan Lal's statement in Login, *John Login*, p. 247.

18  The Logins did, of course, develop affection for Duleep Singh. At one point, Login wrote to his wife that he expected Duleep Singh to look upon her as

his mother (Login, *John Login*, p. 214), and as early as July 1850, he was considering prospective brides for the maharajah (ibid., p. 220).
19. Login, *John Login*, p. 277
20. Sir Henry Elliott quoted in Login, *John Login*, p. 266.
21. Baird, *Letters*, p. 248.
22. Ibid., p. 249.
23. Lord Dalhousie quoted in Login, *John Login*, p. 307.
24. Baird, *Letters*, p. 156. Of course, almost at once, a nephew, son of Maharajah Sher Singh, who had ruled before Duleep Singh, tried to claim the title, for whatever it was worth. Dalhousie, however, made it clear that the maharajah's conversion did not negate his title. Yet, Dalhousie would not even let Duleep Singh take a Sikh wife, so as to to dilute his status—a case of eating his cake and having it too. Login, *John Login*, p. 230.
25. Baird, *Letters*, p. 249. Emphasis added.
26. His age may have had something to do with this. When sent to India, Dalhousie was only in his thirties.
27. In celebrating the takeover of Punjab, for instance, Dalhousie presented it as much as a matter of pride for Britain as being for 'the future good' of Indians now subject to the Company, thanking also 'Almighty God' for this 'brilliant success'. See Baird, *Letters*, pp. 62–63.
28. This is not to say that religious interference was the sole cause of the 1857 Rebellion. There were multiple other grievances also around economic and political displacement.
29. Josiah Bateman, *The Life of the Right Rev. Daniel Wilson*, Vol. 2 (London: John Murray, 1860), p. 119.
30. Ibid.
31. One might see here a variant of the American concept of 'manifest destiny'.
32. Carson, *The East India Company and Religion*, pp. 7–8. See also Veevers, *Origins*, pp. 83–84, p. 95, p. 138.
33. Carson, *The East India Company and Religion*, p. 14.
34. See, for instance, Joshua Marshman, *Advantages of Christianity in Promoting the Establishment and Prosperity of the British Government in India* (London: Smith's Printing Office, 1813), p. 6, where we read that 'the most effectual means of perpetuating British power' was the 'steady and constant diffusion of christian [sic] light among the natives'.
35. For a critique of a disinterested Christianity, see William Wilberforce, *A Practical View of the Prevailing Religious System of Professed Christians in the Higher and Middle Classes in this Country, Contrasted with Real Christianity* (London: T. Cadell, 1797). Correspondingly, after the defeat of Napoleon some years later, British triumph was advertised as confirmation of god's blessings for Protestantism and its propagation.
36. Quoted in Carson, *The East India Company and Religion*, p. 21. And this sense of duty was sincerely absorbed. As one CMS missionary would wonder

in 1838, 'the thought of 800 millions [in India] passing into eternity every 30 years without a ray of hope often overwhelms me, then I ask myself the question, am I doing my part to avert these dire consequences?' Quoted in Antony Copley, *Religions in Conflict: Ideology, Cultural Contact and Conversion in Late-Colonial India* (Delhi: Oxford University Press, 1997), p. 9.

37  And indeed, many saw sin in Calcutta. See Karen Chancey, 'The Star in the East: The Controversy over Christian Missions to India, 1805–1813', pp. 510–11, in *Historian* 60, 3 (1998): 507–22.

38  'The Indian Army', in *Blackwood's Edinburgh Magazine*, Vol. 21 (London: T. Cadell, 1827), p. 563.

39  See Bearce, *British Attitudes*, pp. 39–40.

40  Carson, *The East India Company and Religion*, p. 46.

41  For instance, as the Third Report dated 13 May 1802 of the Religious Tract Society put it: 'We live in an age and in a country distinguished by those inventions and improvements which indicate a highly polished state of Society'. But these would be 'advantageous or prejudicial according to the principle which directs the use of them. The art of Printing, for example' could be used to disseminate 'truth, justice, purity and happiness' but also 'Infidelity and Debauchery'. See *Proceedings of the First Twenty Years of the Religious Tract Society* (London: Benjamin Bensley, 1820), p. 32.

42  On this trend of individual Christians becoming the means of throwing open salvation to non-Christians, see Joseph Stubenrauch, *The Evangelical Age of Ingenuity in Industrial Britain* (Oxford: Oxford University Press, 2016), pp. 29–40. See also Bearce, *British Attitudes*, p. 5, and Copley, *Religions in Conflict*, p. 10, and Alison Twells, *The Civilising Mission and the English Middle Class, 1792–1850: The 'Heathen' at Home and Overseas* (Basingstoke: Palgrave Macmillan, 2009).

43  In this context, see also Cox's reference to a 'geo-religious triumphalism'. Jeffrey Cox, *Imperial Fault Lines: Christianity and Colonial Power in India, 1818–1940* (Stanford: Stanford University Press, 2002), p. 23.

44  Ainslie Thomas Embree, *Charles Grant and British Rule in India* (London: George Allen & Unwin, 1962), p. 118.

45  Oddie, *Imagined Hinduism*, p. 71.

46  Charles Grant, 'A Proposal for Establishing a Protestant Mission in Bengal and Behar', 17 September 1787, in Henry Morris, *The Life of Charles Grant* (London: John Murray, 1904), pp. 108–14.

47  Lord Cornwallis to Henry Dundas, 4 April 1790 in Charles Ross ed., *Correspondence of Charles, First Marquis Cornwallis*, Vol. 2 (London: John Murray, 1859), p. 19.

48  John Shore to Charles Grant, 5 May 1794 in Charles John Shore, *Memoir of the Life and Correspondence of John Lord Teignmouth* (London: Hatchard & Son, 1843), pp. 291–92.

49. For British anxieties over 'native' troops—including fear that training them well might one day allow them to turn on the Company—see G.J. Bryant, 'Indigenous Mercenaries in the Service of European Imperialists: The Case of the Sepoys in the Early British Indian Army, 1750–1800', *War in History* 7, 1 (2000): 2–28.
50. Cox, *Imperial Fault Lines*, p. 24. See also Jean Comaroff and John Comaroff, *Of Revelation and Revolution: Christianity, Colonialism, and Consciousness in South Africa*, Vol. 1 (Chicago: University of Chicago Press, 1991), pp. 51–52, where we find how Sydney Smith (1771–1845), himself a cleric, criticized evangelicals as 'quite insane' for exposing 'our whole Eastern empire to destruction, for the sake of converting half a dozen Brahmans'. 'Upon the whole,' he added, 'it appears to us hardly possible to push the business of proselytism in India . . . without incurring the utmost risk of losing our empire.'
51. Charles Grant, *Observations on the State of Society among the Asiatic Subjects of Great Britain, Particularly with Respect to Morals; and on the Means of Improving It* (1797).
52. Ibid., p. ii.
53. And ironically, Grant had written a rather moving account as a younger man of the great famine in Bengal. See Embree, *Charles Grant*, pp. 35–36.
54. Grant, *Observations*, p. 45, pp. 47–48, p. 50, p. 52, p. 54.
55. Ibid., p. 78.
56. Ibid., pp. 56–65. This is not to say Grant had nothing meaningful to say: His critique of caste (ibid., pp. 81–82), for instance, stands up better to scrutiny.
57. Carson, *The East India Company and Religion*, p. 4.
58. Ibid., pp. 12–13.
59. Caspar Morris, *The Life of William Wilberforce* (New York: Protestant Episcopal Society for the Promotion of Evangelical Knowledge, 1857), p. 207. Elsewhere Wilberforce would speak of 'Hindu divinities' as 'absolute monsters of lust, injustice, wickedness and cruelty.'
60. As Susan Thorne observes, evangelicals saw the home and foreign lands as 'two fronts of the same war' in promoting faith and Christian values. See Thorne, *Congregational Missions and the Making of an Imperial Culture in Nineteenth-Century England* (Stanford: Stanford University Press, 1999), p. 17.
61. Callum Brown quoted in Stubenrauch, *The Evangelical Age*, p. 135.
62. Stubenrauch, *The Evangelical Age*, p. 101.
63. Ibid., p. 124, p. 139. Or as William Carey wrote in support of missionary activity: '[C]ommerce shall subserve the spread of the gospel.' See Carey, *An Enquiry into the Obligations of Christians to Use Means for the Conversion of the Heathens* (Leicester: Ann Ireland, 1792), p. 68. This idea, however, existed even in the seventeenth century. See Das, *Courting India*, p. 58.
64. Similarly, the first Church of Scotland missionary, Alexander Duff, was the son of a gardener.

65  Quoted in Carson, *The East India Company and Religion*, p. 143. See also Susan Thorne, '"The Conversion of Englishmen and the Conversion of the World Inseparable": Missionary Imperialism and the Language of Class in Early Industrial Britain', p. 244, in Frederick Cooper and Ann Laura Stoler eds., *Tensions of Empire: Colonial Cultures in a Bourgeois World* (Berkeley: University of California Press, 1997), pp. 238–62. One missionary himself wrote how a colleague wanted to go to the West Indies to work as a clerk, with hopes of becoming an officer. When that did not happen, he became a missionary. See Potts, *British Baptist Missionaries in India, 1793–1837*, p. 23. See also Pennington, *Was Hinduism Invented?*, p. 76.

66  Quoted in Cox, *Imperial Fault Lines*, p. 8.

67  For a study, see Gareth Atkins, *Converting Britannia: Evangelicals and British Public Life, 1770–1840* (Woodbridge: The Boydell Press, 2019).

68  Carson, *The East India Company and Religion*, p. 53. Carey and his colleague were also expected to focus primarily on educational and linguistic activities, not proselytism. See Dirks, *Castes of Mind*, p. 26. Indigo also evidently required only a part of the year to be dedicated to it; the calculation was that for the rest of their time, the missionaries could focus on selling religion.

69  Potts, *British Baptist Missionaries*, p. 27.

70  Carson, *The East India Company and Religion*, p. 64.

71  Ibid., p. 65.

72  Oddie, *Imagined Hinduism*, pp. 30–31. Carey even celebrated the French Revolution as god's doing.

73  Carey transferred himself from British territory to Serampore, a Danish enclave, in this time.

74  Report of the Vellore Mutiny Commission dated 9 August 1806 in William Bentinck, *Memorial Addressed to the Honourable Court of Directors Containing an Account of the Mutiny at Vellore with the Causes and Consequences of that Event* (London: John Booth, 1810), p. 71. Grant would dismiss this idea, suggesting that it was solely the dead Tipu Sultan's family, held in Vellore Fort, who orchestrated the revolt. Historical consensus is that religious fears were a final addition to more longstanding general grievances, waiting to come to the fore through violence. Sympathy for Mysore also existed. See Farooqui, *Colonial Subjugation*, pp. 57–59.

75  See, for instance, Thomas Twining, *A Letter to the Chairman of the East India Company on the Danger of Interfering in the Religious Opinions of the Natives of India* (London: J. Ridgway, 1807). See also Emma Minto, *Lord Minto in India: Life and Letters of Gilbert Elliott, First Earl of Minto, from 1807 to 1814* (London: Longmans, Green & Co., 1880), pp. 62–64; Kenneth Ingham, *Reformers in India, 1793–1833: An Account of the Work of Christian Missionaries on Behalf of Social Reform* (Cambridge: Cambridge University Press, 1956), pp. 7–8; and C.A. Bayly, *Origins of Nationality in South Asia: Patriotism and Ethical Government in the Making of Modern India* (Delhi: Oxford University

Press, 1998), p. 79. See also Carson, *The East India Company and Religion*, pp. 76–77, which notes that at least fourteen missionaries were active in south India at the time of the mutiny.

76   See Jorg Fisch, 'A Pamphlet War on Christian Missions in India, 1807–1809', in *Journal of Asian History* 19, No. 1 (1985): 22–70.

77   Court of Directors' despatch dated 29 May 1807 in Minto, *Lord Minto in India*, pp. 62–63.

78   Quoted in Carson, *The East India Company and Religion*, p. 82.

79   Ibid., p. 95, and Bayly, *Origins of Nationality*, pp. 68–69.

80   Or, to quote a later commentator, 'God has . . . given us India in trust for the accomplishment of His grand evangelizing designs concerning it.' See Alexander Duff, *The Indian Rebellion: Its Causes and Results* (New York: Robert Carter & Brothers, 1858), p. 255.

81   Why, 'even the boldest opponents of attempts at evangelization were at times anxious to avoid the accusation of indifference towards missionary enterprise'. See Ingham, *Reformers*, p. 11.

82   Carson, *The East India Company and Religion*, p. 132.

83   Ibid., p. 139. As Ingham, *Reformers*, p. 11, reminds us, this was not a spontaneous show of support but very much a campaign organized and instigated to achieve the goal of influencing lawmakers at that critical moment.

84   See the full clause in Carson, *The East India Company and Religion*, Appendix 4, p. 250. Evidently, through some clever maneuvering the vote on the clause took place late at night, and many opponents had already left. See Ian Copland, 'Christianity as an Arm of Empire: The Ambiguous Case of India under the Company, c. 1813–58', p. 1031, in *The Historical Journal* 49, 4 (2006): 1025–54.

85   It was established by Wellesley. Evidently a good part of Tipu Sultan's library was held here, after his death.

86   Carey agreed: 'Men make themselves idols,' he wrote, 'after their own hearts, and therefore to look for good morals among idolaters is the height of folly'. Quoted in Potts, *British Baptist Missionaries*, p. 6.

87   Claudius Buchanan, *Christian Researches in Asia* (Boston: Samuel T. Armstrong, 1811), p. 44.

88   Ibid., p. 60. Similar unflattering comparisons would continue to be made even decades later. See Y. Vincent Kumaradoss, *Robert Caldwell: A Scholar-Missionary in Colonial South India* (Delhi: ISPCK, 2007), p. 99.

89   Interestingly, as the Portuguese had tried to bind the Nasranis—or Syrian Christians—in Kerala to (Catholic) Rome, Buchanan would now attempt to tie these 'native' Christians to the (Protestant) Church of England. See Buchanan, *Christian Researches*, pp. 103–04.

90   As Pennington writes, 'Much of the missionaries' polemical engagements with Hindus had something to do with their own fight for legitimacy.' See Pennington, *Was Hinduism Invented?*, p. 162.

91  Buchanan, *Christian Researches*, pp. 25–40.
92  Wilbert R. Shenk, '"Ancient Churches" and Modern Missions in the Nineteenth Century', p. 52, in Richard Fox Young ed., *India and the Indianness of Christianity: Essays on Understanding—Historical, Theological, and Bibliographical—in Honor of Robert Eric Frykenberg* (Grand Rapids: Wm. B. Erdmans Publishing, 2009), pp. 41–58. In some accounts we read of this as nine reprints in two years.
93  Oddie, *Imagined Hinduism*, p. 82.
94  Claudius Buchanan, *Memoir of the Expediency of an Ecclesiastical Establishment for British India; Both as the Means of Perpetuating the Christian Religion Among Our Own Countrymen; And as a Foundation for the Ultimate Civilization of the Natives* (London: T. Cadell & W. Davies, 1805), p. 25. Emphasis added.
95  The idea that Hindus fed babies to crocodiles endured. In 1894, when the celebrated monk Swami Vivekananda visited America, at Detroit this was among the questions raised before him. The swami 'in a half serious, half comic manner [replied] how, when he was a baby, his mother took him to the Ganges but that he was "such a fat little baby the crocodiles refused to swallow me".' See Mary Louise Burke, *Vivekananda in the West: New Discoveries* (Calcutta: Advaita Ashram, 1961 ed.), p. 246. I am grateful to Govind Krishnan V. for bringing this nugget to my attention.
96  Buchanan, *Memoir*, p. 40. And indeed, Indians who converted often found that Europeans did not treat them as equals. See Potts, *British Baptist Missionaries*, p. 40 for an example.
97  Buchanan, *Memoir*, p. 65.
98  This is believed to have been Charles Stuart, popularly called 'Hindoo Stuart'.
99  A Bengal Officer (Charles Stuart?), *A Vindication of the Hindoos from the Aspersions of the Reverend Claudius Buchanan* (London: R & J Rodwell, 1808), pp. 9–10.
100  Ibid., p. 57. Jean-Antoine Dubois, the French Catholic missionary, also warned against missionary strategies that appealed only to 'stupid and helpless fellows'. See Dirks, *Castes of Mind*, pp. 24–25. Experience also showed that converts often came over for reasons other than faith. See Potts, *British Baptist Missionaries*, pp. 43–44.
101  *Vindication*, pp. 73–74.
102  'Review of a Bengal Officer's Vindication of the Hindus', pp. 104–05, *The Christian Observer*, Vol. 7, No. 74 (February 1808), pp. 104–23 (London: Ellerton & Byworth, 1809).
103  Or as C.F. Schwartz said, Jesus had commanded the apostles to 'preach the Gospel to *all* nations'. The whole world was the missionary's field of action. Quoted in Copland, Mabett et al., *A History of State and Religion in India*, p. 172.
104  John Pemble quoted in Copley, *Religions in Conflict*, p. 12.

105  I borrow these terms from Trautmann's *Aryans and British India*.
106  Criticism of this was occasionally made by missionaries themselves. In 1840, William Buyers of the LMS dismissed BMS pioneer William Ward's work for too much generalization. His claims, Buyers wrote, were 'no more applicable to the great variety' of people in India than 'a description of the people of Yorkshire would apply to the various nations of Europe'. Quoted in Oddie, *Imagined Hinduism*, p. 273.
107  Jones quoted in Amal Chatterjee, *Representations of India, 1740–1840: The Creation of India in the Colonial Imagination* (London: Macmillan Press, 1998), p. 93. Ziegenbalg also reported similar views.
108  As late as 1852, in all Bengal, there were only 102 European missionaries. See Copley, *Religions in Conflict*, p. 65.
109  Carson, *The East India Company and Religion*, p. 250. See also Penelope Carson, 'Missionaries, Bureaucrats and the People of India', p. 142, in Nancy G. Cassels ed., *Orientalism, Evangelicalism and the Military Cantonment in Early Nineteenth-Century India: A Historiographical Overview* (New York: the Edwin Mellen Press, 1991), pp. 125–55, and Ingham, *Reformers*, p. 11.
110  Carson, *The East India Company and Religion*, pp. 147–55. See also Chancey, 'Star in the East' for an exploration of rivalry between the Church of England and the evangelicals. With regard to the bishop, his successor, Bishop Heber, also disagreed with evangelical portrayal of Hindus as depraved. Heber did not like their religion but did not dismiss their culture or character as terrible. The occasional temple could even move him. See Oddie, *Imagined Hinduism*, p. 86–92, p. 94, and Bearce, *British Attitudes*, pp. 85–87.
111  Carson, *The East India Company and Religion*, p. 165. With textbooks, missionaries subtly managed to inject religious content, nevertheless. See Bayly, *Origins*, p. 280.
112  Lord Bentinck to Daniel Wilson, 6 June 1834 (Letter no. 731) in C.H. Phillips ed., *The Correspondence of Lord William Cavendish Bentinck, Governor-General of India, 1828–1835*, Vol. 2 (Oxford: Oxford University Press, 1977), p. 1288.
113  Tellingly, Wilson's appointment as bishop was enabled by Charles Grant Jr, son of the author of the 1792 *Observations*.
114  Thorne, 'The Conversion of Englishmen', p. 246.
115  Of course, in India, there was cooperation, joint excursions, etc. by missionaries of these societies in the early years. See Potts, *British Baptist Missionaries*, p. 59.
116  Between 1780 and 1830, Britain's reading population rose from an estimated 1.5 million to over 7 million. See Oddie, *Imagined Hinduism*, pp. 203–04.
117  *Missionary Papers*, No. 2, Midsummer, 1816.
118  *Missionary Papers*, No. 5, Lady-Day, 1817.
119  *Missionary Papers*, No. 8, Christmas, 1817.
120  Oddie, *Imagined Hinduism*, p. 208.

121 See Bayly, *Origins*, p. 151.
122 There are still occasional reports. See this 2023 report titled 'Minor boy beheaded in human sacrifice ritual in Dadra and Nagar Haveli; three including juvenile held', *The Hindu*, 11 January 2023: available at https://www.thehindu.com/news/national/other-states/silvassa-minor-boy-beheaded-in-human-sacrifice-ritual-three-including-juvenile-held/article66365833.ece (accessed on 8 August 2024). See also Dirks, *Castes of Mind*, p. 174 on how talk of human sacrifice enabled the expansion of the colonial state into tribal areas.
123 Between 1817 and 1827, 4323 cases of sati were recorded, of a total population in India exceeding 150 million. Most of this was in Bengal, while in Madras and Bombay, between 1815 and 1820, the annual figures were under fifty. See Bayly, *Origins*, p. 153. An orientalist like H.T. Colebrooke noted in the 1790s that 'instances of widow's sacrifices are now rare', adding that asking Indians about sati would show 'how few instances have actually occurred' in their memory. See Colebrooke, *Essays*, p. 75. However, BMS missionaries and Buchanan could get away with declaring that Bengal alone saw 10,000 satis on an annual basis. See Ingham, *Reformers*, p. 47.
124 Jorg Fisch, 'Humanitarian Achievement or Administrative Necessity? Lord William Bentinck and the Abolition of Sati in 1829', p. 118 in *Journal of Asian History* 34, 2 (2000): 109–34. In 1813, thus, one sati was aged two-and-a-half years. It must also be admitted that European horror on actually witnessing satis was genuine. In 1782, in Maharashtra, thus, a woman was about to be burned but was rescued by a party of white men. See Rosalind O'Hanlon, 'Narratives of Penance and Purification in Western India c., 1650-1850', pp. 67–68, in *The Journal of Hindu Studies* 2, 1 (2009): 48-75. The mother of William Jones's pandit, Radhakant, also became a sati, aged eighty. See Rocher, 'The Career of Radhakanta Tarkavagisa', p. 627.
125 Dirks, *Castes of Mind*, p. 174.
126 Oddie, *Imagined Hinduism*, pp. 220–21, p. 180. See also Thorne, 'Missionary Imperialism', p. 245 on how journals were dependent on 'large numbers of small contributors' for survival.
127 As a missionary wrote later in the century, if his fellow religious professionals failed to properly impress 'upon the minds of our hearers in Christian lands' a 'clear and definite conception' of the 'soul-destroying influence of idolatry', how could those readers 'feel the profound sympathy' or pray with 'such earnestness and understanding as the occasion demands'? Besides, the 'promise of interesting information' also 'sometimes secures the attendance at missionary meetings of those who otherwise might not take the trouble to come'. See Mateer, *The Gospel in South India*, pp. 11–13.
128 Oddie, *Imagined Hinduism*, p. 217. Indeed, missionaries were admonished for *not* sending sufficiently graphic accounts for the home readership.

129 Indians noted this in the same period. As *The Brahmunical Magazine* complained in Bengal in 1821, 'missionary gentlemen seldom translate into English the Upanishads, the ancient Smritis, the Tantras quoted by respectable authors, and which have always been regarded'. See Jogendra Chunder Ghose ed., *The English Works of Raja Rammohun Roy*, Vol. 1 (New Delhi: Cosmo Publications, 1982), p. 162.

130 Bateman, *Life of Daniel Wilson*, p. 390. Alexander Duff would also later write how his father exposed him to pictures of Jagannath, with 'copious explanations, well fitted to create a feeling of horror towards idolatry and of compassion towards the poor blinded idolaters'. See Thomas Smith, *Alexander Duff* (London: Hodder & Stoughton, 1883), p. 20.

131 Bayly, *Origins*, p. 153. Missionaries could, amusingly, come up with interesting mathematical calculations. One, noting how the number of Christians in Bengal rose between 1783 and 1800 from six to fifty-six projected future conversions at 392 in 1817, 2744 in 1834, 19,200 in 1851 and so on, until the population was fully Christian. See Potts, *British Baptist Missionaries*, p. 35.

132 See William Ward, *A View of the History, Literature, and Religion of the Hindoos: Including a Minute Description of their Manners and Customs, and Translations from their Principal Works*, Vol. 2 (Serampore: Baptist Mission Press, 1818 ed.).

133 Ibid., p. lxxv. See also Oddie, *Imagined Hinduism*, pp. 33–35, p. 164, where we see missionaries investing in learning about Hindu mythology for reasons ranging from wanting to undermine it to wanting to look more approachable to 'natives'.

134 See figures for 1815–28 in Fisch, 'Humanitarian Achievement or Administrative Necessity?', p. 115. Even considering undercounting, the highest figure in these years was just over 800 in 1818. Later authorities agreed that sati was not a widespread custom. See Elphinstone, *A History of India*, Vol. 1, pp. 364–68.

135 George Mundy, *Christianity and Hindooism Contrasted: Or, A Comparative View of the Evidence by which the Respective Claims to Divine Authority of the Bible and Hindoo Sasters are Supported* (Calcutta: Baptist Mission Press, 1827), p. 3, pp. 10–12, p. 14.

136 Jean-Antoine (Abbe) Dubois, *Description of the Character, Manners, and Customs of the People of India; and of their Institutions, Religious and Civil* (London: Longman, Hurst, Rees, Orme & Brown, 1817), p. 15. On the plagiarism, see Jurgen Osterhammel (Robert Savage trans.), *Unfabling the East: The Enlightenment's Encounter with Asia* (Princeton: Princeton University Press, 2018), pp. 179–80. For a counter that claims of plagiarism are exaggerated, see Jyoti Mohan, 'British and French Ethnographies of India: Dubois and His English Commentators', *French Colonial History* 5 (2004): 229–46.

137 Before the book was published, Dubois made fresh edits and changes, in which he advocated non-intervention in Hindu practices. However, this updated version was not printed in English. It would only appear later, in 1899, in a new translation. See Jean-Antoine (Abbe) Dubois (Henry K. Beauchamp ed.), *Hindu Manners, Customs and Ceremonies* (Oxford: Clarendon Press, 1899), p. 97 and 'Prefatory Note'.

138 Trautmann, *Aryans and British India*, p. 117. For a detailed analysis of the text itself and Mill's intellectual thinking, see Javed Majeed, *Ungoverned Imaginings: James Mill's The History of British India and Orientalism* (Oxford: Clarendon Press, 1992). Copley in *Religions in Conflict*, p. 38 goes further and calls Mill's work 'one of the most condemnatory accounts of another culture ever written'.

139 Mill, of course, was also a creature of context, and there were diverse influences informing his approach to history, India and British rule. He believed, for instance, in history as the march of progress; acknowledging a glorious Hindu past which then declined, as orientalists argued, did not fit this world view. For a study exploring this, see Jeng-Guo Chen, 'James Mill's "History of British India" in Its Intellectual Context', Unpublished PhD dissertation, University of Edinburgh, UK (2000).

140 James Mill, *The History of British India*, Vol. 1 (London: Baldwin, Cradock & Joy, 1817), p. 152. For criticism of Mill and his project from within British ranks, see Dirks, *Castes of Mind*, pp. 37–38. Even though Mill was using this to highlight the crudeness of Hindu culture even in a supposedly past golden age, its effect was very much to tarnish contemporary Hindus. On throwing women to dogs, see also Sharma, *Modern Hindu Thought*, pp. 149–50.

141 See Wagle, 'Kotwal's Papers', pp. 35–36; Gokhale, *Poona*, p. 167. See Mill, *History*, p. 158, where he remarks that adultery with a Brahmin woman brought down punishment worse than that assigned for 'parricide'. Yet, in 1772, among the Marathas—under the government of the Brahmin Peshwa—a man who committed adultery with a Brahmin woman faced only confiscation of property. If anything, it was women who were more strictly punished. See Gokhale, *Poona*, p. 167; Wagle, 'Women', p. 35; and Uma Chakravarty, 'Wifehood, Widowhood, and Adultery: Female Sexuality, Surveillance and the State in 18th Century Maharashtra', pp. 12–13, in *Contributions to Indian Sociology* 29, 1 and 2 (1995): 3–21. In Bengal, in 1807, a woman accused of adultery had to face trial by ordeal but again was spared dog attacks. See Chunder, *Travels of a Hindoo*, p. 47. It is possible there were violent punishments elsewhere, but the point is that Mill's generalizations must be identified as that: generalizations, devoid of context.

142 J. Barton Scott, *Spiritual Despots: Modern Hinduism and the Genealogies of Self-Rule* (Chicago: The University of Chicago Press, 2016), p. 37.

143 Trautmann, *Aryans and British India*, p. 118. Within a few years, Mill would have his son also offered a position by the Company.

144 Mill, *History*, p. 646. David Kopf has gone as far as to suggest that Mill had a 'Hitlerean' prejudice against Hindus. See Kopf, 'European Enlightenment, Hindu Renaissance and the Enrichment of the Hindu Spirit: A History of Historical Writings on British Orientalism', p. 26, in Cassel ed., *Orientalism, Evangelicalism*, pp. 19–53.

145 The orientalist H.H. Wilson stated as much in his preface to subsequent editions of Mill's work. See James Mill (H.H. Wilson ed.), *The History of British India*, Vol. 1 (London: James Madden, 1858), p. xii.

146 John Poynder, *Speech of John Poynder at a General Court of Proprietors of the East India Company* (London: Hatchard & Son, 1837), p. 10. On numbers, see also Ingham, *Reformers*, p. 38. For profits gained by government in Madras from managing temple lands in the decade before 1837, see Franklin A. Presler, *Religion under Bureaucracy: Policy and Administration for Hindu Temples in South India* (Cambridge: Cambridge University Press, 1987), p. 18. For an example of total number of pilgrims in a single city in one year, see Bayly, *Rulers*, p. 153.

147 Poynder, *Speech*, p. 24. See also James Peggs, *Pilgrim Tax in India: Facts and Observations Relative to The Practice of Taxing Pilgrims in Some Parts of India, and of paying a Premium to Those who Collect them for the Worship of Juggernaut, at the Great Temple in Orissa* (London: Seely, Wightman & Cramp, & Mason, 1828), and J.M. Strachan, *Juggernaut: Its Present State under British Patronage and Support* (London: Hatchard & Son, 1842).

148 Kenneth Ingham, 'The English Evangelicals and the Pilgrim Tax in India, 1800–1862', p. 16, in *The Journal of the Royal Asiatic Society of Great Britain and Ireland*, 1–2 (1953): 13–22. See also Mudaliar, *State and Religious Endowments*, p. 39 for a similar pattern in Madras.

149 See Oddie, *Hindu and Christian*, p. 55.

150 Poynder, *Speech*, p. 32. See also Cassels, *Religion and Pilgrim Tax*, pp. 106–09, and Ingham, *Reformers*, p. 41. The Company directors were reluctant to include these sections; they were added by the Board of Control, headed by Charles Grant's son.

151 Quoted in Cassel, *Religion and Pilgrim Tax*, p. 122.

152 In fact, at the Company's training institution at Haileybury in Britain also, clergymen and evangelicals acted as lecturers. See Copland, 'Christianity as an Arm of Empire', p. 1037.

153 When Grant died in India in 1838, a memorial service remembered the 'pure and evangelical piety' that shaped him, and his desire to 'do the will of God' for the 'extension of the Gospel'. Thomas Carr, *A Sermon Preached in St Mary's Church Poonah, on the Occasion of the Death of Sir Robert Grant, Governor of the Presidency of Bombay* (Bombay: American Mission Press, 1838), p. 10.

154 This was Thomas Truebody Thomason. See also Copley, *Religions in Conflict*, p. 119, though he gives the governor's name as John Thomason.

155 Carson, *The East India Company and Religion*, p. 136. See also Gilmour, *The British in India*, p. 47.
156 Potts, *British Baptist Missionaries*, p. 40. Havelock was known for distributing Bibles in the army.
157 Quoted in Carson, *The East India Company and Religion*, pp. 166–67.
158 Hints of this change are visible from the 1810s itself. See, for instance, Kumar, *Political Agenda of Education*, p. 29.
159 W.B. Martin, 'On the Character and Capacity of the Asiaticks, Particularly of the Natives of Hindoostan', p. 113, in *Essays by the Students of the College of Fort William in Bengal, to which are Added the Theses Pronounced at the Public Disputations in the Oriental Languages on the 6th February, 1802* (Calcutta: Company Press, 1802), pp. 109–18. Indian *munshis* (teachers) at the college had also in 1804 objected to a theme for a debate titled: 'The Natives of India would embrace the Gospel as soon as they are able to compare the Christian Precepts with their own books.' The matter went up to the governor general, who asked that the topic be changed. See John Clark Marshman, *The Life and Times of Carey, Marshman, and Ward: Embracing the History of the Serampore Mission*, Vol. 1 (London: Longman, Brown, Green, Longmans & Roberts, 1859), pp. 191–92. See also Sisir Kumar Das, *Sahibs and Munshis: An Account of the College of Fort William* (Calcutta: Orion Publications, 1978), p. 7, which tells how 'Christian principles' were enshrined in the college's statutes.
160 Carson, *The East India Company and Religion*, pp. 171–72. See also Mackenzie, *Christianity in Travancore*, pp. 50–51; Menon, *History of Travancore*, p. 397; Koji Kawashima, *Missionaries and a Hindu State: Travancore, 1858–1936* (Delhi: Oxford University Press, 1998), pp. 55–57; and Kooiman, *Conversion and Social Equality*, p. 55. For Munro making his case to his superiors—and being rebuffed—see correspondence in IOR/F/4/616/15311. These efforts to turn the old community of 'native' Nasrani Christians into Company dependents—and bring them to Protestantism—would, in fact, birth cleavages with local Hindus. See Susan Bayly, 'Hindu Kingship and the Origin of Community: Religion, State and Society in Kerala, 1750–1850', in *Modern Asian Studies* 18, 2 (1984): 177–213. This was, in fact, welcomed by missionaries, because it would draw the Nasranis well into the embrace of the 'English clergyman'. See W.S. Hunt, *The Anglican Church in Travancore and Cochin, 1816–1916: Operations of the Church Missionary Society in South-West India*, Vol. I (Kottayam: CMS Press, 1920), p. 15, p. 57. For a study of how the Protestantization proceeded, see Gary Robert McKee, 'Benjamin Bailey and the CMS in the Ecclesiastical Development of Kerala', Unpublished PhD dissertation, University of Leeds, UK (2018).
161 John Bradshaw, *Sir Thomas Munro and the British Settlement of the Madras Presidency* (Oxford: Clarendon Press, 1894), pp. 183–84. In 1832, the same man, in a survey of officials about the pilgrim tax, was among the few

advocating its abolition. See Carson, *The East India Company and Religion*, p. 191.

162 Mahmood, *History of English Education in India*, pp. 58–59. In the governor's view, the Bible was 'the only means I know of giving to the Natives a practical knowledge of the sources from whence arise all those high qualities which they admire so much in the character of those whom Providence has placed to rule over them.' Even missionaries thought this move 'rash'. See Frykenberg, 'Modern Education', p. 59. It was London that staved off the proposal.

163 Oddie, *Hindu and Christian*, pp. 47–55.

164 Copland, 'Christianity as an Arm of Empire', p. 1033.

165 Oddie, *Hindu and Christian*, p. 61. See also Carson, *The East India Company and Religion*, pp. 166–67. Liddle, *The Broken Script*, p. 90, reports how even the Mughal emperor's stipend from the Company was delayed if the first of the month happened to be a Sunday, thanks to an official who refused to work Sundays.

166 Robert Nelson to the Secretary, Court of Directors, 16 March 1838 in Anonymous ('A Late Resident in India'), *The Connexion of the East-India Company's Government with the Superstitious and Idolatrous Customs and Rites of the Natives of India* (London: Hatchard & Son; Nisbet; Seeleys; Crofts, 1838), pp. 142–43.

167 Fisch, 'Humanitarian Achievement or Administrative Necessity?', p. 119.

168 See Ingham, *Reformers*, p. 14

169 See Carson, *The East India Company and Religion*, p. 208 and Cox, *Imperial Fault Lines*, p. 32. This happened in Travancore also, where if John Munro was friendly to missionaries, his successor was not. In 1846, in the Madras Presidency, similarly, 100 men arrested for violence against 'native' Christians were acquitted when two anti-missionary judges disagreed with their colleague, a pro-missionary judge. All three judges were eventually sacked by the governor. See Frykenberg, 'Modern Education in South India', pp. 59–60.

170 See also Knights, *Trust and Distrust*, chapter two for how this extended even to issues of interaction with Indians. Gift-giving and gift-taking could be branded corruption now, and separation rather than engagement (on Indians' terms at any rate) was preferred.

171 Carson, *The East India Company and Religion*, p. 214.

172 I borrow the phrase from John William Kaye, *Christianity in India: An Historical Narrative* (London: Smith, Elder & Co., 1859), p. 381.

173 Carson, *The East India Company and Religion*, pp. 216–17.

174 Oddie, *Hindu and Christian*, pp. 64–65.

175 Mudaliar, *State and Religious Endowments*, pp. 34–37. But unsupervised control of shrines, many with substantial assets, led to complaints—from Indians themselves—of corruption and embezzlement; by the early-

twentieth-century government would step back in as custodians of Hindu shrines across Madras. See Presler, *Religion under Bureaucracy*, pp. 23–30.
176  Carson, *The East India Company and Religion*, p. 191. See also Hudson, 'Life and Times of H.A. Krishna Pillai', pp. 165–67 for complaints in south India from others also about this shift in government servants' attitude.
177  And as one scholar tells in the context of missionaries, 'Anything that stood in the way of the propagation of the gospel was denounced as sin.' See Copley, *Religions in Conflict*, p. 11.
178  Copland, Mabett et al., *A History of State and Religion in India*, p. 173. See also p. 170 for another officer, obliged to protect the claims of Brahmins, personally feeling conflicted about the injustice this caused to other Hindu groups. The Company, essentially, seemed to be endorsing caste.
179  Carson, *The East India Company and Religion*, p. 214. See also Copland, Mabett et al., *A History of State and Religion in India*, p. 176 for similar remarks from a Madras councillor.
180  Carson, *The East India Company and Religion*, pp. 224–25. This was the right granted to converts to retain inheritance and claims in their families. Conversion, that is, could not be cited to deny them a share of property—something that sounds reasonable now, but at the time overturned the logic of caste and family.
181  Bhau Mahajan quoted in J.V. Naik (Murali Ranganthan ed.), *The Collected Works of J.V. Naik: Reform and Renaissance in Nineteenth-Century Maharashtra* (Mumbai: Asiatic Society of Mumbai, 2016), p. 114.
182  Anonymous ('B'), *The First Hindoo Convert: A Memoir of Krishna Pal, A Preacher of the Gospel to his Countrymen More than Twenty Years* (Philadelphia: American Baptist Publication Society, 1852), p. 13.
183  Oddie, *Hindu and Christian*, p. 17. Ironically, even late in the nineteenth century, there were Protestant converts unwilling to give up caste, who wished to retain 'Brahman habits and customs'. ibid., p. 147 and Hudson, *Protestant Origins*, p. 182. See also Carson, 'Missionaries, Bureaucrats', p. 141, where she notes that by 1833, there were thrice as many Protestant missions in India as Catholic, but there was 'no similar correlation in baptisms'.
184  Quoted in Potts, *British Baptist Missionaries*, p. 35.
185  Reference is to Joshua Marshman. See ibid., p. 20. Much later, the missionary Robert Caldwell would also write from south India about his 'spiritual fishing':

> What varied interest and excitement there is in spiritual fishing!—were it not that I fear to make sacred comparison walk on all fours, I could tell how often I am tantalized with 'nibbles', how excited I feel when I get a 'bite', how I exult when a fish is safely landed, and how sometimes when an innocent perch is quietly nibbling at my bait, a great old pike, the persecutor of his neighbourhood, makes a rush at him and swallows

him up. Though my fishing is on a small scale, the proportion of the fish I catch that seem fit only to be cast away is as large, I fear, as if I caught thousands at a time. I rarely indeed cast any away, for the proper time for doing so is yet to come, but I notice now and again, on scrutinizing what I have got, certain unwholesome looking fish, or slippery, slimy creatures, half fish, half snake, which are not likely to fare well when the angels sit down on the eternal shore and separate the good from bad. Not frequently, indeed, fish of that sort do not wait to be rejected, but find their way into the water as fast as they came out of it.

Quoted in Kumaradoss, *Robert Caldwell*, p. 55.

186 Marshman, *The Life and Times of Carey, Marshman, and Ward*, Vol. 1, p. 138.

187 Quoted in Potts, *British Baptist Missionaries*, p. 91. Carey also wanted Serampore to become a 'Christian Benares' with missionaries investing in Sanskrit—chiefly to use that language to turn the tide of Sanskrit literature 'completely on the side of Christianity'. Sanskrit, he believed, was like a 'golden casket' filled with pebbles; the missionary proposal was to replace those pebbles with Christian riches. Quoted in Richard Fox Young, *Resistant Hinduism: Sanskrit Sources on Anti-Christian Apologetics in Early Nineteenth-Century India* (Vienna: De Nobili Research Library, 1981), p. 35. See also Oddie, *Imagined Hinduism*, p. 156. See also Laird, 'The Contribution of Christian Missionaries', p. 309, where we read how they wished for Sanskrit as a language itself to be disconnected from Hinduism, so that its beauties could be 'cultivated in subservience to divine revelation'.

188 George Smith, *The Life of William Carey: Shoemaker and Missionary* (London: J.M. Dent & Sons, 1909), p. 190.

189 Pratap Narayan Mishra quoted in Dalmia, *Nationalization*, p. 112. Emphasis added. For criticism in a similar vein by the novelist Bankimchandra Chatterjee, see his *Letters on Hinduism* (Calcutta: M.M. Bose, 1940 ed.), p. 45. See also Richard Fox Young, 'Hindu–Christian Debates in the Eighteenth and Nineteenth Centuries', p. 133 in Bauman and Voss Roberts eds., *The Routedge Handbook of Hindu–Christian Relations*, pp. 127–38, for another instance.

190 C.B. Leupolt, *Recollections of an Indian Missionary* (London: SPCK, 1843), pp. 108–09. See also p. 110 for another similar remark. Of course, equally there were difficulties also, including insincere conversions. As late as 1831, there were converts who threatened to give up the faith if not paid. See Potts, *British Baptist Missionaries*, pp. 45–46. So too Protestant missionaries often had to tolerate caste differences, even if not to the same degree as Catholics. See Oddie, *Hindu and Christian*, p. 175.

191 Nasranis, or 'Syrian Christians' as they were called, in Kerala were also harassed by Protestant missionaries who saw in their rites and customs too much 'heathenism' and 'vile papistry'. Nasranis maintained rituals of purity

like high-caste Hindus; Protestant missionaries now began to appear at their festivals, denouncing their practices, and 'then intentionally laying hands' on them. 'The crowds would flee in order to avoid the defiling touch of the foreigner, and the missionaries reported gleefully on their ability to break up whole festivals in this way.' See Bayly, *Saints, Goddesses and Kings*, p. 299.

192  Oddie, *Hindu and Christian*, p. 190. See another instance from Travancore in Hunt, *The Anglican Church*, p. 142, and from Bombay in Baba Padmanji (J. Murray Mitchell ed.), *Once Hindu, Now Christian: The Early Life of Baba Padmanji, An Autobiography* (London: James Nisbet & Co., 1890), p. 63, and Carey's remarks on the 'torrents of abuse and obscenity', in Kopf, *British Orientalism*, p. 126. 'Native' converts received even more violent abuse, compared to white missionaries. See Copley, *Religions in Conflict*, p. 16, and also p. 68, p. 85, p. 100 and p. 121 for instances in north India, and p. 153 for one from south India. See also Kawashima, *Missionaries and a Hindu State*, p. 68.

193  Carson, *The East India Company and Religion*, p. 172. See also Kooiman, *Conversion and Social Equality*, p. 145.

194  Reference is to Umapati Mudaliar's *The Padris' Secrets Disclosed*. See Fox Young, 'Hindu-Christian Debates in the Eighteenth and Nineteenth Centuries', pp. 134–35. The template for this story is older, however, and in an earlier iteration was used by Vaishnavas to target Saivas in intra-Hindu polemics. See Doniger, *On Hinduism*, p. 57.

195  Leupolt, *Recollections*, pp. 61–64. Leupolt, though a CMS man, was of German origin.

196  Ibid., pp. 34–35.

197  Ibid., p. 36. See also Copley, *Religions in Conflict*, p. 45. For another discussion between a missionary and a Brahmin in Rajpur in Bengal, see ibid., p. 80.

198  Leupolt, *Recollections*, p. 109. As Dubois had written earlier, 'native Christians were never more than vain phantoms . . . for in embracing the Christian religion they never entirely renounce their superstitions towards which they always kept a secret bent . . . there is no unfeigned, undisguised Christian among these Indians'. Quoted in Mohan, 'British and French Ethnographies', p. 237. However as Copley notes in *Religions in Conflict*, p. 54, quite a few Indians were attracted to Christianity even if they did not actually convert. See also ibid., p. 70.

199  In this context, see also Cox, *Imperial Fault Lines*, pp. 160–61.

200  On this, see also J. Murray Mitchell, *Letters to Indian Youth on the Evidences of the Christian Religion* (Bombay: Thomas Graham, 1857), p. 97.

201  *Oriental Christian Spectator*, June 1830, in *The Oriental Christian Spectator*, Vol. 1 (1830) (Bombay: American Mission Press, 1830), pp. 185–95. See also Fox Young, *Resistant Hinduism*, pp. 25–26.

202  This too was a general habit: as one missionary in Orissa suggested, using 'pertinent quotations from their own books' not only drew people to listen,

but also 'increases their respect for your character'. Quoted in John Murdoch, *The Indian Missionary Manual: Or, Hints to Young Missionaries in India* (Madras: Graves, Cookson & Co., 1864), p. 136.

203 George Smith, *The Life of John Wilson: For Fifty Years Philanthropist and Scholar in the East* (London: John Murray, 1879), pp. 62–66.

204 Of course, comical moments also emerged. Once a Christian catechist accused a Hindu religious figure of profiting from the public's gullibility, only to be accused of 'preaching for a livelihood' rather than any loftier purpose. 'Who,' it was asked, had *really* 'seen Heaven or Hell?' See Kooiman, *Conversion and Social Equality*, p. 188.

205 Dandekar, *Hindudharmasthapana* translated in John Wilson, *An Exposure of the Hindu Religion in Reply to Mora Bhatta Dandekara, to which is Prefixed a Translation of the Bhatta's Tract* (Bombay: American Mission Press, 1832), p. 16.

206 Ibid., pp. 17–18.

207 Ibid., p. 22.

208 Brahmins in the earlier debate with Wilson's associate also made this point, declaring that if Christians had Jesus as a great saintly figure, Hindus had quite a few such who hadn't needed to die to 'save' them. See Fox Young, 'Hindu–Christian Debates in the Eighteenth and Nineteenth Centuries', p. 130.

209 Dandekar, *Hindudharmasthapana*, p. 23.

210 Ibid., p. 25.

211 Ibid., p. 28.

212 See Wilson, *Exposure*, p. 29 onwards.

213 Dandekar provided editorial assistance and guidance.

214 Fox Young, *Resistant Hinduism*, p. 28.

215 Quoted in Wilson, *A Second Exposure of the Hindu Religion, in Reply to Narayana Rao of Satara, Including Strictures on the Vedanta* (Bombay: W. Chapman & Ambrolie, 1834), pp. 85–99.

216 Fox Young, *Resistant Hinduism*, pp. 14–15. Muir also published English versions of his *Matapariksa*.

217 Fox Young, 'Hindu–Christian Debates in the Eighteenth and Nineteenth Centuries', pp. 133–34.

218 See Frank F. Conlon, 'The Polemic Process in Nineteenth-Century Maharashtra', in Kenneth Jones ed., *Religious Controversy in British India: Dialogues in South Asian Languages* (New York: State University of New York Press, 1992), pp. 5–26.

219 Ibid., p. 18. The complete exchange, translated for the English press, is available in George Bowen, *Discussions by the Sea-Side* (Bombay: Bombay Track and Book Society, 1857). See also Copley, *Religions in Conflict*, p. 68 for an instance where it is the missionary whose wit and sense of humour comes to his aid. For a published volume containing (in Marathi)

Vishnubawa's polemics against Christianity, see Vishnubawa Brahmachari, *Vedoktadharmacha Vichar va Christimatakhandan* (Mumbai: Nirnayasagar, 1874).

220 But this likely had other reasons: up north, the Great Rebellion had begun. Such debates occurred between missionaries and Muslims too. See Avril Ann Powell, *Muslims and Missionaries in Pre-Mutiny India* (Surrey: Curzon Press, 1993). For a continuation of such debates in print as late as the 1890s, see, for example, Durga Prasad, *The Defence of Manu, against the Calumny of Christian Priests* (Lahore: Virajanand Press, 1891). This too accuses Christians of degrading women, drinking, priestcraft and belief in demons but significantly carries a section called 'European Opinions about the Bible', quoting *white* critics of the Christian religion, such as Thomas Paine. For debates between Buddhists and Christian missionaries in colonial Ceylon (Sri Lanka), see Young and Somaratna, *Buddhist–Christian Controversies*.

221 'Nilakantha Goreh: A Traditional Pandit Takes on the Missionaries', in Rachel Fell McDermott, Leonard A. Gordon, Ainslie T. Embree, Frances W. Pritchett and Dennis Dalton eds., *Sources of Indian Traditions*, Vol. 2 (Gurgaon: Penguin, 2014), p. 83.

222 C.E. Gardner, *Life of Father Goreh* (London: Longmans, Green & Co., 1900), pp. 35–36.

223 Ibid., p. 37.

224 Jan Peter Schouten (Henry and Lucy Jansen trans.), *Jesus as Guru: The Image of Christ among Hindus and Christians in India (*Amsterdam: Rodopi, 2008), p. 39. See also Fox Young, 'Hindu–Christian Debates in the Eighteenth and Nineteenth Centuries', pp. 134–35.

225 See 'Nilakantha Goreh', in *Sources of Indian Traditions*, Vol. 2, pp. 84–85.

226 Quoted in Gardner, *Life of Father Goreh*, p. 38.

227 See Jon Keune, 'The Intra and Inter-Religious Conversions of Nehemiah Nilakantha Goreh', in *Journal of Hindu–Christian Studies* 17, 8 (2004): 45–54 for a succinct account of Goreh's spiritual yearnings.

228 Schoten, *Jesus as Guru*, p. 43.

229 This was originally in Hindi. For the English translation see, Nehemiah Nilakantha Sastri Goreh (Fitz-Edward Hall trans.), *A Rational Refutation of the Hindu Philosophical Systems* (London: The Christian Literature Society for India, 1897).

230 For the story of another Brahmin convert from 1849, see Deepra Dandekar, *The Subhedar's Son: A Narrative of Brahmin–Christian Conversion from Nineteenth-Century Maharashtra* (New Delhi: Oxford University Press, 2019), pp. xl–xliv.

231 S. Satthianadhan, *Sketches of Indian Christians: Collected from Different Sources* (London and Madras: The Christian Literature Society for India, 1896), pp. 69–75. In the 1870s again, in Kerala, this time in Travancore, there were rumours that the British Resident's sister was attempting to convert

the ranis of the state. See *The Friend of India*, 28 August 1875. The senior rani's husband would later confess that he had 'somehow' grown fond of Christianity. See Pillai, *False Allies*, p. 211.

232  Not that it fit converts from marginalized groups always either. See Sathianathan Clarke, 'Conversion to Christianity in Tamil Nadu: Conscious and Constitutive Community Mobilization towards a Different Symbolic World Vision', p. 337, in Robinson and Clarke eds., *Religious Conversion in India*, pp. 323–50. Equally, many *did* also convert for gains of a non-spiritual nature. In Travancore, thus, one missionary saw much keenness, only to realize that the intending converts hoped he would use his connections with the local rajah to help them. See Kooiman, *Conversion and Social Equality*, p. 75. In Tamil country, shepherds offered to 'think about Christianity' if paid Rs 5 each. See Copley, *Religions in Conflict*, p. 152. See also George Pettitt, *The Tinnevelly Mission of the Church Missionary Society* (London: Seeleys, 1851), pp. 515–16 for how some missionaries addressed this issue.

233  For some other cases of elite Hindu converts from Bengal as well as south India, see Antony Copley, 'The Conversion Experience of India's Christian Elite in the Mid-Nineteenth Century', *The Journal of Religious History* 18, 1 (1994): 52–74. For an autobiographical account from western India, see Padmanji, *Once Hindu, Now Christian*, and a study on a Tamil high-caste convert, see Hudson, 'Life and Times of H.A. Krishna Pillai', p. 214 onwards.

234  Kumaradoss, *Robert Caldwell*, p. 180. See also Cox, *Imperial Fault Lines*, p. 120, for a remark by a late-nineteenth-century missionary about how conversions largely of low-caste persons was akin to 'raking in rubbish into the church'.

235  Oddie, *Hindu and Christian*, p. 147. See also Clarke, 'Conversion to Christianity', p. 340, p. 344, and James Kerr, *The Domestic Life, Character, and Customs of the Natives of India* (London: W.H. Allen & Co., 1865), p. 353. The same applied to other high-caste, non-Brahmin Hindus. See Copley, *Religions in Conflict*, pp. 188–90, for instance.

236  Dandekar, *The Subhedar's Son*, pp. 9–10. Race appears even in the Catholic church's and Catholic missionaries' dealings with old Indian Christian groups such as the Nasranis, who had rites and a culture alien to Europeans. A late-eighteenth-century memoir by a Nasrani not only laments the loss of his community's autonomy from the Portuguese period onwards, but also complications born of their being placed under spiritual leaders of a different race. At one point he even uses the word 'slavery'. See Thomman Paremmakkal (J. Podipara trans.), *The Varthamanappusthakam: An Account of the History of the Malabar Church between the years 1773 and 1786 with Special Emphasis on the Events Connected with the Journey from Malabar and Roma via Lisbon and Back Undertaken by Malpan Mar Joseph Cariattil and Cathanar Thomman Paremmakkal* (Rome: Pont. Institutum Orientalium Studiorum,

1971), p. 35, pp. 39–41, pp. 49–51, p. 62, p. 64, p. 80, pp. 107–08, and p. 138. In Delhi, after the 1857 Rebellion, when one figure, on receiving a blow from a passing British officer, cried out that he was a Christian, he was rewarded with abuse and told he was 'as black as a jet'. See Liddle, *The Broken Script*, p. 343. See also Kawashima, *Missionaries and a Hindu State*, p. 58; Hudson, 'Life and Times of H.A. Krishna Pillai', p. 241, pp. 249–50; and Mateer, *The Gospel in South India*, pp. 36–39.

237 In 1847, the American Madura Mission 'debarred from the Lord's Table' as many as seventy-two Indian Christians who refused to drink tea with lower-caste men. See M.S. Pandian, *Brahmin and Non-Brahmin: Genealogies of the Tamil Political Present* (Ranikhet: Permanent Black, 2017 ed. [2007]), p. 25. This may be why men like Muir urged patience and a conciliatory tone. See Fox Young, *Resistant Hinduism*, p. 57. Meanwhile, Muslim converts also often made it a point to retain their Persianate attire and habits. See Powell, *Muslims and Missionaries*, p. 114. For past instances from earlier centuries of 'Brahmin Christians', see Hudson, *Protestant Origins*, pp. 8–9. See also Cox, *Imperial Fault Lines*, pp. 39–40, p. 65.

238 Quoted in Murali Ranganathan, 'Introduction', p. 16 in Naik, *Collected Works*, pp. 1–42. In Calcutta, two decades before, the editor of the *Calcutta Journal* also got into trouble for publishing criticism of the Company. The British passed press regulations in this period. In 1835, the rules would be relaxed, resulting in a spurt in newspaper production as well as energetic debate.

239 *Bombay Gazette*, 30 July 1841.
240 Ibid.
241 *Bombay Gazette*, 10 August 1841. In this, Pandurang long preceded better-known critics like B.G. Tilak, who we will meet in the last chapter. See also another economic critique, in Marathi, published not long after these letters from Pandurang, in Ramkrishna Vishwanath, *Hindustanachi Prachin Va Sampratchi Sthiti Va Pudhe Kaay Tyacha Parinam Honarey, Hyavishayi Vichar* (Mumbai: Prabhakar Press, 1843), p. 24.
242 *Bombay Gazette*, 10 August 1841.
243 *Bombay Gazette*, 30 July 1841. Emphasis added.
244 *Bombay Gazette*, 13 August 1841.
245 *Bombay Gazette*, 20 August 1841.
246 *Bombay Gazette*, 10 August 1841.
247 *Bombay Gazette*, 20 August 1841.
248 *Bombay Gazette*, 16 September 1841.
249 Pandurang's critique, in fact, straddled a variety of themes: political injustice towards 'native' rulers; economic exploitation, including the milking of China, through the opium trade; foreign policy, such as British interference in Afghan affairs and the Company system, which seemed rigged, letting partisan interests prevail. But its principal quality was that it turned the

language of morality against the colonizer, using their own standards and religion to spotlight imperial sins. India's woes, thus, stemmed from a single cause: that so 'great an Empire' was 'given in monopoly to a body of voracious Merchants'. Nothing in history, our writer declared, 'could approximate' to this travesty (*Bombay Gazette*, 20 August 1841) a line of argument that, interestingly, mirrored those of the Company's early critics like Edmund Burke. On a concise summarization of the letters and their import, see also Naik, *Collected Works*, pp. 57–78.

250 Copley, *Religions in Conflict*, p. 104. See also Liddle, *The Broken Script*, p. 78, for how Begum Samru of Sardhana once entertained British guests with a play in which a Company prize agent, in freshly conquered territory, deprives a starving peasant, who has nothing else to give, of the only thing he has: hair.

251 Leupolt, *Recollections*, pp. 44–45.

252 Preface, *The Brahmunical Magazine, or The Missionary and the Brahmun* (No. 4, Calcutta, 1823) in *The English Works of Raja Rammohun Roy*, Vol. 1, p. 179. We shall read more about the writer in the next chapter.

253 B.S. Jambhekar in *Bombay Durpan*, 13 July 1832, quoted in Deepak Kumar, 'Science and Society in Colonial India: Exploring an Agenda', p. 29, in *Social Scientist* 28, 5–6 (2000): 24–46. Emphasis added.

254 Quoted in Ranganathan, 'Introduction', p. 8, in Naik, *Collected Works*, pp. 1–42. Interestingly, by 1849, the idea of a parliament of Indians—'the smartest men of all castes'—with English representation, would emerge from an Indian's pen. See Gopal Hari Deshmukh (Shripad Ramchandra Tikekar ed.), *Lokahitawadinchi Shatapatre* (Aundh: Usha Prakashan, 1940), Letter no. 60, p. 358.

255 Velu Tampi's Kundara Proclamation in Aiya, *Travancore State Manual*, Vol. 1, pp. 434–36. A similar claim was made in 1803 by the Islamic scholar Shah Abdul Aziz in Delhi, where he declared how '[f]rom here to Calcutta the Christians are in complete control'. See Liddle, *The Broken Script*, p. 24.

256 Letter dated 10 April 1809 from the Chief Secretary, Bengal, to the Chief Secretary, Madras, in IOR/P/317/28.

257 Letter dated 17 September 1811 from the British Resident to the Chief Secretary, Madras in IOR/P/317/45.

258 On the eve of the mutiny, the Bengal Army was made up of 27,000 Brahmins, 28,000 Rajputs, 16,000 'middle' Hindu castes and 13,000 Muslims. It was a largely high-caste Hindu army, and its Muslims too were drawn from elite backgrounds. See Farooqui, *Colonial Subjugation*, pp. 86–87.

259 See, for example, Nana Saheb's proclamation dated 5 June 1857 which also, in detail, explains the prevailing impression of the supposed British conspiracy to convert in 'Proclamations of Nana Sahib', pp. 59–60, in Crispin Bates and Marina Carter eds., *Mutiny at the Margins: New Perspectives on the Indian Uprising of 1857*, Vol. 7 (New Delhi: SAGE Publications, 2017), pp. 57–60.

260 See Copley, *Religions in Conflict*, p. 100 for how villagers in northern India often mistook missionaries as government employees sent out to distribute tracts; and Pettitt, *The Tinnevelly Mission*, p. 251 for how even in south India, there were fears that missionaries were plotting 'some secret measures for the overthrow of Hindooism.' Even Jesuits disapproved of the Protestant style of street preaching, with its 'irreverent gesture and vehement language'. See H. Strickland and T.W.M. Marshall, *Catholic Missions in Southern India to 1865* (London: Longmans, Green & Co., 1865), p. 148.

261 Copley, *Religions in Conflict*, p. 69, p. 99. See also Hudson, 'Life and Times of H.A. Krishna Pillai', p. 155.

262 Copland, Mabett et al., *A History of State and Religion in India*, p. 166. Cow slaughter was a point of conflict as far back as Thomas Roe's time in the seventeenth century. See Das, *Courting India*, p. 83. Similarly, in 1911, when an English official was assassinated in Tirunelveli, the Brahmin assassin carried on his person a note referring to the British king as a 'cow-meat eating' barbarian. See Pandian, *Brahmin and Non-Brahmin*, p. 32.

263 John Bruce Norton, *The Rebellion in India: How to Prevent Another* (London: Richardson Brothers, 1857), p. 96. See also Rudrangshu Mukherjee, *Awadh in Revolt, 1857-1858: A Study of Popular Resistance* (London: Anthem Press, 2002), p. 80. Norton was among several British critics of the Company's government of India. See Priyamvada Gopal, *Insurgent Empire: Anticolonial Resistance and British Dissent* (New Delhi: Simon & Schuster India, 2019).

264 Rudrangshu Mukherjee, *The Year of Blood: Essays on the Revolt of 1857* (Abingdon: Routledge, 2018), p. 12. Contemporary observers said as much too: 'The very bread had been torn out of the mouths of men who knew no other profession than that of the sword,' wrote one, referring to the Company's disbanding of the Awadh army. See the 'Narrative of Mainodin', p. 38, in Charles Theophilus Metcalfe, *Two Native Narratives of the Mutiny in Delhi* (London: Archibald Constable & Co., 1898).

265 On the theme of peasant resistance, see Eric Stokes, *The Peasant and the Raj: Studies in Agrarian Society and Peasant Rebellion in Colonial India* (Cambridge: Cambridge University Press, 1978).

266 See Badri Narayan Tiwari, 'Identity and Narratives: Dalits and Memories of 1857', in Crispin Bates ed., *Mutiny at the Margins: New Perspectives on the Indian Uprising of 1857*, Vol. 5 (New Delhi: SAGE Publications, 2014), pp. 1–16. On tribal participation, see Shashank S. Sinha, '1857 and the adivasis of Chotanagpur', and Sanjukta Das Gupta, 'Remembering Gonoo: The Profile of an Adivasi Rebel of 1857' in Biswamoy Pati ed., *The Great Rebellion in India: Exploring Transgressions and Diversities* (Abingdon: Routledge, 2010), pp. 16–31 and pp. 32–45.

267 The fragmentation of political authority was one source of these imperfections. See, for example, Nupur Chaudhuri and Rajat Kanta Ray, '"We" and "They"

in an Altered Ecumene: The Mutiny from the Mutineers' Mouths', p. 39, in Bates, *Mutiny at the Margins*, Vol. 5, pp. 36–48.

268 This comes through in a contrast rebel documents draw between the conduct of the Company in earlier times when it was better behaved, and its subsequent 'boastful, arrogant' actions, 'pride', 'religious fanaticism' and tendency to act 'without consultation'. See 'Advice of the Royal Army', in Bates and Carter eds., *Mutiny at the Margins*, Vol. 7, pp. 67–68. See also Vishwanath, *Vichar*, p. 22.

269 Pandey, *From Sepoy to Subedar*, p. 165.

270 Mukherjee, *Year of Blood*, p. 68. Some rebels were themselves, in fact, deified into local gods. Tiwari, 'Identity and Narratives', p. 1.

271 Mukherjee, *Year of Blood*, p. 68. See a similar remark in Chaudhuri and Ray, "'We' and 'They'", p. 38.

272 *Abstract of the Twenty-Third Annual Report of the American Madura Mission for 1857* (Madras: American Mission Press, 1858), p. 23.

273 Mukherjee, *Year of Blood*, pp. 68–69. See also Liddle, *The Broken Script*, pp. 311–13.

274 The Azamgarh Proclamation in *Sources of Indian Traditions*, Vol. 2, pp. 98–101. See also Vishwanath, *Vichar*, p. 23, where he notes, fifteen years before the rebellion, in a different part of India, that despite animosity between Hindus and Muslim powers in the past, by the British era, Muslims had found common ground with Hindus.

275 Quoted in *Sources of Indian Traditions*, Vol. 2, pp. 151–52. See also p. 154 for the more directly political content of the proclamation.

276 Andre Fuller, *The Works of the Rev. Andrew Fuller*, Vol. 3 (New Haven: S. Converse, 1824), p. 213. See also Liddle, *The Broken Script*, p. 337, where at the subsequent 'trial' of the Mughal emperor also, British officials were surprised that Indians, who had seemed 'utterly discordant on the score of religion', somehow united to fight a 'common crusade against a faith'.

277 Iqbal Husain, 'The Rebels' Cause in 1857: From their own Spokesmen', p. 551 in *Proceedings of the Indian History Congress* 57 (1996), pp. 547–55. Or as has been noted, the rebellion was 'psychically and emotionally, a step towards the articulation of "the Indian nation"' that would emerge later in the century. See Chaudhuri and Ray, ' "We" and "They"', p. 47. See also another poem from the period in Bates and Carter eds., *Mutiny at the Margins*, Vol. 7, pp. 84–85, and Liddle, *The Broken Script*, pp. 288–89. See also Farooqui, *Colonial Subjugation*, p. 160, for remarks by Engels on the matter.

278 See 'Statement and Appeal from the General Conference of Missionaries Convened at Ootacamund', May 1858, p. xii, in the Appendix, *Proceedings of the South India Missionary Conference held at Ootacamund* (Madras: Society for Promoting Christian Knowledge, 1858). See also Copley, *Religions in Conflict*, p. 111.

279   So much so that a scholar studying Hindu violence against Christians encountered in the twenty-first century the 'head of a prominent south Indian mission agency' who told him: 'When you proclaim the gospel, the disturbance in society is natural . . . Violence is the natural result when you are preaching the truth.' See Chad M. Bauman, *Anti-Christian Violence in India* (Ithaca & London: Cornell University Press, 2020), p. 19.

## Six: 'Native Luthers'

1   Raja Ram Mohun Roy to Lord Minto, 12 April 1809, in Rammohun Roy (Bruce Carlisle Robertson ed.), *The Essential Writings of Raja Rammohan Ray* (Delhi: Oxford University Press, 1999), pp. 267–70.
2   There continues to be debate on whether he was born in 1772 or 1774.
3   Shomik Dasgupta, 'Ethics, Distance and Accountability: The Political Thought of Rammohun Roy, c. 1803–32', Unpublished PhD dissertation, King's College London (2016), pp. 90–91. The source of his wealth would become a cause of controversy among future biographers, with some hinting at corruption. See Brian A. Hatcher, *Hinduism before Reform* (Cambridge: Harvard University Press, 2020), pp. 181–82.
4   Biographical details about Roy may be found in Roy, 'Autobiographical Sketch', in *Essential Writings*, pp. 272–74; Dermot Killingley, *Rammohun Roy in Hindu and Christian Tradition: The Teape Lectures 1990* (Newcastle upon Tyne: Grevatt & Grevatt, 1993); and Bruce Carlisle Robertson, *Raja Rammohan Ray: The Father of Modern India* (New Delhi: Oxford University Press, 2001). For his time in Britain, see Lynn Zastoupil, *Rammohun Roy and the Making of Victorian Britain* (New York: Palgrave Macmillan, 2010).
5   Roy, 'Autobiographical Sketch', pp. 272–73. See also Sophia Dobson Collet (Hem Chandra Sarkar ed.), *The Life and Letters of Raja Rammohun Roy* (Calcutta: A.C. Sarkar, 1914), p. 6.
6   It is generally believed that Roy's mother tried to disinherit him. See Robertson, *Raja Rammohan Ray*, pp. 13–14. That it was a different kind of property dispute is clear from Killingley, *Rammohun Roy*, p. 8, and Noel Salmond, *Hindu Iconoclasts: Rammohun Roy, Dayananda Sarasvati, and Nineteenth-Century Polemics Against Idolatry* (Ontario: Wilfrid Laurier University Press, 2004), p. 94. See also Amiya P. Sen, *Rammohun Roy: A Critical Biography* (New Delhi: Penguin Viking, 2012), pp. 57–59 on how Roy's religious views generated family tension.
7   R.S. Sugirtharajah, *The Brahmin and His Bible: Rammohan Roy's Precepts of Jesus 200 Years On* (London: T&T Clark, 2019), p. 2. Killingley calls him the 'first Indian intellectual to be internationally known while still living'. See Dermot Killingley, 'Rammohun Roy', p. 297, in Bauman and Voss Roberts eds., *The Routledge Handbook*, pp. 297–306. See also Sen, *Rammohun Roy*, p. 6.
8   Zastoupil, *Rammohun Roy*, p. 2.

9   Ibid., p. 90.
10  Roy, 'Autobiographical Sketch', p. 273. See also Sugirtharajah, *The Brahmin and His Bible*, p. 90. One wonders if this aversion had something to do with his father's financial difficulties—which led to him being jailed twice—and such unpleasant dealings with the British authorities. See Sen, *Rammohun Roy*, pp. 39–40.
11  Roy's ethical programme and conceptualization of religion forms the key thrust of Dasgupta's study, 'Ethics, Distance and Accountability'.
12  Roy, 'Anti-Suttee Petition to the House of Commons', *Essential Writings*, pp. 161–62.
13  Or as he wrote:

> Should the Christian attempt to ridicule some part of the ritual of the Veds I shall of course feel myself justified in referring to ceremonies of a similar characters in the Christian Scriptures; and if he dwell on the corrupt notions introduced into Hindooism in modern times, I shall also remind him of the corruptions introduced by various sects into Christianity.

See *The English Works of Raja Rammohun Roy: With an English Translation of 'Tuhfatul Muwahhiddin'* (Allahabad: The Panini Office, 1906), p. 907.

14  See Sugirtharajah, *The Brahmin and His Bible*, p. 3, p. 10. Or as Roy wrote once:

> Having read about the rise and progress of Christianity in apostolic times, and its corruption in succeeding ages, and then of the Christian Reformation which shook off these corruptions . . . I began to think that something similar might have taken place in India, and similar results might follow from a reformation of the popular idolatry.

While there was an admission of crisis in Hinduism here, it yet denounced Catholicism as degraded. Quoted in Collet, *Life and Letters*, p. 162.

15  Killingley, *Rammohun Roy*, p. 118. He also later objected to a painting that depicted Christ with pale skin.
16  This excludes, of course, a work he claimed to have written in his teens, which was never published.
17  Rammohun Roy, 'A Present to the Believers in One God: Being a Translation of Tuhfatul Muwahhiddin', *English Works*, pp. 941–58.
18  There is a question to be asked as to why Roy never translated the *Tuhfat* into English, as he did with his later Bengali works. See also Sen, *Rammohun Roy*, p. 24.
19  One translator even titled the text in English as *A Gift to Deists*. Enlightenment-era radicals and those who challenged religious orthodoxy were often lumped under the term 'Deists'.
20  See Dasgupta, 'Ethics, Distance and Accountability' particularly on the likely influence of the *Akhlaq-I Nasiri* on Roy's thought. See also Rudrangshu

Mukherjee, 'Rammohun Roy's "Gift": His First Published Piece' at https://www.theindiaforum.in/article/rammohun-roys-gift; and Killingley, *Rammohun Roy*, p. 48.

21 Killingley, *Rammohun Roy*, p. 52. Roy himself cited these thinkers. See Roy, 'A Defence of Hindu Theism' (1917), *English Works*, p. 96; and 'Humble Suggestions to his Countrymen who Believe in the One True God' (1823), ibid., p. 211. Nanak is also mentioned in the *Tuhfat*. See 'A Present to the Believers', p. 955. Interestingly, British observers found Deist parallels in the 'religion of well-educated Hindus' elsewhere also. See Fanny Parkes, *Wanderings of a Pilgrim in Search of the Picturesque: Four-and-Twenty Years in the East; with Revelations of Life in the Zenana*, Vol. 2 (London: Pelham Richardson, 1850), p. 288.

22 Robertson, *Raja Rammohan Ray*, p. 20, p. 27.

23 See, for example, Rammohun Roy ('A Friend to Truth'), *An Appeal to the Christian Public in Defence of the 'Precepts of Jesus'* (New York: B. Bates, 1825), which makes this point.

24 As Roy argued, if sati were divine in origin, it would have been universal, whereas it was not even universal in India. Besides, sati offered very material incentives for men under the 'cloak of religion': the 'destruction of the widow' removed her claim to a share of property. See Roy, 'Some Remarks in Vindication of the Resolution Passed by the Government of Bengal in 1829 Abolishing the Practice of Female Sacrifice in India' (1832), in *Essential Writings*, p. 167. See also 'Translation of a Conference between an Advocate for, and an Opponent of, the Practice of Burning Widows Alive' (1818) in ibid., p. 120. It must be noted, however, that Roy's alternative—a life of romantic self-denial for widows—won't be particularly pleasing to today's readers either.

25 There are subtle differences between the Bengali originals and English versions, given that these were intended for different audiences. Importantly, Roy's Bengali writings also 'contributed meaningfully to the development of modern Bengali prose'. See Sen, *Rammohun Roy*, p. 4. See also ibid., p. 15.

26 He himself notes this. See, for instance, 'Translation of an Abridgment of the Vedant' (1816), in *Essential Writings*, p. 3, and 'A Second Defence of the Monotheistical System of the Vedas', ibid., pp. 83–84. And recent scholarship suggests he succeeded in this, achieving considerable popularity. See Dasgupta, 'Ethics, Distance and Accountability', p. 128, pp. 134–41. In fact, Dasgupta notes, though their content was anti-missionary, even the BMS press produced hundreds of copies of his writings later, because they had a lucrative market. See also Hatcher, *Hinduism before Reform*, p. 206 for how in the 1820s, Roy was being discussed even in Gujarat. On the count of language, however, it has been observed that Roy's Bengali was still a 'learned' kind, and not the ordinary Bengali of the masses. See Killingley, *Rammohun Roy*, pp. 40–41.

27   Rammohun Roy, 'Abstract of The Arguments Regarding the Burning of Widows, Considered as Religious Rite' (1830), in *English Works*, p. 367.
28   For example, Roy wrote of his debt to H.H. Wilson's dictionaries in doing his translations from Sanskrit. See Roy, 'Translation of the Ishopanishad', *Essential Writings*, p. 22. He also collaborated with the BMS missionaries in attempting a Bengali translation of the Bible. See Sugirtharajah, *The Brahmin and His Bible*, p. 1. By this time, his English language skills were also strong. See Killingley, 'Rammohun Roy', p. 298, in Bauman and Voss Roberts eds., *The Routledge Handbook*.
29   Or as Sen writes, 'Hindus were quick to realize that "reform" was not just about altering beliefs or practices, but invariably touched upon deeper questions of self-identity.' See Amiya P. Sen ed., *Social and Religious Reform: The Hindus of British India* (New Delhi: Oxford University Press, 2003), 'Introduction', p. 3.
30   See Ragaviah, 'Refutations of Mr Newnham's Charges'. See also Bayly, *Empire and Information*, p. 213.
31   Roy, 'Translation of an Abridgment of the Vedant' (1816), pp. 2–3.
32   On this category of 'religion' itself, and the assumption that it is universal category, recognizable to all people everywhere, see Mandair, *Religion and the Specter of the West*, pp. 6–15.
33   Copley, *Religions in Conflict*, p. 128.
34   S. Radhakrishnan, *The Hindu View of Life: Upton Lectures Delivered at Manchester College, Oxford 1926* (London: George Allen & Unwin, 1927), p. 19.
35   In this respect, see Arvind Sharma, *Modern Hindu Thought*, p. 41 for how, conservatives looking for a divine origin for caste distinctions might find it in a certain Rig Vedic verse; but modernizers, if they wished to claim that caste is a gradual evolution—and, thus, could be reversed—might cite another ancient verse from the Yajur Vedic corpus to back *their* argument. Similarly, in the *Vajrasuchi Upanishad*, we find an argument against birth-based caste. See K. Narayanasvami Aiyar, *Thirty Minor Upanishads* (Madras, 1914), pp. 110–12. Importantly, Roy's critics also cited Vedic and other Sanskrit verses to back their arguments. See Roy's own 'Translation of a Conference', *Essential Writings*, pp. 114–18. See also Arvind Sharma, 'The Hindus as a Textual Community', p. 5 on the idea of 'lost Vedas'—that is Vedas in addition to the extant four—and that any practices for which direct authority from the existing Vedas cannot be found could be ascribed to the 'lost' ones. This made room for acknowledging other faiths also. See also K. Satchidananda Murty, *Revelation and Reason in Advaita Vedanta* (Waltair: Andhra University, 1959), p. 234.
36   Roy, 'A Defence of Hindoo Theism' (1827), *Essential Writings*, pp. 70–71.
37   Robertson, *Raja Rammohan Ray*, p. 84. See also Sen, *Rammohun Roy*, p. 53, where we read that Roy could also 'read into Hinduism perspectives . . . that were only tenuously present in it'.

38  See, for instance, Colebrooke, *Essays*, p. 56.
39  See Killingley, *Rammohun Roy*, p. 87, and F. Max Müller, *Biographical Essays*, p. 21 on Roy's unfamiliarity with the Vedic samhitas. See also Dasgupta, 'Ethics, Distance and Accountability', p. 179 onwards for how Roy did not just translate but injected his own ideas—influenced by his Persianate education—into these texts; and Sen, *Rammohun Roy*, pp. 70–71.
40  Killingley, *Rammohun Roy*, p. 92. See also Sen, *Rammohun Roy*, p. 51, where we read that even finding Vedic manuscripts was tough in Bengal; and Gelders and Balagangadhara, 'Rethinking Orientalism', p. 104.
41  Roy in an 1828 letter, quoted in Collet, *Life and Letters*, p. 124.
42  See D.H. Killingley, 'Vedanta and Modernity', in C.H. Philips and Mary Doreen Wainwright eds., *Indian Society and the Beginnings of Modernisation, c. 1830–1850* (London: SOAS, 1976), pp. 127–40; and Sen, *Rammohun Roy*, p. 50.
43  Robert A. Yelle, *The Language of Disenchantment: Protestant Literalism and Colonial Discourse in British India* (New York: Oxford University Press, 2013), p. 77 citing Sharada Sugirtharajah. See also Dasgupta, 'Ethics, Distance and Accountability', p. 190, p. 199, where Roy declares how his translations were intended to take scripture to *sarvasadharan lok*, ordinary people.
44  See in this regard Scott, *Spiritual Despots*.
45  Roy, 'Translation of an Abridgement', p. 2.
46  Roy, 'Translation of the Ishopanishad' (1816), in *Essential Writings*, p. 25. See also 'A Defence of Hindoo Theism' (1827), ibid., p. 71, and 'Translation of the Kut'h-Opunishad' (1819), ibid., p. 36, where he refers to Brahmins as 'self-interested leaders'.
47  Roy, 'A Defence of Hindu Theism', *Essential Writings*, p. 78. See also 'A Second Defence of the Monotheistical System of the Vedas', ibid., p. 87, p. 100, and Sen, *Rammohun Roy*, pp. 79–80, where we note that such attacks on Hindu gods occurred more in Roy's English writings than in the Bengali.
48  Roy, 'A Second Defence', ibid., p. 101. In this context, see also Raf Gelders and William Derde, 'Mantras of Anti-Brahmanism: Colonial Experience of Indian Intellectuals', *Economic and Political Weekly* 38, 43 (2003): 4611–17. At one point, in fact, missionaries believed Roy to be a potential convert. See Dasgupta, 'Ethics, Distance and Accountability', p. 318, and Killingley, 'Rammohun Roy', p. 304, in Bauman and Voss Roberts eds., *The Routledge Handbook*, pp. 297–306.
49  Roy, 'Translation of the Kut'h-Opunishad', p. 36.
50  Roy, 'Translation of the Moonduk-Opunishad', p. 51.
51  For more see, Pennington, *Was Hinduism Invented?*, pp. 170–72.
52  O'Hanlon, *Caste, Conflict, and Ideology*, p. 224.
53  Roy himself noted that his version of Hinduism was 'well-known' to 'learned Brahmans' even now, when most Hindus had forgotten their actual religion: a hint that his innovations were not entirely alien. See Killingley, 'Rammohun

Roy', p. 297, in Bauman and Voss Roberts eds., *The Routledge Handbook*, pp. 297–306. On philosophical diversity in Hinduism, see Andrew Nicholson, *Unifying Hinduism: Philosophy and Identity in Indian Intellectual History* (New York: Columbia University Press, 2010), pp. 24–29.

54  As Jaiswal notes, in Hinduism 'orthodoxy is to be proved in the realm of ritual and social behaviour' such as caste practices, temple worship, etc., 'but there is no such insistence in the realm of ideas'. Roy, that is, could believe what he wanted—so long as he did not attack the *practice* of Hinduism. See Suvira Jaiswal, 'Semitising Hinduism: Changing Paradigms of Brahmanical Integration', p. 20, in *Social Scientist* 19, 12 (1991): 20–32.

55  This is a more nuanced position from the claim that modern Hinduism simply appropriated Western ideas and gave it a Hindu provenance. The ideas were not, as such a Western monopoly, even if it was under British domination that Indians arranged them a certain way. Or as Weiss puts it, 'rich resources for modernization' existed within Hinduism. See Richard S. Weiss, *The Emergence of Modern Hinduism: Religion on the Margins of Colonialism* (Oakland: University of California Press, 2019), p. 17. Brian Hatcher also emphasizes not the impact of the West on Hinduism but a 'convergence' of Western ideas with Hindu ones. See also Killingley, 'Vedanta and Modernity', p. 127, where he notes how this was the time when 'Hinduism became aware of itself as a religion'. Contemporaries also sensed this, as seen in these disapproving but telling words by Governor General Hastings: 'Since their [Hindus'] intercourse with us they have endeavoured to connect and reconcile their legends . . . to find something abstrusely emblematic in the nonsense.' Quoted in Chatterjee, *Representations of India*, p. 99.

56  Of course, the same saints might sometimes treat god as *sagun*—with qualities—and sometimes as *nirgun*—without relatable qualities: proof again of how both trends existed in India.

57  Sumit Sarkar, *Essays of a Lifetime: Reformers, Nationalists, Subalterns* (Albany: State University of New York Press, 2019), p. 6. See also Sen, *Rammohun Roy*, pp. 73–78.

58  As Sen writes, 'reform was perceived as an interventionist act in which a historical figure was acutely aware of his moral and social roles', and in this case, particularly with the hope that he 'could replicate a European-style reformation in colonial India'. See Sen, *Rammohun Roy*, p. 5.

59  For what translation represented, see Dirks, *Castes of Mind*, pp. 145–46.

60  See in this context Dasgupta, 'Ethics, Distance and Accountability', p. 322, where we see how Roy demonstrated that he was a far better judge of what India was ready for compared to missionaries; the latter sold something unsuited to Indian soil, while he identified what might work. See also Sen, *Rammohun Roy*, p. 20 for how, despite all this, there were young Bengalis who saw Roy as too cautious.

61 Padmanji, *Once Hindu, Now Christian*, p. 4, pp. 6–7, p. 26, p. 34, p. 37, p. 55. Later scholars have also, sadly, been susceptible to such thinking. See, for example, V.T. Samuel, *One Caste, One Religion, One God: A Study of Sree Narayana Guru* (New Delhi: Sterling Publishers, 1977), p. 16, which describes Kerala's religious practices as an 'incongruous mixture'—as if congruity is a necessary universal standard.

62 Wendy Doniger cited in Pennington, *Was Hinduism Invented?*, pp. 169–70.

63 Not all missionaries though. Caldwell, although without admiration, accurately wrote, for example, some decades later:

> . . . it is the peculiar policy of the Brahmans to render all religious systems of India subservient to their purpose by making friends of them all. Brahmanism repudiates exclusiveness; it incorporates all creeds, assimilates all, consecrates all. People are permitted to entertain any opinions they please, and to practice any ceremonies they please, provided only that the supremacy of the Vedas and of the Brahmans is duly acknowledged. When that acknowledgment has been duly made, the new heterodoxy becomes another new authoritative orthodoxy, especially revealed by the Supreme Being himself for the enlightenment and salvation of the particular class of people amongst whom it has become popular. Thus Brahmanism yields and conquers; and hence, though the demon worship of Tinnevelly is as far as possible repugnant to the genius of orthodox Hinduism, and was not only independent of it in origin but, as I believe, long anterior to it, yet even it has received a place in the cunningly-devised mosaic of the Brahmans, and the devils have got themselves regarded as abnormal developments of the gods.

See Robert Caldwell, *Lectures on the Tinnevelly Missions: Descriptive of the Field, the Work, and the Results* (London: Bell & Daldy, 1857), p. 42.

64 Retrospective because in the immediate years after his death, his name and ideas dissipated. Only many years later was Roy and the Brahmo Samaj properly revived, receiving patronage and support from new members with their own ideas. See Brian A. Hatcher, *Bourgeois Hinduism, or the Faith of the Modern Vedantists: Rare Discourses from Early Colonial Bengal* (New York: Oxford University Press, 2008), p. 5.

65 'Trust Deed of the Brahma Samaj' (1830), *Essential Writings*, p. 105.

66 See in this regard Bayly, *Indian Society*, pp. 163–64. Numerically also, Brahmoism remained small: in 1881, out of over 187 million Indians, less than 1150 Hindus returned themselves formally in the census as Brahmos. See Weiss, *Emergence of Modern Hinduism*, p. 6. Brahmoism may have had more influence than these numbers suggest but even so, its overall impact was modest.

67 Robertson, *Raja Rammohan Ray*, p. 12, and Sen, *Rammohun Roy*, p. 48.

68  Roy, *The Precepts of Jesus: The Guide to Peace and Happiness; Extracted from the Books of the New Testament* (Calcutta: Baptist Mission Press, 1820), p. xxviii. Others noticed this too. 'The Hindoos,' one commentator wrote, 'never doubt any part of the miracles and prophecies of our scripture . . . the only thing that surprises them is, that they should be so much less wonderful than those of their own scriptures . . . If a Christian of respectability were to tell a Hindoo, that . . . St Paul had brought the sun and moon down upon the earth . . . he would immediately be put in mind of something still more extraordinary that Krishna did . . .' See W.H. Sleeman, *Rambles and Recollections of an Indian Official*, Vol. 2 (London: J. Hatchard & Son, 1844), pp. 51–52.

69  See Sugirtharajah, *The Brahmin and His Bible* for more. Marshman, the BMS man, was Roy's chief critic at this time in the first half of the 1820s. Interestingly, Roy's stance won him supporters among Unitarians—who also took a rationalist approach to the Bible—in Britain and America both, helping build his celebrity abroad.

70  Two generations later, Chattampi Swamikal (1853–1924) in Kerala would employ a similar formula in his *Kristhumatha Chedanam*, where contradictions, inconsistencies and logical failings within Christian scripture are highlighted to negate its claims.

71  This was later done in western India also, during debates between Hindus and missionaries. See, for example, Young, *Resistant Hinduism*, p. 26.

72  On this, see also Sharma, *Modern Hindu Thought*, pp. 99–105.

73  Sugirtharajah, *The Brahmin and His Bible*, pp. 36–45. This stance would become popular. See for example Rajnarayan Bose's lecture, 'Superiority of Hinduism to other Prevailing Religions', summarized in *Allen's Indian Mail*, 28 October 1872.

74  Quoted in Sugirtharajah, *The Brahmin and His Bible*, p. 57. Roy also remarked once to someone who thought he would convert: 'My Lord, you are under a mistake. I have not laid down one superstition to take up another.' See Sen, *Rammohun Roy*, p. 86. See also David Kopf, *The Brahmo Samaj and the Shaping of the Modern Indian Mind* (Princeton: Princeton University Press, 1979), p. 13.

75  Vishnubawa Brahmachari, who we met in the previous chapter, made similar claims. See Conlon, 'The Polemic Process', p. 14.

76  Roy, *English Works*, p. 882. Missionaries had noted this difference, of course, while conceding that behind the diverse practices was 'some sort of cohesion or basic unity'. See Oddie, *Imagined Hinduism*, pp. 150–51. See also Davis, *Lives of Indian Images*, p. 48.

77  Bankim Chandra Chatterjee, *Letters on Hinduism* (Calcutta: Prabasi Press, 1940 ed.), p. 12.

78  Ibid., p. 11. Amusingly, Chatterjee's words proved prophetic: in 1908, a Bengali prince, wrote of his 'rude shock' in Italy, where the Catholic church,

he wrote, 'instead of enlightening their flocks . . . teaching them the Truth of Religion' fed people 'a form of idolatry' centred on the Madonna. See the epilogue to this book.

79  Chatterjee, *Letters on Hinduism*, p. 16.
80  For more on Chatterjee, his background and intellectual influences, see Tapan Raychaudhuri, *Europe Reconsidered: Perceptions of the West in Nineteenth-Century Bengal* (Delhi: Oxford University Press, 1988), chapter three. For his stressing of a Hindu identity in his work, see Bhagat-Kennedy, 'Imagining Bharat', chapter two.
81  Chatterjee, *Letters on Hinduism*, pp. 45–46. See also, Basu, *Hindutva as Political Monotheism*, p. 112, where we read of Bankim's 'disinterest' in an 'austere and esoteric Vedic monotheism', which is too 'abstract . . . to animate a flock and a nation'. Instead, he desired a 'rational transcription of Puranic cultures and institutions'. Another writer in 1894 also argued that while Vedic Hindus were not idolaters, post-Vedic Hindus were; a situation that 'would hardly be called progress' by Western standards. And yet it was the latter who were 'more advanced than the Vedic Hindus in literature, science, arts and manufactures'. Idolatry, that is, was not by itself proof of decline or corruption. See Pramatha Nath Bose, *A History of Hindu Civilisation During British Rule*, Vol. 1 (New Delhi: Asian Publication Services, 1978 [1894]), p. ii.
82  Not permanently, evidently. In 1846, the remains were removed again and cremated in Calcutta. The shrine at Arnos Vale cemetery still stands, however, and receives pilgrims even now. See Sen, *Rammohun Roy*, p. 166.
83  Dayanand Sarasvati (Durga Prasad trans.), *An English Translation of the Satyarth Prakash of Maharshi Swami Dayanand Saraswati, Being A Guide to Vedic Hermeneutics* (Lahore: Virjanand Press, 1908), p. 1. Hereafter 'Satyarth Prakash'.
84  Chamupati, *Glimpses of Dayananda* (Delhi: Sharada Mandir Limited, 1937), p. 2, and J.N. Farquhar, *Modern Religious Movements in India* (New Delhi: Munshiram Manoharlal Publishers Ltd., 1977), p. 108. Farquhar also notes that Dayananda may have been influenced by Jain monks in Kathiawar who questioned idol worship. Kathiawar also had other Hindu religious figures who made similar arguments. See J.T.F. Jordens, *Dayananda Sarasvati: His Life and Ideas* (Delhi: Oxford University Press, 1960), p. 10.
85  Satthianadhan, *Sketches of Indian Christians*, p. 70.
86  For this title, see Salmond, *Hindu Iconoclasts*, p. 2, and George Chemparathy, 'Some Observations on Dayananda Sarasvati's Conception of the Veda', p. 250, in *Vienna Journal of South Asian Studies* 38 (1994): 231–50.
87  *Satyarth Prakash*, pp. 3–7; Salmond, *Hindu Iconoclasts*, pp. 66–67; and Jordens, *Dayananda Sarasvati*, p. 3, p. 6, p. 19, p. 133. Some have identified a certain family and town, but as Jordens notes, much of this is guesswork. On renunciation and renunciant culture, which is alive to this day—and through

which we can still recognise many of the feelings Dayananda experienced—see Sondra L. Hausner's fascinating *Wandering with Sadhus: Ascetics in the Hindu Himalayas* (Bloomington: Indiana University Press, 2007).

88   Interestingly, however, we have one account which reports that, aged fourteen, Roy also did consider becoming a sanyasi but was dissuaded by his mother. See Collett, *Life and Letters*, p. 5.

89   Farquhar, *Modern Religious Movements*, 108; Kenneth W. Jones, *Arya Dharm: Hindu Consciousness in 19th-Century Punjab* (Berkeley: University of California Press, 1976), p. 34; and Salmond, *Hindu Iconoclasts*, p. 70.

90   *Satyarth Prakash*, pp. 8–11.

91   For Roy's travels, see Robertson, *Essential Writings*, pp. xv–xvi.

92   Jordens, *Dayananda Sarasvati*, pp. 28–29. See also *Satyarth Prakash*, p. 13.

93   *Satyarth Prakash*, p. 9.

94   Ibid., p. 13.

95   Ibid., p. 12.

96   His name was Swami Virajananda. For details of his own travels and career, see Har Bilas Sarda, *Life of Dayanand Saraswati: World Teacher* (Ajmer: Vedic Yantralaya, 1946), pp. 20–39.

97   Chamupati, *Glimpses*, p. 18.

98   Sarda, *Life of Dayanand Saraswati*, p. cxviii.

99   Jordens, *Dayananda Sarasvati*, pp. 31–38.

100  Ibid., pp. 37–38. See also Sarda, *Life of Dayanand Saraswati*, pp. 38–39.

101  Sarda, *Life of Dayanand Saraswati*, p. xl, p. 22.

102  This discomfort with sensuality in religious literature became a general trend. In the twentieth century, one critic would ask if, for example, Kshetrayya's seventeenth-century verses were 'proper or safe' now? There was also a tendency to suggest that the erotic represented higher meaning and not anything *really* sensual. See Ramanujan, Rao and Shulman, *When God Is a Customer*, pp. 28–29.

103  Weiss, *Emergence of Modern Hinduism*, p. 99. Among Shaktas—goddess worshippers—too we find this: some who held that 'true' Shaktas eschewed animal sacrifice and took a more philosophical view of the goddess. See June McDaniel, *Offering Flowers, Feeding Skulls*, p. 18.

104  See Weiss for a thought-provoking study on Ramalinga as well as his chief competitor in reforming Saivism. See also Lloyd I. Rudolph and Susan Hoeber Rudolph, *The Modernity of Tradition: Political Development in India* (Chicago: University of Chicago Press, 1967) for a broader study of the interplay between modernity and tradition, not as two watertight categories but as enmeshed forces; on how tradition played a bigger role than is accepted in the making of modernity.

105  See Anncharlot Eschmann, 'Mahima Dharma: An Autochthonous Hindu Reform Movement', in Eschmann, Hermann Kulke and Gaya Charan Tripathi eds., *The Cult of Jagannath and The Regional Tradition of Orissa*

(New Delhi: Manohar, 1978), pp. 375–410; Lidia Guzy, 'The Poly-culture of Mahima Dharma: On Babas and Alekh Shamans in an Ascetic Religious Movement', in Marine Carrin and Lidia Guzy eds., *Voices from the Periphery: Subalternity and Empowerment in India* (New Delhi: Routledge, 2012), pp. 155–81; and Kenneth W. Jones, *Socio-Religious Reform Movements in British India* (Cambridge: Cambridge University Press, 1989), pp. 131–35. For a similar movement in south India, see M.S.S. Pandian, 'Meanings of "colonialism" and "nationalism": An Essay on Vaikunda Swamy Cult', in *Studies in History* 8, 2 (1992): 167–85, and P. Johnson, 'Vaikunda Swamikal: Harbinger of Social Change in Kerala', in S. Sivadasan ed., *Renaissance in Kerala: A Revisit* (Thiruvananthapuram: Modern Book Centre, 2021 ed.), pp. 121–36. Something similar would transpire with Christians too. Low-caste converts in Travancore, for instance, were discriminated against even in missionary establishments. Poyikayil Yohannan (1879–1939) set up his own sect blending Christian principles with the cultural practices of his people. Missionaries called him a heretic, while his followers saw in him a prophet. By the 1950s, he would be deified. See Mohan, *Modernity of Slavery*, chapter four.

106  Jordens, *Dayananda Sarasvati*, p. 51 notes that in the late 1860s, he still did not speak Hindi and had to manage with Sanskrit.
107  *Satyarth Prakash*, p. 25.
108  Jordens, *Dayananda Sarasvati*, pp. 46–47.
109  Ibid., p. 56.
110  Ibid., pp. 65–66.
111  Hatcher, *Hinduism before Reform*, pp. 220–24.
112  Ibid., p. 161.
113  Reginald Heber, *Narrative of a Journey through the Upper Provinces of India, from Calcutta to Bombay, 1824–1825*, Vol. 2 (London: John Murray, 1873), p. 106.
114  And it worked: if in 1823 he had 1,00,000 followers, today membership of the Swaminarayan sect numbers in the millions. For a study, see Raymond B. Williams, *A New Face of Hinduism: The Swaminarayan Religion* (Cambridge: Cambridge University Press, 1984).
115  He would even write a critique. See Sarda, *Life of Dayanand Saraswati*, p. 128, and *Satyarth Prakash*, pp. 372–75.
116  William, *A New Face of Hinduism*, pp. 39–40.
117  Muller, *Biographical Essays*, p. 168.
118  Or as Muller wrote, 'He took his stand on the Vedas . . . One might almost say he was possessed by the Vedas.' See *Times of India*, 11 January 1884.
119  Salmond, *Hindu Iconoclasts*, p. 71, and *Satyarth Prakash*, p. 208, p. 315. See also ibid., pp. 299–300, where Dayananda argues that sacrifices conducted out of Vedic inspiration emerged from a misreading of the true meaning of certain terms. Asvamedha, or horse sacrifice, for instance was merely about

good government. For criticism, see T. Williams, *Exposure of Dayananda Sarasvati and His Followers Both as to Their Deliberate Falsification of the Rgveda and Their Immorality* (Delhi: Imperial Medical Hall Press, 1889).

120 Quoted in John E. Cort, 'Indology as authoritative knowledge: Jain debates about icons and history in colonial India', p. 146, in Dodson and Hatcher eds., *Trans-Colonial Modernities*, pp. 137–61. See also Chemparathy, 'Some Observations', p. 232 on how Dayananda did indeed 'interpret the Vedic texts in such a way as to make them suit his own ideas'. Even now, there are Hindu-run websites angrily 'exposing' Dayananda.

121 *Satyarth Prakash*, p. 67, p. 123. See also p. 234, where he dismisses the Brahmana section of the Vedas as only commentaries, not part of the original texts. See also p. 337, where he adds that if there was truth in the Puranas, those parts must have come from the Vedas; the rest was falsehood.

122 Ibid., p. 291. America is equated with Patala—the netherworld—in *Satyarth Prakash*. This idea was later expanded on by Chaman Lal in *Hindu America: Revealing the Story of the Romance of the Surya Vanshi Hindus and Depicting the Imprints of Hindu Culture on the Two Americas* (Bombay: New Book Co., 1940), with the hope that Hindus would one day 'reclaim America'. Interestingly, the book carries an image of Gandhi at the start and was published with endorsements from two future Indian presidents: Sarvepalli Radhakrishnan and Rajendra Prasad, in addition to other major public figures.

123 *Satyarth Prakash*, pp. 294–96. Dayananda's guru also saw the great war of the Mahabharata as a historical cut-off point to distinguish between pure Hindu learning and corrupted, inferior scriptural production. See also Jones, *Arya Dharm*, pp. 32–33.

124 Supporters also reveal this attitude, when, for example they describe Brahmins as 'monopolists of religion'. See Sarda, *Life of Dayanand Saraswati*, p. lvii. See also Salmond, *Hindu Iconoclasts*, pp. 84–85.

125 *Satyarth Prakash*, p. 311, p. 319, p. 341.

126 Jordens, *Dayananda Sarasvati*, p. 71.

127 Ibid., p. 312, p. 317, p. 436, p. 475, p. 501. With Islam, Dayananda specifically meant the Black Stone (al-Ḥajar al-Aswad) at the Kaaba. He did not, however, have adequate knowledge of Jainism and often mixed it with Buddhism: a tendency that invited criticism. Rectifying this, he cited more Jain sources in the second edition of *Satyarth Prakash*. See Cort, 'Indology as authoritative knowledge'. For more on Dayananda's polemics against Christianity, including a lampooning of circumcision, of Jesus's disciples 'eating' their guru and of Jesus being a carpenter, see Kenneth W. Jones, 'Swami Dayananda Saraswati's "Critique of Christianity"', in Kenneth W. Jones ed., *Religious Controversy in British India: Dialogues in South Asian Languages* (New York: State University of New York Press, 1992), pp. 52–74. The attacks on Christianity and Islam do not exist in the first edition of

*Satyarth Prakash*, but as Jordens, *Dayananda Sarasvati*, p. 97 shows, this was only to avoid a delay in publication; those sections had already been written and would be carried in the updated edition.

128 Some of his supporters would later explain that this was all done in a constructive spirit; in any case, it is argued that Dayananda's statements met the needs of his time, whereas in the twentieth century, conditions changed. See Sarda, *Life of Dayanand Saraswati*, pp. lxxxviii–xc.

129 Jordens, *Dayananda Sarasvati*, pp. 78–79. See also Jones, *Arya Dharm*, p. 34.

130 Jordens, *Dayananda Sarasvati*, pp. 79–81. Evidently, it was also here that a Brahmo leader suggested that he cease preaching in Sanskrit and use Hindi instead. Urban India also brought Dayananda in contact with interesting people: R.C. Dutt, for example, who became a future Indian National Congress president; the revolutionary Shyamji Krishna Varma, etc. Ironically, later in life, Dayananda would have a falling out with the Brahmo Samaj in Punjab. See Jones, *Arya Dharm*, pp. 40–42.

131 Jordens, *Dayananda Sarasvati*, p. 149.

132 M.G. Ranade quoted in Richard P. Tucker, *Ranade and the Roots of Indian Nationalism* (Bombay: Popular Prakash, 1977), p. 83.

133 Salmond, *Hindu Iconoclasts*, p. 69. Sometimes, though, Dayananda's supporters in turn attacked his critics. See Sarda, *Life of Dayanand Saraswati*, p. li.

134 Tucker, *Ranade*, p. 83.

135 Chamupati, *Glimpses*, p. 154. For other violent attacks, see Sarda, *Life of Dayanand Saraswati*, p. xlix, and Jones, *Arya Dharm*, p. 40.

136 Chamupati, *Glimpses*, p. 76.

137 Sarda's *Life of Dayanand Saraswati* even includes instances where Dayananda divines events and things, much to the surprise of his enemies and followers both.

138 Cited in Pandit Ram Bhaj Datta, *Agnihotri Demolished: Being a Thorough Refutation of His Dayanand Unveiled and Its Rejoinder* (Lahore: Virajanand Press, 1892), pp. 1–2.

139 Henry Martin Clark, *The Principles and Teaching of the Arya Samaj: The Vedic Doctrine of Sacrifice* (Amritsar: Punjab Religious Book Society, 1888), p. 2, p. 4.

140 Williams, *Exposure*, p. 18. Emphasis added. In time, Christian missionaries would publish books attempting to disprove, with scholarly citations and a 'true' picture of the Vedic religion, the Arya Samaj idea that there could ever be a return to that system, or that it could be India's 'national' faith. See, for example, *Vedic Hinduism and the Arya Samaj: An Appeal to Educated Hindus* (London and Madras: The Christian Literature Society for India, 1902).

141 Muller, *Biographical Essays*, p. 170. See *Satyarth Prakash*, p. 282, where we read about Krishna travelling by a steamer. See also Sharma, *Modern Hindu Thought*, p. 65 on how 'Modern Hinduism seeks to relate science

142  *Satyarth Prakash*, pp. 292–93.
143  A.C. Bouquet, *Hinduism* (London: Hutchinson's University Library, 1956), p. 129.
144  *Satyarth Prakash*, p. 293. See also Jordens, *Dayananda Sarasvati*, p. 179 quoting Dayananda who once declared that Western scholars were 'not God that we should accept . . . what they have written'; nor were 'they greater' than Vedic sages.
145  *Satyarth Prakash*, p. 28.
146  John Robson, *Hinduism and Its Relations to Christianity* (Edinburgh & London: Oliphant Anderson & Ferrier, 1893), p. 219. It appears that some of his own followers attempted to take a less determined position on the Vedas, though without success. See Lajpat Rai, *The Arya Samaj: An Account of Its Origin, Doctrines, and Activities, with a Biographical Sketch of the Founder* (London: Longmans, Green & Co., 1915), p. 106. For a defence of Dayananda, see Sarda, *Life of Dayanand Saraswati*, pp. lxxv–lxxviii.
147  Jones, *Arya Dharm*, 36.
148  Jordens, *Dayananda Sarasvati*, p. 230; Sarda, *Life of Dayanand Saraswati*, p. l.
149  Chamupati, *Glimpses*, pp. 136–37.
150  The maharajah's brother, Sir Pratap Singh of Idar, does seem to have absorbed Dayananda's views. As he would later write, Puranic Hinduism represented a 'Dark Age' when Hindus ceased being attentive to 'their true religious scriptures', the Vedas, and reduced their faith to 'a collection of grotesque fancies and a bundle of superstitions' worthy of 'ridicule'. The 'later-day Brahmins' were blamed for this, caring for their 'self-interest' and fabricating all kinds of nonsense. However, 'purified of these later accretions', the Vedic religion was capable of commanding 'the approbation of the thoughtful' including, of course, 'scholars of the West'. See R.B. Van Wart, *The Life of Liuet.-General Sir Pratap Singh* (London: Oxford University Press, 1926), pp. 191–92.
151  Chamupati, *Glimpses*, p. 138.
152  Jordens, *Dayananda Sarasvati*, p. 243.
153  Or as one scholar writes, 'the cow-protection movement was indicative of certain Hindus identifying with others *as* Hindus'. See Peter Robb, 'The Challenge of Gau-Mata: British Policy and Religious Change in India, 1880–1916', pp. 291–92, in *Modern Asian Studies* 20, 2 (1986): 285–319. As for Hindu unity, as an Arya Samaj member would write, 'The chief weakness of Hinduism lay in it being a vast sea of contradictory doctrines and beliefs, which made it an impossible religion for active propaganda work and which laid it open to the attacks of those who aimed in India to convert Hindus.' See Rai, *The Arya Samaj*, p. 113.

154 He once declared: 'What can be a more heartrending pain than the fact that this country is being ruined by the sighs of the widows, the piercing cries of the orphans, and the slaughter of cows?' See Sarda, *Life of Dayanand Saraswati*, p. lv.

155 Dayananda Sarasvati (Durga Prasad trans.), *The Ocean of Mercy: An English Translation of Maharshi Swami Dayanand Saraswati's 'Gocaruna Nidhi'* (Lahore: Virajanand Press, 1889), pp. 16–18. He also raised such issues in personal discussions, evidently, with British officials. See Sarda, *Life of Dayanand Saraswati*, p. 47, p. 57.

156 See instances in Robb, 'The Challenge of Gau-Mata', p. 296. See also songs sung at Hindu festivals in western India in the 1890s, urging Hindus to abandon shared links with Muslims, and to return to the faith of the cow in Cashman, *The Myth of the Lokamanya*, p. 78, pp. 83–84.

157 Sandria B. Freitag, 'Sacred Symbol as Mobilizing Ideology: The North Indian Search for a "Hindu" Community', p. 607, in *Comparative Studies in Society and History* 22, 4 (1980): 597–625.

158 Ibid., p. 606.

159 Robb, 'The Challenge of Gau-Mata', p. 295. Put another way, in 'symbolic terms, the figure of the cow could unite popular and high culture; it could serve reformist and traditionalist ends; it could reach the hearts of townsmen and peasants alike.' See Sandria B. Freitag, 'Contesting in Public: Colonial Legacies and Contemporary Communalism', p. 218, in David Ludden ed., *Making India Hindu: Community and the Politics of Democracy in India* (New Delhi: Oxford University Press, 2005), pp. 211–35. The Samaj would also have ten principles, which were general enough to ensure that 'no Hindu, at any rate, should have any difficulty in subscribing' to them. See Rai, *The Arya Samaj*, p. 103.

160 Quoted in Robb, 'The Challenge of Gau-Mata', p. 303. This was not new. Cow-protection had been political for long, and in 1806, in upper India, the Company themselves banned it to 'silenc[e] the clamors of the adversaries of the British' who painted them as cow-killers. They were referring also to Jaswant Rao Holkar, the Maratha ruler of Indore, who around 1805 attempted to build an anti-British alliance of states, using cow-protection as a plank. See Sugata Ray, 'In the Name of Krishna: The Cultural Landscape of a North Indian Pilgrimage Town', Unpublished PhD dissertation, University of Minnesota (2012), pp. 127–40.

161 See C.S. Adcock, *The Limits of Tolerance: Indian Secularism and the Politics of Religious Freedom* (Oxford: Oxford University Press, 2014), chapter four.

162 *Times of India*, 11 January 1884.

163 For a comparison of the two Samajs as early as 1893, see Salmond, *Hindu Iconoclasts*, p. 65.

164 Dayananda even criticized Brahmo Samajists for being too fond of English and of British habits. See Jones, *Arya Dharm*, p. 40.

165 Sidney Webb in Rai, *The Arya Samaj*, p. xii. See also Jaiswal, 'Semitising Hinduism', p. 27; Jordens, *Dayananda Sarasvati*, pp. 160–64; and Jones, *Arya Dharm* on the social background of Dayananda's Punjabi followers, and why his message was attractive. Among those impressed with the Arya Samaj was a schoolteacher called Krishn Behari Vajpayee, whose son, Atal, would in time become India's first prime minister from the Hindu nationalist Bharatiya Janata Party (BJP). The BJP's predecessor, the Jana Sangh, was also, interestingly, inaugurated in an Arya Samaj school in Delhi. See Abhishek Choudhary, *Vajpayee: The Ascent of the Hindu Right, 1924–1977* (New Delhi: Picador India, 2023), p. 6, p. 13, p. 90.

166 Cox, *Imperial Fault Lines*, p. 66.

167 Frank Lillingston, *The Brahmo Samaj and Arya Samaj in Their Bearing upon Christianity: A Study in Indian Theism* (London: Macmillan & Co., 1901), p. 112. Besides, for practical reasons, the Samaj became more tolerant of Puranic Hinduism; as a missionary observed, in western India, while it still emphasized the Vedas, 'it does not oppose itself in practice to traditional customs. Hence, membership in the Samaj does not mean breaking away from the past.' See J.E. Abbott in *Report of the Fourth Decennial Indian Missionary Conference* (London: Christian Literature Society, 1903), p. 285.

168 Quoted in Sharma, *Hinduism as a Missionary Religion*, p. 53.

169 Ian Copland, *State, Community and Neighbourhood in Princely North India, c. 1900–1950* (New York: Palgrave Macmillan, 2005), p. 83. See also Jaiswal, 'Semitising Hinduism', p. 29. Re-conversion appears to have been favourably looked upon by Dayananda early in his career. See Sarda, *Life of Dayanand Saraswati*, p. 54. See also Jordens, *Dayananda Sarasvati*, pp. 169–70. See also Jones, *Arya Dharm*, pp. 47–49. There are stray instances from Indian history where this was done earlier also: the Maratha general Netaji Palkar converted to Islam and served the Mughals, only to return to the Hindu fold in due course. See also other instances in Hirozhi Fukazawa, *The Medieval Deccan: Peasants, Social Systems and States: Sixteenth to Eighteenth Centuries* (Bombay: Oxford University Press, 1991), pp. 96–97; and, including of a Brahmin, in O'Hanlon, 'Narratives of Penance', pp. 62–64.

170 This did not please everyone. As Gandhi wrote, Dayananda had 'made . . . Hinduism narrow'. Quoted in Sharma, *Hinduism as a Missionary Religion*, pp. 36–37. See also Sharma, *Modern Hindu Thought*, p. 183 for a remark by Gandhi that he could not 'let a scriptural text supersede my reason'. On my use of the term 'evangelical' here: the Samaj also, in time, began to 'include the conversion of non-Hindus and even those whose ancestors had never been Hindus'. Many Sikhs, for example, began to see the Samaj as a threat to their own identity. See Kenneth W. Jones, 'Communalism in Punjab: The Arya Samaj Contribution', pp. 47–50, in *The Journal of Asian Studies* 28, 1 (1968): 39–54. Of course, there were those within the Arya Samaj who were

scandalized by *shuddhi* schemes in which low-caste groups were welcomed into the fold, this sometimes leading to violence. See Lee, *Deceptive Majority*, p. 87, p. 92.

171 It is not entirely without reason that admirers of Dayananda highlight not only his spiritual achievements but also his bodily strength, which could terrify, we read, wrestlers, princes and even the occasional wild animal. Many of these appear in Sarda, *Life of Dayanand Saraswati*, emphasizing the 'masculine' religion Dayananda promoted.

172 Jordens, *Dayananda Sarasvati*, p. 136.

173 For biographical details, see O'Hanlon, *Caste, Conflict, and Ideology*, p. 106. See also Bhaskar Lakshman Bhole (Sudhakar Marathe trans.), *Mahatma Jotirao Phule* (Delhi: Sahitya Akademi, 2011).

174 Braj Ranjan Mani, 'Introduction', p. 6, in Braj Ranjan Mani and Pamela Sardar eds., *A Forgotten Liberator: The Life and Struggle of Savitribai Phule* (New Delhi: Mountain Peak, 2008), pp. 1–13. See also Dhananjay Keer, *Mahatma Jotirao Phooley: Father of the Indian Social Revolution* (Bombay: Popular Prakashan, 1960 ed.).

175 'Sudrasiromani'. See Vishnu Krushna Chiplunkar, *Nibandhamala* (Pune: Chitrashala, 1917), p. 470. He also refers to Phule elsewhere as 'jagatguru' (word teacher), 'mahajnani' (enlightened soul), 'mahapandit' (great scholar) and so on—all in snark.

176 This struggle itself, as Kumar, notes was old. Colonialism just offered fresh agency to lower-caste groups. See Kumar, *Political Agenda of Education*, p. 98.

177 For one anecdote where former low-caste servants of a landlord, after conversion, assumed a tone of equality and 'impertinence' and began even to dress as equals, see Menon, *A History of Travancore*, p. 507. Similarly, K. Natarajan of the *Indian Social Reformer* would write: 'The fear of the Christian missionary has been the beginning of much social wisdom [in India].' Quoted in Fred B. Fisher, *India's Silent Revolution* (New York: The Macmillan Company, 1920), p. 92. See also Lee, *Deceptive Majority*, p. 46, p. 49. Or as Mohan writes, 'Missionary engagement with colonial societies was a complex process' and 'approaching them with a one cap fits all framework will not help us in analyzing their role in colonial societies'. See Mohan, *Modernity of Slavery*, p. 19. See also ibid., pp. 68–69, where we find how colonial conditions allowed slave castes to 'speak'. And that missionaries were willing to 'listen' was empowering in its own way.

178 Ingham, *Reformers*, p. 63.

179 Jana Tschurenev and Sumeet Mhaskar, '"Wake up for education": Colonialism, Social Transformation, and the Beginnings of the Anti-Caste Movement in India', p. 5, in *Paedagogica Historica* (2021): 1–19. See also *Adam's Report*, p. 75 on the general view that Brahmins were better students and 'more intelligent'.

180  Alexander Duff, *Female Education in India: Being the Substance of an Address Delivered at the Annual Meeting of the Scottish Ladies' Association* (Edinburgh: John Johnstone, 1839), p. 38.
181  Quoted in Hayden J.A. Bellenoit, *Missionary Education and Empire in Late Colonial India, 1860-1920* (London: Pickering and Chatto, 2007), pp. 25–26. See also Padmanji, *Once Hindu, Now Christian*, p. 65, where we read how in his classroom also 'there was continually some reference to religion'. See also O'Hanlon, *Caste, Conflict, and Ideology*, p. 108. Some did, however, recognize this. As one figure in the south put it, the Bible 'is a book which no man can read without being entangled'. See Hudson, 'Life and Times of H.A. Krishna Pillai', p. 224.
182  Cox, *Imperial Fault Lines*, p. 191; Hudson, 'Life and Times of H.A. Krishna Pillai', p. 280.
183  Phule famously defended the 1880s conversion of the Brahmin woman, Pandita Ramabai (1858–1922). See O'Hanlon, *Caste, Conflict, and Ideology*, p. 268.
184  Or as one scholar puts it, 'Jotirao Phule's writings against Brahminism utilized forms of speech and rhetorical styles associated with the rustic language of peasants but infused them with demands for human rights and social equality that bore the influence of nonconformist Christianity to produce a unique discourse of caste radicalism.' See Anupama Rao, *The Caste Question: Dalits and the Politics of Modern India* (Berkeley: University of California Press, 2009), p. 39.
185  O'Hanlon, *Caste, Conflict, and Ideology*, p. 111. In Kerala, decades later, the anti-caste movement would draw inspiration from Booker T. Washington's *Up from Slavery*. See Mohan, *Modernity of Slavery*, p. 50.
186  Tschurenev and Mhaskar, 'Wake up for Education', p. 2, in fact, call her 'the first published woman poet in modern India'. It is also said that given their childlessness, when Phule's father asked him to take a second wife, he refused. He would later write how if women were not awarded matching rights, men had no business taking more than one spouse either. See Phule, *Sarvajanik Satyadharma Pustak* ('Universal Religion of Truth'), p. 470, in *Samagra Vangmay*, pp. 443–560.
187  'Ingraji Mauli'. See poem 28 in Savitribai Phule (M.G. Mali ed.), *Savitribai Phule Samagra Vangmay* (Mumbai: Maharashtra Rajya Sahitya ani Sanskruti Mandal, 2011 ed.). See also poems 32 and 38. For a survey of studies on English education's disruptive power, see Bellenoit, *Missionary Education and Empire*, p. 3. See also Kooiman, *Conversion and Social Equality*, pp. 98–99 for reports from the south about the 'immense scope for self improvement' that knowledge of English offered.
188  O'Hanlon, *Caste, Conflict, and Ideology*, pp. 111–12.
189  Tschurenev and Mhaskar, 'Wake up for Education', p. 8.
190  Ibid., pp. 10–11.

191 Savitribai to Jotirao Phule, October 1856, in Sunil Sardar, 'Love Letters Unlike Any Other: Three Letters to Jotiba', pp. 41–43, in Mani and Sardar eds., *A Forgotten Liberator*, pp. 39–47.

192 O'Hanlon, *Caste, Conflict, and Ideology*, p. 118. O'Hanlon refers only to Phule being presented a shawl but Savitribai was also evidently honoured, though probably not in a public ceremony.

193 Cynthia Stephen, 'The Stuff Legends Are Made Of', pp. 17–18, in Mani and Sardar eds., *A Forgotten Liberator*, pp. 14–27.

194 Savitribai to Jotirao Phule, 19 August 1868 in Sardar, 'Love Letters', pp. 44–45.

195 See Chiplunkar, *Nibandhamala*, p. 465. In 1887, Phule would, incensed by an intellectual's critique of Christianity, attack the latter as 'a drunkard and a fool', suggesting a strategic sympathy with missionaries. See Rahul Sarwate, 'Reimagining the Modern Hindu Self: Caste, Untouchability and Hindu Theology in Colonial South Asia, 1899–1948', Unpublished PhD dissertation, Columbia University (2020), p. 37. As late as 1925, a Marathi polemicist, G.M. Nalwade, was able to write a book titled *Satyashodhak ka Christasevak* (*Truthseeker or Servant of Christ?*) (Pune: G.N. Nalwade, 1925), with a foreword by Phule's own relative, calling him both a traitor to his faith and his country. Another relative, Baburao Phule, would accuse Jotirao of being a Christian convert. In the book's foreword, we also read a line suggesting how were one to consume the book without knowledge of its author, one might think it was authored by a missionary. But Phule was hardly alone in his views. In 1876, Bholanath Chakravarti, in Bengal, for instance, declared British rule India's 'good fortune'—though for him this was because the British saved Hindus from Muslim 'oppressions'. We will see more of this line of thinking in the next chapter. See Chatterjee, *Nation and Its Fragments*, p. 94. The Tamil lower-caste intellectual Iyothee Thass Pandithar (1845–1914) would also be seen as a loyalist of the Raj. See, for example, A.R. Venkatachalapathy, *Swadeshi Steam: V.O. Chidambaram Pillai and the Battle against the British Maritime Empire* (Gurugram: Allen Lane, 2023), pp. 345–46.

196 O'Hanlon, *Caste, Conflict, and Ideology*, p. 110. See also Phule, *Gulamgiri* ('Slavery'), p. 187, in Jotirao Phule (Dhananjay Keer, S.G. Malshe and Yashwant Dinkar Phadke eds.), *Mahatma Phule Samagra Vangmay* (Mumbai: Maharashtra Rajya Sahitya ani Sanskruti Mandal, 2006 ed.), pp. 119–201.

197 'Aapmatlabi banavati dharma'. See *Sarvajanik Satyadharma Pustak*, p. 493.

198 Phule, in fact, expressed relief that the British prevailed during the Great Rebellion. See *Gulamgiri*, p. 188.

199 Sharma, *Modern Hindu Thought*, p. 156. See also ibid., p. 139, where we read how Hinduism's 'primary thrust is to secure order in the midst of anarchic pluralism ... rather than to secure justice within an already established order. It may be simply too busy establishing order to do so'. See also Parekh, 'Some Reflections', p. 20, where we read how Hindus saw society 'not [as]

a collection of individuals but a community of communities'. For a critique and the limitations of this pattern, see Tagore, *Nationalism*, pp. 137–38.
200 *Gulamgiri*, p. 124.
201 Tscherenev and Mhaskar, 'Wake up for Education', p. 13.
202 Phule, *Brahmanache Kasab* (*Priestcraft Exposed*), p. 102, in *Samagra Vangmay*, pp. 91–118.
203 Quoted in G. Aloysius, *Nationalism Without a Nation in India* (New Delhi: Oxford University Press, 1997), pp. 81–82. Elsewhere Phule addresses the queen as 'Aaisaheb' (respected mother). See *Sarvajanik Satyadharma Pustak*, p. 523.
204 Phule, *Trutiya Ratna* (*Third Jewel*) in *Samagra Vangmay*, pp. 1–33. This formula—where the missionary and English education save the downtrodden—appears in the same era elsewhere in India also, for instance, in Potheri Kunhambu's Malayalam novel *Saraswati Vijayan* (1892). Kunhambu also, like Phule, saw Brahmins as the root of much evil in Hindu society. See Dilip M. Menon, 'Caste and Colonial Modernity: Reading *Saraswativijayam*', in *Studies in History* 13, 2 (1997): 291–312.
205 Phule, *Memorial Addressed to the Education Commission*, p. 247, in *Samagra Vangmay*, pp. 243–54.
206 See for instance Zvelebil, *The Poets of the Powers*, p. 69.
207 See O'Hanlon, *Caste, Conflict, and Ideology*, p. 41.
208 Quoted in Richard M. Eaton, *A Social History of the Deccan, 1300–1761: Eight Indian Lives* (Cambridge: Cambridge University Press, 2005), p. 129. Elsewhere he wrote:

> Pride of caste has never made any man holy . . . The untouchables have crossed the ocean of life by God-devotion . . . Gora, the potter, Rohidasa, the shoe-maker, Kabira, the Muslim, Sena, the barber, Kanhopatra, the concubine . . . Chokhamela, the outcast . . . Janabai, the maid, have all become unified with God by their devotion. The Vedas and the Sastras have said that for the service of god, castes do not matter.

Quoted in R.D. Ranade, *Mysticism in India: The Poet–Saints of Maharashtra* (Albany: State University of New York Press, 1983), p. 326.
209 This is also linked to O'Hanlon's point that missionaries alone could not have provoked such changes and calls for reform unilaterally. See O'Hanlon, *Caste, Conflict, and Ideology*, p. 52.
210 As Zelliot notes, even if Dalit 'grievances were voiced chiefly against the Brahmin', it was the non-Brahmin Maratha peasantry that 'dominated at the village level'. See Eleanor Zelliot, 'Learning the Use of Political Means: The Mahars of Maharashtra', p. 44, in Rajni Kothari ed., *Caste in Indian Politics* (New York: Gordon & Breach, 1970), pp. 29–69. This was an obstacle in Phule's creation of a broad-based Sudra identity. See also Gail Omvedt, *Cultural Revolt in a Colonial Society: The Non Brahman Movement in Western India, 1873–1930* (Bombay: Scientific Socialist Education Trust, 1976), pp. 110–11.

211  See Fukazawa, *The Medieval Deccan*, pp. 91–113.
212  The Peshwas themselves, for example, came from the Chitpavan sub-caste of Brahmins, who were looked down upon until the eighteenth century by other Brahmins, and 'ran errands and were also cooks'. See Keer, *Mahatma Jotirao Phooley*, p. 124. See also O'Hanlon, *Caste, Conflict, and Ideology*, p. 208, where she notes that Phule did not in any case wish to provide a 'detached description' of Brahmins but to imagine the past in a way that would 'supply . . . the ideological needs of a popular movement'. See also Prachi Deshpande, *Creative Pasts: Historical Memory and Identity in Western India, 1700–1960* (New York: Columbia University Press, 2006), p. 179.
213  Poem 30, *Savitribai Phule Samagra Vangmay*.
214  O'Hanlon, *Caste, Conflict, and Ideology*, p. 143. See also Omvedt, *Cultural Revolt*, p. 103.
215  *Gulamgiri*, pp. 127–33. See also *Sarvajanik Satyadharma Pustak*, p. 476. He may have been influenced by John Wilson's *India Three Thousand Years Ago* (1858) in making this argument. See O'Hanlon, *Caste, Conflict, and Ideology*, pp. 80–81.
216  *Gulamgiri*, p. 138.
217  Phule, *Shetkaryacha Asud* (*Cultivator's Whip-Cord*), pp. 267–75, in *Samagra Vangmay*, pp. 255–343.
218  *Gulamgiri*, p. 137; *Shetkaryacha Asud*, p. 277.
219  Rao, *The Caste Question*, p. 12.
220  *Shetkaryacha Asud*, p. 276.
221  *Gulamgiri*, p. 176, and *Sarvajanik Satyadharma Pustak*, p. 478, p. 518. Phule also expresses respect for William Jones and orientalist researchers for 'opening the eyes' of Sudra Indians. See ibid., p. 519. Additionally, he blames Brahmin saints like Ramdas (seventeenth century) for misleading Hindu kings like Shivaji and causing them to fight Muslims. See ibid., p. 495.
222  *Sarvajanik Satyadharma Pustak*, p. 525. See also Bhole, *Mahatma Jotirao Phule*, p. 18 for an extract from an essay written by a Dalit girl from one of Phule's schools, where she thanks the British for giving them such simple freedoms as visiting the public market; and O'Hanlon, *Caste, Conflict, and Ideology*, p. 198, p. 204.
223  *Gulamgiri*, pp. 150–51.
224  Ibid., p. 158.
225  Ibid., p. 171.
226  *Sarvajanik Satyadharma Pustak*, p. 488. This kind of writing would be continued by committed Phuleites. A 1925 polemic, for instance, somewhat crassly questions the paternity of several Brahmin Peshwas. See 'Satyashodhak' Dinkarrao Javalkar, *Deshache Dushman* (Pune: Sumedh Prakashan, 2005 ed. [1925]), pp. 13–14.
227  *Gulamgiri*, p. 165, p. 174.

228 Ibid., p. 187. See also O'Hanlon, *Caste, Conflict, and Ideology*, pp. 75–76 for an actual 1845 case where a Christian 'untouchable''s use of a well caused local Hindus to purify it by pouring in cow's urine.

229 *Gulamgiri*, pp. 158–59. See also p. 165, where we read that the term 'raksasa', which is used for demons in Sanskrit texts, was derived from 'raksaka' (protector), which referred again to the original inhabitants and rulers of India, and *Sarvajanik Satyadharma Pustak*, p. 475, p. 487. See also O'Hanlon, *Caste, Conflict, and Ideology*, pp. 152–60, and Omvedt, *Cultural Revolt*, p. 115. Phule may, in this, have picked up one something truly felt in marginalized communities. In Kerala too, for example, Dalit communities spoke 'about their former free and elevated position'; of having once been rulers. See Kooiman, *Conversion and Social Equality*, p. 77.

230 For other criticism, see Deshpande, *Creative Pasts*, p. 112.

231 For Narayana Guru's critique of caste and religion, see his *Jatimimamsa* and *Matamimamsa*, respectively. The guru also quipped: 'If caste is necessary, let everyone be a Brahmin.' Quoted in C.N. Somarajan, 'Sree Narayana Guru and Vaikom Satyagraha', p. 15, in S. Sivadasan ed., *Renaissance in Kerala*, pp. 13-22.

232 S. Omana, 'Devotion and Dissent in Narayana Guru', p. 359, in Vijaya Ramaswamy ed., *Devotion and Dissent in Indian History* (New Delhi: Foundation Books, 2014), pp. 348–69. See also P.F. Gopakumar, 'Sree Narayana Guru and the "Installation" of Renaissance', pp. 4–5, in S. Sivadasan ed., *Renaissance in Kerala*, pp. 3–12. In defiantly consecrating temples, the guru was preceded, however, in 1854 and 1855, it is said, by another Ezhava radical, Arattupuzha Velayudha Panikkar.

233 Udaya Kumar, 'Sree Narayanan Guru's Idiom of the Spiritual and the Worldly', p. 374, in Ramaswamy ed., *Devotion and Dissent*, pp. 370–79. See also p. 372, where we see the guru endorse British rule as a positive for marginalized castes. A key disciple, the poet Kumaran Asan, also asked what swaraj, or political liberty, meant when Indians—'mad with caste prejudices'—fought among themselves. See T.K. Ravindran, *Asan and Social Revolution in Kerala: A Study of His Assembly Speeches* (Trivandrum: Kerala Historical Society, 1972), p. xxii.

234 V.T. Samuel, *One Caste, One Religion, One God: A Study of Sree Narayana Guru* (New Delhi: Sterling Publishers, 1977), pp. 60–61, p. 377. See also Gopakumar, 'Sree Narayana Guru', p. 8.

235 C.P. Sivadasan, 'Sree Narayana Guru', p. 211, in M. Govind ed., *Poetry and Renaissance: Asan Birth Centenary Volume* (Madras: Sameeksha, 1974), pp. 209–16; Filippo Osella and Caroline Osella, *Social Mobility in Kerala: Modernity and Identity in Conflict* (London: Pluto Press, 2000), pp. 155–56; A. Aiyappan, *Social Revolution in a Kerala Village: A study in Culture Change* (New Delhi: Asia Publishing House, 1965), pp. 147–48. See also Nataraja Guru, *The Word of the Guru: An Outline of the Life and Teachings of the Guru*

*Narayana* (Ernakulam: Paico Publishing House, 1968 ed.), p. 26, where we read of how a 'dirty' shrine was demolished and replaced with something more acceptable; and Samuel, *One Caste, One Religion, One God*, p. 378. This has links with processes in Maharashtra also: Four decades after Phule died, the Dalit Mahar community also resolved to stop eating 'the flesh of dead cattle' and 'of sacrificial chicken and goats'; to avoid alcohol at religious ceremonies; to greet one another using high-caste forms; to cremate the dead, in the fashion of upper-caste groups, instead of burying them and so on. See Oliver Mendelsohn and Marika Vicziany, *The Untouchables: Subordination, Poverty and the State in Modern India* (Cambridge: Cambridge University Press, 1998), p. 98. For Gandhi later promoting a similar approach, see Lee, *Deceptive Majority*, p. 155. Earlier, from the 1820s, in Chhattisgarh, Chamars, a low-ritual status group, also adopted vegetarianism and so-called 'pure' habits, by this claiming a higher position for their caste. See Pandey, *Construction of Communalism*, p. 89.

236 Omana, 'Devotion and Dissent', p. 360.
237 Or as Ravindran puts it, the guru 'felt no necessity or urge for reforming the Hindu religion. He only restated [its] fundamental principles'. See Ravindran, *Asan and Social Revolution*, p. xxx.
238 See, for instance, Toshie Awaya, 'Some Aspects of the Tiyyas' "Caste" Movement with Special Reference to British Malabar', p. 153, in H. Kotani ed., *Caste System, Untouchability and the Depressed* (New Delhi: Manohar, 1997), pp. 139–68. The same happened with his contemporary, Chattampi Swamikal (1853–1924), who was popular with the Nair community. See, for instance, tales recorded in K.P.K. Menon, *Chattambi Swamigal: The Great Scholar–Saint of Kerala* (Trivandrum: P.G. Narayana Pillai, 1967), where we read about snakes coiling up comfortably round his arm, of ferocious dogs and tigers rendered tame in his presence and of sceptics overpowered by his magical energies (not to speak of his immense stamina).
239 Posthumously, of course, as has often happened with radical ideologies in India before, Phule's legacy was tamed somewhat when his successors cast him as a truer defender of Hinduism. For example, see Javalkar, *Deshache Dushman*, p. 25.
240 O'Hanlon, *Caste, Conflict, and Ideology*, pp. 120–21 for an instance as early as the 1850s.
241 *Gulamgiri*, p. 133. See also O'Hanlon, *Caste, Conflict, and Ideology*, p. 7.
242 Ramasswami, *Viswaguna Darsana*, p. 46. The *Sahyadrikanda* of the *Skandapurana* also speaks of a 'curse' on the Chitpavan Brahmins of Maharashtra whereby they would have to serve Sudras. See Deshpande, 'Ksatriyas in the Kali Age', p. 112.
243 This claim, interestingly, has something of a precedent from south India, where as early as the seventeenth century, lower-caste representatives complained of Brahmins holding most important posts under the British,

preventing others' voices from reaching their rulers. See Kruijtzer, *Xenophobia*, pp. 135–36.
244 *Gulamgiri*, p. 134; *Shetkaryacha Asud*, p. 263.
245 *Gulamgiri*, pp. 135–36. For the Madras University figures, see Pillai, *False Allies*, p. 459. Brahmin domination in government employment was a major issue in south India in the late nineteenth and early twentieth centuries, including in princely states such as Travancore and Mysore.
246 'Memorial Addressed to the Education Commission', p. 248.
247 *Gulamgiri*, p. 137. See also *Sarvajanik Satyadharma Pustak*, p. 524. As Bellenoit, *Missionary Education and Empire*, p. 5 notes, Indians were capable of 'reproducing their own social, religious and caste ethoses within a transformed institutional structure' created under colonial conditions.
248 *Gulamgiri*, p. 137. See also p. 199, and O'Hanlon, *Caste, Conflict, and Ideology*, p. 215.
249 'Kalam-kasai'. *Gulamgiri*, p. 177, p. 180.
250 O'Hanlon, *Caste, Conflict, and Ideology*, p. 110. There is also a story about how, when attending the wedding of a Brahmin classmate from his mission school, Phule, used to a mixing of castes in the classroom, got a jolt when, for the first time, he was insulted on account of his caste by Brahmins.
251 Quoted in Omvedt, *Cultural Revolt*, p. 101.
252 Parimala V. Rao, 'Educating Women and Non-Brahmins as "Loss of Nationality": Bal Gangadhar Tilak and the Nationalist Agenda in Maharashtra', Centre for Women's Development Studies (2008) 11, p. 13 at https://www.cwds.ac.in/wp-content/uploads/2016/09/EducatingWomen.pdf.
253 Ibid., pp. 19–20, p. 24.
254 Ibid., pp. 25–26.
255 Ibid., pp. 5–6. In the south, the Theosophical Society also took a similar position when it suggested that 'untouchable' castes be given 'useful and practical training' instead of being prepared for university. Besides, if they were born into a low caste, it was—as per the theory of karma—due to their own 'misdeeds in a former birth'. See Pandian, *Brahmin and Non-Brahmin*, pp. 36–37.
256 Rao, 'Educating Women and Non-Brahmins', p. 8.
257 Mani, 'Introduction', p. 3. Incidentally, Gandhi took a similar view romanticizing the peasant.

> A peasant earns his bread honestly. He has ordinary knowledge of the world . . . He understands and observes the rules of morality. But he cannot write his own name. What do you propose to do by giving him a knowledge of letters? Will you add an inch to his happiness? Do you wish to make him discontented with his cottage or his lot? . . . Carried away by the flood of western thought, we came to the conclusion that we should give this kind of education to the people.

See M.K. Gandhi, *Hind Swaraj: or Indian Home Rule* (Madras: G.A. Natesan, 1921 ed.), p. 88.

258 Keer, *Mahatma Jotirao Phooley*, p. 127. However, according to another authority, while these men were 'sympathisers', Phule did not permit them to become members of the Samaj. See M.S. Gore, 'Social Movements and the Paradigm of Functional Analysis: With Reference to the Non-Brahman Movement in Maharashtra', p. 933, in *Economic and Political Weekly* 24, 17 (1989): 928–36.

259 Padmanji, *Once Hindu, Now Christian*, pp. 78–79, pp. 83–84.

260 Vasant K. Kshire, *Lokahitawadi's Thought: A Critical Study* (Poona: University of Poona, 1977), p. 10. They evidently graduated in time to eating beef and drinking wine. See Omvedt, *Cultural Revolt*, p. 101.

261 See G.H. Deshmukh (Shripad Ramachandran Tikekar ed.), *Lokahitavadinchi Shatapatre* (Aundh: Usha Prakashan, 1940), p. 62, p. 74, p. 167, p. 286, p. 314, p. 412.

262 Ibid., p. 356. See also O'Hanlon, *Caste, Conflict, and Ideology*, pp. 93–94.

263 Omvedt, *Cultural Revolt*, pp. 106–07.

264 Keer, *Mahatma Jotirao Phooley*, pp. 130–31. See also *Sarvajanik Satyadharma Pustak*, pp. 520–21, p. 523 for Phule's critique of the nationalist claims of such organizations, including the Indian National Congress.

265 In this, he shared the fate of his hero, Thomas Paine, who had also died in economic distress.

266 O'Hanlon, *Caste, Conflict, and Ideology*, p. 135, p. 256.

267 Bayly, *Caste, Society and Politics*, p. 241.

268 This was Sayajirao Gaekwad III of Baroda, who considered Phule India's own Booker T. Washington. Phule's work also impacted the young Maharajah Shahu of Kolhapur, a state where in future there would be major Brahmin-non-Brahmin conflicts, with the ruler siding with the non-Brahmins. For a concise account, see Omvedt, *Cultural Revolt*, chapter seven.

269 O'Hanlon, *Caste, Conflict, and Ideology*, pp. 232–33, pp. 241–42, pp. 278–80.

270 See *Sarvajanik Satyadharma Pustak*, especially pp. 459–70, p. 473, p. 488, p. 493, pp. 511–12, pp. 526–30, pp. 531–32, p. 533, pp. 558–59.

271 Poem 34, *Savitribai Phule Samagra Vangmay*. Fittingly, the University of Pune (Poona) is today named after Savitribai. The emphasis on education was also perhaps a response to a somewhat smug critic's remark that lower castes could have no way to access education without Brahmins' support; and that, therefore, Phule should be more circumspect in his criticism. See Naregal, *Language Politics, Elites, and the Public Sphere*, p. 258. See also Mohan, *Modernity of Slavery*, pp. 242–43 for an instance from the south where low-caste girls insisting on going to school were flogged. Education, it was clear to high-caste groups, was also about political resistance.

272 Sen, *Social and Religious Reform*, p. 4.

273 Ambedkar was the man who would tell Gandhi:

> Gandhiji I have no homeland . . . How can I call this land my own wherein we are treated worse than cats and dogs, wherein we cannot get water to drink? No self-respecting Untouchable worth the name will be proud of this land . . . If in my endeavour to secure human rights for my people who have been trampled upon in this country for ages I do any disservice to this country, it would not be a sin; and if any harm does not come to this country thorough my action, it may be due to my conscience.

Quoted in Rao, *The Caste Question*, p. 159. Like Phule, Ambedkar also did not hesitate to lampoon Hindu gods such as Rama and Krishna. See, for instance, Vasant Moon ed., *Dr Babasaheb Ambedkar: Writings and Speeches*, Vol. 4 (New Delhi: Ambedkar Foundation, 2014 ed.), pp. 323–43 available at https://www.mea.gov.in/Images/attach/amb/Volume_04.pdf. Ambedkar's father was also an associate of Phule's. See Aakash Singh Rathore, *Becoming Babasaheb: The Life and Times of Bhimrao Ramji Ambedkar*, Vol. 1 (Gurugram: HarperCollins, 2023), p. 88.

## Seven: Drawing Blood

1. *Bombay Gazette*, 25 July 1908.
2. Letter dated 5 August 1908 from the Officiating Director, Criminal Intelligence to Officiating Secretary, Home Dept, GOI in Files No. 149–69, Home Dept (Political-A), December 1908, National Archives of India (NAI). The ages of the dead boys are from *Bombay Gazette* cited above.
3. *Bombay Gazette*, 25 July 1908.
4. Letter dated 8 August 1908 from the Secretary, Judicial Dept, Bombay to Secretary, Home Dept, GOI in Files No. 113-118, Home Dept (Political-B), January 1909.
5. Letter dated 27 August 1908 from Commissioner of Police, Bombay to Secretary, Judicial Dept, Bombay, in *Source Material for a History of the Freedom Movement in India: Collected from Bombay Government Records*, Vol. 2 (1885–1920) (Bombay: Director, Government Printing, Publications and Stationery, 1958), p. 275. The millworkers were predominantly from Ratnagiri, which also supplied the bulk of the Bombay Police.
6. *Bombay Gazette*, 24 July 1908; *Times of India*, 24 July 1908.
7. This is how Tilak was described in an affidavit by a supporter during his trial. See N.C. Kelkar ed., *Full and Authentic Report of the Tilak Trial* (1908) (Bombay: N.C. Kelkar, 1908), p.12. Hereafter 'Tilak Trial'.
8. Letter dated 27 August 1908 from Commissioner of Police, Bombay, to Secretary, Judicial Dept, Bombay, in *Source Material*, Vol. 2, p. 269. See also Ram Gopal, *Lokamanya Tilak: A Biography* (Bombay: Asia Publishing House, 1956), p. 320 for a newspaper quote on the 'religious fervour' Tilak attracted.

9 Telegram dated 4 July 1908 from the Government of Bombay to the Government of India in Files No. 61–103, Home Dept (Political-A), October 1908, NAI.
10 Letter dated 27 July 1908 from Governor of Bombay to the Viceroy in Files No. 61–103, Home Dept (Political-A), October 1908, NAI.
11 Exhibit C in *Tilak Trial*.
12 *Kesari*, 28 May 1907 and 16 July 1907 in Ravindra Kumar ed., *Selected Documents of Lokamanya Tilak*, Vol. 1 (New Delhi: Anmol Publications, 1992), pp. 41–42, pp. 49–50. Tilak was also an admirer of the Irish Sinn Fein.
13 See also *Samagra Lokamanya Tilak, Khanda 6: Jeevan Dhyeya* (Pune: Kesari Prakashan, 1976), p. 730, where Tilak brands the British in India worse than Russia, and *Samagra Lokamanya Tilak, Khanda 4: Nave Netrutva* (Pune: Kesari Prakashan, 1976), p. 810.
14 Exhibit D in *Tilak Trial*.
15 *Tilak Trial*, p. 169.
16 Letter dated 27 August 1908 from Commissioner of Police, Bombay to Secretary, Judicial Dept, Bombay in *Source Material*, Vol. 2, p. 271.
17 *Tilak's Trial*, p. 98. In another 1908 editorial, Tilak also noted how the British were content to grant Indians Western degrees and titles, but not gun licenses. See *Samagra Lokamanya Tilak*, Vol. 6, p. 436. As regards journalism, as far back as 1892, in fact, he had complained that the pro-British press lobby saw treason anytime 'natives' aired any grievances. See *Samagra Lokamanya Tilak*, Vol. 4, p. 611.
18 *Tilak's Trial*, p. 166.
19 Ibid., p. 195, p. 197.
20 Quoted in Gopal, *Lokamanya Tilak*, p. 327. The Director of Criminal Intelligence also believed that without being able to directly connect Tilak with the bombs, the Bombay government had acted prematurely. See letter dated 5 August 1908 from the Officiating Director, Criminal Intelligence to Officiating Secretary, Home Dept, GOI in Files No. 149–69, Home Dept (Political-A), December 1908, NAI.
21 Tilak to Dadasaheb Khaparde, 20 May 1909, in S.V. Bapat ed., *Reminiscences and Anecdotes of Lokamanya Tilak*, Vol. 3 (Poona: S.V. Bapat, 1928), pp. 194–95. See also ibid., p. 107 for a similar response in 1897.
22 Tilak's petition dated 25 November 1909 in File No. 59, Home Dept (Political), July 1910, NAI.
23 Letter dated 3 October 1912 from the Bombay Judicial Dept to the Secretary of State in *Source Material*, Vol. 2, p. 278.
24 Extract from a July 1909 letter addressed to the Government of Burma by the commissioner of Mandalay in ibid., p. 281.
25 Confidential Circular dated 26 June 1914, Special Dept, in ibid., p. 303. See also Files No. 135–38, Home Dept (Political-A), July 1914, NAI.

26 Stanley A. Wolpert, *Tilak and Gokhale: Revolution and Reform in the Making of Modern India* (Berkeley: University of California Press, 1961), p. 263. A contemporary also wrote how 'by his examples, by his sufferings, by his courage, by his defiance' Tilak 'taught us to be *men*'. See Bapat, *Reminiscences*, p. 47.

27 Secretary of State quoted in Gopal, *Lokamanya Tilak*, p. 398.

28 See V.I. Lenin (M. Levin trans.), *The National-Liberation Movement in the East* (Moscow: Foreign Languages Publishing House, 1962 ed.), pp. 14–15. Lenin's praise for Tilak came after his arrest in 1908.

29 T. Prakasam's recollection in Bapat, *Reminiscences*, p. 65.

30 B.G. Tilak (B.S. Sukthankar trans.), *Sri Bhagavadgita-Rahasya or Karma-Yoga-Sastra: English Translation*, Vol. 1 (Poona: R.B. Tilak, 1935), p. 554. See also Naik, 'British Secret Official View of Tilak's *Gitarahasya* (M.S.)'. The removal of a thorn with a thorn is ascribed as a quote to Ramdas, the seventeenth-century Maharashtrian Brahmin saint, and appears in his *Dasbodh*.

31 Quoted in Bhupendra Yadav, 'Tilak: Communalist or Political Pragmatist', p. 42, in Biswamoy Pati ed., *Bal Gangadhar Tilak: Popular Readings* (Delhi: Primus Books, 2011), pp. 39–64. One of Tilak's close associates recollected discussing with him the 'insanity, stupidity, and the rest of it' of Gandhi's approach. See Wolpert, *Tilak and Gokhale*, pp. 294–95. Of course, Gandhi would prove himself perfectly astute in the years ahead. Gandhi was also present at Tilak's funeral, shouldering the bier. He would later call himself Tilak's disciple, adding, however, 'that my method is not Mr Tilak's method'.

32 B.G. Tilak, *Bal Gangadhar Tilak: His Writings and Speeches* (Madras: Ganesh & Co., 1919), p. 160.

33 Quoted in Tilak, *Sri Bhagavadgita-Rahasya*, Vol. 1, p. 524. See also the 'rajakarana' section in Samarth Ramdas, *Shridasbodh: Shri Samarthanche Charitra Va Shikavan Yansaha* (Pune: Bhat ani Mandali, 1945), pp. 411–12.

34 Quoted in S.G. Kashikar, 'The Political Thought of Samarth Ramdas Swami', p. 151, in *The Indian Journal of Political Science* 24, 2 (1963): 148–52.

35 See Jayashree Gokhale-Turner, 'Regional and Regionalism in the Study of Indian Politics: The Case of Maharashtra', p. 94, in N.K Wagle ed., *Images of Maharashtra: A Regional Profile of India* (London: Curzon Press, 1980), pp. 88–101. Emphasis added. See also N.K. Behere, *The Background of Maratha Renaissance in the 17th Century: Historical Survey of the Social, Religious and Political Movements of the Marathas* (Bangalore: Bangalore Press, 1946), chapter twenty-two; Bayly, *Origins of Nationality*, p. 24; and V.P. Bokil, *Rajguru Ramdas* (Poona: Kamalesh Bokil, 1979), p. 159. See also Laine, *Shivaji*, pp. 59–60 for stories where Ramdas himself pushes back against both Islam as a religion and Islamic political power.

36 For a succinct history of the evolution of this idea of 'Maharashtra dharma', see Irina Glushkova, 'A Philological Approach to Regional Ideologies', in

Rajendra Vora and Anne Feldhaus eds., *Region, Culture, and Politics in India* (New Delhi: Manohar, 2006), pp. 51–82. A presaging of this tone towards political Islam might also be traced in the *Gurucharitra* of the fifteenth century, centred on the sage Narasimha Saraswati.

37  See Omvedt, *Cultural Revolt*, p. 56. See also Laine and Bahulkar eds., *Sivabharata*, p. 27 (hereafter 'Sivabharata'), where we read how even if Shivaji never saw Ramdas as his guru, the latter might have intellectually buttressed the former. Some sources place their first meeting in the 1640s; others in the 1670s. The issue remains controversial. See Laine, *Shivaji*, p. 52.

38  This was the Nizam Shahi—a kingdom governed by Shia Muslim dynasty of Brahmin descent—which fell in the 1630s, and which Shivaji's father had defended. For a history of the sultanate, see Pillai, *Rebel Sultans*.

39  In the *Sabhasad Bakhar*, thus, one of the oldest sources on Maratha history, we find Shivaji declare 'I am not a servant of the badshah', i.e., the sultan of Bijapur. See Surendranath Sen ed., *Siva Chhatrapati: Being a Translation of Sabhasad Bakhar with Extracts from Chitnis and Sivadijvijaya, with Notes* (Calcutta: University of Calcutta, 1920), p. 163. For a general consciousness, already existent by this time, of Maharashtra as a distinct cultural zone, see Anne Feldhaus, 'Maharashtra as a Holy Land: A Sectarian Tradition', in *Bulletin of the School of Oriental and African Studies* 49, 3 (1986): 532–48.

40  *Sivabharata*, p. 209. This line, as we saw in chapter five, was also used by Vishnubawa Brahmachari in his debate with missionaries.

41  See for instance, Deshpande, *Creative Pasts*, pp. 43–44, and Ravinder Kumar, *Western India in the Nineteenth Century: A Study in the Social History of Maharashtra* (Canberra: Australian National University Press, 1968), p. 13.

42  Though, of course, the sultanate's cultural influences persisted. See Laine, *Shivaji*, p. 31.

43  One historian, in fact, declares that 'a thousand years had passed since such a ceremony was last performed'. See Govind Sakharam Sardesai, *New History of the Marathas: Shivaji and His Line*, Vol. 1 (Bombay: Phoenix Publications, 1946), p. 208.

44  *Sabhasad Bakhar*, p. 187. See also *Sivabharata*, pp. 91–93, p. 115. Note, however, that this was only one way in which Shivaji conceptualized kingship, for one audience. In practice he could also play down religion, and focus on a *regional* patriotism, in which a neighbouring sultan—the Qutb Shah of Golconda—was a legitimate ally. See Kruijtzer, *Xenophobia*, pp. 157–58, pp. 169–71, pp. 184–85.

45  Reference is to Agrindas's *Afzal-Khan-Vadh*. See an English translation in Harry Arbuthnot Acworth, *Ballads of the Marathas: Rendered into English Verse from the Marathi Originals* (London: Longmans, Green & Co., 1894), pp. 1–13.

46 The *Sabhasad Bakhar*, p. 184, thus shows him as led by the goddess, while in the *Sivabharata*, p. 45, p. 88, pp. 91–93, we find Shivaji described as Vishnu incarnate. Afzal Khan himself becomes a kind of sacrificial offering.

47 *Sivabharata*, pp. 51–52, pp. 77–79, p. 84. Arguably, this also maintained ideological space for Shivaji to engage with some Muslims without compromising his broader ideology.

48 Ibid., p. 56. See also note 189 to the Introduction of this book for other sources such as the Maratha *bakhars*.

49 Kruijtzer, *Xenophobia*, p. 267. See also Laine, *Shivaji*, p. 41 for another example of Shivaji's appeal to religion. Shivaji's deeds also inspired people elsewhere; an eighteenth-century Hindi panegyric to Chattrasal Bundela, a younger contemporary of the Maratha hero, presents Shivaji telling the former: 'Go back home and defeat the Mughals.' The Bundela king is accordingly roused and goes to war. See Allison Busch, ' "Unhitching the Oxcart of Delhi": A Mughal-Period Hindu Account of Political Insurgency', p. 429, p. 434, in *Journal of the Royal Asiatic Society* 28 (Series 3), 3 (2018), pp. 415–39. See also for a similar pattern in Nepal, Richard Burghart, 'The Category "Hindu" in the Political Discourse of Nepal', in Vasudha Dalmia and Heinrich von Stietencron eds., *Representing Hinduism: The Construction of Religious Traditions and National Identity* (New Delhi: SAGE Publications, 1995), pp. 129–41.

50 To quote Kruijtzer, the closing years of Shivaji's career down until 1687 is where the 'roots of modern communalism' might be found. See Kruijtzer, *Xenophobia*, pp. 8–9.

51 Or as Tilak stated in a 1917 speech, Indians permitted the Raj to stay in their 'house'; but in the end, brown men remained its legal masters. See Tilak, *Writings and Speeches*, p. 276.

52 As early as 1881, Tilak's paper was described as 'unfriendly to Government' and was urging 'agitation' and 'moral courage' on Indians. See Gopal, *Lokamanya Tilak*, pp. 28–29. See also Robert E. Upton, '"Take out a thorn with a thorn": B.G. Tilak's legitimization of political violence', p. 13, in *Global Intellectual History* (2017), pp. 1–21.

53 Dinker Vishnu Gokhale, *Inaugural Addresses by Presidents of the Indian National Congress: With Charles Bradlaugh's Speech* (Bombay: N.M. & Co., 1895), p. 7. See also Pillai, *False Allies*, pp. 347–49 for more context.

54 In 1899, a leading Congressman quipped how he behaved as if 'he is the coming Saviour of India'. Quoted in Cashman, *The Myth of the Lokamanya*, p. 170.

55 Quoted in ibid., p. 79.

56 See Andrew Gailey, *The Lost Imperialist: Lord Dufferin, Memory and Mythmaking in an Age of Celebrity* (London: John Murray, 2015), p. 414.

57 Gopal, *Lokamanya Tilak*, p. 209.

58 Letter dated 6 December 1904 from Tilak to Dadabhai Naoroji in *Selected Documents*, p. 17. See also *Samagra Lokamanya Tilak*, Vol. 4, p. 244, and

Gopal, *Lokamanya Tilak*, pp. 129–30 for an 1897 comment by Tilak where he ridicules those who viewed politics as a 'holiday recreation' rather than an 'everyday duty'—a reference to moderates. For a criticism of the politics of petitions, see also *Samagra Lokamanya Tilak*, Vol. 6, pp. 417–18.

59    *Kesari* quoted in Gopal, *Lokamanya Tilak*, p. 87.
60    *Samagra Lokamanya Tilak*, Vol. 4, p. 17.
61    The Peshwas in Pune did have a grand celebration for Ganapati, however; this ceased after their fall in 1818.
62    Cashman, *Myth of the Lokamanya*, p. 80.
63    Gopal, *Lokamanya Tilak*, p. 87.
64    *Samagra Lokamanya Tilak*, Vol. 6, p. 695.
65    Gopal, *Lokamanya Tilak*, p. 90. The idea for a public Ganapati festival was given to Tilak by Vinayak Ramachandra Patwardhan, better known as Annasaheb (1847–1917) 'whom Tilak regarded as his *moksha guru*.' See Wolpert, *Tilak and Gokhale*, p. 67. See also Cashman, *Myth of the Lokamanya*, p. 81.
66    *Kesari* quoted in Cashman, *Myth of the Lokamanya*, p. 98. See also *Samagra Lokamanya Tilak*, Vol. 4, p. 36, and Wolpert, *Tilak and Gokhale*, p. 19, where we find one of Tilak's papers refer to 'the nation of Shivaji' as far back as the early 1880s.
67    Letter published in *Kesari*, 28 May 1895 in *Report on Native Papers Published in the Bombay Presidency for the Week ending 1st June 1895*, South Asia Open Archives, IOR, https://www.jstor.org/stable/saoa.crl.25636076. The neglect of Shivaji's samadhi was first highlighted in 1883 by James Douglas in his *A Book of Bombay*.
68    Cashman, *Myth of the Lokamanya*, p. 107. See also *Samagra Lokamanya Tilak*, Vol. 4, pp. 29–32.
69    'Account of the Proceedings of Wasudeo Balwant Phadke', in *Source Material for a History of the Freedom Movement in India: Collected from Bombay Government* Records, Vol. 1 (1818–1885) (Bombay: Director, Government Printing, Publications and Stationery, 1957), pp. 81–83.
70    See reports from *The Shivaji*, 29 November 1879, and *Bodha Sudhakar*, 13 December 1879 in *Source Material*, Vol. 1, pp. 126–28. He also appears to have presented himself as a second Shivaji. See letter dated 9 July 1879 from the Governor of Bombay to the Viceroy in G.R.G. Hambly, 'Mahratta nationalism before Tilak: Two Unpublished Letters of Sir Richard Temple on the State of Bombay Deccan, 1879', p. 156, in *Journal of the Royal Central Asian Society* 49, 2 (1962), pp. 144–60. Tilak did not agree: Phadke's revolt was to him 'the hare-brained attempt of a misguided person'. Quoted in Parimala Rao, 'Religious Identity and Conflict in the Nationalist Agenda of Bal Gangadhar Tilak', p. 13 in Pati ed., *Bal Gangadhar Tilak*, pp. 11–38.
71    Quoted in Wolpert, *Tilak and Gokhale*, p. 80.

72   Damodar Hari Chapekar, 'Autobiography', p. 992 in *Source Material*, Vol. 2, pp. 955–1015.
73   Wolpert, *Tilak and Gokhale*, pp. 81–82. See also *Samagra Lokamanya Tilak*, Vol. 4, p. 36 where Tilak argues that all nations need heroes, and Shivaji was Maharashtra's great hero.
74   Letter published in *Kesari*, 28 May 1895 in *Report on Native Papers published in the Bombay Presidency for the Week ending 1st June 1895*, South Asia Open Archives, IOR, at https://www.jstor.org/stable/saoa.crl.25636076. The Bengali writer—and future Congress president—R.C. Dutt, in an 1878 novel, *Maharashtra Jiban Prabhat*, also praised Shivaji, hoping that a revival of such a national hero would spark patriotic feelings.
75   See Bhagat-Kennedy, 'Imagining Bharat', p. 199.
76   Quoted in Anil Samarth, *Shivaji and the Indian National Movement: Saga of a Living Legend* (Bombay: Somaiya Publications, 1975), p. 37.
77   Quoted in Gopal, *Lokamanya Tilak*, p. 107. See also ibid., pp. 89–90 for an 1896 press quote on how Ganapati songs had 'a strong undercurrent of politics' and were 'spreading political knowledge'.
78   *Poona Vaibhav* dated 26 May 1895 in *Report on Native Papers Published in the Bombay Presidency for the Week ending 1st June 1895*, South Asia Open Archives, IOR, https://www.jstor.org/stable/saoa.crl.25636076.
79   The *Indu Prakash* dated 20 April 1896, in *Report on Native Papers Published in the Bombay Presidency for the Week ending April 25 1896*, South Asia Open Archives, IOR, https://www.jstor.org/stable/saoa.crl.25636123.
80   Chapekar, 'Autobiography', p. 993. See also Gopal, *Lokamanya Tilak*, pp. 147–48 for a song published in the *Kesari* wherein Shivaji laments the present state of his country, and persecution of Indians by foreigners.
81   The *Indu Prakash* dated 20 April 1896, refers to these prints being carried in processions. In time, the British would try to prohibit carrying images of historical figures in Ganapati processions.
82   Wolpert, *Tilak and Gokhale*, p. 82.
83   *Sedition Committee Report* (Calcutta: Superintendent Government Printing, 1918), p. 3.
84   The near contemporary *Afzal-Khan-Vadh* has Khan first attempt to stab Shivaji, who disembowels him in self-defence. See Acworth, *Ballads of the Marathas*, p. 10.
85   Quoted in Wolpert, *Tilak and Gokhale*, p. 86. Or as Tilak would state in 1905, Shivaji killed Afzal Khan not from personal hatred but because he stood in the way of progress. See *Samagra Lokamanya Tilak*, Vol. 6, p. 941.
86   *Sedition Committee Report*, p. 3. See also Upton, 'Take out a thorn with a thorn', p. 11. For a similar reading of the Gita in Bengal, see Sukla Sanyan, 'Legitimizing Violence: Seditious Propaganda and Revolutionary Pamphlets in Bengal, 1908–1918', in *The Journal of Asian Studies* 67, 3 (2008): 759–

87. See also *Sedition Committee Report*, p. 23, where the Gita is seen as a 'textbook' in the 'mental training of revolutionary recruits'.

87  Interestingly, a 1920s print would cause controversy by depicting Tilak in the position of Krishna, giving Arjuna of the Mahabharata this lesson. See Sarwate, 'Reimagining the Modern Hindu Self', p. 87.

88  Quoted in Wolpert, *Tilak and Gokhale*, p. 84. For other criticism of British plague policy, see *Samagra Lokamanya Tilak*, Vol. 4, pp. 715–22.

89  Amusingly, when the plague broke out in Bombay soon after, some orthodox Hindus blamed it on this insult to royalty! See E. Washburn Hopkins, 'The Divinity of Kings', p. 314, in *Journal of the American Oriental Society* 51, 4 (1931): 309–16.

90  He was not entirely wrong. A Protestant missionary, wrote in 1868 how 'education de-Hinduizes the Hindu, breaks down idolatry, and inspires him with a distaste for it, and a latent desire to be free from it'. Boys trained at mission schools and government institutions were 'scandalized by idolatry, and are somewhat ashamed of it'. Indeed, 'there is not one who does not hold Hinduism with a lighter and looser grasp than formerly' than he whose mind had been 'expanded and benefited by the education he has received'. See M.A. Sherring, *The Sacred City of the Hindus: An Account of Benares in Ancient and Modern Times* (London: Trubner & Co., 1868), p. 350.

91  On this, a scholar writes: 'The intensity of the resentment toward all reformers manifested in [Chapekar's autobiography] has no equal in the published records of the period.' See Charles H. Heimsath, *Indian Nationalism and Hindu Social Reform* (Princeton: Princeton University Press, 1964), p. 213.

92  Chapekar, 'Autobiography', p. 964, pp. 965–66, pp. 976–77, p. 980, p. 982, pp. 994–95.

93  Letter dated 10 January 1896 from Tilak to Shyamji Krishna Varma in *Selected Documents*, Vol. 1, p. 6.

94  See Wolpert, *Tilak and Gokhale*, pp. 90–97 for a summary of what is known and of the gaps. For newspaper columns, Tilak wrote after the assassination, see *Samagra Lokamanya Tilak*, Vol. 4, pp. 617–44.

95  Letter dated 30 May 1916 from A. Montgomerie I.C.S. to Secretary, Government of Bombay in *Selected Documents*, Vol. 2, p. 241. See also Gopal, *Lokamanya Tilak*, p. 150 for a reference to *Times of India*—a paper hostile to Tilak—which too hinted he had something to do with the murder.

96  The *Madras Times* quoted in Gopal, *Lokamanya Tilak*, p. 186. For the full judgment, see *Queen-Empress vs. Bal Gangadhar Tilak and Keshav Mahadev Bal* in *Indian Law Reports (Bombay Series)*, Vol. 22, pp. 112–51. His sentence was for eighteen months, but he was granted early release. Interestingly, one of his lawyers in this case, Dinshaw Davar, later became the judge who sentenced him in his 1908 sedition case. In that second case, one of Tilak's lawyers was M.A. Jinnah (1876–1948), who later founded Pakistan.

97  Damodar Chapekar, despite the tone of his autobiography, did submit in 1898 a petition professing innocence and claiming to have been framed. See petition dated 8 March 1898 in *Source Material*, Vol. 2, pp. 353–59.

98  See S.L. Karandikar, *Lokamanya Bal Gangadhar Tilak: The Hercules and Prometheus of Modern India* (Poona: S.L. Karandikar, 1957), p. 161. They were housed in the same jail. See also Vikram Sampath, *Savarkar: Echoes from a Forgotten Past: 1883–1924* (Gurgaon: Penguin Viking, 2019), p. 36.

99  See Upton, 'Take out a thorn with a thorn', p. 2. In later years too, Tilak would insist he was speaking of the 'spirit' of Shivaji's deeds, and not literally. See, for example, Tilak, *Writings and Speeches*, p. 46, p. 50 and p. 70. Yet, as Kapila writes, Tilak's thought 'did make violence possible, plausible and conceivable'. See Shruti Kapila, 'A History of Violence', p. 180, in Devji and Kapila eds., *Political Thought in Action*, pp. 177–99. Interestingly in the 1940s, a viceroy would note that a 'double-tongued' Gandhi too made 'vaguely worded' pronouncements that could be 'interpreted in whatever sense best suits him at a later stage'.

100  Letter dated 18 September 1908 from the Judicial Dept, Bombay, to the Secretary of State in *Selected Documents*, Vol. 1, p. 139.

101  Letter dated 5 August 1908 from the Officiating Director, Criminal Intelligence to the Officiating Secretary, Home Dept, GOI in Files No. 149–69, Home Dept (Political-A), December 1908, NAI.

102  Note dated 10 March 1909 by the Director, Criminal Intelligence in File No. 4, Home Dept (Political), April 1909, NAI.

103  Letter dated 23 December 1909 from District Superintendent of Police to Secretary, Judicial Dept, Bombay in Files No. 87–106, Home Dept (Political-A), March 1910, NAI. See also letter dated 18 September 1908 from the Bombay Judicial Department to the Secretary of State, where the investigation of some men in Kolhapur for making bombs is described. 'Their proceedings if not directly due to Tilak's instigation, are at least natural results of his teachings.' See *Selected Documents*, Vol. 1, p. 140.

104  Reference is to Vishnu Mahadev Bhat. See judgment in Special Tribunal Cases No. 2, 3 and 4 of 1919, High Court of Bombay, in the Nasik Conspiracy Case in Files No. 21–67, Home Dept (Political-A), April 1911, NAI.

105  See documents in File No. 6, Home Dept (Political-B), September 1910, NAI. These men were from the Arya Samaj. And Tilak, it may be noted, while suspicious of most reform movements, was accepting of the Arya Samaj. See Wolpert, *Tilak and Gokhale*, p. 136. See also Files No. 2–23, Home Dept (Political-A), August 1912, NAI for details of the 'Dhaka Conspiracy Case' of 1912, where too the arrested men had images of Tilak. In the south, V.O. Chidambaram Pillai, who set up an Indian shipping company to break a British monopoly, and who would be sentenced for sedition, too was influenced by Tilak. See Venkatachalapathy, *Swadeshi Steam*, p. 150, p. 192, for instance.

106 Letter dated 12 August 1908 from Secretary, Judicial Dept, Bombay to Secretary, Home Dept, GOI in Files No. 113–18, Home Dept (Political-B), January 1909, NAI. See also Gopal, *Lokamanya Tilak*, p. 246, where we read how in some places Tilak was being celebrated as a second Shivaji.

107 Note dated 10 March 1909 by the Director of Criminal Intelligence. It was added that 'Tilak is the central head of the general movement but does not personally control [its] activities'.

108 The unflattering epithet appears in Valentine Chirol's *Indian Unrest* (London: Macmillan & Co., 1910), p. 41. After his release from prison, Tilak would sue Chirol for libelous assertions in the book.

109 Tilak in Arvind Sharma ed., *Modern Hindu Thought: The Essential Texts* (New Delhi: Oxford University Press, 2002), p. 211. See also Heimsath, *Indian Nationalism*, p. 141.

110 Gopal, *Lokamanya Tilak*, p. 216. See also his June 1906 speech in *Writings and Speeches*, pp. 45–46, where he speaks of 'how to build a nation on Indian soil' and the need to 'raise a nation on this soil'; and Sampath, *Echoes*, p. 27, where he is quoted as stating that India was 'made up of different smaller nations' that had to be brought together.

111 Tilak in Sharma ed., *Modern Hindu Thought*, p. 211. We also find Tilak use the term *Hindupana* in Marathi, which can also be translated as Hinduness. See *Samagra Lokamanya Tilak, Khanda 5: Samaj Va Sanskruti* (Pune: Kesari Prakashan, 1976), p. 279.

112 Monier Williams, *Indian Wisdom: Or, Examples of the Religious, Philosophical, and Ethical Doctrines of the Hindus* (London: W.H. Allen, 1876), pp. xvi–xvii.

113 Tilak, *Writings and Speeches*, p. 37. See also Karandikar, *Lokamanya Bal Gangadhar Tilak*, p. 198, for writings from 1904 where Tilak states: 'Every reform must aim at the awakening of national consciousness. The only consciousness which we as a nation can proudly retain and foster ought to have its springs in Hindutva.'

114 Quoted in Wolpert, *Tilak and Gokhale*, pp. 134–35.

115 *Samagra Lokamanya Tilak*, Vol. 6, p. 792. Of course, one could quibble with Tilak here that Hindustan originally used to refer to northern India—specifically the Gangetic heartland—only. But that is to miss his point.

116 *Samagra Lokamanya Tilak*, Vol. 5, p. 276.

117 Tilak, *Writings and Speeches*, pp. 35–36. The Hindus were one body, he would add, not disconnected limbs, and the term 'Hindu' represented a single emotion and motivation. See *Samagra Lokamanya Tilak*, Vol. 6, p. 807. For a similar definition from 1888 emerging from south India, see Pandian, *Brahmin and Non-Brahmin*, pp. 54–55.

118 *Samagra Lokamanya Tilak*, Vol. 5, p. 278. See also Wolpert, *Tilak and Gokhale*, p. 136. Later alongside acceptance of the Vedas, he would also throw in veneration of the Gita and the Ramayana. See Tilak, *Writings and Speeches*, pp. 35–36. Tilak denied other ways of defining Hindus. Caste,

for instance: even Christian converts retained caste, so this could not be a defining parameter of Hinduism. Hindu law was another: Hindus had been around long before the British courts began operating Hindu law. Even philosophical definitions were not satisfactory. See *Samagra Lokamanya Tilak*, Vol. 5, pp. 278–84, and Vol. 6, p. 789.

119  *Samagra Lokamanya Tilak*, Vol. 6, p. 788.
120  Ibid., p. 808.
121  *Samagra Lokamanya Tilak*, Vol. 5, pp. 297–99.
122  For one, as much as Tilak wished Hindus to assert power as one community, our firebrand was less keen to upset hierarchies within. On social reform, as alluded before, while a degree of change was tolerable—in the 1890s Tilak himself caused scandal by taking tea with Europeans—a more fundamental questioning was suspect. (Heimsath, *Indian Nationalism*, p. 24.) Decades later, when asked why he did not eat with non-Hindus and Hindus of other castes, Tilak would say: '[Y]ou see my work is amongst the people of Maharashtra. I must respect their prejudices . . . If I adopt the heterodox ways, I would not be in a position to influence them to the same extent as I could do by keeping to my orthodox ways.' (See Bapat, *Reminiscences*, pp. 7–8.) This selective approach to change continued: when asked how he could go abroad when it was banned for good Hindus by tradition, Tilak quipped: 'We Maratha Brahmans do not allow our religion to interfere with our politics.' (Quoted in Wolpert, *Tilak and Gokhale*, p. 283. Tilak appears to have inherited this approach from his mentor, Vishnushastri Krushnashastri Chiplunkar. See Deshpande, *Creative Pasts*, p. 113.) He offered logic: reform excited an English-educated minority while most Hindus were orthodox. 'Social reform,' then, 'can never be popular'. (Quoted in Gopal, *Lokamanya Tilak*, p. 110.) Nationalism had to win over all Hindus, and this could not be done while also assaulting their beliefs. To him, thus, 'there [was] no inherent connection between social reform and national regeneration'; insistence on reform might even sink the anti-British movement. (Gopal, *Lokamanya Tilak*, p. 214.) Or as he wrote,

> One party [his own] wishes to draw to the Congress as large a portion of the public as it possibly can, irrespective of the question of Social Reform; the other does not wish to go much beyond the circle of friends of reform. The real point at issue is whether the Congress . . . is to be a Congress of the people or of a particular section of it.

This was the opposite of a leader like C. Sankaran Nair, who in 1897 said that 'even greater' than 'political emancipation' was 'the necessity for social and religious reform'. (See Heimsath, *Indian Nationalism*, p. 216.) This also set Tilak apart from other Hindu leaders such as M.G. Ranade (1842–1901), who, not unlike Roy in Bengal, interpreted reform as a return to purity. The social evils reformers were fighting, thus, were to Ranade 'excrescences upon the healthy system of ancient Hindu Society'. He also did not believe government intervention was bad: a 'diseased corruption' in the body politic needed not small pills but a 'sharp surgical operation'. (See Ranade, *Miscellaneous Writings*, p. 81.) Tilak countered mulishly by calling them misrepresentations. 'If you don't know how to interpret the Shastras correctly, then at least try to remain silent.' (Quoted in Wolpert, *Tilak and Gokhale*, p. 55. See also *Samagra Lokamanya Tilak*, Vol. 5, p. 253, where he accuses reformers of picking and choosing fragments from the sastras to suit their reformist agenda.)

123 See R.B. Bhagat, 'Census and the Construction of Communalism in India', p. 4354, in *Economic and Political Weekly* 36, 46–47 (2001): 4352–56. See also Lee, *Deceptive Majority*.

124 As a formula this is not without precedent in India. Saivas in the medieval period, who had their own internal differences and various sects, clarified their common identity *as Saivas* by pushing a 'negative representation of Jains' as the Other. See Peterson, 'Sramanas against the Tamil Way'.

125 *Samagra Lokamanya Tilak*, Vol. 5, pp. 293–94.

126 Ibid., pp. 492–94. See also Kosambi, *Pandita Ramabai*, p. 209. Tilak's dislike of Ramabai was old: as early as 1882, when she began reform work among women, Tilak's *Kesari* disapproved. See ibid., p. 29. Her conversion to Christianity made things worse; unsurprisingly, figures like Phule supported her on this.

127 *Samagra Lokamanya Tilak*, Vol. 6, p. 732.

128 Tilak himself notes the practice. See *Samagra Lokamanya Tilak*, Vol. 4, p. 17. It was not just Hindus. Though strictly speaking, Sunni Muslims were not to participate in this Shia affair, in practice Sunnis across India did. See Pandey, *Construction of Communalism*, p. 34. Notably, in the seventeenth century, a Brahmin minister in Hyderabad was noted as sponsoring lavish Muharram functions, though this was put down to a desire to 'increase his fame'—in private he 'mock[ed]' the proceedings. See Kruijtzer, *Xenophobia*, p. 248.

129 See Amar Khoday, 'The Lokamanya and the Sardar: Two Generations of Congress "Communalism"', Unpublished MA thesis, Concordia University (2000), p. 44.

130 Cited in a letter dated 30 May 1916 from A. Montgomerie I.C.S. to Secretary, Government of Bombay in *Selected Documents*, Vol. 2, p. 230. Tilak himself had in 1888 written of harmony between Hindus and Muslims. See Rao, 'Religious Identity', p. 18.

131 For some of his Marathi writings on the riots, see *Samagra Lokamanya Tilak*, Vol. 5, pp. 329–62.

132 Khoday, 'The Lokamanya and the Sardar', p. 35.

133 Quoted in ibid., p. 36. Emphasis added.

134 Letter dated 30 May 1916 from A. Montgomerie I.C.S. to Secretary, Government of Bombay in *Selected Documents*, Vol. 2, p. 230. See also Gopal, *Lokamanya Tilak*, p. 80.

135  Gopal, *Lokamanya Tilak*, p. 88. See also *Samagra Lokamanya Tilak*, Vol. 4, pp. 17–18, and Vol. 5, p. 388.
136  *Samagra Lokamanya Tilak*, Vol. 5, p. 386.
137  Not everywhere though. In the same period, in Karnataka, the Sringeri Matha—a major Hindu institution—began sponsoring the local Muharram. See Prasad, *Poetics of Conduct*, p. 36.
138  Letter dated 30 May 1916 from A. Montgomerie I.C.S. to Secretary, Government of Bombay in *Selected Documents*, Vol. 2, p. 228. The same complaint is made today about India's secular state by the Hindu right. See also Khoday, 'The Lokamanya and the Sardar', p. 40, and Rao, 'Religious Identity', pp. 18–19.
139  Wolpert, *Gokhale and Tilak*, p. 69.
140  Letter dated 30 May 1916 from A. Montgomerie I.C.S. to Secretary, Government of Bombay in *Selected Documents*, Vol. 2, pp. 228–29. See also Khoday, 'The Lokamanya and the Sardar', p. 35; and Rao, 'Religious Identity', p. 24, for another instance where mosques burned during riots were dismissed by Tilak, who instead accused Muslims of 'constantly violating the sanctity of Hindu temples'.
141  Quoted in Cashman, *Myth of the Lokamanya*, p. 78. See also ibid., pp. 83–84, and Samarth, *Shivaji*, p. 54.
142  Quoted in Khoday, 'The Lokamanya and the Sardar', p. 54.
143  *Kesari*, 28 May 1895 in *Report on Native Papers . . . 1st June 1895*.
144  *Indu Prakash*, 20 April 1896 in *Report on Native Papers . . . 25 April 1896*.
145  Valentine Chirol in Bapat, *Reminiscences*, p. 142.
146  A point highlighted in *Gujarati*, 24 June 1906 in *Report on Native Papers Published in the Bombay Presidency for the Week ending June 23 1906*, South Asia Open Archives, IOR, https://www.jstor.org/stable/saoa.crl.25636548.
147  *Samagra Lokamanya Tilak*, Vol. 5, p. 378.
148  Ibid., p. 383.
149  Ibid.
150  Ibid., p. 361, p. 374–75.
151  The Marathas' liberation of India on behalf of Hindus from Islamic rule was accepted even by Tilak's liberal opponents. See, for instance, Ranade, *Rise of the Maratha Power*, pp. 4–6.
152  Omvedt, 'Non-Brahmans and Nationalists', p. 203.
153  Quoted in Parnal Chirmuley, 'Appropriating the Past: European Indology and Conflicting Notions of History in Nineteenth Century Maharashtra', Unpublished PhD dissertation, Jawaharlal Nehru University, New Delhi (2002), pp. 54–55.
154  Quoted in Wolpert, *Tilak and Gokhale*, pp. 50–51, p. 54
155  Quoted in Heimsath, *Indian Nationalism*, pp. 173–74.
156  Khoday, 'The Lokamanya and the Sardar', p. 34. And Wolpert, *Tilak and Gokhale*, pp. 37–38, where, in another matter also, Tilak accuses the

government of trying to 'castrate' Hinduism, demanding that they cease 'interfer[ing] with our customs which have been carried on . . . from time immemorial.'

157 Omvedt, 'Non-Brahmans and Nationalists', p. 203.
158 Tilak, *Writings and Speeches*, pp. 48–50.
159 Quoted in Samarth, *Shivaji*, p. 67. This is very different from his tone in a 1907 article where he describes Shivaji as 'a Hindu king with a deep yearning for religious freedom fighting against the galling oppression of Mohammedan rulers'. Quoted in Rao, 'Religious Identity', p. 30.
160 Tilak, *Writings and Speeches*, p. 174. See also ibid., p. 46 for a 1906 speech where Tilak speaks of how love of the nation was 'one's first duty.' Religion came second. See also *Samagra Lokamanya Tilak*, Vol. 6, p. 485.
161 Tilak, *Writings and Speeches*, pp. 141–42. Tilak added in this speech that even white men who were devoted to India were not alien. Read another way, however, this equates 'good' Muslims with 'good' Englishmen—but not with Hindus on whom no requirement of 'doing good' is placed as a test of Indianness. See also *Samagra Lokamanya Tilak*, Vol. 6, p. 466, p. 475. See also Bhagat-Kennedy, 'Imagining Bharat', pp. 67–68 for how in an earlier time, Bankim Chandra Chattopadhyay in Bengal also, in using the term 'Bengali' applied it to Hindus alone.
162 He also played a key role in enabling the 'Lucknow Pact', seen as critical to making Congress acceptable to Muslims. See also Yadav, 'Tilak', p. 48, pp. 51–55.
163 Quoted in Cashman, *Myth of the Lokamanya*, Appendix 3, p. 227. This was targeted specifically at his rival, G.K. Gokhale. See also Wolpert, *Tilak and Gokhale*, p. 230, and Sarwate, 'Reimagining the Modern Hindu Self', pp. 55–56.
164 See Tilak, *Writings and Speeches*, pp. 379–81. See also Wolpert, *Tilak and Gokhale*, p. 200 for Tilak's dismissal of 'constitutional politics', on the ground that India had no constitution to start with; and Gopal, *Lokamanya Tilak*, p. 275, where he compares moderates to Shivaji's father, who continued to serve the sultanates even as his son rebelled and launched an independent kingdom.
165 Quoted in Bapat, *Reminiscences*, p. 34. The irony is that this endorsement comes from Jinnah—the man who, in a few decades, would cleave out the state of Pakistan, convinced that Muslims could never be equal citizens in a Hindu-governed India. See also Khoday, 'The Lokamanya and the Sardar', p. 51, p. 55.
166 Quoted in Sarwate, 'Reimagining the Modern Hindu Self', p. 83.
167 See *Samagra Lokamanya Tilak*, Vol. 4, p. 18, where as early as 1894, he notes efforts to undermine Hindu unity by pushing divisions between Brahmins and other castes.
168 Note here that 'Brahmins' refers to professional classes of Brahmins for most part, while non-Brahmins too is a somewhat vague category in which *dominant* non-Brahmins claimed to speak for *all* non-Brahmins.

169  C.U. Aitchison, *Report of the Public Service Commission, 1886–87* (Calcutta: Superintendent of Government Printing, 1888), pp. 39–40. See also Kumar, *Western India*, pp. 282–83. See also Pandian, *Brahmin and Non-Brahmin*, p. 67, and ibid., p. 76 for nineteenth-century criticism that Brahmins in positions of official authority also imported traditional caste stigmas and prejudices into these positions; and Rao, *Beyond Macaulay*, p. 117, p. 197, p. 238 for how in education, under the Raj, Brahmins became dominant as teachers.

170  Quoted in Cashman, *Myth of the Lokamanya*, p. 201. See also Pandian, *Brahmin and Non-Brahmin*, pp. 70–71 for a similar statement from Madras in 1919, which suggests that peaceful, nation-building Brahmins were better leaders than non-Brahmins who had 'more sinews than brains'.

171  Gopal, *Lokamanya Tilak*, p. 401.

172  Quoted in Khoday, 'The Lokamanya and the Sardar', p. 57. Tilak appears later to have changed his mind on the question of Indian participation in the British Army, using this as a means to negotiate for self-government and also to obtain for Indians weapons training. See *Samagra Lokamanya Tilak*, Vol. 6, pp. 757–65.

173  Writing in 1879 the Governor of Bombay observed that educated Brahmins 'preach "unity" among Hindoos . . . as may subordinate caste distinctions to political necessity . . . But elder Brahmins of a stiffer disposition . . . would not surrender their Brahminism even for the sake of expelling the British'. Tilak seemed to combine both positions. See letter dated 9 July 1879 from the Governor of Bombay to the Viceroy in Hambly, 'Mahratta nationalism before Tilak', p. 156. For a similar view of Tamil Brahmins, see N.K. Venkateswaran, *Glimpses of Travancore* (Trivandrum: S. Gnanaskanda Iyer, 1926), where we read:

> Progressive in politics and retrogressive in religion, [the Tamil Brahmin] often yet appears to be unreligious and illiberal. He will not dig up his roots from the old world nor cut off his shoots from the new. He is, therefore, a contradiction and an enigma . . . While he keeps open house for the ideas of these times, he is unreasonably reluctant to abandon the crude notions of a bygone age.

The Dalit leader Ambedkar, in fact, described Tilak as 'one of those social tories and political radicals with whom India abounds'. See B.R. Ambedkar, *What Congress and Gandhi Have Done to the Untouchables* (Bombay: Thacker & Co., 1945), p. 13.

174  See Javalkar, *Deshache Dushman*, p. 9, p. 11, pp. 17–18, p. 28.

175  Quoted in O'Hanlon, *Caste, Conflict, and Ideology*, p. 31. See also Gail Omvedt, 'Non-Brahmans and Nationalists in Poona', p. 202, in *Economic and Political Weekly* 9, 6–8 (1974): 201–16 for accounts of how in later times also, Brahmins in Poona tended to address even wealthy non-Brahmins of

rank in a tone of superiority. See also Mountstuart Elphinstone, *The History of India*, Vol. 1 (London: John Murray, 1843, Second ed.), p. 108 for another relatively early nineteenth century note on animosity towards Brahmins among Marathas.

176  Letter dated 9 July 1879 from the Governor of Bombay to the Viceroy in Hambly, 'Mahratta nationalism before Tilak', pp. 153–60.

177  See letters in Files No. 93–98, Home Dept (Political-B), January 1911, NAI. For a similar suspicion of Brahmins in Madras, see Eugene F. Irschick, *Politics and Social Conflict in South India: The Non-Brahman Movement and Tamil Separatism, 1916–1929* (Bombay: Oxford University Press, 1969), p. 20.

178  We speak here primarily of the Chitpavan Brahmins of Maharashtra who rose under the Peshwas. In this they displaced the Deshastha Brahmins—an older elite and rival Brahmin subcaste—and it was Deshasthas who assisted the East India Company, as described in Chapter 3. That said, the Brahmins of the Deccan as a whole were suspected not just by the British but older imperial powers also; the first Nizam of Hyderabad (a subordinate of the Mughal emperor) in the eighteenth century declared that they were only 'fit to be killed and [have] their heads severed'. See Guha, 'Serving the Barbarian', p. 521.

179  Letter dated 17 September 1910 from the Sec., General Dept, Bombay to Sec., Home, Government of India in Files No. 93–98, Home Dept (Political-B), January 1911, NAI.

180  As late as 1911, there were newspaper debates on whether Chitpavans should even be accepted as proper Brahmins. See *Indu Prakash*, 12 April 1911, in *Report on Native Papers Published in the Bombay Presidency for the Week Ending 15th April 1911*, South Asia Open Archives, IOR at https://www.jstor.org/stable/saoa.crl.25636799. In his early journalistic career, Tilak also tried to encourage unity among Brahmins through intermarriage between subcastes. See *Samagra Lokamanya Tilak*, Vol. 5, pp. 3–18.

181  *Samagra Lokamanya Tilak*, Vol. 5, p. 197.

182  Ibid., p. 194.

183  See *Non-Brahmin Manifesto* of 1916 quoted in Irschick, *Politics and Social Conflict*, p. 48, and Ibid., pp. 51–52.

184  See *Samagra Lokamanya Tilak*, Vol. 6, p. 698.

185  *Samagra Lokamanya Tilak*, Vol. 5, p. 138.

186  See Pillai, *False Allies*, chapter four for more.

187  Bapat, *Reminiscences*, p. 176. Emphasis added.

188  A.G. Widgery ed., *Speeches and Addresses of His Highness Sayaji Rao III, Maharaja of Baroda*, Vol. 2 (Cambridge: Cambridge University Press, 1927), p. 375. See also Tagore, *Nationalism*, p. 135, pp. 145–46.

189  Orthodox Brahmins believed there were no Kshatriyas in the kali yuga—or as one writer put it, the Kshatriya was 'an extinct animal like the Mammoth'.

See Chunder, *The Travels of a Hindoo*, Vol. 1 (London: N. Trubner & Co., 1869), p. 159.
190 See Phadke, *Shahu Chhatrapati Ani Lokamanya*, pp. 45–117.
191 See *Samagra Lokamanya Tilak*, Vol. 5, pp. 148–54.
192 Quoted in Dhananjay Keer, *Shahu Chhatrapati: A Royal Revolutionary* (Bombay: Popular Prakashan, 1976), p. 37.
193 Cashman, *Myth of the Lokamanya*, pp. 115–18. See also Keer, *Shahu Chhatrapati*, p. 145 for an account of a 1907 meeting between Tilak and Shahu. Tilak was willing to acknowledge Shahu as a Kshatriya in his capacity as king of the Marathas, but not his wider caste group. In his dispute with Brahmins, Kolhapur's ruler was also encouraged by colonial officers. See Cashman, *Myth of the Lokamanya*, p. 118. See also Phadke, *Shahu Chhatrapati Ani Lokamanya*, pp. 104–05.
194 In 1894, Kolhapur had sixty Brahmins to eleven non-Brahmin officers—this when Brahmins numbered only a few thousand among a million subjects. Keer, *Shahu Chhatrapati*, p. 41. Shahu's attitude was also noted by Damodar Chapekar when his brother applied for a job in Kolhapur. The maharajah evidently said that he did not employ Poona Brahmins. Chapekar writes sarcastically: 'As soon as these precious words fell from their lips, (my brother) formed an estimate of their Kshatriya origin.' See 'Autobiography', p. 968. For an account of what Shahu represents today, see Gail Omvedt, 'Maharashtra: Politics of Culture: "Rajarshree Shahu University (Pune)"', in *Economic and Political Weekly* 29, 33 (1994): 2128–29. See also Ian Copland, 'The Maharaja of Kolhapur and the Non-Brahmin Movement, 1902–10', in *Modern Asian Studies* 7, 2 (1973): 209–25.
195 Partly under Phule's influence, he had long ago limited expenditure on the ritual feeding of Brahmins. He had no desire, he would remark, for encouraging 'laziness' in 'able-bodied persons'. See the maharajah's 1926 speech in Widgery, *Speeches and Addresses*, pp. 509–10.
196 Tilak, in fact, believed that Hinduism's diversity depended on caste; that caste in principle allowed each component of the wider whole its own space to thrive. See *Samagra Lokamanya Tilak*, Vol. 5, p. 143.
197 Tilak, of course, would have responded by arguing that reform was welcome but slowly and incrementally. His critics would have countered by questioning how he could opt for radicalism in politics and moderation in social affairs. Or as B.R. Ambedkar noted, 'It is foolish to take solace in the fact that because the Congress is fighting for the freedom of India, it is, therefore, fighting for the freedom of the people of India and of the lowest of the low.'
198 Omvedt, 'Non-Brahmans and Nationalists', p. 207.
199 Reference is to Sir M. Visvesvaraya, who presented the issue as one of 'merit'. See M. Visvesvaraya, *Memoirs of My Working Life* (Bangalore: M. Visvesvaraya, 1951), pp. 86–87, and Pillai, *False Allies*, chapter six.

200  Quoted in Irschick, *Politics and Social Conflict*, p. 20. See also D.A. Washbrook, *The Emergence of Provincial Politics: The Madras Presidency, 1870–1920* (Cambridge: Cambridge University Press, 1976), chapters six and seven. Pandian, *Brahmin and Non-Brahmin*, pp. 93–94 notes also how the Congress in Madras, dominated by Brahmins, was sarcastically compared to an *agraharam* (Brahmin colony).

201  Anita Diehl, *E.V. Ramaswami Naicker: Periyar: A Study of the Influence of a Personality in Contemporary South India* (Lund: Scandinavian University Books, 1977), p. 41. There are many parallels between Phule and Periyar, including in language used when criticizing Puranic Hinduism.

202  V.K. Bhave quoted in Sarwate, 'Reimagining the Modern Hindu Self', p. 66.

203  Keshavrao Thakare quoted in Sarwate, 'Reimagining the Modern Hindu Self', p. 44. Sarwate examines the idea of non-Brahmin 'Hinduness', with its own internal debates, in his dissertation, particularly chapter one.

204  Ibid., pp. 28–29, pp. 37–38.

205  Quoted in Rao, 'Religious Identity', p. 14.

206  Javalkar, *Deshache Dushman*, p. 40. Emphasis added.

207  On bullets being fired, see Gajanan Pandurang Parchure, *Mulanche Tatyarao Savarkar* (Mumbai: Ramkrushna Prakashan, 1941), p. 10. On the story of having swum for days, see Sampath, *Echoes*, p. 386. For a newspaper account of the events, see *Pioneer*, 24 July 1910.

208  Letter dated 18 July 1910 from the French Ambassador to the Secretary of State for Foreign Affairs in IOR/L/PJ/6/994.

209  Minute by Secretary of State for Home Affairs dated 28 July 1910, ibid.

210  Enclosure 9 on a meeting dated 4 August 1910 in ibid.

211  See documents in IOR/L/PJ/6/1060, File No. 359. The Permanent Court of Arbitration was established in 1899.

212  Sampath, *Echoes*, p. 5.

213  Ibid., p. 41.

214  Vikram Sampath, *Savarkar: A Contested Legacy:1924-1966* (Gurugram: Penguin Random House, 2021), p. 546. See also Vinayak Chaturvedi, *Hindutva and Violence: V.D. Savarkar and the Politics of History* (Albany: SUNY Press, 2022), p. 291 for a 1931 quote by Savarkar who claimed that as a child he was influenced by 'revolution'.

215  Quoted in Janaki Bakhle, *Savarkar and the Making of Hindutva* (Princeton and Oxford: Princeton University Press, 2024), pp. 248–49.

216  Quoted in Sampath, *Echoes*, p. 98.

217  Quoted in ibid., p. 78.

218  Ibid., p. 25.

219  Bakhle, *Savarkar*, p. 280.

220  And of which this writer is also an alumnus.

221  Its origins evidently lie in the Mitra Mela, an organization Savarkar founded in Nasik in his teens. Savarkar's fascination for secret mobilization also

comes across in his first book. See V.D. Savarkar ('An Indian Nationalist'), *The Indian War of Independence of 1857* (1909), chapter 7.
222  This was a translation of a selection of the Italian revolutionary Giuseppe Mazzini's writings.
223  Quoted in Wolpert, *Tilak and Gokhale*, p. 169. See also Sampath, *Echoes*, pp. 87–88. Savarkar in his own application wrote: 'Independence and Liberty I look upon as the very pulse and breath of [my] nation.'
224  Sampath, *Echoes*, p. 291. Or as Bakhle, *Savarkar*, p. 2 writes: 'He went to London to study law only to have the Metropolitan Police decide he was breaking it.'
225  Chaturvedi, *Hindutva and Violence*, p. 48. One of these three books, a history of the Sikhs, was confiscated by the British and lost forever.
226  Ibid., p. 95.
227  Ibid., pp. 50–52.
228  Quoted in Sampath, *Echoes*, p. 115. And they were not wrong: Savarkar himself wrote that his goal was to inspire Indians to follow in Mazzini's path. See Chaturvedi, *Hindutva and Violence*, p. 57.
229  See full text of 'O! Martyrs' in Appendix I, Sampath, *Echoes*, pp. 447–50.
230  Bakhle, *Savarkar*, p. 55.
231  Ibid., p. 53.
232  Jawaharlal Nehru, *Selected Works of Jawaharlal Nehru*, Vol. 3 (Delhi: B.R. Publishing Corporation, 1988), p. 394. And as with Tilak's pictures, Savarkar's book became a popular possession with revolutionaries across India. See for example report dated 29 December 1914 by the Director of Criminal Intelligence in Files No. 278–82, Home Dept (Political-B), January 1915, NAI, where a revolutionary in Punjab was found with a copy. Even after Savarkar's anti-Muslim turn, the Muslim leader Asaf Ali would in the late 1920s present a copy to his wife. 'I was thrilled by it,' Aruna Asaf Ali wrote. 'It politicized me.' See T.C.A. Raghavan, *Circles of Freedom: Friendship, Love and Loyalty in the Indian National Struggle* (New Delhi: Juggernaut, 2024), p. 173. For a brief discussion of its historiographical infirmities, see Wagner, *The Great Fear*, pp. 12–14.
233  On Savarkar being a successor of sorts to Tilak, an admirer would write: 'Tilak and Savarkar held identical views. In fact, Savarkar would go a step ahead of Tilak.' See Nathuram Godse (Gopal Godse ed.), *May It Please Your Honour* (Delhi: Surya Prakashan, 1989), p. 15. Savarkar himself also wrote that while Tilak's work was not revolutionary, it was 'conducive to revolution'. See V.D. Savarkar (S.T. Godbole trans.), *Six Glorious Epochs of Indian History* (Bombay: Bal Savarkar, 1971), p. 468.
234  See Appendix: Criminal Intelligence Office, 'The Revolutionary Group, India House, London' in Files No. 133–35, Home Dept (Political-A), May 1910, NAI.
235  G.N.S. Raghavan, *M. Asaf Ali's Memoirs: The Emergence of Modern India* (Delhi: Ajanta, 1994), p. 69.

236  Bakhle, *Savarkar*, p. 50.
237  Quoted in Sampath, *Echoes*, p. 118. See also Chaturvedi, *Hindutva and Violence*, pp. 83–84 for a longer discussion on Gandhi and Savarkar's engagement in this period.
238  Sampath, *Echoes*, p. 107. Dhingra's original target had been Lord Curzon, ex-viceroy of India, whose partition of the province of Bengal along religious lines caused umbrage among Indian nationalists. See also V.N. Datta, *Madanlal Dhingra and the Revolutionary Movement* (New Delhi: Vikas Publishing House, 1978).
239  See Dhingra's full statement in *Proceedings of the Central Criminal Court*, 19 July 1909, at https://www.oldbaileyonline.org/record/t19090719-55?text=dhingra.
240  M.K. Gandhi, *The Collected Works of Mahatma Gandhi*, Vol. 9 (Ahmedabad: Navjivan Trust, 1963), p. 302. See also Gandhi (Anthony J. Parel ed.), *Hind Swaraj and Other Writings* (Cambridge: Cambridge University Press, 1997), pp. 77–78.
241  British intelligence report quoted in Chaturvedi, *Hindutva and Violence*, p. 83. The evening where Gandhi publicly disagreed with Savarkar's attitude is described—minus details available in the intelligence report—in *Collected Works*, pp. 498–99.
242  On the Gita's influence on Savarkar, see Chaturvedi, *Hindutva and Violence*, pp. 70–71. Gandhi disagreed with this reading of the Gita, observing how 'Savarkar and others used to tell me that the Gita and the Ramayana taught quite the opposite of what I said they did.' See Gandhi, *Hind Swaraj*, p. xxvii.
243  Quoted in Datta, *Madanlal Dhingra*, p. 64.
244  Appendix: Criminal Intelligence Office, 'The Revolutionary Group, India House, London'. See also Sampath, *Echoes*, pp. 140–41, pp. 151–52, pp. 192–95; Parchure, *Tatyarao Savarkar*, p. 7, p. 9. See also Bakhle, *Savarkar*, p. 47 for how in the 1950s, Savarkar would admit that in going to England, his real goal had always been to 'learn about bombmaking'.
245  Sampath, *Echoes*, p. 198.
246  Chaturvedi, *Hindutva and Violence*, p. 114. See also Sampath, *Echoes*, p. 246.
247  Director of Criminal Intelligence in 1911 quoted in Bakhle, *Savarkar*, p. 60.
248  Sampath, *Echoes*, p. 211. Ironically, Tilak's *Kesari* also denounced Savarkar at this time, though this may well have been due to Tilak's own imprisonment in Burma, which had softened his paper's tone.
249  Quoted in Sampath, *Echoes*, p. 242.
250  The Andamans were also where many rebels from 1857, interestingly, were sent to serve their sentences.
251  V.D. Savarkar, *Majhi Janmathep* (Mumbai: Parchure Prakashan Mandir, 2018 [1927]), pp. 43–44.
252  Quoted in ibid., p. 45. See also ibid., p. 258.

253  Quoted in Sampath, *Echoes*, p. 316. In fact, as late as 1934, Savarkar showed no signs of a 'change of heart' according to British officials. See Bakhle, *Savarkar*, p. 79.

254  Savarkar, *Majhi Janmathep*, pp. 115–16; Parchure, *Tatyarao Savarkar*, p. 13. In the words of another inmate, 'One week [doing oil-grinding and coir-pounding] would be sufficient to make [one] feel what [Jesus] felt on the cross.' See Barindra Kumar Ghose, *The Tale of My Exile* (Pondicherry: Arya Office, 1922), p. 50.

255  Savarkar, *Majhi Janmathep*, pp. 117–19, pp. 177–78, p. 279. See also pp. 174–75, where we read how prisoners would try and deliberately fall ill so to be spared the cruel everyday work in prison. Some pretended even to be mad, eating their excreta to prove it.

256  Savarkar's account makes it appear as if he became a kind of prison leader. Ghose, however, does not single out Savarkar as a special inmate, and mentions him only once in passing in his prison memoirs. Yet another source reports that after 1915, Savarkar was actively docile in his relations with the prison authorities. See Dhirendra K. Jha, *Gandhi's Assassin: The Making of Nathuram Godse and His Idea of India* (Gurugram: Vintage, 2021), p. 22.

257  Savarkar, *Majhi Janmathep*, p. 90, p. 116. See also Ghose, *Tale of My Exile*, p. 77.

258  Sampath, *Echoes*, p. 317. For similar protests by others, see Ghose, *Tale of My Exile*, pp. 90–92.

259  Sampath, *Echoes*, Appendix 3, p. 456. Savarkar had already in 1911 submitted a now-untraceable petition.

260  Ibid., p. 457.

261  Savarkar's October 1914 petition in File No. 245, Home Dept (Political-B), November 1914, NAI.

262  Sampath, *Echoes*, Appendix 3, p. 470. See also ibid., p. 82, where, interestingly, as early as 1906, a government report notes that he was 'ruining his own life for he is yet but a raw boy not fitted to preach opinions which he scarcely understands'. Tilak had also issued similar warnings. See ibid., p. 72. Savarkar's younger brother also made efforts for his release. See correspondence in File No. 354, Home Dept (Political), 1921, NAI, for instance.

263  Sampath, *Echoes*, p. 355. See also ibid., p. 312.

264  Savarkar seems to have been embarrassed by this. After all, he once told colleagues that their path was 'bloody'; there would tortures 'to break your will'. Revolution was for those who could bear it. See Sampath, *Echoes*, p. 71. With his own will broken, his line changed. In his prison memoirs, he notes how conditions in prison tended to make men forget their values. But they must be respected for 'past service, patriotism and self-sacrifice'. See Savarkar, *Majhi Janmathep*, p. 79. Parchure's hagiographical *Tatyarao Savarkar* also makes no mention of his petitions to the British, again suggesting awkwardness.

265 Bakhle, for instance, concludes that Savarkar was 'playing a political game' and 'wrote whatever he thought might help get him back to India and the political arena'. See Bakhle, *Savarkar*, p. 62, p. 65. But even if he was just fed up, that would be understandable. Just poor health in prison could break people. In the 1940s, for instance, the Congress leader Syed Mahmud would also write an ingratiating letter to the British, after which he too was released. See Raghavan, *Circles of Freedom*, pp. 250–51.

266 In 1921, thus, Savarkar had already been moved from the Andamans back to mainland India. His final prison, interestingly, was at Yerwada in Pune, which once housed both Tilak and the Chapekars.

267 Letter dated 17 January 1924 from Secretary, Home Dept, Bombay to Secretary, Home Dept, GOI in File No. 25, Home Dept (Political), January 1924, NAI.

268 See Press Note attached to Letter dated 15 January 1924 from Secretary, Home Dept, Bombay to Secretary, Home Dept, GOI in File No. 8, Home Dept (Political), 1924, NAI. Parchure, *Tatyarao Savarkar*, p. 19, however, though not surprisingly, claims Savarkar made no such promise eschewing violence.

269 See File No. 381-F, Foreign and Political Dept, 1925, NAI.

270 M.K. Gandhi, *Young India: 1919–1922* (Madras: S. Ganesan, 1922), pp. 94–98.

271 Letter dated 6 April 1925 from Savarkar to the Deputy Secretary, Home Dept, Bombay in File No. 91/I, Home Dept (Political), 1925, NAI. See also Chaturvedi, *Hindutva and Violence*, p. 212.

272 Quoted in Chaturvedi, *Hindutva and Violence*, p. 211.

273 Ibid., p. 213. This caused one official to remark that Savarkar 'accepts the letter [of the conditions laid down] for his own safety, but never respects the spirit'. Quoted in Sampath, *Contested Legacy*, p. 17. In 1934, he was also once detained, and his house searched. See ibid., p. 157.

274 Ibid., pp. 261–62, p. 274. As late as the 1940s, even books *about* Savarkar were prohibited. See ibid., p. 314.

275 Ibid., pp. 277–89. Chaturvedi suggests that Savarkar himself authored this, while others like Sampath believe it was a close associate. Savarkar is, again, often lampooned for praising himself in a biography he likely wrote, but as Chaturvedi shows, the anonymous authorship was a product of his context.

276 See Bakhle, *Savarkar*, pp. 68–75, pp. 106–07.

277 Quoted in Sampath, *Contested Legacy*, p. 72.

278 Savarkar, *War of Independence*, pp. vii–viii, pp. 62–63.

279 Ibid., p. 10, p. 444.

280 Ibid., pp. 62–63, p. 162. An earlier Bengali writer, Bhudeb Mukhopadhyay, accepted Muslims, stating that while Hindus were born of India's womb, Muslims were India's foster-children. Here again, we see that combination of acceptance with rejection, noted in the Introduction. See Chakrabarti, *Local Selfhood*, p. 204, and Chatterjee, *Nation and Its Fragments*, p. 111.

281 Savarkar, *War of Independence*, p. 443. In this, Savarkar echoes Ranade, who saw the failure of the Marathas—motivated by a desire to assert 'Hindu nationality'—in a previous generation as an 'education'. See Ranade, *Rise*, p. iv.
282 Savarkar in a speech quoted in Sampath, *Echoes*, p. 90.
283 Yet, even in this phase, he did occasionally slip into anti-Muslim rhetoric. See Bakhle, *Savarkar*, p. 47. It could also be argued that Savarkar's friendlier language for Muslims coincides with such a turn in the same period with his preceptor, Tilak. That is, it stemmed more from political expediency than sincerity.
284 Bakhle, *Savarkar*, p. 5. It was in subsequent editions retitled *Hindutva: Who Is a Hindu?*
285 V.D. Savarkar, *Hindutva: Who Is a Hindu?* (Bombay: Veer Savarkar Prakashan, 1969 [1923]), p. 81.
286 Ibid., p. 113, pp. 100–01. The reverse also applied in that seeing India purely as one's 'holyland' was not adequate—Chinese and Japanese Buddhists, then, might claim Hinduness. India also had to be one's fatherland. See V.D. Savarkar, *Hindu Rashtra Darshan: A Collection of the Presidential Speeches Delivered from the Hindu Mahasabha Platform* (Bombay: Laxman Ganesh Khare, 1949), p. 5.
287 Bakhle, *Savarkar*, p. 147.
288 Quoted in Ibid., p. 83. Emphasis added.
289 Ibid., p. 113.
290 Chandranath Basu—a Bengali conservative who used the term in 1892—also chose a theological explanation. Chaturvedi, *Hindutva and Violence*, p. 138. This was also different from an earlier, nineteenth-century imagining of the term 'Hindu' by Bharatendu Harishchandra (1850–85) in Benares as encompassing *everyone* living in India, though this too was contingent on Muslims being willing to accept the label. See Dalmia, *The Nationalization of Hindu Traditions*, p. 26.
291 Savarkar, *Majhi Janmathep*, p. 225. We see these ideas repeated in his foreword to Savitri Devi's book *A Warning to the Hindus* (Calcutta: Hindu Mission, 1939), p. vii, where Savarkar writes that Hindus had been 'fed on inertia-producing thoughts' which left them good for seeking spiritual release—an 'escape from this world'—without learning to actually live *in* this world. This was one cause of India's 'continuous enslavement'.
292 Or as he noted, internecine wars existed among the British, French, Germans and even in America. 'Are they still a people, a nation . . .? If they do, the Hindus do.' See Savarkar, *Hindutva*, p. 95. And such intra-Hindu disputes continue to this day. See, for example, a 2023 case around the Swaminarayan sect discussed in the previous chapter: Mahesh Langa, 'A "spiritual strife" between Swaminarayan sect, other Hindu outfits in Gujarat', *The Hindu*, 6 September 2023, https://www.thehindu.com/news/cities/Delhi/a-

spiritual-strife-between-swaminarayan-sect-other-hindu-outfits-in-gujarat/article67275042.ece

293 See also Savarkar, *Hindutva*, p. 3, where he states that 'Hindutva is not a word but a history', and p. 95. See also Savarkar, *Hindu Rashtra Darshan*, p. 16; and Bakhle, *Savarkar*, p. 7, where she notes that we see in Savarkar 'no desire to return to the Vedas, or any support for Hindu ritual'.

294 Christophe Jaffrelot, 'Hindutva', pp. 109–10 in Gita Dharampal-Frick, Monika Kirloskar-Steinbach, Rachel Dwyer and Jahnavi Ohalkey eds., *Key Concepts in Modern Indian Studies* (New York: New York University Press, 2015), pp. 108–10. See also Basu, *Hindutva as Political Monotheism*, p. 5, where we read how Hindutva seeks 'a unifying ethnocultural consistency rather than a theological unity'.

295 Of course, groundwork for this was also laid by wider debates in Maharashtra, which created an intellectual environment open to Savarkar's Hindutva. See Sarwate, 'Reimagining the Modern Hindu Self', p. 110. Nor does this mean he dismissed Hinduism. On the contrary, he declared, 'Hinduism and [political] independence were interdependent.' Quoted in Bakhle, *Savarkar*, p. 83.

296 Or as Chaturvedi writes in *Hindutva and Violence*, p. 25: 'Savarkar was clear that his purpose was never to produce academic scholarship.' One is also reminded here of Sheldon Pollock's line: 'We have always known that people make their stories from their histories, and recently we have come to appreciate the degree to which people make their histories from their stories.' See Pollock, 'Deep Orientalism', p. 102.

297 Savarkar, *War of Independence*, p. 5, p. 7.

298 Quoted in Chaturvedi, *Hindutva and Violence*, p. 57. See also ibid., p. 222, p. 238.

299 Savarkar, *Hindutva*, p. 8. See also Chaturvedi, *Hindutva and Violence*, p. 164. As Chaturvedi notes in ibid., p. 338, Savarkar tended to accept Western interpretations of Indian history 'when it suits his objectives' while dismissing all that was 'critical of Hindu history'.

300 Chaturvedi, *Hindutva and Violence*, p. 168. Emphasis added. See also ibid., p. 240.

301 Savarkar, *War of Independence*, p. vii.

302 Much of Savarkar's attitude appears already in older writings. See Tarinicharan Chattopadhyay's work, for example, in Chatterjee, *Nation and Its Fragments*, pp. 103–04. One is also reminded of similar efforts in Bengal, using 'strategic anachronisms'. See Monica R. Bhagat-Kennedy, 'Imagining Bharat'. Opposing views also existed, of course. As P.N. Bose wrote in 1894, while there was patriotism, Hindus 'were patriotic more for the honour of their race and their class than from a love of their countrymen generally'. See Bose, *A History of Hindu Civilisation*, Vol. 1, p. xvii.

303 Savarkar, *Hindutva*, p. 18.

304  Ibid., p. 44. Hindu nationalists are also sometimes accused—and with reason—of succumbing to James Mill's notorious periodization of Indian history into Hindu, Islamic and British periods, these coinciding with the ancient, medieval and modern eras. However, in the eighteenth century, before Mill, a Maratha writer took a somewhat similar line when he declared how India had been 'under Hindu control since the days of the Mahabharata'. But when Hindu kings 'lost their old vigour' and yielded to Muslims, the latter became powerful, until unseated by Marathas centuries later. See G.S. Sardesai, *The Main Currents of Maratha History* (Bombay: Keshav Bhikaji Dhavle, 1933), pp. 9–10. That is, there were the voices within India who might have agreed with Mill's categorizations.

305  Even in his journalism and speeches, he 'frequently took facts ... and mixed them with fiction ... only to assert a general historical argument.' See Bakhle, *Savarkar*, p. 125, pp. 128–30, p. 134. See also p. 295, where we read how Savarkar's was 'an overtly political, polemical, and instrumental hijacking of history as memory work, with a particularly idiosyncratic use of "fact"'.

306  V.D. Savarkar, *Hindu-Pad-Padshahi: Or, A Review of the Hindu Empire of Maharashtra* (New Delhi: Bharti Sahitya Sadan, [1925]), p. 32.

307  Ibid., p. 91, p. 199.

308  Ibid., pp. 207–10.

309  Ibid., p. 216.

310  Jadunath Sarkar quoted in Chaturvedi, *Hindutva and Violence*, pp. 218–19.

311  As Bakhle notes, his books continue to be read '*as* histories'. See Bakhle, *Savarkar*, p. 20. The emotional appeal is explained also because such feelings were not new. In the *Viswagunadarsana*, p. 47, for instance, while Maratha flaws are acknowledged, their conquests are yet accepted as 'bitter medicine' for expelling Muslim power and restoring Hindu deities. Similarly, in making the case for Indian nationalism as a legitimate force, the statesman K.M. Panikkar also described 'the unity of India' as the 'very soul' of Maratha power and expansion. See Panikkar, *Indian Nationalism*, p. 12. For at a broader level, 'struggles about stories of the past may also be struggles over the proper shape of society in the present.' See Bruce Lincoln, *Discourse and the Construction of Society: Comparative Studies of Myth, Ritual, and Classification* (New York: Oxford University Press, 1989), p. 32.

312  Quoted in Sampath, *Contested Legacy*, p. 12.

313  Bakhle, *Savarkar*, p. 153. See also ibid., p. 160, where she notes this as the uniting of all castes in a super-caste.

314  See Tilak, *Writings and Speeches*, pp. 39–40. He also opposed a 1918 bill that would have allowed inter-caste marriage. See Bakhle, *Savarkar*, pp. 165–66.

315  Sampath, *Contested Legacy*, p. 60. Parchure in *Tatyarao Savarkar*, p. 27 goes to the extent of asserting that many Dalits began to see Savarkar as a living god. Savarkar's tone here is reminiscent of the Arya Samaj. As an 1897 editorial in the *Arya Patrika* put it, 'For our Upadeshaks [preachers] to

compete with Christians, they must give up Chhut Chhat [untouchability] and caste restrictions.' See Graham, 'The Arya Samaj', p. 473.
316   Quoted in Bakhle, *Savarkar*, p. 157, p. 181.
317   Sampath, *Contested Legacy*, p. 57. See also Parchure, *Tatyarao Savarkar*, pp. 24–26. Years later, B.R. Ambedkar, leader of the 'depressed classes' would observe that if Dalits went over to in Islam or Christianity, this would 'denationalize' them; if they became Sikhs, they would be out of Hinduism, but not 'Hindu culture'. Quoted in Keith Meadowcroft, 'The All-Indian Hindu Mahasabha, Untouchable Politics, and "denationalizing" conversions: the Moonje-Ambedkar Pact', p. 17, in *South Asia: Journal of South Asian Studies* 29, 1 (2006): 9–41.
318   Sampath, *Contested Legacy*, p. 65, p. 74, and Parchure, *Tatyarao Savarkar*, p. 22, p. 28, pp. 30–31.
319   See Sarwate, 'Reimagining the Modern Hindu Self', pp. 100–10.
320   Quoted in Sampath, *Echoes*, pp. 422–23. Indeed, where intellectuals like Ambedkar saw 'Hindu' and 'Brahmin' as synonymous, Savarkar went with the non-Brahmin idea that 'one became a better Hindu if one shed Brahminism's useless ritualism and illogical beliefs.' See Bakhle, *Savarkar*, p. 170. He also lampooned those who saw modern science in ancient texts. 'As soon as coal-fired trains get going, they start hearing the sound of railway engines in the Vedas.' Quoted in ibid., p. 184.
321   Quoted in Chaturvedi, *Hindutva and Violence*, p. 339.
322   Sampath, *Contested Legacy*, p. 63, and Parchure, *Tatyarao Savarkar*, p. 29.
323   This meant also, for example, that where Tilak not just venerated the cow but urged others to view the 'mother country [also as] a great cow', Savarkar approached the cow from a more utilitarian perspective. See Wolpert, *Tilak and Gokhale*, p. 279, and Sampath, *Echoes*, pp. 429–32. At one point, he even wrote, almost in a Phule-like tone, how the orthodox 'filled their cupped palms with cow urine' but refused to accept even sacred Ganga water from the hands of a Dalit. They worshipped the cow, but why not the pig given that Vishnu had also taken an avatar as a boar? See Bakhle, *Savarkar*, pp. 198–200, p. 218.
324   Savarkar, *Hindutva*, p. 43.
325   Savarkar, *Hindu-Pad-Padshahi*, pp. 19–20.
326   December 1937 speech cited in Appendix A: 'Notes on the Rashtriya Swayam Sewak Sangh' by E.J. Beveridge in File No. 28/8/42, Home Dept (Political-I), 1942, NAI. See also Bakhle, *Savarkar*, p. 116.
327   See Sampath, *Contested Legacy*, p. 329. In a discussion with an American diplomat, Savarkar, in the context of the Muslim demand for a separate state (Pakistan) to be carved out of India, also asked 'what would be the reaction of the average American if the negro minority in the United States were to claim the right to establish an independent State of Mississippi or Alabama'. See letter dated 9 February 1944 from the American

Consul in Bombay to the Secretary of State at https://sangraha.net/s80/NBImages/15001/2019/03/20/2_11_12_01_Consul_1.pdf.

328  Of his two immediate predecessors there, one was an Arya Samajist and the other an associate of Tilak.

329  Quoted in Sampath, *Contested Legacy*, p. 33.

330  Prabhu Bapu, *Hindu Mahasabha in Colonial North India, 1915–1930: Constructing Nation and History* (Abingdon: Routledge, 2013), p. 41. See also p. 37 for how, though the Mahasabha's origins lay in upper India, through the 1920s, its leadership came to be dominated by Tilakite Maharashtrians. In 1939, Savarkar's younger brother in a speech also identified three 'enemies of Hinduism': the British, Congress and Muslims. See 'Notes on the Rashtriya Swayam Sewak Sangh'. The *rashtriya hijade* (eunuchs) line is from Bakhle, *Savarkar*, p. 81.

331  Savarkar, *Majhi Janmathep*, pp. 71–72.

332  Ghose in *Tale of My Exile*, pp. 66–67, 78, pp. 141–42 hints at religious segregation, even if not with Savarkar's bitterness. Muslims and Sikhs were allowed to retain beards, for example, but Brahmins were forced to surrender the sacred thread they wore.

333  Savarkar, *Majhi Janmathep*, p. 230, p. 232, pp. 237–38, p. 243. See also Ghosh, *Tale of My Exile*, p. 73.

334  He reiterates this point in colourful prose in *Six Glorious Epochs*, p. 169.

335  See also Savarkar, *Majhi Janmathep*, p. 418, where Savarkar triumphantly claims that if when he came to the Andamans, the prison was under a 'Pathan Raj', thanks to his strikes and efforts to unite Hindu prisoners, by the end the equation was no longer lopsided. See also Parchure, *Tatyarao Savarkar*, pp. 16–17.

336  In this respect, see also Shraddhananda Sanyasi, *Hindu Sanghatan: Saviour of the Dying Race* (1926).

337  On this, see also Kaviraj, *The Imaginary Institution of India*, with its discussion on 'fuzzy' communities and their transformation into 'enumerated' ones.

338  Cited in Bapu, *Hindu Mahasabha*, p. 15. Reference is to Punjab. See also Lee, *Deceptive Majority*, pp. 42–43.

339  Letter dated 11 March 1932 from Gandhi to Secretary of State for India in IOR/L/PO/6/77. See also Lee, *Deceptive Majority*, pp. 125–26, p. 130.

340  In 1910, thus, the then census commissioner wondered if these sections of Hindus society should really be classed under that tag. It sparked protests and claims that the British were seeking to 'amputate' the Hindu majority. See Bapu, *Hindu Mahasabha*, p. 15.

341  See also Savarkar, *Hindu Rashtra Darshan*, p. 61. Before him Arya Samajists like Lala Lajpat Rai had also made similar arguments. See, for example, his 'The Depressed Classes' (1909), in Christophe Jaffrelot ed., *Hindu Nationalism: A Reader* (Princeton: Princeton University Press, 2007), pp. 235–44.

342  See Pillai, *Ivory Throne*, pp. 396–405. This Hindu character was also used to prevent giving the state's people representative government, on the ground that non-Hindus would also be able to determine political decisions. See Menon, *Triumph and Tragedy*, p. 276. See also Savarkar, *Hindu Rashtra Darshan*, p. 71. And the Mahasabha was quick to seek an alliance with Hindu princes, seeing in them a source of both financial and moral sustenance for their cause. See Manu Bhagavan, 'Princely States and the Hindu Imaginary: Exploring the Cartography of Hindu Nationalism in Colonial India', in *Journal of Asian Studies* 67, 3 (2008): 881–915. See also Chaturvedi, *Hindutva and Violence*, p. 195; and Ian Copland, *State, Community and Neighbourhood in Princely North India, c. 1900–1950* (New York: Palgrave Macmillan, 2005), pp. 103–05.

343  Savarkar, *War of Independence*, pp. 46–47.

344  As one scholar puts it, Hindu and Muslim communal politics emerged in an 'interactive relation'. 'Each side fed off the angers and fears excited by the other.' See Keith Meadowcroft, 'The emergence, crystallization and shattering of a right-wing alternative to Congress nationalism—the All-India Hindu Mahasabha, 1937–52', Unpublished PhD dissertation, Concordia University (2003), p. 7. See also K.M. Munshi, *Akhand Hindustan* (Bombay: New Book Co., 1942), pp. 11–12.

345  Ayesha Jalal, *The Sole Spokesman: Jinnah, the Muslim League and the Demand for Pakistan* (Cambridge: Cambridge university Press, 1985), p. 52. Savarkar also in 1937 described 'two antagonistic nations living side by side in India'; that 'there are two nations in the main' in the country. See Savarkar, *Hindu Rashtra Darshan*, p. 26. But as Chaturvedi observes, Savarkar's admission of two nations did not mean he was willing to concede two *states*, as the League desired. Instead, as one critic noted, his goal was a Hindu 'empire over Muslims'. See *Hindutva and Violence*, p. 333.

346  Address dated 1 October 1906 in Ram Gopal, *Indian Muslims: A Political History* (1858–1947) (Bombay: Asia Publishing House, 1964 ed.), pp. 98–99.

347  A point made by Hindu traditionalists within Congress also: the idea of regional and linguistic affinities triumphing religion. See, for example, Munshi, *Akhand Hindustan*, p. 54.

348  Quoted in Ian Copland, 'The Abdullah Factor: Kashmiri Muslims and the Crisis of 1947', p. 223, in D.A. Low ed., *The Political Inheritance of Pakistan* (New York: Palgrave Macmillan, 1991), pp. 218–54. Similar opinions existed about the mass of Bengali Muslims also. See Ahmed, *The Bengal Muslims*, pp. 6–7.

349  Savarkar, *Hindu Rashtra Darshan*, p. 13. To this was added a mocking of Gandhian non-violence: it was an 'immoral creed' with a 'queer belief in self-tortures'. See Savarkar's statement dated 24 June 1941 in File No. 214, Home Dept (Political-I), 1941, NAI. Elsewhere he also asked: 'If a fast is so effective, why doesn't Churchill fast against Hitler?' See Sampath, *Contested Legacy*, p. 329.

350  Savarkar, *Hindu Rashtra Darshan*, p. 55.
351  Ibid., p. 14. See also Savarkar, *Majhi Janmathep*, p. 292, where early on he accuses Muslims of being unable to think of themselves as Indians first, and *Hindu-Pad-Padshahi*, pp. 197–98 where he speaks of their 'theocratic patriotism'.
352  Savarkar, *Majhi Janmathep*, p. 235. See also ibid., p. 243.
353  Savarkar's foreword to Indra Prakash, *A Review of the History and Work of the Hindu Mahasabha and the Hindu Sanghatan Movement* (New Delhi: Akhil Bharatiya Hindu Mahasabha, 1938), p. xii.
354  Quoted in *Roy's Weekly*, 5 December 1943.
355  Savarkar's statement in File No. 87, Home Dept (Political-I), 1943, NAI. The government investigated and found Savarkar's claims about Muslims converting famine victims untrue.
356  Savarkar, *War of Independence*, pp. 62–63. See also Savarkar, *Hindu-Pad-Padshahi*, p. 21.
357  Ibid, p. 220.
358  Ibid., pp. 234–35.
359  B.B. Gudi's note dated 13 May 1942, Central Intelligence Office, Bombay in File No. 222, Home Dept (Political-I), 1942, NAI.
360  It must be stated that several Congressmen also harboured similar feelings. See, for instance, Madan Mohan Malaviya's 1923 remarks in Jaffrelot, *Hindu Nationalism*, pp. 65–66.
361  In the 1920s also the Mahasabha had asserted that they were the right body to negotiate with the League, given that they openly represented Hindus, as opposed to the Congress. See Meadowcroft, 'Hindu Mahasabha', p. 13.
362  Draft of Resolution for Hindu Mahasabha meeting dated 10 May 1942 in File No. 222, Home Dept (Political-I), 1942, NAI. Emphasis added. This was a longstanding woe. Historically also, Savarkar argued, that Hindus were always bending backwards to assuage Muslim demands. See Bakhle, *Savarkar*, p. 144.
363  See Intelligence Bureau report dated 26 August 1941 in File No. 243, Home Dept (Political-I), 1941, NAI.
364  B.B. Gudi's note. See also Secret Report dated 2 April 1942 in ibid., where also Savarkar states that the 'integral unity of India as a whole has been an accomplished fact of Hindu thought throughout the ages'. The Mahasabha could never 'be a party to proposals aiming at the dismemberment of India'.
365  Savarkar, *Hindu Rashtra Darshan*, p. 36.
366  In the 1945–46 central and provincial elections in India it was wiped out. In 1940, Savarkar himself admonished south Indian Hindus for not being particularly interested in the Mahasabha and its ideology. 'As a Hindu you should feel the pain of Hindus anywhere.' Just because the south did not see polarized relations between Hindus and Muslims, that should not prevent

Hindu consolidation, he argued. Quoted in Sampath, *Contested Legacy*, p. 263.

367  Just as Tilak had subordinated addressing caste inequalities to Hindu consolidation, Gandhi in 1930s highlighted ejecting the British as the first goal, with Hindu–Muslim unity subordinated as something to follow, not precede, this. See, for example, Raghavan, *Circles of Freedom*, p. 190. See also ibid., p. 231, and also Pratinav Anil, *Another India: The Making of the World's Largest Muslim Minority, 1947–77* (London: C. Hurst & Co., 2023), Part One.

368  Quoted in Meadowcroft, 'Hindu Mahasabha', p. 182.

369  For the complicated internal dynamics as well as Savarkar's willingness to ally with the Raj, see ibid., pp. 100–250.

370  Savarkar, *Hindu Rashtra Darshan*, p. 64.

371  Quoted in Chaturvedi, *Hindutva and Violence*, p. 334.

372  Quoted in Meadowcroft, 'Hindu Mahasabha', p. 82.

373  Quoted in Marzia Casolari, *In the Shadow of the Swastika: The Relationships between Indian Radical Nationalism, Italian Fascism and Nazism* (Abingdon: Routledge, 2020), p. 88. Germany also reciprocated Savarkar's interest in Nazism, by translating his book on the 1857 rebellion into German in 1940. See Chaturvedi, *Hindutva and Violence*, pp. 23–24. Savarkar, meanwhile, even in his last book wrote positively about Hitler. See *Six Glorious Epochs*, p. 470.

374  Quoted in Meadowcroft, 'Hindu Mahasabha', p. 97. Reference is to A.S. Bhide.

375  Sampath, *Contested Legacy*, p. 484.

376  Chaturvedi, *Hindutva and Violence*, p. 320.

377  Savarkar played down the connection, but even sympathetic biographers believe this to be disingenuous. See Sampath, *Contested Legacy*, p. 498.

378  Chaturvedi, *Hindutva and Violence*, p. 319.

379  Godse, *May It Please Your Honour*, p. 45. For more on Godse and his story, see Jha, *Gandhi's Assassin*.

380  S.P. Mukherjee, who succeeded him as Mahasabha president in 1945, actually reoriented the organization to work *with* the Congress. In 1950 Savarkar would resign from membership of the Mahasabha.

381  For Savarkar's statement in court see, File No. 54/8, Ministry of Home Affairs (Political Section), 1949. For a recent investigation into the plot, see Appu Esthose Suresh and Priyanka Kotamraju, *The Murderer, The Monarch, and the Fakir* (Noida: HarperCollins India, 2021).

382  Interestingly, in 1934 after a shooting in Bombay, Savarkar had similarly distanced himself from the act by stating that the men involved were 'known to him' only in that they attended some of his 'anti-caste dinners' but beyond that there was no overlap in 'criminal design[s]'. Quoted in Bakhle, *Savarkar*, p. 80.

383 Bakhle, *Savarkar*, p. 5.
384 Quoted in Sampath, *Contested Legacy*, pp. 387–88.
385 This tendency appears elsewhere also. See Bakhle, *Savarkar*, p. 202.
386 Savarkar, *Six Glorious Epochs*, pp. 60–61.
387 Ibid., p. 130. See also ibid., p. 161, pp. 212–13 for all kinds of bizarre theories on how Christians converted Hindus in Kerala, such as by secretly making them lose caste and thereby left with no option but to renounce Hinduism. Even if such events occurred elsewhere, there is no evidence for their having occurred in Kerala.
388 Ibid., pp. 179–80. See also Bakhle, *Savarkar*, p. 349, where we read how Savarkar's view of history required 'the taking of sides'; p. 354 where we find how for him 'Nativism overrode all other criteria for judging historical actors'; and pp. 120–21 for another quote on asserting Hindu might over Muslims.
389 As Bakhle writes, 'Savarkar never doubted that he was a legendary leader of global significance'. See *Savarkar*, p. 14.
390 Savarkar, *Six Glorious Epochs*, p. 224.

## Epilogue: What Is Hinduism?

1 W.H. Findlay, 'The Revival of Hinduism: What does it Mean', p. 423, in *Harvest Field* 9, 2 (1889): 422–25.
2 A very different reality from original hopes where one evangelical voice expected 'multitudes of Hindoos flying to Christ as doves to their windows'. See George Buder's 1795 address in Richard Lovett, *The History of the London Missionary Society: 1795–1895*, Vol. 1 (London: Henry Frowde, 1899), p. 21.
3 See Ashis Nandy, *The Intimate Enemy: Loss and Recovery of Self Under Colonialism* (Delhi: Oxford University press, 1989), p. 3.
4 Sharpe, *The Universal Gita*, p. xi.
5 For a study of this selective appropriation and the historical and philosophical questions involved, see Brian A. Hatcher, *Eclecticism and Modern Hindu Discourse* (Oxford: Oxford University Press, 1999).
6 See, for instance, Heinrich von Stietencron, 'Religious Configurations in Pre-Muslim India and the Modern Concept of Hinduism', in Dalmia and Stietencron eds., *Representing Hinduism*, pp. 51–81.
7 One could, in fact, argue that it is this innate fluidity that allows Hinduism to take new forms as needed. See also Pennington, *Was Hinduism Invented?*, pp. 5–6.
8 Alam, 'Competition and Co-Existence', p. 48.
9 See also Nicholson, *Unifying Hinduism*, where the development of a united Hindu religion is placed between the twelfth and sixteenth centuries.
10 So just as there are Puranas which elevate Vishnu or Siva over one another, there are other Puranas, such as the *Markandeyapurana*, that equate and reconcile them as forms of the same supreme being.

11  Savarkar was not wrong, in this sense, when he wrote: 'Hindutva is not a word but a history.'
12  On this, see also note 119 to Chapter 1, and note 124 to Chapter 7.
13  As early as 1347, we find the Vijayanagara rulers appropriate the word 'Hindu' for themselves. See Pillai, *Rebel Sultans*, p. 80. And in the 1379 *Candayan*, a Delhi sultan is praised 'for treating Hindus and Turks equally'. See Busch, 'Unhitching the Oxcart', pp. 436–37. In the same period, that is, in different parts of India, we find expression of the existence of two identities. See also Pollock, 'Deep Orientalism', pp. 105–06.
14  And all religions, historically, have defined themselves against an 'Other'. To define 'us', there is also a necessity to point to a 'them'. Within religions too—if Catholic–Protestant polemics are any indication—self-definition in good measure derives not only from identifying what one is but also what one is not.
15  See Truschke, 'Hindu: A History'.
16  In parts of Kerala in the south too, the sarong-like *mundu* is also worn in different styles, with Hindus tucking it in on the right, and Muslims on the left. I was first alerted to this custom by a temple priest who, noting I had preferred the left side, asked why I was wearing the mundu 'Muslim style'.
17  Kruijtzer, *Xenophobia*, p. 6, p. 269. The right side, in general, is considered more honourable than the left, and under British rule, for instance, we see their political agents in Indian courts often insisting on sitting on the right of the throne rather than the left, where some 'native' rulers deliberately placed them.
18  See Pillai, *Rebel Sultans*. And as late as the twentieth century, there were in India people who styled themselves 'Mohammedan Hindus', showing also how boundaries could be porous. See Basu, *Hindutva as Political Monotheism*, p. 97. See also Pandey, *Construction of Communalism*, pp. 83–84 for a reference to 'Muslim Rajputs'.
19  See also Kruijtzer, *Xenophobia*, p. 198, p. 247. See also Busch, 'Unhitching the Oxcart'.
20  See Kabir (Linda Hess & Sukhdeo Singh trans.), *The Bijak of Kabir* (New York: Oxford University Press, 2002), pp. 50–51, p. 69, p. 79. Vidyapati, Eknath, etc. do much the same. For a courtly eighteenth-century work that speaks of two different faiths, see Busch, 'Unhitching the Oxcart', p. 419, p. 434, where we read: 'Hindus and Turks have been considered two religions, constantly at odds. They are like the gods and demons.'
21  As Basu writes, 'The genesis of Hinduism was therefore not as far back in time as Hindu nationalists would suggest, nor was it as recent as the nineteenth century, as modernists would aver.' See Basu, *Hindutva as Political Monotheism*, p. 91. And as O'Hanlon and Washbrook observe as a general point, 'pre-colonial Indian culture had its own, often very important, forms of cultural essentialization and reification'; not everything was born of colonial dynamics and Orientalism, for 'Indian cultures had and have their

own forms of objectification and essentialism.' See Rosalind O'Hanlon and David Washbrooke, 'Histories in Transition: Approaches to the Study of Colonialism and Culture in India', p. 121, p. 122, in *History Workshop Journal* 32, 1 (1991): 110–27. On Hinduness fortifying itself into Hinduism: this has parallels with Savarkar's statement that 'Hinduism is only a derivative, a fraction, a part of Hindutva.'

22  We can find other examples too of Indians attempting to systematically unite different strands of tradition, with little no influence from the West. For instance, Tulsi Sahib Hathrasi (c. 1760–1843) presented north Indian bhakti saints as part of one single broader tradition. See Karina Schomer, 'Introduction: The Sant Tradition in Perspective', p. 7, in Karine Schomer and W.H. McLeod, *The Sants: Studies in a Devotional Tradition of India* (Delhi: Motilal Banarsidass, 1987), pp. 1–20. The impulse to unite existed in India, that is, even before sustained interaction with the unitary religions of the West.

23  A.J. Droge, 'Self-definition vis-à-vis the Graeco-Roman world', p. 230, in Margaret M. Mitchell and Frances M. Young eds., *The Cambridge History of Christianity: Origins to Constantine* (Cambridge: Cambridge University Press, 2006, pp. 230-244.

24  See David Brakke, 'Self-differentiation among Christian groups: the Gnostics and the opponents', pp. 245–46 in ibid., pp. 245–60. Writing about South Africa, Comaroff and Comaroff observe similarly how

> Even as they are encompassed by the European capitalist system . . . 'natives' of other worlds often seek to seize its symbols, to question their authority and integrity, and to reconstruct them in their own image. Sometimes they do so in open defiance; sometimes through strikingly imaginative acts of cultural subversion and re-presentation; sometimes in silent, sullen resistance.

See Comaroff and Comaroff, *Of Revelation and Revolution*, Vol. 1, p. xii.

25  Thomas F.X. Noble and Julia M.H. Smith eds., *The Cambridge History of Christianity: Early Medieval Christianities, c. 600–c. 1100* (Cambridge: Cambridge University Press, 2008), p. xvi. Meanwhile, it also formed its sense of self in contrast with other faiths and groups: Jews, Graeco-Roman culture and Islam. Or as Lieu writes, 'To speak of early Christian self-definition is to recognise that the sense of self always implies differentiation from one or more "others".' See Judith Lieu, 'Self-definition vis-à-vis the Jewish matrix', p. 214 in Mitchell and Young eds., *The Cambridge History of Christianity: Origins to Constantine*, pp. 214–29.

26  Edward Terry quoted in Kruijtzer, *Xenophobia*, pp. 59–60.

27  See ibid., pp. 68–69. Emphasis added. This is, of course, not to say that Protestant–Catholic rivalries did not break out in India ever. We know they did, as seen at the end of Chapter 1.

28  This is a general point worthy of notice: the fact that as much as the colonial encounter modified the societies of those who were colonized, it also altered the colonizer and his own society.

29  The preference for the Brahminical can, of course, be explained partly by Brahmin dominance in the spheres of reform, administration, nationalism and in those in dialogue with the colonial state. But additionally, in a diverse country like India, historically also—as we saw in the Introduction—the Brahminical offered unifying elements. This served Hindu intellectuals well in the intersection between religion, nationalism and the assertion of pan-Indian identity.

30  As Pandey writes, '"religion" is also not fixed for all time, unchanging, unchangeable. Rather, new issues gain importance, new questions become central, the "preservation of religion" acquires different meanings in different social and political contexts.' See Pandey, *The Construction of Communalism*, p. 83. All identity itself is, to quote Judith Lieu, about 'experienced continuity amidst the constant change and decay' that comes naturally with time. See Judith M. Lieu, *Christian Identity in the Jewish and Graeco-Roman World* (Oxford: Oxford University Press, 2004), pp. 21–22.

31  They held the Mughal rank of *panch-hazari* and, in the 1790s, the rajah confirmed his 'obedience' to Delhi, even if this was largely ceremonial. See letter dated 18 November 1795 from the Governor of Bombay to Governor General in IOR/F/4/9/711, and B. Sobhanan, *Rama Varma of Travancore: His Role in the Consolidation of British Power in South India* (Calicut: Sandhya Publications, 1977), pp. 14–15. This fits into Bayly's lowest rung of the Mughal order, with its 'nominal allegiance' to the emperor. See Bayly, *Indian Society*, p. 23. It was in 1813 that, when it was suggested that endorsement of his title be obtained from the emperor, that the British vetoed it, stating that it was to the British 'alone [that] the support and protection of the state of Travancore belonged'. See Governor of Madras to Court of Directors, 4 February 1814, IOR/F/4/443/10660.

32  Menon, *History of Travancore*, p. 267. The missionary who reports that the rajah spoke English in the 1780s, of course, could not help but add that despite all this and his 'many good moral qualities', he 'cannot perceive the value of the Christian religion'. See ibid., p. 264. That the rajah spoke English is also confirmed in the Governor of Bombay's letter dated 18 November 1875 cited above.

33  See Pillai, *False Allies*, p. 36, and chapter one of the book more broadly.

34  To recall Benedict Anderson, all communities and identities are 'imagined' and made what they are.

35  Or as Roy wrote, 'The ground which I took in all my controversies was, not that of opposition to Brahminism, but to a perversion of it.' See Roy, *Translation of Several Principal Books, Passages, and Texts of the Veds, and of Some Controversial Works on Brahmunical Theology* (Calcutta: Society for the Resuscitation of Indian Literature, 1903 ed.), pp. vi–vii.

36 As did the idea that contemporary Brahmins were not quite as good as the ideal. The sixteenth-century saint Eknath's writings feature a dialogue in which a Dalit mounts a critique of what Europeans might call priestcraft. 'They say that they are Brahmins, but they don't bathe, pray to the sun, or read the Vedas. They do harm with this chanting, trying to kill and bind, to fascinate and subjugate.' Quoted in Christian Lee Novetzke, 'The Brahmin double: the Brahminical construction of anti-Brahminism and anti-caste sentiment in the religious cultures of precolonial Maharashtra', p. 241, in *South Asian History and Culture* 2, 2 (2011): 232–52.

37 See Günther-Dietz Sontheimer, 'The Erosion of Folk Religion in Modern India', p. 396, in Dalmia and Stitencron eds., *Representing Hinduism*, pp. 389–98. To this might be added the pull of Sanskritization among non-Brahmin leaders as well, who also, to augment the status of their caste or group, frowned on popular religion. Here too, then, we find a complex interplay of the modern with the traditional.

38 Or as Pollock writes, 'If there was a British "Brahmanizing tendency," then, it may largely have recapitulated a precolonial Brahmanizing tendency on the part of medieval ruling elites.' See Pollock, 'Deep Orientalism', p. 101. We see Hindu rulers promoting Brahminical ideas along with actual Brahmins in positions of influence in Vijayanagara, Travancore, Mysore, among the Marathas, etc. Of course, they encouraged this often for their own purposes of statecraft and state-building, but the trend itself was not new.

39 Or as Basu poses the question, is Hinduism 'a garb that modernity throws over Brahminism'? See Basu, *Hindutva as Political Monotheism*, p. 92.

40 Cherian, *Merchants of Virtue*, p. 4, p. 85.

41 Lee, *Deceptive Majority*, p. 36. For instance, in Eknath's famous sixteenth-century 'Hindu-Turk Samvad' (dialogue) also, the 'Hindu' is a Brahmin.

42 Lee, *Deceptive Majority*, p. 42, p. 70, and H.A. Rose, *Census of India, 1901 (Vol. 17): The Punjab, Its Feudatories, and the North-West Frontier Province, Part 1: The Report on the Census* (Simla: Government of India, 1902), p. 113. Similar protests were made in 1891 and 1911 as well. In the Travancore census of 1891, the Brahmin author of its report uses the term Hindus freely when speaking of high-caste groups but throws it in inverted commas when referring to 'lower orders'. See Aiya, *Report on the Census of Travancore*, p. 327.

43 Quoted in Lee, *Deceptive Majority*, p. 69.

44 Quoted in ibid.

45 Quoted in ibid., p. 85.

46 Kancha Ilaiah, *Why I Am Not a Hindu: A Sudra Critique of Hindtva, Philosophy, Culture and Political Economy* (Calcutta, Samya, 1996), p. xi.

47 Dalits too saw themselves often as separate. In religious songs sung by Chuhras in north India, thus, we find lines like: 'The Hindu has his temple, the Muslim his mosque, but I give to you this altar of mud.' Here, Dalits themselves applied the term 'Hindu' exclusively to upper-caste communities.

Quoted in Lee, *Deceptive Majority*, pp. 61–62. See also ibid., pp. 33–34, p. 69.

48  Basu, *Hindutva as Political Monotheism*, p. 2.

49  See B.R. Ambedkar, *What Congress and Gandhi Have Done to the Untouchables* (Bombay: Thacker and Co, 1945), p. 188.

50  For instance, when Mahars in the Konkan demanded that Brahmins serve them as priests; to have Brahmins attend to their rites was always a mark of higher, less 'polluting' status. See Fukazawa, *The Medieval Deccan*, p. 106.

51  Kooiman, *Conversion and Social Equality*, p. 103. It was another matter that high-caste converts looked down on low-caste converts *within* the Christian fold.

52  Quoted in Pandey, *Construction of Communalism*, p. 90. This is, of course, not to forget that casteism did carry itself into Christianity as well, and there were equally cases where conversion did *not* lead to dignity. The Dalit Christian leader Poyikayil Yohannan, for example, moved from a Nasrani church to the two foreign missions only to find them all saddled with caste biases. He eventually fathered his own spiritual and social movement. See Mohan, *Modernity of Slavery*, chapter four.

53  Quoted in Joel Lee, *Deceptive Majority*, p. 77. See also 'Discussion with B.R. Ambedkar, February 4, 1933' at Gandhi - Ambedkar Correspondence, https://www.mkgandhi.org/Selected%20Letters/amb-gandhi%20corr.php.

54  To Ambedkar, even if Dalits believed in the same religion, politically and socially they were separate. Or as he wrote:

> If religion was a circumstance from which social union was made the only permissible inference, then the fact that the Italians, French, Germans and Slavs in Europe, the Negroes and the Whites in the U.S.A and the Indian Christians, Europeans, and Anglo-Indians in India do not form a single community although they all profess the same religion, is enough to negative such a contention.

See Ambedkar, *What Congress and Gandhi Have Done to the Untouchables*, pp. 185–86.

55  Lee, *Deceptive Majority*, p. 92 refers to ever the murder of an Arya Samaj activist at the hands of upper caste groups.

56  Swami Shraddhanad quoted in ibid., p. 95. See also ibid., p. 85, p. 103. See also Bauman, *Anti-Christian Violence*, 'Introduction', for a summarization of some of the problems involved in implicitly assuming that Dalits were always considered Hindu.

57  1928 Arya Samaj tract quoted in Lee, *Deceptive Majority*, p. 77.

58  Ibid., parts 2 and 3.

59  Sampath, *A Contested Legacy*, p. 53.

60  Kanhaiya Mittal quoted in (and translated by) Amrita Singh, 'Passive Voice: Kanhaiya Kumar's new avatar as a Rahul Gandhi clone', in *Caravan*, 27 May

2024 at https://caravanmagazine.in/politics/kanhaiya-kumar-avatar-rahul-gandhi-clone.
61   B.C. Mahtab, *Impressions: The Diary of a European Tour* (London: St Catherine Press, 1908), p. vii.
62   Ibid., pp. 3–4.
63   Ibid., pp. 27–28, pp. 41–42. He adds that this reminded him of the 'lower forms' of Hinduism. But the difference was that while 'every true-thinking Indian is now trying his best to shake himself free', in Europe, the Pope himself was 'but a tool to be used by the influential camarilla of priests', unable to see the 'anti-christian things' and the 'growth of paganism' in his church. India and Hindus, that is, were progressing; but here in the very seat of Christianity in Europe, there was regression.

# INDEX

*A Grammar of the Bengal Language*,
  Halhed 144
Abdali, Ahmad Shah 365n84
*Abhijnanasakuntalam* as *Sacontala*
  142–43, 444n99
Abhinav Bharat 290, 292
Acquaviva, Rodolfo 1–5, 7, 26, 32;
  murder of 4–5, 9, 23, 26
adultery, with Brahmin woman
  474n141
*Aesop's Fables* 55, 135, 137, 251
Age of Enlightenment 65, 72
Agni xx, 81
Aiyanar xxiv
Ajnapatra 91
Akbar, Emperor xliv, 1–6, 14, 34,
  65, 72, 100, 126, 278; 'house of
  worship' 2; image xlii; Jesuit friends
  32; rebellion against 3; *sulhi-kul* 2;
  wives 4
Alagappa ('Aleppa') 54
Alam, Muzaffar 316

Alfred E. Hamill Fund 211
Ambedkar, B.R. 258, 324, 529n197;
  on 'Hindu' and 'Brahmin' 538n320;
  on Tilak 527n173
Anglo–French rivalries 91
anti-Brahminism 253
anti-British agitation 150, 181, 297
anti-casteism 287
Aradhya Brahmins, burials among
  341n76
Arjuna xxxi, 149
Art Institute of Chicago 211
Arya Dharma 235
Arya Samaj 237, 240–42, 244, 275–76,
  302–3, 305, 323–24, 500n140
Aryans xvii, 235, 250, 252; invasion
  xix, 250
Asan, Kumaran 509n233
Ashoka, Emperor xix, 141–42, 147
atheism 72
Auckland, Lord 193
Augustine, Saint 8

Augustinians 25
Aurangzeb, Emperor 22, 66–67, 428n184
avatars, theory of xxii
Awadh, annexation 209
Ay king xxx
Azevedo, Agostinho de 67

Bahadur, Rana Jung of Nepal xiii
Bajirao II 117–18
Bakhle, Janaki 298
*Bande Mataram* 226
banians 407n9
baptism 28, 30, 53, 170
Baptist Missionary Society (BMS) 179–80, 187, 196, 215, 245; first convert, image 196; Hindi-language Bible 197; missionaries 491n28; press 181
barbarians (*Mlechchhas/mlecchas*) xvii–xix, xl, 13, 204, 266, 333n22-23
Barbosa, Duarte 30
Basava xxxii, 222–23, 332n16
*Basavapurana* xxxv
Bassingh, Adolph 13
Battle of Plassey 85, 92, 96, 102, 308
beef eating 208, 240, 275
Benares College 155
Benares xxxix, 68, 122, 133–34, 136, 151–53, 197–98, 206, 238; image 152
Bengal 90–95, 99, 102–7, 110, 112, 156, 158–59, 164, 180, 183, 190, 195, 260–61; army 207, 485n258; Famine 305; system 415-16n91
Bernier, Francois 51, 68
Bhagat-Kennedy, Monika 150
*Bhagavad Gita* 148–50, 185, 224, 272–73, 292
*Bhagavatapurana* 344n99
*bhakti* xxix–xxxi, xxxiv, 59, 78, 82, 347n121; as movement 348n129; poets 223, 249

*Bhavishyapurana* xxiii
Bhonsle II of Tanjore, Rajah Serfoji 128
Bible 36–37, 42, 45–46, 69–75, 81, 83–84, 148, 150, 164, 166, 168, 170, 182, 184, 201–2, 477n162; Bengali translation of 491n28; printed by Ziegenbalg 387n37; vernacularization of 221
Bijaganita 154
blasphemies 25
Bombay, millworkers 259
Bradlaugh, Charles 166
Brahma, image 320
Brahmachari, Vishnubawa 201
*Brahmanache Kasab* ('Priestcraft Exposed,' Phule 249
Brahma-Samaj 242
Brahmin Raj 120
Brahmin(s) xvi–xx, xxii–xxiii, xxv–xxviii, xxxv–xxxvii, xxxix–xl, 30–31, 38–40, 49–50, 60–62, 65–70, 81–85, 87–88, 109–14, 118–20, 122–23, 151–54, 215–17, 247–55, 282–87, 321–23; accountants vs village headmen 253–54; for administrative support 31, 282; in Benal Army 485n258; Bengali 120–21; Chitpavans 283, 289, 433n232; Deshastha 528n178; English-speaking 219, 246; contempt for non-Brahmins 283; converts 68, 203; *dakshina* 415n86; designed nationalism 283; elites/intellectuals xviii, xxvii, xxxvii, 254; Europeans and 375n180; in executive posts 119; Gaud Saraswat 391n83; golden cow ritual xix; of Gujarat as tribal descent 341n80; Italian 38, 40, 64; Maga xxv; and non-Brahmin conflicts 512n268; meat consumption by 340-41n75; Namboodiri xxv, 340n75, 392n91;

INDEX 553

objection to Jain temples 351n153; pandits/priests xv, xxv, 14, 114; rites to re-convert 26; Saiva, image 52; scripture 67; Sanskrit use in Bengal 446n113; signs of, image 63; Sinai 375n179; Smarta 341-42n81; Tamil 108, 221, 419n116; Telugu 119; texts xvii, 405n232; theories xxx; writers 70, 84

Brahminhood xxv, 255

Brahminical 109, 256, 303, 316–17, 322; authority 110, 252; culture xxii, 232; Hinduism 233, 253, 322; ideologies xviii–xix, xxvii, 137; order xviii, xxiv; ritualism 222

Brahminism/Brahmanism xxiv, xxxvii, xli, 84, 251, 256, 286, 298, 303, 494n62; *janeu* or sacred thread in 339n62

Brahmo Samaj 224–25, 237, 242, 494n64

Brahmoism 494n66

British 90–107, 113–26, 128–32, 134–38, 146–47, 149–50, 152–58, 170–76, 182–88, 190–98, 204–11, 240–42, 245–51, 260–64, 267–69, 271–73, 276–80, 282–83, 288–95, 307–10; law 248; officials, image 106; rule 44, 105, 122, 150, 156, 204–5, 216, 248, 255, 260, 278

Britto, John de 64

brown: Christians 23, 43; intellectuals 160; men 145–47, 154, 203, 206, 213, 223, 225, 313, 316, 319, 326, *see also* white men

Buchanan, Claudius 182–85, 190, 193–94

Buddha, enlightenment of xxxiv

Buddhism xvii, xix, xxii, xxviii, xliv, 141, 233; spread of xix

Buddhists xix, xxviii, xxx, xxxii–xxxiv, xxxviii, 59, 141, 297, 316; shrines xxxiv; text xix, xxxvii

Burhan, Shaikh, sufi 354n189
Butler, William 169

Calcutta School Society 164
Calmette, Jean 68–69, 75–76
Carey, William 179–80, 194, 196, 446n112
Carson, Penelope 187
Carter H. Harrison Fund 211
caste/castes xxxiv–xxxv, 84, 108–9, 111, 233–34, 240, 248, 250–52, 254–55, 268–69, 283–84, 286–87, 300–301, 323, 325, 424n157, 491n35; assemblies 426n171; in Deccan 109; groups xviii; Jaiswal on 493n54; Kshatriyas xviii–xix, 122, 284; Paravars 28; Parayars 41, 62, 323; renounce 198; Sudras xviii–xix, 71, 250–53, 284
catechism 26
Catholic: celibacy 25; church 21, 69, 71, 236; missionaries 35, 67; suzerainty 24
Catholicism 37, 39, 69, 77, 319
Catholics 23–24, 27, 32, 36, 38, 40, 43–44, 69–70, 74, 77, 196, 203; as Hindu-Christians 42; low-caste 41; Tamil 42
Chakravarti, Bholanath 506n195
Chandragupta, Emperor 142
Chapekar, Balakrishna 272–73, 289–91
Chapekar, Damodar 272–73, 289–91
Chatterjee, Bankim Chandra 226–27
Chattopadhyay, Bankim Chandra 450n144
Cherian, Divya 323
Chhatrapati, Shahu 529n193
Chidambaram Pillai, V.O. 521n105
Chola emperors 130
Christ, Jesus 1–5, 7, 28, 30, 32, 35, 38, 40, 42, 45, 50, 170, 197–98,

200–201, 225–26; as Prophet for Muslims 4
Christian Enlightenment 165
Christian Missionaries 176, 200, 324; image 199
Christian Missions 132, 245
Christianity xliv–xlv, 8–9, 41–42, 64–65, 71–72, 76, 165–66, 170–71, 176, 185–86, 200–203, 209, 218, 223–26, 313–14, 318–19; Hinduized 42, 97
Christianization 26, 40, 172, 174, 184, 206
Christians 23–24, 26–28, 37–39, 41–43, 49–51, 53–54, 56–57, 173–74, 177, 196–98, 200–203, 274–75, 297–98, 318, 323–24; in Bengal 473n131; brown 43, (*see also* brown men); native 25, 41, 128, 182; saints 19, 27, 42; texts 1, (*see also* Bible); violence against native 477n167
Christopher, St 12
Church Missionary Society (CMS) 188, 194, 197–98, 202
Churchill, Winston 288
Clive, Robert 92, 96, 102, 308; image 92
Cohn, Bernard 124
Colebrooke, H.T. 143–45
colonialism xliii–xliv, xlvi, 220, 223, 233, 245, 248, 254, 257, 315–16, 322
Conti, Nicolo de 12
conversion xxxvi, 54, 64, 164–65, 167, 170–71, 196, 203, 209, 245–46, 303, 465n24; in Kerala 543n387; Smith on 467n50
Cornwallis, Gov.Gen. 93, 97, 177
corruption xvii, 36, 71, 77, 84, 102, 186, 216, 255, 489n13
Couto, Diogo do 68
cow: ceremony 332n16; image 243; slaughter xli, 241, 486n262, (*see also* beaf eating); societies for protection of 276; travel to West xiii; worship 275
culture xxviii, xxxv, 27, 133, 140, 187
Cunningham, Alexander 448n127
Curzon, Lord xxxiv
customs 25, 40, 51, 97, 105, 111, 163, 190–91, 219

Dalhousie, Lord 168, 170–73, 194
Dalits 246–50, 283, 323–24; Mahars 510n235; numerical loyalties 324; temple entry 303; as 'untouchables' 323, *see also* castes
Dandekar, Morobhat 200–201, 206
Danish East India Company 48, 91, 174; lease of Tranquebar 54
Datta, Akshay Kumar 163
Dayananda Saraswati 228–42, 244, 248, 250, 252, 255, 258, 298, 318; Arya Samaj 290; death of 241; Gandhi on 503n170; *Satyarth Prakash* 235
Dayanandism 239
deities xxvi, xxviii–xxx, xxxiii, xxxvi, xxxix, 8–9, 11–12, 21–22, 26–27, 31–32, 60, 75, 77–78, 95–96, 320–22; vegetarian xxvi
Demo, Linschoten on 9
Demo, Varthema on 11
demons 336n44, (*see also* satan/sathanas); Deumo (image) 11
Deshmukh, G.H. 255
Deumo, Devil of Calicut, image 11
Deumo, Malayalam deivam 9
*devadasis* 7–8, 46
Devadevan, Manu xxx
devils 8–9, 16, 19, 30–31, 56, 60–61, 73
devotees xxxi, 12–13
devotionalism xxix, xxxi; democratizing xxxv; *see also* bhakti; worship
*Dharmavivechan*, Pandurang 162

INDEX 555

Dhingra, Madanlal 292
Dominicans 25
Doniger, Wendy xxiii
Doré, Gustave 211
Dow, Alexander 84, 103
Dravidian language group 141
Drayton, Richard 140
Dubois, Jean-Antoine 191, 470n100
Dutch 9, 34, 61–62, 91; into Calicut 33; quarrels between Portuguese and 88

Eaton, Richard xxxviii
Eck, Diana L. xxxi
Edward VII xv, 325
Eknath xl
Ellis, F.W. 139–41, 144
Ellora xxxiv
Elphinstone, Mountstuart 100–102, 172, 193, 245; image 100
Emmanuel, Victor 300
English college 160
English East India Company xliv, 44, 85, 87, 90, 96, 105, 118, 120, 154, 183, 205, 209; fortifying Calcutta base 91; in Pudukkottai 120; tax policies 209
English: education 132, 160, 245, 272, 507n204; printing-press 128
Enlightenment 65, 72–73, 86, 107, 165, 174
Europeans xxiv, 19, 21, 24–25, 36–37, 51, 53, 61, 64–65, 78–79, 84, 133–34, 136–37, 218–19, 315–16; missionaries 180
evangelical missions 168
evangelicalism 179, 190, 194, 233
evangelicals 179–81, 185, 187, 192–93, 195–97, 203, 208, 210, 219, 223
*Ezourvedam* 74–77, 85, 148

fakirs 198, and 'Ashmen' 14, *see also* sadhus
fanaticism 195, 266
Fatehpur Sikri 5; chief mosque 3
female divinity, menstruation rites of 97, *see also* goddesses
female infanticide 109, *see also* sati
female missionary, lynching of 259
female poisoners 13; *see also* sati
Fenicio, Giacomo 31–33, 43
festivals xxvi, 5, 12, 14, 62, 136, 195, 208, 271, 276; Akbar celebrating Hindu xxxix; death of devotees during 12–13, (*see also* sacrifice, human); Durga Puja 407n10; Ganapati xxii, xli, 32, 268–69, 271, 277–78, 290; Holi 5; Kunde Habba (Ass festival) xxvi; Muharram 224, 276–78; pay to celebrate 23; Sanskrit recitations in 404n226; sharing 27; Tanjore 195
Findlay, W.H. 313–15
Firangis [British] 211
folk deities, Khandoba 252
Franciscans 25
French Jesuits 75
French Revolution 179, 271

Gaekwad III, Maharajah Sayajirao xiii, 284; image 285
Gama, Vasco da 19–20
Gandhi, Mahatma 149, 242, 244, 252, 263, 291–92, 295, 297, 299, 303–4, 307–8; murder by Savarkar's followers 292; murder of 310
Ganga xiv, 120
Gaurakshini Sabha ('Cow-Protection Association') 241
*Genealogy of the South-Indian Gods*, Ziegenbalg 56
Gentoos 87, 111, 121, 174
Germans 48, 292, 307–8
Gibbon 252
Goa 4, 9, 20–28, 33, 35, 37, 39–40, 42, 62, 116, 125; Christian

INDEX 556

converts 27; Christianization of 42; destructions of worship places 24; Portuguese enclave 1; temple 5
goddesses xxiv, xxvi, xxix, xxxi, 7, 16, 19, 22, 42, 53, 62, 97; androgynous xxvi; Bhavani 278; Kali 25, 215, 222, 225; and Catholic devotees 27; *gramadevatas* (village gods) 42, 56; Manat of Arabia 352n167; of smallpox 60; tribal 343n61; worship 420n120
gods: animal xxii; local 16, 31, 391n87; Pattinattar on 404n223
Godse, Nathuram 308, *see also* Gandhi, murder of
Goncalves, Diogo 33, 68
Grant, Charles 176–78, 193, 212
Great Rebellion of 1857, 119, 126, 149, 173, 194, 207, 210–11, 291, 299, 306–7; as 'holy war' 209
Greeks xix, 128, 143, 161
Gupta dynasty xxii
Guru Granth Sahib 171
Gwalior, statues at 5

Halhed, Nathaniel Brassey, image 113–14, 120, 144
Hamilton, Frederick 213, 215
Hanuman, birth places of 344n95
Hastings, Warren 102–4, 107, 109, 111–13, 116, 121–22, 140, 147–48, 151, 191, 194; innovations 124; image 103
Hathrasi, Tulsi Sahib 545n22
Havelock, General Henry 193
heathens 18, 24, 26, 28, 35, 48–49, 51, 54, 56–58, 176, 179
Heber, Reginald 126, 128, 151
Henn, Alexander 23
Henriquez, Francis 1, 4
Henry VIII 18
Hindoo/Hindu College 153, 160
Hindu Empire 286
Hindu Law 107–9, 112, 114–16, 120, 122–23, 129–30, 140, 142, 144, 153, 178
Hindu Mahasabha 302, 304, 307–9
Hindu(s)/Hindoos 417n98; Barbosa on 30; consolidation 277, 300; converts from Bengal 483; culture xxvii, xlvi, 9, 35–36, 62, 97, 185, 191, 321, 474n140; customs 39, 56, 61, 99, 319; gods 9, 22, 56, 118, 200; deities xv, 22, 56, 60, 97, 179, 227, 267; Harishchandra on 535n290; ideas 31, 65, 73, 99, 201, 203; identity 54, 219, 244, 258, 277, 300, 304, 323–24; mythology 31–32; nation xliii, 276, 287, 299; nationalism xviii, xxviii, xliv, 274, 277, 286, 289, 295, 297, 305, 309; nationalists 27, 42, 240, 267, 278, 308, 325, 537n304; persecution by an alien race 25; philosophy xlvii, 64–65, 79, 224, 252; powers 33, 41; practices xvii, 5, 90; priests blessing British flag, image 121; reformers 85, 257; shrines, 'Idoles' in 9; temples xxx, 40, 196, 278; traditions 83, 199, 220, 266, 315
*Hindudharmasthapana* (*The Foundations of Hinduism*), Dandekar 200
Hinduism xvii–xviii, xxvi–xxviii, xliv–xlvii, 41–43, 54–62, 64–65, 67–69, 81–83, 85–86, 164–67, 185–86, 216–20, 222–26, 231–33, 235–38, 250–52, 257, 274–77, 297–98, 313–22; amorphous system 220; European ideas of xlv; mass 84; modern xlvi, 58–59, 149, 220, 316, 322, 324, 493n55; political 26; polytheistic 59; Protestantization of 71; Puranic xxiv, 60, 77, 222, 231, 236; rebranding of 314; as Western 'invention' xliv

## INDEX 557

Hindu–Muslim 210, 278, 286, 297, 318; axis xxxii; encounter xl–xliii, 356n202; riots 276; strife 308; unity 542n367; violence 295
Hinduness 258, 274–75, 278, 282, 286–87, 297, 299, 318, 321, 324, 535n286, 545n21; consciousness 317; non-Brahmin 530n202
Hindutva xliv, 275, 282, 285–87, 295, 297–98, 303, 305, 309–11, 325
Holkar, Jaswant Rao 502n160
Holkars, Maratha, plundering temple towns 356-7n204
Holwell, John 76
Humboldt 148

*ibadat khana* 2–3
idolatry 21, 23, 26, 28, 31–32, 43, 59, 61, 64–65, 70, 73–74, 192–93, 196, 233, 236, 472n127, 496n81; in Christianity 326; Dayanand Saraswati and 231
idols/image xxxvi, xli, 7–8, 13–14, 22, 26, 30, 59, 62, 199, 201, 217, 228; of Christ 40; Mattiussi on 11; worship 34, 55–56, 83, 203, 222, 233, 255–56, 405n233
imperialism 93, 98, 118, 204, 264
incarnations xxii, 78, 199, 251
Indian National Congress 267
Indian Nationalism 246, 307
Indo-Aryan: ancestors xx; culture xvii, 141
Indo-Scythians xix
Indra xx
Indraji, Bhagwanlal 448n128
Industrial Revolution 176
infidels xxxvi, xli, 24, 28
Ingersoll, Robert 166
interreligious dialogue 55
Islam xxxv–xxxvii, xxxix–xl, xliii–xlv, xlvii, 4, 236, 242, 276, 278, 297, 300, 303–5; egalitarianism xxxvii

Islamic power xxxix, 251, 266–67, 278, 317; temple-smashing and xxxviii

Jadrup, Gosain (Chitrup), image xliii
Jaffrelot, Christophe 298
Jagannath 95, 130, 183, 188, 190, 193, 225; in exile 22; temple of 95; temple image 96
Jahangir, Emperor xliii, 88, 318
Jainism xvii, xix, xxii, xxx, xliv, 144, 236; decline of 346-47n117
Jains xxiv, xxviii, xxx, xxxii–xxxiv, xxxviii, 2, 71, 115, 236, 297, 316; monasteries xxxiv; sites in Karnataka xxxiv; temple xxxiv
Jaipur, maharajah of xiii
Jambhekar, B.S. 162–63
Jesuits 2–7, 18, 25, 31–35, 37–38, 40–41, 43–44, 49, 54, 61, 67, 73, 76; arrival of 1–2; encyclopaedia 7; Madurai 46; Nasranis against 375n178; observing Hindu practice 5
John III ('John the Pious') 21
John xxII, Pope 371n141
Johnson, W.J. 148
Jones, William, Sir 142–43, 145–46, 148, 150, 154, 178, 186; image 142

Kabir, saint xxxix, 318, 357n56
*kali yuga* xvii–xviii, xxvii, 84, 433n234
Kalidasa 147; *Meghaduta* 144; *Sakuntala* 145
Kaviraj, Sudipta 150
Kerala xxiv–xxv, xxx, xxxiv–xxxvi, xl, 12, 19–20, 24, 33, 35, 68, 108; Brahminical authority in 110; Christians 24–25; Malabarians 49–50; matriliny in 341n77
Khan, Afzal 265–66, 271
Khandoba, deity, Muslim veneration of xxxix
Kizhar, Arisil, on Chera king 342n84

Krishna xxxi, 32, 149, 221, 231, 234; Swaminarayan veneration of 235
*Kristapurana* ('Christ Purana'), Stephens 36
*Kristhumatha Chedanam* 495n70
Kruijtzer, Gijs 317
Kunhambu, Potheri 507n204
*Kurava Vetham* 380n222

Le Baron Henrion, M. 175
Lee, Joel 324
Leni, Alesandro 36
Leupolt, Charles 198, 206
Linschoten, Jan Huyghen van 9, 11–13, 30
Login, John 171
London Missionary Society (LMS) 180, 187, 194, 245
Luther, Martin 69, 224, 275

Macaulay, Lord 137, 161, 193–94
Mackenzie, Colin 146; image 147
Magas, as mlecchas 341-42n81
Mahabharata xx, xxvii, xxxi, 81, 149, 235, 272; translation into Persian xxxix
Mahima Dharma 232–33
Mahima Swami 232–33
Mahmud II, Ottomon Sultan 457n217
Mahmud of Ghazni, raids of xxxvi
Mahtab, Bijay Chand 325
Malcolm, John 99, 122, 172, 208
Malla, Jayasthiti 423n152
Mantena, Rama Sundari 146
Manuel I 20
*Manusmriti* 334-35n30, 335n37, 405-6n236, *see also* castes
Marathas/Mahrattas 90, 95, 97–99, 112, 117–18, 128, 130, 138, 153, 192, 265, 271, 276, 300–301, 412n54; kingdom 266; expansion 119

marriages xv, xxvi, xxix, 25, 90, 108, 111, 123, 219, 235, 279
Marshman, Joshua 194
Mary and Jesus 5; veneration of 3
massacre 26, 226; of 1583 26; of English 211, *see also* Great Rebellion of 1857
*Matapariksa*, Muir 202
Mattiussi, Odoric, traveler 11–12, 24
Mauryan empire xix
Max Müller, F. 166–67, 233, 239, 241
Mazzini, Giuseppe 291, 299
Megasthenes xix
Menon, Dilip xxvi
Mill, James 191, 219, 221
minorities 28, 60, 112, 124, 277, 282, 301–2, 324
miracles 43, 72, 225, 232, 238
missionaries 25–28, 35–37, 48–49, 54–58, 68–69, 74–76, 164–67, 178, 181–82, 185–88, 193–94, 196–97, 200–203, 205–7, 209–11, 215–16, 218–19, 244–46, 248–50, 275–76, 313, 321–22; attack in Pandharpur 273, (*see also* Acquaviva, Rodolfo, murder of); education and caste 461n2631; and schools 459n239
Mitter, Partha 7
Modak, B.P. 162
modernity xxv, 137, 223, 284, 315
monotheism xxxvi, 31, 49, 55, 59–61, 65, 67–68, 73–74, 76, 226, 234, 314
Monserrate, Antonio 1–4
Mughal court 2, 4; Dabistan-i-Mazahib of 349n137; Jesuits in 5
Mughals xiii, 1, 19, 22, 32–33, 53, 60, 76, 90, 93–95, 97–98, 100, 105, 120, 122, 126, 128, 208–9, 265–67, 318, 321, 430n203
Muhammad xxxv, xxxix, 4
Muir, John 201
Mukherjee, Rudrangshu 209

Mundy, George 191
Munro, Thomas 100–102, 104, 172, 208
Murtaza, as Mrityunjaya xxxix
Muslim League 304, 308
Muslims/Mahommedan/ Muhammadans /Mussalmans xxxvii, xxxvi–xxxvii, xxxix–xli, xliii, 4–5, 104–5, 110–12, 124, 209–11, 240–41, 266–67, 274–75, 277–80, 285–86, 297–98, 300–10, 317–19, 323; in Bengal 112; burial in 436n259; Deccan xl; dynasties xxxviii, 266; goddess 348n133, 420n120; in Kerala xxxvi; matrilineal in Kerala xl; Mullahs 324; powers xxxvi–xxxviii, xl, 21, 95, 97; re-Brahminized 112; in Sanskrit narratives xl; Sunni vs Shia 524n127; and superstition 6
Mysore 90, 94, 119, 286
mythologies 56

Nair, Savithri Preetha 136
Nairs, as polyandrous 14
Nalwade, G.M. 506n195
Namboodiripad, E.M.S. 390n82
Namdev 222–23
Nammalvar 78–79; bhakti 79; devotee of Vishnu 78; poetry 82
*Narada Sutras* 82
Narasimha 10, 251; form of Vishnu 9
Narayana Guru 252, 322
*Narayansabdanirukti* 338n56
Nasranis 25, 33, 37, 39, 41, 43, 371n142, 381n245; Kerala as home for 24; against Jesuits 375n178
nationalism 116, 120, 219, 246, 257, 267–68, 274, 285, 287, 291, 297, 304–5, 307; militant 290, *see also* Hindu nationalism
natives 40, 43–44, 54–55, 59–60, 77–78, 100, 102–5, 113–14, 140–41, 144–45, 147–48, 150–51, 154–59, 161–63, 183–84, 186, 196, 204–8, 213, 215–16; de Britto on 64; minds xlv, 157, 319; resist 197; states 119, 174; troops 97, 177, 180
nawabs 91–92; of Bengal 90; Carnatic 119;
Nayakas 130, 135
Nazis 307–8
Nehru, Jawaharlal 291
Nepal, casteism into Newars 347n117
*Nilakantha Goreh*, Muir 201
de Nobili, Roberto 34–37, 39–42, 56, 61, 64–65, 68, 75, 77, 83, 196, 198, 203, 319; innovations of 37–38;
*Nyayasara* 71

Oddie, Geoffrey 188
Orientalism 142, 146–47, 166–67
Ovington, John 14

Padmagarbha (lotus-womb) 62; replacing cow 332n16
pagans 6, 8–9, 18, 20–21, 30–31, 37, 39–40, 51, 57, 182, 187
Paine, Hume 201
Paine, Thomas 201, 246
Palas xxx
Pallavas xxx
*Panchatantra* 55
Pandurang, Bhaskar 204–5
Pandurang, Dadoba 204; image 162
pantheon 8
Paramahansa Mandali 254–55
Parangi Margam ('Parangi faith') 36–40
patriotism 263, 295
peacock murders 110–11
Pemble, John 185
Persian text xxxviii
Peshwas 98, 110, 112, 117–18, 249–50, 283, 289; system 425n161
Peterson, Indira Viswanathan 133

Peterson, Viswanathan 136
Phadke, Vasudev Balwant 269
Phule, Jotiba, 244, 246–48, 250–58, 269, 275, 282, 285–86, 299, 322, 506n194; against Puranic Hinduism 251; anti-caste activism 245–46, 257; denouncing Brahminical Hinduism 322; education to Dalits 248–49; education for marginalized 247; and girls education 254; image 247, 256; life 245, 253; night schools 249
Phule, Savitribai 246–47, 250; memorial image 256; 'Mother English' 246; poem of 257; subaltern reformer 252
Pier, Roberto 34–35
pilgrim: economy 95; tax 192–93, 195, see also under taxes
Pluralism xliii, xlvii
Plütschau, Heinrich 48–49, 57
political power 19, 42, 304–5
Polo, Marco 7, 11–12
polytheism 30, 59–60, 226, 315
Poona 110, 117, 153, 238, 244, 255–56, 268, 277, 280, 289–90; Peshwa regime in 112
Portuguese 4, 20–27, 33–34, 36, 39–41, 43, 48, 88, 91, 100, 104; arrival of 19; dominions 4; monopoly 34; patronage 41; Zamorin of Calicut on 408n19
Poynder, John 192–93
prejudices xlvi, 19, 55, 100, 144, 153, 158–59, 194, 207
priests xiv, xvi, xxx, 22, 25, 53, 60, 77, 87, 109, 179; celibacy of 25; in Goa 23
Prinsep, James 141
Print and Drawing Club Fund 211
prohibition, of going abroad xiv
proselytism 174, 303

Protestantism 70
Protestants 23, 32, 43–44, 65, 69, 174, 180, 196, 203, 221, 235; missionaries 46, 48, 137; movement xxxii, 21; propaganda 43; Reformation 65
Pudukkottai 120
Puranas xxii–xxiii, xxvii, xxxvi, 36, 68, 77, 82, 133, 153, 201–2, 235
Puranic: age xliv; cultures xxvi; religion xxii, 226; stories xxvii, xxxi; system xxxiv; texts xxvi
Puranic Hinduism xxiv, 60, 77, 221–22, 225, 231, 236, 251; Dayananda on 501n150
Puri 13, 95–96, 182, 190, 192, 225, 233; temple chariot wheel 13, 182, 233

Quran 4, 32, 53, 304

racism 204
Radhakant 146
*Rajaboli* (*Story of Kings*) 141
Rajputs 109, 147, 255, 317–18; story of women 13
Rama xiv–xv, xxvii, xxxi, 200
Ramabai, Pandita 276, 524n126
Ramachandra, Master 162
Ramalinga 232, 238
Ramanuja, St. xxxii
Ramaswami Naicker, E.V. 286
Ramayana xxiv, xxxi, 82, 90, 205, 299; BMS project of translating 197
Ramdas 264–65, 291, 293
Rand, W.C. 272–73
Rao, Narayan 201
Rao, Parimala 160
Ravana, imgae 89
rebellion 3, 207, 209–10, 297, 299, 307
rebirth: into asses 333n23; through golden yoni 332n16
reform xxii, 102, 177, 191, 216, 219, 232–34, 258, 275, 284, 318

Reformation 39, 43, 72, 218; anti-Catholic 21, *see also* Protestantism
religion xx; European influences xxiv; vs caste 325; supremacism of 304
Religious Tract Society 179
Renaissance 65, 143, 161, 239
revolutionaries 150, 260, 262, 273, 295
*Rights of Man* 246
Roe, Thomas 88, 318
Rogerius, Abraham 61–62, 68, 83
Roy, Ram Mohun xiii, 215–28, 230, 233–38, 242, 250, 257, 298, 314–15; as anti-idol 222; on Brahmins and idolatry 221; image 214; reform agenda for Hinduism 218; on religion 222; Vedic extracts and 221; veneration, of Upanishads 223
Rubiés, Joan-Pau 19

sacrifices: animal 8, 83; blood 50; buffalo 62; cock 24–25; human xxv, 18, 188, 194; image 189
sadhus/ 'Ashmen' 14, 16, 236, 264; image 17
Sahajanand Swami 234
Saivas xxxii–xxxv, xxxviii, 59, 62, 68, 79, 297, 316, 524n124; and Vaisnavas, rivalries between 394-95n109
Saiva-Vaishnava animosity 349n91
Saivism xxxiii, xxxv
*Sakuntala*, Kalidasa 145–46
salvation 35, 50, 53, 78, 118, 199
Sandracottus 142
Sankara xxviii, 222–23, 231; and image worship 345n105, *see also* idol worship
Sankaracharya 363n57
Sankaran Nair, C., on reform 523n122
*Sankarasmriti* 423n149
Sanskrit College 152–53, 158, 160
Sanskrit xxxvii, xxxix, 78–79, 84–85, 87, 113–14, 140–44, 149, 152–55, 157–58, 161, 201–2, 230, 233; corpus xxii, 68, 220; masters xxiii, 99
Sanskritists 166, 290
*sanyasi* 37, 67, 230, 239–40, 242, 252, *see also* sadhus
Saraswat Brahmins, as fish eaters 340-41n75, *see also under* Brahmins
Sarvesvara kovil, Sarukani 41
Sastri, Vedanayakam 134
satan/sathanas 8, 188, 197; Linschoten on 11
sati stones 363n60
sati/ *suttee*/widow-burning 12–13, 15, 61–62, 182, 185, 188, 190, 195, 205, 216, 218, 399n171, 436n258, 472n123; image 15, 183; interpretation of 13; Roy on 491n24
Satya Pir xxxix
*Satyarth Prakash* 237, 239
Satyashodhak ('Truth-Seeking') Samaj 254
Savarkar, Vinayak Damodar 287–94, 297–303, 305–9, 311, 317, 325; anti-caste activism 324–25; appeals for clemency 294; birth of 289; commemorative stamp 310; death of 310; image 289, 296, 306; in jail 291, 293–94; *Life of Barrister Savarkar* 295; teachings of 292; and territorial nationalism 304;
Savarkarism 308
Schwartz, C.F. 130, 132, 134, 159
sects xliv, 2, 21, 51, 79, 83, 150, 225, 233–34, 240, 316
Serampore, as 'Christian Benares'479n187
Serfoji II, of Tanjore, 129–40, 142, 146, 148, 151–53, 155, 159–61, 182, 184, 195; *Devendra Kuravanji* 133; kuravanji play 133; library 139; royal procession (image) 127, 131

Seths, Jagat 92
Shahu I ('Nero of Tanjore') 438n13
Shahu II 284; Maharajah, image 285
Shakti xxviii, xxxi; image xxix
Sharpe, Eric 315
*Shastah, Chartah Bhade* 76
Shekhawats, birth of 354n189
Shivaji, Chhatrapati 88, 99, 265–67, 269, 271–73, 278–80, 284–85, 290, 295, 317, 516n39; festival 271, 273; image 270; killing of Afzal Khan 271; as Vishnu manifestation xxxix;
shrines xxix–xxx, xxxii, xxxiv, xxxviii, 5, 8, 14, 18, 21, 26, 30, 33, 192–93, 344n101; to Virgin 42
Shukoh, Dara 66–67; portrait image 66
Sikhs 90, 115, 168, 170–73, 211, 274, 297
Singh II, Madho xiv–xvi, xxxiii, 325; to Europe xvii; in London xv
Singh, Duleep 168–70, 172, 194
Singh, Jai, maharajah 453n181
Singh, Ranjeet 168, 172–73
*Sisupalavadha* 145
Sita, as Jain nun 340n72
Siva xx, xxviii–xxx, xxxii–xxxiv, xxxix, 16, 49, 53, 56, 59, 62, 225, 228, 232; Bull image 229; image xxi; incarnation and Buddha xxviii; *ishtalingams* xxxii; wife of xxvi, xxxi; Zupanov on 16
*Sivadharmottara* brands Vedic 82
*Sivapurana* xxii
*Sivavakkiyam* 55
Skanda Purana xxiii
slavery (*Gulamgiri*) 177–78, 211, 248–49
Smith, Adam 93
Smith, Sydney 467n50
social: justice 253–54; reform 279–80, 282, 284, 295, 301

Society for Promotion of Christian Knowledge (SPCK)—Society 174
Society of Jesus 1, 7, 28, *see also* Jesuits
Somnath temple, Gujarat xxxvi; Muslims pay respect on way to Mecca xxxix
Sonnerat, Pierre xxi, xxix, 77
Sontheimer, Günther-Dietz 322
Sramanic xix–xx, xxxiv; monks xxx; religions xxxiii–xxxiv; religions 345n106; rivals xxxiii; traditions xix, xxix
SS *Olympia* xiv
St Thomas Christians 370n135, 371n141, 371n145
Stephens, Thomas 36
stereotypes xxxii, 7, 12, 20, 31, 37, 146, 176
Sthala Puranas xxiii
Stuart, James 97
Sultan, Tipu 129; as patron of shrines xxxviii
sultans xxxviii, 119, 267, 316; adopting Hindu practices 353–54n185; coins with Sanskrit inscriptions xxxviii
superstitions 4, 6, 30, 43, 137, 144, 164, 170, 175, 184, 188
Surat, port of 5
Surya (sun god), image 6
suzerains 90
Swamikal, Chattampi 495n70
Swaminarayan sect 234

Tamils xxxi, 40, 49, 58, 68, 78–79, 109–10, 127, 132, 135, 232; pilgrimage centres 62; plundering shrine of 22; texts 55, 82, 139
Tanjore Enlightenment 131
Tanjore Renaissance 131, 138
Tanjore xvi, 54, 123, 126–30, 134–36, 138, 151, 153, 182; rajahs 54, 126, 162; Siva temple in 130; temple-tower image 138

taxes 151, 207; on pilgrims 475n147; refuse to pay 27
temple(s): burning of 23; culture xxxii, 298; demolished 26; dancer (*See devadasis*); towns 133; worship xvii, xl, 200
*The Open Door to Hitherto Concealed Heathenism,* Rogerius 61–62, 68
Tibet, 'discovery' of 4
Tilak Lokamanya, B.G. xli, 254, 260–65, 267–69, 272–80, 282–87, 290, 292–93, 295, 300–301, 307, 458n231; against education to all 254; anti-Christian feeling 276; anti-sedition laws 271; 'Brahmin imperialism' and 282; Brahminness 282; cultural nationalism 287; death of 263, 285; deportation to Burma 263; Ganapati gatherings of 269; Hindutva 275, 298; image 281, 287; in Mandalay 293; nationalism 282, 291; in prison 260, 264
*Tirukkural* 55
Tirunal, Swathi 159, 162
Tod, James 147
tolerance xix–xx, xxxviii, xli, 3, 27, 50, 100, 195, 303, 306; religious 277
*Tolkappiyam* 55
Tranquebar 48, 53–54, 57, 156, 174
Tranquebar Mission 55, 129
Trautmann, Thomas 191
Travancore rajahs 119, 162, 321
tribal: carnivorous forest gods xxvi; cults xliv, 42; of Dantewada xxxi; goddess 343n61; groups 208; priests xxv
tribes xvii, xix, xxii, xxvi, xliv, 28, 42, 51, 204, 208, 232–33
Truschke, Audrey 85
Tughluq, Muhammad bin, in favour to Jains 353-54n185

Tuhfat-ul-Muwahhidin 217–19, 225

unity in diversity xxxi
untouchability xxxv, xl, 157, 208, 246, 323, 325; and training based on *karma* 511n255
Upanishads xx, 67, 79, 81, 220, 222–23, 235
'Us and Them' xl
Uthram Tirunal, Rajah 162

Vaishnavas xxxii–xxxiv, xxxviii, 50, 62, 202, 240, 297, 316, 321, 337n51; Jaiswal on 337n49; and Saiva 'sectarianism 403n213
Vaishyas xviii
Valignano, Alessandro 385n2
Varma , Martanda 408n19; temple attack of 356
Varma, Raja Ravi 80, 243, 270–71
Varma, Shyamji Krishna 290–91
Varthema, Ludovico di 9, 11, 19–20
Vatican 35, 39
Vedas xviii, xx, xxv–xxvii, xxxv, xxxvii, 65–71, 74–85, 166–67, 169, 220–22, 231, 233, 235, 239, 297–98; as Gita 398n151; into Persian xxxix; Muslim patron 81; in Tamil 78–79, 82
Vedic: experts xxvii, 221; gods xx; Hindus 496n81; religion xvii, 143; religion to Puranic Hinduism 336n45; revivalism 275; sacrifices (*yaagams*) 333n25 333; supremacy 223, 275; texts xxvii, 59, 76
vegetarianism 40, 224
Venkata II 34, 36, 61
Venkata, Cavelly, 448n126
Verma, Hoti Lal 273
Victoria, Queen xxiii, 127, 209, 240, 249, 271; proclamation of 1858 209
Vidyasagar, Iswar Chandra 163

Vijayanagara 12, 20, 34, 130
violence xiv, xxxiv, xxxvii, xli, 26, 54, 250, 258, 260–61, 272, 279, (*see also* massacre); gospel and 488n279
Virasaivas xxxii, 349n116
Vishnu/Visnu xx, xxii, xxiv, xxvi, xxviii–xxxiv, xxxix, 56, 60, 62, 74, 78–79, 220; avatar xxiv–xxv; fish incarnation image 80; image xxi; Jain image as xxxiv; Mohini as feminine form 340n71; as Narasimha (image) 10; Sri Padmanabhaswamy 321
Vishnukundina ruler xxx
Vishnupurana xxii
Vitthal xxiv
Vivekananda, Swami 257
Voltaire 73–76, 85, 104, 201, 315; image 73

Ward, William 190, 193, 219
Washington, George 250, 269
*Wealth of Nations*, Smith 93
Wellesley, Lord 87, 94–96, 130
Western education 165, 206, 253, *see also* English education
white men xlv, 24, 56, 58–59, 61, 111, 114–16, 160, 163, 207, 210, 223, 226, *see also* Europeans
widow burning, *see* sati
Wilberforce 178–79
Wilkins, Charles 148–50

Wilson, Daniel, Bishop 144, 153, 166, 173–74, 190, 199, 201, 206
Wilson, H.H. 144, 216
Wilson, John 198
women: as murderous wives 13, (*see also* sati); Ovington on 14; rights 255, 279; 'secluded ladies' 14; stereotypes on 14
World War: First 294, 297; Second 307
worship xxiv, xxix–xxx, 2, 16, 24, 38, 51, 54, 60, 69, 72, 418n113; Dilip Menon on xxvi; idolatrous 195; of iron gun at Mandu 5; of Juggernaut 475n147; polytheistic image xxxvi

Xavier, Francis 28–31, 33, 37, 42–43, 64, 67, 70, 221, 242; image 29

Yamunacharya, for renouncing Saivism 348n133
*yogis* 16, 55
Yohannan, Poyikayil 498n105

zamindars 417n103
Zelaldinus Equebar (Jalaluddin Akbar). *See* Akbar, Emperor
Ziegenbalg, Bartholomäus 46, 48–51, 53–58, 61, 64, 68–70, 73, 111, 129, 156, 174; birth of 46; image 47
Zoroastrians 2, 400n188; holy fire 3
Zupanov, Ines G. 16, 39

Scan QR code to access the
Penguin Random House India website